MOON HANDBOOKS

SOUTH CAROLINA

D1111374

MOON HANDBOOKS

SOUTH CAROLINA

INCLUDING CHARLESTON, HILTON HEAD, THE BLUE RIDGE, AND HELL HOLE SWAMP

FIRST EDITION

MIKE SIGALAS

AVALON
TRAVEL

MOON HANDBOOKS:SOUTH CAROLINA
FIRST EDITION

Published by
Avalon Travel Publishing
5855 Beaudry St.
Emeryville, CA 94608, USA

© Text and photographs copyright Mike Sigalas, 1999.
All rights reserved.

© Illustrations and maps copyright Moon Publications, Inc.,
1999.
All rights reserved.

ISBN: 1-56691-153-2
ISSN: 1522-3469

Please send all comments,
corrections, additions,
amendments, and critiques to:

MOON HANDBOOKS: SOUTH CAROLINA
Avalon Travel Publishing
5855 BEAUDRY ST.
EMERYVILLE, CA 94608, USA
e-mail: atpfeedback@avalonpub.com
website: www.moon.com

Printing History
1st edition—September 1999
5 4 3 2

Editors: Gregor Johnson Krause, and Jeannie Trizzino
Map Editor: Gina Wilson Birtcil
Production & Design: Carey Wilson
Cartography: Mike Morgenfeld
Index: Sondra Nation

Front cover photo: The Battery, Charleston. © Steve Murray/Picturesque, 1999

All photos by Mike Sigalas unless otherwise noted.
All illustrations by Bob Race unless otherwise noted.

Distributed by Publishers Group West

Printed in the USA by Bertlesmann Services, Inc.

For my wife, Kristin, and the late James Dickey, author, poet, teacher.

CONTENTS

MAPS

HELP MAKE THIS A BETTER BOOK

It's unavoidable: between the time this book goes to print and the moment you read this, a handful of the businesses noted in these pages will undoubtedly change prices, move, or close their doors forever. Other worthy attractions will open for the first time. If you see anything that needs updating, clarification, or correction, or if you have a favorite gem you'd like to see included in the next edition, I'd appreciate it if you drop me a line.

Address comments to:

Moon Handbooks: South Carolina
c/o Avalon Travel Publishing
5855 Beaudry St.
Emeryville, CA 94608
USA
e-mail: atpfeedback@avalonpub.com

(please put "South Carolina"
in the subject line of your e-mail)

ACCOMMODATIONS RATINGS

based on high-season, double-occupancy rates

Budget . . . . under $35
Inexpensive $35-60
Moderate $60-85
Expensive. $85-110
Deluxe $110-150
Luxury . . . . $150+

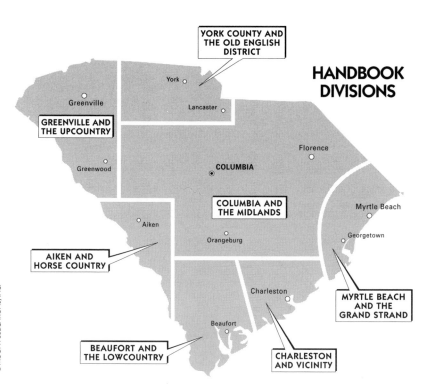

HANDBOOK DIVISIONS

YORK COUNTY AND THE OLD ENGLISH DISTRICT

York

Lancaster

Greenville

GREENVILLE AND THE UPCOUNTRY

Florence

Greenwood

COLUMBIA

Myrtle Beach

COLUMBIA AND THE MIDLANDS

Aiken

Georgetown

Orangeburg

AIKEN AND HORSE COUNTRY

MYRTLE BEACH AND THE GRAND STRAND

Charleston

BEAUFORT AND THE LOWCOUNTRY

Beaufort

CHARLESTON AND VICINITY

© MOON PUBLICATIONS, INC.

MAP SYMBOLS

═══ Superhighway	⬡ U.S. Interstate	◉ State Capitol
══ Primary Road	⬠ U.S. Highway	○ City
── Secondary Road	◯ State Highway	○ Town
─ ─ ─ State Boundary	☐ County Road	★ Point of Interest
┄┄┄ County Boundary	✕ International Airport	▪ Other Location
┄┄┄┄ Intracoastal Waterway	▲ State Park	

INTRODUCTION

I like the sense of continuity, the sense of human family that is part of being Southern. There's a sense here of your life meaning something, a sense of consequentiality. Those are the things about the South that appeal most to me.

—James Dickey,
interviewed in Charlotte, April 1977

In a 1998 letter to the editor of the Charleston *Post and Courier,* Genevieve Peterkin explained the allure of the Grand Strand's Brookgreen Gardens:

Brookgreen Gardens is not about "change," or needless embellishment. It is about tranquility, constancy, and, indeed, the absence of change, especially in the present climate of rapid change.

For anyone trying to understand the appeal of South Carolina to the modern mind, this letter is not a bad place to start. While Carolina possesses numerous other attractions, perhaps none is as celebrated as its reputation as "The Land That Time Forgot."

But there is a danger in this: mistaking the state's timelessness for backwardness. All this stasis amid a hurricane of change has not come by accident. To assume that South Carolina needs to "catch up" shows a misunderstanding of its goals. Like the Amish and the Navajo, South Carolinians have chosen a different path from the rest of the U.S., creating, in many ways, an alternative America.

And therein lies the state's allure for the cultural adventurer: South Carolina is a visit to an America the way it might have been. The way it might have been if we'd said "No" sometimes when we said, "Yes"; if we'd turned right occasionally when we actually turned left; if we'd stayed put at times instead of leaping forward. It's not always a better America, but it's intriguingly different.

It is, for instance, an America that on the whole refused to pare down its families to fit the mobility requirements of the Industrial Revolution. It is an America that has never fully bought the Enlightenment sanctification of human wisdom, an America that still allows its preacher up there in the ivory tower with its professor, an America that has never fully discarded its skepticism of Rousseau's theories about the innate goodness of humankind and, thus, never truly believed (as did the New England Romantics) that humanity—and thus, society—was perfectible.

Now, to some this may sound like a description of hell. But to many others, South Carolina's stay-puttedness—the fact that most South Carolinians (quite unlike most of America) view life through the shadows of their ancestors' gravestones—is intriguing. And those who appreciate this side of South Carolina approach the state in the same way that they approach the Pennsylvania Dutch or a Cherokee reservation—with curiosity, and with the respect that any thoughtful traveler bears for an unfamiliar culture.

THE LAND

THE THREE HISTORIC REGIONS OF SOUTH CAROLINA

Since at least the 16th century, South Carolinians have traditionally seen their state as consisting of three regions: the Lowcountry, the Midcountry or Midlands, and the Upcountry (or Back Country). If you know these terms, you've come a long way in grasping the way the state understands itself.

The **Lowcountry** was the first region settled by Europeans and today features some of the state's foremost attractions: Charleston, Beaufort, Myrtle Beach, and Hilton Head Island. Long dominated by rice and indigo plantations, this is the region of the state in which slavery was most prominent. Not coincidentally, this is also the place where you'll find the highest number of remnants of the state's famed antebellum "high" culture. The aristocratic structure of the plantation system, because it condemned many slaves to mind-numbing labor, also freed time—and provided the wealth—for the few fortunates at the top to study arts, architecture, medicine, and poetry; to put on plays, attend school in England, serve as political leaders, and essentially do the things reserved for the "leisure" classes until technology eased the burdens of daily living for the rest of us in the late 19th and 20th centuries. Because it quickly proved such a fruitful plain, it was the Lowcountry that enjoyed the densest—and wealthiest—European settlements, and hence provided most of South Carolina's state and national leadership from the earliest Colonial days up through the Civil War.

For many years, the **Midlands** existed as a sort of no-man's land between the Lowcountry and Upcountry. Certainly, people lived in the region—the Royal Colonial governor had seen to that, offering astonishing amounts of land to anyone who dared to take on the then-frontier between the Lowcountry estuaries and the fall line (the point near the middle of the state where the resistant crystalline rocks of the Piedmont region run into the softer sedimentary rocks of the coastal plain, resulting in rock outcroppings, which in turn create waterfalls and rapids, making commercial navigation impossible). But nobody knew quite what to *call* it. In John Drayton's 1802 *A View of South Carolina,* Drayton refers to South Carolina's "lower, middle, and upper country," but while the first and final terms continue to be well-used even today, "Middlecountry" never came into the common parlance. As late as 1941, the WPA's *South Carolina, A Guide to the Pal-*

SOUTH CAROLINA SYMBOLS AND EMBLEMS

Animal: white-tailed deer
Beverage: milk
Bird: Carolina wren
Butterfly: tiger swallowtail
Dance: the shag
Dog: Boykin spaniel
Fish: striped bass
Flower: yellow jessamine
Folk dance: square dance
Fruit: peach
Gem: amethyst
Insect: praying mantis
Reptile: loggerhead turtle
Shell: lettered olive
Songs: "Carolina" and "South Carolina on My Mind"
Stone: blue granite
Tree: palmetto
Wild game bird: wild turkey

a Lowcountry salt marsh

metto State, in describing the "typical" South Carolinian, claimed that he "is a Low Country-man or an Up Countryman, with the native of the mid-section having characteristics of both." The "Midlands" tag has come about relatively recently: according to Kovacik and Winberry's *South Carolina: A Geography,* Henry Cauthen, editor of Columbia's *The State* newspaper, coined the term in the 1950s.

Carolinians call the upper third of the state the **Upcountry.** Here, in the higher elevations of the Piedmont region and the Blue Ridge Mountains above the fall line, scrappy, independent-minded Scotch-Irish Calvinist Presbyterians and German-Swiss Lutherans settled after coming down from Pennsylvania and other northern states in search of kinder soils and gentler winters. Because the rugged land and fast, largely unnavigable rivers made a plantation economy impossible to transplant to this region, the two areas developed quite differently. While relatively sophisticated cities such as Charleston, Beaufort, and Georgetown sprang up along the coast, farmers only 100 or 200 miles away in the Back Country lived like pioneers—hard, largely self-sufficient subsistence existences on small plots of land—on what was then the edge of the American Frontier. Cotton came later to the Upcountry, and industry still later, making use of the strong clear rivers to produce textiles. Today, the Upcountry is South Carolina's primary manufacturing region. In the early 1990s, when BMW opened its first (and, thus far,

only) non-German plant near Rock Hill, it joined a long list of other foreign manufacturers taking advantage of the Upcountry's cheap labor and strong work ethic.

GEOLOGY

According to many scientists, South Carolina's Blue Ridge Mountains formed hundreds of millions of years ago when igneous and sedimentary rocks met up with tremendous heat and pressure underground. Some 500 million years ago, during the late Precambrian era, the Piedmont region was an island floating off the coast of North America. Around 470 million years ago, the island slammed into North America, raising up the Blue Ridge and ruining a lot of perfectly good oceanfront property in Tennessee. As these new mountains proceeded to drain down to the new coast they deposited sediments, forming the Piedmont region of Greenville and the sandhills regions just above Columbia.

Meanwhile, however, North America—with the Piedmont region as its cutting edge—was still barreling toward northwest Africa. The two collided about 350 million years ago to form the supercontinent Pangaea.

Had things stayed this way, airfares between Charleston and Capetown would have been very low indeed. Unfortunately, the scientists tell us that a mere 125 million years later, these two continents went the way of Lennon and Mc-

SOUTH CAROLINA

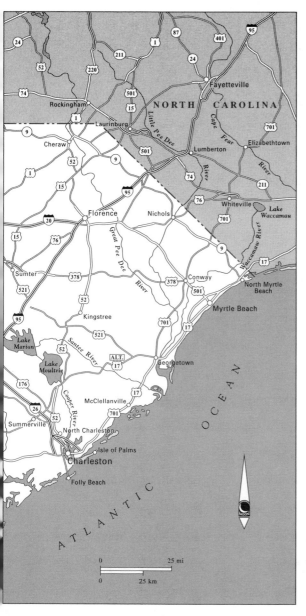

Cartney; North America headed northwest until it reached its current location, taking with it a residue of land formerly belonging to Africa.

When comparing the shape and size of the Blue Ridge Mountains to, say, the Sierras in the western U.S., it's evident that the smaller, more-rounded look of the Blue Ridge results from its 350 million years of exposure to rain, sleet, and snow. The Sierra Nevada, for instance—that several-million-year-old geological spring chicken to the west—is predictably much taller, and more jagged, than the Blue Ridge.

GEOGRAPHY

For a wonderful source of information on South Carolina's geography, see Kovacik and Winberry's *South Carolina: A Geography,* published in 1989. The following section owes much to their work.

Size and Area

The mass of land we humans have taken to calling the state of South Carolina encompasses 31,113 square miles, nearly 500 of which are covered with water. It ranks 40th in size among the 50 U.S. states, placing it right between Maine and West Virginia. You could fit three South Carolinas into the state of Oregon, though I suppose you'd have to fill out a fairly hefty Environmental Impact Report to do it. Or, if you want to consider South Carolina as an independent country—as it has at times considered itself—the state ranks somewhere between Ireland and Austria for size.

THE TWO CAROLINAS

Because it had no deepwater port and only one river that ran directly to the ocean (most others ran through modern-day South Carolina first), the northern part of Carolina developed quite differently from its southern sister, becoming home primarily to small Welsh and Scottish farmers rather than the type of wealthy English planters found in the Lowcountry. By 1712, the northern half of Carolina was granted its own governor and officially named "North Carolina."

Due to its greater development, South Carolina was the part of Carolina most Europeans meant when they spoke of "Carolina." Even so, the region south of North Carolina came to be known as "South Carolina."

Elevation

South Carolina is generally low-lying: the average elevation hovers around 350 feet. The highest spot is 3,560 feet—the top of Sassafras Mountain in the rugged northeast corner of the state, a huge mountain bearing the North/South Carolina borderline like an invisible tow rope slung over one granite shoulder. The state's lowest elevation is sea level, all along the coast.

The state generally slopes northwest to southeast, from the granite outcroppings of the Blue Ridge Mountains in Oconee, Pickens, and Greenville Counties through the foothill or Piedmont region around Spartanburg and Rock Hill, the sandy, still-rolling Midlands sandhills around Columbia, and on through the swamps to the coastal plain of the Lowcountry. South Carolina slopes toward the sea, 285 miles east to west and 225 miles north to south. The California cities of Los Angeles and San Francisco are about a hundred miles farther apart than the farthest borders of South Carolina.

Population

At the 1990 census, 3,486,703 people called South Carolina home, ranking it smack dab in the middle of U.S. states for population. This marked an 11.7% increase since 1980—a rate of increase slightly above the middle of the pack among American states for the decade. As far as Deep South states go, South Carolina is downright urbanized, with 115.4 persons per square mile. Mississippi, by contrast, boasts less than half that concentration. But lest you start worrying that South Carolina's becoming overcrowded, consider that even on a slow day at Disney World, the state of Florida packs in twice as many people per square mile as South Carolina. And New Jersey crams in nearly 10 times as many people per square mile as the Palmetto State.

To look at it on an international level, South Carolina covers more than twice as much land as Switzerland but holds only half as many people.

In fact, the secret to South Carolina's low-key, small-town feeling comes from its wealth of small and midsized communities. This means that while your travels in South Carolina might take you quite a distance from the nearest supermall, you're never too far from the nearest town square. Even the biggest cities in South Carolina—Charleston, Columbia, Greenville—don't hold much more than a hundred thousand people apiece.

This is not to say that it's all banjos and double-wides. South Carolina has always been—since the early days when Charleston's Dock Street Theater debuted as the nation's first permanent theater—a fairly "sophisticated" state. But the sophistication rarely leads to the type of impersonal atmosphere one associates with major urban areas—largely because the state lacks any single great metropolitan center on the level of a Boston, Dublin, Zurich, or Atlanta. More people live in the teeming metropolis of Oklahoma City, Oklahoma, in fact, than in the four biggest cities in South Carolina combined.

OCEAN

Many non-Southern visitors are surprised to learn that South Carolina perceives itself largely as a coastal state. But South Carolina offers the visitor 185 miles of coastline—twice as much coastline, in fact, as the Hawaiian island of Kauai. Even the official state nickname—the Palmetto State—refers to the tree indigenous to South Carolina's Sea Islands. And, according to the latest statistics, 55% of tourists in South Carolina say they come for the beaches. From the white sands of North Myrtle Beach to the Gullah Sea Islands at the Georgia border, South Carolina's beaches are a national treasure, and certainly (with the possible exception of central Myrtle Beach) a vast improvement over the overbuilt strips farther south in Florida.

The Grand Strand

South Carolina's most famous stretch of coastline is the "Grand Strand," a 60-mile stretch reaching from the North Carolina border south to Winyah Bay below Georgetown, paralleled by the Waccamaw River to the north. Some scientists say the strand is built on a 100,000-year-old barrier sand formation.

This region is marked by erosion; despite "beach nourishment" programs, big storms bring out the sandbagging teams, who try to protect oceanfront hotels and other structures.

The Santee Delta

The Santee Delta is a 20-mile zone stretching down the coast from Winyah Harbor south to Cape Romain. The largest delta on the east coast, it has retreated 1,000 or more feet since the 1940s, when Lakes Moultrie and Marion were created upriver, slowing the flow of the mighty river and causing it to drop the bulk of its sedimentary load long before reaching the coast. Newer reservoirs along the river's tributaries and diversions of Santee waters into the Cooper River have further exacerbated the problem.

The Sea Islands

South of the delta, the Sea Islands begin. Biggest is Hilton Head Island, the largest Sea Island south of New Jersey. Some, such as Sullivan's and Edisto Islands, have been inhabited by European-Americans for centuries; others, including Hilton Head and Kiawah, took on tile-roofed condos and putting greens in the 1960s and 1970s; still others, including Seabrook Island and Fripp Island (home of novelist Pat Conroy), are just now being dragged down the path of Disneyfication.

Prime pristine island experiences include Hunting Island and Bull Island—both protected by law from the developers' axes.

RIVERS, SWAMPS, AND LAKES

South Carolina is rich in water. Over 31 billion gallons of water a day flow into the Atlantic Ocean from South Carolina's rivers. To understand the changing character of South Carolina's waterways is to begin to grasp the traditional patterns of human life in the state. South Carolina's three major water systems—the Pee Dee, Santee, and Savannah—all follow the downward northwest-to-southeast slope of the state, beginning as clear, narrow, swift-moving Upcountry streams and rivers, then widening in the Midland region into red, muddy rivers before winding through the Lowcountry and becoming (stained by the tannic acid from cypress and other roots) slow-moving black rivers.

To know South Carolina's rivers is to know her history. First Americans established villages

Spanish moss hangs heavy in a South Carolina swamp.

generally along rivers and streams. Colonialist intrusion into the state followed from the coast up Lowcountry rivers; even the state's capital, Columbia, was purposely built at the confluence where the Upstate's Broad and Saluda Rivers conjoined to form the mighty Congaree. Later in the 19th century, textile factories arose around the Upcountry to take advantage of the powerful river currents there and brought the state out of is post-Civil War poverty.

Even today, you could follow the Reedy River through the heart of Greenville and southeast until it joins the Saluda, which, in turn, marries the Broad River off the shores of Columbia, and then pushes through a pair of large man-made recreation/electrical generation lakes—Marion and Moultrie—before changing its name to the Cooper, that quintessential Lowcountry river caressing the northeast cusp of the Charleston Peninsula before meeting the independent Ashley at the Battery to (so Charlestonians insist) form the Atlantic Ocean.

The **Pee Dee** is the northernmost of the river systems, consisting of the Lynches, Great Pee Dee, and Little Pee Dee Rivers, which join with the Black River and Waccamaw at the head of Winyah Bay near Georgetown. Alone of the major rivers, the Pee Dee has not been dammed to create hydroelectric power—though this seems about to change. In 1999, the U.S. Army Corps of Engineers announced plans to select the site for a new lake that would allow water to be stored, then released into the Great Pee Dee River when the water level is low. Politicos in Dillon County believe that the lake will provide additional water to the Great Pee Dee River, allowing industries to locate there. And industries mean jobs. Thus, they're going to change the landscape of the region so that those who live there already don't have to move, even though traditionally, it's not the local residents who get the new jobs brought by new industry—normally the jobs go to imported labor. Opponents say it would ruin scenic swamps and encourage increased industrial dumping of more pollutants into the system. The six dams in *North* Carolina are the reason for the Great Pee Dee's water level drop. However, the Corps says that increasing the level of the Pee Dee could actually help fish and wildlife by diluting the pollutants already in the river and by restoring and extending wetlands.

Whether the lake will actually come about is anyone's guess at the time I'm writing this. Nonetheless, the Corps is considering 14 different sites, including ones in Cheraw State Park; Spot Mill Creek, near the Chesterfield-Darlington county line; White's Creek, four miles north of Cheraw; Thompson Creek, about two miles south of Cheraw; and Back Swamp, about two miles north of I-95 near Florence.

The largest of the state's river systems, the **Santee,** is formed by the coming together of the Wateree and the Congaree Rivers. It drains nearly 40% of the entire state before finishing its run as a slow-moving black river sliding out between coastal islands into the Atlantic. The **Savannah** river system drains the southwestern reaches of the state, as well as northwestern Georgia.

Black Rivers

As opposed to the large rivers draining the Piedmont region, Lowcountry-born black rivers form at a much lower elevation, normally at the foot of the sandhills in the center of the state's coastal plain. As a result, the larger rivers carry sedimentary loads and are often colored a milky reddish-yellow (about the color of coffee with a lot of cream), while the slower, non-sediment-carrying Lowcountry rivers receive their coloring exclusively from the tannic acid that emanates from the decaying coastal plain trees and tree roots along its shores. The color of these rivers is black—about that of thin, unadulterated coffee.

A TURN FOR THE WORSE: THE COSTLY SANTEE-COOPER DIVERSION

We humans have a way of playing with nature's rules. In the 1930s, to help generate more electrical power along the outer coastal plain, Santee waters were diverted to the Cooper River to increase its flow. This increased flow did generate more electricity, but it also enabled the Cooper to carry more sediment, with which it dutifully began to fill Charleston Harbor, the state's premier shipping port.

A costly rediversion built in 1985 carries about 80% of the Santee's water back to the Santee after it has done its job of generating electricity.

CAROLINA'S BAYS

No, these oval or elliptically shaped depressions didn't get their name because they look like little self-contained bays, but because of the bay trees that usually grow around them. Look hard enough and you'll find nearly half a million Carolina bays in the coastal plain from Maryland to Florida, but you'll find them most commonly in South and North Carolina. If you drive by one (and you will), you might assume it's just an isolated swamp, but from the air, or on a topographic map, their distinctive shapes make them easy to identify.

So where did they come from? That's what scientists would like to know. Here are the facts: All of South Carolina's bays face in a northwest-southeast direction. Sometimes a sandy ridge will encircle the bay, but almost always only on the southeastern rim.

Is it possible that these bays are the result of a single catastrophic event? Some scientists believe the bays are scars from a meteorite that exploded into thousands of pieces just before hitting the earth. If a meteor hit the earth headed in a northwesterly direction, this would explain the identical direction of the bays and would explain the oblong shape—as meterorite pieces burrowed to a stop in the ground.

It's a fine theory. Unfortunately, no one has found any remnants of a meteor anywhere around the bays, nor have they detected the magnetism normally found around remnant areas.

A second theory, less exciting, argues that the bays' unique shape comes from the area's constant exposure to prevailing southwesterly winds. The ridge of sand around the southeast rim of many of the bays might be the result of occasional strong northwesterly winds from rare winter storms.

Nobody knows for sure. But wherever they come from, the bays are worth visiting. The smallest bays are around four or five acres in area, some serving as private ponds. The largest is Big Swamp in the Manchester State Forest in Sumter County. The best place to see a picture-postcard bay is probably **Woods Bay State Park,** which preserves a three-mile-long, one-mile-wide bay near the town of Olanta, near where Hwy. 378 crosses I-95 in Florence County.

The Edisto River, which runs from the center of the state through Orangeburg's beautiful Edisto Gardens and on out to the coast, is the longest blackwater river in the world. The Edisto, along with other smaller rivers such as the Ashley and Combahee, combine to drain about 20% of the state.

The large, sediment-carrying rivers tend to drop their loads right at a river's end, creating river deltas. On the other hand, black rivers, with their slight but steady water flow and very little sediment, dig estuaries and deep embayments, such as Charleston Harbor and Port Royal Sound near Beaufort.

Lakes

All of South Carolina's large lakes are man-made, including Wateree, Wiley, Murray, Greenwood, Marion and Moultrie, J. Strom Thurmond, Hartwell, Keowee, Jocassee, and Russell—all created as fringe benefits of power generation.

The linked Santee-Cooper Lakes of Marion and Moultrie combine to provide 171,000 acres of water for various recreational purposes. The stumps and timber left behind beneath the new lake also offer a furnished home for striped bass, bream, largemouth bass, white bass, and crappie. The fishing here is legendary. Fishermen have pulled a world record 109.4-pound catfish and a 58-pound channel catfish from these waters.

Near Columbia, on the Saluda River, Lake Murray offers 50,000 acres of water surface and 525 miles of shoreline, and lots of fishing for stripers, bass, bream, and crappie.

In the Old 96 District in the southwest corner of the state, the Savannah River has been dammed to form the "Freshwater Coast" (a federally reserved nickname), resulting in a large lake recently renamed for J. Strom Thurmond but still called by many (including those in Georgia) by its old name, Clarks Hill Lake.

MOUNTAINS

Piedmont

Carolina's foothill region is about 100 miles wide and ranges in elevation from 300 feet at the base of the sandhills region, around Columbia, to 1,200 feet at the northwest edge, near the mountains proper. Though the Piedmont's hills aren't very tall, they are fairly rugged, with granite outcroppings leading to sheer cliffs—and beautiful views. Kings Mountain, up near Blacksburg, is one of these outcroppings. Perhaps the most famous and most beautiful is Caesars Head on US 276.

Blue Ridge

Only about 600 square miles of South Carolina belong to the Blue Ridge Mountains, itself a small part of the Appalachian system running from Georgia to Maine. But South Carolina's are 600 spectacular square miles.

A good place to see the state's mountains is along the Cherokee Scenic Highway, Hwy. 11, between I-26 and Walhalla. Admittedly, however, this drive pales a bit in comparison to North Carolina's Blue Ridge Parkway.

The mountains in the small extreme northern parts of Oconee, Pickens, and Greenville Counties contain the state's highest peaks—ranging 1,400-3,500 feet. The tallest is Sassafras Mountain, at 3,554 feet. But since half of Sassafras lies in North Carolina, Pinnacle Mountain (3,425 feet) wins for the highest mountain completely within the state.

CLIMATE

When to Visit

Most Carolinians will tell you that the best times to see South Carolina are in the autumn and in the spring. In fact, some Charleston inns consider midsummer and winter to be off-season. And there's some sense to this.

In autumn, the crops are in—meaning roadside stands are packed with fresh fruits and vegetables—and the temperature and humidity are down. In fact, in South Carolina (as in much of the South) most state fairs and county fairs are held in the fall rather than midsummer, to capitalize on the more merciful weather. Of course, on the coast, fall is also hurricane season—but hurricanes only come along a handful of times each century, while *every* fall features some beautiful cool weather.

In the spring, the dogwood and azalea blossoms are out and the weather is a blessed mix:

> *Carolina is in the spring a paradise, in the summer a hell, and in the autumn a hospital.*
> —*Colonial American saying*

not too cold, not too hot, but just right. In the mountains, swollen rivers hurtle off the sides of granite cliffs in spectacular waterfalls.

Even in this age of air-conditioning, South Carolina summers—particularly inland—are just too hot and humid for many people. Temperatures can rise to over 100° F, with humidity above 50% (and sometimes much higher). A 100° temperature with 100% humidity is about right for a hot shower, but not a vacation. Average temperatures in the Midlands around Columbia range from a high of 92° to a low of 70°; at Caesars Head in the Upcountry, they're considerably lower, ranging from 80° to 63°. On the coast, count on it being somewhere between 88° and 75° on a July day.

In truth, though, for people without limitations on their breathing, summer in South Carolina is not all that bad, and it has its own likable nuances. The ocean and lakes are warm and swimmable. The kids are out of school and fill the playgrounds at the parks. And there is something to be said for being able to say you've experienced the South's legendary humidity at its high-water mark.

It's also true that a midsummer lightning storm over the Midlands, or over the salt marshes of the Lowcountry, is an experience not to be missed. And those looking to understand the heart of South Carolina culture have only to live through a hot week in August to understand where the slow speech and languid pace of Carolinians comes from. I've woken up plenty of summer mornings with a plateful of goals for the day, but when it's that hot and that humid—when just getting out of bed coats your back with sweat—you don't really feel much like taking on the world. Sitting out on the shady porch with a pitcher of sweet tea sounds like the only reasonable thing to do.

So if you're planning a lot of sightseeing—as opposed to just lolling by the pool, on the lake, or at the beach—then think twice before visiting between June and September. And this is doubly true if you're planning on camping and hiking, both of which at this time of year become more of a life struggle against the insect kingdom than a time of relaxation. If you're already familiar with the South or come from a place that enjoys a similar climate, then you won't have a problem. But if you're flying in from London or San Francisco and stepping off the plane into the heat of a Carolina August, you're going to need at least a few days (and possibly some grief counseling) to adjust.

Winter in South Carolina is a much different experience in the northeast part of the state than it is in lower climes such as Charleston. The water will be too cold to swim in the lakes and at the beach—though surfers brave it with wet suits—but the high number of evergreen pines throughout the state keeps the foliage looking generally full year round. If you have the option, you should make an effort to visit Charleston—or many of the state's wonderful small towns—while the Christmas lights are up and the carolers are singing on the street corners. A genuine treat.

Precipitation

First-time visitors to the American South always comment on "how green everything is." The South in general, and South Carolina in particular, are very damp places. Even the hottest day of the year might have a rain shower. In fact, some parts of South Carolina receive as much as 81 inches of rain annually (most of Hawaii gets only 45 inches). The statewide average is around 49 inches of rain annually.

One thing that many non-Southerners don't realize is that summer is the rainy season in South Carolina. Convectional rain comes on humid days in the summer. As the sun heats the earth, the earth in turn warms the air layers just above it. Pretty soon you've got convection currents—movements of warmed air pushing its way upward through cooler air. Eventually, this rising moisture reaches an elevation where it begins to cool and condense, creating cumulus clouds. As the clouds thicken and continue to cool, they create the dark thunderclouds that send picnickers and beach-goers scurrying for cover.

In a land this humid, every sunny day holds a chance for "scattered showers." Bring an umbrella; if you're camping, consider tarping your tent and gear before leaving for any long hike—

you don't want to return to a soggy sleeping bag and waterlogged supplies. If you get hit by a particularly heavy storm while driving, do what the locals do: pull off under an overpass and wait it out. These types of heavy torrents don't usually last more than a few minutes. As one Carolinian said it, "When God wants to show off like that, I pull over and let Him do it."

As opposed to convectional precipitation—always a warm-weather phenomenon—frontal precipitation nearly always takes place during the winter. Frontal precipitation also differs in its general lack of drama—instead of a rapidly forming and short-lived torrent, it normally takes the form of a steady rain or drizzle, with little or no lightning and thunder. It almost always means chilly—and sometimes polar—air masses, but most cold fronts coming down from the north are diverted by the Blue Ridge Mountains. Warm air from the Caribbean often can keep the thermostat at a bearably warm level in the winter.

Frontal precipitation brings what little snow comes to South Carolina. Snow, hail, and sleet do occasionally make an appearance in the state, particularly in the Upcountry. The Midlands get a sprinkling of snow about once every year—when they do, cars fishtail, schools close, and everyone gets out the Instamatic to take snapshots for posterity. Charleston has received snow in the past, but if you're only heading to the Lowcountry, you can feel fairly safe leaving your snowshoes home.

Hurricanes

Hugo. Hazel. It seems as if every generation of South Carolinians has its own Day 1, its own hurricane from which to date the events of their lives. As in, "Our Honda's only a couple years old. But we've had that old truck since before Hugo." In 1991, I had the following conversation:

ME: So Hugo really gave you a hard time, eh?

MOUNT PLEASANT SHOP OWNER: Oh no. The fellow down the street, his place got ruined—terrible. Nothing left. But other than losing the roof, we-all here didn't have any damage.

ME: Other than losing the roof?

> *After 1893 storm, Colonel Ward take me and Peter Carr, us two and a horse, take that shore to Little River. Search for all them what been drowned. Find a trunk to Myrtle Beach. Have all kinda things in 'em: comb for you hair, thing you put on your wrist. Found a dead horse, cow, ox, turkey, fowl—everything. Gracious God! Don't want to see no more thing like that!*
>
> *Find two them children way down at Dick Pond what drowned to Magnolia Beach . . . all that family drown out, because they wouldn't go to this lady's house on higher ground. Wouldn't let none of the rest go. Servants all drowned: Betsy, Kit, Mom Adele. Couldn't identify who lost from who was saved 'til the next morning. Found old Doctor's body by his vest sticking out of the mud. Fetched the Doctor's body to shore and his watch was still a-ticking.*
>
> *—1937 WPA interview*
> *with Ben Horry of Murrells Inlet*

Hurricanes have undoubtedly struck the South Carolina coast ever since there *was* a South Carolina coast, but the first one recorded in history books hit in late 1561, when three of four Spanish ships set on settling the Port Royal region were lost. Twenty-six men drowned.

In 1686, a hurricane blasted the same section of coastline, just in time to stop a marauding army of Spaniards who had already slaughtered the Scottish settlement in Beaufort and were mauling their way to Charleston.

Three more hurricanes hit the coast in the first half of the 18th century, but a 1752 hurricane nailed Charleston dead center, hurling harbor ships into city streets, flattening homes and trees, and killing at least 28 people.

In 1885, just as South Carolina was shaking off the bonds of Reconstruction and attempting to salvage its economy, a 125-mph hurricane smashed into Charleston, killing 21 people and damaging or destroying nine of every 10 homes in the city.

And then the fun really began. On August 23, 1893, a hurricane swept up from Savannah through Charleston and the Sea Islands, killing at least 1,000 people. Another devastating hurricane followed the same October. Others followed in 1894, 1898, 1906, 1910, and 1911.

Hurricane Hazel of 1954 and Hugo of 1989 are the two hurricanes that stick out in the minds of many living Carolinians. Hazel killed 95 people from South Carolina to New York, not to mention perhaps as many as 1,000 in Haiti and an additional 78 in Canada. Less deadly but costlier was Hugo, which featured 135-mph winds and a 20-foot storm surge. The storm devastated the state for 200 miles inland, causing over $5 billion worth of damage. Hugo claimed 79 people overall (49 in the U.S.), but—though it passed through the heavily populated Charleston area—only 17 people died in the state.

Nearly every year brings two or three hurricane watches, but this doesn't keep people from building expensive multimillion-dollar homes right on the waterfront. And why should it? The Housing and Urban Development Act of 1968 (amended in 1969 and 1972) made federal flood insurance available to homeowners and developers, subsidized by taxpayer money. Thus it was that after Hugo, homeowners replaced the old rambling beach houses of yesteryear with beachfront mansions on stilts.

Tornadoes

Much more common than hurricanes are tornadoes. South Carolina gets about 10 tornadoes a year, more than any other South Atlantic state.

When a tornado comes along, try to be somewhere else. About a third of all of South Carolina's tornadoes form in April and May. In 1924, in the worst tornado season on record, 77 people in the Piedmont and Midlands died when two series of tornadoes tore their way through the state, injuring eight hundred.

Put together 10 tornadoes a year, and the fact that South Carolina sports the U.S.'s highest percentage of population living in mobile homes (16%), and you've got a recipe for trouble.

Earthquakes, Too?

It's August 31, 1886, a warm St. Louis evening on the banks of the Mississippi River. You stand on the silent dock, awaiting the whistle of a steamboat, but hear only the sounds of cicadas drifting out over the silent brown water.

And then the surface of the river ripples. The dock quivers, drops you to your knees. What could it be? Then the movement's over and you rise again, thankful the earthquake was minor.

But 1,000 miles away, near the quake's epicenter, all hell has broken loose in Charleston. Buildings 200 years old have crumbled; brick facades topple forward onto passersby in the street.

All those retaining bolts you see in old Charleston buildings aren't there for hurricanes. The 1886 quake here did more damage than Sherman, and another's always lurking. Experts estimate that the 1886 quake ran a 7.7 on the Richter scale and a 10 on the 12-point Mercalli scale of earthquake intensity. It left 60-92 dead (accounts vary) and caused an estimated $23 million damage. Even today, more than 100 years later, South Carolina is rated as a major earthquake risk area, based almost entirely on the 1886 incident and the 351 smaller jolts that followed over the next 27 years. After "The Shake," Charleston homeowners inserted long rods between the walls of their houses to brace them. You can still see the unique plates today.

FLORA AND FAUNA

For the following information I owe much to Audubon International; to the fine *Landscape Restoration Handbook,* by Donald F. Harker, Gary Libby, Kay Harker, Sherri Evans, and Marc Evans; and to George Sigalas III, horticulturist at Reynolds Plantation resort in Greensboro, Georgia.

LOWCOUNTRY FLORA

You get your first palm tree in South Carolina.
—Ratso (Dustin Hoffman)
Midnight Cowboy

Coastal Vegetation
Among the native vegetation you'll see along the coast are the state tree, the cabbage palmetto *(Sabal palmetto),* along with dwarf palmetto *(Sabal minor)* and the groundsel bush *(Baccharis halimifolia),* covered with what look like tiny white paintbrushes in late summer and fall. You'll also see grand live oak *(Quercus virginica)* and laurel oak *(Quercus laurifolia)* shading the coastal cities.

Many of these trees hang thick with Spanish moss *(Tillandsia usneoides),* which is not, as many people believe, parasitic. Instead, it's an epiphyte, similar to bromeliads and orchids. These plants attain their nutrients from the air, not from their host plants. Many oaks are also adorned with resurrection fern *(Polypodium polypodioides),* which looks shriveled up and often blends in with the bark of the tree it is climbing. When it rains, however, the fern unfolds, and its dark green fronds glisten like green strands of jewels.

Sea oats *(Uniola paniculata)* grow among the sand dunes on the coast. Waving in the ocean breezes, they look like something out of a scenic calendar. Because of their important role in reducing sea erosion, sea oats are protected by state law.

Freshwater Marsh
The South Carolina coast has many freshwater marshes, characteristically thick with rushes, sedges, grasses, and cattails. Many of the marshes and associated swamps were diked, impounded, and converted to rice fields during the 18th and 19th centuries; today many of these impoundments provide habitat for waterfowl. Characteristic plant species include swamp sawgrass *(Cladium mariscus),* spike-rush, bulrush, duck-potato, cordgrass, cattail, wild rice *(Zizania aquatica),* southern wax myrtle *(Myrica cerifera),* and bald cypress *(Taxodium distichum).*

MIDLANDS FLORA

Southern Floodplain Forest
Southern floodplain forest occurs throughout the coastal plain along large and medium-size rivers. A large part of the floodplain lies saturated during the winter and spring—about 20-30% of the year. In these areas you'll find abundant amounts of laurel oak and probably willow oak *(Quercus phellos),* sweet gum *(Liquidambar sturaciflua),* green ash *(Fraxinus pennsylvanica),* and tulip tree *(Liriodendron tulipifera)* as well.

In higher areas on the coastal plain, swamp chestnut oak *(Quercus michauxii)* and cherrybark oak *(Quercus pagoda)* dominate; in lower areas, you're more likely to find bald cypress, water tupelo *(Nyssa aquatica)* and swamp tupelo *(Nyssa biflora),* along with southern magnolia *(Magnolia grandiflora),* American beautyberry *(Callicarpa americana),* common papaw *(Asimina triloba),* southern wax myrtle, dwarf palmetto, trumpet creeper *(Campsis radicans),* groundsel bush, Virginia sweetspire *(Itea virginica),* cinnamon fern *(Osmunda cinnamomea),* sensitive fern *(Onoclea sensibilis),* and the carnivorous pitcher plant.

Sandhills Pine Forest
The sandhills region stretches across South Carolina in a belt that includes Chesterfield, Columbia, and Augusta, Georgia. The dominant trees are longleaf pine *(Pinus palustris),* slash pine *(Pinus elliottii),* and loblolly pine *(Pinus taeda).* Other vegetation includes water oak *(Quercus nigra),* sweet bay magnolia *(Magnolia virginiana),* wax myrtles, dwarf palmettos, swamp cyrilla *(Cyrilla racemiflora),* spanglegrasses, and panic grasses.

KUDZU: THE VINE THAT ATE THE SOUTH

Though Asians have harvested kudzu for well over 2,000 years, using it for medicinal teas, cloth, paper, and as a baking starch and thickening agent, the fast-growing vine wasn't introduced to the U.S. until it appeared at the Philadelphia Centennial Exposition of 1876, and Southern farmers really first became acquainted with it when they visited the Japanese pavilion at the New Orleans Exposition of 1884-86. For some 50 years afterward, though some visionaries proclaimed the vine as the long-awaited economic savior of the South, most Southerners thought of it largely as a garden ornamental. They called it "porch vine," since many used it to climb trellises and provide shade for swings.

After the boll weevil infestation of the 1920s wiped out South Carolina cotton crops, and years of single-crop farming began to take their toll on the soils of the South, the U.S. Department of Agriculture under Franklin D. Roosevelt imported vast amounts of kudzu from Japan, and the CCC planted some 50,000 acres of the vine for erosion control and soil restoration. Down-and-out farmers could make as much as $8 an acre planting kudzu, and in the midst of the Depression, few could refuse the offer.

And that was the last time many of those acres saw sunlight. The problem, it seems, is that kudzu's insect nemeses had no interest in immigrating to America along with the vine, so kudzu actually grew better in the U.S. than in Asia—often a foot or more a day. Soon, kudzu had covered fences, old cars, and small houses. It swallowed whole trees, depriving their leaves of sunlight and killing them. And this at about the time that many farmers realized it was loblolly pine timber, not kudzu, that could bring them back to prosperity.

Today, a wiser Department of Agriculture categorizes kudzu as a weed. Millions of dollars are spent each year trying to eradicate the stubborn vine, whose roots survive the South's mild frosts and most available herbicides. Some say it covers more than two million acres across the South, though just over 10,000 acres in South Carolina.

Read any Southern newspaper long enough and you'll run across a dozen varieties of the same story: *Kudzu May Contain Cure for X*. Nobody can believe that the plant could be as annoying as it is without also providing some major benefit to humanity. One thing we do know for sure: as a member of the bean family (Fabaceae), kudzu's roots contain bacteria that fix atmospheric nitrogen and thus help increase soil fertility.

And South Carolinians know how to make the best of things. Up in Walhalla, Nancy Basket creates kudzu paper and then uses it in multicolored collages celebrating rural life and Native American themes. Others weave thick baskets from the mighty vine. Some farmers have experimented with grazing goats and other livestock on kudzu, which not only provides free food for the animals, but also seems to be one of the few dependable ways to constrain the plant.

Though there may be less kudzu in the state than there was a few years ago, don't worry—you'll still find kudzu all across the South Carolina, climbing and covering trees, inching toward the edge of the road. It's everywhere. Are you parked on a Carolina roadside as you're reading this? Reach over, open your glove box, and you'll probably find some kudzu.

If you'd like to find out more about the "vine that ate the South," go to the Web site www.cptr.ua.edu/kudzu.html, which will in turn lead you to a number of other sites dealing with the vine. A documentary, *The Amazing Story of Kudzu*, has been distributed to public TV stations nationwide, so watch your local listings to see when it might be broadcast in your town. Or you can purchase a copy of the video by calling (800) 463-8825 (Mon.-Fri. 8 a.m.-5 p.m. central time). Tapes run about $21.

UPCOUNTRY FLORA

Mixed Hardwood Forest

Up until the 1800s, short-leaf pine and stands of hardwood covered the Piedmont. But when cotton-growing became the cash crop in this region, down came the trees, burned away and replaced by cotton rows. However, between 1945 and the 1970s, with improved farming methods creating increased yields per acre, the amount of cultivated land in the Piedmont was cut by over 50%, strengthening cotton prices and allowing the now-abandoned fields to begin the long process of regrowth.

Consequently, as you drive through the Piedmont today, you'll find countless one-time farmlands in various stages of regrowth. Dog fennel *(Eupatorium compositifolium)* and rabbit tobacco *(Gnaphalium obtusifolium)* are usually the first to thrive in an abandoned field, enjoying the direct sun. You'll also find the tall, quick-growing, long-trunked loblolly pine abundant in old farm fields. It's a transplant from the Lowcountry, brought up here by timber interests. Indigenous forest in this area consists of oak, hickory, and pine. The dominant trees are hickories, shortleaf pine *(Pinus echinata)*, white oak *(Quercus alba)*, and scarlet oak *(Quercus coccinea)*.

Other vegetation you'll find in these forests includes red maples *(Acer rubrum)*, eastern red cedar *(Juniperus virginiana)*, common persimmon *(Diospyros virginiana)*, and black walnut *(Juglans nigra)*.

The tulip tree *(Liriodendron tulipifera)* found in this region features beautiful orange and green tulip-like flowers in early spring, though you'll rarely see them because they often bloom 200 feet in the air. The tulip tree is in fact the tallest growing broadleaf tree in eastern North America. Other Piedmont vegetation

includes flowering dogwood *(Cornus floridus)*, painted buckeye *(Aesculus sylvatica)*, common papaw (called the poor man's banana for its delicious custard-like fruit), sourwood *(Oxydendron arboreum)*, mountain azaleas, viburnums, poison oak *(Toxicodendron pubescens)*, broomsedge *(Andropogon virginicus)*, pink lady's slipper, joe-pye weed, and mountain mint.

Appalachian Oak Forest

Before chestnut blight eliminated the American chestnut in the early 20th century, it was one of the more important canopy trees in the region. Today, the remaining vegetation includes white oak, chestnut oak *(Quercus prinus)*, hickories, flowering dogwood, American witch hazel *(Hamemelis virginiana)*, downy serviceberry *(Amelanchier arborea)*, eastern hemlock *(Tsuga canadensis)*, sassafras *(Sassafras albidum)*, and blueberry.

Appalachian Forests

In the highest reaches of South Carolina's Blue Ridge Mountains grows hardwood forest, the tail end of a similar forest type that reaches all the way up to New England. In the beginning of the 20th century, a fungus killed off the American chestnut trees that characterized this area; you may find rotten bits of these trees by the trailside. Chestnut oaks and other oaks stepped up to fill the void. Up here you'll also find hemlock, white pine, yellow birch, and colorful azaleas and rhododendron.

This whole region gets beautiful color in the autumn; for many Carolinians, a drive up through the Upcountry and onto the Appalachian Parkway through the mountains of southwestern North Carolina is an annual tradition.

flowering dogwood

MAMMALS

Scientists have claimed that in ancient days great bison, camels, and even elephants roamed South Carolina, but you won't find any there today. In the mountains it's possible—but unlikely—that you'll encounter a black bear. And panther encounters are even more rare.

However, if you're hiking in the upper parts of the state, you may well see white-tailed deer, raccoons, badgers, beavers, possums, and a variety of squirrels, though you'll need a flashlight to catch the nocturnal flying squirrel. River otters, beavers, and the seldom-seen bobcat also dwell in the forests, as does the rare red fox, currently being reintroduced into the Francis Marion National Forest north of Charleston.

Ocean mammals include the playful bottle-nosed dolphin and the rare, gentle manatee, which attempts to dwell peacefully in the coastal inlets but often ends up playing speed bump to the many leisure craft swarming the waters.

AQUATIC LIFE

Featuring everything from clear mountain streams to saltwater marshes and the Atlantic itself, South Carolina's diverse waters provide a correspondingly wide variety of fish and other sea life.

Freshwater
The nonindigenous rainbow and brown trout inhabit the 200 miles of creeks and rivers in the mountains, having effectively chased out the native brook trout, which live on nowadays only in the headwaters of various Carolina rivers, and only because the other two species find it impossible to live there.

As you move down through the Piedmont and into the sandhills and Midlands, you'll find striped, largemouth, and white bass; blue gill; crappie; perch; red-eye bass; redbreast; pickerel; pike; and several kinds of catfish in the lakes, rivers, and freshwater creeks.

Coastal and Ocean
The tidal rivers and inlets teem with flounder, sea bass, croaker, drum, and spot. Deep-sea fishing—particularly as you head out toward the Gulf Stream—includes bluefish, striper, flounder, drum, Spanish and king mackerel, cobia, amberjack, shad, and marlin, to name only a few.

Other sea life includes numerous types of jellyfish, starfish, conch (pronounced "conk"), sand dollars, sea turtles, numerous species of shark (many of them edible), rays, shrimp, and Atlantic blue crabs. You'll also find oyster beds along the coast, though, due to pollutants, most of these are no longer safe for consumption.

REPTILES AND AMPHIBIANS

The Palmetto State hosts a large population of one of the most feared reptiles—the **alligator.** Generally inhabiting the low-lying areas of the coastal plain, they prefer fresh water; only very

two of the attractions at Myrtle Beach's Alligator Adventure

rarely will you find them in the ocean—a fact for which the coastal tourism industry is eminently grateful. Although South Carolina alligators are not nearly as large as their counterparts in Florida, they can reach up to six feet or so, plenty big enough to do damage to a human being. While alligator attacks on people are very rare, exercise caution if you see one— these log-like creatures can move mighty quick when food is involved.

Water brown snakes often grow as long as four feet. You'll find them in the lower two-thirds of the state. The water brown is also a tree-climbing snake; sometimes you'll see them enjoying the sun on tree limbs overhanging rivers, streams, and swamps. They feed mainly on catfish. In blackwater swamps you'll find **black swamp snakes,** usually just over a foot long.

But these aren't the kinds of snakes most visitors have on their minds when they're hiking in South Carolina. The Palmetto State, after all, leads the nation in its variety of **poisonous snakes,** containing six different slithering creatures that can bring on trouble with a bite: copperhead, canebrake rattlesnake, eastern diamondback rattlesnake, pigmy rattlesnake, cottonmouth (water moccasin), and the eastern coral snake. Fortunately, none of these animals are aggressive toward humans; you'll probably never even see one while in South Carolina.

BIRDS

Although South Carolina ranks as one of the nation's smaller states, within its boundaries you'll find more than 375 different species of birds—over 40% of the bird species found on the continent. In the Upcountry you may well see the yellow warbler, chestnut-sided warblers, cedar waxwing, ruffled grouse, brown thrasher, house finch, peregrine falcon, dark-eyed junco, scarlet tanager, bald eagle, Louisiana waterthrush, red-breasted nuthatch, and the golden-crowned kinglet. Favorite birding sites include Clemson's **South Carolina Botanical Gardens,** the **Mountain**

brown thrasher

Bridge Wilderness Area, Table Rock State Park, Lake Jocassee and Devils Fork State Park, and **Sumter National Forest.**

Down toward the Old 96 District in Abbeville, Edgefield, Greenwood, and McCormick Counties, you may also see the wild turkey, Bachman's sparrow, various neotropical migrants, grasshopper sparrow, red-shouldered hawk, pileated woodpecker, American woodcock, Bonaparte's goal, and the double-crested cormorant. The better birding sites in this area include **Calhoun Falls State Park, Sumter National Forest,** in Abbeville County, and the **Ninety Six National Historic Site.**

The Midlands host many of the same species, along with the red-headed woodpecker, hooded warbler, yellow-billed cuckoo, osprey, Mississippi kite, king rail, brown creeper, and the great blue heron, among others. Popular birding sites include **Aiken State Park, Aiken's Hitchcock Woods, Edisto Memorial Gardens** in downtown Orangeburg, **Santee State Park, Carolina Sandhills National Wildlife Refuge,** and **Congaree Swamp National Monument** near Columbia.

In the Lowcountry, look for various wading birds, shorebirds, the wood stork, swallow-tailed kite, brown pelican, marsh hen, painted bunting, seaside sparrow, migrant ducks and waterfowl, black-necked stilt, white ibis, the marsh wren, and the yellow-crowned night heron. Popular birding sites include **ACE Basin National Wildlife Refuge, Brookgreen Gardens,** and **Huntington Beach State Park,** south of Myrtle Beach; **Cape Romain National Wildlife Refuge, Edisto Island State Park, Francis Marion National Forest,** including the Swamp Fox section of the Palmetto Trail starting in McClellanville; **Magnolia Plantation and Gardens** (near Charleston), the National Audubon Society's **Francis Beidler Forest Sanctuary,** and the **Pinckney Island National Wildlife Refuge,** near Hilton Head; and the **Savannah National Wildlife Refuge,** near Hardeeville.

For more information on birding, contact the South Carolina Department of Parks, Recreation and Tourism and request the pamphlet

Birding the South Carolina Heritage Corridor, or contact the South Carolina chapters of the National Audubon Society at (803) 471-2821 (North Augusta) or (803) 748-9066 (Columbia).

Or pick up a copy of *Finding Birds in South Carolina,* by Robin Carter, USC Press, 1993.

INSECTS

The members of South Carolina's vast insect population that you'll want to know about include **fireflies, mosquitoes,** and **no-see-ums.** The first of these are an exotic sight for those who haven't seen them before; people traveling with kids might want to ask around to find out where they can hope to spot some fireflies come sundown.

Don't worry about where to find mosquitoes and no-see-ums—they'll find you. If you're visiting between spring and late fall and plan to spend any time outdoors, bring insect repellent.

ENVIRONMENTAL ISSUES

As opposed to, say, most parts of California, where landscapers must intentionally plant grass and trees—along with artificial watering systems—South Carolina is so fertile that at times it seems that if you don't hack nature back, it might swallow you up. Farmers complain about "wet" summers here. Grass grows to the very edge of the highways. Pine trees grow everywhere they haven't been cut down, and kudzu grows over everything not in motion.

Consequently, while there have always been a number of farsighted environmentalists in the state, many South Carolinians have been slow to see a need for conserving natural resources and preserving places of wild scenic beauty. A common Carolina practice when building a home, for instance, is: a) clear-cut the entire property of native scrub pine; b) build the home; c) plant a lawn, along with a few nursery-bought oaks or willows for shade.

But this view of Nature-as-adversary is slowly changing. The popularity of Adopt-a-Highway programs, the increased traffic to South Carolina's excellent state parks, and the huge number

of Carolinians from industry, government, and the private sector currently pitching in to build the Palmetto Trail—a hike/bike path across the entire state—are all signs boding well for the future of South Carolina's remaining wilderness.

A more immediate danger to the general well-being is the state's numerous industrial plants using and/or producing dangerous materials. The Deep South is the closest thing the U.S. has to a third-world economy, where a depressed, generally undereducated population gladly trades the community's safety for a little prosperity.

But (and I say this warily) the tide seems to be turning. For instance, for years, folks around Rock Hill have been watching—and profiting—as rampant growth from Charlotte, North Carolina, spilled down into South Carolina. But recently, concerned citizens have taken steps to preserve the rural nature of the area. In April 1998, Chester County created South Carolina's first "river preservation district," providing for a 100-foot buffer along the Catawba riverbank. Granted, it's a minimal protection, but it's a sign that somebody is thinking about the future. Farther upriver in York County, the York County Council set a goal of preserving one acre of natural land for every one acre developed. Around the same time, the Nation Ford Land Trust acquired 219 acres across the river from Landsford Canal State Park, protecting the view from the park, as well as the endangered Rocky Shoals spider lily, which grows there.

In 1997, Senator Arthur Ravenel helped get some acres in Georgetown, Horry, and Marion Counties established as the Waccamaw National Wildlife Refuge. The state also began acquiring the beautiful Jocassee Gorges property upstate for preservation and public use. The South Carolina Coastal Conservation League and Charleston Mayor Joe Riley called for establishing greenbelts around Lowcountry urban areas, and a number of Lowcountry General Plans began to require industry clustering (getting industries to locate near each other to preserve natural space) and also—when possible—to use each other's waste products in their own manufacturing.

In a 1998 runoff election, long-time Folly Beach Mayor Bob Linville was voted out and replaced by Vernon Knox, of the South Carolina Department of Natural Resources, largely because Linville was viewed as soft in his enforcement of development codes. The *Post and Courier* quoted a Knox voter as saying she'd voted for Knox because she was afraid that Folly Beach would turn into another Myrtle Beach otherwise.

There was a time when many Carolinians *dreamed* that someday their town, too, would have the wealth and material expanse of Myrtle Beach. Maybe things really are changing.

The Savannah River Project
The Savannah River Site covers about the southeast third of Barnwell County, churning out nuclear weapons—and the inescapable waste material, which was dumped along with radioactive waste collected from around the country into the U.S.'s No. 1 nuclear waste facility. Though Governor Carroll Campbell had signed legislation to close the dump in 1994, the movement stalled during the Beasley years. As of early 1998, many Carolinians were hoping for proactive measures by Governor James Hodges.

HISTORY

In the long sweep of history, South Carolina has been one of the most contentious states of the union.
—Louis B. Wright, South Carolina, A Bicentennial History (1976)

When most out-of-staters think about history in South Carolina, they think of Fort Sumter, the bloodless initial battle in what would become the bloodiest of American wars. But by the time Beauregard had Anderson holed up in Charleston Harbor, South Carolina itself was already one of the most noted of American historical regions. It was settled originally by numerous indigenous tribes, including the Muskogee, Cherokee, and Creek. They were followed by the Spanish and the French, and eventually the British and their African slaves. South Carolina in the Colonial period witnessed a number of Native American uprisings, culminating in the Yamassee War of the early 1700s. By the time the indigenous peoples had finally been vanquished—largely by disease and forced removal—the British faced such pirates as Blackbeard and Stede Bonnet, who had begun to threaten Carolina seaports.

Later that same century, South Carolina's importance in the American Revolution was perhaps matched only by that of Massachusetts and Virginia—the Declaration of Independence was commissioned while a South Carolinian chaired the Continental Congress, and several important battles took place in both Upcountry and Lowcountry South Carolina.

After the Revolution, Charleston bloomed as the arts center of the South. Such actresses as the English-born Elizabeth Arnold Poe (Edgar Allan's mother) entertained Lowcountry audiences at the Dock Street Theater (still an operating theater today). By 1830, the "Best Friend of Charleston" began the world's first regularly scheduled railway service, linking Charleston and Augusta, Georgia. Then, in 1832-33, the Nullification Crisis focused the nation's eyes upon the Palmetto State as President Andrew Jackson and his former vice president, South Carolina senator John C. Calhoun, debated whether a state government could overrule a federal law within state boundaries—an important step in a long series of attempts to define the relative powers of the states and the federal government.

So by the time cadets from the Citadel fired the first shot of the Civil War—at a federal ship in Charleston Harbor—South Carolina was already a treasury of American history. And today, its cultural center, Charleston, is arguably the best-preserved major Colonial city in the United States, putting such painted sisters as Boston, St. Augustine, and New Orleans to shame.

FIRST ARRIVALS

Ethnologists estimate the number of indigenous Americans present in South Carolina at the time of European contact at around 15,000; by 1715, this number had been halved by European diseases and war. And by the time of the American

Revolution, the population was a small fraction of its former size. Two hundred years later, the 1980 census would report only a few thousand unassimilated Native Americans living in South Carolina, mostly in a last-ditch coalition on the Catawba Reservation in the northern part of the state.

In the two decades since that census, however, a growing celebration of Indian heritage has drawn a number of Carolinians with aboriginal blood to come out of the genetic shadows and request to be recognized as members of various indigenous tribes.

Prehistoric Peoples

If these people had only known they'd end up lumped for all eternity into a dimly lit category called "prehistory," they no doubt would have taken better notes for posterity. What many scientists theorize based on the little existing evidence is that migrating peoples reached South Carolina some 15,000 years ago. This was still at the end of the Ice Age, but they found megafauna such as mammoth, mastodon, and great bison. All we know about these early people is that they were primitive tool makers and crude hunters.

Toward the end of the Pleistocene epoch, the Paleo-Indian appeared—which is to say, descendants of the same Indians, but with better tools. The culture—primarily defined by its use of Clovis points used on spears—spread apparently from the Great Plains toward the Atlantic. The Paleo-Indians were the first great big-game hunters of South Carolina. They went after mammoth and mastodon; one of their tricks was to burn the marsh or woods, driving the animals that hid within to slaughter. They may have also added some gathering to their prodigious hunting efforts.

When the Ice Age finally ended, South Carolina's physical environment went through some predictably large changes in the region's flora and fauna. The early Americans adapted to these changes, creating a society fed on fish, shellfish, small mammals, and fowl. With the greater abundance of game, and the resulting leisure time, you might think that a "high" culture would have developed at this point, but the living was so easy, and apparently the existing philosophies were so comfortable, that little change is noticeable in the artifacts of these cultures, though they're separated by thousands of years.

During this, the Archaic period, South Carolinians apparently spent spring and summer near a major body of water—a river, marsh, or the Atlantic; shell middens and shell rings identify these sites. The people would move to higher regions to hunt white-tailed deer in the fall, returning to their waterside digs for the winter. Trade may have also begun during this period: tools made of Piedmont materials have been found in the Lowcountry; coastal plain materials have been found at Archaic sites in the mountains.

Pottery some experts date to between 2500 B.C.E. and 1000 B.C.E. first appeared along the Savannah River around the time Moses and the Israelites were waiting for a ferry on the shore of the Red Sea. Archaeologists have found these simple ceramics around the shell middens along the coast.

During the late Archaic period, domestication of such plants as beans, squash, sunflower, and sumpweed began, though apparently corn was not a big crop in the Southeast until much later.

During the Woodland period—1000 B.C.E. to 1000 C.E.—Native Americans began to rely increasingly upon agriculture. Farming both permitted and required a less mobile lifestyle, which in turn gave rise to further development of ceramics (now that nobody had to lug the pots across the state anymore) and permanent structures. Being tied to one area also meant that hunters needed to be able to kill more of an area's available wildlife instead of moving on to easier pickings elsewhere; to that end, the bow and arrow—developed around this time—came in handy.

The Mississippian period (named because this type of culture seems to have first appeared in the middle Mississippi Valley region) was a time of great advances. Cultural nuances such as ritual burial practices, platform mounds, and a hierarchical structure organized under village chiefs suggest a sophisticated religio-socio-political system. Just over the border near Macon, Georgia, you can find temple pyramids. Along South Carolina's fall line, in the decades after 1150 or so, as the French were constructing Chartres Cathedral, Mississippians were battling their way eastward into the pristine world of the well-established Woodland Indians.

Because the Mississippians were an invading force, their early sites in the state feature encircling palisades—defensive structures for pro-

DOVER PUBLICATIONS, INC.

typical shell gorget from Mississippian period

tecting themselves against the invading Woodland peoples. Eventually, the Mississippians, and the Mississippian way of life, won out.

Mississippians tended to plant their crops in the rich bottomlands beside rivers, building their villages up on the bluffs overlooking them. One of the best—and only—descriptions of one of these "towns" comes from Hernando de Soto. When de Soto explored western South Carolina in 1540 (on his way to discovering the Mississippi River), he encountered Cofitachequi, an important Mississippian town on the banks of the Wateree River in today's Kershaw County. Ruled by a female chief, Cofitachequi consisted of temple mounds and a number of rectangular, wattle-and-daub, thatched-roof houses, with storehouses of clothing, thread, deerskins, and pearls.

The pearls suggest that the good folks of Cofitachequi traded with coastal Indians—an interpretation further bolstered by the fact that they were well versed in the existence of the Spanish, whose only other presence in the region had been established 14 years earlier, on the coast, at the failed colony of San Miguel de Gualdape.

All the Native Americans who dwelt in South Carolina at the time of the European invasion derived from Iroquoian, Siouan, Algonquian, and Muskogean language groups. Northeast of the Catawba-Santee waterway lived the numerous Siouan tribes, the southern portion of the Sioux nation extending to the Potomac River near what would later become Washington, D.C. At the coast, where the living was easy, tribes tended to be small but plentiful: the Combahee, Edisto, Kiawah, Etiwan, Wando, and Waccamaw. The fewer tribes of the Upcountry were larger and stronger.

For instance, the most powerful tribe, the Cherokee, ruled a 40,000-square-mile region—the northwestern third of modern-day South Carolina—though they were constantly at battle with the more warlike Creeks and the Chickasaws of northern Mississippi and western Tennessee, and the Choctaw in the southern Mississippi region. Only with the Cherokees' help did the Carolinian colony survive.

South Carolinian Indians contributed many things to the Carolinian way of life, most notably place-names. Whether you're sunning on Edisto Island, watching a football game at Wando High School in Mount Pleasant, fishing the Saluda or Congaree River, or doing time in Pee Dee Federal Penitentiary, take time to reflect on the Native Americans who gave the name to your location. Also, the next time you sit down to a plate of grits or barbecue—*barbacoa*—thank those who first developed them.

BRITISH PROPRIETARY PERIOD

Though the 16th century brought a handful of reconnaissance missions and attempts at colonization by Spain and France, the Spanish and the French had nearly all disappeared by the turn of the following century. Except for a handful of Spanish Jesuit priests, South Carolina was left again to the indigenous Americans. For 83 years. (After a generation or two without them, the tales of armies of marauding white men must have seemed like myths to young Chicoras and Sewees.)

But this didn't mean that Europeans had forgotten about South Carolina. By the second quarter of the 17th century, Spain's power had declined to the point where British monarch Charles I began to assert England's historic claims to the coast, founded on the discoveries of the Cabots. The king was prompted by his need to do something with the French Huguenots who had taken refuge in England. In 1629, he granted his attorney general, Sir Robert Heath, a charter to everything between latitudes 36 and 31 (more or less from the present-day Georgia-Florida line to the North Carolina-Virginia line) and all the way west to the Pacific. In the charter, Charles lists the name of the region as "Carolana," a transmogrification of "Charles." Despite one failed attempt (the famed *Mayflower* miscalculated and landed its French Huguenot passengers in Virginia), no one ever settled in South Carolina under the Heath Charter.

Establishment of the Lords Proprietors
While the Heath Charter was gathering dust, Cromwell and the Puritans beheaded Charles I and took control of England. Upon Cromwell's death, Charles II was restored to the throne, largely due to the efforts of the English nobility. The king was short of funds but wanted to show his gratitude to his allies, so in 1663 he re-granted most of the Heath Charter lands to a group of eight noblemen: his cousin Edward, the Earl of Clarendon; his cousin and counselor George Monck, Duke of Albemarle; William, the Earl of Craven; John Lord Berkeley; Anthony Ashley-Cooper; Sir George Carteret; Sir John Colleton; and Sir William Berkeley. This grant was expanded in 1665 into an even larger swath encompassing everything from 65 miles north of Saint Augustine to the bottom of Virginia.

Of course, the successors of Robert Heath had a legal right to Carolina (Charles II had changed the "a" to an "i"). To mollify them, the king promised future lands, which eventually turned out to be 100,000 acres in interior New York. The original grants were made null and void, and Carolina thereby gained eight lords proprietors.

The term "lords proprietors" does a good job of explaining both the nobles' roles and their motives in the early settlement of Carolina. As

"lords," they had penultimate say over what life would be like for settlers in this new land. As "proprietors," they had an almost purely financial interest in the venture. Certainly none of them came to Carolina to live. The weaknesses inherent in this government-by-the-barely-interested were to become apparent before long.

The Barbadians
Britain already had a highly profitable colony in Barbados, so the lords were overjoyed when a number of British Barbadians showed interest in exchanging the West Indies' hurricanes, tropical illnesses, unbearable humidity, and already overcrowded conditions for the chance to settle Carolina. The lords sent the self-named "Barbados Adventurers" an enthusiastic letter promising to assist them "by all way and means," and asking them to spread the word about Carolina among their planter neighbors.

The influence these Barbadians and other planters from the West Indies would eventually have over the structure and flavor of Carolina culture is hard to overstate. They brought the socially stratified European feudalism upon which the Lowcountry was founded; their experience raising rice largely determined the economy of the Lowcountry through the Civil War; and their preference for West African slave labor would shape Carolina society into the 21st century.

In 1663, the eager Barbadians sent William Hilton sailing along the Carolina coast, looking for a good site for settlement, but other than his discovery and naming of Hilton Head Island, nothing much came of the expedition. The Barbadians established a short-lived colony at the mouth of the Cape Fear River in modern-day North Carolina and sent a ship, captained by Robert Sandford, southward to explore the Port Royal area. Sandford visited with the friendly Edisto Indians. When the ship left for Cape Fear, Dr. Henry Woodward stayed behind to explore the interior and study the native languages.

The Treacherous First Passage
After many, many delays, in August 1669 the first three ships (the *Mayflowers* of South Carolina, if you will), named *Carolina, Port Royal,* and *Albemarle,* sailed from England to Barbados, arriving in late fall. Actually, the *Albemarle* turned out to be the *Santa Maria* of the journey—it sank off

Barbados. After gathering up proprietor-prescribed farming supplies, *Carolina* and *Port Royal* set sail again, with the sloop *Three Brothers* replacing *Albemarle*. Not long afterwards, the ships were separated by a storm. *Port Royal* drifted, lost, for six weeks (running out of drinking water in the process) before finally wrecking in the Bahamas. Though 44 persons made it safely to shore, many of them died before the captain was able to build a new vessel to get them to the nearest settlement. On the new craft, they reached New Providence, where the captain hired another boat that took most of the surviving passengers to Bermuda. There, they caught up with the *Carolina*.

In Bermuda, an 80-year-old Puritan Bermudan colonist, Colonel William Sayle, was named governor of Carolina. Under Sayle, the colonists finally reached Port Royal—on March 15, 1670. As Nicholas Carteret reported, the Indians who greeted the settlers on shore made fires and approached them,

> *whooping in their own tongue and manner, making signs also where we should best land, and when we came ashore they stroked us on the shoulders with their hands, saying "Bony Conraro, Angles," knowing us to be English by our color.*

These Indians spoke broken Spanish—a grim reminder that Spain still considered Carolina its land. The main Spanish base, in St. Augustine, was not all that far away.

Running across overgrown remnants of Spanish forts on Santa Elena island and remembering the not-so-long-ago Spanish massacre of a French colony there no doubt made the English leery of settling at the hard-to-defend Port Royal. Neither did the Edistoes seem thrilled to have the English settle there permanently. Fortunately, the cassique (chief) of the Kiawah Indians, who lived farther north along the coast, arrived to invite the English to settle among his people, in exchange for help in beating back the ever-threatening Spanish and their Westo Indian allies.

The settlers agreed to the terms and sailed for the region now called West Ashley, just south of Charleston Peninsula. There, in early April at Albemarle Point on the shores of the Ashley (the site of present-day Charlestown Landing), they founded Charles Town—named, of course, for their king.

On May 23, the *Three Brothers* struggled into Charles Town Bay, minus 11 or 12 of its passengers, who had gone ashore for water and provisions at St. Catherine's Island, Georgia, and run into Indians allied with the Spanish. In fact, of all the several hundred who had begun the journey from England or Barbados, only 148 survivors stepped ashore at Charles Town Landing. Three were African slaves.

Carving Out a Home

The settlers immediately set about protecting themselves against the Spanish and their Indian allies, and this was not a moment too soon. In August, the Spanish at St. Augustine sent forth Indians to destroy Charles Town. Fortunately, Dr. Henry Woodward, who had been left behind by Sandford four years earlier, was now able to help. When the Spanish and Indians arrived, Woodward had just returned from a diplomatic journey throughout the region, in which he had convinced the many small tribes to unite with the English into a single, powerful defense league against the hated Spanish.

Facing the united tribes, and a British militia well warned of its coming, the arriving Spanish and Westoes decided they didn't really want to attack after all. The Spaniards went back to St. Augustine and decided to get serious about making that a permanent, well-fortified city.

THE COLONY BLOSSOMS

By the following February, 86 Barbadians had joined the settlement. Shortly after that, steady old Governor Sayle died, replaced by the temporary Governor Joseph West, one of the state's most capable Colonial-era leaders. On September 1, 1671, Barbadian Governor Sir John Yeamans showed up with nearly 50 more Barbadians. Yeamans eventually replaced West as governor.

In its earliest days, the young colony's economy depended largely on trade with the Indians. To coax the continent's furs from the indigenous peoples, Indian traders went deep into the territory—some as far as the Mississippi River—bearing metal tools, weapons, and other things for which the Native Americans were willing to trade pelts.

WHERE THE BOYS ARE

If any maid or single woman have a desire to go over, they will think themselves in the golden age, when men paid a dowry for their wives; for, if they be but civil and under 50 years of age, some honest man or other will purchase them for their wives.

—From Robert Horne's 1666 pamphlet Brief Description of Carolina

Carolina grew quickly in population and in prosperity. By 1700, it was inarguably the crown jewel of England's North American colonies. However, with so much land, and a crop system that required a great amount of labor, the bulk of South Carolina's first immigrants came as indentured servants or slaves to work for those Barbadians already building plantations among the coastal Sea Islands and up the rivers. Since they could legally be kept as slaves for life, and because many of them had experience growing rice back in their native country, West Africans were the preferred import.

Yet while the traders were penetrating the interior as they bartered with the Indians, and the sheer logistics of the growing plantation economy meant that planters had to spread out, Kovacik and Winberry estimate that even as late as 1715, 90% of South Carolina's European/African population lived within 30 miles of Charles Town. The danger from the Spanish and Westoes was simply too great for most would-be pioneers to venture farther.

Those whites who did live out on the plantations lived largely among their own slaves, with African-American bond servants outnumbering free persons often as much as 10 to 1 in some districts. The voices of whites who warned that planters were setting themselves up for an insurrection were lost amid the clinking of gold in the planters' coffers. The Barbadians had turned a wild land into a boom economy before, and they were certain that slavery was the way to do it.

The proprietors, who were all for government by the elite, weren't too concerned about the preponderance of slavery in Carolina. Neither were the royals, since slavery was yet legal in the British empire. What they *were* concerned with was Carolina's exports: Carolinian rice (and, after 1740, indigo) was extremely valuable to the empire; in the 1730s, England even made a point of settling Georgia to act as a buffer zone between the prized plantations of Carolina and the Spanish at St. Augustine.

By 1680 the settlers had decided that the Albemarle Point spot was too unhealthy and hard to defend; some settlers began moving north to Oyster Point, site of the present-day Charleston Battery. The white-shell point at the end of a narrow-necked peninsula was much easier to defend—there was no question about which direction a ground attack might come from, and anybody attacking from the harbor would be visible a long ways off. In May of 1680, the lords proprietors instructed the governor and his council to resettle Charles Town at Oyster Point.

It really *was* a better spot. Because it was low on the peninsula, coastal planters both north and south of the town could easily transport their goods to Charleston's port using tidal creeks.

The French Huguenot Protestants began arriving by the boatload in 1680; France's 1685 repeal of religious freedoms for non-Catholics accelerated this process.

In 1686, though the Spanish had agreed to the English settlement at Charles Town, they forbade any further encroachment to the south. In 1684, a group of Scottish religious dissenters had tried to start up a community at Port Royal, but the Spanish raided it and slaughtered most of the residents. In 1686, 100 Spanish, free blacks, and Indians landed at Edisto Island and broke into Governor Joseph Morton's house, stealing his valuables and kidnapping and then murdering his brother-in-law. They also kidnapped/liberated/stole 13 of Morton's slaves. Normally the Spanish offered liberty to escaped English slaves. In this case, though, whatever they offered these 13 didn't appeal to two of them; they escaped and returned to their master.

By 1695, Charles Town citizens (or rather, their slaves) had built thick stone walls and six bastions, making the city into an armed fortress. By 1702, England was embroiled in Queen Anne's War with France and Spain. Since the French were now in the Mississippi Valley to the west, and the Spanish in Florida to the south, the penned-in Carolinians decided to be proactive and attack the Spanish stronghold of St. Augustine. Unfortunately, though Moore's men were able to clean out smaller Spanish settlements between the rival capitals, the War of Augustino ended in failure—the Spanish would stay in control of Florida until the U.S. purchased it from them in 1819.

The first part of the 18th century brought numerous problems—pirates and the Yamassee War principal among them—to the young colony. In both cases, when the colonists pleaded with England for help, the proprietors took a deep breath, rolled up their puffy sleeves, and . . . did nothing. Thus, in both cases, the Carolinians ended up using their own abilities to solve the crises. Consequently, though they certainly didn't mean to do it, it was the proprietors who convinced the Carolinian settlers that they didn't need lords proprietors at all.

"DOWN WITH THE LORDS, UP WITH THE KING": END OF THE PROPRIETORS' ERA

It was time for a revolution, South Carolina style. It was a very polite and orderly revolution. Everyone said "please," "thank you," and "yes, ma'am." No one was killed.

In a sense, the Carolina Revolution of 1719 was the opposite of the Revolution of 1776. Colonists in 1776 tended to feel some fidelity to the distant King George, even while hating the governors and soldiers he had installed over them. But the Revolutionists of 1719—which, again, unlike 1776, included just about everyone—very much respected Proprietary Governor Robert Johnson, who had, after all, just saved Charles Town from the pirates. But Johnson wasn't popular enough to atone for the sins of the lords proprietors back home. In November 1719, Carolina elected James Moore as governor and sent an emissary to England to ask the king to make Carolina a royal province with a royal governor and direct recourse to the English government.

The royal government—which had interest in Carolina's exports and realized that the lords proprietors were not up to the task of protecting the colony—agreed. While this was all worked out, Carolina was a self-ruling nation for

two years. At the end of this time, Carolinians elected Robert Johnson—the old proprietary governor—as the first royal governor.

Now that the boundaries of South Carolina were more or less defined (though disputes with Georgia over the exact border extended into the 1980s), Johnson set about trying to encourage settlement in the western frontier—both to make Charles Town's shipping more profitable and to provide a buffer against whomever might next want to cause the Carolinians grief. The western frontier at this point meant just about everything beyond the coastal inlets and river mouths.

Birth of the Midlands

To encourage immigration, Carolina arranged for a fund to lure European Protestants. Each family would receive free land, based on the number of people they brought over—including slaves. Every 100 families that settled together would be declared a parish and given two representatives in the state assembly. Within 10 years, eight townships formed, all along navigable streams. This middle country had, in a sense, the worst of both worlds. While it was out of the reach of the easily navigated Lowcountry waterways (essential for shipping produce and goods), it also suffered from the lack of ocean breezes. Nonetheless, Germans, Scots, Irish, and Welsh, in various configurations, founded such towns as Orangeburg and Saxe-Gotha (later Cayce). Charlestonians considered these settlers the first line of defense against Indian attack, and reservists against the threat of a slave uprising.

Birth of the Upcountry

By the 1750s, the hills or Piedmont region above the fall line began to fill up with frontier families from the colonies up north, who fled the greater Indian threats and the harsher winters for a safer, warmer life. The philosophical differences between the Calvinist subsistence farmers of the Upcountry and the Anglican aristocrat planters of the Lowcountry soon spilled over into large distrust and animosity between the regions.

By the time of the Revolution, the Back Country contained nearly half the white population of South Carolina—20,000-30,000 pioneer farmers, nearly all of them "dissenters" (i.e., non-Anglicans); despite the promises of the initial constitutions, the Anglican planters had gone ahead and established the Anglican church as the official state church of South Carolina. Though Governor Francis Nicholson had sought to pacify the Cherokee—the dominant Upcountry tribe—with gifts and trade preferences, they had nonetheless grown discontent with the arrangements. In 1730, Sir Alexander Cuming negotiated with the Cherokee and arranged for them to open up their lands for settlement. By 1753, however, the Cherokees' animosities with the neighboring Creek led Governor James Glenn to act as Jimmy Carter at Camp David, stepping in to bring peace between the two. The Cherokee rewarded Glenn by granting South Carolina a few thousand acres of land, on which the Carolinians built Fort Prince George on the Keowee River as a British outpost to protect British citizens and interests in the area and to protect the Cherokee from the Creek. Two years later, Old Hop, top Cherokee chief, sat down with Glenn at Saluda Old Town, midway between Charles Town and the Indians' town of Keowee, and deeded the Carolinians the 96 District, a region that now includes parts of 10 separate counties.

By January 19, 1760, the Cherokee, angered at British encroachments and broken promises, began massacring white settlers in the Upcountry, an uprising referred to as The Cherokee War. Carolinians acted quickly, spreading their own brand of terror into the Cherokee villages and burning out their crops and winter stores. In 1761, a number of Cherokee chiefs led by Attakullakulla petitioned for peace.

With the Cherokee finally "pacified," new settlers—including the future parents of one-day president Andrew Jackson, born in 1767—flooded into the Upcountry through the Waxhaws in (now) Lancaster County. As in most frontier communities, lawlessness soon ensued. Robbery, arson, and looting became common.

Unfortunately, South Carolina's sole court of law held forth in Charles Town. Without any real formal law to protect them, Upcountry residents formed a group of "Regulators"—vigilantes—who took the law into their own hands.

Now home to more than 50% of the state's white population, the Upcountry sent representative Patrick Calhoun and others before the Charles Town state legislature to appeal for rep-

resentation, courts, roads, and provisions for churches and schools. Fortunately, fairer minds prevailed in Charles Town and before long, Calhoun and Moses Kirkland were sitting in the legislature as Upcountry representatives.

By 1775, the colony contained an estimated 60,000 European-Americans (fully one-half of whom lived in the Upcountry) and 80,000 African-Americans—nearly all working the rice and indigo plantations of the Lowcountry.

No other American colony enjoyed the amount of wealth now concentrated in the Lowcountry. Plantations generated over one million pounds annually, allowing planters to hire private tutors for their children and to send their sons to England for further education. It was these well-educated planters' sons—familiar with, but not unduly impressed by the subtleties of English law—who would eventually lead the charge for the colony's independence from the mother country.

Of course, if only a handful of elites had wanted revolution, the Revolution would never have taken place. But while the wealthy were essentially being raised to lead, the colony's constant battles with Indians, the French, and the Spanish were enhancing the average colonist's feelings of military competence and independence.

"DOWN WITH THE KING, UP WITH 'LIBERTY'": THE AMERICAN REVOLUTION IN SOUTH CAROLINA

Prerevolutionary Agitations

At first glance, most South Carolinians had little reason to want to go to war with England. As a British colony, South Carolina had prospered more than any other. However, the Lowcountry elites had ruled the colony for so long that when an impoverished Crown began taxing the American colonies to raise revenues, the rulers felt put upon. To protest the Stamp Act, South Carolina sent wealthy rice planter Thomas Lynch, 26-year-old lawyer John Rutledge, and Christopher Gadsden to the Stamp Act Congress, held in New York in 1765. Historians commonly group the hot-headed Gadsden—leader of Charles Town's pro-Independence "Liberty Boys" (akin to Boston's Sons of Liberty)—together with Massachusetts' James Otis and Patrick Henry as one

The famous "Don't Tread on Me" flag, whose snake features one rattle for each of the 13 colonies, was designed by South Carolina's hotheaded Christopher Gadsden, leader of Charles Town's pro-Independence "Liberty Boys."

of the three prime agitators for American independence. It's Gadsden who designed the famous "Don't Tread on Me" flag, first hoisted on John Paul "I Have Not Yet Begun to Fight" Jones' *Alfred* on December 3, 1775. The flag features a rattlesnake with 13 rattles, each representing an American colony.

When the 1767 Townsend Acts laid new taxes on glass, wine, oil, paper, tea, and other goods, Gadsden led the opposition. Even when the British removed the taxes from everything except tea, Charlestonians mirrored their Bostonian brethren by holding a tea party, dumping a shipment into the Cooper River. Other shipments, though allowed to land, were left to rot in Charles Town storehouses.

When delegates from the colonies (excepting Georgia, which refused to send any) came together for the First Continental Congress in 1774, five South Carolinians—including the three who had represented the colony in the Stamp Act Congress—headed for Philadelphia, and South Carolinian Henry Middleton served as president for part of the Congress. The following January, after being disbanded by Royal Governor William Campbell, the South Carolina colonial assembly reformed as the extralegal Provincial Congress. During this and subsequent meetings, in June 1775 and March 1776, the South Carolinians created a temporary government to rule until the colony ironed things out with England. Henry Laurens and, later, John Rutledge were voted "president" (de facto governor) of the state.

Unfortunately for the revolutionaries, not all South Carolinians believed it practical or even moral to separate from the British government. Many of these loyalists—or "Tories"—came from the Upcountry, where domination by the elitist Charles Town planter class in an unsupervised new government sounded worse than continued subservience to the British Crown. In order to win over converts to the "American Cause," Judge William Henry Drayton and the Reverend William Tennent were sent into the Back Country to evangelize for the Lowcountry's General Committee and Provincial Congress. They met with limited success.

In September 1775, the Royal Governor William Campbell dissolved what would be South Carolina's last-ever Royal Assembly, and, declaring, "I never will return to Charleston till I can support the King's authority, and protect his faithful and loyal subjects," was rowed out to the safety of the British warship *Tamar* in Charleston Harbor.

Violence Erupts

The popular conscious has so intertwined the American South with the Civil War that it's often forgotten that the Revolution was also fought down here. It's said that history is written by the victor, and in an odd way, the North's triumph in the Civil War long gave Northern academia—centered in Boston, the self-proclaimed "Athens of America"—the job of telling the whole American story. And in the Northern version, the Revolutionary battles fought in New England

and thereabouts are given all the emphasis. As a result, many people are surprised to find out that South Carolina was the site of any Revolutionary action at all. They're even more surprised when (and if) they learn that 137 significant Revolutionary battles were fought within South Carolina's borders—more than in any other state.

On November 19, 1775, revolutionists (or "Whigs") fought loyalist forces in the old western Cherokee lands at Ninety Six, spilling the first South Carolinian blood of the war. Colonel Richard Richardson rushed a large party of Whigs Upcountry to squelch the uprisings there and to assert the power of the revolutionary General Committee over the entire colony.

The "South First" Strategy, Part I

With war erupting in and around Boston, the British decided that their best strategy was to take advantage of the strong loyalist support in the Southern colonies, beginning a military drive from Charleston that might sweep through the Upcountry, then on through North Carolina and Virginia, gathering men along the way with whom to take on Washington in the North.

When the South Carolinians under William Moultrie brought the British Navy a stunning defeat at the battle of Sullivan's Island in late June 1776, they gave the American army its first major victory. When the news reached the Colonial delegates up in Philadelphia a few days later, it emboldened them to write up and sign a Declaration of Independence from England.

The Sullivan's Island debacle also caused the British to rethink their strategy—and they abandoned the South for nearly three years.

Other Events

The following December, the new state legislature met to complete the state constitution begun the previous October. It de-established the Anglican Church. Meanwhile, in the Upcountry, the British had persuaded the Cherokee to fight on their side. The British officer in charge of this operation ordered the Cherokee to attack only organized bodies of patriot soldiers, but the Cherokee employed a more holistic fighting style. Soon, murder and cabin burnings plagued the frontier. In response, Whigs Andrew Williamson, Andrew Pickens, and James Williams—who for years

had been battling the Tories in the Upcountry—launched a successful campaign against the Cherokee. In 1777, the Cherokee ceded their remaining lands in the region to the South Carolina government.

By 1780, the British were back on the Carolinians' doorstep, and the loyalists and patriots fought the state's first civil war.

The "South First" Strategy, Part II

By 1780, the British had seen enough success up north to attempt the 1776 south-to-north strategy a second time. With George Washington's troops now mired down in the North, the idea was to sandwich them by pushing troops up from the South while Washington tried to defend himself to the North.

British troops moved up from St. Augustine, Florida, landing on John's Island, from where they moved across to James Island and attacked Charles Town. After a two-month siege, General Benjamin Lincoln (who had foolishly allowed his army to get bottled up on the peninsula) was forced to surrender his men—practically every Continental soldier in the Carolinas—to British General Henry Clinton. An army of Continentals under General Gates marched into the state to try to reclaim it for the patriots, but it suffered a devastating defeat at Camden.

This was the low point for the Carolinian revolutionaries. The fence-sitting Carolinians who had finally been persuaded to take the independent government seriously now rubbed their eyes and once again proclaimed allegiance to the King. Even Henry Middleton, one-time president of the First Continental Congress, was forced as a prisoner at Charles Town to take an oath of allegiance to the Crown.

On June 4, 1780, General Clinton gloated,

With the greatest pleasure I further report . . . that the inhabitants form every quarter reparit to the detachments of the army, and to this garrison (Charles-town) to declare their allegiance to the King, and to offer their services in arms for the support of the Government. In many instances they have brought in as prisoners their former oppressors or leaders, and I may venture to assert, that there are few men in South Carolina who are not either our prisoners or in arms with us.

Unfortunately for Clinton, South Carolina President John Rutledge was one of the "few men" still on the loose. Lincoln had begged Rutledge and the rest of the state's council to leave Charles Town while there was still time, and they had. Now Rutledge moved to and fro about the state, encouraging the patriots, printing up proclamations and other state papers on a printing press he'd taken with him, and sending letter after letter demanding that the Continental Congress send the Continental Army for the relief of South Carolina.

Clinton's understanding of South Carolina was that it was an essentially loyalist colony that had been bullied into Revolutionary actions by a small minority of rabble-rousers. Certainly, this was the way the loyalists had presented things. Consequently, Clinton's idea was to increase the British presence over the entire state and win back the confidence of the moderates so that they too would want to fight for the British in the long-planned northern push.

Clinton's idea of turning the Southern militia into loyalists willing to shoot their former comrades might have been a bit dubious, but Clinton's public relation skills were even more so. Rather than spending money on extra arms and soldiers, the British would have been wise now to simply hire a few spin doctors. Instead, Clinton and his men proceeded to do everything they could to turn the Carolinians against them.

How to Lose Friends and Alienate People

The first thing that made erstwhile loyalists blink was Clinton's sending Lieutenant Colonel Banastre Tarleton after Colonel Buford and his body of Virginia patriots. Buford had raced south with the intention of defending Charles Town, but turned back when he realized that they had arrived too late. However, Tarleton was unwilling to let the rebels escape back to the North and gave chase. He caught up with them on May 29, near the present town of Lancaster. The Americans were told to surrender but refused. Soon, they found themselves attacked furiously by the British. Realizing quickly that they had no chance of victory or escape, the Americans finally threw down their arms and begged for quarter, but the British ignored their pleas, butchering the unarmed Americans. Of 350 rebels, only 30 escaped capture, wounding, or death. For the rest of the war, Southern patriots would charge at

their British enemies to the cry of "Tarleton's quarter!"—i.e., "Take no prisoners!"

The second major British blunder was Clinton's revocation of the Carolinians' paroles. To gain leverage in the battle for the hearts and minds of the Carolinians, he reneged on the paroles of Carolinians who had surrendered with the understanding that if they did not actively seek to harass the British government, the British would leave them alone. Clinton's June 3 proclamation notified all prisoners of war that they might have to choose between taking arms up against their fellow Americans or being considered traitors to the Crown. This understandably rankled many of the militiamen, whose pride was already bruised by defeat. Many of them reasoned that if they were going to have to take the chance of getting shot again, they might as well fight for the side they wanted to win.

The third mistake the British made was in harassing the invalid wife and burning the Stateburg home of a rather inconsequential colonel named Thomas Sumter. In his fury at this outrage, "The Gamecock" became one of the fiercest and most devastating guerrilla leaders of the war.

Other Carolinian Whigs took matters into their own hands as well. The Lowcountry partisans fighting under Francis "The Swamp Fox" Marion and the Upcountry partisans fighting under Andrew Pickens (whose home had also been burned) plagued British troops with guerrilla warfare in the swamps, woods, and mountains of the state.

The Tide Turns in the Upcountry

At Kings Mountain on October 7, 1780, British Major Patrick Ferguson and his body of American loyalists were attacked on a hilltop by a body of North and South Carolinians under Pickens. This major victory for the patriots—particularly since it was won by militiamen and not trained Continentals—provided a great swing of momentum for the fence-sitting Uplanders who had grown tired of British brutality. Because of this, it is considered by some to be the turning point of the Revolution—especially since it forced General Cornwallis to split his troops, sending Lieutenant Colonel Banastre "No Quarter" Tarleton into the South Carolina Upcountry to win the area back for the British. This division of his forces made it impossible for Cornwallis to move on his plan for a major push north, since that plan required a loyalist body of troops to stay behind and keep the peace in the Carolinas.

Finally, that December, General Nathanael Greene arrived with an army of Continental troops. Once Greene heard of Tarleton's approach, he sent General Daniel Morgan and his backwoodsmen thundering over the Appalachians to stop him. On January 17, 1781, at a natural enclosure used as a cow pen, the two forces met.

Pickens and his guerrillas joined up with Morgan just before the battle. Morgan felt they were still too weak to take on Tarleton's trained troops and, in order to secure a chance of retreat, wanted to cross a river that would have separated them from the British. Pickens convinced him to stay on the British side of the river, so that they'd have to fight it out. And fight they did, in what some military historians consider the best-planned battle of the entire war. The patriots devastated the redcoats, and later victories at Hobkirk's Hill and Eutaw Springs further weakened the Brits. In December of 1782, the British evacuated Charles Town. Shortly thereafter, jubilant residents changed the name to "Charleston," merely because to their ears it sounded somehow "less British."

One historian notes that some 137 battles, actions, and engagements between the British/Tories/Indians and the American patriots in South Carolina were fought by South Carolinians *alone*. Despite the version presented in U.S. history textbooks, no other state endured as much bloodshed, sacrifice, and suffering during the Revolution as South Carolina.

Writing the United States Constitution

In all of those famous paintings of the Founding Fathers, South Carolinians make up a lot of the faces you see behind Washington, Jefferson, Franklin, and the other big names. In 1787, John Rutledge, Charles Pinckney, Charles Cotesworth Pinckney, and Pierce Butler headed up to Philadelphia, where the Constitutional convention was cobbling together the Constitution. Just 30 years old, Charles Pinckney had long been a critic of the weak Articles of Confederation. Though wealthy by birth and quite the epicurean, Pinckney became the leader of democracy in the state; he was even considered something of a turncoat to his fellow elites. On May 29, 1787, he presented the Convention with a detailed outline that ended up as perhaps the primary template for the U.S. Constitution. John Rutledge also gave valuable input. Ominously, Pierce Butler's sole contribution was the clause for the return of fugitive slaves.

This federal (and Federalist-leaning) Constitution was ratified by the state in 1787, as was the new state constitution in 1790, without the support of the Upcountry. Lowcountry elite—controlling three-quarters of the South Carolina's wealth—still ruled the state, even though the region boasted only a quarter of the state's white inhabitants.

EARLY ANTEBELLUM OLD SOUTH (1790-1827)

In 1786, the Lowcountry rulers (or enough of them, anyway) agreed that to ease the tensions between Upcountry residents and Lowcountry denizens, it made sense to move the state capital from Charleston to a more convenient spot for everyone concerned. With the capital in Charleston, Upcountry citizens had had to travel two days to reach government offices and courts.

The town of Columbia (the first city in America to take that name) was planned and erected. In 1790, the state's politicians moved in, and nobody's been able to dislodge them since. Some state offices remained in Charleston until 1865: the Lowcountry and Upcountry even had separate treasury offices, with separate treasurers.

In 1800, the Santee Canal, connecting the Santee and Cooper Rivers, was completed, making it possible to transport people and goods directly from the new capital to Charleston. In 1801, Columbia's South Carolina College (now the University of South Carolina) was chartered.

It was after the 1793 invention of the cotton gin, however, that a different series of events caused the Upcountry and Lowcountry to see eye to eye. Though the Lowcountry had grown long staple cotton, the short staple cotton supportable by Upcountry soils took too much time to separate by hand. Eli Whitney's invention of the gin (in Georgia, just over the state line) changed all that. Now short staple cotton couldn't be grown quickly enough.

THE SPEECH OF SPECKLED SNAKE

Published in the Savannah *Mercury* in 1829, the following article is rumored to have been written by John Ridge, a young Cherokee named Speckled Snake who had been educated in Connecticut, in protest of Andrew Jackson's proposed moving of the Creeks, Cherokees, and other tribes to the Indian Territory west of the Mississippi. Ten years later, the great removal was completed along the "Trail of Tears." In a grim irony, shortly after the removal Ridge was assassinated by Cherokees for his role in the treaties that gave away their lands.

BROTHERS! We have heard the talk of our great father; it is very kind, he says he loves his red children.

BROTHERS! I have listened to many talks from our great father. When he first came over the wide waters, he was but a little man, and wore a red coat.—Our chiefs met him on the banks of the river Savannah, and smoked with him the pipe of peace. He was then very little. His legs were cramped by sitting long in his big boat, and he begged for a little land to light his fire on. He said he had come over the wide waters to teach Indians new things, and to make them happy. He said he loved his red brothers; he was very kind.

The Muscogees gave the white man land, and kindled him a fire, that he might warm himself; and when his enemies, the pale faces of the south, made war on him, their young men drew the tomahawk, and protected his head from the scalping knife. But when the white man had warmed himself before the Indian's fire, and filled himself with their hominy, he became very large. With a step he bestrode the mountains, and his feet covered the plains and the valleys, and his head rested on the moon. Then he became our Great Father. He loved his red children, and he said, "Get a little further, lest I tread on thee." With one foot he pushed the red man over the Oconee, and with the other he trampled down the graves of his fathers, and the forests where he had so long hunted the deer.—But our Great Father still loved his red children, and he soon made them another talk. He said, "Get a little

further; you are too near me." But there were now some bad men among the Muscogees then, as there are now. They lingered around the graves of their ancestors, till they were crushed beneath the heavy tread of our Great Father. Their teeth pierced his feet, and made him angry. Yet he continued to love his red children; and when he found them too slow in moving, he sent his great guns before him to sweep his path.

BROTHERS! I have listened to a great many talks from our great father. But they have always began and ended in this—"Get a little further; you are too near me."

BROTHERS! Our great father says that "where we now are, our white brothers have always claimed the land." He speaks with a strait tongue, and cannot lie. But when he first came over the wide waters, while he was yet small, and stood before the great chief at the council on Yamacraw Bluff, he said— "Give me a little land, which you can spare, and I will pay you for it."

BROTHERS! When our great father made us a talk, on a former occasion, and said, "Get a little further; go beyond the Oconee, the Ocmulgee; there is a pleasant country," he also said, "It shall be yours forever." I have listened to his present talk. HE says the land where you now live is not yours. Go beyond the Mississippi; there is game; and you may remain while the grass grows or the water runs. BROTHERS! Will not our great father come there also? He loves his red children. He speaks with a strait tongue, and will not lie.

BROTHERS! Our great father says that our bad men have made his heart bleed, for the murder of one of his white children. Yet where are the red children which he loves, once as numerous as the leaves of the forest? How many have been murdered by his warriors? How many have been crushed beneath his own footsteps?

BROTHERS! Our great father says we must go beyond the Mississippi. We shall there be under his care, and experience his kindness. He is very good! We have felt it all before.

BROTHERS! I have done.

For the first time, Upcountry landowners had the chance to escape subsistence-level farming and make their fortunes. Unfortunately, cotton plantations required great numbers of workers, so Upcountry planters began importing large numbers of African and African-American men and women as slaves. Now with its own wealthy planter class, and with a common interest in protecting the institution of slavery against Northern "do-gooders," the Upcountry began to work alongside the Lowcountry more than it had before. Nonetheless, slaveholding in the Upcountry never reached anything like the level in the Lowcountry. (And since it received three-fifths of a vote for each slave, the Lowcountry still managed to politically dominate the state.)

Resentment of the North

In 1811, British ships plundered American ships, inspiring South Carolina's outraged "War Hawk" representatives to push Congress into declaring the War of 1812. During the war, tariffs on exported goods were raised to support America's military efforts, but afterward Northern lawmakers continued to vote for higher and higher levies on exports and imports. These surcharges mainly punished the South for selling its goods in Europe instead of in the North. Not surprisingly, laws also forced the South to buy its manufactured goods from the North.

Concluding that they were at the hot end of the poker, many South Carolinians began to talk of seceding from the union to operate as an independent state with trade laws tailored to its own best interests. Even South Carolina–born vice president John C. Calhoun, who had begun as a Federalist favoring a strong centralized government, began to doubt the wisdom of this vision as he saw the rights of his home state trampled for the "good" of the more powerful North. However, he also saw the political dangers in dissolving South Carolina's union with the other states.

The Nullification Crisis

In 1828, Calhoun decided upon the doctrine he would espouse for the rest of his life—the primacy of "states' rights." He believed that constitutionally, the state government of each state had more power within that state than the federal government. Consequently, if a state deemed it necessary, it had the right to "nullify" any federal law within its state boundaries.

To most Carolinians, this sounded like a sensible compromise. Some in the state, however—such as Joel R. Poinsett (for whom, coincidentally, the poinsettia and Poinsett State Park are named), novelist William Gilmore Simms, and James L. Petigru—believed that while a

> *Their lives are not worth the powder that will blow them out of existence. . . . Their slaveholding Sodom will perish for the lack of five just men, or a single just idea. It must be razed and got out of the way, like any other obstacle to the progress of humanity.*
>
> — New Englander John William Deforest, Miss Ravenel's Conversion from Secession to Loyalty, *1867 (written while Deforest was a Union officer working for the Reconstruction-era Freedmen's Bureau in South Carolina)*

state had the full right to secede from the Union if it chose, it had no right, as long as it remained a part of the Union, to nullify a federal law (this same theory has been codified by millions of parents of teenagers as the "As Long as You're Sleeping Under My Roof" Law).

Not surprisingly, the federal government saw the whole idea of nullification as an attack upon its powers, and when, in 1832, South Carolina's houses quickly "nullified" the hated federally mandated tariffs, President Andrew Jackson (ironically, South Carolina's only native-born president) declared this an act of rebellion and ordered U.S. warships to South Carolina to enforce the law.

In December 1832, Calhoun resigned as Jackson's vice president (making him the only vice president to resign until Spiro Agnew, some 150 years later) so that he could become a senator and stop South Carolina's destructive run toward secession, while solving the problems that had so inflamed his fellow Carolinians.

Fortunately, before federal forces arrived at Charleston, Calhoun and Henry Clay agreed upon a compromise tariff that would lower rates over 10 years. The passage of this tariff pacified everyone just enough to prevent immediate armed conflict. But the debate between the relative importance of states' rights versus federal power became a dividing line between the North—whose majority position gave it power over federal decisions—and the South—which, because it featured a different economy and social structure from the North, knew that it would rarely be in the majority opinion on a federal vote.

The Abolitionist Movement and Southern Response

By this time, the fact that most of the slaves in the Northern states had been freed made it much easier for Northerners to be intolerant toward the sins of their Southern neighbors. Most Abolitionists were Christians who saw the protection of African-Americans—along with any other unfortunates—as a God-given responsibility. Southern slaveholders generally saw their opponents as dangerous, self-righteous meddlers who would be better off tending to their own sins than passing judgment on the choices of others. Pro-slavery apologists argued that Northerners had no place in the debate over the morality of slavery, because they could not own slaves and would therefore not suffer the societal impacts that manumission would mean to the South.

The crux of the debate lay in the question of the extent of the humanity of slaves. Slaveholders contented themselves that Africans, while admittedly sharing many traits of human beings, were somehow less than fully human, which made the slaves' own views about their enslavement unworthy of consideration. Many believed that blacks were on their *way* to becoming "elevated" as a race but needed close interaction with whites (even at gunpoint) to help them along. Hence, Columbia-area plantation mistress Keziah Goodwyn Hopkins Brevard could, on the brink of the War between the States, write, "Those who have come & have had kind masters have been blest—had they been left to this day on Afric's sands there would have been one trouble after another for them—it is only in favoured spots *now* that they are safe from war & slavery in their own country."

The effect of bloody slave rebellions, such as the Vesey revolt of 1822 and John Brown's massacre at Harper's Ferry in 1859, embarrassed more moderate abolitionists into silence—particularly in the South—and pro-slavery Southerners perceived these isolated incidents as indicative of the "true" ends and means of all abolitionists, inflaming and galvanizing Southerners into a reactionary anti-abolitionist stance that effectively ended reasoned debate on the issue. To most abolitionists, the question was one of man's duty to respect other human beings as children of God; to many Southerners, it was a question of defending a state's right to determine what was best for its own people.

Brevard wrote in her journal, "cut throat Abolitionists—I will not call them neighbours—not [sic] they are the selfish & envious . . . not a grain of Christ's charity in their whole body."

The Cult of Slavery: Slavery as Intrinsically Good

South Carolinians had earlier tolerated slavery more or less as a necessary evil. But largely in reaction to the continual sparring with abolitionists, in the last decades before the Civil War many people in South Carolina reached a new height of sophistry, proclaiming slavery a positive good—a benefit to the enslaved, and a proper response to the "natural" differences between whites and blacks. Apologists such as Thomas Harper argued that the wage-employee system of the North was irresponsible—and more exploitive than slavery itself. The Southern slaveholder, after all, paid room and board for a slave even when the slave was too young, too sick, or too old to work. Meanwhile, the Northern capitalist paid his wage earners only for the hours they worked; when they were sick, or when they got too old, or when a new technology came

> *Master had three kinds of punishment for those who disobeyed him. One was the sweat box. That was made the height of the person and no larger. Just large enough so the person didn't have to be squeezed in. The box is nailed, and in summer is put in the hot sun; in winter it is put in the coldest, dampest place. The next is the stock. Wood is nailed on or with the person lying on his back with hands and feet tied with a heavy weight on chest. The third is the Bilbao [or bilbo: foot shackles]. You are placed on a high scaffold for so many hours, and you don't try to keep a level head, you'll fall and you will surely hurt yourself, if your neck isn't broken. Most of the time they were put there so they could break their necks.*
>
> *—Prince Smith,*
> *Wadmalaw Island, WPA interview*

along that they were not trained for, the wage payer could fire the employees, and his responsibility for their welfare was considered finished. (Some historians argue that the average slave was actually paid 90% of his or her life's earnings by the time of death.) Virginian George Fitzhugh, in such 1850s titles as *Sociology for the South* and *Cannibals All!,* argued that slavery, being a humane and efficient system, was destined to regain its popularity throughout the world.

> *These people were educated at Northern schools mostly—read the same books as their Northern contemners, the same daily newspapers, the same Bible—have the same ideas of right and wrong—are highbred, lovely, good, pious, doing their duty as they conceive it. They strive to ameliorate the condition of these Africans in every particular. I say we are no better than our judges North— and no worse. We are human beings of the nineteenth century.*
>
> *—Mary Boykin Chesnut, on slaveholders, November 27, 1861*

So avid had this defense of the indefensible become that by 1856, Governor James Hopkins Adams was recommending a resumption of the Foreign Slave Trade. And a powerful minority of slaveholders always looking for ways to get the rest of the state behind them had begun arguing that every white man should be legally required to become the owner of at least one slave—a measure that would give every male citizen an interest in the issue as well as instilling the sense of responsibility that they believed owning slaves engendered in a man.

Even the Charleston *Mercury,* though, which had long agitated for secession, denounced the return to the slave trade as cruel and divisive. Nonetheless, in 1858 and 1859, a number of newly captured slaves were imported into the state at Charleston—in violation of federal law.

Free Blacks and the Vesey Plot
Since colonial times, South Carolina had always been home to a sizable population of free blacks, many of them descended from mulattoes freed by their white father/owners. Others had been freed because of faithful service or by buying themselves free with portions of their earnings

> *If ever [the slaves'] emancipation be effected, it must be through the Divine agency of the light of reason, not by the sword, bloodshed, and rapine.*
>
> *—Camden, New Jersey, Star, 1822, after exposure of the Vesey conspiracy*

they had been allowed to keep. As long as there had been free blacks, free blacks had made the white population nervous.

In 1822, after free black craftsman and preacher Denmark Vesey was convicted and hanged for having masterminded a plan to overthrow Charlestonian whites by slaves and free blacks, whites established curfews and forbade assembly of large numbers of African-Americans. Forbidden, too, was the education of slaves, though this seems to have been widely flouted.

Since the mere presence of free blacks was seen as dangerous, South Carolina leaders also made it illegal for slaveholders to free their slaves without a special decree from the state legislature.

Like Denmark Vesey, many of South Carolina's free blacks lived in Charleston, where their own subculture—with its own caste system— had developed. Charleston free blacks performed over 50 different occupations, some as artisans. Some African-Americans, such as Sumter cotton-gin maker William Ellison, amassed great fortunes—and did so in the same fashion that most wealthy whites did: through the labor of black slaves. In fact, historian Richard Rollins estimates that a full 25% of all free Southern blacks legally owned slaves. Some were family members purchased by free blacks, but most were purchased to act as the owners' servants or workers. Opinions vary as to whether slaves could normally expect better treatment from a black owner than from a white one. Some free blacks, wanting to demonstrate their fitness to join "white" society, probably felt a special pressure to exert their authority over their slaves. Doubtless, the relative happiness of a slave owned by an African-American was dependent upon the character of the individual owner.

The Mexican War (1846)
The war with Mexico affected South Carolina considerably. For South Carolinians, what was at

stake was the acquisition of additional lands open to slavery—and hence more representation in the U.S. Congress by slaveholding states. Under Pierce M. Butler, J.P. Dickinson, and A.H. Gladden, the Palmetto Regiment's palmetto flag entered Mexico City before any other flag. South Carolina's fighting prowess was once again proven in battle, but, largely due to disease, of 1,100 South Carolinian volunteers who fought in the war only 300 returned alive.

Even with its much smaller population, the South as a whole, in fact, sent and suffered the loss of more soldiers, furnishing 43,232 men in the Mexican War while the North, whose pundits had disapproved of the effort, sent along only 22,136 troops. Hence, the Wilmot Proviso, a proposal by a Pennsylvanian legislator to ban slavery within all territory acquired as a result of the Mexican War, struck South Carolinians as extremely unjust: Southerners who had risked their lives to win over the New Southwest were now being told they could not expect to bring their "property" with them if they settled there. John C. Calhoun attempted to rally the rest of the slaveholding states to oppose Wilmot's plan as yet another effort to tighten the noose around slavery's neck. The Southern-led Senate blocked the bill.

But the question of how to handle the issue of slavery in the new and future acquisitions of an expanding nation was now out in the open. The issues raised by the acquisition of the American West in the Mexican War made plain to Northerners and Southerners their different visions of America's future, and hence accelerated the nation's tailspin toward civil war. In the North, many of those willing to tolerate the cancer of slavery in those states who already practiced it could not with good conscience watch it spread to new lands beneath the shadow of the Stars and Stripes. The South, which had held a hope that territorial expansion and the spread of slavery might allow the South to ascend again to equality or even dominance in national politics, finally had to confront the fact that the North would never willingly allow this to happen. As long as the South remained in the Union, it would always be the oppressed agricultural (and, hence, to Southern perceptions, slaveholding) region, its interests continually overlooked for the interests of the industrialized North.

> *Raids, reprisals, and abductions marked the Revolution in the South, one of the most vicious partisan wars ever waged.*
> —Kent Britt, National Geographic, *April 1975*

South Carolinians had been telling the rest of the South this since the Nullification Crisis 20 years before.

Eruption of Secessionism and the Descent into War

Few South Carolina whites saw general emancipation as an option. If blacks—the vast numerical majority in most parts of the state—were freed, whites feared the "Africanization" of their cherished society and culture, as they had seen happen after slave revolutions in some areas of the West Indies.

Carolinian leaders had long divided up between devoted Unionists, who opposed any sort of secession, and those who believed that secession was a state's right. Calhoun proposed that Congress could not exclude slavery from the territories and that a territory, when it became a state, should be allowed to choose which type of economy it wanted—free labor or slave. But after Calhoun's death, in 1850, South Carolina was left without a leader great enough, both in character and in national standing, to stave off the more militant Carolinian factions' desire to secede immediately.

"THE WAR FOR SOUTHERN INDEPENDENCE"

In 1850 and 1851 South Carolina nearly seceded from the Union all by its lonesome. Andrew Pickens Butler, considered by historian Nathaniel Stephenson "perhaps the ablest South Carolinian then living," argued against fiery Charleston publisher Robert Barnwell Rhett, who advocated immediate and, if necessary, independent secession. Butler won that battle, but Rhett outlived him. By 1860, no strong personality in South Carolina was Rhett's equal.

Several historians argue that South Carolina's "states' rights" demand to be recognized

ARMS-BEARING POPULATION KILLED IN THE AMERICAN WAR OF 1861-65

Northern states	5%
Southern states	10%
South Carolina	23%

as an independent, autonomous entity was not simply a rationalization for slavery but rather a protest integral to its nature and understanding of itself. As Stephenson wrote:

In South Carolina all things conspired to uphold and strengthen the sense of the State as an object of veneration, as something over and above the mere social order, as the sacred embodiment of the ideals of the community. Thus it is fair to say that what has animated the heroic little countries of the Old World—Switzerland and Serbia and everglorious Belgium—with their passion to remain themselves, animated South Carolina in 1861. Just as Serbia was willing to fight to the death rather than merge her identity in the mosaic of the Austrian Empire, so this little American community saw nothing of happiness in any future that did not secure its virtual independence.

When Lincoln was elected, a number of conventions around the Deep South organized to discuss their options. South Carolina's assembly met first, at Columbia on December 17, 1860. States with strong pro-secession movements like Alabama and Mississippi sent delegates to the convention, where they advised the Carolinians to "take the lead and secede at once."

The Truth is the whole army is burning with an insatiable desire to wreak vengeance upon South Carolina. I almost tremble at her fate, but feel that she deserves all that is in store for her.

—Gen. William T. Sherman, December 24, 1864, writing to another Union general

Thus it was that on December 20, 1860, South Carolinians in Charleston (where the convention had moved following an outbreak of smallpox in Columbia) voted to secede from the Union. The hot-blooded delegate from Edisto Island declared that if South Carolina didn't secede, Edisto Island would secede all by itself.

Six days later, on the day after Christmas, Major Robert Anderson, commander of the U.S. garrisons in Charleston, withdrew his men against orders into the island fortress of Fort Sumter, in the midst of Charleston Harbor. South Carolina militia swarmed over the abandoned mainland batteries and trained their guns on the island. Sumter was the key position to preventing a sea invasion of Charleston, so Carolina could not afford to allow the Federals to remain there indefinitely. Rumors spread that Yankee forces were on their way down to seize the port city, making the locals even itchier to get their own troops behind Sumter's guns.

Meanwhile, the secessionists' plan worked. Mississippi seceded only a few weeks after South Carolina, and the rest of the lower South followed. On February 4, a congress of southern states met in Montgomery, Alabama, and approved a new constitution—which, among other things, prohibited the African slave trade.

So excited was Florence-born bard Henry Timrod that he was moved to write what many consider his greatest poem, "Ethnogenesis," in honor of the convention, which includes the hopeful lines:

HATH not the morning dawned with added light?
And shall not evening call another star
Out of the infinite regions of the night,
To mark this day in Heaven? At last, we are
A nation among nations; and thee world
Shall soon behold in many a distant port
Another flag unfurled!

Unfortunately for Timrod, Lincoln argued that the United States were "one nation, *indivisible,*" and denied the Southern states' right to secede. It looked as if a war were imminent. Upper Southern states such as Virginia and North Carolina—which had not yet seceded—called a peace conference. This came and went without making a dent against the accumulated bitterness on both sides of the Mason-Dixon line.

Anticipating the battles to come, Timrod wrote:

We shall not shrink, my brothers, but go forth
To meet them, marshalled by the Lord of
* Hosts,*
And overshadowed by the mighty ghosts
Of Moultrie and of Eutaw—who shall foil
Auxiliars such as these?

When, on January 9, 1861, the U.S. ship *Star of the West* approached to reprovision the soldiers in the fort, two Citadel cadets fired what was arguably the first shot of the War between the States in Charleston Harbor—a cannon shot meant to warn the vessel off. One of the ship's officers quipped, "The people of Charleston pride themselves on their hospitality. They gave us several balls before we landed."

Then, for the rest of the month, nothing happened. Finally, Virginian orator Roger Pryor barreled into Charleston, proclaiming that the only way to get Old Dominion to join the Confederacy—and thus bring along the other border states—was for South Carolina to instigate war with the United States. The obvious place to start was right in the midst of Charleston Harbor.

On April 10, the *Mercury* reprinted stories from New York papers that told of a naval expedition that had been sent southward toward Charleston. The Carolinians could wait no longer if they hoped to take the fort without having to take on the U.S. Navy at the same time. Some 6,000 men were now stationed around the rim of the harbor, ready to take on the 60 men in Fort Sumter. At 4:30 a.m. on April 12, after days of intense negotiations, and with Union ships just outside the harbor, the firing began. Thirty-four hours later, Anderson's men raised the white flag and were allowed to leave the fort with colors flying and drums beating, saluting the U.S. flag with a 50-gun salute before taking it down. During this salute, one of the guns exploded, killing a young soldier—the only casualty of the bombardment and the first casualty of the war.

Again, South Carolina's instigation persuaded others to join the Confederacy: Virginia, North Carolina, Arkansas, and Tennessee—now cer-

tain that Lincoln meant to use force to keep their fellow Southern states under federal rule—seceded, one by one.

Even so, the outgunned, outmanned, and virtually Navy-less South had no chance against the North. Federal ships sailed south, sealing off one important port after another. As early as November, Union troops occupied the Sea Islands in the Beaufort area, establishing an important base for the ships and men who would stymie the ports at Charleston and Savannah. When the plantation owners—many of them already off with the Confederate Army elsewhere—fled the area, the Sea Island slaves became the first "freedmen" of the war, and the Sea Islands became the laboratory for Northern plans to educate the African-Americans for their eventual role as full American citizens.

Despite Carolina's important role in the start of the war, and a long, unsuccessful attempt by Federals to take Charleston from 1863 onward, few military engagements occurred within the state's borders until 1865, when Sherman's Army, having already completed its infamous March to the Sea in Savannah, marched north to Columbia and leveled most of the town, as well as a number of towns along the way and afterward.

South Carolina lost 12,922 men to the war—23% of its white male population of fighting age, and the highest percentage of any state in the nation. Sherman's 1865 march through the Carolinas resulted in the burning of Columbia and numerous other towns. Poverty would mark the state for generations to come.

On February 21, 1865, with the Confederate forces finally evacuated from Charleston, the black 55th Massachusetts Regiment marched through the city. To most of the white citizens—those few who hadn't fled—this must have looked like Armageddon. To the African-Americans of the city, however, it was the Day of Jubilee. As one of the regiment's colonels recalled:

Men and women crowded to shake hands
with men and officers. . . . On through the
streets of the rebel city passed the column,
on through the chief seat of that slave power,
tottering to fall. Its walls rung to the chorus of
manly voices singing "John Brown," "Babylon
is Falling," and the "Battle-Cry of Freedom."

It's hard to conceive of how unbelievable Emancipation must have seemed for these men and women people born into slavery.

At a ceremony at which the U.S. flag was once again raised over Fort Sumter, former fort commander Robert Anderson was joined on the platform by two men: African-American Union hero Robert Smalls and the son of Denmark Vesey.

RECONSTRUCTION

Though they had long made up the majority of the state's population, African-Americans played a prominent role in South Carolina government for the first time when federal troops occupied the state from 1866 to 1877. Despite the anti-Northern fury of their prewar and wartime politics, most Carolinians—including South Carolina's opinion maker, Wade Hampton III, believed that white Carolinians would do well to accept President Andrew Johnson's terms for re-entry to full participation in the Union. However, when the powerful "radical" anti-Southern Congress seized control of the Reconstruction process, things got harder for white Carolinians. The idea of these Republicans was to establish a solidly Republican South by convincing blacks to vote Republican and then keeping former Confederates from voting for as long as possible.

The federally mandated new Constitution of 1868 brought democratic reforms, but by now most whites viewed the Republican government as representative of black interests only and were largely unsupportive. Laws forbidding former Confederates (virtually the entire native-white male population) from bearing arms only exacerbated the tensions, especially as rifle-bearing black militia units began drilling in the streets of Carolina towns.

THE RED SHIRTS' *PLAN FOR THE CAMPAIGN OF 1876*

The Red Shirts were founded by General Martin W. Gary of Edgefield, who distributed his *Plan for the Campaign of 1876* to various counties around the state. The plan featured a number of fairly predictable political tactics—encouraging Democrats to get weak or incapacitated Democrats to the ballot box and to prevent nonvalid Republican voters from voting and valid ones from voting more than once, but it also included the following:

12. Every Democrat must feel honor bound to control the vote of at least one negro, by intimidation, purchase, keeping him away or as each individual may determine, [sic] how he may best accomplish it.

13. We must attend every Radical meeting that we hear of. . . . Democrats must go in as large numbers as they can get together, and well armed, behave at *first* with great courtesy and assure the ignorant negroes that you mean them no harm and so soon as their *leaders* or speakers begin to speak and make false statements of facts, tell them *then* and *there* to their faces that they are liars, thieves and rascals and are only trying to mislead the ignorant negroes and if you get a chance get upon the platform and address the negroes.

14. In speeches to negroes you must remember that argument has no effect upon them: they can only be influenced by their *fears,* superstition and cupidity. . . . Treat them so as to show them, you are the superior race, and that their natural position is that of subordination to the white man.

and, finally, ominously:

15. Let it be generally known that if any blood is shed, houses burnt, votes repeated, ballot boxes stuffed, false counting of votes, or any acts on their part that are in violation of Law and Order! that we will hold the leaders of the Radical Party personally responsible, whether they were present at the time of the commission of the offense or crime or not; beginning first with the white men, second the mulatto men and third with the black leaders. . . .

The draft Gary gave to his secretary contained several items he had reconsidered and marked "omit," including number 16: "Never threaten a man individually if he deserves to be threatened. The necessities of the times require that he should die."

Added to the brewing interracial animosity was many whites' sense that their former slaves had betrayed them. Before the war, most slaveholders had convinced themselves that they were treating their slaves well and had thus earned their slaves' loyalty. Understandably, most slaves had been happy to give their masters the impression that they were, indeed, devoted to the household. Hence, when the Union Army rolled in and slaves deserted by the thousands (though many did not), slaveholders took it as a personal affront.

And thus went Reconstruction: the black population scrambled to enjoy and preserve its new rights while the white population attempted to claw its way back to the top of the social ladder by denying blacks those same rights.

Perhaps predictably, Ku Klux Klan raids began shortly thereafter, terrorizing blacks and black sympathizers in an attempt to reestablish white supremacy. Most of the state's "better element" showed little tolerance for such violence—especially when undertaken anonymously—and largely squelched the movement locally after a few years. In 1876, Piedmont towns were the site of numerous demonstrations by the Red Shirts—white Democrats determined to win the upcoming elections through any means possible. Named for their trademark red shirts (worn to mock the histrionic "waving of the bloody shirt" of the radical Republicans), the Red Shirts turned the tide in South Carolina, convincing whites that, after 11 years of military rule, this could indeed be the year they could regain control. Before the election, concerned Republican Governor Chamberlain asked Washington for assistance and was sent 1,100 federal troops by President Ulysses S. Grant to keep order and ensure a "fair" election.

Even so, the hard-fought and bitter political campaign of 1876 ended in a deadlock, as Hampton won the official vote but Chamberlain and his followers claimed—accurately, the record seems to show—that the Democrats' "victory" was the result of massive voter fraud and coercion by the Red Shirts. In Edgefield and Laurens Counties, for instance, Hampton and other Democratic candidates received more votes than the total number of registered voters in both parties.

Both parties claimed victory, and for a while, two separate state assemblies did business side by side on the floor of the state house (their Speakers shared the Speaker's desk, but each had his own gavel) until the Democrats moved to another building, where they continued to pass resolutions and hold forth with the state's business, just as the Republicans were doing. The Republican State Assembly tossed out the results of the tainted election and re-elected Chamberlain governor. A week later, General Wade Hampton III took the oath of office for the Democrats. Finally, after months of this nonsense—not to mention a couple of near shoot-outs—in April 1877, President Rutherford B. Hayes—in return for the South's support in his own convoluted presidential "victory" over Samuel Tilden—withdrew federal troops from Columbia, at which point the Republican government dissolved, and Governor Chamberlain headed back north.

The white elites were back in charge of South Carolina, in the person of General Wade Hampton III. Hampton's election marked the establishment of a 99-year hold on the State House by the Democrats—the next Republican governor of South Carolina was James Burrows Edwards, in 1975. The normal American two-party system was thrown off balance because the Democratic Party, in those years, was the "white" party in South Carolina, and whites successfully kept blacks away from the ballot boxes through various Jim Crow laws.

But this by no means resulted in unanimity amongst South Carolina's fiery electorate. Hampton and other wealthy former Confederate officers—known as "Bourbons"—ruled the state, but the farmers of the Upcountry were in no mood to return to the aristocratic leadership that had led them into destruction. Finally, at the

> *The Negro in the country districts must be made to understand what he has already been taught in the city, that freedom does not mean idleness. On the other hand, the late master should specially be made to understand that the spirit of slavery must go to the grave with the thing itself. It will not be an easy work to teach either class its chief lesson. We must have patience.*
>
> *—New Yorker Sidney Andrews,*
> The South Since the War, *1886*

> The South, the poor South!
>
> —John C. Calhoun, last words, 1850

1890 election of the great populist and advocate of agriculture, Edgefield's Ben "Pitchfork" Tillman, the Upcountry made its long-awaited ascent to state leadership. But Tillman realized that the divided white electorate made it possible that a united black electorate could again gain control of the state. Therefore, in 1892, after his reelection as governor, Tillman led the charge to hold a new state constitutional convention to draw up a new constitution that would disenfranchise blacks.

He succeeded.

THE NEW SOUTH

In 1886, Atlanta newspaper publisher Henry W. Grady, speaking before a New York audience, proclaimed his vision of a "New South"—a South, that is, based on the Northern economic model. By now, the idea had already struck some enterprising South Carolinians that all that cotton they were sending north at cut rates could be processed just as well down in South Carolina. By the end of the 19th century, the textile industry was exploding across the state—but particularly upstate, with its powerful turbine-turning rivers—at last bringing relief from the depressed sharecropper economy.

For whites, anyway, things were looking up. In 1902, the Lowcountry hosted the Charleston Exposition, drawing visitors from around the world, hoping to impress on them the idea that the state was on the rebound. On April 9, President Theodore Roosevelt—whose mother had attended school in Columbia—even made an appearance, smoothing over the still simmering animosities between North and South by declaring:

The wounds left by the great Civil War ... have healed. ... The devotion, the self-sacrifice, the steadfast resolution and lofty daring, the high devotion to the right as each man saw it ... all these qualities of the men and women of the early sixties now shine luminous and brilliant before our eyes, while the mists of anger and hatred that once dimmed them have passed away forever.

Northerners had long made this kind of reconciliatory talk—the sort of easy generosity possible to the victor, especially if the victor needs the loser's cooperation to have a successful economy. But now—in economics, if not in civil liberties—South Carolina truly did seem to be improving, and things continued to improve, even after the Tillman era ended with the election of progressive Governor Richard I. Manning in 1914.

Unfortunately, the invasion of the boll weevil, beginning in 1919, destroyed the cotton crop, which, though it hadn't paid well since before the Civil War, was nonetheless the state's primary crop. Thus, just as it was coming out of its post-Civil War slump, South Carolina—with other cotton states—led the nation's topple into the Great Depression. Blacks and low-income whites left the state in droves for better jobs up north. Only the expansion of military bases during World War II, as well as domestic and foreign investment in manufacturing in more recent decades, have revitalized the state.

EMANCIPATION

G radual emancipation had worked smoothly in many Northern states, but the Union Army's instantaneous emancipation of Southern slaves into a war-ravaged economy left some African-American Carolinians nearly as bitter as their white counterparts:

Honey, us wasn't ready for the big change that come. Us had no education, no land, no mule, no cow, not a pig, nor a chicken, to set up housekeeping. ...

The Yankees sure throwed us in the briar patch ... [A]ll us had to thank them for was a hungry belly and Freedom. Something us had no more use for then, than I have today for one of them airplanes I hears flying round the sky, right now.

—Violet Guntharpe of Winnsboro, WPA interview

DESEGREGATION

Compared to hot spots such as Mississippi and Alabama, desegregation went relatively smoothly during the 1950s and 1960s in South Carolina. The tragic shooting at Orangeburg in 1968 made one great exception—three students were killed and more than 30 others were shot by police overreacting to the students' violence. Up in Rock Hill in 1961, nine black Friendship College students took seats at the whites-only lunch counter at McCrory's (now Vantell Variety, on Main St.) and refused to leave. When police arrested them, the students were given the choice of paying $200 fines or serving 30 days of hard labor in the York County jail. The "Friendship Nine" chose the latter, becoming the first sit-in protesters of the Civil Rights Movement to suffer imprisonment.

When Clemson was forced to allow Harvey Gantt into its classes in 1962, making it the first public college in the state to be integrated, word went out from influential whites that no violence or otherwise unseemly behavior would be tolerated. Gantt's entrance into school there went without incident. Gantt himself had his own explanation for this: "If you can't appeal to the morals of a South Carolinian," he said, "you can appeal to his manners."

In 1964, Barry Goldwater's platform galvanized South Carolina's conservative Democrats and led to major defections into the Grand Old Party, most notably by Senator Strom Thurmond.

By 1970, when South Carolina celebrated its Tricentennial, more than 80% of its residents had been born in the state. Since then, however, Northerners have discovered South Carolina's golf courses and beaches, and the state—particularly the coastal areas, but increasingly inland as well—has become more popular as the nation's collective memories of race riots and lynchings in the South continue to dim. Even some descendants of black Carolinians who moved out of the South during the Jim Crow years have moved back. Even still, the number of native-born Carolinians in the state hovers around 69%.

RECENT DEVELOPMENTS

In the 1970s, South Carolina elected its first Republican governor since Reconstruction. In 1987 and 1991, the state elected and reelected Governor Carroll Campbell, another Republican. Republican David Beasley—a former Democrat who claimed to have undergone a spiritual rebirth that caused him to reconsider his views, ran for governor as a Republican and won. As governor, Beasley surprised everyone and risked the wrath of Southern traditionalists by announcing, in 1996, that as a Christian he could not justify keeping the Confederate flag flying over the State House knowing that it offended black South Carolinians. Many praised Beasley for his turnaround; critics claimed he was positioning himself for a possible future run at the White House.

Beasley cruised into the 1998 elections with such an edge in popularity that the top two Democratic candidates didn't even bother to run. Amazingly, Beasley was brought down by the third string—Lancaster State Assemblyman Jim Hodges, a former opponent of legalized gambling who now attacked Beasley's opposition to the creation of a state lottery and to the continued growth of video gaming in the state, which Hodges painted as the salvation tax base for public education.

Though Beasley opposed the flying of the Confederate flag over the Capitol and Hodges refused to pledge *his* opposition to it, 90% of African-American Carolinians voted for Hodges, enough to swing the election his way. Gambling interests were elated, including the Collins Company, makers of video gambling machines (which by some estimates had tucked a whopping $7 million into Hodges' campaign purse). In January 1999, after Hodges took office, *USA Today* completed and published a study it had made of the election. The independent paper—ordinarily no friend of the Republican Party—determined that Hodges had indeed been given at least $3.5 million in donations from the gambling industry.

Time will tell if Hodges will be able to work the magic he has promised with South Carolina schools, but, given that they're usually ranked just above Mississippi's (and sometimes just below), there's nowhere to go but up.

ECONOMY

Rich and Poor

Since the Civil War, South Carolina has consistently ranked as one of the two or three poorest per capita states in the Union. Part of this can be attributed to the ruin of the moneyed class by the Civil War and Reconstruction. Before that, South Carolina's per capita income was one of the top two in the United States. Since then, it has never climbed back into the top 40.

Another part may be the flight of middle-class blacks during the Jim Crow years. Blacks were traditionally on the bottom of the economic ladder; as soon as many African-American families climbed a rung or two up that ladder, they tended to move north, where they found better job opportunities and fewer degradations.

Agriculture

Up through the Civil War, **rice** was South Carolina's most important crop. Rice—not cotton—literally built most of the famed Lowcountry Plantations. After the war, however, though rice remained an important part of Carolinian recipes and diets, it more or less disappeared as a cash crop. Indigo was grown on the lands above the rice fields, on up through the Piedmont, and proved another gold mine for those with the equipment and the (slave) labor to process it. By the 1790s, however, overproduction in India, Louisiana, and Latin America lowered indigo prices, and farmers began looking for an alternative crop, which they found, eventually, in cotton.

The state's major crop today is **tobacco,** though noncarcinogens are popular as well: **soybean** and **cotton** crops make up major parts of the economy. South Carolina farmers also raise **corn, wheat, rye, oats,** and **barley.** What surprises many out-of-staters is South Carolina's tree crops: the state's **peach** industry claimed over four million

trees in the 1980s, and today South Carolina produces more peaches than any other state in the union—including Georgia. Spartanburg and Oconee Counties grow most of the state's considerable **apple** crop—mostly Red Delicious.

Truck crops such as **tomatoes, cucumbers,** and **watermelons** are grown in the Lowcountry or lower Midlands.

Poultry is the most common **livestock** raised in South Carolina, though the cattle industry is not insignificant. The Upcountry is home to most of South Carolina's cattle ranches, which operate as cattle nurseries: most of their calves are shipped off to Western states for fattening and slaughter.

Industry

More than a third of South Carolina's workforce

FORREST GUMP SLEPT HERE

One of the first movies filmed in South Carolina was *Ride the Wild Wind,* an early John Wayne pirate film.

But in recent years, South Carolina has come into its own, filmwise. The state has done a phenomenal job of luring Hollywood types to the Lowcountry over the years. In 1995, tiny South Carolina ranked eighth among American states in film revenue, raking in more than $54 million. *The Great Santini, The Big Chill, Forrest Gump, The Prince of Tides, Shag: The Movie, Rich in Love, Paradise,* and *Bastard out of Carolina* have all been set and shot here.

Others have used South Carolina locales to stand in for other locations. In *Die Hard III: Die Hard with a Vengeance,* the Ashley-Cooper Bridges were supposed to be in New York City, and for Disney's live-action *Jungle Book,* Hunting and Fripp Islands posed as Asian jungles. Disney's horse epic *Wild Hearts Can't Be Broken* was filmed in part at the Orangeburg Fairgrounds. And Columbia posed as both a generic Southern college town and an ugly Northern industrial city in *The Program.* The film's most infamous scene, in which the football players lie along the center divider of a busy street as a test of courage (after inspiring imitation that resulted in real-life tragedy, the scene was removed from the film prior to its release on video), took place across the river in West Columbia.

Ironically, Michael J. Fox's *Doc Hollywood,* set in fictional "Grady, South Carolina," was filmed in Florida.

works in **manufacturing,** and the principal products are textiles, chemicals, plastics, and paper goods. The single biggest industry is the textile industry, centered in the Upcountry: South Carolina mills weave more than four billion yards of cloth annually, enough to circle the Earth 80 times. Fortunately, since doing this is not necessary, the companies are able to sell the cloth instead, providing a great boon to the state's economy.

Mining is also somewhat significant—some 500 mines operate in South Carolina today. The state ranks at the top, or nearly so, in U.S. production of marl, kaolin, vermiculite, and crushed granite. **Timber** and **fishing** operations are also of note in various parts of the state.

Tourism

Tourism in South Carolina is rising: up 25% since 1991. In 1996, despite hurricanes and competition for regional visitors from the Atlanta Olympics, South Carolina enjoyed an increase in its number of overall visitors to 32 million, its fifth straight year of growth. According to the South Carolina Department of Parks, Recreation and Tourism, out-of-staters made up 78% of this number: North Carolina and Georgia each sent over five million visitors; New York, Pennsylvania, Virginia, and Florida each sent between one and five million; California, Massachusetts, Connecticut, New Jersey, West Virginia, Tennessee, Alabama, Kentucky, Michigan, Wisconsin, Illinois, Indiana, and Texas each contributed 100,000 to 1 million visitors. A million people came from Washington, D.C., alone, and another million from New York City.

What drew these people to the state? Over 8.4 million of 1996's visitors listed shopping as their primary leisure activity while in South Carolina. Another eight million—in a hurricane year—came for the beaches; 3.8 million came to backpack, mountain bike, fish, boat, or enjoy other forms of outdoor recreation. Over three million visitors said they were attracted primarily by Carolina's museums and historical sites. Some 2.2 million came for the abundant golf and tennis, and 1.5 million came specifically to enjoy one of the state's many festivals.

THE PEOPLE

Despite all its physical beauty, despite its music, its food, and the salty scent of the coastal marshes, the very best thing about South Carolina is its people. Remove South Carolina's people, replace them with New Yorkers, give it five years, and what would you have? Florida.

Make no mistake: it's South Carolinians who make South Carolina the unique place it is. Despite Charlestonians' legendary pridefulness, by and large South Carolinians are a meek lot, humbled by the mistakes of their past in a way that Northerners and Westerners are not.

Unless they leave home, South Carolinians cannot escape their past: a white Middleton may well share a classroom with two black Middletons, likely descendants of his great-great-great-grandfather's slaves—and possibly distant cousins.

A lot of Southerners see Northerners as the finger-pointing husbands who quit cheating on their wives and immediately became crusaders against adultery. Westerners are the husbands who ditched their wives and kids and headed to the coast with their secretaries. Southerners are the husbands who have been caught in the act, been half-forgiven, and now live on in a town where—no matter what other accomplishments they may muster—their sin will never be forgotten. And it is because of this that white South Carolinians tend to evince an odd mixture of defensiveness, good nature, and perhaps a little more understanding of human nature than other folks. And perhaps because so much of their history has been spent withstanding the tugs and blows of other regions that commanded them to change, Carolinians are none too quick to equate change with progress. Which, granted,

> *In sacred memorials to those who gave their lives in the Confederate cause we find central expressions of the unofficial state religion.*
>
> *—Kevin Lewis, "Religion in South Carolina Addresses the Public Order," in* Religion in South Carolina, *1993*

One treat for South Carolina visitors is being able to watch a craftsperson, such as this Lowcountry basketmaker, hand-construct an item that you can then buy.

I met little Ben Lance, a mountain boy who had just driven his cows into that wild mountain pasture. . . .

"Ben," I said to my small companion, "You often see the sunrise from this pasture, don't you?"

"I calculate," he said, with his quaint drawl, "That she will be here just the same time I is. I is late sometimes, but the sunrise she ain't never late. I guess that's because God manages that."

I pondered the child's words as we looked together at the flaming waves of heliotrope that were fringing the mountain crest. Every tree on the skyline of those tremendous slopes stood out vividly; dark lay the valleys beneath.

"What do you know about God, Ben?"

"I know He made everything," he said; "and He watches how we behave. I like to be here when the sun comes up," he went on; "it makes me feel how great God is, and then I ain't skeered of nothing."

Childish ramblings, some would call them; yet to me they brought a heartening message. Here was a lonely little lad who felt God in the sunrise; who knew in his own way the meaning of communion. Ben Lance had learned by himself the most interesting thing that all Nature has to teach us.

—Archibald Rutledge,
Peace in the Heart, 1923

can make them a bit slow to acknowledge even a good change when it comes about. The state only formally ratified the 19th Amendment, allowing women the vote, in 1969.

This understanding of people as intrinsically flawed creatures also makes South Carolinians value traditions and manners more than many—for in a culture where human nature is seen as inherently flawed, "self-expression" and "doing what

I've always respected a white Southerner more than a white Northerner. A white Northerner is one who says openly that he has no prejudice and yet practices it every day of his life. The white Southerner is the one who says, "I am prejudiced, but I have certain friends I would do anything in the world for." In other words, one is a hypocrite and the other is bluntly honest.

—African-American New York Congressman
Adam Clayton Powell

you feel" are not necessarily good things. To Carolinians, some parts of the self are . . . well . . . just selfish. Hence, Carolinians use ritualized courtesies copiously to smooth the rough edges of humanity. Carolinians are taught to say "yes, ma'am," "no, sir," "please," and "thank you," whether or not their inner children feel like it.

One of the most charming things about South Carolinians is how they're nearly always genuinely surprised to hear that non-Southerners have bothered to come all this way just to see their little state. They know that South Carolina is a gem but won't know how you found out about it. Most Carolinians are proud of where they live and usually quite happy to show you around.

Church Homecomings

To many South Carolinians, belonging to a church is like belonging to a spiritual family,

> "With all due respect, why should we entertain the opinion of a white southern male?"
> I leaned forward and whispered, "Because, Doctor, when I'm not eating roots and berries, when I'm not screwing mules from the tops of stumps, and when I'm not slaughtering pigs out back at the still, I'm a very smart man."
>
> —Pat Conroy, The Prince of Tides

wherein shared hopes and commitment to divine principles and promises form bonds with others deeper than those forged anywhere else. This is why church homecomings are such a big deal—once-a-year events, wherein like Japanese city dwellers returning to their ancestral villages, people return to their hometowns and home churches to renew friendships, patch up others, and bask in their deepest-felt identity.

Language

One of the things outsiders often notice about Southerners is the Southern way with figurative language. To some degree this is derived from the strong Biblical tradition of the region; for centuries, Southern evangelical Christians have naturally striven to illustrate the intangibles of life with easy-to-visualize parables, following the example of Jesus, who used illustrations drawn from situations familiar to his unschooled first-century audiences (a shepherd's concern for his sheep, wheat planted amongst briars, a disobedient son returning home) to explain complex theological doctrines.

Hence, if you're butting into a conflict between two South Carolinians, you may be reminded that "y'all don't have a dog in this fight." If you think a person is smart just because he went to school, you're forgetting that "livin' in a garage don't make you a Ford." My personal favorite, though I only heard it once, describes a thought-

FAMOUS SOUTH CAROLINIANS

LITERATURE

Hervey Allen (Charleston), author of *Anthony Adverse,* Charleston schoolteacher

Mary Boykin Chesnut (Camden, Columbia), famous Civil War diarist

Pat Conroy (Beaufort), best-selling author of *The Prince of Tides, Beach Music, The Great Santini, Lords of Discipline,* and others

James Dickey (Columbia), longtime USC professor, author of *Deliverance, To the White Sea,* other novels, and several books of poetry

Dubose Heyward, author of *Porgy* (basis of subsequent Gershwin opera *Porgy and Bess*)

MOVIES AND TELEVISION

Helen Chandler (Charleston), actress, Bela Lugosi's *Dracula*

Stanley Donen (Charleston), director, *Singin' in the Rain* and many other films

Leeza Gibbons (Hartsville), USC grad, *Entertainment Tonight* reporter and sometime co-anchor, eponymous host of *Leeza!* talk show

Bo Hopkins (Greenwood), actor, *The Wild Bunch, American Graffiti, The Getaway,* and many others

Nina McKinney (Lancaster), groundbreaking black actress

Andie MacDowell (Gaffney), actress, *Sex, Lies, and Videotape; Object of Beauty; Groundhog Day; Three Weddings and a Funeral;* and others

Chris Rock (Georgetown), comedian, actor, *Saturday Night Live*

Vanna White (North Charleston), letter turner, *Wheel of Fortune*

MUSIC

Pink Anderson (Spartanburg), important blues stylist; origin of first part of the name of group Pink Floyd.

James Brown (Barnwell), the Godfather of Soul

Peabo Bryson (Greenville), singer, Grammy Award-winner

Chubby Checker (Spring Gully); his "The Twist" is one of the biggest records ever

Dixie Hummingbirds (Greenville, Spartanburg), Seminal Gospel quartet founded in Greenville and fronted by a Spartanburg native

Hootie and the Blowfish (Columbia), record-breaking pop artists

ful person who, apparently, was "sweeter than sugar cubes in syrup." Makes you want to brush your teeth just hearing it.

South Carolinians don't think or figure, they "reckon." They don't get ready, they "fix," as in, "I'm fixing to head down to Charleston." They don't push buttons, they "mash" them. They "cut" lights on and off, "carry" people around in their cars, accomplish urgent tasks in a "skinny minute," and push shopping "buggies" around the Winn-Dixie. If a South Carolinian is a stranger to a subject, she "doesn't know 'boo'" about it. If she's never met you before, she doesn't know you from "Adam's house cat." If she *does* know you and sees you, she won't just hug you, she'll "hug your neck." And if a Carolinian says he really needs to "take a powder," it probably just means he has a headache and is taking a dose of Goody's powder (a regional remedy—essentially crushed aspirin). If he tells you he's "like to pass out," it means he's very tired, not drunk.

South Carolinians never pop in to say "hello" or "hi"—they stop by to say "hey." In fact, you'll rarely hear "hi," in public—it's usually "hey."

Fairly well known is the preference for "y'all," or the more formal "you-all." (Some Carolinians argue that "y'all" is actually more politically correct than the Yankee "you guys," since it's not gender-exclusive.) It's usually the first linguistic nuance you'll pick up when you're in the state, and it's one of the hardest for displaced Carolinians to mask when they're outside of Dixie. It just sounds friendlier. If you meet more than one person walking together on the street, it's proper and friendly to say, "hey, you-all."

You may also hear (usually) white South Carolinian males call each other "Bo," the way males in other American subcultures might call one another "Homes" or "Dude": "Hey, Bo—can I borrow your johnboat?" "Sure, Bo."

Pronunciation counts, too. Though there's not the space to go into all the regional varia-

---

Eartha Kitt (North), famous torch singer, one-time Catwoman on *Batman* TV show

Marshall Tucker Band (Spartanburg), country rock pioneers

Sparkletones (Spartanburg); their "Black Slacks" was an early rockabilly classic

Swinging Medallions (Greenwood); *Rolling Stone* magazine called their "Double Shot of My Baby's Love" the "Greatest Party Song of the 1960s"

Aaron Tippin (Spartanburg), "Working Man" country star

POLITICS

Preston Brooks (Edgefield), congressman most famous for beating abolitionist Massachusetts Senator Charles Sumner with a cane on the U.S. Senate floor in May 1856

John C. Calhoun (Clemson), foremost "states' rights" advocate, two-time vice president, Supreme Court justice, secretary of state

Andrew Jackson (Lancaster County), U.S. president and war hero

Jesse Jackson (Greenville), long-time civil rights leader, sometime presidential candidate

Andrew Johnson (Laurens), U.S. president (1865-69)

Henry Martyn Robert (Roberts), protocol expert, author of *Robert's Rules of Order*

Strom Thurmond (Edgefield), famous as segregationist-turned-integrationist, Democrat-turned-Republican

Colonel William Travis (Saluda County), legendary Alamo hero.

Woodrow Wilson (Columbia), U.S. president

SCIENCE

Alexander Garden (Charleston), Colonial-era botanist (the gardenia is named in his honor)

Joel Poinsett (Charleston), former U.S. ambassador to Mexico (the poinsettia is named in his honor)

SPORTS

Joe Frazier (Beaufort), former heavyweight boxing champion

Shoeless Joe Jackson (Greenville), famous and infamous member of 1919 "Black Sox"

Sugar Ray Leonard (Mullins), former welterweight boxing champion, Olympic champion

Bobby Richardson (Sumter), 1950-60s star infielder of New York Yankees

Mookie Wilson (Bamberg), 1980s star of New York Mets

A SOUTH CAROLINA SYLLABUS

BOOKS

- **Rich in Love** (1989)—Josephine Humphries. Set in Mount Pleasant, Humphries' book gives you one of the best portrayals of real-world, shopping-mall-and-public-school modern-day South Carolina. If the book has a weakness, it may be in that it tries to be *so* strident in asserting its "modern" viewpoint that it becomes a bit sappy and moralistic. Still, the book's loaded with memorable Lowcountry characters, and full of human warmth.

- **The Prince of Tides** (1986)—Pat Conroy. A lumbering novel set in both Lowcountry South Carolina and in New York City. A novel of the American South in the modern world. Perhaps the single best book about the Southerner in the post-Faulknerian era.

- **The Boo**—Pat Conroy (1970). Conroy's first book, written shortly after he left the Citadel, about the man called "The Bear" in *The Lords of Discipline.* When I taught at the Citadel, I found this book much more accurate in its descriptions and tone than that other Conroy epic. It's more accurate and less sensationalistic than *Lords.*

- **Miss Ravenel's Conversion from Secession to Loyalty**—John William DeForest (1867). One of Hemingway's favorites; the one great war novel published by a participant in the Civil War. Fascinating for its Northerner view of South Carolinians.

- **Porgy**—Dubose Heyward (1925). The novel on which Dubose based his Pulitzer Prize-winning play, *Porgy and Bess,* later made into the opera by George Gershwin.

- **The Civil War Diary of Mary Boykin Chesnut.** This sharp-quilled woman was there, backstage, in the Confederate circles of power during the Civil War. Fascinating reading.

- **The Orangeburg Massacre**—Jack Bass (1970). Though regarded as something of an exposé when it came out, just two years after the shootings, Jack Bass's moment-by-moment account of the title tragedy strikes the modern reader as an admirably restrained bit of objective reporting that helps the reader to understand how things like this can happen.

- **The Yemasee**—William Gilmore Simms (1835). The greatest of Simm's historical romances, which earned him the title "The Southern Cooper." Strong in its account of the true-life Colonial-era Yamassee War. In this early novel, you'll notice Simms' already playing the apologist for slavery, but even this is fascinating and informative for those who have always wondered how the sensitive, well-educated Southern mind was able to live with itself.

- **Mama Day**—Gloria Naylor (1989). A Lowcountry resident herself, Gloria Naylor's fictional island of Willow Springs is home to a small group of black families who have lived there since the time of Sapphira Wade, a "true conjure woman" who may or may not, as legend has it, have murdered the white landowner who was first her owner and then her husband. A good insight into Gullah culture, set on the South Carolina-Georgia border.

- **Southern Fried** (1962) and *Southern Fried Plus 6* (1968)—William Price Fox. In the 1960s, Fox caused quite a stir with these collections of humorous stories from the low-income white burgs around Columbia. *The Oxford Guide to American Literature* likens him to Mark Twain. Fox's fiction gives a great taste of South Carolinian culture, especially of the low-income white variety.

- **Deliverance**—James Dickey (1971). Set in Georgia, but in the northeast corner of Georgia, along the Chattooga, which draws the border between Upcountry South Carolina, Georgia, and North Carolina. Most people remember the book and the movie for one very disturbing scene, but the book is truly about seeking deliverance from modern society in the wild and embracing nature with all its defects and perils.

- **Scarlet Sister Mary**—Julia Peterkin (1928). The Pulitzer Prize-winning novel about the life of a Gullah woman. Peterkin's husband worked as a plantation manager, allowing her some insight into the daily lives of the Gullah people.

- **Before Freedom: When I Just Can Remember**—ed. Belinda Hurmence (1997). A fascinating compilation of WPA narratives from South Carolinian ex-slaves.

For more great South Carolina–themed reading, see the **Booklist** at the end of this book.

FILMS

- **Shag—The Movie** (1991). In the summer of 1963, four recent high school graduates head from their homes in Spartanburg for a weekend of romance, drinking, and shagging at Myrtle Beach. Okay, so it's not *Citizen Kane*, but it's not *Beach Blanket Bingo*, either. Notably accurate in overall tone and cultural nuances. Great soundtrack, realistic accents, and fine shagging! Fiftysomethings who were cruising Ocean Blvd. back in '63 tell me the filmmakers get it right. South Carolina shagging czar Barry Thigpen makes a guest appearance as the emcee of the big dance contest at the end.

- **Gone With The Wind** (1939). Sure it all takes place in Georgia, but this romantic epic belongs to all of the South and is essential for grasping the white South's romantic understanding of its past. And Rhett Butler, you'll remember, hails from the wickedly worldly city of Charleston.

- **The Great Santini** (1985). Set in Beaufort, based largely on author Pat Conroy's childhood there. Some great shots of Beaufort. The same waterfront house later doubled as Harold and Sarah Cooper's house in *The Big Chill*.

- **Rich In Love** (1990). In this movie, based upon Josephine Humphrey's novel, Albert Finney makes this movie, with his on-the-money portrayal of a Mount Pleasant man struggling to his feet after his wife abandons his family. A little heavy-handed in its philosophizing, but not a bad first hour and a half.

- **Conrack** (1971). Jon Voight in Pat Conroy's autobiographical recounting of his time spent on St. Helena Island teaching English to Gullah children.

- **Deliverance** (1973). See this if only to remind yourself why you put off coming to the South for so long. In writing *Deliverance*, the late James Dickey may have single-handedly curbed emigration into the Southeast for at least a decade. Great shots of the Chattooga River, which crosses into South Carolina's Upcountry, and a fine guest appearance in the film's closing moments by Dickey himself as Sheriff Bullard.

- **Glory** (1989). The powerful dramatization of the story of the 54th Massachusetts, the first black regiment to see combat in the Civil War. Most of the battles the regiment engages in take place in South Carolina; the climactic Battle of Fort Wagner was fought on Morris Island, just south of Charleston and north of Folly Beach.

- **Paradise** (1991). Then-married Don Johnson and Melanie Griffith (now real-world divorced) play a couple whose wounded marriage heals with the visit of a sensitive young boy (Elijah Wood). Okay, so maybe nobody in the film bothered to sit down with a voice coach (Johnson apparently figured his Missouri twang was close enough to a Lowcountry lilt), but the film does capture some great shots of the shrimping culture around McClellanville. Actually a remake of a European film, the English-language script was originally set in a Washington state fishing village before the South Carolina Film Commission lured the filmmakers to McClellanville.

- **Prince of Tides** (1988). At least she didn't make it a musical. See this only if you don't let it keep you from reading Pat Conroy's novel, since director Barbra Streisand's script favors the New York-based subplot of the story. Still, some good performances, realistic accents, and nice location footage shot in and around Beaufort.

- **The Apostle** (1998). Though set in Texas and Louisiana, this is worth seeing for the unique insight it provides. It's one of the only literate studies of the highly influential Christian Fundamentalist/Pentecostal subculture of South Carolina and other Southern states.

tions, just remember that no one watches television in South Carolina; they watch "the TEE-vee." And cautious Carolinians buy "IN-surance" on their house, which will pay for the family to stay in a "HO-tel" if the house burns down.

In the Upcountry particularly, the "s" on the ends of plurals is often dropped, as in, "That Co-Cola is sixty-five cent."

Terms of Address
One of the most admirable qualities of Southern culture is its resistance to the Cult of Youth. South Carolina is a place where it's not against the law to get old (ask Senator Strom Thurmond). Here, age is generally still respected, and one way of showing and reinforcing this respect is the customary respectful way of referring to elders as "ma'am" and "sir." For example: "Excuse me, ma'am, but could

Mr. Rufus Oates and Miss Esther, sometime operators of North Myrtle Beach's beach music mecca, Judy's House of Oldies

you tell me where to find the trailhead?" "Didn't y'all see the sign back away? Where the two magnolia used to be?" "No, ma'am."

Granted, there is some classism involved. Bosses and the wealthy tend to hear themselves addressed as "sir" or "ma'am" more often than, say, gardeners or house cleaners. "Aunt" and "uncle" are familiar terms used by whites toward elder African-Americans, although almost completely absent in all but the oldest generations.

Note that visitors don't *have* to say "ma'am" and "sir"—Southerners expect non-Southerners to be ill-mannered, anyway—but doing so might help you blend in a little better.

Children address adults normally with "Mr.," "Miss," or "Mrs." attached to either the adult's first name or last name. Family friends or other adult friends are often addressed by the first name, preceded by either Mr. or Miss—whether or not the woman in question is married. Hence, to the children of some of our friends in Orangeburg, my wife and I became "Miss Kristin and Mr. Mike." It's much more genuine than the automatic uncle or aunt status some parents elsewhere are always trying to confer upon you. It's a typically South Carolinian compromise, reinforcing societal roles and responsibilities by keeping the generations separate, yet also encouraging intimacy with first names.

Note, too, that if a large age difference exists between you and another (older) person, it's still proper to address an elder as Mr., Ms., Mrs., or Miss; among the 20 graduate English students in James Dickey's Poetry Workshop at USC, I never heard one of us address him (even in private) as anything but "Mr. Dickey."

Southern Subtleties:
How to Read through Southern Manners

Let's say that you and your travel companion meet a nice Carolinian couple, who invite you to their home for dinner. You eat, you adjourn to the porch for beverages, and then you sit around, talking. It gets a little late, but your hosts seem so eager to continue the conversation that you linger. It gets later. You really *should* go, but as you rise, your hosts offer another round of drinks. Finally, you decide you must go. You leave, while your hosts openly grieve your departure. You're begged to return again when "y'all can stay a little longer."

What the average unsuspecting non-Southerners don't realize is that they have just committed a major faux pas. Though you of course had no way of knowing, your hosts were ready for you to leave right after dessert, but offered drinks on the porch only because you showed no signs of leaving, and they wanted to be polite.

So what's the rule of thumb when visiting with South Carolinians you don't know very well? Leave about when you first suspect you should, only an hour earlier.

ON THE ROAD
OUTDOOR ACTIVITIES

There is a wicked lie that keeps people like my father trapped in southern California: I have to live here—where else can you go the mountains and the beach in the same day?

Of course, folks in Virginia, Georgia, and, for that matter, northern California, can easily provide an answer. South Carolina is another such place. In fact, one spring break, my wife and I got sunburned lying out at Edisto Island one day and awoke a day later in snow at our campsite in the Blue Ridge Mountains. Since it's hard to be more than 230 miles away from anywhere in South Carolina without leaving the state, it's quite possible to eat rainbow trout for breakfast on the Chattooga River and go to sleep that night with the roar of the Atlantic in your ears and Lowcountry shrimp in your belly.

PUBLIC LANDS

South Carolina offers some of the least-crowded outdoor recreation facilities in the United States. The National Park Service manages **Congaree Swamp National Monument, ACE Basin National Wildlife Refuge, Cape Romain National Wildlife Refuge, Carolina Sandhills National Wildlife Refuge, Pinckney Island National Wildlife Refuge, Santee National Wildlife Refuge, Savannah National Wildlife Refuge,** and the **Chattooga National Wild and Scenic River.** You'll find each of these detailed elsewhere in the book. Recreation choices differ from park to park, but commonly include wildlife viewing, hiking, backcountry camping, paddling, and fishing. On the coast they also include shrimping and crabbing.

The Park Service also operates a number of national monuments and historic sites and battlefields in South Carolina. These include **Fort Sumter National Monument, Charles Pinckney National Historic Site, Ninety Six National Historic Site, Cowpens National Battlefield,** and **Kings Mountain National Military Park.** None of these offers camping, though most include short interpretive trails, and visitors to Kings Mountain can camp at the adjacent state park.

Some NPS-administered sites in South Carolina charge nominal entry fees—usually $1-3 per person or $3-10 per vehicle. The NPS also offers several special entrance passes, available at any fee-charging national site.

National Park Passports

The government has established the discount Golden Eagle, Golden Age, and Golden Access Passports. These allow purchasers to enter fee areas without additional charge. This is very convenient when traveling to several areas that charge entrance fees. (Note that the passports are nontransferable. The pass belongs to the person who signs it and cannot be loaned to someone else.)

The **Golden Eagle Passport** gives you entry to those national parks, monuments, historic sites, recreation areas, and national wildlife refuges that charge an entrance fee. The Golden Eagle Passport costs $50 and is valid for one year from date of purchase. The Golden Eagle Passport admits the pass holder and any accompanying passengers in a private vehicle. If you're traveling by bus or in some way other than a private vehicle, the passport admits you, your spouse, children, and parents.

The Golden Eagle Passport covers entrance fees only. It doesn't cover or reduce extra fees for camping, swimming, parking, boat launching, or tours. You may purchase a Golden Eagle Passport at any NPS entrance fee area or by mail. To purchase by mail, send a $50 check or money order (do not send cash) to the attention of Golden Eagle Passport, National Park Service, 1100 Ohio Dr. SW, Room 138, Washington, DC 20242.

Practically speaking, unless you're traveling with three or more family members, or planning to visit most or all of the NPS properties in South Carolina—or a few of them repeatedly within the year—the Golden Eagle won't mean much of a savings, if any. If you're planning to travel to other states, then it may be well worth it.

The **Golden Age Passport** is a lifetime entrance pass for those 62 years or older. It carries a one-time processing charge of $10. You must purchase a Golden Age Passport in person (it is not available by mail or telephone). This can be done at any NPS entrance fee area. At time of purchase you must show proof of age (be 62 years or older) and be a citizen or permanent resident of the United States.

The Golden Age Passport admits the pass holder and any accompanying passengers in a private vehicle. Where entry is not by private vehicle, the passport admits the pass holder, spouse, children, and parents.

The Golden Age Passport also provides a 50% discount on federal use fees charged for facilities and services such as fees for camping, swimming, parking, boat launching, or cave tours. It does not cover or reduce special recreation permit fees or fees charged by concessionaires.

The **Golden Access Passport** is a *free* lifetime entrance pass for persons who are blind or permanently disabled. It is available to citizens or permanent residents of the United States, regardless of age, who have been determined to be blind or permanently disabled. You may obtain a Golden Access Passport at any entrance fee area by showing proof of medically determined disability and eligibility for receiving benefits under federal law.

SIGHTSEEING HIGHLIGHTS

Beaufort
• Historic District

Charleston
• Fort Sumter National Monument
• Historic District
• Magnolia Plantation and Gardens

Columbia
• South Carolina State Museum
• Riverbanks Zoo and Botanical Garden
• The Horseshoe, University of South Carolina
• State Capitol
• Congaree Swamp National Monument (nearby)

Greenville
• Mountain Bridge State Natural Area (above town)

Myrtle Beach
• Brookgreen Gardens
• Huntington Beach State Park

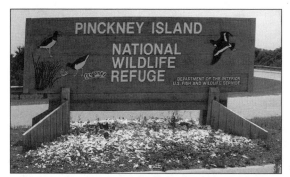

The Golden Access Passport admits the pass holder and any accompanying passengers in a private vehicle. Where entry is not by private vehicle, the passport admits the pass holder, spouse, children, and parents.

The Golden Access Passport also provides a 50% discount on federal use fees charged for facilities and services such as fees for camping, swimming, parking, boat launching, or cave tours. It does not cover or reduce special recreation permit fees or fees charged by concessionaires.

Finally, a Park Pass can be purchased from specific NPS-administered sites for $10-15 and allows unlimited entry to that particular site for one calendar year.

State Parks

South Carolina's state park system is one of the nation's best. Its 48 developed parks and eight additional properties take up some 81,000 acres across the state. Many of the developed parks date to, and feature structures built by, the Depression-era Civilian Conservation Corps. You'll find one within a half hour of just about any town in the state. Most of the state's most pristine shoreline—both ocean and lake—lies within the boundaries of the state parks. Between them, the parks hold thousands of miles of hiking, biking, and equestrian trails. All but a few of the parks offer camping facilities, and most include water and electricity.

If you've camped in the American West, you'll find many of South Carolina's parks relatively "resorty," featuring rental cabins or "villas," snack shops and/or restaurants, general stores, staffed swimming beaches, canoe and boat rentals, car-

pet golf, archery courses, and, at Cheraw, Goodale, and Hickory Knob, a full-size 9- or 18-hole golf course as well. Hickory Knob, Santee, and Table Rock also include restaurants.

Things are changing, however, as environmentalists push for "less-improved" parks that allow public access to pristine areas without paving or sodding them in the process—Woods Bay State Park near Olanta is a good example. Standout state parks of the old school include **Edisto Island State Park, Hunting Island State Park,** and **Oconee State Park,** with a tip of the hat also to **Sesquicentennial State Park** for providing a fine forest experience not far from urban Columbia. For a complete listing of state parks, call any state park listed in this book and staff will gladly send you one.

Entrance to many state parks costs nothing, but some charge a parking fee ranging $3-4 per car per day. Generally, inland parks cost less than coastal parks. Huntington Beach costs $3 per *adult;* Charles Town Landing costs $5 per adult, half price for kids 6-14. South Carolina senior citizens and kids under 5 get in free to all parks.

If you plan to visit several South Carolina state parks, invest $40 or so for the annual Parks Passport, which allows unlimited park entry for all passengers (up to 15) in your vehicle. For all of these parks, camping fees are additional.

You can purchase a pass in person at any fee-charging state park, or by mail or phone from the South Carolina State Parks, 1205 Pendleton St., Columbia, SC 29201, tel. (888) 887-2757 or (803) 734-0156, fax (803) 734-1017, or visit online at www.sccsi.com/sc/Parks/index.html.

Though some of the busier parks have office hours 9 a.m.-5 p.m., most park offices are open only 11 a.m.-noon. Those with cabins are also open 4-5 p.m.

National Forests

The state's two National Forest Service properties, **Francis Marion National Forest** and **Sumter National Forest,** were both named after the Revolutionary War guerrillas who once used the respective forests as hideouts and striking areas against British armies. Together their holdings total over 600,000 acres, more than the total acreage of all the Wal-Mart parking lots in America.

So far.

Since the lands were purchased from individual owners during the 1930s, the nearly clear-cut forests have regrown. Together they offer nearly 500 campsites and over a hundred picnic sites, along with nearly 200 miles of hiking trails. For maps or information contact the Supervisor's Office, Strom Thurmond Federal Building, 1835 Assembly St. (P.O. Box 2227), Columbia, SC 29202, tel. (803) 765-5222.

OCEAN SPORTS

Surfing

Yes, South Carolina has surfing. What's even more startling to some first-time visitors is that the state hosts a full-blown surf subculture as well. The enthusiasm for the sport runs high along the coast—much higher than the waves, in fact. The single best, most dependable surf spot in the Charleston area, if not in the entire state, is **The Washout,** at the end of E. Ashley Ave. in Folly Beach. If the waves are small everywhere else, they may still be decent here. If they're good everywhere else, here they'll be pounding. Of course, if the swell's good, it's also going to be crowded here, and while the localism among area surfers is nowhere near Hawaii or California levels, you might want to let the tube-starved locals enjoy themselves. The Washout hosts the state's surfing championships every year. To get there, take Hwy. 17 south of Charleston, then take Hwy. 171 until it dead-ends at the Holiday Inn. Turn left at East Ashley and keep going.

Another popular spot at Folly is **10th Street,** where you can count on smaller—but often cleaner and less-crowded—waves than you'll find up at the Washout. The **Folly Beach Pier,** beside the Holiday Inn at E. Atlantic Ave., sometimes offers cleaner waves and longer rides than The Washout, but keep an eye out for The Law: though not always enforced, it's illegal to surf within 200 feet of the pier.

Over in East Cooper, a lot of folks enjoy surfing at the **Sea Cabins Pier,** right at 21st and Palm Blvd. on Isle of Palms. If the wind's blowing out of the northeast, you may want to head over here, or to **Bert's** at Station 22, Sullivan's Island. Named in honor of the venerable bar out on Middle St., this is one of the best places to surf at low tide.

In Myrtle Beach, you'll find the best surf between 20th Ave. N and 20th Ave. S, but that's not saying much; 29th Ave. S and 38th Ave. N are especially popular. Surf shops are good spots to pick up tips on where the "big" ones are breaking and/or to rent boards or wet suits. These include **Surf City Surfboards,** with three locations, 1103 N. Kings Hwy., tel. (843) 626-7919; Myrtle Square Mall, tel. (843) 626-5412; and N. Myrtle Beach, tel. (843) 272-1090. **Village Surf Shoppe,** 30 years old and an institution on the Strand, offers rentals from two locations: 500 Atlantic Ave., Garden City, tel. (843) 651-6396; and 2016 N. Kings Hwy., Myrtle Beach, tel. (843) 626-8176. Finally, **Xtreme Surf and Skateboard Co.** over at 515 E. Hwy. 501, tel. (843) 626-2262, makes custom surf- and skateboards, as well as renting sticks to the visiting gremmies.

When you hit the surf in the Myrtle Beach area, make sure you wear your leash and stay at least 400 feet away from all piers—in Horry County, it's the law.

McKevlin's Surf Shop offers a 24-hour surf report on Charleston-area beaches, tel. (843) 588-2261. It's updated several times throughout the day. The Charleston *Post and Courier* offers its own **InfoLine Surf Report,** updated a minimum of three times a day, tel. (843) 937-6000, ext. 7873.

Recently, a website opened up featuring South Carolina surfing updates: http://www.angelfire.com/sc/surfextreme2/index.html.

Diving

The South Carolina coast's long history of shipwrecks makes the offshore waters a virtual wonderland for divers. However, if you're here in the winter, rough, cold waters can make offshore diving pretty inhospitable between October and May.

But people dive in the historic rivers year-round; one Lowcountry favorite is the Cooper River, filled with fossilized giant shark's teeth, bones, and mammal teeth, as well as colonial and prehistoric artifacts. Expect water temperatures in the 50s.

Contact **Charleston Scuba,** 335 Savannah Hwy., tel. (843) 763-3483 (www.charlestonscuba.com), or the **Wet Shop,** 5121 Rivers Ave., tel. (843) 744-5641, also in Charleston. Down in Hilton Head, the folks at **Island Scuba Dive and Travel,** 130 Matthews Dr., tel. (843) 689-3244, offer local river diving, classes, and eco-river tours. In Beaufort, call **Outfar Diving Charters,** tel. (843) 522-0151, to arrange a trip.

Up the coast on the Grand Strand, **Coastal Scuba,** 1626 Hwy. 17 S, N. Myrtle Beach, tel. (843) 361-3323, claims the area's largest, most comfortable dive boat, offering dive charters to Civil War and WW II wrecks, along with rentals, repair, and instruction. **Mermaid Diving Adventures,** 4123 Bus. Hwy. 17, Murrells Inlet, tel. (843) 357-3483, and **The Scuba Syndrome,** 515-A Hwy. 501, tel. (843) 626-3483, Myrtle Beach, also provide diving instruction, equipment rentals, and charters.

Inland, you'll find **Columbia Scuba,** 1234 St. Andrews Rd., tel. (803) 561-9500, which offers complete lessons and equipment rentals, as does the **Wateree Dive Center Inc.,** 1767 Burning Tree Dr., tel. (803) 731-9344. These businesses are always getting together groups to probe the depths of South Carolina's lakes and rivers, and will even take you on down to the coast, where a wealth of sunken ships awaits. A third alternative is **Sunset Scuba** at 5339 Sunset Blvd., tel. (803) 808-3483.

In the Upcountry, **All Water Sports,** 105 E. Butler Rd., Mauldin, tel. (843) 288-9339, provides rentals, diving excursions, and lessons, as do **Scuba Diving Downunder,** 21 Rushmore Dr., Greenville, tel. (843) 244-3373; **Premier Scuba and Water Sports,** 2005 E. Greenville St., Anderson, tel. (843) 226-1660; **Scuba Connection,** 16 W. Lee Rd. in Taylors, tel. (843) 244-5282; and **Scuba Ocean Sports,** 110 N.W. Main St., Easley, tel. (843) 306-3483.

Other Water Sports

Sailing, parasailing, windsurfing, and **catamaran sailing** are all popular along the South Carolina coast. You'll find plenty of great places to **water-ski** and **jet-ski** in South Carolina, both on the coast and inland in the state's many lakes. For information on outfitters for all of these sports, see the listings under individual destinations.

CANOEING/KAYAKING

South Carolina is a paddler's paradise, offering everything from challenging clear mountain whitewater to peaceful blackwater rivers oozing through swamps and wave-challenging Atlantic beach paddles. In the Lowcountry, perhaps the place to start is **Hunting Island State Park,** which offers ocean and inlet kayaking around pristine subtropical islands.

Or contact **Coastal Expeditions,** 514-B Mill St., Mount Pleasant, tel. (843) 884-7684, and set up a sea-kayak trip to the uninhabited, well-regulated **Bull Island,** just north of Charleston. If you're a nature lover, it may well be the best experience of your Lowcountry life. Fantastic scenery and birding.

In the Midlands, **Congaree Swamp National Monument**'s 27-mile designated canoe trail provides unbeatable views of this primeval wonderland. In the Upcountry, it's hard to beat the **Chattooga River** for whitewater excitement; the river includes the Class V rapids that gave Burt Reynolds such grief in *Deliverance.*

In the Upcountry, you'll find great day trips and overnighters with **Nantahala Outdoor Center** in Mountain Rest, tel. (800) 232-7238 or (864) 647-9014, and other outfitters.

In the Lowcountry between Charleston and Hilton Head you'll find the **Edisto River Trail,** which takes in some 56 peaceful Lowcountry miles along the Edisto River. You'll find guided canoe and kayak tours of the ACE Basin National Wildlife Refuge and the Edisto River Canoe and Kayak Trail offered by **Carolina Heritage Outfitters** in Canadys, tel. (843) 563-5051 or (800) 563-5053; **Outside Hilton Head** on Hilton Head Island, tel. (843) 686-6996 or (800) 686-6996; **The Kayak Farm** on St. Helena Island, tel. (843) 838-2008; **Time Out** in Charleston, tel. (843) 577-5979 (kayak trips only); Georgetown's **Black River Expeditions,** tel. (843) 546-4840, Myrtle Beach's **Wind N Sea Outfitters,** tel. (843) 272-4420 (kayaking only). The same businesses are the places to look for rental options.

Midlands outfits providing tours include **Adventure Carolina,** tel. (803) 796-4505, and **River Runner Outdoor Center,** tel. (803) 771-0353, both in Columbia. Upcountry tour providers include **Chattooga Whitewater Shop,** tel. (864)

647-9083, in Long Creek; **Chattooga River Adventures,** tel. (864) 647-0365, in Mountain Rest; and **Sunrift Adventures,** tel. (864) 834-3019 in Travelers Rest.

If you're planning a trip into the area and would like to meet other people interested in exploring the state's waterways with you, contact the **Palmetto Paddlers Club,** tel. (803) 771-4329 which promotes the use and preservation of both urban and wild rivers and waterways.

RAFTING

As with canoeing and kayaking, the birth of whitewater rafting's popularity can be traced to the Chattooga River, where the film *Deliverance* was filmed (for an excellent blow-by-blow account of the shooting, see Christopher Dickey's 1998 book *Summer of Deliverance*) in South Carolina's northeast corner (as well as northwest Georgia). Dropping an average of 49.3 feet per mile, the **Chattooga National Wild and Scenic River** runs for 40 miles as a cascading, boiling dividing line between South Carolina and Georgia. If you want to experience this famous stretch of whitewater but don't have canoeing or kayaking experience, consider a guided raft tour. They're relatively safe and sometimes these things are more fun when you share the experience with a group. For guided raft tours, contact **Wildwater Ltd.,** tel. (800) 451-9972 or (864) 647-9587, or **Nantahala Outdoor Center** in Mountain Rest, at (800) 232-7238 or (864) 647-9014.

Paddlers around the world revere the Chattooga River for its Class IV and V rapids.

If you're new to rafting, a Class IV rapid is one that requires safety helmets. Class V requires sedatives. (Niagara Falls is considered a Class VI, so you see where we're headed here.)

FISHING

The person who invents the all-in-one driving iron and fishing pole will make a quick fortune in South Carolina—beyond golfing, Carolinians like most to fish.

The Lowcountry features Gulf Stream fishing for marlin, sailfish, tuna, dolphin, and wahoo. Closer in, you can still hope to land mackerel, blackfin tuna, cobia, and shark. Surf and jetty fishing includes spottail bass, flounder, croakers, and whiting. The Midlands' streams and marshes teem with fish, including blue catfish, striped bass, crappie, bream, and white and largemouth bass.

Licenses
Nonresidents 14 or older must have a license to fish in any fresh waters. South Carolina has a reciprocal fishing agreement with Georgia only. Licenses are generally available at hardware and tackle shops. You won't need a license to fish in the ocean, unless you fish from a private boat.

SHRIMPING

How To
For shrimping, you'll need a cast net and an ice chest or some saltwater. A cast net is round, with weights all along the rim; you throw a cast net somewhat the way you'd throw a Frisbee, though in truth it flies closer to the way an uncooked pizza would. Which is one way of saying this might take you a little practice. But what's a half hour or hour's practice when it teaches you how to catch shrimp?

After you've thrown a perfect loop—so that the net hits the water as a circle, its weights bringing the net down in a perfect dome over the unsuspecting shrimp—wait for the weights to hit the bottom. This is something you just have to sense, since you can't see or feel it. Now jerk on the center line that draws the weights together, closing the bottom of the dome into a sphere, and trapping the shrimp.

You can rent a small johnboat or outboard, or you can throw from some inlet bridges; it's up to you, but most people seem to feel that ebb tide is the time to throw, since this is when the shrimp, who spend high tide spread out and frolicking in the marsh grasses, are the most concentrated in the creek beds. Cast your net toward the side of a waterway, just on the edge of the grasses, and you may well snag a number of these mobile crustaceans.

CRABBING

How To

Crabbing has to be one of the easiest ways to catch some of the best food found in the ocean. Oh, you can charter your boats far out to sea, slaphappy on Dramamine, but you'll find *me* in the shallows with a bucket, a string, a sinker, a net, and some ripe chicken backs. That's pretty much all you need to land a good supper's worth of **blue crab** in South Carolina.

1. Tie the string to a piece of chicken and the sinker.
2. Wade out in the water about waist-high.
3. Hold onto one end of the string, and drop the chicken and sinker into the water.
4. Wait for the crabs to come scuttling over for supper.
5. When you feel a tug on the chicken, pull up on the string and swoop beneath the crab with your net.

A few rules here:
- If the crabs have yellow eggs (roe) on the underside, the law requires you to toss them back.
- If the crab is less than five inches wide across its back, you'll need to toss it back, too.

Drop the "lucky" ones who pass these two tests into an ice chest and keep them cold until you cook them.

When you've got an ice chest full of blue crabs, only one step remains:

6. Call me; invite me over for dinner.

HUNTING

South Carolina has one of the longest hunting seasons in the United States. For many Carolinians, a crisp fall day just isn't complete without the blast of a rifle and the "thunk" of metal tearing flesh.

And who can blame them?

Granted, the only animal I ever shot was tin and had a bull's-eye painted between its forepaws. And granted, irresponsible hunters who kill something as beautiful as a buck only to

strap a new pair of antlers to their Blazer should be forced to wear the antlers and a fur coat to the next PETA convention. But few instincts seem to be as ingrained in humans as the instinct to hunt prey, and the activity ("sport" seems somewhat misleading—as if the animals had to kick in a league fee to join the fun) has a long history in the South, and in the cultures from which modern-day Southerners descend.

You'll find white-tailed deer, wild turkey, ruffed grouse, quail, squirrels, and other small mammals just a-beggin' to be gunned down across the state in national and state forests, national wildlife refuges, and wildlife management areas.

Get the specifics from the South Carolina Department of Natural Resources, P.O. Box 167, Columbia, SC 29202-0167, tel. (803) 734-3938.

HIKING, BACKPACKING, AND BIKING

South Carolina features a number of excellent hiking trails, including the soon-to-be-completed **Palmetto Trail,** stretching across the entire state.

Though it won't help your wildlife-viewing any, during hunting season, try to wear some fluorescent orange. Better yet, you'll find plenty of great trails in hunting-free state parks and nature preserves to keep you busy until the smoke clears at the end of hunting season. Just to be safe, however, it won't hurt to wear some orange here also—to keep safe against poachers.

If you're hiking with a dog, make sure Fido's wearing some orange, too.

The Foothills Trail

This is a spectacular, often rugged, 85-mile deep-woods path winding over the steep ridges of the North Carolina border from Table Rock to Oconee State Park. You'll find primitive campsites along the trail. Call Caesars Head at (864) 836-6115 for information.

Other Trails

Go online to www.sctrails.net/Trails/ for a very helpful searchable database of nearly 200 South Carolina trails. Go on to the links area for a great listing of Trails and Outdoor Resources on the Web.

Biking

Much of the Palmetto Trail, and many other SC trails, allow mountain bikes. In the coastal areas particularly, you'll find good rides abounding. A very dependable ride is to simply take your bike along the hard-packed sand on the beach. See individual chapters for specifics.

TENNIS

Both Hilton Head and Myrtle Beach are amazing tennis resorts. See individual regional chapters for specific resorts.

As for watching tennis, the **Family Circle Magazine Cup,** one of the country's top professional women's tennis tournaments on the Corel WTA Tour, takes place in late March or early April on Hilton Head Island. Call (800) 677-2293 for information.

GOLF

South Carolina offers some 250 golf courses to the public. (That means that for every Waffle House you see in South Carolina, the state offers two public golf courses.) Golf contributes $650 million and 14,000 jobs annually to the South Carolina economy.

Because of a solemn vow I once made to a dying Dutch/Hawaiian uncle, I don't personally golf on courses without concrete volcanoes or miniature windmills located somewhere on the course. But don't let my scruples keep *you* from enjoying South Carolina's world-class links: I've enlisted the aid of dedicated duffer Kendall Buckendahl of Mount Pleasant—manager of Pro Golf of Charleston—to lend his insights into the state's offerings.

Classic Courses

In 1998, when *Golf* magazine put out a list of the top 100 courses the average person can play in the U.S., **Harbour Town Links** (Hilton Head) and **The Ocean Course** (Charleston) ranked in the top 10. **Wild Dunes' Links Course** (Charleston), **The Dunes** (Myrtle Beach), and **Tidewater** (Myrtle Beach) all ranked in the top 40.

Caladonia in Pawleys Island came in at a very respectable No. 85.

Other Stellar Courses

South Carolina courses offer a lot of diversity, scenery-wise: from mountain courses to seafront links. **Tidewater** in Myrtle is a good one. Also, Kiawah Island's refurbished **Cougar Point** is getting a lot of praise. In Charleston, **Charleston National** is a great one that is relatively moderate in price, and the ocean course is the tops by far for ocean scenery. In the Upcountry, **Cliffs of Glassy** is another jewel—it's pretty exclusive, but if you have the money, you can probably get in. Truly a gem in the mountains.

Values

If you want to golf inexpensively, keep a couple of things in mind. One is the time of year. Spring and fall are high season, and "high season" equals "high prices."

Head to Myrtle Beach in the winter and dead of summer for great price specials. The Grand Strand offers the highest concentration of golf courses in the country. It is really *the* golf destination of the South, if not the nation.

Other values come from areas that have resorts close by, such as Hilton Head and Charleston. The well-cared-for grounds at the resorts force the public courses in the surrounding area to upgrade their grounds for competition's sake; the value comes from not having to pay the resort's high prices for a resort-grade course.

In Charleston, **Charleston National** as well as **Dunes West, Coosaw Creek,** and **Crowfield** all have great layouts and cost under $100 to play, even in the high season. At **Hilton Head,** a couple of names that stand out value-wise include: **Palmetto Dunes, Shipyard,** and **Whispering Pines.**

To Find Out More

South Carolina offers an excellent booklet, the *South Carolina Golf Guide,* published annually; pick one up at one of the state's visitors centers, or call (800) 682-5553 for a copy.

WINTER SPORTS

Downhill Skiing

Okay, I will admit that to downhill ski, you actually do need to leave South Carolina—but not by much. Beech Mountain, Sugar Mountain, and Hawksnest all lie just over the North Carolina border.

If you're looking for the best skiing in the entire Southeast, you'll want to head to **Winterplace,** in West Virginia.

SPECTATOR SPORTS

Football

Though the NFL's Carolina Panthers, based up in border town Charlotte, North Carolina, were carefully named to represent (and, thus, draw) fans from both Carolinas, it's *college* football that still dominates South Carolina. Even people who never got around to completing eighth grade take intercollegiate ball very seriously.

How seriously? Think of it as religion instead of football, and of Northern Ireland instead of South Carolina. But instead of Roman Catholicism vs. Protestantism, here we have USC Gamecockism vs. Clemson Tigerism. True believers of either faith can live anywhere in the state, though loyalties grow predictably more fierce near the home coliseums. Signs of devotion can include anything from class rings and ball caps to 40-foot motor homes painted with tiger paws. Yes, other South Carolina colleges have notable football programs (the Citadel Bulldogs are perhaps the third-largest "denomination" available—and the state is home, too, to a number of dissenters who support North Carolina's Duke), but that doesn't

In South Carolina, even Barbie's got football fever.

mean you can answer "Wofford" when asked who you're *for* on USC/Clemson game day. On that day, in either Columbia or Clemson (it alternates yearly), caravans of color-coordinated trucks, cars, and RVs pour into the game town bearing hordes of the opposing team's faithful. If the game's on a Sunday, sermons end early. Streets are deserted, and an eerie silence pervades the town, broken only by synchronized cheers erupting from a thousand bars and living rooms whenever the home team scores.

Minor League Baseball

It's hard for a lot of fans to take Major League Baseball seriously these days; it's hard to see much drama in a game when you're looking out at a diamond full of players who, win or lose, are cumulatively worth more than the GM Board of Directors. If you've grown weary of high ticket prices and multimillionaire players, be sure to catch a minor league game while you're in state. Watching these 18- and 19-year-olds—who are being paid less than a middle manager at Hardee's—battle it out for a chance at the bigs just might help you remember why you fell in love with the game in the first place. South Carolina is blessed with *three* single-A baseball teams. The first two, Columbia's **Capital City Bombers** and the **Charleston River Dogs,** compete in the South Atlantic (or "Sallie") League. Both play in first-rate stadiums, with maybe a tip of the cap

> *The titanic clashes of annual football rivals in huge stadiums, drawing as they do legions of pilgrim followers garbed in totemic tribal colors to these holy sites, pouring out libations to the gods at ritual tailgating activities, screaming anathemas at their evil opponents while imploring the spotless host of their own team, praying for redemption—all this has the aspect of a public religious observance, perhaps an exorcism, perhaps a collective pursuit of spirit-filled ecstatic trance. In South Carolina such recurring rites are difficult to ignore or to avoid.*
>
> —Kevin Lewis, "Religion in South Carolina Addresses the Public Order," in Religion in South Carolina, *1993*

going to Charleston's classic style, designed by the same people who created groundbreaking Camden Yards in Baltimore.

By the time you read this, a new $16 million ballpark should be completed in Myrtle Beach for the single-A Carolina League farm team for the Atlanta Braves.

Up in Greenville, you'll find the AA Braves—another Atlanta farm team. Over in Fort Mill, you'll find the AAA **Charlotte Knights** playing their home games at the top-notch Knights Castle.

Professional Soccer

The **Charleston Battery** plays fine USISL minor league soccer over in their new 5,600-seat stadium on Daniel Island. The Battery has played in Charleston since 1993 when the team joined the USISL, a conglomeration of nearly 150 teams in five separate leagues. The Battery has placed toward the top of their division every year since 1994, including winning in the USISL finals in 1996. They play about 20 games a year in Daniel Island Stadium, located right off the Mark Clark Expressway (I-126), tel. (843) 740-7787. Tickets run $8-10 for adults, less for kids. Be sure to bring the kids (under 16 years) up to an hour before game time, when the Fun Zone, an "interactive soccer theme park" (which overstates it a bit) is open, including a soccer bounce, various games, a playground for the kids, and a picnic area for kids. See the Battery online at www.bb-service.com/battery. The Grand Strand now has the **Myrtle Beach Sea Dawgs,** tel. (803) 236-7767, Web site: www.seadawgs.com.

Minor League Hockey

All of a sudden, there are three professional hockey teams in South Carolina: the **South Carolina Stingrays, Pee Dee Pride,** and the **Greenville Grrrowl.** All three teams play in the East Coast Hockey League.

The Stingrays, affiliated with the Buffalo Sabres in the NHL and the Rochester Americans in the AHL, have done battle at the North Charleston Coliseum since first skating their way into the hearts of Charlestonians in 1993. Check them out online at www.stingrayshockey.com. The independent Pride plays in Florence at the Florence County Civic Center, a.k.a. "The Lion's Den" or "The Jungle." This is their second year in South Carolina. Before moving here they

were known as the Knoxville Cherokees. Their Web site is www.peedeepride.com.

Greenville, affiliated with the NHL Boston Bruins and the AHL Providence Bruins, plays at the Bi-Lo Center in Greenville.

A fierce rivalry has already sprung up between the rival South Carolinian teams, which vie each year for the All Tell Cup (formerly the Palmetto Cup). The rivalry is greatest between the Rays and the Pride; according to one fan, the Rays have been known to "misprint" "Pee Wee Pride" on tickets for home games against the Pride.

Auto Racing

If you're new to South Carolina and the South in general, you may be surprised to discover that cereal boxes, billboards, and fast food commercials often feature the likes of Dale Earnhardt, Richard Petty, and Jeff Gordon—auto racers all. Among other events, Darlington's **Darlington Raceway** is site of the NASCAR TranSouth Financial 400 stock car race each spring and the high-stakes Mountain Dew Southern 500 on Labor Day weekend. Call (843) 395-8821 for information. Auto racing fans will want to visit the **Joe Weatherly NMPA Stock Car Hall of Fame,** next door. Call (843) 395-8821 for information.

Horse Racing

Each spring, the **Aiken Triple Crown Horse Races** extend over three consecutive weekends, normally the last three weekends in March, and draw an average of 20,000 people to little Aiken. They provide viewers with the chance to watch three separate events. The first race is the Trials, held since 1942 on the Aiken Training Track, the first public viewing of some of the finest thoroughbreds in the world. Nominal admission. Bring tailgating goodies and join the crowds that always gather to party/picnic down in the parking lot before the races. The Steeplechase is run at Conger Field the following weekend, complete with a massive tent party. The final weekend features harness racing at the Aiken Mile Track. For information, contact the Aiken Chamber of Commerce at 400 Laurens St. NW, tel. (800) 542-4536 or (803) 641-1111, fax (803) 641-4174.

In November, Camden's prestigious **Colonial Cup steeplechase race** usually determines the champion and winner of NSA's Eclipse award. Call (803) 432-6513 for information.

Rodeo
Credit Tant Ehrhardt of Orangeburg with one of the best reviews ever given of a second-rate rodeo: "I think the animals won." Granted, South Carolina is not the first state that comes to mind when you think of rodeo, but the western two-thirds of the state was part of America's first frontier, and a strong equestrian subculture remains, even if some of the trappings of South Carolinian rodeos are imported from points west.

Blacksburg hosts the **Ed Brown Rodeo** in August, complete with bareback and saddle bronc riding, calf roping, steer wrestling, barrel racing, and bull riding. Call Ed himself at (864) 839-5646, for information. In mid-September you can attend two full-scale rodeos at the **Congaree Western Weekend** in West Columbia, tel. (803) 755-2512, and at the **Ruby Rodeo** in the town of Ruby, tel. (803) 283-3302. Smaller (and often less complete) rodeos take place in rural towns throughout the year; keep an eye on the telephone poles beside two-lane roads for flyers telling when and where.

ENTERTAINMENT AND EVENTS

MUSEUMS

You'd better believe that a state as interested in culture and in its own history as South Carolina can offer a number of stellar museums to peruse. Below I've discussed some of the most noteworthy, but note that these do not count the many small museums found at the state's myriad historic sites.

Historical/Cultural
Nearly every town in South Carolina features a local museum of some sort. Often, these are little more than collections of historic objects, with very little interpretation involved. The interpreting usually comes from the volunteer seated by the door.

That said, South Carolina features some of the finest contemporary museums in the South. Historic Charleston—a living history museum in itself—is the place to start. The **Charleston Museum**—oldest museum in the United States—interprets the natural and cultural history of the Lowcountry. **African-American National Heritage Museum**—actually, a collection of sites in the Charleston area, with its hub at the **Slave Mart Museum** on Chalmers St.—is one of the nation's premier museums exploring the origins and contributions of African-American culture in the U.S. For the other side of the story, visit the **Daughters of the Confederacy Museum** upstairs above the Old City Market. One of my favorite smaller museums—featuring the "Hurricane Hugo Revisited" exhibit—is the **Museum on the Common** over in Mount Pleasant. Nearby, off Hwy. 17, you'll find **Patriots Point Naval and Maritime Museum,** which includes as one of its exhibits a little thing called the aircraft carrier **USS Yorktown.** Those fascinated by things nautical can also tour a submarine, a destroyer, and a re-creation of a Vietnam naval support base. Columbia's **State Museum** also includes a very strong history section.

Fine Arts
You'll find scores of art museums throughout the state: can't-misses include the **State Museum** in Columbia and Charleston's **Gibbes Museum of Art,** which both showcase collections of American art and portraits with connections to Southern history.

Brookgreen Gardens, south of Myrtle Beach, is the world's largest outdoor sculpture showcase, containing 550 19th- and 20th-century pieces, landscaped with 2,000 species of plants. In Greenville, **Bob Jones University Museum and Gallery** provides arguably the best collection of Dutch, Spanish, and Italian masters in America, including works from Dolci, Rembrandt, Rubens, Titian, and Van Dyck.

Botanical Gardens, Zoo, and Aquariums
Columbia's nationally ranked Riverbanks Zoo and Botanical Gardens constitutes a double whammy to those interested in carbon-based life forms. Greenville also features a zoo, and Clemson University is home to the beautiful South Carolina State Botanical Garden. In the past few years, South Carolina has sprouted two huge aquariums, Myrtle Beach's entertainment-oriented but still educational **Ripley's Aquarium** and Charleston's education-oriented but still entertaining **South Carolina Aquarium.**

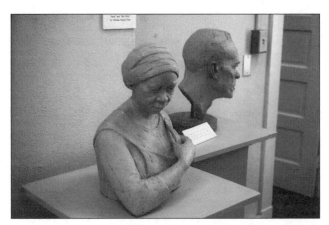

sculptor Thomas Clark's "Sam" and "His Wife"

WINETASTING

If you've come to South Carolina primarily for its winetasting offerings, your travel agent somewhere has given you a bum steer. McCormick County's Bordeaux community, founded by French Huguenots in 1764, *was* the first commercial winery in the U.S., but at press time for this book, South Carolina was home to only two active wineries. In the Upcountry, **Cruse Vineyards and Winery,** Woods Rd., off Hwy. 72, about four miles north of Chester, tel. (803) 377-3944, offers tasting of their reds, whites, and blushes on Friday and Saturday afternoons. Just 2.5 miles east of Aiken on Hwy. 78, you'll find **Montmorenci Vineyards,** tel. (803) 649-4870. Open for tours and tastings Wed.-Sat. 10 a.m.-6 p.m., year-round.

A few other wineries are planned for various spots around the state. Check with one of the state's visitors centers for updated information, or watch for the next edition of this book.

PLANTATIONS

Most non-Southerners don't really feel that they've visited the South until they tour a real plantation. Well, if it's antebellum splendor you're seeking, you'll find it in South Carolina. Probably the most outstanding examples of plantation grounds are **Magnolia Plantation** and **Middle-**

ton Place, though in both cases, the main house has been Shermanized. At Magnolia, you'll find acres and acres of beautiful gardens to explore on foot or by boat, and the Audubon Swamp Garden, where the famous wildlife artist himself once wandered about, sketch pad in hand, as a guest of the Drayton family. At Middleton, an adjoining guest house survived Sherman; it's where the Middletons lived after the war. Remarkable gardens—the oldest formal gardens in North America—here as well.

Drayton Hall, off Ashley River Rd. in North Charleston, still boasts its original main house, a famous example of early Georgian architecture. Though its main plantation house is a 1935 reconstruction of the original, **Boone Hall Plantation** near Mount Pleasant is worth visiting because: 1) it allows you to see what a plantation looked like when it was relatively new; 2) it contains nine original slave cabins, which tell more about slave conditions than all the interpretive exhibits in the world; 3) if you're looking for the type of plantation you saw on TV's *North and South,* Boone Hall Plantation *is* precisely that plantation; it's where that miniseries, and several others, were filmed; and 4) rumor has it that Margaret Mitchell's *Tara* (she finished *Gone With The Wind* in 1936) is modeled after the place—down to the gauntlet of moss-dripping oaks at the entrance. Battle reenactments are performed here in the summer, filling the grounds and mansion with period-dressed soldiers and belles (though oddly, nobody seems to want to come dressed as a slave). For the Civil War buff, there's nothing like it.

Farther north along the coast, the **Hampton Plantation State Park** and **Hopsewee Plantation** are excellently preserved properties rich with historical import.

MUSIC

I used to say that to understand almost everything you need to know about South Carolina's musical tastes, you need only examine the selections on the jukebox in the student lounge at Orangeburg-Calhoun Technical College: one-half rap and soul, one-half country-and-western. The college has removed the divisive jukebox, but the musical cleft still continues, though this split is not completely along racial lines, either—you're quite likely to hear thumping bass and rap lyrics spilling out of a fat-tired four-by-four with Coors cans in the back, driven by Skoal-chewing, ball cap-wearing European-Americans—though it's less common that you'll find urban African-Americans blasting Garth Brooks and Wynonna.

I say *almost* everything because South Carolina's music scene also includes bluegrass, black and white Southern gospel, and Carolina beach music, as well as burgeoning alternative rock scenes in Charleston, Columbia, and Greenville.

Country

Because so many South Carolinians still live in smaller towns, and because, by God, this *is* the American South, you can expect to hear a lot of country-and-western music in South Carolina—with the emphasis on the country, and less emphasis on the western swing tradition. You'll hear country played between innings at baseball games, from the grandstands at the county fairs, in barber shops, and even faintly in the background as you browse some bookstores.

Country music is a major force in South Carolina culture, and South Carolina has been an important force in country music—particularly in the genre's early days. Born in Chesterfield County, **Jimmie Tarlton** of the 1920s act Darby and Tarlton, wrote the now-standard "Birmingham Jail" in 1925 after having been jailed in said

Alabaman city for moonshining. Darby and Tarlton pioneered the blending of black blues vocals (and even Hawaiian slide guitar) with the mountain sound derived from Elizabethan ballads, giving them a bluesy quality that reveals its influence in the birth of modern country. Though the duo quit performing altogether by 1935, they were rediscovered during the 1960s folk revival, during which Jimmie Tarlton recorded a new album, performed at folk clubs, and was interviewed continually by folklorists. He died in 1979.

Darlington's **Dixon Brothers,** Dorsey and Howard, temporarily escaped their lives as Upcountry textile mill workers in the 1930s, creating some of the most creative, socially conscious, and spiritually sensitive music of the era. Their songs reflect their faith ("Wonderful Day," "Not Turning Backward") and social interests ("School House Fire," "Weave Room Blues," "Spinning Room Blues," and "Weaver's Life is Like an Engine"). Perhaps most famous is the compelling "Wreck on the Highway," covered by Roy Acuff and numerous folk groups in the 1960s.

Enoree's **Claude Casey** became famous in the 1930s and 40s touring as front man of the western swing band Claude Casey and the Pine State Cowboys, and went on to make a handful of movies, most notably 1943's *Swing Your Partner* with Dale Evans, and 1949's *Square Dance Jubilee.* His contributions to Upcountry music included his years as host of a TV show in Greenville in the early '50s and the founding and operation of WJES, in Johnston.

Like the Dixon Brothers, **Arthur "Guitar Boogie" Smith** came from the Piedmont-area mill culture. Born in Clinton, he played on Spartanburg radio station WSPA in the 1930s, and brought his Dixieland background into his country guitar stylings. His 1945 "Guitar Boogie" has become a standard. In the 1950s, he and guitarist Don Reno wrote a song called "Feudin' Banjos," which they later proved in court was the basis for Eric Weisberg and Steve Mandel's 1973 *Deliverance* theme song and pop hit "Dueling Banjos."

Whenever you hear the original "Sugarfoot Rag," the twanging guitar solo of Elvis Presley's "Little Sister," or the intro to Patsy Cline's prophetic "I Fall to Pieces," you're listening to the amazing finger work of the Spartanburg area's **Hank "Sugarfoot" Garland,** a major Nashville Cat in the 1940s and '50s, largely sidelined since 1961 by a car accident.

Credit (or blame) banjoist Bob Thompson of Converse with that rapid-fire finger-picking you used to hear at the beginning of TV's *Hee Haw.* That's also him playing during the chase scenes on *Smokey and the Bandit,* and on a number of Monkee records (you really didn't think it was Peter Tork, did you?). Spartanburg County's **Buck Trent** backed up everyone from Porter Waggonner and Dolly Parton to Roy Clark before getting a job on *Hee Haw,* where he became famous as a comedian. Widely credited with having invented the electric banjo, Trent continues as a popular performer today in Branson, Missouri.

Comedian/singer Jim Nesbitt from Bishopville scored with a number of comedic, mild social protest songs in the 1960s and '70s. Country Music Hall of Fame songwriter **Bill Anderson** was born in Columbia but raised in an Atlanta suburb. (Nonetheless, you'll find him in the South Carolina Entertainer's Hall of Fame in North Charleston.) His 1961 hit "Po' Folks" became the name of a Southern restaurant chain, for which he became the spokesman.

In more recent years, South Carolina's contributions to the country music world include Spartanburg's influential country-rock **Marshall Tucker Band,** which had a few pop and country hits in the early to mid-'70s and was a major influence on a number of groups from Garth Brooks and Hank Williams Jr. to the Kentucky Headhunters. In the early 1980s, Aiken-area native **Leon Everette** nailed down a number of hits and a nomination as the Academy of Country Music's Best New Male Vocalist, but by the 1990s he had settled into running a store in Ward. In the early 1990s, Sumter-born USC alumnus **Rob Crosby** had a handful of hits before disappearing from radar, as did **Dixiana,** featuring the powerful vocals of Cindy Murphy.

Probably Greenville's **Aaron Tippin,** who grew up on his father's 120-acre Upcountry farm, is the biggest current South Carolina-bred star in the country-and-western universe. Tippin came out in 1990 sounding like the Voice of the Upcountry with "You've Got to Stand for Something (or You'll Fall for Anything)," at just the right time for the song to be picked up as a kind of anthem for soldiers in and supporters of the Persian Gulf War. Tippin followed this up with one of the greatest car songs in recent memory, "There Ain't Nothing Wrong With the Radio," which went to No. 1 on the country charts, and then proceeded with other self-penned songs documenting and celebrating the rural blue-collar Upcountry heritage, including the pro-Labor, "Working Man's PhD" and the anthemic "I Wouldn't Have It Any Other Way." Rock Hill's **David Ball,** whose "Thinking Problem" rocked country airwaves in 1994, played for years with Spartanburg-born, gone-to-Austin legend Walter Hyatt in Uncle Walt's Band. Hyatt himself was claimed as an inspiration by Lyle Lovett, Jimmie Dale Gilmore, Marshall Chapman, Hal Ketchum, and Junior Brown, all of whom played various memorial concerts for him after Hyatt died with 109 others in the crash of a Valujet DC-9 into the Florida everglades in May 1996.

Misters Tippin and Ball aside, today South Carolina's primary contribution to the country music subculture today seems to be in giving country acts venues to play. With over a half dozen country-themed concert halls, and more on the way, Myrtle Beach has in the past few years become the Branson, Missouri, of the Deep South. Country-rock supergroup **Alabama** made its living for many pre-stardom years in the early 1970s as the house band at the Myrtle Beach beachside bar the Bowery. In the early 1990s, they opened their own eponymous club in North Myrtle. They had a country (and beach music) hit in 1997 with "Dancin', Shaggin' on the Boulevard," a tribute to the band's early years in Myrtle Beach, and to the city that played such a big part in their careers.

Bluegrass

In West Columbia, **Bill's Pickin' Parlor** is the place to go for Friday night sit-in sessions with local musicians. As long as you can have fun without cussing, drinking, and smoking (all forbidden), you'll have yourself a ball. Bring your stringed instrument and join in. In May, head on up to Lancaster for the **Carolina Legends Bluegrass Festival,** featuring the Dewitt "Snuffy" Jenkins Memorial Banjo Competition. In truth, unless a festival is focused on a different tradition—Charleston's Greek Festival, for instance, features little bluegrass—it'll bring out the pickers.

Southern Gospel and Blues

Since 1973, when they sang backup on Paul Simon's pop hit "Loves Me Like a Rock," the **Dixie Hummingbirds** have been gospel's best-known group. More recently, *Ebony* magazine chose them as the greatest black gospel quartet of all time. Formed in 1928 in Greenville, the Birds' distinctive longtime (since 1944) lead singer, Ira Tucker, hails from Spartanburg. Listen to some of the Hummingbirds' hits like the rhythmic "Christian's Automobile" (1957) and fiery "In the Morning" (1961), and you'll see where groups like the Temptations and Four Tops found the fire.

Political folk/gospel/blues giant **Josh White,** from Greenville, had a uniquely diverse career. He spent his musical apprenticeship traveling around the South with a series of blind street singer/guitarists before moving to New York City in the early 1930s and recording gospel songs such as "Joshua White, the Singing Christian," while simultaneously recording blues records as "Pinewood Tom." His performances with Paul Robeson in the show *John Henry* led him to fame; throughout the 1950s and '60s he was revered as a folk singer and was a major influence on Pete Seeger and others.

Born in Laurens in 1896, **Reverend Gary Davis** (who sometimes also performed as Blind Gary Davis) attended a Braille school in Spartanburg before being discovered in 1920s while street singing in Durham, N.C. He was taken to New York City where he recorded and continued street preaching; he began to receive recognition in the 1940s for his guitar stylings. Bob Dylan recorded a number of his songs.

Born just four years after Davis in the same tiny Piedmont town of Laurens was legendary blues guitarist **Alvin "Pink" Anderson.** He went to the streets of Spartanburg to find his musical glory. Somehow, in the 1960s, a copy of Pink Anderson's rare album *Carolina Blues Man* found its way into the hand of a young British musician named Syd Barrett, who was so impressed he ended up naming his blues band—Pink Floyd—after Pink (and North Carolina bluesman Floyd Council). Today, Anderson's son Alvin "Little Pink" Anderson, having done a couple spells in prison, is attempting to build a career on replicating his father's music.

Blues singer **Eartha Kitt** was born in tiny North, South Carolina, near Orangeburg. She moved to New York while still a child and later went on to star on stage and screen, including a turn as TV's Catwoman. Sometime-preacher, sometime-convict Reverend **James Brown** was born in Barnwell, and though he spent much of his early life across the river in Augusta, Georgia, he's now a sometime resident of Aiken.

R&B singer **Peabo Bryson** hails from Greenville as well.

If at all possible, be sure to catch **Marlena Smalls and the Hallelujah Singers,** based in Frogmore on St. Helena Island. They were the gospel group featured in *Forrest Gump*—Smalls played Bubba's mother.

The very unbluesy white gospel singers of the **Blue Ridge Quartet,** based in Spartanburg, recorded more than a hundred albums from the '50s through the '70s, but they were truly etched into the Formica countertop of pop culture in R.E.M.'s song, "Voice of Harold," which begins with the tag, "To Elmo Fagg, founder and leader of the Blue Ridge Quartet."

You'll find blues clubs in all major cities in South Carolina. They're listed in the appropriate destination chapters.

Carolina Beach Music

Outside of the South, beach music is one of the least known and least understood musical genres in America. Part of the confusion lies with those who assume that the term beach music refers to the California vocal surf music of the Beach Boys and Jan and Dean or the instrumental surf music of Dick Dale and the Surfaris. Carolina beach music is a whole different animal, popular on a whole different coast, and one main difference is that it is not primarily music featuring lyrics about the beach or developed to capture

---

CATCH THE "BREEZE"

Listen to Carolina beach music in South Carolina on The Breeze Radio Network, which comprises the following stations:

> 98.9 FM, WWBZ, Charleston
> 99.7 FM, WHBZ, Hilton Head
> 98.5 FM, WLXC, Columbia

You can also visit the network online at www.breezeradio.com.

SHAG CLUBS

Shaggers—practitioners of that South Carolina institution the shag—love getting together to cut a rug. Shag clubs provide a point of contact for other interested shaggers. Most meet regularly to dance, and all are good places to find out about local shagging spots. Below is a list of such clubs throughout the state. For details about clubs in particular towns, call (800) 742-4437 (800-SHAGGER), check the Web site www.shagger.com, or e-mail shagger@shagger.com. The same sources can give you information on expatriate shag clubs located as far west as California and as far north as Rhode Island.

Anderson
• Electric City Shag Club

Charleston
• Charleston Shag Club

Columbia
• Columbia Shag Club
• Palmetto Shag Club

Dillon
• Dillon County Shag Club

Folly Beach
• Islanders Shag Club

Greenville
• Carolina Shag Club

Greenwood
• Greenwood Shag Club

Hilton Head Island
• Hilton Head Island Carolina Shag Club

Lake Wylie
• Lake Wylie Shag Club

Lancaster
• Lancaster Shag Club

North Augusta
• CSRA Shag Club

Orangeburg
• Orangeburg Area Shag Club

Pawley's Island
• South Strand Shag Club

Rock Hill
• Rock Hill Shag Club

Spartanburg
• R & B Shag Club

the rhythms of the ocean (as instrumental West Coast surf music was), nor is it music that is necessarily written and performed by Carolinian or even Southern artists. Some of beach music's greatest stars have probably never known that they were making "beach music" at all.

Beach music is blues music; most of the early performers of beach music were black. All that was needed was an easy-flowing song with four beats to the measure, about 120 beats per minute. Songs like the Drifters' "Under the Boardwalk," the Tams' "What Kinda Fool Do You Think I Am?" and Maurice Williams and the Zodiacs' "Stay" became beach classics. Perhaps the "Johnny B. Goode" for beach music is the Dominoes "Sixty-Minute Man."

If people found that a jukebox song was good to shag to—even if recorded and/or lyrically set hundreds of miles from the Strand—Bob and Earl's "Harlem Shuffle," for instance—it quickly became absorbed as part of the canon of beach music. Later, in the late '60s, '70s and '80s, a few regional groups began to record songs that lyrically celebrated the beach music/shagging subculture, including The Embers' anthemic "I Love Beach Music."

Other songs, such as Band of Oz's "Ocean Boulevard," celebrated Myrtle Beach life. And some paid homage to local values and enthusiasms—General Johnson and Chairmen of the Board's praise for the "good looks/and sweet personality too" of "Carolina Girls," is but one example.

In 1997, country-rock crossover superstars Alabama released "Dancin', Shaggin' on the Boulevard," which paid tribute to the group's early years as house band at a Myrtle Beach bar, The Bowery. In the process, it fondly evoked the Grand Strand of the 1970s.

Of all of the shagging-specific songs, the most popular outside the beach music subculture has been the Tams' "There Ain't Nothing Like Shagging," which surprised everyone when it raced up into the top 20 on the British pop charts in the mid-'80s. And then everyone remembered what "shagging" means in British English and got over their surprise.

Today, any song with the right beat—whether it's country-and-western, gospel, blues, or rock—can make the beach music charts. Such diverse acts as The Cherry Poppin' Daddies, John

Fogerty, Tracy Chapman, and Patti LaBelle have shared the charts.

You'll find shagging nightclubs in almost any good-sized town. To purchase the music, see **www.shagger.com** online, visit **Judy's House of Oldies,** in N. Myrtle Beach, tel. (843) 249-8649, or call **Ripete Records** (pronounced re-PEAT) at (803) 428-3358.

Rock and Soul

It is said that pompadoured pioneer rocker Eskew Reeder, who recorded as **Esquerita** and lived in Greenville across the street from a toddler named Jesse Jackson, was the major influence behind rocker Little Richard's famous style. As recounted by Michael B. Smith in his *Carolina Dreams: The Musical Legacy of Upstate South Carolina,* Reeder, then a touring gospel pianist, met young Richard Penniman at the Macon, Georgia, bus station at three in the morning in 1954. Penniman went on to base much of his onstage image on Reeder. The career of Esquerita—as Columbia Records insisted on billing him—reached its peak with the low-level hit "Rockin' the Joint" in 1958. Reeder continued performing throughout the years but never reached the fame of his protégé. In 1986, he died penniless, of AIDS, in a Harlem hospital.

Before Esquerita's "Rockin' the Joint" made the charts, Spartanburg's teenage rockabillies, the **Sparkletones,** had a nationwide top 10 hit with "Black Slacks," met Elvis Presley in Vegas, and appeared on the Ed Sullivan Show. The Sullivan appearance, band leader Joe Bennett says in *Hub City Music Makers,* was such a major event locally that it cleared out Spartanburg's Sunday night church services, leaving the churchgoing Sparkletones feeling a bit guilty when they heard about it.

In the early 1960s, around the time young folkie Bob Dylan was recording covers of songs by Laurens' Reverend Gary Davis, Spring Gully in the Lowcountry saw Ernest Evans, a.k.a. Chubby Checker, hit the charts with numerous dance hits—most famously, "The Twist," which rocketed to No. 1 in 1961 and then again in 1962. Around the same time, Barnwell-born James Brown—then living in Augusta, Georgia—began to strike gold with a string of soul hits. Greenwood's **Swinging Medallions** recorded what *Rolling Stone* magazine voted the "Greatest Party Song of the 1960s," "Double Shot of My Baby's Love," and the Amazing Johnny C. took the soulful "Boogaloo Down Broadway" into the *Billboard* top 10 in 1968.

Country rock's **Marshall Tucker Band** led the charge of the Carolinians in the 1970s. The band's opening act featured one-time Spartanburg resident Charlie Daniels on the fiddle. Meanwhile, Spartanburg's Artimus Pyle reached fame as drummer for the tragedy-haunted Southern rock supergroup Lynyrd Skynrd.

In the 1980s, the South Carolina rock scene was overshadowed by what was going on just over the border in Athens, Georgia. In fact, the band that met in the USC dorms in 1985—Hootie and the Blowfish—began its musical career playing R.E.M. covers at many a college gig. Nothing prepared South Carolinians for the Hootiemania that struck in the mid-'90s, when Columbia's favorite party band suddenly became a Grammy-winning, chart-topping phenomenon. Many Carolinians can tell you where they were the night Hootie appeared on the Dave Letterman show. Though the band hasn't matched the sales success of its chart-smashing first album, by putting out worthy follow-ups it seems destined for a long career as an adult contemporary pop rock band. For the complete story on the rise of Hootie, see Mike Miller's fine, *Hootie!: How the Blowfish Put Pop Back Into Pop Rock.* As the new century dawns, every up-and-coming alternative band in South Carolina that gets a recording contract—and a number of companies have signed local bands, including Spartanburg's **Albert Hill** and long-time Charleston street performers **Jump Little Children**—has to go through a period of being described as "The Next Hootie!"

The hottest rock scenes in the state are in Columbia, Charleston, Greenville, and Spartanburg. See the destination chapters for club listings.

Other

You'll find most every kind of live music in South Carolina, from church bell choirs to reggae. Check the local listings in whatever town you're visiting. **Jazz** is popular here in Dizzy Gillespie's home state; Charleston and Beaufort are hot spots. Surf music fans thrill to the sounds of Charleston's **Smoky Weiner and the Hot Links,** who churn out pounding guitar surf with titles like "Gunfight on Folly Beach."

SHOPPING

Antiques
Because South Carolina is a relatively old state, and because it was such a relatively wealthy state in the antebellum years, it's not surprising that this is a great state for antique hunters. Charleston's **King St.** is probably the top stretch in the entire state for antique shopping, but you'll find better prices in smaller towns. Landrum, just south of the North Carolina border on I-26, is becoming something of an antiquing town. Charleston's Vista District offers some good stores and auctions.

Music
The best three music stores in the state are Millennium Music on King St. in Charleston (new local music); Papa Jazz in Columbia's Five Points (used music); and Judy's House of Oldies on Ocean Dr., North Myrtle Beach (beach music).

Factory Outlets
With all the interstates crossing through South Carolina, the state has more than its share of freeway-close outlet shops. You'll find factory outlet stores up near Gaffney, Columbia, Rock Hill, on I-95 at Santee, down at Myrtle Beach, up near Greenville, and down by Hilton Head.

ACCOMMODATIONS

HOTELS AND MOTELS

The differences between hotels and motels are basically matters of price, amenities, and, in some cases, location. Hotels are usually more expensive than motels, but the increased price is usually—though not always—represented by better facilities. In addition to the pool, ice machine, and soda machine that you'll usually find at a motel, hotels often offer a restaurant or bar, an exercise room, valet parking, and greater proximity to shopping and places of cultural interest.

Another useful distinction for accommodations is proximity to freeways and highways. Sometimes hotels, sometimes motels, these places cater mostly to overnight travelers who need a place to stay while driving to somewhere else, rather than to extended-stay vacationers who want a relaxing place to spend a week or more. Spend the night at a Motel 6, for instance, and you'll find the parking lot nearly deserted at 9 a.m.

By absolutely no means do these descriptions fit in all, or even most, cases. No class of businesses has a copyright on the words "hotel" or "motel," and any business owner in the country has the right to call an establishment whatever he or she wants, and a lot of motels are confusing the issue by calling themselves inns, lodges, and so on. If you're already in town, it never hurts to just pull into the parking lot and take a look around.

If you are unsure about staying at a motel because you are afraid it will lack the features you want, or about staying at a hotel because you are afraid it will be too expensive, call ahead. You'll probably call anyway for prices and room availability. Consider also what you are looking for in an accommodation. Do you plan to stay more than two nights? Are you in a hurry to get somewhere else, and just need a place to sleep overnight? Do you want a place where you can

If you're looking for the spirit of a place, head for the stove.
—Charles Kuralt

"get away from it all" for weeks at a time? If you correctly assess your expectations you should have no problem finding a satisfactory accommodation, from $25-a-night roadside motels to $300-a-night luxury hotels.

Some well-known hotel/motel chains include:

- **Best Western**—a chain with no consistent style; most are clean but strictly stick-to-the-freeway type accommodations, but others offer luxurious rooms and prime locations. Call (800) 528-1234 in the U.S. and Canada.

- **Days Inn**—over 45 locations in S.C., from Aiken to York, with clean rooms, low prices ($29-79, depending on location). Call (800) 329-7466 in the U.S. and Canada. Often a continental breakfast buffet is served downstairs in the morning. Visit online at www.daysinn.com.

- **Econo Lodge**—usually close to the freeways, Econo Lodges offer average low-priced accommodations. Call (800) 553-2666 in the U.S.

- **Hilton**—luxurious rooms, numerous amenities, and great locations, tel. (800) 445-8667 in the US, (800) 268-9275 in Canada.

- **Holiday Inn**—spacious rooms, quality dining; some offer entertainment, but there is no consistent level of amenities. The phone number is (800) 465-4329 in the U.S. and Canada. See them online at www.holiday-inn.com.

- **Howard Johnson**—a.k.a. "HoJo's"—offers spacious rooms close to the freeways; ask about special prices for seniors and families. The toll-free number is (800) 446-4656 in the U.S. and Canada.

- **Motel 6**—close to the freeways, in the low $20s for a single, kids stay free, tel. (800) 466-8356 in the U.S. The upside is that this is the cheapest chain available. The downside is that, well, this is the cheapest chain available. As you check in late to an urban Motel 6, sliding your money in a tray beneath the bulletproof window to the 24-hour front desk clerk, you may wish you'd spent another $10 to get into a slightly more upscale environment. In most smaller towns, there's nothing to be concerned about. If you're staying in a city with more than one Motel 6, you may find that the one by the local airport (as opposed to the one downtown) is less intriguing, safety-wise.

• **Ramada**—sometimes upscale, sometimes just another hotel. Call (800) 228-9898 in the U.S., (800) 854-7854 in Canada.

BED AND BREAKFASTS

Bed and breakfasts are usually someone's house or a portion of their house opened as a guest accommodation. South Carolina has a worthy selection of these, mostly used as weekend getaways but not inappropriate for longer stays. The proprietors provide breakfast in the mornings (hence the name), and some offer lunch and dinner as well. As with hotels and motels, the name is not always indicative of the features. Sometimes older, smaller, rustic hotels call themselves bed and breakfasts to attract a wealthier clientele.

Bed and breakfasts usually offer personal hospitality and atmospheric, often historic homes to stay in. Perhaps because South Carolina is so rich in both of these, her B&B room rates are cheaper than in a lot of other areas, where the hospitality has to be flown in daily. In many smaller towns, rooms can dip down into the $40 range, which, considering you'll probably spend the same or more for a sanitized, midrange chain out on the highway, is quite a bargain.

Many B&Bs offer one or two different meal plans included with the price. They may offer the European-style continental breakfast, a light meal including coffee and orange juice; some combination of toast, English muffin, or Danish; and sometimes fruit. On the other hand, if you're lucky, you may be offered a Southern-style breakfast and dinner. Expect coffee, eggs or pancakes, grits, biscuits, bacon or ham, and potatoes for breakfast, and fried chicken, steaks, and salads for dinner.

If you've never stayed at a B&B, one thing to keep in mind is your privacy. At some, you'll be given a separate cottage or a room with an exterior entrance, which means you won't have to see the proprietors and other guests except at meals, unless you want to. At other lodgings you may share a bathroom with other guests. Or the homeowner

may have a curfew, after which you will not be allowed back into the house for the night.

CABINS

State parks with cabins include: Barnwell, Cheraw, Devils Fork, Dreher Island, Edisto Beach, Givhans Ferry, Hickory Knob, Hunting Island, Keowee Toxaway, Myrtle Beach, Oconee, Poinsett, Santee, Table Rock. Hickory Knob also has an 80-room lodge.

Cabin reservations will be accepted in each park for the following calendar year beginning the first Monday following January 1. First priority is given to reservation requests made by telephone beginning the first Monday following January 1 through the following Friday. Any reservation request received by mail during this time will be processed after 5 p.m. on Friday. After Friday, reservations may be accepted by telephone, mail, or in person.

Reservations are not confirmed until a deposit has been received. The deposit must be received within 10 working days of the date that the request was made, or the reservation may be voided.

Some parks allow only by the week rentals from Memorial Day to Labor Day. However, sometimes short notice reservations will be accepted for weekend rentals, depending on availability, on the Monday before the weekend desired.

CAMPING AND RV PARKS

The South Carolina State Park System
South Carolina offers over 3,000 campsites at some 50 state parks in its fine state parks system.

Unless specified as a "tent site," all of the sites have electric hookups. Some tenters pack a portable fan and extension cord with the Coleman gear in the summer. If you've camped in the American West, you'll find most of South Carolina's parks relatively "resorty"—meaning rental cabins, snack shops, general stores, monitored swimming beaches, putt putt (miniature golf), and sometimes a full-size 9- or 18-hole golf course or tennis courts as well.

Things are changing, however, as environmentalists push for "less-improved" parks that allow public access to pristine areas without paving it (or sodding it) in the process. Standout state parks of the old school include **Edisto Island State Park, Hunting Island State Park,** and **Oconee State Park,** with a tip of the hat also to **Sesquicentennial State Park** for providing a fine woods experience not far from urban Columbia. For a complete listing of state parks, call any state park listed in this book.

One recent development is that 11 of the most popular parks have recently taken to accepting reservations for some—but not all—of their campsites. You can reserve your spot as early as 11 months in advance, and no later than 24 hours prior to occupancy. To make a reservation, call, write, or visit the park where you'd like to camp. You can reserve a site for a minimum of two nights and a maximum of 14 consecutive nights. You'll pay an additional $1 a night fee for a reserved campsite, and you'll need to pay your camping fee in full within 10 working days of the date you make your request. No reservation will be confirmed until payment in full is received. The maximum number of sites you may reserve is three; however, each site must be reserved in the name of the individual occupying each site. Requests for adjoining or adjacent campsites will be honored subject to availability. Checkout time is no later than 2 p.m. Cancellations must be made in writing 24 hours in advance and may be subject to a handling fee.

The parks taking reservations at press time are: **Calhoun Falls, Devils Fork, Dreher Island, Edisto Beach, Hunting Island, Huntington Beach, Lake Hartwell, Myrtle Beach, Oconee, Santee,** and **Table Rock State Parks.**

Trailside camping is allowed at Jones Gap, Caesars Head, and Keowee-Toxaway. Devils Fork allows boat-in camping. Both trailside and boat-in are $2 per person per night.

Private Campgrounds and RV Parks

For a listing of South Carolina's privately owned campgrounds and RV parks, contact the SC Campground Owners Association at Point South KOA, P.O. Box 1760, Yemasee 29945, tel. (843) 726-5733.

To camp in the Grand Strand area, call (800) 356-3016 for a pamphlet extolling the virtues of camping at Myrtle Beach, *The Camping Capital of the World.*

FOOD AND DRINK

SEAFOOD

Along the coast, seafood is king. South Carolina **shrimp** are everywhere; you can catch them yourself or buy them right off the boats or nearly as fresh from coastal supermarkets. Ditto for the **Carolina soft-shell crab** used mainly for crab cakes and She Crab Soup (along the coast, you'll find lots of places serving crab legs, but these are from imported Alaskan king and Dungeness crabs). Up around Myrtle Beach you'll find a lot of "Calabash seafood," lightly battered and deep-fried. The name comes from the tiny port town of Calabash just north of the North Carolina border, where fishing and shrimping crews used to quickly deep-fry some meals at the end of a long day on the boats. Visitors who came down to the docks to purchase fresh fish from the boats got hungry smelling all this crunchy goodness, and soon they were buying it from quick-thinking vendors, who dubbed the fresh-and-fried style "Calabash." Today, most Calabash seafood restaurants, ironically, are not in Calabash, but rather along Restaurant Row in Myrtle Beach.

MEATS

Barbecue

My brother George, who lives not far over the border in Athens, Georgia, told me recently that he and his wife had become vegetarians. I asked him if he was going to have a hard time giving up barbecue. He reminded me that in the South, barbecue is a vegetable.

People have various theories as to how to spot a good barbecue joint. Some say that the presence of a pig anywhere on the sign is a good omen. Others claim that anyplace open more than three days a week (normally Thursday through Saturday) should be avoided like a Danish pizza parlor. I would add only the following amendment: the fewer windows, the better.

The ideal barbecue joint is built of bricks or cinder blocks, usually on a country road where police cruise-bys are weekly events (unless it's mealtime) and where security alarms would only irritate the possums. Hence, most barbecue owners seem to figure, no windows, no hassle. And who needs windows, anyway? Eating barbecue is a serious business—you're not here to admire the scenery.

There are exceptions to the rule. I have even once or twice been into a decent barbecue with both windows *and* central air-conditioning—but somehow, it felt like camping on Astroturf.

Now the question comes—what is barbecue? The answer varies across the country: in the West, "barbecue" is something you do, not something you eat. You barbecue some ribs or steaks. To tell a Nevadan you're going to eat some "barbecue" is like telling them you're going to eat some "fried." In the Midwest—and Texas—"barbecued" is an adjective and usually comes before "ribs." Most parts of the deep South agree that "barbecue" (the noun) refers to smoked shredded or pulled pork. Where they can't agree is on how that pork should be dressed.

There are three main camps on this issue, and each is represented in South Carolina: the vinegar-based camp, the tomato-based camp, and the mustard-based camp. As Kovacik and Winberry suggest in *South Carolina: The Making of a Landscape*, you'll generally find the tomato variety more prominent as you get closer to the Up-country and to the Georgia border. Mustard-based concoctions predominate in the Midlands on down through the Beaufort/Hilton Head area. And Vinegar and Pepper seems to hold sway in the Grand Strand and Pee Dee regions. Of course, as people (and barbecue chains) move from one region to another, the lines of division are becoming blurred.

Many of the tomato-based sauces are similar to the "barbecue sauce" most non-Carolinians know already. The Vinegar and Pepper is very popular in North Carolina (and on up into parts of Virginia), so perhaps mustard-based barbecue sauce is the most uniquely South Carolinian variety.

MORE CLASSIC SOUTH CAROLINA EATS

You'll want to try **slaw burgers** and **pimento cheeseburgers,** regional variations on the American artery-clogging favorite. **Slaw dogs** are simply hot dogs with coleslaw on top; you'll also find chili slaw dogs offered at many stands. **Fried chicken** is sold everywhere, from gas stations to Chinese restaurants to drive-up carhop restaurants. And most of it's good.

Fried **chicken livers** are offered at most places that sell fried chicken. If you've always publicly admired Native Americans for using up every portion of the animals they killed, here's a chance to walk your talk.

And of course, **chitlins** will give you another such chance. These are the deep-fried small intestines of a pig. If you really decide you like them, or if the idea of large people strutting around makes you giddy, be sure to head over to Salley for the annual "Chitlin' Strut" each Thanksgiving weekend.

Side Dishes

Of course, **biscuits** are important in Carolina country cooking. One surprising place where you'll find good biscuits

Little Joe, mascot of Maurice Bessinger's Original Piggie Park Barbecue, in West Columbia, beckons the Bar-B-Q faithful.

is at Hardee's, but maybe that's not surprising, since Hardee's was founded in the Carolinas.

Folks trying to eat healthy in South Carolina are sometimes stymied by the tendency of Carolinians toward **stewed vegetables,** including spinach, okra, and collard greens, throwing in a slab of fatback for good flavor, and **fried vegetables,** which again seems to miss the point of eating vegetables entirely. But in the case of okra, perhaps it's an improvement.

Grits have become something like the official food of the South (if you eat at Denny's, you'll know you're in the South when they start including grits on the menu). So strong was the association of Southerners and grits that back in 1980, Bob Hope suggested that Georgia's Jimmy Carter and Walter "Fritz" Mondale should run for re-election as "Grits and Fritz." Grits are made from corn or hominy. Most Northerners would mistake them for Cream of Wheat, but don't put sugar and cinnamon on them—while this doesn't taste too bad, the proper way to eat this plain-tasting food is with butter and salt and pepper—or Texas Pete's—and/or mixed in with eggs, ham, and whatever else is on your plate.

Finally, no trip to the South would be complete without a helping of **black-eyed peas.** These are actually beans, not peas—they're called cowpeas in other parts of the country—and they're not particularly tasty. If they were, you wouldn't have to come to the South (or to a northern "soul food" restaurant) to eat them. They became popular Southern food items because, like collards, they were easy to grow and cheap to buy down here, in a region that only recently has recovered from the Civil War.

Hot Boiled Peanuts

Take raw, unshelled peanuts. Add water and salt. Boil for about a decade. Now you have hot boiled peanuts, often spelled "hot boil p-nuts" on roadside signs and pronounced "hot bowled peanuts" by most South Carolinians. If you've never heard of them, they sound almost unimaginable. If you've never eaten them before, they taste a little bit like salted peas. But if you've eaten a handful of them, you're probably hooked for life.

You can find hot boiled peanuts for sale in many convenience stores—usually in a brown paper bag enclosed in a Ziploc resealable bag—outside many Wal-Marts, in front of a flea market,

---

ANITA'S BANANA PUDDING

1 14 oz. can sweetened condensed milk

1 1/2 cups cold water

1 pkg. instant banana-flavored pudding

1 pint heavy whipping cream

2 tablespoons sugar

36 vanilla wafers

3 large bananas

lemon juice to taste

Whisk condensed milk and water. Add pudding mix. Beat. Chill 15 minutes.

Whip whipping cream until stiff. Add sugar and whip 30 seconds more. Fold into the chilled pudding.

Layer 12 wafers, one banana, and one-third of the pudding. Repeat twice more.

Chill 4-6 hours minimum.

---

or—best of all—at roadside stands in the Piedmont and Blue Ridge regions, and at minor league baseball games all across the state.

ALTERNATIVES

Soul Food

With African-Americans making up nearly 50% of the population of the state, you might think there'd be more "soul food" or African-American restaurants in South Carolina. The truth of course is that much of the food you'll find in a soul food restaurant up in New York City is called "country cooking" down in South Carolina.

Mexican Food

Used to be that the average Mexican restaurant in South Carolina would have to feature phonetic spellings and explanations of its items: "*Burrito:* bur-EE-toe: beans, shredded beef, and cheese, wrapped in a flour *tortilla* (see above)." But over the past 5-10 years, coinciding with an increase in the number of Mexican immigrants, numerous Mexican restaurants have opened up in South Carolina. The influx of people from the south has been much happier for everyone involved than that other invasion from the north a while back. And amazingly, to some degree we have Taco Bell to thank for all this good new spicy food; in many small towns (Orangeburg, for instance), Taco Bell was the first Mexican food South Carolinians had ever eaten. Fortunately, this whetted folks' appetites and has opened the way for more extensive and authentic Mexican restaurants to open, many run by first-generation Mexican immigrants. In other towns, chains like Chevy's and Don Pablo's have opened, bringing their experienced Mexican restauranteering into towns that didn't know their *flautas* from a chicken dumpling in 1989.

Though the competition has gotten rougher in the past few years, the best Mexican restaurant I've found in the entire state is still Columbia's **Little Mexico.**

More International Cuisine

Asian restaurants—particularly Chinese ones—have a long history in most South Carolinian towns, partly a result of the Pacific Theater duty many of the state's men saw in WW II. In bigger cities with tourist districts or large transplant populations—Charleston, Columbia, and Greenville—you'll find Indian food, Thai food, just about anything you could want.

Health Food/Vegetarian

If you're dedicated to a low-fat, low-cholesterol diet, you really ought to consider going off it while you're in South Carolina. Otherwise, you'll miss most of the most authentic local cuisine. However, even the most dedicated cultural submersionist may have to come up for some unfried air while in South Carolina on an extended visit. You'll find health food stores and restaurants in all the cities—Greenville, Columbia, Charleston—and wherever non-Southerners have come to live, study, or visit en masse. If nothing else, you can find a Subway or Blimpie's

in most every town of any size; these can turn out a pretty good vegetarian sandwich in a pinch.

BEVERAGES

Tea

The terms "sweet tea" and "ice tea" (no *d*) are nearly synonymous here. At some restaurants, it's served as a matter of course, like coffee at a truck stop diner. The sugar in sweet tea is added while the water's still hot, which allows the sugar to melt and blend more fully into the drink.

If you're at a restaurant—particularly in the country—and you want unsweetened tea, ask for it (quietly) and hope they have it.

Alcohol

If South Carolina's "Blue Laws" haven't managed to keep people from drinking irresponsibly, they have at least helped endow the state's alcohol abusers with better foresight and planning skills than those in other states.

The minimum legal age for drinking in South Carolina is 21. Alcoholic beverages can't be served after midnight Saturday and all day Sunday, except in establishments with special permits in Charleston, Columbia, Edisto Beach, Hilton Head, the Myrtle Beach area, and the I-95 town of Santee.

In South Carolina, alcoholic beverages aren't sold in supermarkets; to buy anything beyond wine and beer, you'll need to visit a package store (also called an "ABC" or "red dot" store), where sales are permitted Monday through Saturday 9 a.m.-7 p.m. You'll notice that the stores do not have the word "alcohol" or "liquor" displayed on the outside—they are marked by the red dot alone, so that only people in the know will frequent them. It also helps make certain that even the illiterate can find the package stores.

It's illegal to have an open container of alcohol in a moving vehicle on South Carolina roads.

12 ESSENTIAL SOUTH CAROLINA DINING EXPERIENCES

I could easily add 10 or 20 more wonderful dining stops to this list, but here's a representative selection of some of the most interesting and tasty spots in the state. You'll find details on each in the appropriate destination chapters.

Beaufort
• Shrimp Shack (outside of town)

Charleston
• Hyman's
• Poogan's Porch
• Robert's of Charleston

Columbia
• Little Mexico
• Maurice's Gourmet Piggie Park Barbecue (West Columbia)
• Yesterday's (Five Points)

Hilton Head Island
• Old Fort Pub

Holly Hill
• Swetman's Barbecue

Mount Pleasant
• See Wee Restaurant (north of town)

Orangeburg
• Duke's Barbecue (any location)

Spartanburg
• Beacon Drive In

Blenheim Ginger Ale

Despite the debut of several local beers around the state, this still gets my vote for the official bottled beverage of South Carolina. This fiery drink (it's available in three different heat levels, like salsa) has been made in the little Pee Dee town of Blenheim for decades. Try it when you find it.

SOUTHERN RESTAURANT CHAINS

Waffle House

Each location of this chain is nearly identical—stools, bright yellow and imitation wood Formica, appalling coffee, a sizzling grill, an order-shouting staff, and a jukebox. A patron of the Waffle House in Orangeburg could easily walk into one in Biloxi, Mississippi, blindfolded, sit down, order, play the jukebox and pay the bill without taking the blindfold off. But the Waffle House serves the needs of Southerners so perfectly that it somehow transcends its chain status.

Founded in an Atlanta suburb in 1955—the same year Disneyland opened—the Waffle House calls itself "America's Place to Eat, America's Place to Work." I've never worked at a Waffle House, other than doing some writing at one, but it does seem to be the one inescapable dining experience in the South. Because it's so common (more than 1,000 locations, seemingly off every other highway exit in the South), and because it's so *available* (open 24 hours every day except Thanksgiving and Christmas), it's become an icon of the South. So beloved is it that the Internet contains several non-official Waffle House sites.

The chain boasts of being the world's leading server of waffles, omelettes, raisin toast, grits, and apple butter. It's also the only place in the world where the jukeboxes play such specially recorded songs as "Waffle Doo-Wop" and "Good Food Fast"—along with standard oldies and country selections.

Try the pork chops and eggs with hash browns and raisin toast. Bert's Chili is also pretty good. Or just order some hash browns with tomatoes, "Scattered, Smothered, Covered, Chunked, Topped and Diced."

A couple of the best Web sites (with links leading to Virtual Waffle Houses, Waffle House FAQ Pages, a Waffle House drinking game, and all sorts of Wafflemania) are: userwww.service.emory.edu/~mangeli/links.html, www.cc.gatech.edu/people/home/fed/WaffleHouse/Home.html, and craigt.home.avana.net/WaffleHouse/.

Cracker Barrel

Don't let it keep you away from the mom and pop restaurants in town, but if you're out on the interstate and in a hurry, or in dire need of a pullover, this chain is a safe bet for good country cooking along the interstate. With rocking chairs out front, a fireplace burning, and old-timey photos on the wall, Cracker Barrels feature a warm ambience that makes an hour's meal seem like a genuine break away from the highway.

Founded in 1969 in Lebanon, Tennessee, each restaurant contains a little gift shop featuring regional knickknacks reflecting the South in general and often the restaurant's location in particular. Before long I imagine these will spread to every state in the Lower 48, but for now they haven't penetrated the West Coast yet. In South Carolina you'll find them in Anderson, Columbia, Florence, Gaffney, Greenville, Hilton Head, Murrells Inlet, North Charleston, North Myrtle Beach (across from Barefoot Landing), Rock Hill, Santee, and Spartanburg. See them online at www.crackerbarrel.com.

Hardee's

Hardee's was founded in Greenville, North Carolina, but its first chain franchise opened in Spartanburg in 1961. Today, Spartanburg has 11 locations, and South Carolina has over 200. And that's not counting 2,900 hundred other branches in 38 other states. Hardee's is usually the first chain restaurant to infect a small Southern town, opening the way for Ronald McDonald and the rest of the coven.

Some time back, the folks at *Consumer's Digest* rated the fast food mongers of America and named Hardee's food No. 2 among all major fast-food chains, but it's hard to see what all the fuss is about. The two things that are worth getting here are the breakfast sandwiches made with fresh biscuits and the seasonal peach shakes.

They seem (with some exceptions) to hire some of the most insolent workers you'll find in America. In 1998, Hardee's was purchased by Carl Karcher Enterprises, owner of the Carl's Jr. chain on the West Coast.

Chick-Fil-A

Don't call it "Chick Feela"—it's pronounced "chick fih-LAY." This is the largest privately owned restaurant chain in America. Georgia's Truett Cathy founded his first restaurant back in 1946; today the company operates nearly 600 restaurants. More than 400 of these are in malls, which means you'll see one in nearly every mall in South Carolina (Cathy pioneered the idea of fast food restaurants in malls). The main thing to get here is a seasoned boneless chicken breast sandwich. Kids love the Chicken Fingers. The food doesn't do much for me, but obviously somebody likes it. Closed on Sunday to allow workers to go to church and spend time with their families, Chick-

Fil-A remains a true Southern phenomenon. See them online at www.chickfila.com.

Bojangles

The dirty rice and Cajun chicken make this Tennessee-based chain a cut above the rest.

Shoneys

Food for people who don't care what they eat, cooked by those who don't care what they cook. Some people praise the breakfast buffet, but there's no dearth of good breakfast places in South Carolina.

BUYING GROCERIES

Farmers' Markets

With all the agriculture in the area, most towns in South Carolina have some sort of farmers' market. Where possible, I've mentioned them in the description of the town. But if you have a certain town in mind, call its chamber of commerce.

The best farmers' market you'll find is in Columbia, across from the USC Williams-Brice Stadium (open Mon.-Sat. 6 a.m.-9 p.m.), with a selection including peaches, turnips, potatoes, and tomatoes.

Charleston's Farmer's Market takes place every Saturday at the Maritime Center on Concord St., down by the South Carolina Aquarium, April 18-Oct. 31.

At the **Pee Dee Farmers Market,** one mile west of I-95 on Hwy. 52 near Florence, you'll also find farm-fresh produce.

Supermarket Chains

You have your **Piggly Wiggly,** the world's first true self-service grocery store, founded in 1916 by a Memphis, Tennessee, entrepreneur named Clarence Saunders, who later went on to pioneer (unsuccessfully) the world's first completely automated store. Where did the name "Piggly Wiggly" come from? Nobody knows. When people used to ask Saunders, he would answer, "So people will ask that very question."

Do note that though the Piggly Wiggly logo looks a lot like Porky Pig wearing a butcher's hat, Piggly predates Porky by 20 years or so. Today there are more than 700 Piggly Wiggly stores stretching from Texas north to Minnesota, south to Florida, and north to Virginia. You'll find one or two in every decent-sized South Carolina town. The Piggly Wiggly store brand is usually a good way to save money—especially their barbecue sauces and peanut butter.

Yes, **Winn-Dixie** sounds like a political statement, but the name actually refers to the 1955 merger of the Winn & Lovett stores from Florida and Georgia, and the Dixie Home Stores of the Carolinas. Now with 12,000 stores in 14 states in the Bahamas, the Sunbelt, and on up to Ohio, Winn-Dixie is building a number of Marketplace Stores, with delis and ATM machines and such.

The new kid on the Southern grocery chain block, North Carolina's **Food Lion** got a lot of bad press a few years back when ABC's television newsmagazine *20/20* sent an undercover reporter to work at one of their stores and exposed some shoddy food-handling practices, including a tendency to re-label outdated meats. Despite successful counter suits that challenged the network's methods, the chain has been troubled since then, though individual locations can be quite good. I don't recommend the Food Lion brand foods, however—they're nothing special.

Kroger stores are a part of a Cincinnati-based chain, but since they're so plentiful in larger South Carolina cities, and because their superstores are often the most comprehensive supermarkets available (including, in many cases, ATM machines), you might want to use them if you're shopping for food while on the road, or while staying at a rental.

If you find a **Publix** in your travels, you've likely stumbled upon a clean, well-lighted place with good produce and fish.

Harris Teeter is probably the high-end choice for groceries. There's a great one located in an old warehouse on East Bay Street in Charleston; for seeing how even chain stores can blend successfully into their environment, it's worth checking out.

GETTING THERE AND AROUND

BY CAR

Five interstates—I-26, I-95, I-20, I-85, and I-77—crisscross South Carolina, making the state quite easy to get to from most anywhere east of the Mississippi. From New York and other parts north, just head south on I-95 (following the historic Fort Lauderdale Trail blazed by generations of spring breakers) until you're blinded by neon. This means you've arrived at South of the Border, are officially in South Carolina, and can now legally play video poker and buy firecrackers.

From Atlanta, just head either northeast on I-85—to get to Greenville and the Upcountry—or west on I-20, where you'll cross into South Carolina just past Augusta. Another worthwhile route from Atlanta—though infinitely more time-consuming—is to take the Atlanta Highway (Hwy. 29) due east through the scenic Piedmont towns of northeast Georgia, including Athens, where if you're lucky you'll run across a member of R.E.M. or the B-52s. If you're really lucky, you'll run across one of my brothers, who live there as well. But as I say, this is the slower, two-lane route, which stops numerous times in small towns all the way across the Piedmont. It's scenic, but don't say I didn't warn you.

If you're up in Charlotte, you'll enter either on I-77 due north of Columbia, or on I-84 as you head southwest toward Greenville. Though it's a relatively small state, enough of South Carolina remains rural that the best way to explore it is by automobile—unless you're planning to restrict your travel to a single metropolitan or resort area.

Rentals
You'll find locations for all the major car rental chains throughout South Carolina, and especially around its major airports. Call Alamo at

---

GETTING DIRECTIONS

S ome folks can give good, quick directions in South Carolina. But as you leave the main highways, you're likely to get a large dose of history along with any practical information you request. A good direction-giver in rural South Carolina will tell you more about where you should *not* turn than where you should, more about what comes up just *after* your turn than what comes up just before it. And of course, since many of the rural roads are poorly marked—and then only with obscure numbers—you should expect to receive a lot of directions by landmark, which are great ways to understand the history of the area. Example:

You head down this road. After a while, you'll get to the Old Dairy. It's where they used to have the dairy, but it got closed down when they opened up the big Winn-Dixie over in town. Nothing there now, but a little white building, no bigger 'n this building here. You see that, you just keep going straight.

Now just let the road carry you down maybe five mile, and then you'll see a big black hole in the ground over on your right, and it looks like there

been a fire. Used to be a Shell station, closed up 'cause the tanks was leaking. Was a Texaco before that, but then the man owned it, Trey Hampton—No! Trey owned the one further up the road a piece, but, anyhow, he sold it to this black fella by the name of Middleton, Duke Middleton, real nice fella, and—Joe . . . Joe Powell was his name, fella that owned the Texaco—and Duke run it as a Shell for maybe five year—done real well. Used to sell bait and tackle out there too, till the state inspector come out and closed him down. Duke didn't have enough money to dig up them tank and fix 'em, and then his wife got cancer, or not cancer, but something with her lung, and then one night a couple year ago, around Christmas, there was a fire, burnt the building to the ground. Emphysema. They reckoned Duke had something to do with it, and I don't think he ever saw a red penny from the insurance, cause he wasn't insured. He moved with his wife down to Charleston, I guess, so she could get treatment.

Anyway, ya'll wanna turn about a half a mile before you see that burned-out station, at the blinking light.

SMALL-TOWN GEMS OF SOUTH CAROLINA

Abbeville
A true uptown square with an opera house providing live shows throughout the week. Two Amish-run restaurants provide some of the best comfort food this side of Mom's house.

Aiken
Whether or not the horses are running, this is a fine place to disappear for a while—especially if you own a horse. Plenty of shops and fine restaurants, and a first-rate brewpub.

Beaufort
A quiet, historic waterfront town made famous in Pat Conroy's *The Great Santini* and *The Prince of Tides*. Lots of historic B&Bs.

Camden
Some of the best Revolutionary-era sites and a number of restored Colonial buildings make Camden—the first inland city in South Carolina—a beautiful place to visit.

Cheraw
Though its downtown still contains a lot of closed-up units, this pleasing antebellum town features a town green, blocks and blocks of splendid homes, and a small museum honoring its famous native son, John Birks "Dizzy" Gillespie.

Chester
Aaron Burr stepped off his horse here and pleaded with Chesterians to let him stay with them. Chester tends to affect people that way. A very quaint, sloping brick downtown that's on the rebound.

Georgetown
Third-oldest city in the state, Georgetown retains its coastal small-town flavor, while containing ample amenities for tourists.

Newberry
With its refurbished and reopened Opera House, Newberry is quickly becoming an artisans' community.

Ocean Drive Beach
Though the high-rises are going up as we speak, North Myrtle Beach's "Old O.D."—ground zero for the shagging subculture—remains a tight-knit beach community devoted to innocent pleasures.

Pendleton
Founded in the 1770s, Pendleton's extensive and well-preserved historic district features numerous antique and specialty shops, as well as restaurants and B&Bs, all in addition to some 40 structures of historical interest.

York
Known by some as "The Charleston of the Upcountry," this cultural-minded town features a beautiful sloping downtown district.

Runners-Up: Bennettsville, Chesterfield, Clemson, Conway, Edgefield, Folly Beach, Fort Mill, Laurens, Lexington, McCormick, Mullins, Saluda, and Walterboro.

Possibly in a Few Years: Bluffton, Daniel Island, Lancaster, Newpoint (St. Helena Island), Orangeburg, and Port Royal.

Other Downtowns Worth Exploring: Market Area, Charleston; Five Points/Shandon and Vista District (Columbia); Greenville, Old Village (Mount Pleasant); and Rock Hill.

(800) 327-9633, Avis at (800) 831-2847, Budget at (800) 353-0600, Enterprise at (800) 325-8007, and Hertz at (800) 654-3131 (www.hertz.com).

Rules of the Road
Americans drive on the right side of the road, the way God intended. If you forget and drive on the left side of the road, other drivers will remind you by driving straight toward you and blaring their horns. A driver's license serves as indispensable identification. In America, you need a driver's license for everything from cashing a check to renting movies.

A driver must be 25 years old and have a valid driver's license to rent a car. You will have the chance to buy insurance coverage for the car and yourself; unless your policy back home covers you, you'll want to go ahead and get

> *Why'd dey have to put da South so far South?*
> —Bugs Bunny

some now. It's illegal to drive without at least liability coverage in the U.S.

Travelers from outside the U.S. must carry an International Driver's Permit as well as a current valid license from their home country.

Note: It's illegal in South Carolina to drive while drinking alcoholic beverages or while under the influence of alcohol.

BY AIR

Charleston, Myrtle Beach, Columbia, and Greenville all have large airports. The **Myrtle Beach International Airport** serves as the commercial airport for the Grand Strand and includes scheduled service from USAir, Atlantic Southeast Airlines, COMAir (for Delta connections), Jet Express, Air Canada, Midway Connection, Spirit, and GP Express/Continental. If you're hunting for cheap tickets and don't mind a few extra miles on the rental car, check out flights into Charlotte, North Carolina; Atlanta, Georgia; or Savannah, Georgia.

BY TRAIN

Most sizable towns in South Carolina are served by Amtrak. For reservations and schedule information, call (800) 872-7245.

BY BUS

Most towns—sizable or not—are served by Greyhound Bus Lines. For reservations and schedule information,call (800) 231-2222.

BY BOAT

For the nautically endowed—those who own boats—South Carolina is very accessible. The Atlantic Intracoastal Waterway, a 1,095-mile nautical pathway from Norfolk, Virginia, south to Miami, Florida, passes behind the coastal islands of South Carolina. Contact the **SC Marina Association,** P.O. Box 24156, Hilton Head Island, SC 29925, tel. (843) 837-9525, for information.

VISAS AND OFFICIALDOM

Entry Requirements
Non-U.S. citizens will need the following for entry to the country:
• Valid passport from a recognized country *or* valid visa
• Roundtrip or return ticket, or proof of sufficient funds to support yourself during your visit and to afford a return ticket. You may be required to purchase a return ticket at the airport before you are given a visa, or you may have to show proof of a return ticket when you are actually applying.
• $13.95 in fees for the services of the immigration, customs, and agricultural inspectors

Passports
Passports are the most common type of travel document used as proof of your identity when crossing an international border. A passport is required for travel into the United States and even for air travel within the country.

It is always easier to travel with a passport than to try to get by with some other type of photo identification.

If you don't already have a passport, you should start the process for acquiring one as soon as possible. Make sure that it is valid for at least six months, preferably a year, after you plan to return home. If the passport issued to you by the government in your country expires while you are in the U.S., you will have to contact an embassy or consulate of your home country to renew it. U.S. passport offices do not provide services to holders of non-U.S. passports.

For extended stays, bring your birth certificate, extra passport photos, and even a photocopy of the original passport. This will help speed the process of replacing a lost or expired passport. If your passport is stolen, report it the police immediately and get a copy of the police report, or at least record the important details contained in it (name and title of the officer, the police precinct number, the file number, etc.). This should also help in replacing your passport.

Visas

Visas are documents, usually a stamp in your passport, that are issued by the government of the country you want to visit. Visas are a precondition for being admitted to a country, but they are not a guarantee of entry. The rules for acquiring a visa are arbitrary and occasionally very strict, but if you plan ahead and follow the rules to the letter, you shouldn't run into any problems.

A very few countries in the world participate with the U.S. in the Visa Waiver Pilot Program. Check with a U.S. embassy or consulate to find out if your country is included in the program. Otherwise, you are required to have a visa. You should always be courteous and respectful to consular, immigration, and customs authorities. If you are applying for a tourist visa to the U.S., you will be required to appear in person at a U.S. consulate or embassy for an interview, as well as meet certain other requirements, including proof that you have a return ticket.

Make sure to find out what the current visa requirements are for travel, or if your country is "officially recognized" by the U.S. government. Visa requirements can change at any time, without notice. If you have already bought nonrefundable air tickets and are denied entry, you'll be out of luck.

The United States charges $13.95 in arrival fees to pay for the services of the customs, immigration, and agricultural inspectors.

State Border Crossings

Part of the evidence that South Carolina and the rest of the Confederacy lost the argument over state sovereignty is the ease with which one can travel between American states. The only restrictions you're likely to encounter involve transporting certain plants or produce across state lines, or transporting illegal substances or guns across state lines.

Border authorities sometimes forbid produce and plants from entering a state because the flora may contain pests or diseases harmful to the native plants or agricultural products of the state. In some cases, if you are carrying produce in your car and are stopped at a state border, you will be asked to dispose of the produce.

Generally forbidden substances include illegal drugs, explosives, or dangerous chemicals. In most states, transporting illegal drugs across the state line increases the legal penalty for possession from a misdemeanor to a felony.

Many counties also have laws governing the amount of alcohol and number of cartons of cigarettes you can bring across their border. If a county border is also a state border and you are carrying alcohol or cigarettes into that county, check its laws concerning alcohol and cigarettes. A pack of cigarettes and a bottle of beer are not cause for legal action, unless the beer is open. A carton of cigarettes and a bottle of whiskey might raise a few eyebrows, but shouldn't cause you any trouble. Twenty cartons of cigarettes and a case of whiskey will get you into trouble in many counties.

If you are carrying a gun, you must have a valid permit. Check with the embassy or consulate where you got your passport if you plan to buy and carry a gun while traveling in the U.S., and understand that foreign visitors requesting information regarding firearms will be viewed with some suspicion.

In 1996, it became legal in South Carolina for a citizen who has taken a safety course to carry a concealed weapon. Consequently, as you a pass through many business doorways you'll see signs forbidding concealed weapons while on the owner's private property. Don't let these signs make you think that everyone in South Carolina is packing heat. The number of people requesting such permits is low indeed. But if you are, you'll need to unpack it—remove the cartridges and put it somewhere where it can't be stolen.

SPECIAL INTERESTS

Travel with Children

South Carolina is very much a family-oriented state. Many parks feature wide, family-size swings; nearly every community event includes children's activities, and most resorts provide thorough programs for youngsters. The only places where children are unwelcome is in nightclubs and bars (obviously), in gambling parlors (no big loss), and in many bed and breakfasts. Still, South Carolina seems to have a higher percentage of "children welcome" B&Bs than most other states. Where possible, I've noted whenever establishments have stated a preference.

One nice thing about automobile travel in South Carolina is that everything in the state is so close together that it's rare you'll find yourself driving very long without the opportunity to stop and let the kids get out and burn off some energy. The enclosed playgrounds now popular at McDonald's and some of its competitors make pretty handy pit stops, even on a rainy day.

Women Travelers

I've never been a woman, despite what my football coach used to yell, so I've asked my wife Kristin to help with this section:

Most women find themselves treated especially politely in South Carolina. Doors will be opened, bus seats offered. There are, however, areas still considered male domains—the same places, generally, considered male domains throughout most of the Western world—honky-tonk bars, hunting clubs, golf clubs (some of them), sports bars. A woman is in no particular danger in most of these places, but her presence there may be interpreted as a desire for male companionship.

Women traveling alone should be aware of their surroundings. When you head for your car, carry your keys in hand and get to and into the car quickly. Drive with your doors locked and your windows rolled up.

If possible, carry a cellular phone—otherwise, a breakdown on the highway will leave you waiting and hoping the first motorist to stop for assistance has good motives.

A sizable number of crimes each year are committed by people impersonating police officers. If you're pulled over—especially at night—don't open your car door or window more than a crack, and then only to demand that a marked patrol car be called. This is well within your rights.

No matter how authentic the uniform looks, demand to see the marked car. They sell police uniforms at costume shops and Army-Navy stores. If the officer can't produce a black and white, move on. Don't hand over your license, which gives your name and address.

If you feel suspicious, ask the officer to follow you to a more-populated, better-lighted area.

Gay/Lesbian Travelers

In recent decades, American gays and lesbians have begun to enjoy an increase in tolerance toward same-sex couples. In South Carolina, larger cities like Charleston and Columbia have their share of gay hangouts and nightclubs, many of them private clubs that require a nominal "membership fee" for admittance. In other areas, gay and lesbian travelers not wanting to draw attention to themselves generally respect the local mores and avoid public displays of affection.

Travelers with Disabilities

Though all of South Carolina's new public buildings provide facilities and access for the physically disabled, many of the state's historic structures and sites have been hard-pressed to do the same. Throughout this book, I've tried to note attractions that may pose special difficulties for the disabled, as well as those that specifically define themselves as wheelchair accessible. If you're uncertain about the accessibility of a specific attraction, be sure to call ahead.

AA, Al-Anon, Other Recovery Programs

Chapters of **Alcoholics Anonymous** hold meetings throughout the Palmetto State, and most welcome visitors. Call (803) 254-5301, for information and help, 24 hours a day. **Narcotics Anonymous**, tel. (800) 922-5305, specializes in helping those with other drug addictions. **Al-Anon** specializes in providing help for the families of alcoholics. It, too, has a 24-hour phone service, tel. (803) 735-9944. You'll find an automated information alcoholism resource at (803) 612-1666, ext. 8030 or 8031.

Churches

Visiting South Carolina without attending a church service is like going to Thailand and not visiting a temple. Church life and the spiritual life (and sometimes the two intersect) are of major importance to most South Carolinians, and it would be hard to get any real grasp on the culture without passing between the white pillars and taking a spot in the pew.

If it's a representative experience you seek, then in the Lowcountry you might want to visit one of Charleston's enormous Episcopalian cathedrals or attend synagogue at America's first reformed temple. Or visit the state's fastest-growing church, Seacoast Community Church in Mount Pleasant, a "seeker" church that began with a marketing survey of the affluent East Cooper area and today packs in several thousand young go-getters each Sunday.

In Columbia, you might attend a service at First Baptist Church, the original sanctuary of which was the site of the first meeting for secession, in 1861, and which was spared from Sherman's wrath only by the quick thinking of an African-American deacon. Or you can attend at the Trinity Episcopal Cathedral, outside of which lie six S.C. governors and Woodrow Wilson's parents.

Of course, for every large, celebrity church, a couple hundred humble congregations of every stripe meet each Sunday. To get a truly representative feel for the spiritual tempo of South Carolina, you might be better off pulling out a Yellow Pages, picking a church that catches your eye, and attending a service.

Compared to most parts of the country, South Carolina churches are still fairly dressy: most women wear dresses or pantsuits (most Carolinian women, visiting a new church, wear a dress or skirt just to play it safe); men wear slacks, shirts, and ties, and often jackets. The general philosophy behind all this finery runs something like this: "You'd dress up to go ask some fellow at the bank for a loan. Doesn't God deserve the same respect?" (Whether it's respectful to treat God as though he thinks as superficially as the average loan officer is another question.) Dress is generally more casual in nondenominational churches and in congregations in coastal communities.

Very few services are significantly integrated—reminding one of Martin Luther King's quote about Sunday morning being the most segregated hours in America. However, very, very few congregations will object to the presence of friendly, well-behaved visitors of a different race, and most will be quite happy to have you there.

*one way to
get around at the beach*

HEALTH AND SAFETY

HEALTH MAINTENANCE

Insect Repellent
Unless you're planning to spend all of your time on city streets, you'll want insect repellent while you're here. The two critters that will trouble you most are no-see-ums (particularly at the coast) and mosquitoes. "No-see-ums" are tiny gnats that bite as if it's personal. The best way to fight them seems to be with Avon's Skin-So-Soft cream. Wear a hat—they'll bite your scalp as well.

Mosquitoes are pleasant companions by comparison, but in swamps and salt marshes they can quickly turn a day hike into a personal purgatory. Skin-So-Soft works with them as well, and so does Deep Woods Off and most Cutter products.

Sunscreens
South Carolina summers can be particularly deceiving; though it's hot, the gray sky overhead can lull you into thinking that your skin's not taking a beating from ultraviolet rays—but it is. To ward off skin cancer, premature wrinkles, and sunburn, use sunscreens with an SPF rating of 15 or more—higher for those with fair skin.

Adjusting to the Humidity
Stepping off a plane into the middle of a South Carolina summer can just about knock you out. If you live in a less humid area and your plans in South Carolina include a lot of physical activity, try to give yourself a day or two to acclimate.

LOCAL DOCTORS

Despite its sometimes high mortality rate, South Carolina has no dearth of qualified physicians for those with the money to pay for them. Neither is the state short of walk-in medical clinics where you can stop in without an appointment. Check the local phone book under "Physicians" to find the address and phone number of physicians in your area, or stop into a shop, explain your situation to a clerk, and ask for a recommendation.

NATURAL HAZARDS

For all its natural beauty, the South does seem to have more than its share of natural hazards—from alligators and poisonous snakes to hurricanes and jellyfish. But 99% of the time these hazards can be avoided with a little foresight and caution.

Lightning Storms
Sociologists throw around a lot of reasons for the fervent spirituality of many South Carolinians, but one overlooked cause may be the prayer-inspiring lightning storms. When the sheet lightning flares across the sky like a flickering fluorescent bar, and the bolts are blasting transformers to either side of the road, even a trip to the local package store can quickly turn into a religious experience.

If you're out on the trail or the golf course when a storm rolls in, seek shelter—though not under a tree, since the tree is likely to get hit, in which case you don't want to be anywhere around it. Electrocution is rarely worth risking—especially since the average summer convectional storm will be over in less than an hour anyway. Go find a cup of coffee somewhere and enjoy the show from safety.

If you're indoors, do as most South Carolinians do—they won't talk on a phone (though cordless phones are okay) or use plumbing when a storm is striking around them, since both phone lines and water can serve as conduits. There are a number of urban legends revolving around a man/woman using the toilet during a lightning storm; ask almost any Carolinian and he or she can fill in the details.

Hurricanes
Hurricanes—and, more commonly, the threat of hurricanes—are simply a factor of life in coastal South Carolina. Annually, the Charleston *Post and Courier* includes a pre-hurricane season insert, providing informative articles that help Carolinians to understand and survive these storms. Local news teams run ads boasting of

their prophetic capabilities, and supermarkets like Piggly Wiggly buy full pages to proclaim themselves "Your Hurricane Stock-Up Store."

Pay attention to the public warnings on the radio and television when you're in the state, especially June-Oct.—hurricane season. The mildest warning is a **Small Craft Advisory,** issued when strong winds—up to 38 mph—strike the coastal waters. This is not the day to rent or charter a fishing boat. Next up is a **Gale Warning,** issued when winds reach 39-54 mph. A **Storm Warning** means winds 55-73 mph. **Hurricane Watches** are issued when hurricane conditions are a real possibility and may threaten coastal or inland areas within 36 hours. A **Hurricane Warning** means a hurricane is expected to hit an area within 24 hours. If you're visiting the coast and a Hurricane Warning is issued, it's time to consider visiting South Carolina's historic Upcountry for a few days. Or call up your old schoolmate in Atlanta and tell him you're coming to visit. One way to stay ahead of the game—or to put off a visit if you haven't left home yet—is to check www.stormalert.com, a Web site run by one of the local news stations.

The two things you *don't* want to do are panic or ignore the warnings. If an evacuation is called, you'll hear about it on the radio and TV. But by this point, you as a traveler should be gone already. Save the spot in the relief shelter for a local resident. Get thee to the Upcountry.

Snakebite

No other state offers the variety of poisonous snakes found in South Carolina. A full six different snakes can make your life complicated here in the Palmetto State, but even the most outdoorsy visitor is unlikely to come across any of them on a visit.

The **copperhead** averages around two to three feet long and normally lives in damp woods, mountainous regions, or in the high ground

in swampy areas—which is to say you'll find it all through South Carolina.

Canebrake or **timber rattlesnakes** are also found throughout the state—usually in deciduous forests or swamps on high ground. These snakes average three to four feet in length and can even reach five.

The **eastern diamondback rattlesnake** runs 3-6 feet and up, with a basic dark brown color and brown/yellow diamonds. They mostly keep to the woods of the Lowcountry.

The **pigmy rattlesnake** is rare and only reaches a bit over a foot long. You'll find them in all but the highest lands of South Carolina. They're dull gray with brown splotches on the back and sides.

The **cottonmouth** or **water moccasin** thrives in wetland areas in the lower two-thirds of the state.

The beautiful black, red, and yellow **eastern coral snake** is rare, found in woods and fields.

Bring a **snake kit,** wear leather boots to protect your ankles, and watch where you step. Several thousand people are bitten by poisonous snakes each year, but less than 10 die in the U.S. annually.

In most cases, snakebite is preventable. More than 50% of poisonous snakebites take place after the victim has seen the snake and had the chance to get away. In fact, most victims are bitten in the attempt to pick up a poisonous snake, harass it, or kill it. The point is simple enough: keep your eyes open when in the woods and stay away from any snake that you're not absolutely certain is nonpoisonous.

If you or someone in your party is bitten by a snake, try not to panic. Even if the snake is poisonous, odds are nearly even that it was a "dry" bite—meaning that no poison was injected into the victim. Nonetheless, don't allow the victim to engage in strenuous physical activity, since this will get the heart pumping faster, thus spreading the poison quicker. Try to safely identify the breed of snake if it's possible, and if it doesn't take too long to do it. Get the victim to the nearest hospital or emergency medical facility as soon as possible.

If local doctors are unsure of the correct snakebite serum to use to treat the bite, tell them to contact the regional Poison Information Center.

Yellowjackets

To avoid most stinging insects, the place to start is in your clothing—bright colors attract, dark ones don't. If you notice yellowjackets about and you're drinking or eating something, be sure to keep checking the food or drink (soda cans are notorious) to make sure no yellowjacket has snuck aboard.

Yellowjacket stings are painful—not unlike being burned by a just-extinguished match. The danger comes in when people have allergic reactions.

How can you tell if it's an allergic reaction? A good rule of thumb is that as long as the reaction is around the site of the bite, you can assume it's a local reaction and needs to be treated with something like an antihistamine and maybe a little topical steroid, if anything. But if you get bitten or stung by an insect and you develop symptoms elsewhere on your body, those are signs of an allergic reaction; you need to get in and see a doctor.

Some of the signs of an allergic reaction are hives; swelling of the lips, tongue, eyelids, internal organs; blocked airways; shock; and low blood pressure.

If you're headed in this direction, your doctor will probably administer epipens, which contain epinephrine and quickly reduce the symptoms of an allergic reaction.

Fire Ants

These ants are extremely aggressive when protecting their nests; if you inadvertently knock over a mound, don't stand around apologizing too long or you may soon find yourself covered with stinging ants. Stings can cause a severe reaction and even death. Watch for their domed mounds, commonly at least 15 inches wide at the base and about six inches high, usually found in damp areas—which includes most all of the American South—particularly under trees, in lawns, or in flower beds.

Winged fire ants originated in South America and first appeared on U.S. soil in Mobile, Alabama, in 1918. Since then they've spread like the kudzu of the animal kingdom to 11 Southern states—including South Carolina—and in the last half of the 1990s made their appearance in Southern California—about the same time as Krispy Kreme doughnuts.

You'll find numerous chemical treatments for ant mounds in any grocery store or hardware store. Some swear that pouring boiling water into the top of an ant mound will do the trick, without harming the local water supply.

Fire ant bites leave a sterile pustule. The urge to scratch or pop the pustule is very tempting, but try not to do it. Scratching or picking at a bite until it becomes open allows it to get infected.

If you're allergic to fire ants, wear shoes and socks—don't go outside barefoot or in sandals.

Jellyfish

If stung by a jellyfish, clean the area carefully. If you have tentacles still stuck to the wound area, don't just pull them off with your hand—they may still have venom sacs attached. Instead, use a credit card to scrape parallel with the skin, pushing the tentacles off sideways. Try not to break any of the venom sacs.

For pain relief, try meat tenderizer, a baking soda and water paste, or vinegar.

Jellyfish stings very rarely cause allergic reactions, but when they do, they can include hives, itching, and swelling on parts of the body that weren't stung. If any of these occur, get to an emergency room.

Stingrays

Stingray wounds are much more rare than jellyfish stings, but they happen. To avoid them, shuffle your feet as you walk in the water.

If you do happen to step on a stingray, it will let you know—it'll swing its mace of a tail around and send you hopping back to shore. Most stingray victims get it on the foot or ankle.

One treatment is to submerge the wound in the hottest water you can stand for 20 or 30 minutes. This seems to neutralize the poison. Most people enjoy noticeable relief within minutes.

Even so, if you've danced with a stingray and

come away stung, you should still see a doctor—you may need an antibiotic.

Sharks

Usually one to three people get attacked by sharks in South Carolina waters each year. A few years back, the number shot up to about 10, mostly in the Grand Strand—which should put to rest those charges of Myrtle Beach visitors having bad taste.

The odds of being bitten are still incredibly low. To make them lower, the experts say:

• Swim in groups, preferably composed of people better-tasting than you are.

• Don't swim too far out—if you see sharks, you want to be close to shore so you can get out fast.

• Avoid swimming in the late afternoon, at night, or in the early morning. This is when sharks feed the most.

• Lose the flashy jewelry. Sharks can't see well in South Carolina's murky waters, but they'll see the glitter from that bracelet or belly ring of yours.

Another thing to remember is that sharks don't watch movies, so they don't know that they're supposed to stick their dorsal fins up out of the water as they cruise toward the beach. Most sharks near the shore usually swim on the bottom, so their victims have no advance warning.

Though the whole U.S. East Coast may only see 40 shark attacks a year (and few if any of these fatal), the number of incidents has been increasing over the past decade and a half—presumably because more folks are hitting the surf than ever. Along the East Coast, practically all shark attacks are "hit and run strikes" by black-tipped or spinner sharks, usually no more than six feet long. The shark bites, realizes that the victim tastes bad, and releases. Most bite victims bleed but don't lose any actual tissue.

Of course, sometimes they do kill people—in 1998, a nine-year-old boy died in Florida from a shark attack. But vengeance is certainly ours: while sharks kill about 100 people a year worldwide, humans annually kill some 100 million sharks.

Poison Ivy

If you've been exposed to poison ivy, you have two or three hours to wash it off and avoid a breakout. If you are out and about and can't take a shower, rubbing the skin with alcohol—even beer—will often help. What you *don't* want to do is touch the unwashed, exposed part of your body with any other part, thus spreading the irritating serum.

Giardia

Ironically, one of the smallest critters in the state causes much more cumulative discomfort across the state than any other. While a lake or stream may appear clean, think twice before taking a sip. You're risking a debilitating sickness by drinking untreated water. The protozoan *Giardia duodenalis* is found in fresh water throughout the state, spread by both humans and animals. Although curable with prescription drugs, giardia's no fun—unless bloating, cramps, and diarrhea are your idea of a good time. Carry safe drinking water on any trip. If your canteen's dry, boiling creek or lake water will kill giardia and other harmful organisms. Some hikers prefer to use water filters made by companies like Mountain Safety Research and Pur, about $50 at most backpacking stores. However, cheaper filters may allow the tiny giardia protozoan (as small as 0.2 microns) to pass through; even the best filters may not always filter out other, smaller organisms. Traditional purifying chemicals like chlorine and iodine are unreliable, taste foul, and can be unhealthy. Boiling's really your best bet.

Unfortunately, it's also possible to get giardia while bathing; be careful not to swallow water while swimming in fresh water; men with mustaches should carefully dry them after leaving the water.

Lyme Disease

Lyme disease is caused by a bacteria transmitted to humans through the bite of the deer tick. Not all ticks carry the disease, but infection rates in certain areas can be quite high. Don't assume that because you are not in a high-infection area you cannot get Lyme disease. Most cases have been reported in the northeast and upper Midwest, but an increasing number of cases are being seen in southeastern states. If you are bitten by a tick anywhere in the U.S., you should get checked for Lyme disease. The disease can be detected by a blood test, and early treatment can cure the disease or lessen the severity of later symptoms.

An early symptom of Lyme disease is a red, circular rash in the area of the bite that usually develops a few days to a few weeks after being bitten. Other symptoms can include flu-like symptoms, headache, stiff neck, fever, and muscle aches. Sometimes, these symptoms will not show up for months. If any of these symptoms appear, even if you don't remember being bitten by a tick, have a doctor check you. Early detection of Lyme disease provides excellent opportunity for treatment (largely with antibiotics).

The three types of ticks known to carry Lyme disease (not necessarily every individual) are the deer tick (most common) in the northeast and north-central U.S., the lone star tick in the South, and the California black-legged tick in the West. If you are bitten by any tick, save the body for later identification if at all possible.

Remove a tick as soon as possible after being bitten. The best way is to grab the tick as close to your skin as possible with a pair of tweezers. The longer a tick has been on your body, the deeper it will bite you to find more blood. The closer to its head you can grab it, the less chance that its mouth parts or head will break off in the wound. If you can't get the whole thing out, go see a doctor. Clean the wound with antiseptic and cover it to avoid infection.

CRIME

South Carolina's crime statistics aren't overly high, relative to other states in the U.S., but of course, when it's late at night and you're on a dicey side of town, this doesn't mean much. A friend of mine from Orangeburg says his daddy gave him three rules for staying safe, and they seem worth repeating:
• Nothing good ever happened after one a.m.
• Don't carry more than you're willing to lose
• There's safety in numbers

One a.m. is when most bars in South Carolina close, after which the streets become populated with drunk folk and those who prey upon them. Rule No. 2 is an important one. If you can't immediately hand over your wallet to a robber and

know you'll be all right, then you need to go through your wallet and remove the "valuable" contents. Rule No. 3 also makes sense. Single people get robbed more often than couples, who get robbed more often than trios, who get robbed more often than quartets, and so on. The bigger the crowd, the better the odds.

In Charleston a few years back, a Georgia tourist walking with a woman was held up at gunpoint by a trio of young men on bicycles. It was after 1 a.m. The man refused to give his wallet to the kids, and one of them shot him dead before they rode off into the darkness.

Police who responded to the scene found several thousand dollars in the victim's wallet.

How to Protect Yourself
• **Don't carry too much money.** How much is too much? Too much is so much that you won't gladly give over your wallet to get a robber to leave you and your travel companions alone.

• **Don't give carjackers time to size you up.** Walk to your car quickly, with your keys in your hand; get in, lock the doors, start up, and drive off. Fix your hair and/or makeup while you're at a *stoplight,* like a good American.

• **When driving—particularly in urban areas—keep your doors locked and your windows rolled up.** Carjackers are generally not the hardest-working individuals you'll ever run across—they're watching for an *easy* mark.

• **Keep your wallet or purse out of sight when you're driving.**

• **If you're involved in an accident that seems suspicious, signal to the other driver to follow you and then drive to a better-lit, more populated area.** A common ploy for carjackers is to bump their victims from behind and then rob them as they get out to inspect the damage to their car.

• **If you're traveling with children and get carjacked, tell the carjacker you've got a child in back and ask if you can take him or her out.** Many times the carjacker—who doesn't want to add a kidnapping charge to all the others he's racking up—will let you get the child out.

- **Park in a central, well-lit area.** In downtown Charleston, you might consider using one of the paid lots, which normally have some sort of supervision. Be aware, though: Sometimes the attendant leaves at sunset, which might leave your car unattended in a dark, deserted parking lot until 2 a.m. Ask the attendant how late the car will be supervised.

- **When in public, wear your money and/or purse close to your body—and wallets in your front pocket.** This will make it harder for pickpockets/purse snatchers to rob you undetected.

- **If you're driving a rental car, make sure there are no identifying markers.** Travelers have, in some places in the U.S.—Florida, most famously—become targets. If there are items that indicate your car is rented—license-plate frames emblazoned with the name of the company, for instance—ask the folks at the rental office if you can remove them while you have the car in your possession.

OTHER ISSUES

Racism
People have found a number of excuses for not loving each other throughout the centuries; one of the most common is racism.

Members of every imaginable race and combination of races live in South Carolina, but the vast majority—well over 95%—consider themselves either "white" or "black." And of course, it is between these two groups that most of the racial tension in South Carolina has traditionally existed.

Most of what passes for racism in South Carolina is, instead, largely "classism." What appears as white/black animosity is instead disguised class hatred: in the most common scenario, "racist" whites attribute to blacks all the traits historically attributed to anyone at the bottom of the social ladder—laziness, low intelligence, dishonesty, envy, criminal habits, and reproductive irresponsibility. "Racist" blacks on the other hand, attribute to whites all the traits underclasses generally hang on an upper class: greed, snobbery, condescension, lack of compassion, hedonism, shallowness, spiritual vacuousness, clubbishness. In each case, the "racist" person is probably right to oppose the

values they attribute to people they dislike. Where they err is in attributing these values to members of a given race.

If you're "white" or "black," it's possible you'll feel some hostility from "the other" while visiting South Carolina. If you are part of an interracial couple, you'll possibly experience some disapproving looks from members of both races, especially as you venture into the country or into the more homogeneous neighborhoods of the major cities. (If you're a non-black person of color, and far from any large town, you may find people scratching their heads, wondering how you ever ended up in South Carolina.)

To an amazing degree, a smile and eye contact break down the walls that most people put up between strangers of the "other" and their better selves. Your goal is to show them that you're an exception, that you don't carry the attitudes they expect to find in someone with your pigmentation.

If this doesn't work, the best thing to do is to cut your losses and move on.

Drugs
South Carolina is not known for its tolerant attitude toward illicit drugs, or for the comfortable nature of its jails. Possession and sale of marijuana is illegal here, as are all the usual mind-altering substances.

Sexually Transmitted Diseases
AIDS is alive and well in South Carolina, as are numerous other debilitating sexually transmitted diseases (STDs), including a couple flavors of hepatitis and genital herpes. The safest thing to do is to not share hypodermic needles and not have sex with anyone you haven't screened first. If a person tells you he or she is HIV-negative, make sure the person hasn't had sex with another partner since that last screening. And since there's a six-month window during which someone who has contracted HIV may still show negative in a HIV test, to be safe you need to know that a person didn't have sex for six months *before* the screening (although some people with HIV have tested negative as late as five years after contracting the virus).

If, given the irresistible attractiveness of most South Carolinians, celibacy seems an impossible task, you should at least reduce the risk by using a latex condom, though these tear easily.

COMMUNICATIONS, MEDIA, AND INFORMATION

POSTAL SERVICES

Sending mail from the United States to anywhere in the world is pretty easy. Almost every town and city in the U.S. that you are likely to visit has at least one post office, or a local business that acts as the local post office. In larger cities you'll also find the major international delivery companies (UPS, Federal Express, and so on). The U.S. Postal Service and the delivery companies will also ship packages for you to many foreign countries.

Charges are based on weight. At publication, a standard U.S. postal stamp costs 33 cents.

The delivery companies and the postal service offer next-day and two-day service to almost anywhere in the world.

If you plan to receive mail in the United States, make sure that the person sending mail addresses the envelope with your name exactly as it appears on your passport. This will help to avoid any questions as to whether the mail is yours. You can also have mail delivered to your hotel. Make sure to provide the person sending you mail with the correct address. Also request that the person sending you mail print or type your address on the envelope to avoid any confusion that might arise because of worldwide differences in writing styles.

Always attach postage yourself to ensure that the proper amount is used.

When shipping large parcels overseas, it's best to pack the item(s) yourself or oversee the job. There are many packaging stores in the United States, offering boxes in various sizes, as well as tape and other packaging material. Many of these stores double as a post office or pickup/dropoff spot for the large delivery companies.

Unfortunately, though the U.S. Postal Service likes to cite Herodotus' quote, "Neither snow, nor rain, nor heat, nor night stays these couriers from the swift completion of their appointed rounds," you'll find that just about any old bank holiday—even Columbus Day—will stay these couriers. Post offices will also close, and any mail you've already sent off will sit for a full day—so be prepared.

TELEPHONE

Public

Public phones are widely available on street corners and outside convenience stores and gas stations. They are maintained by a variety of private companies, which may sometimes charge more than the usual fee of 35 cents. Use any combination of coins; however, in the case of a 35-cent local call, if you use two quarters, change will not be provided. Dialing directions are usually provided on the face of the phone, but when in doubt simply dial "0" for an operator who will direct your call for an added charge of one to three dollars. To place a local or long dis-

tance call, simply dial the number and an automated voice will tell you how much money to deposit. When using a calling card billed to your home account, dial "0" plus the number (including area code) you're calling. You'll hear a tone, then often a voice prompting you to enter your calling card number and Personal Identification Number. For universal calling cards, follow the instructions provided on the back of the card or dial "0" for operator assistance.

Emergency
In an emergency when an ambulance, firefighters, or police are required, you can dial 911 and be instantly connected with an emergency switchboard; otherwise dial "0" for operator. When you dial 911, your number and address are displayed on a viewing screen, enabling the authorities to locate you, even if you yourself don't know where exactly you are.

Long Distance
Prepaid calling cards are the most hassle-free method of making long-distance calls, short of carrying around a cell phone. If you purchase a $10 card, you are given $10 of long-distance credit to spend. You can spend it all on one call, or—more likely—on a series of calls throughout your trip. Best of all, if you lose your card—unlike some other calling cards that give access to your account with your phone company—you can't lose more than the $10 you spent on it. Stores like Kroger and Wal-Mart sell prepaid calling cards.

Phone books are generally available at public phone booths and normally cover everything within the local area code, though frequently they are vandalized. Besides containing phone listings, phone books also carry maps to the local area, zip codes and post offices, information on public transportation systems, and a listing of community services and events.

Area Codes
Used to be you could dial area code 803 for anywhere in South Carolina. But the advent of fax machines and pagers has brought about a division of the state like that visited upon Germany after Potsdam. Now, essentially, the Upcountry is 864, the Midlands (where most of the state agency numbers are) remain 803, and the Lowcountry is 843.

INTERNET ACCESS

By and large, Internet cafés seem to have already run their (short) course in South Carolina, though you will find a couple around the state (listed in the appropriate destination chapters). Some public libraries boast Internet access, and many better business hotels offer separate modem lines.

NEWSPAPERS

Nearly any South Carolina town of any size has its own newspaper; reading these can give you a good feel for the pace of life in a town. The Columbia *State* may just be the paper of record, though the Charleston *Post and Courier* is well thought of and well read. You can find the *Post and Courier* online at www.charlestonnet.com and the *State* online at www.thestate.com.

You'll also find *USA Today* all around the state. The New York *Times* is available in the business districts of major cities.

RADIO

In most of South Carolina, you'll find a wide variety of music, with a heavy emphasis on country but liberal dosings of urban, metal, and pop stations. Contemporary Christian rock music stations have popped up in a couple of the bigger cities. As usual, nearly everywhere in the state, the left end of the FM dial is where you'll find gospel stations and the local South Carolina Public Radio/NPR affiliate, where faithful listeners will find *All Things Considered, Prairie Home Companion,* and *Car Talk,* along with local shows—a few of which highlight regional music.

The AM dial contains gospel music and preaching, country music, some local news and talk shows, and the sonic strip mall that is American syndicated talk radio today.

Classic Radio Stations
WWBZ 98.9 FM, Charleston; WHBZ 99.7 FM, Hilton Head; WLXC 98.5 FM, Columbia ("The Breeze" Radio Network): These three stations (a fourth broadcasts from Wilmington, North

Carolina) play "Beach, Boogie, and Blues," giving you the chance to listen to authentic Carolina beach music and Carolina blues as you drive around most of the state. They'll also keep you up to date with local performances and shagging events.

WBUB 107.5 FM, Charleston: "The Big Bubba" features some lively jingles ("The Big Bubba . . . Uh-*huh!*") and a lot of top 40 country. As such it captures the pulse of a good bit of the Lowcountry, and listening to its "Cryin', Laughin', Lovin' and Leavin'" hour might give you a slight insight into the lives of the people in the next lane at the bowling alley.

WAVF 96 ("WAVE") FM, Charleston: This may not be the state's most-listened-to station, but you'll probably see more bumper stickers for this station on cars (and skateboards, and traffic signs, and park benches) than any other. WAVE is the prime alternative rock station in the state. It features regional bands.

WTMA 1250 AM: Listen to this Charleston standby in the mornings (before the station goes satellite for Rush Limbaugh and the usual talk offerings) to hear Dan Moon, a local celebrity and a Charleston institution, and get a sense of the workings of the city, as he broadcasts live from store openings, flea markets, and just about any event with room for a mobile unit. Libertarian Scott Caysen hosts a local call-in talk show 3-5 p.m., which occasionally touches on local issues.

WVOC 560 AM: Essentially the WTMA of Columbia, this station's greatest strength is its tagline: "WVOC—The station you're hearing *right now.*"

WKCL 91.5 FM: WKCL boasts "100,000 Watts of the Lord's Power, 24 Hours a Day." It's a good place to take a peek into the large Evangelical Christian subculture in the state. Musically, most of the songs, with different lyrics, would be considered adult contemporary.

WPAL 730 AM, 100.9 FM: Bills itself as "The Soul of Charleston," featuring black gospel preaching and music, and electrifying combinations of both.

TELEVISION

For Pete's sake—you're on vacation. Don't watch television.

However, if you must, be sure to watch Joe Pinner, a.k.a. "Mr. Knowzit"—a beloved local children's show—on Saturday mornings in Columbia.

If you're shy about attending a church but would like to see what Southern preaching is about, you can turn on the tube on Sunday and catch all varieties. Be forewarned, though: preachers on TV—with some notable exceptions—tend to be the Johnnie Cochrans of the profession, which can be entertaining, to be sure, but hardly representative.

Another valid use of a television in South Carolina would be to watch a Gamecock or Tiger game—it will give you something to talk about with locals for the next week.

TOURIST INFORMATION

Department of Parks, Recreation and Tourism

Call the South Carolina Department of Parks, Recreation and Tourism at (803) 734-1700 or fax (803) 734-0138 to request a copy of the very helpful and up-to-date *South Carolina Travel Guide,* a travel map of the state, and other materials. Or write to P.O. Box 71, Columbia, SC 29202. Visit the department online at www.travelsc.com.

International visitors from the U.K. can contact the South Carolina Tourism Office at 20 Barclay Rd., Croydon CRO 1JN, United Kingdom, tel. (181) 688-1141, fax (181) 666-0365, e-mail: 100447.657@compuserve.com. Other Europeans should contact the South Carolina Tourism Office, Simensstrasse 9, 63263 Neu-Isenburg, Germany, tel. 6102-722-752, fax 6102-722-409, e-mail: 100753.500@compuserve.com.

International visitors from other regions should contact the **International Marketing Office,** South Carolina Department of Parks, Recreation and Tourism, 1205 Pendleton St., Columbia, SC 29201 USA, tel. (803) 734-0129, fax (803) 734-1163.

Welcome Centers

If you're driving into the state, be sure to stop at one of South Carolina's 10 welcome centers along the major highways at the state borders, as well as one in the middle of the state on Interstate 95 in Santee. The folks are generally very knowledge-

---

A PRONOUNCING GAZETTEER OF SOUTH CAROLINA CITY NAMES

Abbeville	AB-ee-vuhl
Beaufort	BYOO-fort (note, however, that Beaufort, North Carolina, is pronounced BOW-furt)
Blenheim	BLEN-um
Cheraw	chu-RAH
Colleton	COL-ton
Congaree	CON-guh-REE
Huger	HYOO-gee
Kiawah	KEE-a-wuh
Oconee	uh-COE-nee
Pee Dee	PEE-dee
Pocotaligo	POKE-uh-tuh-LEE-go
Saluda	suh-LOO-duh
Santee	san-TEE
Savannah	suh-VAN-uh
Sherman	SAY-tun
St. Helena	saint HELL-en-uh
Wadmalaw	wahd-MALL-ah
Wando	WAHN-doh
Westo	WEST-oh
Yamassee (tribe, war)	YAM-uh-see
Yemasee (town)	YEM-uh-see

---

able and helpful about the state's recreational opportunities and can help you plan your time in South Carolina to get the most possible out of your stay. They also dispense free maps and about a zillion pamphlets from every region of the state. They can even help you set up tee times.

MONEY

The U.S. dollar is divided into 100 cents. Paper notes include $1, $2, $5, $10, $20, and $100; the $2 bill is rarely seen but perfectly legal. Coin denominations are one cent (penny), five cents (nickel), 10 cents (dime), 25 cents (quarter), 50 cents (the rare half dollar), and the $1 coin (even more rare). Unfortunately, there are many counterfeit bills in circulation, usually hundreds or twenties.

In the late 1990s, the old $100, $50, and $20 bills were replaced with new bills featuring much larger portraits on the front side. If you're hand-ed one of the earlier forms of bills, rest assured that they're still accepted as legal tender.

Banks

It's best to carry traveler's checks in U.S. dollar denominations. Most businesses and tourist-related services accept traveler's checks. Only in very small towns will you run into problems with traveler's checks, or exchanging foreign money. The solution? Drive to a larger town. It's not a very big state.

Most major banks in big cities are open 9 a.m.-5 p.m. Hours for branches in smaller towns vary. Banks are usually closed on Saturday, Sunday, and most national and some religious holidays. However, some larger banks open for limited hours on Saturday, frequently 9 a.m.-1 p.m. Branch offices are becoming more omnipresent in the U.S., popping up in grocery stores and shopping malls across the state. But typically only major commercial banks have the ability to exchange foreign currency. Though banks are your best bet, other good places to obtain U.S. dollars include international airports (Charleston, Columbia, and Greenville, as well as Atlanta, Georgia, and Charlotte, North Carolina), and American Express offices. Check the local phone book Yellow Pages for addresses and phone numbers. Many banks have toll-free numbers answered by an automated voice, which gives options for various numbers. Stay on the line or press the appropriate number to speak to a human.

Most businesses accept major credit cards—MasterCard, Visa, and American Express. On occasion, in very small towns and rural areas, cash (US$) will be the only accepted form of money. It's also possible to get cash advances from your credit card at designated automated-teller machines (ATMs). ATM machines are omnipresent in the U.S. You'll see them in grocery stores, shopping malls, sometimes at festivals or fairs, sporting events, street corners, and, of course, at most banks. In Charleston, the police department got proactive about the number of incidents occurring around ATM machines and installed one inside the lobby of the police building.

In many supermarkets, it's now possible to pay for your groceries with a credit card or a debit card, which deducts the amount directly from your checking or savings account. Often this method incurs a small transaction fee; check with your bank for details. For you to use ATMs and debit cards, your bank must be affiliated with one of the several ATM networks. The most common affiliations are Star, Cirrus, Plus, and Interlink.

Taxes
Expect to pay 6% sales tax on anything you buy—except food at the grocery store. You'll also pay a room tax at lodging establishments.

Tipping
It's standard in South Carolina to tip your waitperson 15% of the bill for acceptable service. If you're at a breakfast place, where the bills are lower but the staff is often just as hardworking as those at more expensive dinner spots, you may wish to tip at least 20%. Never tip the regular amount to reward rude or inattentive service—it only encourages more of the same.

Tip airport skycaps $1 a bag; the same for hotel bellhops.

READING

Libraries
The single-best library in the state is the Thomas Cooper Library at the University of South Carolina in Columbia. It's amazing the books that they allow to stay in the stacks—it's quite possible to pull a book printed in the mid-1800s off the shelf and—if you're a student or faculty—check it out. For South Carolina and Southern/Confederate titles, one of the top places to go in the world is USC's Caroliniana Library, on the Horseshoe.

As far as public libraries, it's clear that South Carolina takes its public libraries seriously. One of the finest is the **Richland Public Library** in Columbia, but the Main Charleston County Library at 68 Calhoun St. has a fine selection as well. Probably the coolest little library in the state is the Edgar Allan Poe Library, built into the old fort works on Sullivan's Island.

You'll find all of these libraries listed in the appropriate destination chapters.

Bookstores
No matter what the SAT scores say, South Carolina has a literate population that likes to read, and thus you won't have trouble finding a book-store in nearly any town. Though Barnes and Noble, Books a Million, and other discount book-sellers have arrived on the scene in the state, you'll also find numerous quality independent bookstores like Charleston's **Chapter Two** and Columbia's **The Happy Bookseller,** in addition to a worthy bookstore at the University of South Carolina. Most larger cities have used bookstores, though about half of these feature genre fiction. Two of the best are **Atlantic Books** in Charleston (two locations) and **The Book Dispensary** (multiple locations) in Columbia.

Publishing Houses
South Carolina is blessed with two prolific presses dedicated to Southern and South Carolinian titles. The first is **University of South Carolina Press,** 718 Devine St., Columbia, SC 29208, tel. (800) 768-2500, fax (800) 868-0740, based in Columbia near the university. They'll be glad to send you a catalog. Visit the press Web site at www.sc.edu/uscpress. The books tend a bit more toward academic titles—including USC professor Matthew Bruccoli's fine scholarship on F. Scott Fitzgerald—but also include cookbooks and Civil War titles.

Sandlapper Publishing, Inc. is based in downtown Orangeburg, of all places. Request a catalog at P.O. Box 730, Orangeburg, SC 29116-0730, tel. (800) 849-7263, fax (800) 337-9420, tel. (803) 531-1658, fax. (803) 534-5223. Or stop by its little store at 1281 Amelia St. NE, in Orangeburg. Until 1982 the company was owned by the folks who publish *Sandlapper Magazine,* but since then it's been a separate entity and now features literally hundreds of different books on South Carolina. Sandlapper is a great resource for native Carolina literature—the company has republished much of the work of William Gilmore Simms, Julia Peterkin, Archibald Rutledge, and William Price Fox. It also publishes historical maps and videotapes, including a Gullah version of Heyward Dubose's *Porgy.*

Magazines and Newsletters
Sandlapper: The Magazine of South Carolina is a fine, professional glossy quarterly published out of Lexington by Sandlapper Society, Inc. Each issue includes articles about some hidden treasure in the state—good pre-reading before a visit. You'll find the magazine on sale at

better newsstands for $5, or you can contact Dolly Patton, the executive director of the society, at P.O. Box 1108, Lexington, SC 29071, tel. (803) 359-9954, about becoming a "member" of the society—for which you will receive a subscription to *Sandlapper*. See the magazine's site at www.sandlapper.org or send e-mail to sandlap@alltel.net.

Southern Living is another good place to read ahead on South Carolina.

HOLIDAYS

South Carolina celebrates the common holidays and memorial and observation days observed throughout the United States and adds a few of its own.

January 1—New Year's Day: First day of the Gregorian year: many Carolinians spend the morning watching Pasadena, California's, televised Rose Bowl Parade, a mammoth, moving spectacle in which all of the floats are decorated with flowers or flora of some kind. Afterward follows the famous Rose Bowl football game between two top college teams. Several other college bowl games keep most football fans in front of the television until late at night. Otherwise, the day is generally spent recovering from New Year's Eve parties and reconsidering New Year's resolutions. An old South Carolinian tradition—presumed to have come over from Africa with the slaves—is to eat black-eyed peas for good luck on this day. They're usually served with collard greens and cornbread.

Late January—Super Bowl Sunday: Not a legal holiday, but a major cultural event, as professional football's two top teams play for the sport's world championship. Marked locally by football parties in homes and bars.

Third Monday in January—Rev. Martin Luther King Jr's. Birthday (observed): Celebrates the birthday of the Georgia-born civil rights leader.

February 14—Valentine's Day: Saint Valentine, the Roman Catholic patron saint of lovers, is memorialized on this increasingly superficial holiday by the exchange of greeting cards, flowers, and candy. Generally a day to celebrate love and affection between romantically inclined couples.

Third Monday in February—Presidents' Day: celebrates the birthdays of Abraham Lincoln (February 12, 1809) and George Washington (February 22, 1732). Lincoln, the 16th president, authored the Emancipation Proclamation freeing the slaves and is considered the man who preserved the Union in the Civil War. Washington, commander of the American forces during the Revolution and first president of the United States, is often called "the father of our country."

March 17—Saint Patrick's Day: Celebrates the Roman Catholic patron saint of Ireland, a Brit or Norman (historians disagree) kidnapped and placed in slavery in Druid Ireland. Patrick escaped back home, was converted to Christianity, and returned to evangelize his former captors and eventually all of Ireland. He used the ubiquitous three-leaf clover to help explain the Christian conception of the Trinitarian nature of God; to this day, the clover and its color (Kelly green) are closely associated with both Patrick and Ireland. In America, St. Patrick's Day mainly celebrates

Myrtle Beach's Sun Fun Festival

FESTIVAL AND EVENT HIGHLIGHTS

Nothing makes the delights of a small town (or even a bigger city) more accessible than a public festival, and South Carolina offers bushels of them—the list below represents only a sampling.

If you're planning to visit a region on a given weekend, check ahead of time with the respective tourism department or chamber of commerce on upcoming events. Remember, too, that once you're in South Carolina, you're no more than six hours away from any festival anywhere in the state.

JANUARY

Grand American Coon Hunt (Orangeburg) is the largest coon dog field trial in the U.S., and about as Southern as you get. Call (803) 534-6821 for information.

Lowcountry Oyster Festival (Charleston) features buckets of oysters, live music, kids' events, and a shucking contest. Call (843) 577-4030 for information.

FEBRUARY

Africa Alive (Rock Hill) is a feast of storytelling, dance, music, and crafts celebrating all things African. Call (803) 329-2121, ext. 136, for information.

Battle of Aiken (Aiken) gives re-enactors the chance to bring to life the 1865 battle, with cavalry, artillery, gunfire, shouts—everything but the killing and maiming. Call (803) 649-9273 for information.

MARCH

Andrews Gospel Music and Storytelling Festival (Andrews) offers a fine opportunity to experience the cultural by-products of rural life in the South. Call (843) 264-3471 for information.

Edisto Indian Cultural Festival (Summerville), held in a quaint Charleston-area town, celebrates Native American culture with lots of authentic dance demonstrations, as well as dance and craft competitions. Call (843) 871-2126 for information.

Festival of Houses and Gardens (Charleston). For over 50 years, this festival has allowed common folk to tour the port city's historic manses and private gardens. Throw in some oyster roasts and you've got yourself a quintessential Charleston experience. Call (843) 723-1623 for information.

Spring Tours of Homes (Beaufort), self-guided, showcase beautiful Lowcountry homes and plantations—a 40-year tradition. Call (843) 524-0363 for information.

APRIL

Blessing of the Fleet and Seafood Festival (Mount Pleasant) combines seafood, crafts, entertainment. Simply shrimpalicious. For information, call (843) 849-2061.

Governor's Frog Jump and Egg Striking Contest (Springfield). In addition to the two powerhouse events noted in its name, this quintessential small-town festival features something for everyone: a street dance, horseshoe competitions, Easter egg hunts, and more. Call (803) 258-3152 for information.

South Carolina Festival of Roses (Orangeburg) is one of the state's biggies, held in Edisto Memorial Gardens on the banks of the slow-moving North Fork of the black Edisto River. Features arts and crafts, a 10K race, entertainment, canoe/kayak races, and rows and rows of beautiful roses.

Stone Soup Storytelling Festival (Woodruff) brings storytellers from around the country to this little town southwest of Spartanburg on the 221 to perform and take part in storytelling workshops. Call (864) 476-3123 for information.

World Grits Festival (St. George). The name says it all: grits-themed contests, and a chance to sample unique grits-based recipes highlight this festival held in this handsome town southeast of Orangeburg. Call (843) 563-4366 for information.

MAY

Hell Hole Swamp Festival (Jamestown) is a combination snake and reptile show, parade, greased-pole climb, beauty pageant, and more. Call (843) 257-2234 for information.

Gullah Festival (Beaufort) is a cultural event featuring storytelling, fine art, dance, music, and special events in celebration of the cultural traditions of the Sea Islands. Call (843) 525-0628 for information.

Carolina Legend Bluegrass Festival (Lancaster). Old-time country, bluegrass, and gospel music fills the air; highlights include the Dewittt "Snuffy"

Jenkins Memorial Banjo Competition. Call (803) 285-7451 for information.

Blue Crab Festival (Little River) is a fun, crabmeat-filled festival in a small fishing town north of Myrtle Beach. Call (800) 356-3016 for more information.

Spoleto Festival USA and Piccolo Spoleto (Charleston) are the premier arts festivals in the state; see the Charleston chapter for a description. Call (843) 722-2764 for information on Spoleto, (843) 724-7305 for Piccolo Spoleto specifics.

JUNE

Sun Fun Festival (Myrtle Beach) is Myrtle Beach at its Myrtle Beachiest. A parade, beauty pageants, live music, sand sculpture competitions, and more. Call (843) 626-7444 for more information.

South Carolina Festival of Flowers (Greenwood) celebrates the arrival of summer with this four-weekend festival, featuring tours of Park Seed Company's trial gardens and processing plant, the town garden, and historic homes; arts and crafts demonstrations, sporting events, and live music—usually including classical recitals and a major beach music act (not infrequently the locally grown Swinging Medallions). For information, call (864) 223-8411.

Harborwalk Festival (Georgetown) brings cultural arts, local crafts, and live music to the streets of this pretty river town each June, making it an even more intriguing destination than usual. Call (843) 546-1511 for information.

JULY

Festival on the Fourth (Charleston). Since it was the headquarters of Revolutionary activity in the South, Charleston's a fitting place to spend the Fourth. Look for live music and fireworks over the harbor. Call (843) 724-7305 for information.

Watermelon Festival (Pageland) includes parades, a rodeo, a beauty pageant, and gargantuan produce. It's a perfect festival for experiencing small-town Carolina. Little Pageland is on SC 9 between Lancaster and Chesterfield. Call (843) 672-5257 for information.

AUGUST

S.C. Peanut Party (Pelion) celebrates the wonder of peanuts with a parade, a car show, a cooking contest, a carnival, live music, and lots of boiled peanuts. If you're a peanut fan, a small-town connoisseur, or just really miss the Jimmy Carter era, you'll want to catch this. Pelion is on SC 302 southwest of Columbia. Call (803) 263-4167 for information.

Summerfest (York). It doesn't take much to get me up to visit this charming hill town, but the Summerfest is a great excuse. Attractions include a fun-run, kids' activities, crafts, food, a car show, and York itself. Call (803) 684-2590 for more information.

SEPTEMBER

Scottish Games and Highland Gathering (Charleston), held at beautiful Tara-esque Boone Hall Plantation, is a gathering of the kilts that includes medieval competitions, Scottish dancing, and, yes, bagpipes. Call (800) 868-8118 for information.

Autumnfest (Columbia) shows off the capital city at its best for this celebration, featuring live music and often outdoor dancing. Call (803) 343-8750 for information.

OCTOBER

Apple Harvest Festival (York) features apple cider-making and butter-churning, hayrides, scarecrow stuffing, live music, and more. A great chance to experience this pleasant, historic hill town. For information call (803) 775-0908.

South Carolina State Fair (Columbia) showcases major (or once-major, anyway) musical acts, crafts, a giant rocket, corndogs, elephant ears, rollercoasters anchored by cinderblocks, and teenaged trios cruising for the opposite sex. If this doesn't sound like a good time, you've strayed too long from the fair. Call (803) 799-3387 for information.

NOVEMBER

Holiday Festival of Lights (Charleston). Head over to James Island County Park at night to experience a drive-through wonderland of miniature light displays. Begins the second Friday in November through New Year's; admission runs about $10 per carload. Once you've done the drive, get out and explore the Christmas gift shops, and have some hot chocolate at the concessions area. Call (843) 795-7275 for information.

(continues on next page)

FESTIVAL AND EVENT HIGHLIGHTS

(continued)

Chitlin' Strut (Salley) is a raucous celebration of this dubious member of meat group. Amusements include a parade, live music, a hilarious "Strut" contest, and all the chitlins you can stomach. Held the Saturday after Thanksgiving. Call (803) 258-3485 for information.

DECEMBER

Catfish Stomp (Elgin). Rest assured, this does *not* involve stepping on catfish. However, it does usually involve ingesting great quantities of the bewhiskered critters—usually after they've been fried or slipped into a zesty stew. A carnival and parade will help you pace yourself between servings. Set in tiny Elgin, on US 521 south of Lancaster. Call (803) 438-5766 for information.

Lights Before Christmas (Riverbanks Zoo, Columbia). While the animals sleep, humans stalk the paths of Riverbanks, wearing scarves and mittens, sipping hot cider, and ogling the fascinating light displays throughout the complex. A fun holiday tradition. Call (803) 779-8717 for information.

First Night (Greenville, Columbia, Charleston). Ring in the new year in with these alcohol-free street celebrations, which seem to be catching on around the South. Fireworks replace the giant ball they have up north. Call (843) 853-8000 for information about First Night Charleston, (803) 799-3115 for First Night Columbia, and (864) 370-1795 for First Night Greenville.

Irish-Americans and their contributions to American culture. It's a lighthearted holiday for most, marked by parades, green clothing (forget to wear some and you may get pinched), and the overconsumption of green beer and green eggs at bars (which open extra early for the occasion). Columbia and nearby Savannah, Georgia, have famously raucous celebrations.

March or April—Easter Sunday: Celebrating Jesus of Nazareth's resurrection from the dead—for Christians, the single-most important event in the history of the universe: the final evidence that Jesus was indeed the long-awaited Christ of the Hebrew prophets, the day that eternal life became possible for human beings, and the ultimate historical proof of God's sovereignty over death and evil. Through the centuries, this celebration has become merged in spirit with pagan regeneration festivals celebrating the Earth's waking from its winter sleep. Consequently, rabbits and eggs (both symbols of regeneration, for obvious reasons) are today as commonly associated with Easter Sunday as an empty tomb.

In South Carolina you'll find Easter celebrated with outdoor sunrise church services (including one held at the ominous Sheldon Church ruins near Beaufort), children's egg hunts in public parks, and unusually crowded church services attended by families in new Easter clothes. Noteworthy Carolina public celebrations include Lexington's "L'Eggsington Easter Eggstravaganza"; the tiny town of Springfield, east of Aiken, holds the famed **Governor's Frog Jump and Egg Striking Contest,** featuring a parade, egg hunt, street dance, a frog jumping contest, and an egg striking event. In Charleston, dozens of local and nationally known gospel music acts appear at **Gospel Fest.**

April 1—April Fool's Day: Early Europeans were sometimes fooled by the weather into thinking that summer had arrived early. Those more experienced with the changing seasons knew better than to believe summer had arrived in April, and their foolish neighbors became a source of great humor and were often sent on "fool's errands." April Fool's Day in South Carolina is marked by false news stories in the media and practical jokes between friends, family members, and coworkers.

May 5—Cinco de Mayo: Marks the day in 1862 when Mexico repulsed a French invasion. In the United States it's become a celebration of things Mexican. In South Carolina this is largely limited to specials at Mexican restaurants.

May 10—Confederate Memorial Day: Long celebrated in lieu of the Federal Memorial Day—which was seen locally as a Yankee holiday. At publication, this is considered an "optional" state holiday, meaning that schools and government offices are not required to close on this day.

Some have proposed that both this and Martin Luther King Day (also presently "optional") be made official holidays.

As it is, look for the day to be marked by ceremonies held in Confederate graveyards.

Second Sunday in May—Mother's Day: Celebrating Mom and her influence on the lives of her children. Marked by gifts of flowers, candy, and greeting cards, and taking Mom to her favorite restaurant.

Last Monday in May—Memorial Day: Honors Americans killed in war. In South Carolina, look for ceremonies held at military graveyards. For a long time, Southerners saw this (rightly) as a holiday established by Abraham Lincoln to honor the Union war dead, but since WW II it has become more commonly celebrated south of the Mason-Dixon line.

Third Sunday in June—Father's Day: Celebrating Dad the same way we celebrate Mom in May. In South Carolina, golf courses tend to overflow with reservations.

July 4—Independence Day: The day, in 1776, when the Declaration of Independence was signed, the Founding Fathers' formal proclamation that the American Colonies were severing their ties with England—essentially the birth of the United States. In practice, the celebration of all things American, marked by patriotic parades, barbecues and picnics, flag-waving, and at night, fireworks. Traditional foods include hamburgers, hot dogs, watermelon, and apple pie.

First Monday in September—Labor Day: Though it sounds like another variation of Mother's Day, Labor Day actually celebrates working folks—mothers or not—who are rewarded with a day without labor. Predictably, management takes the day off, too.

October 12—Columbus Day: Observed on the second Monday in October. Celebrating the day when Christopher Columbus "discovered" America for Europeans. Marked increasingly by counterdemonstrations protesting the effects of this discovery upon Native Americans.

October 31—Halloween: This holiday, whose name is a contraction of "Hallows' Evening," is based in the early European tradition of leaving gifts outside one's front door overnight to ward off evil spirits, who were believed to come out in large numbers on this night, the eve before the Roman Catholic feast day for All Hallows—all

dead Christian believers—dating back to the time of Christ. It was believed that failure to leave a gift would cause the spirit to play a "trick" on the occupant of the house. Today children dress up in costumes and go from home to home, ringing the bell and shouting "Trick or treat!" when homeowners open the door. Adults dutifully offer these spooky "spirits" some treats—almost invariably candy. Adults also celebrate by dressing up in a variety of costumes and going to parties.

Some of South Carolina's Christian churches, uncomfortable with the idea of a holiday that seems to them increasingly to celebrate the forces of evil, hold counter "Harvest" celebrations on this night, to give thanks for God's blessings—and help the kids forget they're not out trick-or-treating. Many of these celebrations invite children to dress up as their favorite biblical character or other (non-evil) hero, and include candy, apple cider, pumpkin pie, bobbing for apples, and many of the same autumnal trappings as the average Halloween party, sans the cardboard skeletons, mummies, and vampires.

First Tuesday after the first Monday in November—Election Day: Not really a holiday, but a day to which a lot of attention is paid by the American public and the media.

November 11—Veterans Day: A day to honor war veterans. Traditionally marked by parades of veterans, but as romantic ideas of soldiery dissipate in the post-Vietnam era, and the days of legitimate military threats to U.S. sovereignty become more distant, some look with increasing apathy and even disdain upon the Armed Forces.

Fourth Thursday in November—Thanksgiving Day: Historically the day when the Puritan pilgrims (the first English persons to settle in what is now the eastern United States) gave thanks to God for their survival and prosperity in the "New World." Today families get together and eat huge meals—usually turkey, cranberries, mashed potatoes, and (down here) cornbread stuffing—and reflect and give thanks for their blessings during the past year.

Many Americans watch New York City's Macy's Thanksgiving Day Parade on television in the morning. Increasingly, this is also a day when family members spend the afternoon (before and after the turkey) watching college football bowl games together.

The day after Thanksgiving is heralded as the first day of the Christmas shopping season—resulting in big sales and crowded shops.

Mid-late December—Hanukkah (also Chanukah or Chanuka): An eight-day Jewish holiday commemorating the victory of Judah the Maccabee and his four brothers over the Syrian-Greeks in 165 B.C., thus restoring the right of Jews in Palestine to perform Jewish religious rituals and remain free of the paganism of the Hellenistic world.

Though Hanukkah celebrates an important milestone in Jewish history, it remained a fairly little-marked holiday until recently, when Jews living in predominantly Christian societies wished to celebrate more elaborately so that their children would not feel they were missing out by not celebrating Christmas. Now, for many South Carolinian Jews, each night the traditional menorah lighting is followed by gift-giving. The word "Chanukah" means "rededication," referring to the victorious Jews' reconsecration of the temple of Jerusalem to Yaweh after its conversion to a pagan shrine under the Syrian King Aniochus IV.

December 24—Christmas Eve: The weeks before Christmas are marked by various parades, concerts, home tours, and light displays, culminating in Christmas Eve, which, for many, has become as much an event as Christmas itself. Marked by last-minute shopping, caroling in the streets, gift-giving, and little children staying up late to get a peek of "Santa Claus"—the U.S. transposition of the European St. Nicholas tradition—dropping down the chimney with a sackful of toys. On this night, many Roman Catholics and liturgical Protestants attend once-a-year candle-lit or midnight services.

December 25—Christmas Day: Celebration of the birth of Jesus Christ. Marked by gift-giving, Christmas trees, caroling, and large family dinners.

December 31—New Year's Eve: The last day of the year on the Gregorian calendar. Marked by huge parties, the countdown, the midnight kiss, and noisemakers of any kind. The downtowns of Charleston, Columbia, and Greenville ring in the New Year with "First Night" (shouldn't it be "Last Night"?), a downtown, alcohol-free (except in the bars) street party marked by music and fireworks. In other towns, the action centers on nightclubs and private gatherings. Because of the high number of drunken drivers on the roads, most people who don't have to drive on this night don't.

ODDS AND ENDS

Photo Etiquette

You will see quaint homes in South Carolina. You will want to take pictures of them.

If you're in downtown Charleston, and the house is one of the famous old Charleston houses along the Battery or on Rainbow Row, then go ahead and snap away. If you're up in a tiny Upcountry town and you want to take a picture of a private citizen's house, then you might try to get permission first. It's not really a legal requirement, just a courtesy. And courtesy goes a long way in South Carolina.

Some of the savvy basketweaving Gullah women you'll see in Charleston and along Hwy. 17 north of Mount Pleasant will charge you $5 or more to take their picture.

Camping Gear

With rain showers so unpredictable—particularly in summer—you'll want a tarp over your tent as well as beneath it. If you're car-camping, consider a screen canopy, inside of which you'll be able to sip your hot cocoa without enduring mosquito and no-see-um bites. If you'll be hiking long distances from a car that can get you to a doctor, then bring a snakebite kit.

WEIGHTS AND MEASURES

South Carolina (like all other states in the U.S.) does not use the metric system. For help converting weights, distances, and temperatures, see the table at the back of this book.

Electricity

Despite what Hollywood may have led you to believe, it's rare to find anywhere in the South that doesn't vibrate with electrical power. Electrical outlets in the U.S. run on a 110 or 120V AC. Most plugs are either two flat prongs or two flat and one round. Adapters for 220V appliances are available in hardware or electronic stores.

Time Zone

South Carolina rests within eastern time zone, the same one used by New York City, Boston, and Florida. It is three hours ahead of Los Angeles.

VACCINATIONS

The United States currently has no vaccination requirements for any international traveler. Check with the U.S. embassy or consulate in your country and request an update on this information before you leave.

The International Health Regulations (IHR) adopted by the World Health Organization (WHO) state that countries may require an International Certificate of Vaccination (ICV) against yellow fever. An ICV can also be required if you are traveling from an infected area. For current information, look up the Web site for WHO, at www.who.ch, or the Centers for Disease Control, at www.cdc.gov.travel/travel.html.

MYRTLE BEACH AND THE GRAND STRAND

The 60-mile stretch of coast running from Georgetown to the northern border of South Carolina is often called the Grand Strand, but the term more aptly describes the area between Murrells Inlet to the south and Little River to the north. The city of Myrtle Beach—named for the many wax myrtles once found along the shore—is today the centerpiece of a region that draws more visitors than any other single South Carolina destination.

But unfortunately, Myrtle Beach suffers from its reputation. Imagine New Yorkers without the wherewithal to drive to Miami. Imagine the Dukes of Hazzard at the beach. Now, imagine a pleasure land custom-built for these constituencies. You get the idea. We're talking miles of chain restaurants, cartoonish miniature golf courses, and beachwear shops specializing in genitalia-joke T-shirts.

This is the reputation. It's also the truth—one real, regrettable side of it, anyway. But the Grand Strand didn't become the state's top destination by accident: the local white sand beaches *are* gor-

geous; Barefoot Landing, a marketplace built on stilts amid a scenic salt marsh, *is* a memorable shopping experience (and has enjoyed the distinction of being the state's No. 1 tourist attraction for much of the '90s); and such venues as the Carolina Opry, Alabama (owned by the famous country rock band of the same name), and Gatlin Brothers Theatre justify promoters' claims that Myrtle Beach is now the country-and-western music capital of the Deep South. In fact, Myrtle Beach ranks as the nation's second most popular destination for bus tours, behind only Nashville—and just ahead of Branson, Missouri.

The Grand Strand is also an international destination for golfers and tennis players. In a state with seemingly more space allotted to fairways than to roadways, the Greater Myrtle Beach area alone boasts more than 100 golf courses. You could almost tee off at a different Grand Strand hole every morning for two and a half years and never play the same hole twice.

In fact, the allure of Myrtle Beach is such that today, the city claims rank as the second-fastest-growing metropolitan area in the United States. You'll see a lot of former Northerners and non-coastal Southerners here in tennis whites, sunglasses, and perfect tans—folks who vacationed in Myrtle Beach for years before finally sinking permanent roots into the region's fine white sand. In addition to the retirees, many younger folk of less patient generations have moved here to profit off the boom—and to enjoy the sun and fun now, not later.

This immigration is both a blessing and a curse to the Strand. On the positive side, the local economy—even after the devastating 1992 closure of the Myrtle Beach Air Force Base—is booming. But while people who readily leave behind family and friends for warm weather and a laid-back lifestyle tend to be very friendly, they don't normally become dedicated environmentalists or historical preservationists once they arrive. For most of these folks, Myrtle Beach is all about pleasure, pleasure, pleasure—now, now, now. Tellingly, the city's most important city festival doesn't celebrate the area's Revolutionary War heroes or founding families. Instead, the Sun Fun Festival celebrates, yes, sun and fun. But this is fitting—all good South Carolina towns

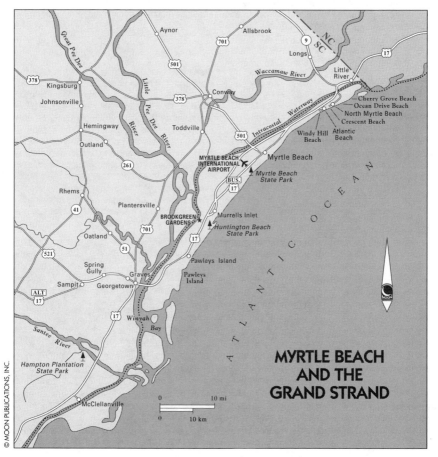

MYRTLE BEACH
AND THE
GRAND STRAND

hold festivals in honor of its most famous local product. In Salley, the product is chitlins. In Pageland, it's watermelons. In Myrtle Beach, it's sun-baked hedonism.

Head north or south of Myrtle Beach to enjoy fresh seafood in the quaint fishing villages of Little River and Murrells Inlet. Or drive north to the 1950s beach-town ambience of Ocean Drive Beach, longtime mecca for shaggers and beach music aficionados from around the world. **Huntington Beach State Park,** just south of town, provides picnicking and camping on some of the most pristine marshland and beachfront on the Carolina coast, and right across Hwy. 17 from Huntington stand the gates to **Brookgreen Gardens,** the world's largest outdoor sculpture garden and one of the most beautiful places in the entire South. Farther south on Hwy. 17 lie the "arrogantly shabby" vacation town of Pawleys Island; Georgetown, one of the state's most historic and scenic riverfront towns; the beautiful and historic Hopsewee and Hampton plantations; and the quaint fishing village of McClellanville, head of the state's new Palmetto Trail.

The majority of Myrtle Beach's vacationers have always been South Carolinians. Generations of spring breakers and summer vacationers have trekked to the myriad hotels and motels and cruised the Strand to see and be seen. For some 60 years, young Carolinians have taken their dates to ride the rickety Swamp Fox roller coaster; dine on fried shrimp, slaw burgers, and elephant ears chased with sweet tea;

and then head over to the Pavilion in their Weejuns to shag on the sand or on the sandy, sagging wood floor of The Pad, to beach music by bands like the Tams, the Drifters, and Maurice Williams and the Zodiacs. The shagging subculture is an important part of 20th-century Carolina. What Lafayette is to Cajun music, Myrtle Beach is to Carolina's own unique beach, or shagging, music.

Yes, Myrtle Beach's primary function is as a vacation town. But if you want to understand a people you really need to understand how it lets its hair down. And anyway, perhaps providing relaxation and family memories is a noble enough function for any community.

LAND

Starting at Little River near the North Carolina state line, a thin sliver of land between the Atlantic Ocean and the Waccamaw River runs on down to Winyah Bay at Georgetown. This sliver is known as Waccamaw Neck. Horry County encompasses this region and beyond, continuing west to the Little Pee Dee River. In today's world of drained swamps and hardly-notice-it concrete bridges, it's easy to underestimate how isolated Horry County was just 100 years ago. Folks liked to speak of "The Independent Republic of Horry County"; the rugged farmers and woodsmen who lived in the woods and swamps got along pretty much on their own.

Myrtle Beach, South Carolina

GRAND STRAND HIGHLIGHTS

Alligator Adventure
This is not your father's alligator farm. Instead, it's got a professional, eco-friendly demeanor and under-stated natural wood architecture—but it still offers plenty of chances to get close to more alligators than you can count.

Barefoot Landing
The classiest modern shopping experience in South Carolina, with a number of interesting restaurants; repeatedly voted the state's No. 1 tourist attraction.

Brookgreen Gardens/Huntington Beach
Either of these would make the list by themselves, but considering that they're just across Hwy. 17 from each other and share a common history, there's no reason to only visit one. Brookgreen contains a wonderful set of aviaries in addition to its exquisitely landscaped gardens, accented by the world's largest outdoor sculpture collection.

Huntington Beach is one of the most pristine coastal stretches in South Carolina—great for shelling, solitary walks, and wildlife viewing. The Huntingtons' Spanish Moorish home, Atalaya, is worth a tour as well.

Carolina Opry
Calvin Gilmore and the gang put on a show worthy of Nashville; of the region's many showcases, this is the one to catch.

Conway
This charming riverfront town is worth the drive in-land from Myrtle Beach.

Georgetown's Harborwalk
South Carolina's second-oldest city offers a slow-paced and scenic downtown, lots of historic B&Bs, and waterfront dining.

Murrells Inlet
More good seafood places (including standout Oliv-er's Lodge) than you can shake a shell-cracker at, and enough residual authenticity to make this a welcome change from Myrtle Beach.

Ocean Drive Beach
Both the Holy Land and ground zero for the shag explosion. Pop into any shagging club for an eye-ful—and a chance to join the slow-motion jitterbug.

The Pavilion
The bass-pumping, cat-calling heart of Myrtle Beach; if you're 16, you'll be in heaven; if you're not, this may be worth a quick visit just to remember how it felt. And if you're a cheesy T-shirt vendor, you prob-ably already live here.

Pawleys Island and the Pawleys Island Shops
Ever-serene Pawleys Island itself is worth a visit, but don't dismiss the shops. A Pawleys Island ham-mock will make a perfect souvenir or gift.

You also won't want to miss:
• The shopping and entertainment complex Broad-way at the Beach
• Hampton Plantation
• The Swamp Fox section of the Palmetto Trail (McClellanville)
• Ripley's Aquarium
• Sea Captain's House restaurant

Horry is South Carolina's largest county, larg-er than the state of Rhode Island in area. Most of this land is rural farmland, though the massive development of the county's oceanfront strip has rewritten the coast into a different story. But no matter what you might think of the Strand's prostituting its natural resources, Horry is pro-nounced with a silent "h," as in "O-ree." South of the Strand (and Horry County) proper is George-town County.

Here's something to keep in mind: the Strand proper is 60 miles long. If your show starts at 8 p.m. at Barefoot Landing in North Myrtle Beach, and you've made dinner reservations at 6 p.m.

down at Murrells Inlet, you may have planned out a pretty breakneck night for yourself, partic-ularly on a busy weekend, when both Hwy. 17 and the Hwy. 17 Bypass promise bumper to bumper traffic.

CLIMATE

January temperatures see an average high of 59° F and a low of 40° F; July and August see highs of 89° F and lows of 74° F. Rainfall during January averages just 4.03 inches; July, the rainiest month, sees an average of 6.41 inches. When I was here one June, it was raining and 95°. Humidity was up around 85%. So if you're expecting cold coastal breezes, you may have another think coming.

HISTORY

Though many historians suspect that Lucas Vasquez de Ayllon's short-lived 16th-century colony of San Miguel, the first European settlement in continental North America, was set somewhere in the present-day Hobcaw Barony north of Georgetown, this is only speculation. What's certain is that Georgetown was the third permanent city founded in South Carolina—after Charleston and Beaufort—and named after the German-born Prince George II. After its founding in 1735, Georgetown and the surrounding area became a hotbed for rice and later indigo, and grew into one of the richest cities in Colonial America.

During the Civil War, the Confederates established a fort up by Cherry Grove, surrounded by a ditch 10 feet wide and five feet deep. In January 1863, U.S. Navy Lieutenant William B. Cushing and 25 men captured the fort to use as an overlook while searching for Confederate boats attempting to run the Union blockade. Cushing and his men held the fort only briefly; before long they ran out of ammunition and made a hasty retreat.

After the Civil War broke most of the plantation owners, the land was bought up by members of Northern industrialist families with names like Ford, Vanderbilt, and Huntington, for summer retreats. In 1893, the region weathered a deadly hurricane.

To see an eerie reminder of the storm's handiwork, head out at low tide to where 42nd Ave. reaches the ocean. You can make out the wreck of the *Freeda A. Wyley,* a 507-ton ship carrying pine lumber from Mississippi to New York when she was caught in the storm and hit by lightning. The ship caught fire and burned clear down to the waterline before sinking, but amazingly, the crew was able to escape to shore.

At the time of the hurricane, the present-day town of Myrtle Beach consisted of two things: myrtle and beach. But in the last decade of the 19th century, Conway's F. G. Burroughs cut a swath from Conway to the sea, laying tracks as

he went, and building a lumber mill three-quarters of the way at Pine Island. He timbered the land between Conway and the ocean and used his new railroad, The Conway Seashore, to move this lumber to Conway where it could be loaded on barges and floated down the Waccamaw to Georgetown. He founded a new town at the ocean end of the railroad and, in a momentary lack of imagination, called it New Town. By 1900, he'd changed the name to Myrtle Beach. Local families got into the habit of riding the lumber trains down to the ocean, and by 1901, Burroughs had built an inn for the visitors.

For quite a while, though, the place didn't really catch on with anyone but the locals. In 1926, Greenville businessman John T. Woodside bought up a lot of the area around town and laid out streets. He built a major hotel, the Ocean Forest Hotel, and began advertising the beaches around Myrtle Beach as "America's Grandest Strand." The following years made Myrtle Beach a respectable player in the East Coast beach-town parade, but since Myrtle had little to offer that wasn't already available in Miami, Virginia Beach, or even Atlantic City, most of the people it drew continued to be locals: pleasure-seeking folks from the Midlands, Upcountry, and North Carolina. It wasn't until the late '60s that a local businessman built two golf courses and invented the "golf package," which allowed visiting golfers to receive special deals and preferences on lodging and golf by paying for them together as one "package." Before long, tourists wearing plaid pants and funny hats had begun to linger far beyond the summer months.

In fact, over the past 20 years, an alarming number of duffers and others have chosen to linger till death do them part. Development after development, faux plantation after plantation goes up, and retiree after retiree, tan entrepreneurial young couple after tan entrepreneurial young couple move down to feast on the good life they once tasted for only a week a year.

In 1992, as government officials downscaled the U.S. military, the Myrtle Beach Air Force Base was closed, leaving unemployed the largest body of workers in the county. What the county should do with the former base immediately became, and remains, a matter of some debate. Various business and community leaders have proposed a theme park, an expanded airport, and an industrial complex. Time will tell.

Meanwhile, the arrival of the massive shopping/entertainment complex Barefoot Landing signaled a positive change in the quality and tone of construction in the area; for the first time in a long time, something had been built here that contained an extended concept, a larger vision. And the public responded very positively, quickly turning Barefoot Landing into the state's top attraction, bar none. If other Myrtle Beach building followed suit, the "beachy" bric-a-brac street fronts could be on the way out, and an era of buildings more worthy of their location might be on its way in. Myrtle Beach might begin to attract more of the aesthetically sensitive visitors repelled by the gaudy tack.

But it was not to be. The addition of the even more massive shopping/entertainment complex Broadway at the Beach in the early '90s seemed, at first, to signal another step in the right direction, with its coherent, classic theme. But then came the chain tourist town eyesores: Hard Rock Café built a pyramid—a *pyramid*—just slightly out of theme for the New Orleans-themed area of Broadway at the Beach's Celebrity Square. And then, worst of all (so far), Planet Hollywood built its worthy-of-Vegas globe building, stuck right out on the Hwy. 17 Bypass where you can't miss it, no matter how hard you may try.

SIGHTS

ORIENTATION

Murrells Inlet

Mainly a strip of restaurants along the inlet named for a pirate (Captain Murrell) who made this his home base. Over the past decades, this fishing town with a 3,300 population has increasingly become a tourist draw, almost entirely for the fresh seafood and water sports along the inlet. Crime novelist Mickey "Mike Hammer" Spillane lives here. Pick up the local paper and you may see the name of his wife, Jane Spillane, an Inlet native who's active in area politics.

Downtown Myrtle Beach (the Pavilion Area)

This describes most everything near the Pavilion at 9th Ave., for about 20 blocks in either direction. On the south side of 1st Ave., the streets intersecting Hwy. 17 and Ocean Blvd. contain an "S" in their names, as in "19th Ave. S." North of 1st Ave., they receive an "N," as in 12th Ave. N. The downtown area encompasses the famed Pavilion area, center of spring break activities and the teenage cruise scene, and home to two midsize amusement parks and myriad miniature golf courses.

Broadway at the Beach

With the huge success of Barefoot Landing, that tastefully designed 100-acre complex north of town, it didn't take long for the next Big Thing to come to town. Broadway at the Beach opened in the early '90s between 21st Ave. N and 29th Ave. N, southeast of the Hwy. 17 Bypass, and takes up 350 acres, featuring a park, a 23-acre lake, theaters, nightclubs, 16 restaurants, and 100 specialty shops. The design is admirable, and it includes the worthwhile Ripley's Aquarium, but BATB has also attracted such garish Vegas-esque tourist-town inescapables as Bullwinkle's, Hard Rock Café, and Planet Hollywood. For better and worse, this is the new heart of Myrtle Beach. For information, call (800) 386-4662 or (803) 444-3200, or see the Web site at www.broadwayatthebeach.com.

Restaurant Row

Sometime in the 1970s, folks began building restaurants up here just beyond where Hwy. 17 and the Hwy. 17 Bypass rejoin north of town, and ending somewhere around the Briarcliffe Mall. Today you'll still find many fine restaurants up here, including Thoroughbred's and Garcia's, but with the hip new restaurants at Barefoot Landing and Broadway at the Beach, this is no longer the only place to eat in Myrtle Beach.

Barefoot Landing

This 100-acre complex, built along the Intracoastal Waterway and around a 27-acre freshwater lake, is perennially named South Carolina's single-most popular attraction, entertain-

SHAG: THE DANCE

The shag is best performed on a hot summer night, on a wooden dance floor sparkling and gritty with beach sand. The humidity needs to be eighty percent or above. The crowd should be thick, the temperature near the jukebox, almost insufferable. The dancers need to feel fully justified in sweating.

—Bo Bryan,
Shag: The Legendary Dance of the South

South Carolina has an official state dance, and it's not the Charleston. In the years just after WW II, a uniquely Southern phenomenon evolved along the Carolina coast. As author Bo Bryan explains it, as the rest of the nation worked off its postwar exuberance doing a violent, provocative dance called the "flying jitterbug," Southern couples on the Grand Strand moved a bit slower, and a bit more conservatively. The women—young Southern ladies, after all—were not quite so willing to have their thighs

(and underwear) exposed as they flew over their partner's shoulders or wrapped their legs around his torso. And the young men on the dance floor, young Southern gentlemen that they were, could not ask their partners to do it. And besides, it was hotter than Hades in Grand Strand dance clubs in the middle of summer: slower tempos and more intricate, subtle movements only made sense.

And thus was born the "subtle wildness" called the shag. Most South Carolinians will tell you that the dance developed in the late 1940s in Myrtle Beach. Some North Carolinians argue that the whole "shag scene" first appeared in Carolina Beach, near Wilmington, and moved down to the Grand Strand only after the Carolina Beach police department cracked down on the rowdy dancers. A third theory has the "birth" of the shag (i.e., the moment that the Northern jitterbug met South Carolinian understatement) taking place at the old Folly Beach Pavilion near conservative Charleston.

Wherever it began, the shag has been *the* dance of coastal Carolina for more than 50 years—and increasingly of the lower South as a whole. The music the first shaggers danced to was "race music"—blues and soul—of a certain tempo—approximately 120 beats a minute, to be precise. The Dominoes' 1951 R&B hit "Sixty Minute Man," Maurice Williams and the Zodiacs' "Stay," and the Drifters' "Under the Boardwalk" all had the right feel, and all became classic examples of what was called, from the 1940s onward, "beach music." Though unplayed on white radio stations, records by black R&B artists filled beach jukeboxes throughout the 1940s and early 1950s.

If the birthplace of the shag is disputed, nobody debates the historic headquarters: Ocean Drive Beach north of Myrtle Beach (now a part of North Myrtle Beach) became the mecca of shaggers from 1954 on—after Hurricane Hazel leveled a number of popular Myrtle Beach dance spots and left standing a dumpy old Ocean Drive house that was converted into "The Pad," the Strand's dive of dives and the holy of holies for shaggers. The floor was dirt at first and then later an uneven plank floor, and the walls and bare rafters were covered with shagger graffiti. But from the 1950s through the early 1990s—when it was regrettably torn down—"The Pad" was the center of action, and a kind of rite of passage for "Bos" and "Sugs" (as in "Sugar").

shagging at Fat Harold's

The whole Bohemian ambience of the place was not something proper Southern girls immersed themselves in in the late 1950s and early 1960s. And, as one fiftysomething shagger told me, it certainly wasn't something you told your father about beforehand. As this Pad alumnus puts it, there was something "naughty" about The Pad and the whole shagging scene that made it especially attractive to white Southerners of the pre-Vietnam era—it was the chance to break free from social taboos, dance to "race" music—often with sexually provocative lyrics ("Sixty Minute Man," for example, is little else but a sexual boast with a great beat), drink too much beer, and generally do all the things they'd feel terrible about in church come Sunday morning.

In the late 1970s, some of the now-middle-aged former shaggers began to talk about getting the old crowd back together. Thus was born the first Society of Shaggers festival in Ocean Drive. The SOS continues to meet several times each year, during which time the rooms book up at Ocean Drive and the floors at Fat Harold's, Ducks, Ducks Too, and the Spanish Galleon pack out. You'll find a shaggers' Walk of Fame on Main St. in Ocean Drive in front of Fat Harold's—and across the street, there's even a store specializing in shag-themed art. In 1984, Governor Dick Riley signed a bill declaring the shag the official South Carolina state dance.

For a superficial but accurate peek into shag culture, circa 1963, check out the 1989 movie *Shag,* with Bridget Fonda and Phoebe Cates. Or head online to www.shagger.com for more information or to order beach music and shag "how-to" videos.

ing over seven million people annually with its 100 specialty and retail shops, 15 waterfront restaurants, and 14 factory outlet stores. The area also includes the Barefoot Princess side paddlewheeler, the Alligator Adventure Live Reptile Zoo, the Alabama Theatre, and Dan Aykroyd's blues club, House of Blues. For information, call (800) 272-2320 or (843) 272-8349, fax (843) 272-1052, or visit the Barefoot Landing Web site at www.bflanding.com.

Ocean Drive

"Old O.D.," as beach music icons the Embers called it, is one of the northernmost beaches on the Strand. It was up here in little hangouts like The Pad that the whole shagging/beach music subculture was born, and it's here shaggers return each year for various contests and festivals. The sidewalk on the north side of Main Street contains the Shagger's Walk of Fame, which has honored famous shag dancers, beach musicians, disc jockeys, and other shag-related personalities since the 1980s. Judy's House of Oldies, also on Main Street, is arguably the best place in the world to pick up beach music or shagging instructional tapes.

Little River

The quaint fishing village of Little River is a good place to get away from the crowds of the Grand Strand. The town draws a lot of people who come for the deep-sea fishing charters that de-part from here. Others come for the annual Blue Crab Festival.

The Outlets and Fantasy Harbour

Up Hwy. 501 on the way west to Conway you'll come across the Myrtle Beach Outlet Mall and the Waccamaw Pottery Shops, good places to look for new merchandise at good prices. Fantasy Harbour contains some of the newer entertainment houses in the area, from Big Band at the Savoy to the Gatlin Brothers Theatre.

Conway

This is probably the best inland day trip from the Strand; head inland on Hwy. 501 to reach the well-preserved river town of Conway, with antique shops and a number of good restaurants.

MUSEUMS AND GARDENS

Brookgreen Gardens

This preserve, on Hwy. 17 three miles south of Murrells Inlet, tel. (800) 849-1931 or (843) 237-4218, ext. 250, is Myrtle Beach's one must-see attraction. It's America's largest outdoor sculpture display, 9,127 acres in all, including the beautiful gardens shaded by gigantic oaks, a wildlife park, two aviaries, and indoor art galleries.

The history of Brookgreen is an interesting one. What is now called Brookgreen Gardens was once four different plantations. George

*near the Pavilion,
Myrtle Beach*

Washington spent the night at the Brookgreen plantation on his southern tour in 1791, the guest of Dr. Henry Collins Flagg, a surgeon during the Revolution, and his wife, Rachel Moore Allston Flagg. Joseph Alston, who inherited the plantation next, married Theodosia Burr, daughter of Vice President Aaron Burr, and generally considered one of the most educated women of her era. In 1812, after her husband's election as governor of South Carolina, Theodosia sailed from Georgetown on the schooner *Patriot* to visit her father in New York. The ship disappeared forever off the North Carolina coast during a terrific storm.

Early in the 1900s, Archer Huntington—son of 19th-century railroad magnate (and one of California's "Big Four" robber barons) Collis Huntington—having grown up in mansions and riches, and assured of a life of ease, was not quite as motivated a capitalist as his father. He didn't want to take over the family business and instead became a poet. In his middle age, he met middle-aged Anna Hyatt, by this time a self-supporting artist.

Huntington bought a huge plot of land made up of the four former Waccamaw Neck plantations and built a huge summer home styled as a Moorish castle. As Anna continued with her sculptures, she needed a place to show her work, and she wanted to support the work of other artists as well. Hence, Brookgreen Gardens was born. Later additions include a 50-acre wildlife park and 90-foot-high aviary, and excursions on the Waccamaw River. Open daily

9:30 a.m.-4:45 p.m., longer hours in summer. Admission runs $8.50 for adults, $4 children. Best time to go is in April when everything seems to be abloom, but as long as you avoid the hotter months of summer—when you just won't feel like enjoying the swamp trails—any time is a good time to visit. Closed Christmas.

Southern Living readers recently named this one of the South's five favorite public gardens.

Vereen Memorial Historical Gardens
Up north of Myrtle Beach, on Hwy. 17 just 1.4 miles before you reach Little River, you'll see a sign for Vereen Memorial Historical Gardens, named after one of the founding families in the area. Here you'll find a 115-acre natural park with a 1.25-mile self-guided nature trail that winds past the Vereen farmhouse and a Revolutionary War cemetery.

Ripley's Aquarium
When I first heard that Ripley's—of "Believe It Or Not!" fame—and the "Believe It Or Not!" museum chain opened a $37 million aquarium, I was a little concerned: I kept imagining two-headed sea bass and sharks. But Ripley's Aquarium is an admirable balance of science and show business. It offers visitors the chance to stand face-to-face with deep-sea life that they were probably never even supposed to know about.

The 74,000-square-foot aquarium, the first of seven that Ripley's plans to open worldwide over the next few years, is designed so that the path taken by the visitor replicates the experience of submerging in the water to the ocean's depths, then re-emerging. You start out at a display called Rio Amazon, where you get a look at a cross section of a simulated Amazon River, featuring various indigenous fish, including piranhas. From Rio Amazon you move down a winding ramp "below the surface" to Rainbow Rock, which features more than 119 colorful species of fish from the Indo-Pacific region in a 10-by-40-foot viewing window. As you continue down "underwater," you actually end up literally underwater at Dangerous Reef, the world's longest clear acrylic underwater tunnel, the best of its type that I've seen. Normally, these tunnels are never as impressive as I think they'll be, perhaps because you're carted through the tunnel on a conveyor belt, which helps with the traffic flow but always makes me feel as if I'm being given the bum's rush. To stand still on these other belts, I need to sidestep those being pulled toward me. Fortunately, the Ripley's conveyor moves very slowly through the 310-foot-long tunnel. Best of all, staying on the moving belt is optional—at any time, you're free to take a step to the right and stand on carpet firma, giving yourself more time to commune with the shark, fish, eel, or ray of your choice.

As you ascend up out of Dangerous Reef, the nearby crashing waterfall is meant to suggest to you the feeling of surfacing from the deeps—nice touch. On your way up and out you'll see the Monterey Wharf exhibit, featuring rockfishes and starfish. The jellyfish displays and living coral are enough to make you want to rent some scuba equipment and head out for some diving. Up here on the surface you'll find Ray Bay.

And speaking of rays, one thing you may notice if you've visited aquariums in other states is that Ripley's has no mammals—no dolphins, no whales, no seals, no walruses. Which is to say, it has none of the cute, cuddly, money-making critters that places like California's Monterey Aquarium depend upon to generate plush toy sales, otter book bags, and the like. This is no oversight on Ripley's part: it's actually against the law to keep an aquatic mammal in captivity in South Carolina. What the marketing folks here have done in their stead, you'll notice, is start a campaign to change the public image of the ray family. Though many of us have grown up afraid

of being stung by stingrays, the folks at Ripley's point out that only a handful of the roughly 100 species of rays can harm humans. Caribbean-island–themed Ray Bay is an interactive spot where guests can pet rays (the Southern stingrays have had their stingers removed). In the gift shop you'll find plush stingrays for the kids.

The kids will probably also enjoy the Sea-for-Yourself Discovery Center, where you and they can learn more about the creatures they've been gawking at. And finally, you'll find the Feeding Frenzy fast food restaurant upstairs, where you can pick up a veggie burger—you probably won't feel much like a fish sandwich.

Why did Ripley's decide to build the aquarium here in Myrtle Beach? It's not because it was close to the ocean. After all, the second Ripley's Aquarium was scheduled to open in December 1999 in Gatlinburg, Tennessee. No, it was Myrtle Beach's unique year-round tourist-based economy—which Ripley's has experienced through its Believe It Or Not Museum down by the Pavilion for some 20 years.

But there's a difference between luring sun-dizzy tourists into a modern-day freak show like the Believe It Or Not Museum and enticing them into—no matter how it's packaged—an educational experience like the aquarium. Sure Ripley's has built it—will people come?

Consider this: The aquarium opened in June 1997. On April 24, 1998, Gerald Pomery from Maryland stepped through the turnstiles to become the aquarium's millionth visitor. Open 9 a.m.-9 p.m. Admission runs $13.50 for adults, $7.95 ages 5-11, $2.95 ages 2-4. Enjoy your visit. And be sure to pet one of those cute stingrays for me.

South Carolina Hall of Fame
In the lobby of the Myrtle Beach Convention Center, 21st Ave. N and Oak St., tel. (843) 448-4021, this small museum adds members each year, normally one living member and one who has passed on. Members include John C. Calhoun; Apollo 10, 13, and 16 astronaut Charles M. Duke; Andrew Jackson; Federal architect Robert Mills; General William Westmoreland; Dizzy Gillespie; presidential advisor and college founder Mary McLeod Bethune; Cardinal Joseph Bernardin; and Pulitzer Prize-winning novelist Julia Mood Peterkin. Hours are Mon.-Fri. 9 a.m.-5 p.m. Admission free.

THEME PARKS
AND OTHER ADVENTURES

Myrtle Beach Pavilion
Amusement Park and Family Kingdom

Myrtle Beach suffers for its vast wealth of small amusement centers; down by the Pavilion, it seems you can't drive three blocks without seeing a Ferris wheel or concrete volcano. In sheer terms of size or originality, those used to the Disney or Six Flags parks will find neither of the Pavilion area's two main amusement parks—the Myrtle Beach Pavilion Amusement Park, Ocean Blvd. and 9th Ave. N., tel. (843) 448-6456, Web site: www.mbpavilion.com; and Family Kingdom Amusement Park, Ocean Blvd. and 3rd Ave. S., tel. (843) 626-3447—anything to write home to Mom about (unless Mom happens to be a retired carny).

You've seen it all before: the barkers, the cotton candy, the skee ball, the shirt-screening places. But there really is nothing quite like clicking to the top of a seaside roller coaster and looking over at the huge ocean, feeling the coastal breeze in your hair, smelling the salt air, and wondering about the corrosive effects of salt on wood and metal.

Admission to both parks is free; you can purchase all-day unlimited ride passes at the 11-acre, 40-ride Pavilion for $12 and for $14.95 at Family Kingdom (somewhat cheaper rates for children), but unless you're 13 years old and cruising for girls/boys, there's really not much to keep you here all day.

Of course, since Disney is currently building a mock seaside amusement park at its new California Adventure Park in Anaheim, California, the Pavilion and Family Kingdom are not only good representatives of amusement parks past, but of the future as well.

Family Kingdom Oceanfront Water Park, 3rd Ave. S, tel. (843) 916-0400, stands right across from Family Kingdom Amusement Park. It's the only oceanfront water park in town, featuring a 60-foot free-fall slide and a number of different flumes and tubes. You can choose between paying for a one-day pass for $14.50 ($10.95 for children under 48 inches) and buying a "Ride and Slide Combo Pass," which allows admission into both Family Kingdom parks, for

$29.95. If you're interested, look for a coupon-heavy Family Kingdom pamphlet in the racks of your motel/hotel lobby. It'll save you $3 off an all-day pass.

Myrtle Waves Water Park

This is the granddaddy of South Carolina water parks, 20 acres in size and offering more than 30 rides and attractions including water slides and a wave pool—where the surf is often bigger than that of the actual ocean hereabouts. Open June-Aug. 10 a.m.-7 p.m., mid-May through May 31 and Sept. 1 through mid-Sept. 10 a.m.-5 p.m. Closed the rest of the year. Admission is $17.99 per adult for an all-day pass; senior/child discounts available. Discount admissions after 3 p.m. Allow about four hours to get your fill.

Alligator Adventure

This place, tel. (843) 361-0789, surprised me with its quality and cleanliness. Next to House of Blues at Barefoot Landing, the park is attractively staged, with wooden boardwalks, shade areas, and Africa-inspired buildings. I was also surprised by the sheer number of gators here; on the swamp boardwalk I saw perhaps 50 or 60 lying on the ground or swimming in the "river" just a few feet below the boardwalk—all told you're sharing Alligator Adventure's 15 acres with more than 800 alligators, not to mention the snakes and Komodo dragons. You can view rare albino alligators and, in the spirit of "compare-and-contrast," a collection of crocodiles at the park's south end.

Periodic gator feedings and venomous snake demonstrations let you see the often lethargic animals in action and help you learn about these feared but also beautiful and fascinating creatures. You'll also find some giraffes and tropical birds here, blessedly oblivious to the park's population statistics. Give yourself a couple of hours to see it all. Do I need to tell you that kids love it? Just be sure *not* to—for obvious reasons—sit them on the guardrails or put them on your shoulders while viewing the gators. One bump from behind could be tragic.

When you've seen all the critters you care to, head out the South Gate entrance, take the boardwalk to Barefoot Landing, and get yourself something to eat at Mad Boar Restaurant and Brewery.

Carolina Safari Jeep Tours
Here's a different way to get off the paved road and experience the history and natural environment of the Waccamaw Neck region. These three-hour tours promise to take you through three different ecosystems and show you alligators, bald eagles, and a mock rice plantation. Call (843) 497-5330 for details—pickup is available from most Myrtle Beach hotels.

BEACHES

For a city, being named "North Myrtle Beach" must be a lot like being known as "Joe's kid brother." South San Francisco, East St. Louis, North Charleston, North Augusta—none of them grow their own identities; all too often, they become or ever remain incomplete towns, towns without centers, because they are in truth a mere addendum to the town with the famous name.

With this in mind, I can't see why the towns of **Cherry Grove Beach, Ocean Drive Beach, Crescent Beach,** and **Windy Hill** allowed anyone to staple them together to form a single nine-mile-long beach city, under the polyester banner of "North Myrtle Beach." Ocean Drive Beach, in particular, had enjoyed regional notoriety as birthplace and capital city of the shagging world.

Determinedly ducking this civic group-hug was **Atlantic Beach,** five miles south of the new city's border. Known during segregation days as one of the top African-American beaches on the East Coast, Atlantic Beach even today shows no interest in changing the status quo.

Ocean Drive Beach
This little beach, just south of Cherry Grove Beach on Ocean Blvd. S, is where—by some accounts—the whole shagging subculture began. It's also a nice little beach, though some shortsighted planning is allowing high-rises to be built right on the beach, somewhat altering the ambience of the place, and certainly robbing the ocean views from a number of the small beach

houses that have long been the bread and butter of the region. A necessary shrine any shag pilgrim must stop to see is **Judy's House of Oldies,** 300 Main St., N. Myrtle Beach, tel. (843) 249-8649 or (843) 280-0581, a small record store with perhaps the best selection of beach music in the world, run by Judy Collins (no relation), a top DJ at shagger's dances, and occasionally by the knowledgeable Mr. Rufus Oates and Miss Esther.

Huntington Beach State Park
Huntington (Hwy. 17, three miles south of Murrells Inlet, tel. 843-237-4440, Web site: www.prt.state. sc.us/sc) is one of the most beautiful coastal parks in the state, with three miles of virgin, beachcombing sand, untold acres of coastal marsh for crabbing and gator- or birdwatching, and Archer and Anna Hyatt Huntington's intriguing Moorish castle, Atalaya, to tour. This was the coastal section of the Huntingtons' massive landholdings in the area—Brookgreen Gardens, directly across Hwy. 17, made up the rest.

Surf and jetty fishing may net spottail bass, flounder, croakers, and whiting; if you're without tackle, stop by the park office and borrow a rod and reel. The park has two campgrounds.

The critter-watching here is excellent. Besides the ever-present alligators, more than 280 bird species have been recorded here, making it one of the premier birding spots on the entire East Coast. Favorites include whistling swans, bald eagles, and various sandpipers. Call ahead and ask about the various ranger-led programs, ranging from alligator classes to evening "ghost tours" of Atalaya.

Myrtle Beach State Park
This beach on Hwy. 17 south of Myrtle Beach, tel. (843) 238-5325, offers 312 acres of Grand Strand au naturel, with a 700-foot recently reconstructed (after Hugo) fishing pier, a freshwater swimming pool, a nature trail, picnic areas, and 350 campsites. Some sites are first-come, first-served, but some you can reserve ahead of time by calling.

ACCOMMODATIONS, FOOD, AND NIGHTLIFE

For a complete list of accommodations, call the South Carolina Division of Tourism at (803) 734-0122.

HOTELS AND MOTELS

Ocean Drive Beach and Golf Resort
This new ocean-eclipser, 98 N. Ocean Blvd., tel. (800) 438-9590 or (843) 249-1436, fax (843) 249-1437, e-mail: odresort@sccoast.net, advertises itself as "A New Resort of Distinction in Ocean Drive," which seems to miss the laid-back, unpretentious nature of Ocean Drive altogether. Nonetheless, the golf packages and reasonable room rates so far away from the crowds of Myrtle Beach will doubtless fill the ODBGR's beds, particularly during local shaggers' conventions. Inexpensive-Premium.

Kingston Plantation, Featuring an Embassy Suites
The 145-acre Kingston Plantation, 9800 Lake Dr., tel. (800) 333-3333 or (843) 449-0006, fax (803) 497-1110, Web site: www.kingstonplantation.com, a right turn off Hwy. 17 just before it rejoins the bypass north of town, will remind you of Hilton Head. Unfortunately, the private beachfront resort looks little like a true plantation, what with its three towers looming over the Atlantic, but I suppose this is where a modern-day Scarlett O'Hara would choose to stay while in town. If the towers don't interest you, consider the one- to three-room villas offering lakefront, wooded, tennis court, and poolside views. Amenities include a private beach, sport and health club (including clay and hard surface tennis courts), a pool complex, and children's programs. You can still hop in the car and head over to rub elbows with the Myrtle Beach masses if you like, but you could also easily spend all of your trip right here. Expensive-Luxury.

Myrtle Beach Hilton Oceanfront Golf Resort
Nine miles north of Myrtle Beach on Hwy. 17, at 10000 Beach Club Dr., tel. (800) 248-9228 or (843) 449-5000, fax (843) 497-0168, you'll find this 15-story building. All rooms have balconies. Amenities include lighted tennis courts, a rooftop lounge, and the Arcadian Shores Golf Club on-site; suites and golf packages are available. Moderate-Luxury.

Swamp Fox Ocean Resort
The mammoth Swamp Fox, S. 2311 Ocean Blvd., tel. (800) 228-9894 or (843) 448-8373, fax (843) 448-5444, e-mail: swpfox@aol.com, Web site: www.swampfox.com, offers oceanfront efficiencies and tower suites, two indoor and five outdoor pools, whirlpools, and a Lazy River, as well as a steam sauna and an on-site restaurant. Golf packages available. Inexpensive-Luxury.

Chesterfield Inn
When you first see the solidly Georgian-style Chesterfield Inn, you get the impression that if everything in downtown Myrtle Beach were washed away in the next hurricane, the Chesterfield alone would remain, its front porch rocking chairs creaking softly in the retreating winds. Located a coin toss away from the Pavilion at 700 N. Ocean Blvd., tel. (800) 392-3869 or (843) 448-3177, this 1946 brick inn sits nobly placid amid downtown's squalor like a New Hampshire schoolmarm at a love-in. The Chesterfield features a lobby with a fireplace and a warm, informal dining room with wood-paneled walls, a terracotta tile floor, and an unbelievable ocean view. Rooms are decorated in early American, and the complex contains a pool and shuffleboard court. The inn offers a number of different plans, including the popular Modified American Plan, which includes breakfast and evening dinner with the room rate. The menu changes daily, always offers a choice of entrées, fruits and vegetables, and homemade desserts. Given the wealth of dining opportunities in the area, I'd recommend the less expensive European Plan. The wings of motel rooms added in the 1960s allow more rooms with private balconies overlooking the ocean. Golf packages available. No elevators.

The time of your visit greatly affects your room rate—a room that costs $34 in November will cost you $107 in July. Budget-Premium.

Yachtsman Resort

At 1400 N. Ocean Blvd., tel. (800) 868-8886 or (843) 448-1441, fax (843) 626-6261, this all-suite, front-row establishment is a favorite with families. Two shorter towers sit to either side of a 20-story third. All rooms have kitchens and whirlpool baths, and nearly all have full or partial ocean views—though the "city view" rooms do not. Within walking distance of the Pavilion, and with Pier 14 right at its base, this is the kind of place where you might just park for the duration of your stay. Studios, efficiencies, one- and two-bedroom apartments are available. Amenities include indoor and outdoor whirlpools, sauna, weight room, shuffleboard, minigolf, all on grounds. One tip: The only downside of being in the middle of it all is that you're, well, in the middle of it all. During warm weather months, Ocean Blvd. carries a nightly cruise scene with a nearly dusk-till-dawn orchestra of thumping bass, honking horns, and hooting adolescents. Try to get an oceanfront room or one high in the central tower. Golf packages, smoke-free rooms available on request. Moderate-Luxury.

Motels

The **Blake Motel,** 209-211 N. Ocean Blvd., tel. (843) 448-5916, is a funky old place with one- and two-room apartments and a heated pool smack dab between the Pavilion and the Swamp Fox roller coaster. Depending on who else is staying there when you are, it could be a nice, cheap, quiet stay. Budget-Moderate. The Marlowe family owns and runs **Noel Court and Apartments,** 306 N. 6th Ave., tel. (843) 448-6855, much more like staying in a beach house than staying in a motel. Budget-Moderate. Up in Cherry Grove, you'll find the **Inlet Motel,** 5409 N. Ocean Blvd., tel. (800) 968-7975 or (803) 249-1853, fax (843) 249-8661. Nothing special to look at, but it offers a nice, relatively quiet location up there near the Intracoastal Waterway, right across Ocean Blvd. from the ocean, and you're not far from the fishing at the Cherry Grove Pier. Extras include refrigerators in every room, kitchens, tennis courts, and golf privileges. Budget-Moderate.

GUEST AND RENTAL HOUSES AND B&BS

Stella's Guest Home, Little River, South Carolina, tel. (803) 249-1871, e-mail: Stella@scarolina.com, is a nice, relatively quiet place on busy Hwy. 17 in Little River, a homey spot to return to after a long day of fishing or a night at the theater, clubs, and Restaurant Row. The single-story brick ranch home is decorated in antique reproductions; Stella's is warm and friendly, with a view—from one suite's terrace, anyway—of a small lake. Did I mention that it sits on a golf course? All the rooms have private baths, private entrances, and color cable TV. You'll see it on the left as you head north on Hwy. 17. Inexpensive.

If you're looking for something comfortable and low-key, consider Kate and Phil Mullins's **Serendipity Inn,** 71st Ave. N, tel. (843) 449-5268, a motel converted into a Spanish-style bed-and-breakfast inn on a lazy side street, just a block and a half from the sand. With your window open, you can hear the traffic from Kings Highway, but you can't see it. The courtyard includes several fountains, and the breakfast room boasts a fireplace, which can make for a cozy winter's morning. Uniquely decorated rooms and suites are complemented by a breakfast buffet with fresh fruit, breads, and so on. Amenities include a heated pool and whirlpool, and you can use a grill on the grounds to grill up whatever fish you've caught during the day, or whatever meat you've found at the Piggly Wiggly. Children welcome. Inexpensive-Expensive.

Dr. Wendell Brustman's **Brustman House,** 400 25th Ave. S, tel. (843) 448-7699, is a quiet two-story on a wooded lot not far from downtown. All three rooms have private baths with two-seater whirlpool tubs. Homemade breakfasts feature 10-grain pancakes. Smoke-free. Children allowed on case-by-case basis. A two-bedroom suite with kitchen is available for $110 and up. Moderate-Expensive.

Condo and beach-house rentals are a popular way to go here, especially for families and large groups. For a great, restful weekend or week, pick a spot up in Ocean Drive or Cherry Grove, where you'll find a number of small places to eat, dance, and shop. You'll want to reserve far ahead, however, especially during peak season. Fortunately, since most of the area real estate companies work on a multiple listing service, contacting one will give you access to most every rental on the Strand. You might start by calling **Booe Realty,** 7728 N. Kings Hwy., tel. (800) 845-0647 or (843) 449-4477; **Elliott Realty,** 401 Sea Mountain Hwy., N. Myrtle Beach, tel. (800) 525-0225 or (843) 249-1406, Web site: www.northmyrtlebeachtravel.com; or **Sea Breeze Realty,** 1210 N. Waccamaw Dr., tel. (800) 446-4010 or (843) 651-1929, Web site: www.sea-breeze-realty.com, e-mail: c-breeze@worldnet.att.net.

CAMPGROUNDS

Unfortunately, there are no hostels on the Grand Strand, but fortunately, with more than 10,000 sites in the area, camping is always a budget option at Myrtle Beach. Keep in mind, though, that when the weather gets hot, even an occasional coastal breeze isn't going to make you forget that your tent is not an air-conditioned room. Also keep in mind that many people see Myrtle Beach camping more as a way to save beer money than as a chance to commune with nature; pick the wrong neighbors and the campground can get rather loud.

But this is not to say there isn't some fine camping on the Grand Strand. For pristine—or relatively pristine—land and the cheapest rates, go with the public campgrounds at **Myrtle Beach State Park** and **Huntington Beach State Park** (see above). Beyond this, you'll find no less than seven privately owned camper's havens in Myrtle Beach. All are overly geared toward RV campers, which means, in some cases, that you'll find very few shade trees around.

Two of the top choices include the **Apache Family Campground,** 9700 Kings Rd., tel. (800) 553-1749 or (843) 449-7323, on the oceanfront in the Restaurant Row area, which offers the East Coast's longest fishing pier, a restaurant, trading post, and complete hookups (including cable TV). **Barefoot Camping Resort,** 4825 Hwy. 17 S, tel. (800) 272-1790 or (843) 272-1790, is probably the cream of the crop, with oceanfront sites, mobile home rentals, a sauna and a fitness center, as well as indoor and outdoor pools.

For more information on Myrtle Beach's camping options, contact the **Myrtle Beach Family Campground Association,** P.O. Box 2158, Myrtle Beach, SC, 29578-2158.

FOOD

If you're staying somewhere with a kitchen, think about heading over to any of the numerous local grocery stores to stock up on food. This is really a good way to save money so that when you *do* go out, you can afford to hit one of the area's finer restaurants. You'll find a lot of Food Lions and Piggly Wigglies in this region, so don't think you have to shop at one of the overpriced small corner beach markets if you don't want to.

Looking for a restaurant in Myrtle Beach is like looking for sand at the beach. Two local television stations—which you'll likely find on your motel/hotel television—do nothing but advertise area restaurants and interview the owners, 24 hours a day. One way to pick a place to eat is to simply flip on the station and watch until something makes you hungry.

Another way to go is to look for where the locals eat. Of course, since a busy week brings 10 tourists to Myrtle Beach for every resident, finding a true locals' hangout can be a challenge indeed, especially since so many of the bars and restaurants advertise themselves as just this. In general, you'll find three types of restaurants in Myrtle Beach: 1) Tourist-oriented theme restaurants frequented almost solely by out-of-towners; 2) tourist restaurants revered by out-of-towners and locals alike; and 3) places frequented primarily by locals. Now, in my book, since Myrtle Beach is, and was born as, essentially a vacationers' village, there's no shame in frequenting the first group. The downside is that the prices are geared toward those who've come to town to dispense with their discretionary income. Locals generally stay away from most of the restaurants on Restaurant Row, at Barefoot Landing, and at Broadway at the Beach for precisely this reason. But many of these restaurants nonetheless have become traditional spots for families to visit on their annual pilgrimage to the sea. In this group you'll also find the chain theme restaurants lately unloaded at the new complexes, including the House of Blues, Hard Rock Café, and Planet Hollywood.

Seafood and Steaks

Most places in the area—no matter what their theme—serve seafood; these are just ones that make it their specialty.

A cheap way to go in Murrells Inlet is the **Seven Seas Fish Market,** Hwy. 17 Business, tel. (843) 651-1666, where you can pick up a shrimp dinner with fries, slaw, and hush puppies for around $7.

Oliver's Lodge, 4204 Hwy. 17 Business, tel. (843) 651-2963, is the one you should not miss; open since 1910, it has a big screened back porch where you'll want to sit to watch the boats along the waterway. Plan on spending $15-20 for a hearty seafood dinner. Oliver's is simply the kind of been-there-forever place that most of the other places are trying to be.

Nance's Creek Front Restaurant & Original Oyster Roast, Hwy. 17 Business, tel. (843) 651-2696, Web site: www.the-strand.com/nances, combines a nice view with happy hours and an early-bird special wherein you can buy one dinner at full price and receive a second one for half price, 4-5 p.m. daily. Nance's features Alaskan snow crab legs, steak, and fried chicken, in addition to local seafood: oysters, scallops, deviled crab, and so on.

Pier 14, 1304 N. Ocean Blvd., Myrtle Beach, tel. (843) 448-4314, Web site: www.the-strand.com/pier14, is a relaxed restaurant located (surprise) on a pier on 14th Street, directly behind the Yachtsman Resort. Great views, live entertainment nightly March-October. Large outdoor deck, happy hour 4-6 p.m., early-bird specials, and a friendly Canadian ex-patriate owner.

On Kings Highway not far from the Pavilion is **Sir John's Sea Food,** 411 N. Kings Highway, tel. (843) 626-7896, featuring a salad bar, prime rib, and of course, seafood—especially crab legs.

The Sea Captain's House, 3002 N. Ocean Blvd., tel. (843) 448-8082, was built in the 1930s as a private family beach house and opened as a restaurant in 1962. It's something of an institution here with its nice location, just at the northern end of the commercial district blocks as you head north on N. Ocean Drive. Breakfast features brie and bacon omelettes, blueberry pancakes. Late in the day you'll find sautéed crab cakes, avocado and roast beef sandwiches, Carolina shrimp, or Inlet oyster stew. Lots of original specials. Gives the feeling of the kind of place people return to year after year after year with their families. Also one of the only places with a nice view of the water from just about every spot in the place; the restaurant is actually built on pylons over the sand. The food includes innovative variations of local seafood plates; I had a nice crab au gratin for $15. It wasn't overly filling, but where quantity is lacking, quality abounds. If you arrive really hungry, just eat a lot of the hush puppies that come with your meal.

Perhaps the very best time to eat here is in the winter, on a cold foggy day when they've got a fire going in the fireplace. I recommend this place. The food's good, more creative than you might expect; it was voted No. 1 seafood restaurant by *Southern Living* magazine.

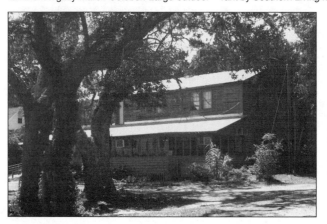

Oliver's Lodge, open since 1910 and boasting a big screened back porch with views of boats along the waterway, is a must-stop for seafood fans.

Thoroughbred's, 9706 Hwy. 17 N, tel. (843) 497-2636, Web site: www.thoroughbredsrest. com/, is perhaps the premier restaurant in Myrtle Beach. The people here just take their jobs seriously. It's also possibly one of the most romantic restaurants in the area, with its candlelit tables, fine linen tablecloths, and dark paneled walls made to resemble the ambience of a horse breeder's den, complete with paintings of famous horses on the walls.

The waiters here wear long-sleeved white shirts with ties, which is about as formal as you'll get on the Strand; nonetheless, this doesn't mean that the patrons dress very formally, though everyone I saw was wearing their long Duckheads rather than their shorts, and at least their very best Izod shirt.

This is a place to dine, not just eat. The bread and herbed butter just about became my main course, I ate so much of it. The appetizers ("The Starting Gate") include some intriguing items, as well as traditionals like shrimp and grits. I had the herb-seared ostrich, a nice-sized cut for an appetizer ($7.95), and it was fabulous. And for those who are wondering, no, it didn't taste like chicken.

As for salads, be sure to go ahead and let your waiter talk you into the house dressing, a fine poppyseed blend. The meat cuts are the specialty, but the seafood's fine as well; I ordered the seafood platter, which, at the then-current market price, came out as a high-ticket item at $24.95. The food was excellent and plentiful. Try the Kentucky Derby pie for dessert. Thoroughbred's is working hard to gain the reputation as Myrtle Beach's finest dining experience, and the warm, attentive service shows it. Even if spending $50 or so for dinner and wine stretches your budget a bit, I'd recommend cutting back on a couple of the all-you-can-eat Calabash seafood lunches to save up for this fine experience.

Giving Thoroughbred's a run for its money is relatively venerable **The Library,** 1212 N. Kings Hwy., Myrtle Beach, tel. (843) 448-4527 or 448-9242, founded way back in 1974. European and continental cuisine. A hushed atmosphere. If you're going to the Library to check things out, be sure to bring your (credit) card. Reservations preferred.

Set in a rebuilt 1885 Methodist church, with stained-glass windows imported from a Baptist church in Mullins, **Parson's Table,** Hwy.17, Little River, tel. (843) 249-3701, Web site: www. the-strand.com/parsons, keeps quietly winning awards up in Little River. Ed and Nancy Murray's beef and seafood place has been ranked as one of the top 50 best overall restaurants in the U.S. by the industry, and as the No. 1 historic restaurant in South Carolina. With a semiformal atmosphere, straight ladder-back chairs, and wood paneling, it specializes in veal, prime rib, steaks, poultry, and seafood. Open for dinner Mon.-Sat. (Sunday, too, in summer). Ask about the early-bird/pre-theater specials. Reservations suggested. Expect to spend around $20 a meal.

American

Olympic Flame Waffle House, 14th Ave. N and Ocean Blvd., tel. (843) 448-2746, offers—if you lean the right way and peer between the towers of the Yachtsman Resort—a view of the beach along with its stellar pancakes, waffles, and other breakfasts. The pecan pancakes are excellent. Breakfast and lunch only.

The **Main Street Grill,** 746 Main St., tel. (843) 946-6149, a couple blocks from and within sight of the Pavilion, is a true locals' spot, with basic Southern cooking and an authentic home-grown atmosphere. Great basic lunches here cost $4.40; try the two tasty pork chops with three sides and cookies thrown in to boot. A great spot to head to if you're tired of spending $12.95 for all you can eat, or if you're simply tired of the tourist culture. Good spot for simple breakfasts as well.

For a raucous time—and possibly a raucous *good* time—I'd recommend **Dick's Last Resort,** 4700 Hwy. 17 S, at Barefoot Landing, tel. (843) 272-7794. The food's pretty good (shrimp, ribs, so on), but that's not what draws people. They come for the 74 different kinds of beer and for the atmosphere, which is—to put it delicately—abusive. Waiters and waitresses are instructed to act surly. Imagine if John Belushi had lived to retire at the beach and open a restaurant, and that's pretty much what you have here. And it's an interesting study; when you know that they're *supposed* to be mean, being mistreated by a rude waitperson can actually be kind of fun. Did I mention it's over the water? You can see alligators and ducks during the day.

Maybe not the place for a romantic date, but a lot of fun with a crowd. Would this be the great job for a cocky young teenager, or what? Live rhythm and blues. Open seven days a week, noon till late.

Carolina Roadhouse is one place, 4617 N. Kings Hwy., tel. (843) 497-9911, you will certainly find locals; it's with-it, owned by the same folks who did so well with California Dreaming. Already locally famous for its tender babyback ribs and seafood platters. Also strong on salads, steaks, chicken, and the "Killer Dog." Happy hour 4-7 p.m. Open for lunch and dinner seven days. Phone ahead or be prepared to wait.

House of Blues, at Barefoot Landing, 4640 Hwy. 17 S, tel. (843) 361-2900, features the ambience and menu of an old Southern Delta home, with such Southern-inspired fare as jambalaya, barbecued chicken, étouffée, and catfish bites. Dan Aykroyd's scrupulously themed chain restaurant honors the culture of poor Southern blacks while its prices keep them away. It features what it calls a "family-oriented" gospel brunch (as opposed to an "adults-only" gospel brunch?), which includes a Southern-style buffet and a live gospel choir. Hours 11 a.m.-2 a.m. A separate concert hall features various types of music.

Italian
Rossi's Fine Italian Cuisine, located in the Galleria shopping center at 9636 N. Kings Hwy., tel. (843) 449-0481, fax (843) 626-4578, Web site: www.the-strand.com/rossis, offers serious Italian seafood, veal, beef, and pasta plates. Cozy little **Mancuso's Italian Restaurant**, 4700 Hwy. 17 Bypass S, tel. (843) 293-3193, focuses on well-prepared southern Italian entrées, with fresh seafood, pasta, and other meats. Casual dress here, dinner only, 5-10 p.m. Expect to spend around $13 a plate. **Angelo's Steak and Pasta**, 2011 S. Kings Hwy., tel. (843) 626-2800, features Italian food and steaks in a casual atmosphere. Early-bird specials. Closed for much of December and January. Dinner only, 4-9:30 p.m. Features a magician some nights. No cover.

Mexican
Rosa Linda's, 4713 Hwy. 17 S, tel. (843) 272-6823, serves up the best Mexican food in Myrtle Beach, which is, believe it or not, saying something. Featuring early-bird specials and a cocktail lounge, Rosa Linda's specializes in Mexican, Italian, and casual American. **Garcia's**, 9600 N.

Kings Hwy., tel. (843) 449-4435, specializes in fajitas and serves up some pretty good authentic northern Mexican cuisine to boot. You'll find it behind the Galleria Mall on Restaurant Row.

Asian
Yamato at Broadway at the Beach, tel. (843) 448-1959, prides itself on its Japanese seafood, sushi, steaks, and showmanship. Columbians constantly vote it the best restaurant—all genres included—on the Strand.

Nakato Japanese Steak House, Seafood and Sushi Bar, 9912 N. Kings Hwy., tel. (843) 449-3344, has prices starting at about $11. Open seven days a week 5-10 p.m.

Burgers
There are dozens of good places to pick up a hearty $6 burger on the Strand. Two that come to mind are **Hamburger Joe's**, 810 Conway St., tel. (843) 272-6834, and the **River City Cafe** over at 404 21st Ave. N, tel. (843) 448-1990. Of course, either of the town's **Sonic Drive-Ins**, located at 1930 10th Ave. N and 200 N. Kings Hwy., will do in a pinch.

Brewpubs
Mad Boar Restaurant & Brewery, Barefoot Landing, 4706 Hwy. 17 S, tel. (843) 272-7000, Web site: www.pubbrew.com/mbbb.html, offers six handcrafted beers on tap and a happy hour 4-7 p.m. every day. Sure, its location at Barefoot Landing makes all the polished wood and olde-style furnishings seem a little forced, but after a couple of pints, you won't notice.

Liberty Steakhouse Brewery, Broadway at the Beach, tel. (843) 626-4677, offers eight different beers, changing weekly. The brewery also features steaks and your standard brew food. I prefer the Mad Boar over at Barefoot Landing for atmosphere; both are pre-fabricated olde neighborhood pubs, but Mad Boar's friendlier. But heck, if you're at Broadway at the Beach and you feel like a beer, and the smarm level is tolerable, go ahead and order the Waccamaw Blonde.

Dinner Theaters
Dolly Parton's **Dixie Stampede**, junction of Hwy.17 and Hwy.17 Bypass, tel. (843) 497-9700, modeled on Parton's Pigeon Forge, Tennessee, complex, features a fun, horse-riding, gun-

shootin' spectacular to watch as you dine on vegetable soup, roasted chicken, hickory smoked ribs, corn on the cob, herb-basted potatoes, homemade Dixie bread, dessert, and bottomless nonalcoholic drinks. It sure beats dinner in front of the motel tube, and at $27.95 ($14.95 ages 4-11), it's actually a bargain over some of the show-only theaters. Shows are at 6 and 8 p.m. nightly. Reservations suggested.

Medieval Times Dinner and Tournament, 2904 Fantasy Way, tel. (800) 436-4386 or (843) 236-8080, is part of a tourist-town chain that features hearty dinners in a replica castle, eaten while Arthurian jousts and various other contests of skill and strength take place. Cost is $27.75 per adult, $15.75 ages 3-12. Reservations required.

CLUBS AND PUBS

In Ocean Drive Beach you'll find a handful of classic shagging spots, great places to practice the state's official dance or just sit with a cold one watching others tear up the floor. The best thing is, most of these spots are within walking distance of one another: **Ducks and Ducks Too,** 229 Main St., N. Myrtle, no cover, tel. (843) 249-3858; **Fat Harold's Beach Club,** 212 Main St., no cover, tel. (843) 249-5779;

SHAGGERS BOUND FOR GLORY RIDE DUCKS' OVERHEAD RAILROAD

Step inside Ducks, at 229 Main St., O.D., and you'll find more than a vintage shaggers' club. Look overhead and you'll notice a small model train circling the dance floor. The trains that run these tracks bear the ashes of veteran shaggers Lee Huggins and Dewey "Tinker" Kennedy, who asked in their wills to be allowed to spend the hereafter chugging along above the dancers. Other shaggers have lined up to request berths when they, too, reach an ashen state. Owner Norfleet Jones says he'll extend the tracks if he needs to in order to accommodate additional glory-bound shaggers.

Spanish Galleon, Main St., no cover Sun.-Thurs., $7 Friday (ladies free), $10 Saturday, tel. (843) 249-1047. **Pirate's Cove Lounge,** 205 Main St., no cover 8 p.m.-closing, tel. (843) 249-8942, has featured Joe Turner, Martha Reeves and the Vandellas, and Clyde McPhatter over the years. Ducks, Fat Harold's, and Pirate's Cove all offer shag lessons at different times during the week; call for details.

For $6-10 cover charge, **2001,** Restaurant Row, tel. (843) 449-9434, offers one of the hipper places to dance and mingle, featuring beach music in its Razzie's Beach Club area and "dance" music in its Pulsations Dance Club. **Studebakers,** 21st Ave. N on Hwy. 17, tel. (843) 448-9747, features a mythic 1950s' theme and one of the largest dance floors on the Strand. Open daily 8 p.m.-2 a.m.

At Broadway at the Beach's Celebrity Square, the New Orleans-style nightclub district offers nine different clubs all within staggering distance of one another: **Celebrations** offers three different themed nightspots in one; **Froggy Bottomz Blues and Beach Music** is important because it contains the Beach Music Hall of Fame and features some good live and recorded music. **Malibu's Surf Bar** is top 40, and **Club Boca** reminds me of a Latin discotheque, with Latin/European cuts mixed in with the top 40. Of course, by the time you get there, one or more of these themes is almost sure to have changed. Next door at **Revolutions Retro Dance Club** the theme, tragically, is disco. Across the way you'll find **Crocodile Rock's Dueling Piano Bar,** 1320 Celebrity Circle, tel. (843) 444-2096, home to a fun and funny dueling pianos act. Lively, rowdy, and featuring some good music. When they play "stump the piano players," you're welcome to come up with a song they don't know. One of the pianists is the son of Kate and Phil Mullins, owners of Serendipity Inn. Cover charge.

Finally, country rock fans should take a pilgrimage to **The Bowery,** 110 9th Ave. N, tel. (843) 626-3445, which offers live music for a $2-5 cover charge. This classic hole-in-the-wall has served them up cold since 1944. But the Bowery became truly famous when its longtime house band, Wildcountry, which played here for tips from 1973 to 1979, changed its name to Alabama and went on to country-rock fame and fortune with such megahits as "Mountain Music," "40 Hour Week," and "Cheap Seats." In 1997, the band saluted its Myrtle Beach roots with the song "Dancin', Shaggin' on the Boulevard."

THEATER AND DANCE VENUES

Okay, granted, my corn tolerance is perhaps higher than most people's, but I think the **Carolina Opry,** the original theater at Myrtle Beach at the junction of Hwy. 17 and Hwy. 17 Bypass, is a hoot. Mostly country music, but with dalliances into everything from Broadway show tunes to gospel and an oldies medley, broken up with some good, family-oriented humor. It helps to have some knowledge of roots country, but if you don't, this might make it all the more exotic for you. The cost is $26.95 a pop, but most area lodging spots can offer you some kind of cut on the price. Most of the performers hail from South Carolina, making this a nice showcase for the state's vocal and dancing talent. If you can swing it, it's a nice place to enjoy an old-style variety show; you'll be wondering why these seasoned performers aren't in Nashville. Reserve your seats ahead of time: tel. (800) 843-6779 or (843) 238-8888, Web site: www.enterpoint/cgp.

Since the venue's owned by country-rock icons Alabama, you might come to *Celebration!* at the Alabama Theatre, 4750 Hwy. 17 S, tel. (800) 342-2262 or (843) 272-1111, Web site:www.alabama-theatre.com, expecting country music, but the focus here is on variety—Broadway, pop, and oldies (as well as country)—and on big, flashy dance numbers. Though the mostly college-age cast can sing and dance, *Celebration!*'s songs are nearly all performed en masse, diluting the numbers' emotive power. It's all good fun, but if you're heading to just one showcase during your stay at Myrtle Beach, make it Carolina Opry. The Alabama Theatre *does* host some major entertainers (including the theater's owners), and if you're here when someone you want to see is performing, by all means get a ticket—this is a fine, intimate place to catch an old favorite.

Up Hwy. 501 at Fantasy Harbour, the **Gatlin Brothers Theatre,** tel. (800) 681-5209 or (843) 236-8500, Web site: www.fantasyharbour.com,

owned by the famous country act, features a handful of different shows throughout the year, both with and without the actual Gatlin Brothers themselves, including a special fall show and a top-notch Christmas show. One show, "Moments to Remember," features Steve Gatlin and includes everything from gospel to country to a Sinatra tribute, dancers, and a "soul-stirring patriotic finale." Call for show times.

Upstart *From Nashville to Broadway,* the show at the **All American Music Theatre,** Fantasy Harbour, tel. (800) 236-8500 or (843) 236-8500, offers two hours of country, big band, and show tunes, with a 23-member cast. Rounding out the show scene is the **Eddie Miles Theatre,** 701 Main St., N. Myrtle Beach, tel. (843) 280-6999, featuring Eddie himself imitating Elvis Presley. The Strand's surrogate King appears Tues.-Sat. at 8 p.m. during the summer; hours vary during the off season. And if that's not enough for you, the Myrtle Beach location of **Legends in Concert,** 301 Hwy. 17 Business S, tel. (800) 960-7469 or (843) 236-7827 offers Elvis, along with Marilyn Monroe, Buddy Holly, and a host of other late-greats who, if they were still alive, would probably be playing lounge venues exactly like this. They're joined by an imitation Dolly Parton, Bette Midler, Neil Diamond, Garth Brooks, and so on.

Most any time you're in town, Broadway at the Beach's **Palace Theatre,** 1420 Celebrity Circle, tel. (800) 905-4228, or (843) 448-0588, will have a beloved old Broadway show up and running. The casts often resemble a veritable Who-Was-Who of American pop culture: heartthrob Rex ("You Take My Breath Away") Smith played Jesus in a recent production of *Godspell;* Barbara "I Dream of Jeannie" Eden starred in *Gentlemen Prefer Blondes,* and Sheena "Morning Train" Easton played the female lead in *Man of La Mancha.* The Palace also hosts other major and second-rung acts; recent performers include the Bolshoi Ballet, B.B. King, Travis Tritt, Liza Minnelli, Clint Black, The Temptations and Four Tops, and a *Dukes of Hazzard* reunion. The theater seats 2,700.

The Palace's summertime entertainment revue, *Pizzazz,* features an orchestra, trained lions and chimps, former Broadway dancers and singers, fireworks, and lasers. It is hosted by Barry Williams

(Greg from TV's *The Brady Bunch*) and Debbie "You Light Up My Life" Boone. Tickets for all shows run $30-38 adults, $18-38 children.

For an enjoyable taste of WW II nostalgia, you may want to head over to **Big Band at the Savoy, starring the Jimmy Dorsey Orchestra,** Fantasy Harbour, Hwy. 501 just west of the Intracoastal Waterway bridge, adjacent to Waccamaw Pottery, tel. (800) 681-5209 or (803) 236-8500, Web site: www.fantasyharbour.com. It's a 1940s' themed night with a USO floor show and dancing to the music of Glenn Miller, Count Basie, Guy Lombardo, the Dorsey Brothers, and Harry James. It's a fun way to remember, or pretend to experience, a decade with far better music and clothes than our own.

CINEMAS

At Broadway at the Beach, you'll find the area's largest—so far—movie theater, the **Carmike Broadway Cinema 16,** tel. (843) 445-1616. It's a top-of-the-line theater, with THX auditoriums and digital sound systems. But while the Carmike has more screens than any other theater in Myrtle Beach, the **IMAX Discovery Theater,** tel. (843) 448-4629, has more *screen*—six stories tall, to be specific—along with an appropriately gargantuan sound system. The specially photographed films vary in topic from the undersea world to the Rolling Stones. Call ahead for movies and times.

SPORTS, RECREATION, AND SHOPPING

ON THE WATER

Surfing

Between 20th Ave. N and 20th Ave. S, you'll find the best surf Myrtle Beach has to offer, which normally isn't much. But this has not kept a full-blown surf culture from blossoming on the Grand Strand. Some surf shops at which to pick up tips for where the big ones—or, here, moderate ones—are breaking and/or rent a board or wet suit from include **Surf City Surfboards,** with three locations: 1103 N. Kings Hwy., tel. (843) 626-7919; Myrtle Square Mall, tel. (843) 626-5412; and N. Myrtle Beach, tel. (843) 272-1090. **Village Surf Shoppe,** 30 years old and an institution on the Strand, offers rentals from two locations: 500 Atlantic Ave., Garden City, tel. (843) 651-6396, and 2016 N. Kings Hwy., Myrtle Beach, tel. (843) 626-8176. Finally, **Xtreme Surf and Skateboard Co.** over at 515 E. Hwy. 501, tel. (843) 626-2262, makes custom surf and skateboards, and also rents sticks to the visiting gremmies.

When you hit the surf, make sure you wear your leash and stay at least 400 feet away from all piers—in Horry County, it's the law.

Windsurfing and Catamaran Sailing

Downwind Sails, located on the beach beside Damons at 29th Ave. S, tel. (843) 448-7245, offers rentals, rides, and lessons on sailboats, jet skis, windsurfers, catamarans, and kayaks April-September. Or check **Surf City Surfboards,** with three locations: 1103 N. Kings Hwy., tel. (843) 626-7919; Myrtle Square Mall, tel. (843) 626-5412; and N. Myrtle Beach, tel. (843) 272-1090, for windsurfer/catamaran rentals.

Parasailing

Parasailing is something of a staple in Myrtle Beach. Two outfits specialize in getting you up above the sea: **Captain Dick's Marina,** Murrells Inlet, tel. (843) 651-3676; and **Marlin Quay Marina,** 1318 S. Waccamaw Dr., Murrells Inlet, tel. (843) 651-4444. Cost at either place is $45 per person; your actual flying time is about 12-15 minutes, but the boat ride out and back (with as many as six people in the boat, each of whom also takes a turn in the harness) lasts up to two hours.

Diving

The folks at **Coastal Scuba,** 1626 Hwy. S, N. Myrtle Beach, tel. (843) 361-3323, advertise the area's largest, most comfortable dive boat, offering dive charters to Civil War and WW II wrecks, along with rentals, repair, and instruction. **Mermaid Diving Adventures,** 4123 Hwy. 17 Business, Murrells Inlet, tel. (843) 357-3483, and **The Scuba Syndrome,** 515-A Hwy. 501, tel. (843) 626-3483, Myrtle Beach, also provide diving instruction, equipment rentals, and charters.

Boat Rentals

Whether you're looking for a jet boat, pontoon boat, jet ski, or even just a lowly kayak, you'll find them at **Barefoot Watersports,** 4898 Hwy. 17 S, at the Barefoot Landing Docks, tel. (843) 272-2255, and at the North Myrtle Beach Marina, tel. (843) 280-0080. **Downwind Sails,** on the beach at 29th Ave. S, tel. (843) 448-7245, offers rentals, rides, and lessons on sailboats, jet skis, windsurfers, and kayaks April-September. Finally, **Myrtle Beach Water Sports,** tel. (843) 497-8848, guarantees its rates as best on the beach for jet ski, pontoon boat, kayak, and canoe rentals, plus jet boats, island trips, and morning nature tours.

Cruises

Taking a nice cruise before or after dinner can be a great way to unwind from the hectic pace of having a good time; try **The Great American Riverboat Company,** located at Barefoot Landing, tel. (843) 272-7743. For something a little faster, hop aboard the hydroplaning **Sea Screamer of Myrtle Beach,** 1 Harbor Place N, tel. (843) 249-0870. Or call **Captain Dick's Explorer Adventures** in Murrells Inlet at (800) 344-3474 or (843) 651-3676.

Fishing Charters

With the Gulf Stream surging by just a few miles off the Carolina coast, a lot of deep-sea fisherfolk find their casting wrists twitching every time they look out to sea. Chartering a boat is very expensive, but if you get five or six other people to go in on it with you, you can usually get it down to around $200 a person, which, for the true angler, is well worth the chance to drop a line into the Gulf Stream. The Grand Strand abounds in charter outfits. **Marlin Quay Marina,** 1398 S. Waccamaw Dr., Garden Beach, tel. (843) 651-4444, fax (843) 651-7795, e-mail: marlinquay@marlinquay.com, Web site: www.marlinquay.com, offers sportfishing charters for half day, three-quarter day, or full day, as well as overnights.

ON LAND

Golfing

The Grand Strand is arguably the very best golf destination in the world, with several courses perennially among *Golf Digest*'s top 50 in the U.S. In a state with seemingly more space allotted to fairways than to roadways, the Greater Myrtle Beach area alone boasts—by one count—more than 100 golf courses. You could tee off at a different Grand Strand hole every Saturday for two years and never play the same course twice.

Some of these courses are must-plays for avid golfers. If this describes you, be sure to call up the desired course before you make your hotel reservations and ask them which hotel's golf packages will enable you to play your Links of Dreams. Then call up one of the hotels and make a reservation there.

To get up to speed on the Grand Strand golfing scene, pick up a free copy of *Myrtle Beach Golf* at an area pro shop, or subscribe by sending $12 for 12 issues to Myrtle Beach Golf, P.O. Box 406, Myrtle Beach, SC 29578-0406. The paper is owned by the *Sun News,* which has a Web site at www.myrtlebeachaccess.com.

Tennis

The Grand Strand claims more than 200 tennis courts. Call the Myrtle Beach Parks and Recreation Department at (843) 918-2280 for a list of public courts. A few privately owned ones where visitors can play for a fee include the **Litchfield Country Club-Racquet Club,** tel. (843) 448-3331; the **Myrtle Beach Tennis and Swim Club,** Hwy. 17 Bypass, tel. (843) 449-4486; the **Riverfront Tennis Center,** 7 Elm St., tel. (843) 248-1710; and the **Sport and Health Club** at Kingston Plantation, tel. (843) 497-2444.

Volleyball

There are few more pleasant ways to spend a day than sitting on the sand with a loved one and a cooler, watching a beach-volleyball tournament. If you're interested in a game yourself, you'll find pickup beach volleyball games all along the Strand. Two good spots to hunt down a game are down on 29th Ave. S at the public nets at Downwind Sails and at the Radisson in Kingston Plantation.

Miniature Golf

The Grand Strand is the Pebble Beach of miniature golf, hosting over 40 courses, more than many U.S. states. Some people call it putt-putt; others call it miniature golf. Yet others call it "championship golf," which seems a little extreme to me. One of the best in town is **Mount**

Mini-golf is serious business along the Grand Strand.

Atlanticus, 707 N. Kings Hwy., tel. (843) 444-1008. You have to see this brand-new course—it's set on a man-made mountain that rises above Kings Hwy. like a . . . well, like a mountain. In September, **Hawaiian Rumble Golf,** 4201 Hwy. 17 N, tel. (843) 449-5555, and **Hawaiian Caverns,** 33rd Ave. S and Hwy. 17, tel. (843) 272-7812, both owned by Bob Getweiller, are home to the Masters of Miniature Golf, which began in 1997 and was covered by both ESPN and *Golf* magazine. Hawaiian Rumble was featured in the 1992 Dennis Hopper flop *Chasers.* You'll see a montage of photos from the shooting inside the office and across the street at the Baskin-Robbins.

If you're interested in joining the international group of putters playing the Masters of Miniature Golf, contact either course, or write Masters Miniature Golf, 4201 N. Kings Hwy., Myrtle Beach, SC 29577. Entry fee is $100; first prize is $5,000.

Myrtle Beach Braves (Baseball)

The Atlanta Braves' single-A affiliate began playing in Myrtle Beach for the 1999 Carolina League season. The brand-new stadium cost $12 million and seats over 5,000, humongous for a single-A ballpark.

The team plays 70 home games over the summer; besides the many between-inning contests that are a staple of minor league baseball, for every home run the Braves hit, Dinger the Homerun Dog—a Labrador retriever—is let loose. (For every double play they hit into, is he swatted with a rolled-up newspaper?) Call (843) 946-7557 for ticket information.

SHOPPING

There are so many malls, so many specialty stores, so many outlet shops, and so many tourist beachware boutiques that you'd think all people do here is shop. Both Broadway at the Beach and Barefoot Landing offer over a hundred specialty stores. You should pretty much avoid the tourist chains like **Eagles, Wings,** and **Bargain Beachware,** out of general principle—they're eyesores on the outside, and on the inside, they're the visual equivalent of too much caffeine. At Ocean Drive, **Beach Memories,** 209 Main St., tel. (843) 249-7215, sells shag-related art.

Outlet Stores

Myrtle Beach Factory Stores, 4635 Hwy. 501, tel. (843) 236-5100, is home to 85 outlet stores, including Harriet & David, Off Fifth Saks Fifth Avenue Outlet, Coach, Nine West, and Lillian Vernon. Most importantly, it offers a **Duck Head Outlet,** where you can buy some true Southern fashions for a reasonable price. Get some shorts, get some shirts. Now you'll fit in at the next shag contest.

The **Waccamaw Factory Shoppes,** Hwy. 501 at the Intracoastal Waterway, tel. (800) 444-8258, is so large it actually comprises four separate malls, connected by shuttles you can pick up outside. It offers stores like Waccamaw Pottery (advertising "Over 3 Football Fields of Unique Items For Your Home!"), Black and Decker, London Fog, Bugle Boy, and American Tourister.

BEST BOOKSTORES

New

You'll find a **Barnes and Noble** at 1145 Seaboard St., tel. (843) 444-4046. Out at the Outlet Park Mall you'll find a spotty but bargain collection at **Book Warehouse,** Outlet Park Mall III, tel. (843) 236-0800. **Readers Outlet** offers a similar selection at Outlet Park II, tel. (843) 236-1571. Those so inclined will find a large collection of Christian and inspirational reading at the earnestly named **Faith Bible Mart,** 1910 Hwy. 17 N, in Surfside Beach, tel. (843) 238-5912.

Used

The Bookstall, tel. (843) 272-2607, tucked away on the left between Briarcliffe Mall and Barefoot Landing as you head north up Kings Hwy., carries over 50,000 books, many bought from estate sales: paperbacks, hardbacks, children's books, fiction, and nonfiction. Hours tend to vary; call ahead.

INFORMATION AND TRANSPORTATION

TOURIST OFFICES, CHAMBER OF COMMERCE

You'll find all the pamphlets, coupon books, and area maps you can carry at **The Greater Myrtle Beach Chamber of Commerce** at 1200 Oak St., tel. (843) 626-7444. The **Little River Chamber of Commerce** is over at 1569 Hwy. 17, tel. (843) 249-6604. Or check online at www.myrtle-beachaccess.com.

HOSPITALS, POLICE, EMERGENCIES

The **Grand Strand Regional Medical Center,** 809 82nd Pkwy., tel. (843) 692-1000, is the place you want to get to in a medical emergency. If it's something non-life-threatening, see the folks at **Care Express,** tel. (843) 692-1770, a walk-in clinic. Or head to **Atlantic Medical Care,** 1410 S. Kings Hwy., just north of 6th Ave., tel. (843) 626-4420, which is open extended hours in the summertime.

If you're down in Georgetown, **Georgetown Memorial Hospital,** tel. (843) 527-7461, would be the place to call.

PUBLIC LIBRARIES

On the hottest day of summer, on the craziest day of Sun Fun weekend, you'll find air-conditioning, quiet, and clean public restrooms just waiting for you at the **Myrtle Beach City Library** at 400 14th Ave. N, tel. (843) 918-1275, and at branches of the **Horry County Library** at 799 2nd Ave. N, in North Myrtle Beach, tel. (843) 249-4164, and 410 Surfside Dr., Surfside Beach, tel. (843) 238-0122.

NEWSPAPERS

The *Sun News* is the paper of record in Myrtle Beach; you'll find it in newsstands all around town. Weekly, it publishes *Kicks!,* where you'll find all the entertainment news you need, including movie listings, special events, and a long list of who's-playing-where in the area. *Alternatives* is the local free arty paper. Look for it in record stores, surf shops, and anywhere else nose rings and tattoos can be found.

GETTING THERE

By Car
Most people who visit Myrtle Beach come by car. From Washington, D.C., and coastal points north, take I-95 south to Hwy. 301 at Dillon. Take the 301 to Hwy. 576 E; this will lead to Hwy. 501 W. Take this on in through Conway and into Myrtle Beach. From Columbia, take Hwy. 378 east through Sumter and Lake City to Conway, where you'll turn onto Hwy. 501 E to Myrtle Beach. From Charleston and Georgetown, just head north on Hwy. 17. Look for the billboards.

By Air
The **Myrtle Beach International Airport,** 1100 Jetport Rd., tel. (843) 448-1589, fax (843) 626-9096, operates a 125,000-square-foot terminal with four gates and one runway.

By Bus
Greyhound Bus Lines serves the Myrtle Beach terminal at 511 7th Ave. N in Myrtle Beach, tel. (800) 231-2222 or (843) 448-2471.

GETTING AROUND

By Bus
The **Coastal Rapid Public Transit Authority,** 1418 3rd Ave., tel. (843) 248-7277 or (843) 626-9138, provides regular local bus service up and down the Strand. Call for schedule and information.

By Taxi
What with all the space between attractions, it's no wonder Myrtle Beach is home to over two dozen cab companies. Some of the more de-

pendable are **Yellow Cab,** tel. (843) 448-5555; **Coastal Cab,** tel. (843) 448-4444; and **Broadway Taxi,** tel. (843) 448-9999. All three offer 24-hour service. A cheaper way to go (sometimes) can be the **Magic Bus,** tel. (843) 361-2467, offering a special $15 multiple-pickup "ride-all-night" deal Thurs.-Sat. operating from Hwy. 501 in Myrtle Beach to Cherry Grove in North Myrtle and along Hwy. 17 and the Hwy. 17 Bypass. Buses are radio dispatched.

VEHICLE RENTALS

Cars
You'll find plenty of rental cars available in the area, and, given the logistics of the place, if you want to do some sightseeing, you'll probably want to take advantage of one if you're here without a car. You'll find full listings in the local Yellow Pages, but some places to start with include **Budget,** 1100 Jetport Rd., tel. (800) 527-0700 or (843) 448-1586, and **Enterprise Rent-a-Car,** 1377 Hwy. 501, tel. (843) 626-4277, or 3108 Terminal Rd., N. Myrtle Beach, tel. (843) 361-0418, toll-free for both locations (800) 736-8222.

Bicycles
The flat terrain of the Grand Strand makes it top-notch biking territory for even the novice biker. If you can't bring your own bike along, you can find one to rent at **Bicycles-N-Gear,** 515 Hwy. 501, tel. (843) 626-2453; **The Bike Shop,** 715 Broadway, tel. (843) 448-5335; and **Full Circle Cycles,** down in Garden City Beach at 2450 Hwy. 17 S, tel. (843) 651-2659.

GEORGETOWN AND VICINITY

The first thing many people (especially those coming up from Charleston) notice about Georgetown is the huge paper mill billowing smoke into the sky. But don't let the smoke fool you—this is one of the friendliest, most historic, most attractive towns in the state. And if you don't believe me, just ask Norman Crampton, whose last two editions of *The Best Small Towns in America* list this slow-paced river town of 9,500 as one of his anointed burgs.

One of the best times to be in Georgetown is during its annual Harborwalk Festival held in late June or early July, when you'll find live music, a shag dance contest, a boat show, a road race, street dance, arts and crafts, and lots of good food available on Front Street and around the Harborwalk, the 1,000-foot walkway that's become the centerpiece (if not, for obvious reasons, the physical center) of Georgetown's newfound tourist district. For more information, contact Peggy Wayne at (843) 546-1511.

In 1965, Grammy-award-winning comedian Chris Rock was born here at Georgetown Memorial Hospital when Rose Rock—raised in Andrews—was in town visiting an ailing grandmother. After the surprisingly quick delivery, she spent two weeks recovering from the birth and then took Chris back up to New York, where she and her husband raised him in Brooklyn.

He was eventually discovered by Eddie Murphy. Rose Rock moved back down to South Carolina in 1992, after the death of her husband, and owns and runs the First Steps Daycare on South Island Road.

Chris occasionally comes to town to visit his mother. His visits are major local news. He's been spotted walking over to the Wendy's for a hamburger.

HISTORY

The story of the six or seven Native American tribes who dwelt in the Georgetown area before the arrival of Europeans is murky, since by the early 1700s illness and war had shrunk the tribes and caused them to either disappear or combine with others. The main Native American legacy in the area is, as it is in so many areas in the U.S., the region's place-names: the Sampit, Pee Dee, Santee and Waccamaw Rivers, for instance.

Georgetown is undoubtedly the third-oldest city in South Carolina—after Charleston and Beaufort—but some historians claim that European-American history actually began in Georgetown County, on what's now called the Hobcaw Barony, just north of Georgetown on Hwy. 17. Lucas Vasquez de Ayllon gathered up about

500 men, women, and children for the colonization effort, establishing San Miguel—the first European settlement in what would become the United States of America.

No one knows precisely where San Miguel was located, but many suspect it may have been in Winyah Bay. Wherever it was, one thing's for sure—San Miguel was no eternal city. The settlers' Native American guide, Francisco Chicorana, abandoned them as soon as they landed, and before three months were up, Ayllon was dead. By the end of that winter, only three in 10 colonists were still alive. Leaving behind little but regret and a lot of graves, the survivors sailed back to Santo Domingo.

Over a century later, after the settlement of Charles Town, the British residents began hankering for new, tillable lands fairly quickly. The area where Georgetown stands today was granted to John and Edward Perrie as early as 1705, and a few hardy souls did leave Charles Town to begin working the land here. In 1721, the royal government granted the designation of a new parish to those who had settled here: "Prince George, Winyah Parish on Black River." But it wasn't until the bloodshed of the Yamassee War had passed, in 1729, that the new community of Georgetown was laid out. With the importation of African slaves to clear the swamps and work the crops, indigo and rice soon became fiercely profitable for parish planters. Three years later, Georgetown became an official port of entry, allowing local planters to cut out Charleston as a middleman and thus reap even bigger profits. In 1757, the first public school between Charles Town and Wilmington, North Carolina, was opened in

> *A Southern river at night is a haunting thing, with great stars hanging like spangles in the dark pines and the ancient water oaks fringing the river shores. Wider flows the dim stream as it moves through the last reaches of the immense coastal plain. Baffling to navigate by broad daylight, the Santee at night is mysterious . . . a huge river that seems to be wandering toward eternity.*
>
> —Archibald Rutledge,
> Peace in the Heart, 1923

Georgetown by the wealthy members of the Winyah Indigo Society.

Wealth brought power to the city and its inhabitants; area planters Thomas Lynch Sr. and Thomas Lynch Jr. both represented the state, and the latter signed the Declaration of Independence. When the Revolution ruined the indigo trade, rice became the main crop in the area; soon, the Georgetown District supplied nearly 50% of the young country's rice crop. The slave population rose to 85% of the area's total population. During and after the Civil War, however, the emancipation of the slaves and hurricanes harmed the rice crops; the area never regained its supremacy in rice.

Georgetown eventually turned to lumber for its chief industry, and this did the region well until the Depression hit. In 1936, the International Paper Company opened what would later become the largest mill in the world here. Later, a steel mill opened here as well. More recently, tourists have become a staple crop cultivated by local merchants, innkeepers, and restaurant owners.

SIGHTS

Rice Museum

This museum at Front and Screven Streets, tel. (843) 546-7423, Web site: www.the-strand.com/rice, is far more interesting than it sounds. Yes, it's about rice cultivation, but since the story of rice cultivation is the background to nearly everything that's happened to Georgetown in the past 200 years, it's an interesting story. Here you'll find maps, dioramas, historical artifacts, and original boats used in the rice fields by slaves and other workers. The museum is in the Old Market Building (1842), which in turn is home to the Town Clock, a four-sided timepiece set atop a tower added to the main building in 1845. Open Mon.-Sat. 9:30 a.m.-4:30 p.m.; closed Sunday and major holidays. Admission is $2 adults, students free, military personnel in uniform 50 cents. If you're lucky, Zella Wilt will be volunteering at the information/entrance desk; she's a transplant from up north, but she's helpful and knows her stuff.

This is a good place to begin a tour of Georgetown's historic district. Pick up a self-guided tour in the Rice Museum annex downstairs in the 1842 **Kaminski Building,** one of the first new Front

Georgetown's Rice Museum is housed in the 1842 Old Market Building, which is also home to the 1845 Town Clock tower.

St. business buildings erected—in brick—after a devastating 1841 fire that wiped out most of the business district. The cast-iron front was created by Daniel Badger of New York. But the Polish-born Kaminski didn't purchase the building until 1869, when he opened a hardware store there.

If the annex is closed, or you're in a hurry, I'll give you an abbreviated tour that will give show you some of the oldest and most historic structures in town:

A Brief Walking Tour

From the Kaminski building, continue southeast

down Front St. to the corner of Queen and Front. On the northeast corner you'll see the circa 1775 **Mary Man House,** a Georgian two-story double house with paired interior chimneys. Mary Man's father owned the Mansfield Plantation outside town; Mary had the home built using her father's timber and slaves.

Continue in the same direction along Church and turn right at Cannon. Here you'll see on your right the circa 1765 **Dr. Charles Fyffe House.** Fyffe was a Scottish doctor forced to flee the country because of the intolerance of his pro-independence neighbors, who resented his loyalty to the royalty. Fyffe returned to Georgetown after the war and repurchased another house, but this one was lost to him forever. Across the street, you'll see the late-18th-century **Red Store Warehouse,** from which one of the state's most educated women, Theodosia Burr Alston (Aaron Burr's daughter and Governor Joseph Alston's wife), boarded the good ship *Patriot,* which disappeared at sea during a storm off the North Carolina coast.

Now head back up to Front, turn right, and walk to the corner of Front and St. James. On the right hand corner nearest you, you'll see the circa 1737 **John and Mary Cleland House,** one of the earliest remaining homes in Georgetown. Turn left on Saint James and walk up two blocks, passing by the circa 1790 **Thomas Hutchinson House,** which originally looked identical to the **Savage Smith House** next door, until Federal soldiers and freed slaves stripped the building during the Civil War.

Turn left on Prince and you'll pass a number of antebellum homes on either side of the street. When you get to the corner of Screven and Prince, you'll see the site of the Masonic Lodge on the northeast corner. George Washington, a Mason himself, visited this lodge on his 1791 Southern tour. Continue across Screven. The circa 1824 **Georgetown County Courthouse** on your left was designed by Robert Mills, the South Carolinian who also designed the Washington Monument. Just beyond the courthouse is the circa 1734 **Thomas Bolem House,** which historians believe was a pre-Revolutionary tavern run by Mr. Bolem himself.

Turn right on Broad and walk a full block until you reach the corner of Highmarket and Broad. On the near right-hand corner stands the circa 1825 **Benjamin King House,** now the King's

Inn B&B. Across the street on the right is one of the town's most beautiful and historic buildings, the circa 1747 **Prince George Winyah Church,** 300 Broad St. at Highmarket St., tel. (843) 546-4358. This edifice was the first major building constructed in Georgetown, and served as a government building as well as a church building during the time when the Church of England was the official religion of the colony of South Carolina. The steeple is a "new" addition, having been added in 1824. The local Episcopal congregation still uses the building weekly for services, making them the envy of other Episcopalians for miles around. The graveyard contains graves dating back to the Colonial period. Open for viewing March-Oct. Mon.-Fri. 11:30 a.m.-4:30 p.m. No admission fee.

Now head back southwest on Broad until you come back to Prince, and turn right. Continue until you've crossed Orange and are nearly to King Street. On your left you'll see the circa 1760 **Joseph Hayne Rainey House,** the home of Rainey, the first African-American member of the U.S. Congress. Rainey lived here during the Civil War.

The next house on the left is the circa 1740 **John Arthur House,** unique because it looks like something you'd see up in New England. Today, this serves as the DuPre House B&B.

Now turn left on King and walk back to Front Street, and head into the Park area. The circa 1769 waterfront **Harold Kaminski House Museum,** 1003 Front St., tel. (843) 546-7706, was owned originally by the prominent Colonial businessman Paul Trapier II, known locally as "The King of Georgetown." Harold Kaminski's widow gave it to the city in 1972.

While you're here, you really ought to tour the home—it contains one of the best collections of antiques in the American Southeast, and the guides here can answer just about any question you might think to ask. Tours given on the hour Mon.-Sat. 10 a.m.-4 p.m., Sunday 1-4 p.m. Admission runs $4 for adults, $2 for kids 6-12.

Also at the park is the circa 1750 **Robert Steward House,** a two-and-a-half-story Georgian on the river, where President George Washington spent the night while in Georgetown in 1792.

Now work your way back down Front Street, eating, drinking, and shopping as you go.

ACCOMMODATIONS

Motels

Carolinian Inn, 706 Church St., tel. (843) 546-5191, is a nice, clean, cheap place to stay. You can walk to dinner at the on-site **Hook, Line, and Sinker,** or across the street to breakfast at **Lafayette Restaurant.** Inexpensive-Moderate.

Days Inn, 210 Church St., tel. (843) 546-8441, offers continental breakfast, an outdoor pool, and an on-site grill and lounge. It's one of the better bargains in town. Inexpensive-Moderate.

Bed and Breakfasts

Ashfield Manor B&B, at 3030 S. Island Rd., tel. (800) 483-5002 or (843) 546-0464, is a two-story, plantation-style inn two miles south of the Hwy. 17 and Hwy. 17A intersection. The manor offers four rooms and a full breakfast on a large screened porch overlooking a lake. Look out in the lake and you may see the resident alligator. No smoking. No pets. Inexpensive.

Innkeeper Marshall Wile's **DuPre House,** 921 Prince St., tel. (800) 921-3877 or (843) 546-0298, fax (843) 520-0771, Web site: www.virtualcities.com/sc/dupre.htm, dates back to 1740, when it was built by John Arthur. This tastefully decorated three-story home offers five bedrooms with private baths. Three rooms offer tubs; the rest offer showers only. Two rooms offer fireplaces. Wile serves a full breakfast and afternoon refreshments. Swimming pool, hot tub. Smoking outdoors only. Moderate-Premium.

The **1790 House,** 630 Highmarket St., tel. (800) 890-7432 or (843) 546-4821, offers six luxurious guest rooms with private baths, wraparound porches, beautiful gardens, and gourmet breakfasts. There's also a romantic cottage with a jacuzzi. Smoke free. Moderate-Premium.

With so many vintage 18th-century homes around, don't let the "newness" of the 1825 **King's Inn at Georgetown,** 230 Broad St., tel. (800) 251-8805 or (843) 527-6937, fax (843) 527-6937, cause you to overlook it. After all, this seven-room, two-story inn, with its original moldings, floors, and chandeliers, was a few years back ranked one of the top 12 inns in the country by *Country Inns.* Private baths, lap pool, no smoking. Moderate-Premium.

Rob and Sandy "Alexandra" Kempe's **Alexandra's Inn,** 620 Prince St., tel. (888) 557-0233 or (843) 527-0233, fax (843) 520-0718, Web site: www.alexandrasinn.com, is set in an 1880 home originally built as an overflow for guests of the Winyah Inn, now the Masonic Lodge. Alexandra's offers five rooms, all with 11-foot ceilings and fireplaces, and each named and themed after a character from *Gone With the Wind.* Scarlett's Room features a jacuzzi (just like in the movie?), three bay windows, and a four-poster bed. Rhett's Room features a king-size sleigh bed and a red velvet settee, with a double jacuzzi and a separate corner shower. When Sandy's not around, maybe you could slip Rob a bill and ask him about "Belle's Room."

Alexandra's carriage house sleeps six and features a full kitchen. Discount rates available for extended stays. No young children allowed inside the main house—not even in Bonnie's Room. Smoke-free except on the porches. Gardens, swimming pool. Premium.

Outside of town on Hwy. 701, you'll come across a sign for Sally and Jim Cahalan's **Mansfield Plantation,** Rt. 8, tel. (800) 355-3223 or (843) 546-6961. Moderate-Premium. Follow the magnificent avenue of oaks onto the 900-acre property to the circa 1800 plantation house. Amenities include access to the Black River for boating and golfing next door. Downtown is only a short drive away. Pets welcome; smokers will be given the chance to spend some private time outdoors.

RESTAURANTS

At 1 Marina Dr., tel. (843) 527-1376, Web site: www.the-strand.com/landsend, **Land's End Restaurant** offers great views of the Marina, the Intracoastal Waterway, and some tasty seafood, chicken, and prime rib. Dine indoors or outside on the covered deck.

Yum's Barbecue, tel. (843) 237-9052, said to be one of best, if not *the* best barbecue joint in the state, hides in its cinderblock shell on the left-hand side of Hwy. 17 north of town. Located on the boardwalk is the **River Room,** 801 Front St., tel. (843) 527-4110. Strong seafood menu; open Mon.-Sat. 11 a.m.-2:30 p.m., 5-10 p.m.

Hook, Line & Sinker, 706 Church St., tel. (843) 546-5191, specializes in seafood, steaks, sausages, pasta, chicken, and more. Located at the Carolinian Inn.

ACTIVITIES

Antiquing
Georgetown contains a number of fascinating antique stores. Stop in at **Augustus & Carolina,** 830 Front St., tel. (843) 545-9000, to take a look at some of the high-end imported French and English antiques. **Aunt Maggie's,** 1032 Front St., tel. (843) 545-5024, usually has some interesting items to browse, as do **Emma Marie's Antique Shoppe,** 827 Church St., tel. (843) 545-8030, and **Tosh Antiques,** 802 Church St., tel. (843) 527-8537. Over on Highmarket St., poke your head into **Grandma's Attic,** 2106 Highmarket St., tel. (843) 546-2607 and **Hill's Used Furniture and Antiques,** 4161 Highmarket St., tel. (843) 546-6610.

Paddling
If you're looking to get onto the river, Winyah Bay, or the Intracoastal Waterway, you need to talk to the folks over at **Black River Expeditions,** 21 Garden Ave., Hwy. 701, three miles north of Georgetown, tel. (843) 546-4840, Web site: www.blackriveroutdoors.com. They'll rent you a canoe or kayak if that's all you need. They also lead day and evening tours of blackwater cypress swamps, rice plantation creeks, saltwater tidal marshes, wildlife refuges, and/or around historic Georgetown Harbor itself. Bring your (waterproof) camera. Half-day guided tours are $40 a person, children under 13 years old $20.

INFORMATION

Visit the **Georgetown County Chamber of Commerce** at Front and King Streets when you first get to town. The folks there will load you up with pamphlets and maps, and they have some good local history books for sale as well. Or call before you leave home at (800) 777-7705 or (843) 546-8436 and ask them to send you a travel guide.

Tours

To really get into the spirit of things, you might want to take a walking tour with **Miss Nell's Tours,** 308 Front St., tel. (843) 546-3975. Miss Nell Cribb, a native Georgetonian, leads tours starting and ending at the Mark Twain Store at 723 Front Street. Departure times are Tues.-Thurs. 10:30 a.m. and 2:30 p.m., Sat.-Sun. and all other times by appointment. A 30-minute tour runs $5, one hour runs $7, and the full 90-minute tour runs $9. Children under 12 years of age accompanying adults get to come along for free, as long as they don't pay attention.

If all that walking sounds a bit too pedestrian, you might consider covering much of the same ground with **Swamp Fox Tours II,** 3525 Choppee Rd., tel. (843) 527-6469, Web site: www.georgetown-sc.com, a 20-year-old outfit recognizable by the blue and white tram the tour operators drive around. Geraldine Jayroe and her cohorts offer tours Mon.-Fri. 10 a.m.-4 p.m. on the hour, departing from 1001 Front St., the Georgetown County Chamber of Commerce Visitor's Center. Cost is $7.50 for adults, children $4.

But if riding around in a tram pulled by a gas engine ruins the 19th-century ambience for you, you may want to consider taking a ride with Ashley Cooper Carriage Co., located on Front St., tel. (843) 546-8727. These horse-drawn carriage tours, offered Mon.-Fri. 10 a.m.-4 p.m., Saturday 10 a.m.-2 p.m., are one hour long and fully narrated.

Yet another possibility is the two-hour historic sailing boat tour with the crew of the **Jolly Rover,** 735 Front St., tel. (843) 546-8822, open Mon.-Saturday.

Books

Harborwalk Books, 723 Front St., tel. (843) 546-8212, with a good collection of local-interest books, is one of the places where I've always got to stop in when I visit Georgetown. The **Mark Twain Store,** 723 Front St., tel. (843) 546-8212, features books on local history as well, along with local art. **Goat Island Mercantile,** 911 Front St., tel. (843) 527-8538, also carries new and used books and unique local gifts. **The Olive Branch,** 829-A Front St., tel. (843) 546-9630, features Christian and inspirational books.

NORTH OF GEORGETOWN: PAWLEYS ISLAND

Pawleys Island, just north of town on Hwy. 17, has been a resort for over 200 years; it's where planters would come during the warm weather to get away from the fevers and mosquitoes, and to take advantage of the beach breezes. Before Hugo, the local bumper stickers proclaiming the town as "Arrogantly Shabby" perfectly described the weatherworn, air-conditioning-free, antebellum houses with their open windows flanked by beaten shutters and sagging porches crisscrossed by the now-famous Pawleys Island hammocks. But by the early 1980s, people started moving in who just didn't "get it." Up went the big new houses. In 1989, Hugo slammed through here, leaving a new inlet, flattening nearly a hundred houses, and paving the way for a host of new air-conditioned beach homes with six- and seven-figure prices. Still, a week on noncommercial Pawleys Island can unknot even the tightest shoulder muscles, and the sight of the remaining old tin-roofed classic Pawleys houses is a delight not to be missed.

Accommodations

On the island itself you'll find 18 airy rooms at the venerable **Sea View Inn,** tel. (843) 237-4253. Luxury. Out on Hwy. 17, you'll find a friendly and nicer-than-average **Ramada Inn,** Hwy. 17 S, tel. (800) 553-7008 or (843) 237-4261, fax (843) 237-9703. Golf packages available. Inexpensive-Expensive.

Litchfield Plantation, King's River Rd., tel. (800) 869-1410 or (843) 237-9322, fax (843) 237-8558, offers a unique chance to stay in the real thing—an authentic 1750 plantation. Once you've entered the 600-acre property, follow the avenue of live oaks up to the Georgian man-

---

The casual dress of Pawleys Island's summer residents astonishes newcomers. Bare feet are the rule, even for bank presidents; girls dance at the Pavilion in sweeping evening gowns but without any shoes or stockings.

—*WPA's* South Carolina:
A Guide to the Palmetto State, 1941

sion. You'll choose from four suites with views of either the oaks or the old rice fields. Swimming pool, tennis courts, golf, oceanfront beach clubhouse. A private restaurant is located on the property. Premium-Luxury.

A lot of golfers like to stay at **Pawleys Plantation Country Club Villas,** Hwy. 17, tel. (843) 237-6100, which is not right on the island, but is right on a golf course. Most units have a fireplace and sleep up to six people. Expensive-Luxury.

To stay on Pawleys itself means you're probably going to need to rent a house. Call **James W. Smith Real Estate,** 1336 Hwy. 17, tel. (800) 476-5651 or (843) 237-4246, or **Pawleys Island Realty,** on Pawleys Island, tel. (800) 937-7352 or (843) 237-4257. Or pick up a phone book and start calling.

Restaurants

You won't find any restaurants on the island itself. On the highway, **Frank's Restaurant and Bar,** 10434 Ocean Hwy., tel. (843) 237-3030, Web site: www.the-strand.com/franks, is an upscale standard in this area, known for its gourmet seafood and extensive wine list. Expect to spend more than $25 a plate. Behind the restaurant you'll find the more casual and less expensive **Frank's Outback,** 10458 Ocean Hwy., tel. (843) 237-1777. Open Tues.-Sat. 6-10 p.m. If the weather's good, eat outside under the oaks.

TO THE WEST: THE CHUBBY CHECKER BIRTHPLACE

Ernest Evans, a.k.a. Chubby Checker, was raised a country boy just down Hwy. 521 in **Spring Gully.** Although his mother now lives in Walterboro, he returns occasionally to visit his aunt and old friends in Spring Gully. Checker (who got his game piece stage name after Dick Clark's wife remarked that he looked like a younger, thinner Fats Domino) attended Great Pleasant Church on Hwy. 521 as a boy, and he has ancestors in the graveyard outside dating back to the 1850s. He also attended the decaying schoolhouse next door. His family moved to Philadelphia when he was just eight, and after high school, when he was toiling as a chicken-plucker, already-discovered schoolmates Frankie Avalon and Fabian brought him

into the recording studio to jump-start his career. There he met Dick Clark, who was looking for someone to re-record a Hank Ballard dance song called "The Twist." It became one of the biggest hits in rock history—the only single ever to rise to No. 1 on the *Billboard* charts, disappear, and then rocket back to the top again the following summer. Chubby also churned out numerous other hit dance tunes, including "Let's Twist Again," "Slow Twisting," "Pony Time," and "Limbo Rock."

Every year, local boy Chubby performs for the home crowd at nearby Andrews' **Good Ole Days festival** in May.

POINTS SOUTH

Hopsewee Plantation

Hopsewee Plantation, 494 Hopsewee Rd., Hwy. 17, 12 miles south of Georgetown, tel. (843) 546-7891, overlooks the Santee River. It's one of the oldest plantation homes still standing, having been built in the 1730s by Thomas Lynch, who attended the Continental Congress. His son, Thomas Jr., signed the Declaration of Independence. This restored home features period furnishings. Open March-Oct. Tues.-Fri. 10 a.m.-4 p.m. Getting on the grounds, which allows you to see the outside of the house and hike a short nature trail, costs $3 a vehicle. Touring the house costs $6 for adults, $2 for kids 5-17.

Hampton Plantation State Park

Turn off Hwy. 17 (a left if you're headed north) and visit this important plantation home at 1950 Rutledge Rd., built circa 1730 and long the chief building on this former rice plantation. When George Washington visited here, he learned that a small young oak in front of the house was soon to be cut down; he convinced the owner to spare the tree, and today the Washington Oak still stands before the house—blocking the view exactly as the building's owner had said it would. Archibald Rutledge, South Carolina's first poet laureate, returned here to his ancestral home after retiring from a career in teaching and devoted himself to his writing and to the restoration of the Hampton Plantation. No admission for grounds, open Thurs.-Mon.; $2 admission for house, open Thurs.-Mon. 1-4 p.m.

McClellanville

McClellanville is a quaint, largely unselfconscious antebellum fishing village between Myrtle Beach and Charleston. It gets little coverage in travel literature, but because of a number of movies recently filmed there (including Don Johnson and Melanie Griffith's 1992 film *Paradise*), a small number of travelers have begun to trickle in. A good place to stay is Cheri and Matthew George's one-room **Village Bed-and-Breakfast,** tel. (843) 887-3266, where you can simply relax. Be sure to stop in at the ancient **Buster Brown's The Country Store** on Pinckney St., tel. (843) 877-3331, where you'll find everything from clothing to tackle to food. The Browns also serve good home-cooked meals here out on the screened porch.

McClellanville is also the easternmost head of the recently begun Palmetto Trail, a 240-mile hiking path reaching from the small coastal town all the way across to the mountainous Oconee State Park near the Georgia border.

A very, very off-the-beaten-path place to stay here is **Laurel Hill Plantation,** a B&B reconstruction of an old two-story Lowcountry home with wraparound porches overlooking the Cape Romain Wildlife Refuge's salt marshes and creeks, and the Atlantic Ocean. Look for the entrance opposite St. James Santee School out on Hwy. 17 four miles south of McClellanville, then turn east and follow the dirt road just over a half mile through the trees until you see the house. There's plenty of birdwatching to do here. Pontoon boat rides, conversation, and lots of porch sitting will make up the rest of your day. Hosts Jackie and Lee Morrison also operate an antique shop on site. Children are allowed at the Morrisons' discretion. Call ahead for a reservation, because once you see the place, you're going to want to move your bags in and stay a spell. Moderate-Expensive.

CHARLESTON AND VICINITY

In writing of Charleston, travel author John Milton Mackie puts his finger on one of the city's greatest charms: "It was pleasant to find an American city not wearing the appearance of having all been built yesterday," he writes. "The whole town looks picturesquely dingy, and the greater number of buildings have assumed something of the appearance of European antiquity." Few who have visited here would disagree. What makes Mackie's opinion interesting is that he wrote these words way back in 1864, when Charleston was already closing in on its bicentennial. Founded in 1670, this is about as old an American city as you'll find.

Charleston's nickname, the "Holy City," refers to the number of cathedral peaks that tower over its streets, not to any especial piety in the populace. The city functions as the Austin, Texas, or San Francisco of South Carolina: it's where the quiet, creative kid at Pickens High disappears to after graduation, to return a year later with tattoos and an independent record deal. It's where interracial couples kiss on the street.

Charleston is a noted player on the international arts scene: the annual Spoleto Festival draws hundreds of thousands of art enthusiasts from around the world. Charleston also overflows with culture of the more organic variety: African, Greek, and Irish-American festivals (among others), Gullah basketweaver stands, Civil War reenactments, black-tie only debutante balls for the daughters of SOBs (wealthy Charlestonians living South of Broad Street), and shrimp boils held by fifth-generation shrimpers. And Charleston has

---

The rest of South Carolina has a keenly developed inferiority complex about Charleston, a complex that Charlestonians feel is richly deserved.

—Pat Conroy,
The Lords of Discipline, 1980

Though the native Charlestonian takes his time to think and to live, he talks with inconsistent rapidity. "Garden" here is characteristically "gyarden," and "car," "cyar," while the "a" of Charleston is fully as distinctive as that of Harvard.

—WPA's South Carolina:
A Guide to the Palmetto State, 1941

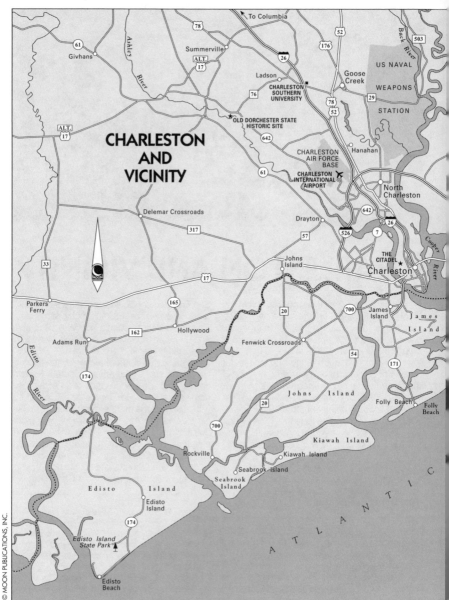

CHARLESTON
AND
VICINITY

To Columbia

Givhans
Summerville
Ladson
CHARLESTON
SOUTHERN
UNIVERSITY
OLD DORCHESTER STATE
HISTORIC SITE
Goose
Creek
US NAVAL
WEAPONS
STATION
Hanahan
CHARLESTON
AIR FORCE
BASE
CHARLESTON
INTERNATIONAL
AIRPORT
North
Charleston
Delemar Crossroads
Drayton
Johns
Island
THE
CITADEL
Charleston
Parkers
Ferry
James
Island
J a m e s
I s l a n d
Adams Run
Hollywood
Fenwick Crossroads
J o h n s   I s l a n d
Folly Beach
Folly
Beach
Rockville
Kiawah Island
Kiawah Island
Seabrook
Island
Seabrook Island
E d i s t o   I s l a n d
Edisto
Island
Edisto Island
State Park
Edisto
Beach
A T L A N T I C
Ashley
River
Edisto
River
Cooper
River
Back
River

© MOON PUBLICATIONS, INC.

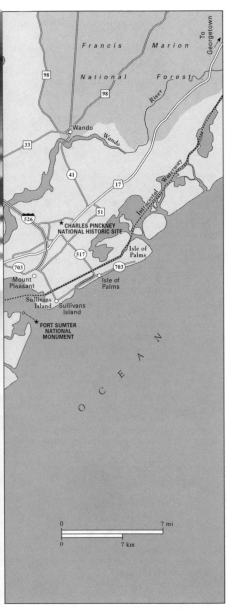

the Citadel, perhaps the most distinctively Southern—and South Carolinian—place on the planet.

Charleston's history is as worthy of veneration as that of any American city: the first decisive American victory of the Revolutionary War was won over at Sullivan's Island in 1776; the first shot of the Civil War was fired here. A lot of people through the years have chided Charleston as a city that worships the past. But all of Charleston's careful primping and long-sighted preservation have paid off; in 1997, *Travel and Leisure* named Charleston the 24th-best city in

---

LOWCOUNTRY SPIRITUALS

The Lowcountry has produced some of America's most popular spirituals. "We Shall Overcome," the anthem of the 1960s' Civil Rights Movement, began as a Johns Island folk song. The even better known (and much-recorded) "Michael Row Your Boat Ashore" had its beginnings in Beaufort. Northern teachers and missionaries present in Beaufort during the Civil War heard the song belted out by African Americans as they rowed the ferry boats from the landing at the foot of Beaufort's Carteret Street across the Beaufort River to the opposite shore of Lady's Island, now known as Whitehall Landing. Some of the missionaries wrote down the words and music, and the song appeared for the first time in the 1867 book *Slave Songs of the United States:*

Michael Row the Boat Ashore

Michael row the boat ashore, hallelujah,
Michael boat a Gospel boat, hallelujah.

Michael boat a music boat hallelujah,
Gabriel blow the trumpet horn, hallelujah.

O you mind your boastin' talk, hallelujah,
Boastin' talk will sink your soul, hallelujah.

Jordan stream is wide and deep, hallelujah,
Jesus stand on th' other side, hallelujah.

Common wisdom has it that the "Michael" of the song is the archangel mentioned in the Bible. Whether he ever worked in the Beaufort area as a boatman is unknown. Why Michael has to row while Gabriel gets to play his horn is also unknown.

The 186-foot steeple atop St. Michael's Episcopal Church—built in 1751, the oldest church building in South Carolina—is visible for blocks.

the world and sixth-best in the United States, handily besting such traveler's favorites as Seattle, Portland, Miami, Las Vegas, Austin, Atlanta, Savannah, Washington, D.C., Philadelphia, and Los Angeles. Of other Southern cities, only New Orleans made the top 25.

In November 1997, readers of *Southern Living* named Charleston the "Premier Shopping Area," "Most Romantic Getaway," and "Most Historic Travel Destination in the South." *Condé Nast Traveler* readers have named it a top 10 domestic destination for years.

Perhaps most telling is the compliment given Charlestonians by Marjabelle Young Stewart, renowned etiquette expert. Over the past 20 years, Charleston has never failed to make her list of the U.S.'s most polite cities. And in five different years, Charleston has ranked number one.

If you're looking for the Old South, you won't find a better urban expression of it than Charleston.

LAND

Charleston stands on a peninsula lying between the Ashley and the Cooper Rivers, a tongue of land pointed at the Old World. Here, Charlestonians like to say, the Ashley and Cooper Rivers meet to form the Atlantic Ocean.

At the southernmost point of the peninsula stands White Point Gardens and the Battery, where pirates were left hanging in the coastal breezes to scare off their scurvy brethren, and where guns fired upon British ships during the War of 1812.

Though the peninsula points southeast, Charlestonians have traditionally seen their city as the center of the world and thus have decided that the area above old Charleston is north; northeast of the Cooper, by Mount Pleasant, becomes "East Cooper"; the islands to the other side are "West Ashley"; and southwest of the Battery is "South." And White Point Gardens is due south.

Thus, the region to the northeast of the Cooper River is called simply "East Cooper," and this encompasses the major town of Mount Pleasant as well as the buffer Sea Islands of Sullivan's Island and Isle of Palms. The area southwest of the peninsula, on the other side of the Ashley, encompassing James Island, John's Island (where slaves composed the hymn that would become the civil rights anthem "We Shall Overcome"), and Folly Beach is called simply "West Ashley." The Charleston Neck region and further northwest are now called "North Charleston."

CLIMATE

Weather on the Charleston coast tends to be mild, with average lows in January still well above freezing at 40° F and average midsummer highs below 90° F. Which doesn't mean things can't get quite sticky in July and August in Charleston, especially downtown, where the standing water from the frequent rain showers adds to the humidity. Things are most always a bit better right on the beach on one of the surrounding islands, when a breeze is blowing.

Hurricane season rolls in from July to October.

HISTORY

History is as palpable in Charleston as the scent of the wood pulp factories, locally called "bread and butter." In 1855, back before most other American cities had even *begun* their histories, Charleston's elites decided to form the South Carolina Historical Society, which today maintains a collection of books, letters, plantation histories, and genealogical records. A number of the local TV and radio stations start off their newscasts with, "And now, from America's *most historic city . . .*"

> *Charles-town is, in the north, what Lima is in the south; both are Capitals of the richest provinces of their respective hemispheres.*
> —*Hector St. John de Crévecoeur,*
> Letters from an American Farmer, 1782

Colonial Powerhouse

South Carolina's first permanent European settlement, Charleston was founded at its current peninsular site only after the original colonists changed their minds twice. Their first choice was Port Royal, site of the former failed French and Spanish colonies and thus the best-documented site for 17th-century European travelers. But when the English colonists under Governor William Sayle arrived at Port Royal on March 15, 1670, they were greeted by Spanish-speaking Indians—a disheartening reminder that the Spanish still considered Carolina their land, and that the Spaniards' base in St. Augustine was not all that far away. Neither did it help that the colonists kept running across the overgrown remains of Spanish forts on Santa Elena Island; they knew well that the Spaniards had massacred French Huguenot settlers in the past, and this low-lying site, surrounded on three sides by woods, was hard to defend. All this made the

British wary. To top it off, the local Edisto Indians weren't really showing them much Southern hospitality (it hadn't been invented yet).

Fortunately, soon after they had landed, the leader of the Kiawah Indians, based north in the present-day Charleston region, sent word that the English would be very welcome in the Kiawah land farther north: they could help the Kiawah fight against the hated Spanish and the Westo Indians, the latter of whom the Kiawah described as "a ranging sort of people reputed to be man-eaters." Joined by a number of Edisto Indians and led by the cassique, the settlers sailed for the region now called West Ashley, just south of Charleston Peninsula. There, in early April, on the shores of the Ashley at Albemarle Point—site of present-day Charles Towne Landing—they founded Charles Town, named after their king.

As rice and later indigo became important local crops, and as Barbadians and Europeans, drawn by the reports drifting back from Carolina of cheap land and high profits, sailed into Charles Town Harbor, the city grew and prospered. By 1700, Charles Town had become inarguably the crown jewel of England's North American colonies.

The bulk of Europeans who emigrated to South Carolina in the early Colonial period came as indentured servants or slaves to work for those already in the colony. With so much land, and a rice economy that required a great amount of labor, indentured servants and slaves soon poured by the boatload into Charleston to be bought by planters who were building plantations among the coastal Sea Islands and up the rivers.

By 1680 the settlers had decided that the Albemarle Point spot was too unhealthy and hard to defend; some settlers began moving over to Oyster Point, site of the present-day Charleston Battery. The white-shell-covered point at the end of a narrow-necked peninsula was much easier to defend—there was no question about which direction a ground attack might come from—and planters both north and south of the port city could easily transport their goods from plantation to town using the natural currents of tidal creeks.

> *In Charleston, more than elsewhere, you get the feeling that the twentieth century is a vast, unconscionable mistake.*
> —*Pat Conroy,* The Lords of Discipline, 1980

PIRATES IN THE CAROLINAS

The very year after the Creeks finally agreed to peace to end the Yamassee War, Charles Town and the Lowcountry became a haven for Caribbean pirates. Pirates had long cruised the Carolina coast—which wasn't too surprising, given that the colony lay between the West Indies and the Cape Fear inlet, two favorite pirate lairs. In many of the new colonies, piracy was fairly well-tolerated, and in some of the less-well-run colonies (North Carolina comes to mind), pirates worked hand in hand with corrupt government officials. But South Carolina drew a line in the seashells early on: as early as the 1680s, Charles Town colonists were hanging pirates at the mouth of Charles Town Harbor as a warning to others.

The fact was that many pirates were just seamen who had been encouraged by their mother countries to attack, loot, and commandeer ships owned by competing imperialist nations. These privateers were paid with whatever they stole, so, in fact, the governments themselves trained a generation of sailors about the joys available to those who combined a little avarice with their violence. When the War of Spanish Succession ended in 1714, it left a lot of well-trained sea robbers very suddenly out of work. Not many of them decided to head ashore and become ministers, bakers, or cobblers. Most became pirates—freelance privateers.

In 1717, Edward "Blackbeard" Teach—one of the most notorious pirates of all time, if not *the* most notorious—anchored just outside the mouth of Charles Town Harbor with four ships. When a ship arrived at the harbor and stopped to await a pilot boat to lead it through the shoals and into the docks, the pirates pounced on it. When the pilot boat arrived, they grabbed that, too. Then they proceeded to rob the next seven or eight ships that came along—ships carrying materials the young colony needed to survive.

Finally, Blackbeard grabbed a ship with a number of Carolina notables on it. He sent messengers ashore to tell the Charles Townians that he was holding their neighbors hostage and would kill them unless he received a shipment of medicine. Given the alternative, the people of Charleston coughed up the requested provisions. The passengers were released unharmed—robbed to their skivvies, but alive.

South Carolina's Governor Robert Johnson complained to the lords proprietors, who took a deep breath, rolled up their puffy sleeves and . . . rang for another snifter of brandy. The English government stepped in, in an indirect sort of way. To their credit, the Brits, realizing their role in creating this predicament, and the difficulty of actually rounding up all these scurvy bilge rats and swinging them from the nearest yardarm, at least tried to be reasonable. In September 1718, the royal government offered amnesty for any piracy committed before the previous January.

Many pirates took advantage of the opportunity to wipe their records clean; they poured into the harbors and turned themselves in, and many began new, reasonably upstanding lives.

The fact that the Crown's offer had come in September was no happenstance. While the summer of 1718 had been quiet piracy-wise, fall was pirate season—with the holds of the colony's ships packed with produce.

In September and October, a new race of meaner, saltier pirates pulled out all the stops. They repeatedly blocked Charles Town harbor for 10 days at a time, capturing every ship that attempted to land there. With his colony still reeling financially from the Yamassee War, Governor Johnson wrote England again, pleading for warships. But he received no response.

Finally, a pirate named Charles Vane looted a slave ship of much of its human cargo just outside the harbor (don't get too happy—the poor Africans were no doubt resold elsewhere), then looted another craft from Boston, and *then* accosted four ships trying to slip *out* of the harbor. Johnson and the rest of the colony had just about had it. Then word came that yet *another* pirate ship was barreling down the coast, headed for Charles Town.

The Citizens' Revenge

With no one to turn to, the Carolinians resolved to help themselves. Johnson put Colonel William Rhett, who had co-led the naval units in the capture of the Yamassee capital of Pocotaligo, in charge of two sloops and a force of 130 men. The sloops took off south after Vane, but to no avail. Still itching for a fight, they tacked northward and sailed past Charles Town toward Cape Fear, in search of the pirates rumored to be on the way. They arrived at Cape

Fear at sunset and espied in the dying light the masts of the infamous pirate Stede Bonnet, commanding an eight-gun sloop, the *Royal James,* and two unarmed trading vessels—recently acquired prizes.

Both groups of men spent the hot, salty August night in the cramped cabins of their respective sloops, preparing for battle at sunrise. At first light, Bonnet raised anchor in an attempt to get his pirate booty out of trouble; Rhett gave chase, but in the excitement—and with all parties in unfamiliar waters, both Bonnet and the two Carolina ships ran upon shoals, fixing the three ships in a kind of still-life chase scene. One of the Carolina ships was stuck out of firing range of the pirates, but Rhett's ship was mired within musket range (in 1718, that was not far away at all).

In a straight-out cannonfest, the better-armed Carolina boat could have won the day handily. But then the tide turned. Or ebbed. Rhett's *Henry* tilted sharply toward Bonnet's, as if to say, "Here—let me help you shoot my crew." At the same time, the *Henry*'s guns were now pointing at water—good for bagging porpoises, but completely useless against the pirates. The unfortunate men on the *Henry*'s deck scrambled for their lives, some diving into the hold, others finding something to give cover, others finding nothing and crumpling as the shots found them. For six straight hours, the pirate guns pounded the daylights out of the top deck. Except for the wounded and dying above decks, Rhett's men huddled down below, awaiting their fate—and praying, no doubt, for high tide. Both crews knew it—if Rhett's men and ship could withstand the barrage until the tide came back in, then the first ship to rise off its shoal would have the other at its mercy.

The tide came in. Slowly, slowly, the battered *Henry* tilted back upright, and slowly her gun barrels rose, rose, rose . . . until they pointed straight at the side of the *Royal James.* The men of the *Henry* staggered from the dank hold where they'd spent the most harrowing day of their lives, and, standing amidst the bodies of 10 shipmates, eyeing their tormentors, they prepared to board the pirate's ship.

Bonnet raised a white flag. Rhett promised to intercede for Bonnet with the governor if Bonnet allowed the Carolinians to board without further bloodshed. With five men already dead and two mortally wounded, Bonnet agreed.

Rhett brought his prisoners back to Charles Town, where they were tossed in prison until trial. Twenty-two of Bonnet's men were tried and executed. Bonnet managed to escape (possibly with outside help) but was recaptured, tried, found guilty of piracy, and sentenced to death by hanging. Remembering his promise, Rhett made a passionate plea for the pirate's life, even offering to sail Bonnet to England to personally plead his case before the king, but Johnson demurred. On December 10, 1718, Bonnet was hanged at what would later become known as the Charleston Battery.

The Pirate Era Ends
Immediately following the capture of Bonnet, another two pirate ships—commanded by a Captain Worley—set up right outside Charles Town harbor. Rhett—angry at having had his word made violate by the governor—refused to take part in any further action against the pirates. So the governor himself decided to lead the operation. Outfitting four vessels with a total of 70 concealed guns, Johnson sailed these mock merchant ships over the bar and deliberately into Worley's trap. When Worley fired upon the four, Johnson's men opened return fire. The shocked pirates tacked and tried to escape, but after a four-hour flight and fight, both pirate ships were sunk—though most hands were saved long enough to be hanged. Fortunately, also rescued were the 106 English convicts (nearly 40 of them women) who had been the cargo of one of Worley's ships.

Only a few days later, on November 22, 1718, Blackbeard was killed in battle by Virginians who had also become disgusted with North Carolina's complacency about pirates. Though piracy would continue in other regions for quite a while, this harsh crackdown largely discouraged its practitioners from troubling South Carolina's waters ever again.

In May of 1680 the lords proprietors formally instructed the governor and his council to resettle Charles Town at Oyster Point.

Meanwhile, the English-African-Indian mix was becoming even more diverse. French Huguenot Protestants began arriving in Charleston by the boatfuls in 1680. French King Louis the XIV's 1685 repeal of religious freedoms for non-Catholics accelerated this process. European Jews, enticed by the colony's tolerant policies on religious freedom, poured in as well—by the end of the 18th century, Charleston had the second-largest Jewish population in the country.

In 1686, though the Spanish had resigned themselves to the idea of a English settlement at Charles Town, they forbade further encroachment to the south. Nonetheless, the increased population of Charles Town required planters to move out away from the city to find enough land for their plantations.

By 1690, the gradual movement of Charles Town to Oyster Point was officially completed. By now the city's population was estimated at around 1,200 people, making Charles Town the fifth-biggest city in all North America. By 1695, Charles Town citizens (or rather, their slaves) had built thick stone walls and six bastions, making the city into an armed fortress.

In 1700, the city established a tax-supported free library, possibly the first in America. On September 2, 1706, joint French and Spanish units attacked Charles Town during Queen Anne's War, but the Carolinian forces captured a French vessel and sent the Papists packing. The Powder Magazine at 79 Cumberland St. and the Pink House Tavern at 17 Chalmers were built in 1710, and the Rhett Mansion went up at 54 Hasell St. in 1712. The city served as a refuge for survivors of the initial Yamassee attacks in Beaufort and the Lowcountry plantations, and in the years leading up to the American Revolution, Charleston served as the Southern center of patriot sentiment.

Although it held off the British Navy at the Battle of Sullivan's Island in 1776, the city was captured by the British in 1780 and remained in British hands until they withdrew at war's end. Charleston was the state's capital until 1788 and served as one of the nation's most important ports, exporting Southern cotton and rice in the early part of the 19th century until protective tar-

THE STONO UPRISING

Just as the fruits of leisure began to bloom in Charles Town, adversity struck again. Ever trying to weaken the English colony in Carolina, Spain sent out operatives who made it known that the country offered freedom to any Carolinian slaves who could reach St. Augustine.

On September 9, 1739, at Stono Creek, a large number of African-American slaves broke open a store from which they took weapons. They killed 21 whites, including women and children, and marched southward, killing every white in their path, encouraging other slaves to come with them, and burning numerous houses along the road. At 11 the next morning, Governor William Bull, riding back to Charles Town from Granville County with four other men, saw this fireball of human rage barreling down the road. Fortunately for him, he spotted them far enough away that he was able to hide until they had passed.

It's unfortunate for the slaves that they hadn't stolen horses as well as guns. Bull rode to give notice to the Charles Town militia, which rode after the walking mob, catching up with them by four o'clock and shooting and hanging 44 of them. The surviving rebels escaped into the dense woods but were hunted down over the following weeks.

The uprising understandably frightened white Carolinians. "If such an attempt is made in a time of peace," Bull wondered, "what might be expected if an enemy should appear upon our frontier with a design to invade us?"

Over the next year, a number of minor insurrections arose across the colony and were put down. A fire burned down most of the waterfront district in 1740. Numerous other plots for rebellion were uncovered, and no doubt many slaves and free blacks were unjustly implicated and tried for plans dreamt up only in the minds of frightened slave owners. Eventually, a law was passed requiring white men to go armed to church, in preparation for slave uprisings.

The slave code became stricter after the Stono uprising, but—talk about your thin silver linings—so did laws against the brutal maltreatment of slaves, which slave owners saw as a factor in the rebellion.

SHELL THE OLD CITY! SHELL!

I.

Shell the old city! shell!
Ye myrmidons of Hell;
Ye serve your master well,
With hellish arts!
Hurl down, with bolt and fire,
The grand old shrines, the spire;
But know, your demon ire
Subdues no hearts!

—William Gilmore Simms

iffs ended the trade. In 1830, to compete with Savannah, which received produce from eastern Carolinian farmers who floated their goods down the Savannah River, a group of Charlestonians built America's first commercial railroad, stretching from Charleston to the newborn Savannah River town of Hamburg (near modern-day North Augusta). When the "Best Friend of Charleston" began taking this run, it was the longest railroad in the world.

The War between the States

In 1860, after being chased out of Columbia by an epidemic, South Carolina leaders passed their Ordinance of Secession here, a major step toward the beginning of the Civil War. The first armed conflict of the war began here the following April with the Confederates firing upon the Union garrison holed up inside Fort Sumter.

During the War between the States, Charleston saw little action after Fort Sumter, though Union boats quickly sealed off the port to all but the most stealth blockade runners. Union forces—including the famed African-American 54th Massachusetts—attempted to take Fort Wagner to the south of the city, but Confederate forces successfully defended it. The world's first "successful" military submarine—the CSS *Hunley*—sailed out from Breach Inlet between Sullivan's Island and Long Island (Isle of Palms) and sank the USS *Housatonic* before sinking itself, with all hands. The war in Charleston ended as Confederate troops fled and the black 55th Massachusetts marched through the streets, shocking white citizens and bringing emancipation to the city's black slaves.

After the War

If ever there was a place that rejected the New South, it was the port city.

—Walter Edgar, South Carolina: A History

The city had been ravaged by long-term bombardment, and it took a long time to recover. The discovery of nearby phosphate deposits brought some life back into the local economy, but the severe "shake" of 1886—an earthquake of an estimated 7.7 on the Richter scale—left 60-92 dead and caused an estimated $23 million damage.

By dredging Charleston Harbor to make room for large trans-Atlantic freighters, the city improved its shipping activity.

Around this time, a number of savvy Charlestonians began to think that perhaps all the postwar poverty had actually been a blessing in disguise, since by impoverishing Gilded Age business interests it had prevented them from initiating new projects, for which the city's historic buildings would have been torn down. In the early 1920s, Charleston devoted itself to expanding its tourism industry, leading to the building of both the Fort Sumter Hotel—now the Fort Sumter House—and the newly revitalized Francis Marion Hotel. With its harbor, and with the construction of the Charleston Naval Yard (spearheaded by North Charleston-raised Chief of the U.S. Armed Services Committee Mendel Rivers), Charleston became an important military installation during both world wars. Though many places shut their doors with the base closures at the end of the Cold War, by then tourism had become the city's chief industry. Today, tourism complements the city's production of paper and wood pulp, asbestos, clothing, cigars, rubber products, fertilizer, and other items.

One of the best things that's happened to Charleston over the past quarter century has

A city of ruins, of desolation, of vacant houses, of widowed women, of rotten wharves, of deserted warehouses, of weed-wild gardens, of miles of grass-grown streets, of acres of pitiful and voice-full barrenness—this is Charleston.

—Sidney Andrews, 1865

been the reign of Citadel graduate Joseph P. Riley as mayor. First elected in 1975, Riley has focused on stimulating new development and restoration of historic downtown Charleston, starting by planting high-end projects—1986's Charleston Place, for instance—in run-down neighborhoods, and then watching as the adjacent neighborhoods rejuvenated themselves. He spearheaded the annexation of Daniel Island and numerous other areas so that Charleston's physical size—and, thus, the size of its tax base—has exploded from 16.7 square miles in 1975 to nearly 90 square miles by the turn of millennium. The River Dogs' new classy riverfront baseball stadium—lovingly named Joseph P. Riley, Jr. Stadium (or "The Joe") in the mayor's honor—is one of Riley's more recent accomplishments, along with the forward-looking,

pedestrian-friendly development of Daniel Island and the new South Carolina Aquarium—placed amid what has been until recently a fairly ugly and certainly not tourist-friendly part of town.

Avid fans or foes of planned developments will want to see Daniel Island off I-526 North. Long an agricultural island farmed by poor blacks, Daniel Island is now being reborn as Riley's dream city, a re-creation of the classic Charleston neighborhoods of yesteryear.

The biggest trial the city has faced lately was Washington's 1992 announcement that it was shutting down Charleston's base and shipyard, which employed some 19% of Charleston's workforce. Fortunately, city leaders worked together to find industries to fill the projected shortfall, and by 1995, some $1.2 billion in capital investment had created more than 8,000 new jobs.

JFK AND THE SPY WHO . . . UM . . . LOVED HIM

FBI files released in 1998 revealed that in 1942, when John Fitzgerald Kennedy was a 24-year-old naval lieutenant living in the Atlantic fleet's intelligence office at 29 East Battery, Charleston, he enjoyed two visits from tall, blonde Inga Arvad Fejos, a former Miss Denmark. But Fejos was also a Nazi sympathizer with ties to Hitler, Goebbels, and Goering.

President Franklin Delano Roosevelt's attorney general was aware of Fejos's background and had set the FBI on her case. When she rented a room at the Fort Sumter Hotel, the FBI promptly bugged it.

Apparently, the lovers set the bug wires aglow with their passionate carryings on. In between, Kennedy was recorded spilling the beans to Fejos about his future military assignments.

Kennedy would have been of interest to the Nazis because of his intimacy with his father, former ambassador to England Joseph Kennedy.

Instead of taking the evidence to the navy, which would probably have resulted in JFK's receiving an assignment swabbing decks, the attorney general unaccountably took it to Joseph Kennedy himself. The elder Kennedy, to save his son's political future, had him shipped off to PT boat duty in the Pacific theater.

The rest of the story is, as they say, history: Kennedy captained PT-109, which was rammed and sunk, but he saved his crew, which made him a hero back home, igniting his political career and eventually leading to the White House.

So there it is—incontrovertible evidence that Charleston's romantic ambience led to JFK's election as president.

SIGHTS

ORIENTATION

Our houses are flirts. Lined up all along the streets, they are approachable and alluring, without the vast front lawns or privacy fencing with which suburban houses shield themselves. These houses are touchable, right from the sidewalk, yet at the same time they are very clearly private.

—*Josephine Humphreys,* Travel Holiday

To understand Charleston's logistics, think "parallels." Parallel rivers—the Ashley to the west and the Cooper to the east—separate the peninsula from the mainland. The primarily suburban area west of the Ashley is called **West Ashley,** and this includes **James Island, Folly Beach, Johns Island, Kiawah Island,** and **Seabrook Island.** East of the Cooper is called **East Cooper,** which includes **Mount Pleasant, Sullivan's Island,** and the **Isle of Palms.** And the area immediately north of Charleston is called **North Charleston.** Who needs Rand McNally? Farther north lie the booming suburbs of **Hanahan, Ladson, Goose Creek,** and **Summerville.**

Parallel Highways 78 (King St.) and 52 (Meeting St.) thread the peninsular spine one block apart from each other. A couple blocks east of Meeting, East Bay St. (Hwy. 52 Spur) follows the southward plunge, turning to East Battery St. after Broad. Over toward the Ashley side of the peninsula, Ashley and Rutledge Streets provide the main artery for traffic, and similarly end up at the south end of the peninsula.

Being as the city of Charleston was founded from the tip of the peninsula and spread its way up, you'll find the very oldest and most historic sections in the southern half of the peninsula. The visitors center on Meeting St. is a good starting point for southbound walking tours, though the Citadel and a few other historic sites north of this point are certainly worth viewing. But if you see nothing else in the area, see downtown Charleston. First off, there are some things you'll want to notice. For instance, you'll see a few streets still paved with stones—but notice there just aren't a whole lot of stones sitting around in the Charleston soil. In fact, most of the stones in the streets were imported as ballast from English ships.

Various Charleston promoters have broken up the historic district itself into various subdistricts, but in practice, all you need to know to successfully navigate downtown Charleston are a handful of landmarks. First of all, know that **The Battery** (a.k.a. White Point Gardens) perches on the very tip of the land tongue that is Charleston Peninsula, and the term in general use refers to the area south of **Broad Street,** which bisects the peninsula partway up. Nearly any route you take between White Point Gardens and Broad Street will take you by some incredible old homes. **St. Michael's Episcopal Church** is another handy landmark, since you can see its steeple for many blocks. It stands at the intersection of Broad and Meeting Streets, also known (and made famous in *Ripley's Believe It or Not!*) as the **Four Corners of Law,** because the buildings on the intersection— St. Michael's, City Hall, the Charleston County

---

CHARLESTON AREA HIGHLIGHTS

- African-American National Heritage Museum
- The Battery and White Point Gardens
- College of Charleston
- Old City Market
- Charleston Museum
- The Citadel
- Fort Sumter National Monument/Fort Moultrie
- Hyman's restaurant
- Magnolia Plantation and Gardens
- Old Exchange Building and Provost Dungeon
- Patriots Point Naval Museum (Mount Pleasant)
- Seewee Restaurant (Awendaw)
- St. Michael's Episcopal Church

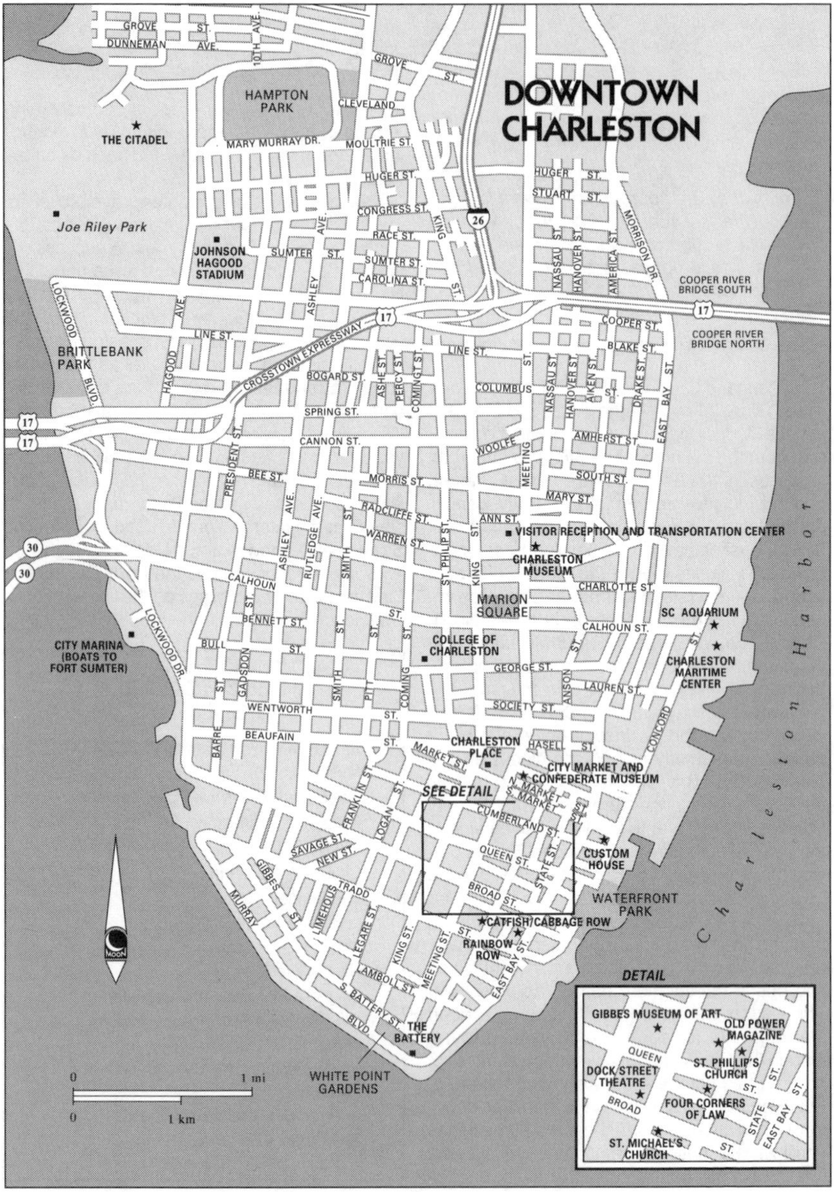

DOWNTOWN CHARLESTON

GROVE ST.
DUNNEMAN AVE.
10TH AVE.
GROVE ST.
HAMPTON PARK
CLEVELAND
★ THE CITADEL
MARY MURRAY DR.
MOULTRIE ST.
HUGER ST.
STUART
KING ST.
Joe Riley Park
CONGRESS ST.
RACE ST.
26
JOHNSON HAGOOD STADIUM
SUMTER ST.
SUMTER ST.
CAROLINA ST.
ASHLEY AVE.
NASSAU
HANOVER ST.
AMERICA
MORRISON DR.
COOPER RIVER BRIDGE SOUTH
17
LINE ST.
17
COOPER ST.
BLAKE ST.
COOPER RIVER BRIDGE NORTH
BRITTLEBANK PARK
HAGOOD
LOCKWOOD BLVD.
CROSSTOWN EXPRESSWAY
BOGARD ST.
ASHE ST.
PERCY ST.
COMING ST.
LINE ST.
COLUMBUS
NASSAU ST.
HANOVER ST.
AIKEN ST.
DRAKE ST.
EAST BAY ST.
17
17
SPRING ST.
CANNON ST.
WOOLFE
MEETING ST.
AMHERST ST.
SOUTH ST.
30
BEE ST.
PRESIDENT ST.
MORRIS ST.
MARY ST.
30
RADCLIFFE ST.
ASHLEY AVE.
RUTLEDGE AVE.
SMITH ST.
PHILIP ST.
WARREN ST.
ANN ST.
★ VISITOR RECEPTION AND TRANSPORTATION CENTER
CALHOUN
★ CHARLESTON MUSEUM
KING ST.
CHARLOTTE ST.
CITY MARINA (BOATS TO FORT SUMTER)
BENNETT ST.
GADSDEN
BULL
SMITH ST.
PITT ST.
COMING ST.
MARION SQUARE
★ COLLEGE OF CHARLESTON
GEORGE ST.
CALHOUN ST.
ANSON ST.
LAUREN ST.
SC AQUARIUM ★
CHARLESTON MARITIME CENTER
WENTWORTH
SOCIETY ST.
BEAUFAIN
BARRE
FRANKLIN ST.
ST. PHILIP ST.
HASELL ST.
CHARLESTON PLACE
N. MARKET ST.
S. MARKET ST.
MARKET ST.
COLCORP
CHARLESTON PLACE
CITY MARKET AND CONFEDERATE MUSEUM
SEE DETAIL
CUMBERLAND ST.
SAVAGE ST.
NEW ST.
LOGAN ST.
QUEEN ST.
STATE ST.
CUSTOM HOUSE
GIBBES
TRADD
BROAD ST.
WATERFRONT PARK
MURRAY
ARCHDALE ST.
LEGARE ST.
KING ST.
MEETING ST.
★ CATFISH/CABBAGE ROW
★ RAINBOW ROW
EAST BAY ST.
Charleston Harbor
LAMBOLL ST.
S. BATTERY ST.
MOON
BLVD.
★ THE BATTERY
WHITE POINT GARDENS
0 ——— 1 mi
0 ——— 1 km

DETAIL

GIBBES MUSEUM OF ART ★
OLD POWER MAGAZINE ★
QUEEN ST.
DOCK STREET THEATRE ★
ST. PHILLIP'S CHURCH ★
BROAD ST.
FOUR CORNERS OF LAW ★
STATE ST.
EAST BAY ST.
ST. MICHAEL'S CHURCH ★

© MOON PUBLICATIONS, INC.

Courthouse, and the U.S. Courthouse and Post Office—each represent a different form of law. Almost due east of the Four Corners you'll find **Waterfront Park,** a beautiful modern facility with swings, fountains, and lots of lawn to nap upon. Just north of here, back toward the center of the peninsula on Meeting Street between North and South Meeting Streets, you'll find **The Old City Market,** or "The Market" in local jargon. If downtown Charleston has a nucleus, this is it; many popular clubs, restaurants, and shops orbit around, including a recently opened Saks Fifth Avenue and **Charleston Place,** the hotel whose opening kickstarted the revival of Old Charleston. The Market is also the place from which many tours leave.

Within a couple blocks north of the Market, the tourist-centered economy thins out and the area can even look a bit dicey, though this is improving. At **Calhoun Street** you'll come across **Francis Marion Square,** which sits right between King St. and Meeting, and is home to many of the city's public events, including the Farmer's Market held every Saturday from April 18 to October 31. Just north of here you'll find the **Charleston Visitors Center.** You'll pass this on your left coming south on Meeting St.; stop in and grab all the pamphlets and coupons you can carry.

On the Ashley River, just south of where the **Hwy. 17 Alternate** cuts across the neck of the peninsula, you'll find the **Charleston,** home to dinner/dancing cruises, Fort Sumter tours, and a number of fine restaurants. North of the Alternate, you'll find **Joe Riley Stadium** and **The Citadel.**

Near the Charleston Visitors Center— North of Calhoun Street

The Charleston Visitors Center, 375 Meeting St., tel. (843) 723-5225, is a great place to stop in and get some background and a bagful of brochures and coupon books. The folks here will also plan out your stay and call hotels to find you a room. Very helpful and, except on extremely busy days during Spoleto, good, fast service. A bookstore also provides some worthwhile titles you may want to read around the pool or out on the balcony of your room. They also offer tickets for an in-house audiovisual show, the 24-minute *Forever Charleston,* which tells the city's story. Admission charged. Not a bad first step if this is your first visit and you're trying to get an overview of what-all's here.

The **Best Friend Museum,** Ann and King Streets, tel. (843) 973-7269, doesn't have too much to recommend it, other than the full-size replica—but only a replica—of the first train in regular passenger service in the U.S., which left from Charleston. Most of the rest of what's here is a gift shop, but if you're going to be over by the visitors center anyway, or if you're a train nut, it's right around the corner, and free.

Between Calhoun and Beaufain/Hasell Streets

The **College of Charleston** is simply one of the most beautiful and historic campuses in America. Situated as it is near the bright lights of downtown Charleston, it's no surprise that COC has long

cobblestone street in Charleston

had a reputation as a party school; even back in the early 1800s, famed pioneer, Mexican War commander, and later U.S. presidential candidate John C. Frémont was booted from the college rolls for his tendency to show up for classes with a hangover—if he showed up at all.

You may recognize the school buildings from the Alexandra Ripley miniseries, *Scarlett,* parts of which were filmed here.

Over at 90 Hasell St. you'll find the large, 1840 Greek Revival **Beth Elohim Synagogue,** tel. (843) 723-1090, second-oldest synagogue in the nation (founded 1749) and the oldest in continuous use. More importantly, in 1824 this became the birthplace of Reform Judaism in the U.S. Worth making a visit. Archives available. Open Sun.-Fri. 10 a.m.-noon. Free.

If you're feeling ecumenical, head across the street to **St. Mary's Church,** 89 Hasell St., tel. (843) 722-7696, the first church in the Carolinas and Georgia. Built in 1839, the church building itself contains a number of beautiful paintings.

Between Beaufain/Hasell and Broad Streets

The 1841 **Old City Market,** on Market St. between Meeting and East Bay, continues today as Charleston's beating heart. A good place to start your visit, it features small shops, restaurants, and a flea market with everything from produce to antiques. You'll find vendors for everything from special homegrown hot rice recipes ("So good you'll double-smack your lips!" brags one sign) to professional photographs of the city. The **Daughters of the Confederacy Museum** in the upstairs building has been closed for renovation, but it should be open again upstairs by the time you get here. Call (843) 723-1541 before noon for information.

In the wake of Indian attacks, early Charles Town residents built the square, low-lying 1703 **Old Powder Magazine,** 23 Cumberland St., tel. (843) 805-6730, as part of the city's fortifications near the northwest bastion. Today, it's the oldest remaining public building in Charleston. Open Mon.-Sat., Sunday afternoons. Admission charged.

St. Philip's Episcopal Church, 142 Church St., tel. (843) 722-7734, was built 1835-38 by Joseph Hyde, though Edward Brickell White later added a tall octagonal steeple. This steeple once held a light for seamen, but this made it a target during the Union bombardment of the city. This church congregation is the first Anglican parish south of Virginia. According to local legends, barristers questioned Reverend White's credibility, since he had in 1682 drunkenly christened a young bear. White went on to remain a pastor for many years, but the bear apparently drifted from the faith.

If you'd like to attend a service in this magnificent structure—and many traveling visitors do—Sunday services are held at 7:45 a.m., 8:45 a.m., and 11 a.m., Wednesday services are 10 a.m. and 5:30 p.m. No bears allowed.

Declaration of Independence-signer Edward Rutledge and John C. Calhoun lie buried out in the church's graveyards, along with Colonel William Rhett, capturer of pirate Stede Bonnet. Both Christopher Gadsden, the maverick Revolutionist, and Charles Pinckney, four-time governor and drafter and signer of the federal Constitution, are also said to be buried here in unmarked graves.

Though the current Gothic **Huguenot Church** at 44 Queen St., tel. (843) 722-4385, is "only" 150-plus years old, it was built on the walls of its predecessor. French Huguenots have worshiped on this site since as early as 1687. Until the early 1900s, the service was conducted in French on certain Sundays, but now it's English only.

The **Circular Congregational Church,** 138 Meeting St., tel. (843) 577-6400, a huge brick Romanesque, was built in 1891 for a congregation founded way back in 1681. The church began with a group of non-Anglican Calvinists from a number of nationalities and was originally known as the Church of Dissenters. Architects designed the present church in the aftermath of the 1886 earthquake, using circular logic. Dr. David Ramsay (1749-1815), author of the definitive early South Carolina history, *History of South Carolina (1789),* and an important early biography of George Washington, is buried among others in the churchyard. Today the church building continues in use for the local congregation of the United Church of Christ.

The historic **Dock Street Theater** at 135 Church Street, tel. (843) 720-3968, is a reconstruction of the 1736 Dock Street Theater—the first building in American designed for purely theatrical purposes—and the 1809 Planters

Hotel. The Dock Street Theater (on Dock St., which was later renamed Queen St., near Church) opened on February 12, 1736, with a performance of *The Recruiting Officer,* by George Farquhar. After a few successful seasons, the theater burned. But Charleston had caught footlight fever, and a second theater opened on the same site on October 7, 1754. Theater became wildly popular with the powdered wig set before the Revolution, so much so that the proprietors built a new, grander theater to replace this second theater on nearly the same site, opening in 1773. Unfortunately, though the theater miraculously survived the heavy bombardments during the Revolution, it burned to the ground shortly thereafter.

In the last decades of the 18th century, theater productions were later banned in Charleston under a particularly harsh blue law, as thespians were officially condemned as antithetical to decent, upright living. But this era was short-lived, and shortly thereafter, productions were taking place in various spots around Charleston, though the Dock Street Theater still lay in ruins. In 1809, a business concern built the **Planters Hotel** around the ruins of the theater. In 1835, to meet popular demand, the hotel was remodeled to include a theater, so that by the theater's centennial, the Dock Street Theater was again up and running. Though the theater was closed by the Civil War, the WPA during the Depression got the theater refurbished and open in time for its bicentennial on February 12, 1936.

Today, the Dock Street Theater continues to offer first-rate theatrical performances through the Charleston Stage Company, the state's largest theater company, producing over 120 performances a year. If you just want to poke your head inside to take a look around this historic building, stop by during business hours. To speak with folks in the box office, call (800) 454-7093 or (843) 965-4032 Mon.-Fri. 9 a.m.-5 p.m. Shows are held Thursday, Friday, and Saturday at 8 p.m., Sunday at 3 p.m.

The Slave Market, 6-8 Chalmers St., is one of the many places where slaves were sold during the days of the slave trade in town.

The intersection of Broad and Meeting Streets is known as the **Four Corners of Law,** because the buildings on each corner represent a different sort of law. On the northeast corner stands City Hall, circa 1801, Meeting and Broad Streets, representing city law. The Charleston County Courthouse, representing legal law, stands on the northwest corner. On the southwest corner, the U.S. Courthouse and Post Office represent federal law. Directly across Broad you'll find St. Michael's Episcopal Church holding down the southeast corner, representing divine law. On most days, the traffic on Meeting Street represents the law of perpetual motion.

Charleston City Hall, on Meeting and Broad Streets, open Mon.-Fri., free admission, was built circa 1801; the City Council Chamber contains valuable works of art, including the John Trumbull portrait of George Washington, dated 1791. The tower above is topped by an Indian weathervane; the Indian is supposed to be King Haigler, a Catawba chief, and saviour of the Camden Quakers in 1753. He fought with the Carolinians against the Cherokee in 1759, but was killed by a Swanee ambush in 1765. The town bell was cast in Philadelphia in 1824. It used to ring out every night at nine o'clock, marking the beginning of curfew hours for slaves.

South of Broad Street
St. Michael's Episcopal Church, 1751, is the oldest church building in South Carolina. During Colonial days, this was the second Anglican church built south of Virginia. The clock toward the top of the 186-foot tower/steeple has kept time for Charlestonians since 1764. Inside the church is grand, with box pews; wealthy Charlestonians would rent these to assure themselves the best—and hence, most prestigious—seats possible on Sundays. How they reconciled this kind of privilege with the teachings of a peasant rabbi who spent most of his time around the downtrodden is beyond me. The graveyard

> *The mansions South of Broad Street form a magnificent archipelago of exclusion. It was not a matter of money that assured access to the charmed region; it was a matter of blood. . . . If you were crass, lowborn, or socially offensive, it would have made no difference to the proud inhabitants South of Broad that you owned France; they would not invite you to their homes.*
>
> —Pat Conroy, The Lords of Discipline, 1980

PORGY IN EXILE

Though based upon a novel written by Charleston's own Dubose Heyward, and set in the city, the classic American opera *Porgy and Bess* was not performed in Charleston until 1970. The interracial cast required to stage the show would have violated segregationist city codes.

beside the church is worth visiting for its many ornate and affecting tombstones. The bells overhead were stolen by the British during the Revolution and carried back to England in 1784, though they came back to Charleston. In 1862, they were shipped to Columbia for safekeeping from Federal shells and stored in a shed on the grounds of the State House—as if that wasn't a target. When the State House was burned in 1865 by Sherman's troops, the bells were partially destroyed. Preservation-minded folks sent the fragments that remained to England in 1866, and they were recast in the original molds. Then the bells made their fifth trip across the Atlantic, landing in Charleston in 1867.

St. Michael's stands on the corner of Broad and Meeting Streets, where the first church in Charleston—St. Philip's—was built in 1681-82. When the growing parish was divided in 1751, the lower half was named St. Michael's. George Washington and Lafayette both worshipped here, and here the first vested boys' choirs in the country began. During the Revolutionary period, Reverend Robert Cooper was forced out of the pulpit—and out of the country—for offering prayers for the King of England. Since the church's steeple provided the highest viewpoint in Charles Town, Peter Timothy, editor of the *Charles Town Gazette,* climbed up there with a spyglass to watch the approaching British troops before the American loss of the town in 1780. Timothy had taken over the paper from his mother, the first woman publisher in the U.S. and a business partner of Benjamin Franklin. To make the steeple less of a target for British guns, Continental Commodore Abram Whipple proposed that someone should paint it black to make it less obvious to the eye. But once it was painted black, against the blue sky, it stuck out far more

than before. Hours are Mon.-Fri. 9 a.m.-5 p.m., Saturday 9 a.m.-noon. Donations accepted. Call (843) 723-0603 for more information. Sunday services are at 8 a.m. and 10:30 a.m.

The **Old Exchange and Provost Dungeon,** 122 E. Bay St., tel. (843) 727-2165, stands on the site of the original British Court of Guards, built in 1680. In 1767 the current exchange and customs house was built right on top of the old building, preserving the basement down below. Admission is $4 for adults.

Today you can visit the basement dungeon, where Stede Bonnet, the pirate, was imprisoned in 1718. The building itself once stored the tea taken during Charleston's version of the Boston Tea Party. When the British had the Carolinians bottled up in the city in 1780, General William Moultrie hid 10,000 pounds of gunpowder in a secret room behind a false wall down in the basement. Though the British moved in and took over the city and the building, they never did find the hidden powder.

In 1791, George Washington stood on the steps of this building to watch a parade given in his honor. That night, Washington tripped the light fantastic at a ball and governor's dinner up in the Exchange Hall.

You'll come to **Cabbage/Catfish Row** at 89-91 Church St., the model for DuBose Heyward's Catfish Row in his novel *Porgy,* the basis for George Gershwin's opera *Porgy and Bess.* Vendors once peddled produce along the street here (hence the name Cabbage Row). In the novel, Heyward relocated *his* row over to E. Bay St. to place it closer to the waterfront (hence Catfish). Not that you'll find many catfish in Charleston Harbor.

Farther south along Church St. you'll come to the **Heyward-Washington House,** circa 1772, 87 Church St., tel. (843) 722-0354, which was the home of Thomas Heyward Jr., whose name you may remember from the bottom portion of the Declaration of Independence. George Washington lived here awhile in Charleston in 1791. The original kitchen building is still there, as well as Charlestonian furniture and a formal garden abloom with plants available in Charleston in the 18th century. Open daily 9 a.m.-5 p.m.; admission $6 adults, $3 children. This home is owned by the Charleston Museum.

The **Nathaniel Russell House,** built for a local prosperous merchant in 1808, the year before Abraham Lincoln was born, stands yet at

51 Meeting St., tel. (843) 724-8481, amidst a large garden. A great example of the Federal style popular after the Revolution, this is a rectangular three-story mansion with a three-story octagonal bay on one side, a free-standing spiral staircase, and ornate moldings. Adams-style furnishings. Guided tours Mon.-Sat. 10 a.m.-5 p.m., Sunday 2-5 p.m. Last tour begins 4:40 p.m. Closed Thanksgiving, Christmas Eve, Christmas. Admission $6, under 6 free. It's possible to buy a combination ticket for Drayton Hall, Edmondston-Alston House, Gibbes Museum of Art, Middleton Place, and the Nathaniel Russell House, all for $29, or $19 for those under 12.

If you're only going to take one home tour, you may want to make it the circa 1828 **Edmondston-Alston House,** 21 East Battery, tel. (843) 722-7171. For one thing, this is one of those beautiful mansions on the Battery that overlook the harbor. It's also a great example of the "golden era" for Charleston antebellum society. Originally built for Charles Edmondston, a wealthy Scottish-born merchant and owner of a lucrative wharf, the home has been owned by Alston family members since 1838. Because members of the Alston family still live here, your 30-minute guided tour ($7, under 6 years old free) will cover only the lower two floors of this stately three-floor Greek Revival. Open Tues.-Sat. 10 a.m.-5 p.m. (last 30-minute tour starts at 4:30) and Sunday and Monday 1-5 p.m. You can buy a combination ticket for Drayton Hall, Edmondston-Alston House, Gibbes Museum of Art, Middleton Place, and the Nathaniel Russell House, all for $29, or $19 for those under 12.

Calhoun Mansion, 16 Meeting St., tel. (843) 722-8205, a 24,000-square-foot Victorian baronial manor house, circa 1876, features a 75-foot domed ceiling with stairwell. John C. Calhoun never lived here, but a kinsman did. Hours are Wed.-Sun. 10 a.m.-4 p.m. (closed January); admission $10 adults, $5 children.

Colonists came to call **The Battery** "White Point" after the oyster shells, which you'll still find on the ground; today it's still called **White Point Gardens.**

Later, a lot of pirates used to hang around here—literally. In 1718, Stede "The Gentleman Pirate" Bonnet and 21 of his men were allowed to hang for quite a while, so that their corpses'

ghastly presence could send a message to other would-be pirates.

But the city long ago cleaned up all the bodies, so don't let this keep you from visiting. However, to keep the same general demeanor of tension in the place, the city has neglected to put any bathrooms here—so plan ahead.

This area got its nickname when it housed guns protecting Charleston Harbor during the War of 1812. The northeast side of the Battery is also called "High Battery." While no one's been executed here in many years, a lot of couples take advantage of the natural beauty here and get married on the gazebo.

In 1923 the city donated land on the Battery for the Fort Sumter Hotel (now the Fort Sumter House, the condo building at 1 Meeting St.). John F. Kennedy and a Swedish woman who was probably a Nazi spy spent some passionate nights here back in February 1942.

PLANTATIONS, GARDENS, AND PARKS

Most South Carolinians, even at the height of antebellum society, never owned a slave. Only a relative handful owned, much less lived on plantations. In fact, more African-Americans lived on plantations than European-Americans ever did—and they lived as slaves. Which means, of course, that the vast majority of people who lived on the famed Southern plantations, with their stately buildings that nearly every new house built in South Carolina seems to emulate, did so unwillingly.

Even still, most non-Southerners don't really feel that they've visited the "real" South until they tour a plantation. And if it's antebellum excess you're seeking, you'll come to the right place in South Carolina. Coastal South Carolina in particular was one of the wealthiest plantation areas in antebellum times, and Charleston was the hub of antebellum Carolinian life—as it is today, in many ways—so you'll find many old plantations here, a number of them open to the public.

Drayton Hall

Drayton Hall, 3380 Ashley River Road (Route 61) in North Charleston, tel. (843) 766-0188, is a red-brick Georgian-Palladian, one of the finest

FOR WHOM
THE GARDENIA IS NAMED

The fragrant white gardenia is named after South Carolinian Dr. Alexander Garden. Born in Scotland around 1730, Garden settled into Charles Town and worked as a physician. But it was in his dedicated dabblings as a naturalist that Garden became most noted. To most of Europe, America was still very much a "new world," and to his many scientist correspondents in distant Old World universities—including the Swedish naturalist Linnaeus—Garden served as a "man in the field," slogging through South Carolina's swamps in search of new species. Garden was welcomed into numerous scientific societies on both sides of the Atlantic and is formally credited with discovering several species, including the congo snake and the mud eel. It was Linnaeus who complimented Garden by naming one of his new plant discoveries the gardenia.

Garden died in London in 1791.

skills—all illegal—while providing them religious instruction. Sherman and Co. Remodelers burned the Magnolia Plantation house to the ground and strung up Adam Bennett, the top-ranking slave, from a nearby (still standing) tree, because he refused to tell them where he'd buried the family treasure. Fortunately, the Boys in Blue remembered at the last moment that they were, after all, supposed to be "God's Truth Marching On," and cut poor Bennett down. After the war was over, Bennett traveled 250 miles on foot to Flat Rock, North Carolina, where Reverend Drayton was hiding out in one of the Draytons' summer homes, having heard that the freed slaves had seized control of the plantation and "taken [it] for their own." Bennett told Drayton everything was ready for his return. Drayton later disassembled his Summerville house and floated it downriver to the plantation, where it stands today on the foundation of the Shermanized house.

The good reverend planted his informal gardens in the 1840s and opened them to the public in 1870 as a way of paying for the upkeep of

picture-perfect bridge at sumptuous Magnolia Gardens

examples of early Georgian architecture in the United States. Not the nicest guy, John Drayton, but then neither was William Randolph Hearst. He was a rich man, the owner of 500 slaves at his death.

Because it was being used as a smallpox hospital at the time, Drayton Hall was the only authentically Colonial structure along the Ashley to survive Shermanization. Just keep in mind that this was the—ahem—"smaller" house of the Draytons. There's no furniture here, which makes it easier to appreciate the architecture, moldings, and flooring.

Magnolia Plantation and Gardens

Of all the Charleston plantations, Magnolia is my personal favorite—and that's saying something. John Drayton's daddy, Thomas Drayton, lived on Magnolia Plantation in the main house, where he was born in 1708. Thomas Drayton Jr., Thomas's father, built the original house in the 1680s. He came here with a group of Barbadian planters in 1671, with (later governor) John Yeamans.

Drayton's great-great-grandson, Reverend Dr. John Drayton, apparently treated his slaves quite well, educating them in reading, writing, and math

mansion at
Magnolia Gardens

the plantation; the magnificent gardens today include a **Biblical Garden,** featuring most of the plant species you grew to love in the Old and New Testaments (unfortunately, the Tree of Eternal Life from Genesis is missing); an herb garden; a Barbados tropical garden; a wildlife refuge; and a petting zoo.

If you feel that your own family tree could stand a little thinning, you might be interested in the quarter-mile *Camellia sasanquas* **maze.** Perhaps most impressive is Magnolia's latest addition, the 60-acre **Audubon Swamp Garden.** For $5 an adult, you can take the "Nature Train"—a tram car, to be more accurate—for an interesting tour of the grounds, but you should take the Swamp-walk (also $5) as well. If you were at the drive-ins in the late 1970s, you saw these swamps featured in the Adrienne Barbeau epic *The Swamp Thing.* Many years before Barbeau slogged through these waters, trailing a residue of acting greatness, no less a personage than John J. Audubon, the famed ornithological artist, wandered about the same area, sketchbook in hand, as a guest of the Reverend Dr. Drayton.

Magnolia Plantation and Gardens, Hwy. 61, tel. (843) 571-1266, Web site: www.magnolia-plantation.com, e-mail: magnolia@internetx.net, is open 8 a.m.-5 p.m. Mon.-Sat.; prices vary according to which of Magnolia's attractions you want to tour, but plan on spending from a minimum of $10 up to about $25 for adults, about half that for children. Senior citizens save a dollar on most admissions. A number of the trails are paved and wheelchair accessible.

Middleton Place
Here you get an idea of Charleston's abundance of floral beauty—drop Middleton Place into the middle of nearly any other region in the country and it would attract visitors from hundreds of miles away. But then, I suppose Middleton Place does that already, and it's just four miles past Magnolia Plantation on Ashley River Road (Hwy. 61), tel. (800) 782-3608 or (843) 556-6020.

And well they *should* come, for Middleton Place holds the nation's oldest landscaped gardens, begun back in the 1740s. Arthur Middleton, signer of the Declaration of Independence, grew up here. A lot of locals prefer Middleton for its lack of hype; a visit here is more like visiting an actual plantation than is a visit to, say, Magnolia, which has been opened for—and shaped by—the demands of paying customers since Reconstruction. Though only a staircase and foundation remain of the main house, for a couple of bucks extra you can tour the "flanker" house, where the Middletons lived after the war. Don't even think about taking a camera inside—the folks at Middleton have gone so far as to construct a row of lockers on the house's front porch, where you may (must) leave your camera before entering the house.

Remarkable gardens here as well, of a more formal, French variety. Unlike Magnolia, these aren't particularly impressive outside of spring—go in June and you'll be mainly touring rows of shrubs.

You'll also find a good Southern-style restaurant here (open Friday and Saturday only) with impeccable atmosphere and moderate prices. You can also take a tour of the authentically appointed guest (now main) house, walk amid a small slave graveyard, or visit an authentic working stable yard. Open daily 9 a.m.-5 p.m. Admission is $14 adults, $7 children.

Cypress Gardens

Up north along the Cooper River, in Moncks Corner, you'll find 163 acres of azaleas, dogwoods, daffodils, wisteria, and dark waterways. Two nature trails offer you good chances to look for wildlife: river otter, woodpeckers, owls, and, of course, our friend the alligator. Springtime's bloom time, and fall is also quite pretty. Summertime is pretty, too—pretty hot, and a pretty good time to bring repellent. Take the glass-bottom boat ride, or canoe yourself and a significant other around. From Charleston, head north on I-26 to Exit 208; follow Hwy. 52 north and look for the signs to Cypress Gardens, 3030 Cypress Gardens Rd., Moncks Corner, tel. (843) 443-0515. Open Mon.-Sat. 8 a.m.-5 p.m. Admission is adults $6, children 6-12 $2, under 6 years admitted free Feb.-April; May-Jan. the price drops to adults $4.

Boone Hall Plantation

Closest to downtown Charleston is Boone Hall Plantation, lying along the Wando River near Mount Pleasant. Though its main plantation house is a 1935 reconstruction of the original, Boone Hall is worth visiting because 1) it allows you to see what a plantation looked like when it was relatively new; 2) it contains nine original slave cabins, which tell more about slave conditions than all the interpretive exhibits in the world; 3) if you're looking for the type of plantation you may have seen in the TV miniseries *North and South,* Boone Hall Plantation *is* where that miniseries and several others were filmed; and 4) rumor has it that Margaret Mitchell's Tara (her *Gone With the Wind* was published in 1936, a year after Boone Hall's renaissance) is modeled after the place—down to the gauntlet of moss-dripping oaks at the entrance. Battle reenact-

ments are performed here in the summer, filling the grounds and mansion with period-dressed soldiers and belles (nobody seems to want to come dressed as a slave). For the Civil War buff, there's nothing like it. Boone Hall Plantation is off Hwy. 17, tel. (843) 884-4371. Open all year 8 a.m.-5 p.m.; admission is $7.50 adults, $5 for senior citizens, $3 for children 6-12. Under 6 admitted free.

Angel Oak Park

Over on John's Island you'll find Angel Oak, 3688 Angel Oak Rd., tel. (843) 559-3496, a massive live oak *(Quercus virginiana)* tree just 65 feet tall but 25.5 feet in circumference and providing some 17,000 square feet of shade. Because live oaks tend toward heart rot, making core samples useless in determining age, nobody knows for sure how old the Angel Oak is, though some estimates—based on the large limbs stretching out up to 89 feet from the trunk and measuring 11.25 feet around—possibly 1,400 years old.

Incidentally, though some have waxed poetic about the way the Angel Oak spreads its angelic, "winglike" branches to the ground, the name actually comes from Justis Angel, who owned the tree and its land in the early 1800s. The South Carolina Agricultural Society rented the tree for $1 a year from the Mutual Land and Development Corporation 1959-64, until another private owner bought the tree and surrounding site. He opened the land to the public, but vandalism and other problems forced him to build a fence around it and start charging a viewing fee.

In 1991, the City of Charleston acquired the Angel Oak and the surrounding property, and opened Angel Oak Park to the public on September 23, 1991. People meet here for picnics, family reunions, weddings, and other special events. Permits are required for large events and for the use of alcoholic beverages.

Charles Towne Landing—1670

At 1500 Old Towne Rd., off Hwy. 171 about three miles northwest of downtown Charleston, tel. (843) 852-4200, this peculiar park rests on the original site of Charleston—the spot the founding folk abandoned when they decided it was safer and healthier to move over to White Point. You can take a guided tram tour of the original 1670 fortification, explore seven miles of pathways through the gigantic shade oaks and lagoons of English Park gardens, and walk through the Animal Forest, where you'll see the same animals the settlers would have seen in 1670, including bison, pumas, bears, wolves, alligators, and bobcats. You're also free to participate in activities in the Settler's Life area, a re-creation of an early South Carolina village. Perhaps most interesting is the full-scale replica of a 17th-century trading vessel moored in Old Towne Creek picnic sites. Unlike the original Charles Town settlement, most everything here's wheelchair accessible. Admission: $5 (15 and older), $2.50 (children 6-14), S.C. senior citizens free. Open daily 9 a.m.-5 a.m.

James Island County Park

This park, at 871 Riverland Dr., is a 640-acre facility with boardwalks, bike and hiking trails, a fishing/crabbing dock, lagoons, a playground for the kids, picnic sites, a campground, rental cabins, and the **Splash Zone** water park, featuring a 200-foot slide, a lazy river, and other attractions.

Palmetto Islands County Park

This beautiful facility on Long Point Rd. in Mount Pleasant features marsh boardwalks, trails, a mile-long canoe trail, a playground, an observation tower, bicycle paths, and fishing docks.

Folly Beach County Park

A neat beach-access park, Folly Beach, on W. Ashley Ave. in Folly Beach, offers 4,000 feet of oceanfront beach and 2,000 feet of riverfront beach. Lifeguards are on duty during the high season. Plenty of parking, dressing areas, showers, public restrooms, and picnic tables.

Francis Marion National Forest

Francis Marion comprises 250,000 acres of forest north of Charleston, offering picnicking and camping sites; boat ramps; fishing; and horseback, bicycle, and motorcycle trails. Head north on Hwy. 17 and look for the signs.

Seewee Visitor and Environmental Education Center

This center, at Hwy. 17 N, Awendaw, tel. (843) 928-3368, is open Tues.-Sun. 9 a.m.-5 p.m. The center focuses on the natural history of the Low-country, featuring hands-on displays, a live birds-of-prey area, and a red wolf education area.

MUSEUMS, HISTORY, AND ART

Charleston Museum

You can't miss this museum, at 360 Meeting St., tel. (843) 722-2996, fax (843) 722-1784, as you head south toward the Market and Battery off Hwy. 17 or I-26 along Meeting St.; it's on the east side of the street, a modern-looking brick building fronted by a large model of the CSS *Hunley.* The oldest museum in all North America, this is one of the best, first places to stop and get a handle on Lowcountry culture and history. Kids will enjoy the interactive "Discover Me" room upstairs, and history buffs will enjoy the collection of small-press historical books in the gift shop downstairs. The museum also operates the historic Heyward-Washington and Joseph Manigault Houses. No flash photography. Open Mon.-Sat. 9 a.m.-5 p.m., Sunday 1-5 p.m. Admission to any one of the museum's sites (the museum or either house) is $7 adults, $4 ages 3-12; admission to two is $12 adults, $8 children; admission to all three is $18 adults, $12 children.

Joseph Manigault House

As long as you're here, you might as well head across John St. to this house at 350 Meeting St., tel. (843) 723-2926, a national historical landmark also owned by the Charleston Museum. Many consider this house, built in 1803 by amateur architect Gabriel Manigault, the premier example of Adams-style architecture in the country. Open daily, $6 if visited individually, $3 children.

Aiken-Rhett House

And while you're over *there,* why not take in the Aiken-Rhett House, 48 Elizabeth St., tel. (843) 723-1159, begun in 1817. The former home of Governor William Aiken Jr., this unique three-story home also served as headquarters for C.S.A. General P.G.T. Beauregard during the war. This house has been preserved pretty much as it was during the Aiken-Rhett days, with the original wallpaper, paint colors, and many of the original furnishings still there. Ask the staff at the museum for directions to the house. Admission to the Aiken-Rhett house is $7 adults, free for children; admission to the Aiken-Rhett and the Samuel Russell House (as well as the Powder Magazine) is $12 adults. Open Mon.-Sat. 10 a.m.-5 p.m. (last 40-minute tour starts at 4:15), Sunday 2-5 p.m. (last tour at 4:15).

African-American
National Heritage Museum

This is actually a collection of sites in the Charleston area, with its hub at the **Slave Mart Museum** on Chalmers Street. Fittingly—given the city's prominent role in slave importation— this is one of the nation's premier museums exploring the origins and contributions of African-American culture in the U.S. Other museum properties include the reconstructed **McLeod Plantation,** tel. (843) 723-1623, where you can find a complex of antebellum home, farm structures, and slave dwellings. Open by advance appointment only, so call ahead.

Daughters of the Confederacy Museum

For the other side of the story, visit this facility, upstairs above the Old City Market. It has been closed for renovation, but it should be open again by the time you get here. Call (843) 723-1541 before noon for information.

Museum on the Common

This is one of my favorite smaller museums. It features the "Hurricane Hugo Revisited" exhibit. Find it at 217 Lucast St., Shem Creek Village, Mount Pleasant, tel. (843) 849-9000.

Gibbes Museum of Art

This museum, at 135 Meeting St., tel. (843) 722-2706, has presented outstanding collections of American art to the public since 1905, with an emphasis on portraits relating to Southern history. Artists represented include Benjamin West, Thomas Sully, and Rembrandt. The museum also includes Japanese wood-block prints and one of the world's best collections of miniatures, with over 7,000 pieces to view. Each year, the Gibbes presents dozens of exhibitions by regional, national, and internationally known artists.

If you come for nothing else, come for the local artwork; Alice Ravenel Huger Smith, Anna Heyward Taylor, and other Lowcountry artists have created an impressive body of work focused on the Holy City.

The museum also offers films, lectures, videos, talks, and symposia on the works and on the arts in general. Art classes for all ages are also held here quarterly, in case viewing all this fine work makes your palette hand twitch.

Allow yourself time to browse the museum shop as well. The building itself was erected as a memorial to James Shoolbred Gibbes; it's Charleston's best example of beaux arts architecture. Open Tues.-Sat. 10 a.m.-5 p.m., Sunday 1-5 p.m. Admission $5 adults, $3 children, $4 seniors. Find parking on nearby Queen and Cumberland Streets. For a guided tour, call ahead and ask for the Education Department. Photography prohibited. Handicapped accessible.

Avery Research Center for African-
American History and Culture

Even if the College of Charleston (125 Bull St.) wasn't one of the most beautiful college campuses in America, the Avery Research Center, tel. (843) 727-2009, Web site: www.cofc.edu/library/avery/avery.html, would make it worth a visit. The research center, set in the restored 1868 Avery Normal School for freedpersons, is a research center for documenting and preserving the history and culture of Lowcountry African-Americans. Includes the John's Island Collection of historical photographs and taped gospel music. Reading room and archives. Open Mon.-Sat. noon-5 p.m. Walk-in tours are offered Mon.-Fri. 2-4 p.m., Sunday noon-5 p.m. Donation requested.

American Military Museum

Here, at 40 Pinckney St., tel. (843) 723-9620, you'll find uniforms and other artifacts from every U.S. war and from every branch of the service.

Patriots Point Naval and Maritime Museum

Among the exhibits here, tel. (843) 884-2727, across the harbor from the city, you'll find a little thing called the aircraft carrier **USS Yorktown.** Those fascinated by things nautical—or easily bullied by those who are—can also tour a submarine, a destroyer, and a re-creation of a Vietnam naval support base.

Clanging your way around these ships can be fascinating, though you should note that most of the tours are inaccessible to the wheelchair-bound, and anyone may find the climbing from deck to deck something of a challenge, especially on a hot day. Also, claustrophobes should think twice before descending into the *Clagamore* submarine.

On the hangar deck of the USS *Yorktown,* you'll find the **Congressional Medal of Honor Museum,** 40 Patriots Point Rd., tel. (843) 884-8862, headquarters of the Congressional Medal of Honor Society. The Medal of Honor, of course, is the highest award for valor in action that the U.S.A. awards to servicemen and -women. The museum divides up into the eight eras of U.S. military history: the Civil War, Indian Campaigns, Wars of American Expansion, Peacetime, World War I, World War II, Korea, and Vietnam. Some of the recipients' names you'll probably recognize—Audie Murphy, Sergeant Alvin York—while

---

ELIZA LUCAS PINCKNEY

When Charleston's Eliza Lucas Pinckney died of cancer in Philadelphia in 1793, President George Washington—at his own request—served as one of her pallbearers. This was a fitting finale to the life of one of America's most accomplished 18th-century women.

Born in the West Indies around 1722, Eliza came to Carolina with her family in 1738, at the age of fifteen. Her father, Major George Lucas, owned a large plantation overlooking Wappoo Creek "seventeen miles by land and six by water" from Charleston. The Lucases owned other plantations around the colony. In 1739, the political conflicts between Spain and England required the elder Lucas to return to his military post in Antigua. With her brothers schooling in England and her mother an invalid, Eliza was left to supervise the 600-acre Wappoo plantation (including its 20 slaves) and to maintain correspondence with the overseers who managed the plantations on the Combahee and Waccamaw.

Since many of the rice markets were unavailable now that they were at war with Spain, at her father's suggestion Eliza began methodically experimenting with raising indigo. In 1740, 1741, and on through 1744 she experimented with raising a promising grade of indigo. By the end of 1744 she had impressed the British government—which wanted the dark blue dye for their uniforms.

By 1745, the Lucases were making a large income from the crop. The sales saved the family's Wappoo plantation. In 1744 she married Charles Pinckney, South Carolina's first native lawyer, a widower more than twice her age. He built her a home in Charleston overlooking the harbor, and they also lived on the Belmont Plantation on the Cooper River. Eliza bore four children, three of whom lived to adulthood; her daughter, Harriet, ended up marrying into the Horry family of Hampton Plantation and competently managed that plantation after her husband died. Eliza's two sons, Charles

Cotesworth and Thomas, became important American leaders during the Revolutionary period. After spending five years living in England, the family returned to the colonies in 1758, whereupon the elder Charles immediately was stuck with malaria. He died in Mount Pleasant and is buried in St. Philip's churchyard.

Eliza survived her grief and went on to take care of the family's long-neglected Belmont Plantation, along with the islands they owned near Hilton Head (today known as Pinckney Island), the Pinckney Plains plantation west of the upper Ashley, the 1,000-acre Auckland tract on the Ashepoo River, and several others. She also oversaw two homes on East Bay Street in Charleston.

During the Revolution, Eliza's slaves deserted the plantation for the British camps, where they were promised freedom, though smallpox immediately broke out there and many died. Charles Cotesworth Pinckney became a brigadier general by war's end and was elected to the General Assembly in 1782. He was named one of South Carolina's delegates to the national Constitutional Convention in 1787. That same year Thomas had been elected governor of the state, and the following year he presided at the State Convention that ratified the Constitution. Both men were national candidates for the Federalist party; when President Washington made a tour of the South in 1791, he stopped at Hampton Plantation for breakfast with the Pinckneys and Horrys.

Just a year later, Eliza journeyed to Philadelphia to consult a doctor famous for cancer cures. She died there on May 26, 1793, and was buried the next day, with President Washington as one of her pallbearers. She was 70 years old.

The Letterbook of Eliza Lucas Pinckney includes a fascinating collection of letters, most from her indigo-experimenting years, but spanning in all 1739-1762. You can pick up a copy in most any South Carolina library, as well as from Sandlapper Publishing.

others you may not, such as Marcario Garcia, who single-handedly assaulted two German machine-gun emplacements during WW II, and Brent Woods, one of the African-American Indian fighters dubbed "buffalo soldiers" by their foes. Admission: $10 adults, $5 children. Open daily.

Fort Sumter National Monument

To access Fort Sumter, the spot where Union Major Robert Anderson holed up with his garrison and awaited relief from the North, sparking the first shots of the Civil War, you'll need to take a boat either from Patriots Point or the City Marina. Call (843) 722-1691 for rates and schedules.

Charles Pinckney National Historic Site

Take Hwy. 17 north through Mount Pleasant proper, past the Isle of Palms Connector, and you'll come to the point where Long Point Rd. tees onto Hwy. 17 at Christ Church, a Colonial-era, still-active Episcopal church. Turn left, following the brown National Park Service signs, go up a mile or so, and you'll arrive at Charles Pinckney National Historic Site, 1254 Long Point Rd., tel. (843) 881-5516, a 28-acre spot preserved from the former 715-acre Snee Farm, a plantation owned by Charles Pinckney (1757-1824), framer of the U.S. Constitution, four-time South Carolina governor, and U.S. Ambassador to Spain under President Jefferson, 1801-05. Pinckney is one of those guys in the background of all the famous historical paintings like Louis S. Glanzman's *Signing of the Constitution,* where you can see Pinckney rubbing elbows with George Washington, James Madison, and other varsity squad Founding Fathers.

One of the things about historic sites like this one, and Fort Moultrie across the marshes over on Sullivan's Island, is that they are not nearly as imposing as most NPS properties tend to be. It's a good spot to spend a couple of hours, though—George Washington did so back in 1791, while making his triumphant presidential tour of the South. Though no standing structures remain from the Pinckney era, the folks in the National Park Service have turned a circa-1820 Lowcountry home into a nice visitors center and museum. It includes a display of the archaeological work going on here (more than 150,000 artifacts have been recovered thus far), as well as exhibits showing the efforts of the

African-American slaves (and, later, sharecroppers) who made Snee Farm a successful farm.

The South Carolina Aquarium

Slated to open in spring 2000, this 93,000-square-foot marvel will feature some 10,000 animals and 5,000 plants, representing some 500 animal species indigenous to the state. The aquarium's more than 60 exhibits will focus on the state's water life, beginning with the Blue Ridge ecosystems of the northeast, then moving on to include life forms found in the state's rivers, swamps, and salt marshes, and off its shores. The aquarium actually sticks some 200 feet out over the Cooper River, reinforcing the aquatic theme and giving guests the chance to spot the dolphins who frequent the waters. Since state law forbids the impounding of marine mammals, this is as close as visitors will get to this particular species.

Built in a former industrial area—part of it a federal Superfund site—the aquarium is the centerpiece of Joe Riley's master plan for this part of the Cooper River. That plan will also eventually include, among other things, a new departure marina for the boats to Fort Sumter. The total improvement to the area should cost well over $100 million, but the project is bound to push Charleston's ratings as a desirable vacation and relocation destination even higher.

Admission prices will apparently come in at just under $15 for adults, with probable discounts and/or specials for state residents. Call (843) 720-1990, e-mail Tara Stewart at tstewart@ scaquarium.org., or see the Web site www. scaquarium.org. for the latest news.

The Citadel:
The Military College of South Carolina

Located at 171 Moultrie St., tel. (800) 868-3294 (868-DAWG) or (843) 953-6726, the Citadel Military College moved over here across from Charles Town Landing back in 1922, after 80

[The Citadel] is still one of the last places in America where a Brooklyn boy can learn to become a southerner and where a southerner can learn to become a Confederate.

—Pat Conroy

When cadet Pat Conroy attended the Citadel in the late 1960s, and when I taught there briefly in the mid-1990s, we spent most of our time in Capers Hall (home of the English Department), named for one of the most distinguished graduates of the Citadel, Confederate General, Episcopal Bishop, and Sewanee Chancellor Ellison Capers, class of 1857.

Apparently, Capers was always a man of deep spiritual devotion. The following prayer is attributed to him while he was a cadet here. Tom Law, one of Capers' fellow cadets, recorded the prayer thus:

Lord of love
Look from above
Upon this tainted ham;
And give us meat
That's fit to eat
For this ain't worth a damn.

years at Marion Square in the Old Citadel. The Old Citadel building was originally built in 1822 after the Vesey conspiracy was uncovered, as a place for whites to hole up in the event of another slave uprising. Though originally this first building kept a standing army of professional soldiers—as did the Arsenal, now the Governor's House, in Columbia—Governor Peter Richardson suggested in 1842 that it would be cheaper and smarter to replace the professional soldiers with young men who could both provide protection and receive military and "practical" training. By 1861, the two schools merged into the single South Carolina Military Academy.

On January 9, 1861, Citadel cadets stationed on Morris Island fired the first shot of the War for Southern Independence, firing on the Union steamer *Star of the West* as it attempted to reprovision the Union soldiers garrisoned at Fort Sumter. After the war, Union soldiers occupied the old campus until 1881, after which the South Carolina Military Academy reopened under the state's jurisdiction and quickly became the training ground for the state's business and political leaders. In 1919, the City of Charleston donated the present 200-acre site to the college, which was in need of expansion.

When you get there, just tell the cadet at the gate to direct you to the museum. You'll find the

Citadel Museum, 171 Moultrie St., tel. (843) 953-6846, on the third floor of the Daniel Library, the first building to your right inside the main gate. The museum features the history of the Citadel, with photographs highlighting exhibits that attempt to document the military, academic, social, and athletic aspects of cadet life. Open Sun.-Fri. 2-5 p.m., Saturday noon-5 p.m. No admission. Closed when the college is.

Next to the library is the Summerall Chapel. If you go inside, walk quietly—the poor harassed first-year cadets ("knobs") sometimes sneak in here to take a nap on a pew. If it's Christmastime, ask around and see when they've scheduled the candlelight service, a memorable spectacle that you'll want to catch, if possible.

Of course, the most famous Citadel graduate of the past 40 years is novelist Pat Conroy, who drew upon his experiences here to write two of his earliest books: 1970's *The Boo,* a nonfiction biography of Thomas Nugent "The Boo" Courvoisie, the Commandant of Cadets during Conroy's time there, and 1980's fictional *The Lords of Discipline,* also set at the Citadel. In *Lords,* Conroy changes the school's name to "The Institute," and changes The Boo's name to "The Bear."

Folks at the Citadel don't generally take to the latter book, which revolves around corruption in the ranks of the cadets and the school administration. In fact, when *Lords* was made into a movie, the filmmakers had to film the campus scenes at an institute up north.

Continue along to Mark Clark Hall, where you'll find a canteen and gift shop, both open to civilians. To find out about Citadel events, including Bulldogs games, call (800) 868-DAWGS or (843) 953-6726.

The campus looked as though a squad of thin, humorless colonels had designed it. . . . There was a perfect, almost heartbreaking, congruence to its furious orthodoxy. To an unromantic eye, the Institute had the look of a Spanish prison or a fortress beleaguered not by an invading force but by the more threatening anarchy of the twentieth century buzzing insensately outside the Gates of Legrand.

—Pat Conroy, The Lords of Discipline, 1980

> *The US population is 271 million. . . . They estimate that next year they will add 2.3 million people. I think half of them are moving to Mount Pleasant.*
>
> —Woody Windham, 1998

MOUNT PLEASANT

The East Cooper area includes beautiful antebellum Mount Pleasant, fun-and-sun Isle of Palms, and historic Sullivan's Island. Mount Pleasant is a subtly beautiful Lowcountry town founded in 1680. Erase the cars parked on the sides of the narrow streets, and you can well imagine that it's 1859 here. Not surprisingly, even many island dwellers consider a move inland to Mount Pleasant a move "up." Novelists Bret Lott and Josephine Humphries and former Milwaukee Brewers star Gorman Thomas all call the town home.

Other than the Patriots Point Naval and Maritime Museum, Hurricane Hugo Museum, and Boone Hall Plantation (see above), one of the best things to do in Mount Pleasant is to walk around the Old Village.

ISLE OF PALMS AND SULLIVAN'S ISLAND

On the north lip of Charleston Harbor, Sullivan's Island is a beautiful southern beach retreat, home of Fort Moultrie, which was the site of a famous Revolutionary battle, the burial place of great Seminole chief Osceola (who died while incarcerated here), and sometime home of Edgar Allan Poe (who, while stationed here, found the settings for such famous stories as "The Gold Bug," and, some argue, "Fall of the House of Usher") and Lieutenant (later General) William Tecumseh Sherman. Along with Fort Wagner on the southern side of the harbor, Fort Moultrie was designed to work in unison with Fort Sumter in providing protection for Charleston Harbor. Hence it's doubly ironic that Moultrie's guns were used for firing upon the Union-held Sumter at the start of the Civil War.

Today, besides some pretty good surfing, Sullivan's Island is best known for its unpretentious but expensive homes (some built in former military bunkers), a handful of nice seafood restaurants, and Fort Moultrie, now part of Fort Sumter National Monument. Isle of Palms was developed relatively recently—around the turn of the century—and for a long time was accessible only by ferry. In the early 1900s it became a tourist destination, with a giant pavilion and the second-largest Ferris wheel in the world spinning high overhead. Hurricanes inspired renovation of the town's layout, and today the Isle of Palms, while still a tourist destination, largely serves as the beach for East Cooper residents and a favorite dinner destination for Charlestonians. The north part of the island, untouched jungle until the 1970s, is now the home of the Wild Dunes Resort, a megaplex of jungle condos, bungalows, and golf courses. Wild Dunes is a popular destination for people boating the East Coast along the Intracoastal Waterway.

History

The Breach Inlet between Isle of Palms and Sullivan's Island has made the history books twice. First, during the American Revolution, British General Cornwallis landed a regiment of troops on Isle of Palms and tried to sneak them south across the shallow inlet and onto the north end of

> *[Sullivan's] island is a very singular one. It consists of little else than the sea sand, and is about three miles long. Its breadth at no point exceeds a quarter of a mile. It is separated from the mainland by a scarcely perceptible creek, oozing its way through a wilderness of reeds and slime, a favorite resort of the marsh-hen. The vegetation, as might be supposed, is scant, or at least dwarfish. No trees of any magnitude are to be seen. Near the western extremity, where Fort Moultrie stands, and where are some miserable frame buildings, tenanted, during summer, by the fugitives from Charleston dust and fever, may be found, indeed, the bristly palmetto; but the whole island, with the exception of this western point, and a line of hard, white beach on the sea-coast, is covered with a dense undergrowth of the sweet myrtle so much prized by the horticulturists of England.*
>
> —Edgar Allan Poe, "The Gold Bug," 1828

Sullivan's Island. They hoped to rear-surprise the Americans holding down the palmetto-log fortress on Sullivan's southern tip, but unfortunately for Cornwallis, the inlet proved treacherous. While attempting to march across its swift currents, dozens of his men drowned or were picked off midstream by American sharpshooters. The British retreated.

In the 1860s Confederate soldiers launched the *Hunley*—claimed by some as the world's first successful submarine—from Breach Inlet's shore. Pedaled by one man and steered by another, the sub slipped southward around Sullivan's Island and successfully planted and exploded a bomb on one of the Union ships blockading Charleston Harbor, but sank itself (with both hands) in the process. The wreck of this pioneer sub was finally discovered in 1995 by a team headed by popular novelist Clive Cussler. It turned out to be much smaller than historians had believed. At publication, authorities were still arguing over whether the ship could or should be raised.

Pencil-thin for protection from winds, this lighthouse stands on Sullivan's Island.

Sights

Fort Moultrie, 1214 Middle St., Sullivan's Island, tel. (843) 883-3123, Web site: www.nps.gov/fomo is officially a part—the larger part—of Fort Sumter National Monument, featuring a visitors center where you should take time to watch the short but worthwhile film giving the history of the fort. The present-day Fort Moultrie is in a sense the third fort to occupy the south end of Sullivan's. The first was the palmetto-log fort that took a beating, but, held during a fierce June 28, 1776, battle against nine British warships. The current fort, its 15-foot walls encompassing 1.5 acres, was completed in 1809, though improvements—including radar—continued on through WW II. During the Civil War, Fort Moultrie held some 40 guns and 500 Confederate soldiers, who weathered a 20-month siege that began in 1863. In 1947, when new technological advances made the fort obsolete, Fort Moultrie was deactivated, after 171 years of service. Since its adoption as a national park site in 1961, the interior of the fort has been restored with various weapons and fortifications spanning from the 1820s through WW II.

Fort Moultrie is open daily 9 a.m.-5 p.m. with extended hours in summer. No fee to tour the visitors center, but a small fee—usually $2—is charged to enter the fort. Closed Christmas Day. Partially wheelchair accessible.

Stella Maris Catholic Church, near the fort, is an interesting old church, which, rather than featuring a large crucifix above the altar, features a statue of Mary holding the baby Jesus. Every October, the local parishioners hold a Halloween carnival that's worth stopping by for the village ambience.

One other thing to see before you leave the island: down on I'On street you'll see some interesting homes, but by far the most interesting ones are those built in the old bunkers. To see one of these, head over to Middleton Street. It's private property, so be sure to stay out on the street.

BEACHES

My favorite beach in this region is Isle of Palms—but then, I never pack a lunch, so being close to a number of good lunch spots is important to me. If you're looking for a beach-beach, meaning

THE BATTLE OF SULLIVAN'S ISLAND

With war erupting in and around Boston, the British decided their best strategy was to take advantage of the strong loyalist support in the Southern colonies, beginning a military drive from Charles Town that might sweep through the Upcountry, gathering men, and then on through North Carolina and Virginia to sandwich Washington in the north.

Realizing this, the Continentals sent English professional soldier General Charles Lee down to Charles Town to oversee the defense of the town. After inspecting the palmetto log fort at the southern tip of Sullivan's Island, protecting the mouth of the harbor, and after noting that its isolation left its defenders no avenue of retreat, he declared it a "slaughterhouse" and ordered it closed. The stubborn Colonel William Moultrie said he and his men could hold the fort, even if the British guns blasted away the earthworks and the Americans had to hide behind the piles of rubble to await the landing party. And so South Carolina President Rutledge refused to evacuate it. And so it was that on June 18, 1776, as British troop ships sailed to Charles Town, prepared to first seize Sullivan's Island and then the town, they found the fort expertly manned by Colonel William Moultrie and a garrison of men who fought as though their lives depended on it.

Sir Henry Clinton landed 2,000-3,000 men on Long Island (now Isle of Palms), just a narrow inlet to the north of Sullivan's. The plan was that at the same moment the nine British ships began shelling the fort, these trained soldiers would rush across the shallow Breach Inlet, overtake the Americans guarding the opposite shore, and proceed southward down the island to overtake the fort.

Unfortunately for the plan, the Breach Inlet was five feet deeper than British intelligence had said it was. The Brits could not "rush" across, but would have to be ferried across by longboat. The extra time it would take to row vs. wade would slow down the process considerably, since there were only boats enough for 600 redcoats to cross at once, and since 780 Americans under Colonel William Thomson had dug into reinforcements on the opposite shore to prevent just such an attack.

Communication broke down. The infantry on Long Island were as surprised as the Americans when the British ships swooped in closer and opened fire. Uncertain as to what exactly the navy had in mind, and facing severe losses if they tried the assault, the infantry decided to wait until the ships had silenced the Carolinian guns before attempting the crossing. A captain of the British 37th regiment assigned to Long Island wrote, "Very fortunately for us it was not attempted, for in the opinion of all present, from what we have since learned, the first embarkations must have fallen a sacrifice."

Around 11 a.m., the British ships continued on to a point 300 yards (900 yards, according to one British source) from shore, dropped anchor, and opened fire. Moultrie and his 400-plus South Carolinians had little powder and had to ration their shots, but to everyone's surprise—including the relieved Carolinians—the spongy palmetto logs absorbed the British shots. Still, some shots got through, eventually killing 11 Carolinians and wounding 50.

"I never experienced a hotter fire," General Charles Lee, who visited the fort midbattle, later wrote General Washington. But his description reveals that despite 12 hours of this unrelenting barrage, Moultrie's men held out with typical Carolinian obstinance:

The noble fellows who were mortally wounded conjured their brethren never to abandon the standard of liberty. Those who lost their limbs deserted not their posts.

Upon the whole, they acted like Romans in the third century.

No one's quite sure why the British decided they needed to overtake Sullivan's Island first before taking Charleston; possibly they feared entering the harbor and thus exposing themselves to both the guns set up on the southern side of the harbor as well as Moultrie's. Presumably, had they won Sullivan's Island, they would have established a base of operations on the relatively secure site, from which they might begin the taking of Charleston.

When the British troops on Long Island awoke the next day, they saw that their British boats had disappeared. In truth, the British ships had lost hundreds of men, including Royal Governor William Campbell. A few weeks later, complaining that "The heat of the weather now is almost become intolerable," the sweltering Brits were picked up by British ships and taken north to other perils.

This key victory caused the British to rethink their strategy and abandon the South for nearly three years.

DOVER PUBLICATIONS, INC.

attack on Fort Moultrie

crowd; it's a great place to join a pickup game of volleyball or watch one of the recurring tournaments.

Isle of Palms is really a great little beachy sort of beach, with its hamburger shops and beach bars right there on the water, although the arrival of a new hotel may change things a bit.

Sullivan's Island

Named for Captain Florence O'-Sullivan, captain of the *Carolina,* Sullivan's today has some of the better surf in the area, right down by 21st Street. This area has become one of the pricier addresses in the Charleston area; if you can't afford to buy on the Battery, you might just have to settle for ocean-front on Sullivan's. The challenge of going to the beach here is the lack of a parking lot; just park on a residential street, but make sure no signs forbid it. At the south end of the island (down by Fort Moultrie) swimming's prohibited. And a good thing, too—it's dangerous there. But don't let that stop you from heading down after a day at

bikini shops, hamburger stands, and board rentals, then you'll want to hit either Isle of Palms—right around the Isle of Palms County Park at the end of the Isle of Palms Connector—or Folly Beach.

Isle of Palms

One of the reasons that Isle of Palms is now so easy to reach—via the 1994 Isle of Palms Connector—is because the owner of the Windjammer bar campaigned to get the road built and then immediately began broadcasting to all the young party animals of Charleston how easy it was to get out to Isle of Palms. When he was the first person mugged by unsavory youth drawn by the "easy access" and good times, a lot of people had a hard time feeling sorry for him. But all that aside, Charleston County has built a nice recreational facility on the water at Isle of Palms. This is for the loud, tan, bikini-and-bathing suit

the beach to visit Fort Moultrie and walk along the beach where you'll have a great view of Fort Sumter and, if you're fortunate, a huge ship that passes by like a city block on water.

Folly Beach

Folly Beach has always had great bumper stickers. It calls itself "The Edge of America." After Hugo, when most of the beach's famed white sands were swept away, a new bumper sticker began to appear: "Where's the Beach?" Now with beach renourishment programs, the beach is back, though no one thinks it will be here very long. Better see it while you can.

Folly Beach has served many roles in its history: from Civil War killing field to Southern Coney Island, from archaeological excavation site to countercultural refuge, and, increasingly, to upscale Charleston oceanfront suburb.

The island first appears on history's radar during the Civil War, when Union troops stationed at

Hilton Head waded through waist-high water onto the south end of Folly Beach as part of their attempt to capture Fort Wagner, the nearly impregnable Confederate fort on Morris Island, north of Folly Beach. In the 1930s and 1940s, the Folly Pavilion provided great dancing; an amusement park drew the kids. Ira Gershwin stayed down here to pick up local flavor while writing the score to *Porgy and Bess*. But tide, time, and storms have taken all of those away from Folly, though in the last few years a new fishing pier has opened, and the Holiday Inn has become a favorite place for local shaggers.

If Hurricane Hugo (1989) had a good side, it is that in passing through it ripped open the sands enough to expose some long-hidden archaeological remnants from the Union encampments on Folly Island. Five months after the storm, a number of Folly residents and beachcombers called to report that they'd found bones on the beaten-up island. Archaeologists raced out and quickly identified the bones as cattle bones. Big deal.

Fortunately, Rod O'Conner, a former Folly Beach policeman, shortly thereafter notified the Charleston Museum that he'd found not just bones, but leather remnants. Local members of the Underwater Archaeological Division, South Carolina Institute of Archaeology and Anthropology, headed out to the scene, collected what they could, and got the U.S. Coast Guard, which controlled the land, to allow a dig to take place immediately. Time was running out—the sand in which the artifacts lay was daily being lost to the ocean.

From April 24 through November, archaeologists removed as many artifacts as they could, while the ocean ate away at the dig site. By November, the remaining land yielded little. The site was officially closed.

Fortunately, two years later, when the Coast Guard prepared to relinquish control of the property, federal laws required them to commission an archaeological survey of the entire area. A private archaeological firm located remnants of the assault batteries and other important occupation-era features on the island. They recommended that the land be preserved as an historic park, and most of it has been acquired by the Department of Parks, Recreation and Tourism with plans to preserve it as a park.

Partly because it had had some of the tackiest pre-Hugo buildings, Folly took one of the worst hits from the storm, and took the longest to recover. You could walk here for years after Hugo and find telephones and food processors still buried in the Folly sand. But when the buildings finally went back up, they began reflecting the increased value of the oceanfront property. As *Post and Courier* reporter Linda L. Meggett reported, prices had begun to climb significantly by early 1998. A vacant lot assessed for $45,400 in 1993, for example, sold for $100,000 in March 1996. The starting sale price of the villas in the new 96-unit complex on West Arctic Ave. opened at $169,000 in 1997. By early 1998, it had climbed to $240,000. For a villa, mind you—essentially a condo.

The dreadlocks seem to be headed out and the dread Yuppies are on their way in, paying too much for houses and thus pushing up everyone's assessments and, thus, their property taxes.

Kiawah's Beachwalker Park

This is the only public beach on Kiawah Island; it's a beautiful stretch of beach—about 300 feet worth—with restrooms, dressing areas, outdoor showers, a snack bar, picnic area, and parking. It's on Beachwalker Drive, at the west end of the island, tel. (843) 762-2172. Unfortunately, the rest of the island is privately owned.

COLLEGES

With nearly 11,000 students, the **College of Charleston,** a.k.a. University of Charleston, is the largest in the area, offering both BA and MA degrees. It has something of a reputation as a creative school, and as a party school. It's also one of the most beautiful campuses in America. It was used in the filming of TV's *Scarlett,* the alleged sequel to *Gone With the Wind*—but don't hold that against it. Founded in 1770, chartered in 1785, opened in 1790, and made a municipal college in 1837, this is the oldest municipal college in America. Attendance used to be free to Charleston students—it was considered a natural extension of the K-12 free education. It's a wonderful place to walk around, though the area can get a little dicey at night.

The College of Charleston **Robert Scott Small Library** is open for varying hours throughout the year. **The Avery Research Center,** tel. (843) 953-7609, is open Mon.-Sat. noon-5 p.m., closed Sunday. Open before noon by appointment only.

Charleston Southern University is a private Baptist school lodged deep in North Charleston. Its campus is modern but still reasonably attractive, and the basketball team is top-notch.

ACCOMMODATIONS

Charleston is full of charming places to stay, from quaint B&Bs to world-class hotels, from seaside cottages to beautiful campsites overlooking the undulating golden salt marshes. And there are also a number of cheaper, more practical motels for those who would rather spend their money at the restaurants and clubs than at the hotel desk.

My listings here are necessarily incomplete; I've given you a sampling of the different types of lodgings available, but feel free to stop into the visitors center on the way into town and browse the racks of pamphlets by the many different businesses offering a place to sleep in the Holy City. If you stumble upon a really first-rate place I've failed to mention, drop me a line about it so we can tip off other folks who would appreciate the things it has to offer. This way you can be more sure it will still be around next time you come to town.

There are a couple different ways you might approach lodging in Charleston. One is to find somewhere quiet off in the wilderness not 25 minutes away from the downtown historic district. Another approach is to grab a room at one of the local beaches, making daily or nightly trips into the Holy City for sightseeing and entertainment.

Approach number three is to find a cheaper place on the outskirts, in Summerville or North Charleston, or maybe over in West Ashley. The upside of this is that you can save some money. The downside is that you probably won't save *that* much money from the better-value downtown spots, and you'll be spending your evenings staring at the glare of a Shoney's or Waffle House sign rather than the quaint flickering gaslights of the historic district.

Which brings me to approach number four, which is to stay downtown as cheaply as possible. This is usually my strategy. There's just nothing like waking up early and strolling down Market or King until the smell from some coffeehouse or bakery yanks me in off the street.

And if it's possible to fall in love with a city, I can pinpoint the moment I fell in love with Charleston for the first time: it was 7 a.m. and I stumbled downstairs from the King Charles Inn and sat out in front of Fulford and Egan (since closed) on Meeting Street, sipping a mocha as the dawn stretched over the weathered storefronts and wet, deserted streets.

Approach number five is paying whatever it costs to stay wherever you want in the quaint spots downtown. This isn't normally an option for me, but if it's an option for you, skip ahead to the "Luxury" section below.

One note: High seasons for many Charleston lodging spots are spring and fall, meaning that you'll find low season (with rate reductions of up to 50%) in the heat of summer—after Spoleto—as well as in the chill of winter. And winter is not always that chilly either. December temperatures often sneak up into the 70s.

HISTORIC DISTRICT

Moderate ($60-85)
I like the **Best Western King Charles Inn,** right downtown at 237 Meeting St., tel. (843) 723-7451. Sure, your balcony (if you get one) probably doesn't look out over much, but it's an excellent base to head out from and return to each day, and the rooms are spacious and reasonably priced. Since a lot of business travelers stay here, you can sometimes get pretty good rates on the weekends. Recently, the inn underwent a major renovation, with the entire eastern facade replaced with a stucco surface, a secondary lobby added, and the guest rooms enlarged. Now it fits into the neighborhood even better than before.

The new-on-the-block **Hampton Inn: Historic District,** 345 Meeting St., tel. (800) 426-7866 or (843) 723-4000, fax (843) 722-3725, sits beside the Charleston Visitors Center, in itself a reasonable walk from the Market area, though you can take one of the Center trams, which are always heading down into the historic district. Though it's relatively new, this place seems like it's been here forever; it features antique reproductions in the rooms and lobby. Offers a nice, gated pool and an exercise room. This might be perfect for you if you don't mind being right on top of things.

When I'm not feeling particularly wealthy or adventurous, I usually find Days Inns to be a safe bet. If you're looking for a clean bed and decent service; downtown you might want to head over to **Days Inn: Historic District,** 155 Meeting St., tel. (843) 722-8411. Call (800) DAYS INN to get the central reservations number, or go online to www.daysinn.com. The facility here looks like a revamped motel, but you can't beat the location, right next door to the Meeting Street Inn.

For my money—or, for that matter, for your money—**Meeting Street Inn,** 173 Meeting St., tel. (800) 842-8022 or (843) 723-1882, fax (843) 577-0851, is one of the most romantic spots to stay in the city. It features a very nice courtyard with a number of fountains and tables, and large, beautiful rooms with wallpaper, West Indian architecture, four-poster rice beds (in most rooms), armoires, and wood shutters on the windows. Ask for a room on the ground floor so your view will look out into the courtyard and not over the courtyard wall and into the Days Inn parking lot. If no first-floor rooms are available, then ask for a room on an upper floor (there are four) in the high numbers—you'll be able to step out onto your back balcony and see the main entrance to Charleston Place, beautifully lit at night. A stellar staff here, and room rates include continental breakfast and an afternoon wine-and-cheese reception.

Premium ($100-150)
One of the most intimate spots in Charleston is the **Elliott House,** 78 Queen St., tel. (843) 723-1855, with a charming, fully enclosed courtyard, built on the site of original buildings designed by Robert Mills. If you call, ask about the packages—the "Get Away" includes three nights in a queen room with parking, a horse-drawn tour for two, and a tour of Sumter, all for $383. Summer and winter "low-season" rates run about $94. Expect to pay about 50% more for high season. Room rates here include use of the hotel's many bikes—perfect for exploring the nooks and crannies of the historic district.

A nice spot right up by the College of Charleston is **Barksdale House Inn,** 27 George St., tel. (843) 577-4800. Only 14 rooms here, so the feeling is intimate. Nice floral prints on the walls, armoires, four-poster beds. You'll discover a bottle of wine or champagne in the room every night, teas and sherry on the back porch in the afternoon. Located right in the midst of the historic district. $69-150 single or double. Children 7 and older only.

Battery Carriage House Inn is right down on the Battery, tel. (843) 727-3100 or (800) 775-5575, fax (843) 727-3130, with 11 rooms featuring four-poster beds, hardwood floors, quilted bedspreads, and so on. Continental breakfast only, unfortunately—down here on the Battery, it's not like you can walk around the corner and get shrimp and grits.

Rooms at the **Indigo Inn,** 1 Maiden Ln., tel. (843) 577-5900 or (800) 845-7639, fax (843) 577-0378 face an interior courtyard with a fountain.

The four-story circa 1844 **Planters Inn,** Market at Meeting St., tel. (843) 722-2345 or (800) 845-7082, fax (843) 577-2125, offers 62 rooms and a number of suites with fireplaces and whirlpool baths.

Farther up the peninsula, at Citadel Square you'll find the **Francis Marion Hotel,** 387 King st., tel. (843) 722-0600, built in 1924 as part of a push to turn Charleston into a tourism center. The Francis Marion was hit hard by Hugo and underwent a major $12 million renovation by the Westin Company in the 1990s as part of Mayor Joe Riley's effort to bring a renaissance to this stretch of King Street.

Luxury ($150 and up)
And the waterfront was darkness, and the spirit of the South Bronx ran too and fro across the face of the peninsula.

This is how things were before the Omni, renamed **Charleston Place,** corner of King and Meeting Streets, tel. (843) 722-4900, (800) 611-5545, opened up in 1986. Today, it's owned by the same folks who own and run the famous Orient Express. A couple years back, *Travel and Leisure* rated Charleston Place the 54th best hotel in *the world,* placing it above such also-rans as New York's Ritz-Carlton (72), London's The Ritz (81), Los Angeles' Hotel Bel-Air (87), and the Four Seasons hotels in Boston (76),

New York (97), and London (100). Of hotels in the continental U.S., Charleston Place ranked 20th. *Condé Nast Traveler* ranked it as one of the U.S.A.'s top 10.

While the Francis Marion Hotel was under refurbishment during the 1990s, another exceptional renovation took place about the same time across Calhoun Square at the original Citadel Building. After months of work, the **Embassy Suites,** 337 Meeting St., tel. (800) 362-2779 or (843) 723-6900, emerged, offering elegant two-room units, 12 rooms with whirlpools, and a complimentary full breakfast.

The **Mills House,** 115 Meeting St., is a fine reconstruction of a famed antebellum inn, right downtown at the corner of Queen and Meeting, tel. (800) 874-9600 or (843) 577-2400. Robert E. Lee and Teddy Roosevelt both raved about it.

Of course, if Bob and Teddy aren't big enough names, you might want to head over to the **John Rutledge House Inn,** 116 Broad St., tel. (843) 723-7999, where no less than George Washington once sat down to breakfast. And traveling writers take note: the former owner, John Rutledge, brainstormed on a little thing called the U.S. Constitution in one of the inn's rooms. Wine and sherry are offered each evening in the ballroom.

A new spot down in the nighttime quiet by Waterfront Park is the appropriately named **HarbourView Inn,** 2 Vendue Range, tel. (800) 853-8439 or (843) 853-8439. A little farther back up the street is the very romantic 18th-century **Vendue Inn,** 19 Vendue Range, tel. (800) 845-7900 or (843) 577-7970. Fireplaces in some rooms, a beautiful restaurant, and a rooftop bar. This building was once home to a print shop financed by Benjamin Franklin; when the printer, Lewis Timothy, died, his widow took over and capably managed the business, becoming the first female publisher in the United States. She later handed over the business to her son, Peter Timothy, who daringly used to climb up into the bell tower of St. Michael's and spy on the British troops camped over at James Island.

BED AND BREAKFASTS

Charleston overflows with historic B&Bs. When you stop by the visitors center, be sure to pick up the booklet *Historic Charleston Bed and Break-*

fasts to get the full selection. Below I've listed some of the more interesting and diverse options.

If you'd like to stay in an authentic Charleston Single House, the **1837 Bed and Breakfast,** 126 Wentworth St., tel. (843) 723-7166, gives you just that opportunity—and for under $100 a night (sometimes much under), which includes a full breakfast. This is a bit off the beaten path but still in the old, historic part of Charleston. Eight rooms in all, including some in the carriage house.

Two Meeting Street Inn is a favorite, a pretty Queen Anne Victorian down on the Battery, at 2 Meeting St., tel. (843) 723-7322, facing White Point Gardens, Charleston Harbor, Fort Sumter, and, if your eyes are really good, western England. Afternoon tea and sherry; continental breakfasts.

Built back in 1734, **36 Meeting Street** is at (sensing a pattern?) 36 Meeting St., tel. (843) 722-1034. The lodging offers a private walled garden, authentic Lowcountry rice beds, and kitchenettes.

King's Courtyard Inn, 198 King St., tel. (843) 723-7000, is a very private, very inviting place to stay. Beautiful courtyard, elegant rooms. Best of all, step outside the courtyard and you're right on King St., with a multitude of great places to eat and intriguing antique stores to explore.

Over in the Old Village section of Mount Pleasant, **Guilds Inn Bed and Breakfast,** 101 Pitt St., tel. (800) 331-0510 or (843) 881-0510, is set in an 1888 home with six large rooms/suites with private whirlpool baths, telephones, TVs, and continental breakfast. Next door is the fine Captain Guild's Cafe.

EAST COOPER

Moderate ($60-85)

Before my wife and I moved out to Isle of Palms, we used to stay at the **Ocean Inn,** 1100 Pavilion Blvd., tel. (843) 886-4687, Web site: www.awod.com/oceaninn, e-mail: wwall@awod.com, just a block off the ocean. It's a small place with a laid-back ambience and a little pathway running back to the convenience store out on Palm where you can get late-night munchies. Reasonable rates, especially in the off season, as well as weekly rates. Some rooms feature kitchenettes, which, with all the shrimp you're going to catch while here, would be a good idea.

Last time I was out on the island they were just opening up the 51-room **Seaside Inn**, 1004 Ocean Blvd., tel. (888) 999-6516 or (843) 886-7000, right on the waterfront, amid the bars and beach traffic, but also right on the sand. No pool, but the inn does have a hot tub. You'll find a microwave and refrigerator in every room. Free parking here, which will mean something to you if you're coming during the busy warm-weather months.

Another, catacomby way to go is to rent one of the **Sea Cabins** right beside the county park. These are small and not exactly private, but staying here *does* give you access to private tennis courts, a pool, and a fishing pier. They also (unlike the condos down at Wild Dunes) put you within walking distance of the island's restaurants and shops. Choose between one- or two-bedroom villas. Call Island Realty at (800) 707-6429 or (843) 886-8144, Canada (800) 876-8144 to get a nice, thick brochure.

About as close as you can be to the Isle of Palms without actually being *on* the Isle of Palms is **Hampton Inn & Suites** right at the foot of the Isle of Palms Connector on Hwy. 17 in Mount Pleasant, tel. (843) 856-3900. It sports a tropical, sugarcane-plantation look, with Bermuda shutters; Canary Island date palms; hardwood, stone or woven matted floors; and teak, mahogany and rattan furniture. Forty of the 121 rooms are two-room suites including a full kitchen.

Days Inn: Charleston Patriots Point is at 261 Johnnie Dodds Blvd., Georgetown Exit, Mount Pleasant, tel. (800) 329-7466.

Holiday Inn: Mt. Pleasant is at 250 Johnnie Dodds Blvd., Mount Pleasant, tel. (843) 884-6000.

Premium ($100-150)

If a little bit of city bustle goes a long way with you, consider staying at the **Charleston Harbor Hilton Resort Patriots Point,** 20 Patriots Point Rd., Mount Pleasant, tel. (843) 856-0028, is a new, deluxe resort offering a great across-the-harbor view of Charleston's steepled skyline and blinking lights. Though swimming in the harbor is forbidden (not to mention a bad idea) because of harbor mouth currents, the resort has pools and a nice sand beach to relax on. When I was there they were building some wa-

terside cottages perfect for families; call and ask for rates. You're also a cart-ride away from the Patriots Point Golf Course. The best thing about this place is that the hotel-front water taxi that takes you right over to Waterfront Park and the heart of Charleston's historic district actually makes you closer, time-wise, at the Hilton than you would be at some of the drive-to hotels in West Ashley and East Cooper—especially if you consider the time you won't have to spend looking for parking.

One more additional plus—you can watch the big freight ships pass by your window, something like watching a New York City street slide by.

Or head farther east to the north end of Isle of Palms to **The Boardwalk Inn** at Wild Dunes, 5757 Palm Blvd., tel. (800) 845-8880, ext. 1, or (843) 886-2260, fax (800) 665-0190, Web site: www.wilddunes.com. They've painted these pastel colors in an imitation of Rainbow Row. If you want to golf while in Charleston, this is the place to stay, since it includes the world-ranked Wild Dunes Links, as well as the Harbor Course.

There's also the seaside Grand Pavilion, a mock turn-of-the-century boardwalk without the rides and carnies. Really, it's a charming place, nicer and cleaner than it could be if it were open to the general public—which I guess is the point.

WEST ASHLEY

Moderate
Holiday Inn: On the Beach, 1 Center St., at Folly Beach, tel. (843) 588-6464, Web site: www.holiday-inn.com, is one of several nice Holiday Inn locations. Another is up on the Savannah Highway—**Holiday Inn: Riverview,** 301 Savannah Hwy., tel. (843) 556-7100—and a third is over in Mount Pleasant.

RENTAL HOUSES

You'll find rental houses a-plenty in the beach cities. You might call **Ravenel Associates** for a free 28-page guide on one of the Charleston area's many beach resorts, offering information on lodging rates, golf packages, tours, and more. Call for information on rentals on: Isle of Palms, tel. (800) 365-6114; Kiawah Island, tel. (800) 845-3911; Wild Dunes, tel. (800) 346-0606; Seabrook Island, tel. (800) 845-2233; or Sullivan's Island, tel. (800) 247-5050. For more historic establishments in Charleston itself, call **Carriage House Vacation Accommodations,** 11 New Orleans Rd., tel. (800) 845-6132.

If you're thinking about staying on Folly Beach, consider calling **Fred Holland Realty,** tel. (843) 588-2325; **Seashell Realty,** 34 Center St., Folly Beach, tel. (843) 588-2932; or **Sellers Shelters,** 104 W. Ashley Ave., Folly Beach, tel. (843) 588-2269, ext. 9.

For Kiawah Island rentals, one major player is **Beachwalker Rentals, Inc.** 3690 Bohicket Rd., Suite 4-D, tel. (800) 334-6308 or (843) 768-1777, Web site: www.aesir.com/Beachwalker.

Good places to find a rental on the Isle of Palms or Sullivan's Island are **Carroll Realty, Inc.,** 103 Palm Blvd., Isle of Palms, tel. (800) 845-7718 or (843) 886-9600; **Dunes Properties of Charleston,** 1400 Palm Blvd., tel. (888) 843-2322 or (843) 886-5600; and **Island Realty,** 1304 Palm Blvd., tel. (800) 707-6430 or (843) 886-8144.

CAMPGROUNDS

Unlike most major cities, Charleston offers a number of fine campgrounds within 20 minutes of downtown. As long as it's not high summer, so that you won't be essentially camping in a bug-infested sauna, if you're trying to save your money for the restaurants rather than for your bed, you might want to give it a try. Of area campgrounds, **The Campground at James Island County Park** certainly bears the most inflated name. For Pete's sake—we're talking about a *campground* here. What's next? "The Convenience Store at Isle of Palms"? "The Solid Waste Dump at Orangeburg"?

But I digress. TCAJICP is a neat campground at a nice park, with 125 RV sites, full hookups, 24-hour security, an activity center, the **Splash Zone** water park for the kids, and a roundtrip shuttle service to the historic district and Folly Beach. Reservations recommended. Rates are $24 for sites with full hookup, $22 for water and electricity, $18 for tent sites. TCAJICP, 871 Riverland Dr., James Island, tel. (843) 795-7275 (795-PARK), also offers 10 modern vacation cottages overlooking the Stono River marsh. Each sleeps up to eight and includes a kitchen, TV, and telephone. Rates for the cottages are $99.50 a night, $557 a week. There's a two-night minimum and a two-week maximum stay, and Memorial Day through Labor Day they rent only by the week. (Prices do not include tax.)

In East Cooper, right around the northernmost (so far) tract developments of Mount Pleasant along Hwy. 17, the newish **KOA Mt. Pleasant-Charleston,** 3157 N. Hwy. 17, Mount Pleasant, tel. (843) 849-5177, is a beautiful spot surrounded by pines, set on a pond, and next door to a golf course. Of course, like most KOAs, it's managed to mow down every semblance of a shade tree in the midst of the campground itself, but this one's definitely better than most, while still offering the KOA standard features that have made them so popular: a swimming pool, playground, boat rentals, and so on. A cute little campstore there will keep you from having to run into town for hot cocoa and such. It also has little air-conditioned Kamping Kabins if you forgot to bring your tent, or if it's just too dang-blasted hot to camp properly. Not a bad choice if you just want out of the urbane. Sites and Kamping Kabins (for two) run about $25-35.

There's another **KOA** up Hwy. 178 (just off I-26) in Ladson, south of Summerville, at 9494 Hwy. 78, tel. (843) 797-1045 or (800) 489-4293—not a bad place to stop if you're coming into the area late in the day and don't feel up to taking on Charleston quite yet; it offers pretty much what the Mt. Pleasant one offers. Sites and Kamping Kabins (for two) both run about $20-25.

FOOD

CHARLESTON PROPER

Charleston is one of the best restaurant cities in the United States; to avoid overwhelming you, I've listed 25 or so here that are personal favorites. You won't go wrong if you eat from one of the places on this list, but if you find a spot that's not mentioned here, and it looks good, go ahead and give it a whirl.

Seafood/Lowcountry Cuisine
Hyman's, 215 Meeting Street, tel. (843) 723-6000, is my favorite place for seafood. It's warm, with bright wood paneling and wooden floors, a friendly staff, hot boiled peanuts at your table, healthy meal choices, reasonable prices, and fresh fish daily.

Unfortunately, we made the mistake of telling a few friends, and they apparently told a few friends, and so on, and so on. Now this place is a serious institution: in 1997, *Southern Living* readers from 18 states (from Delaware to Texas) voted on the best seafood houses in all the American South; Hyman's was named No. 2 overall and No. 1 in all of South Carolina. The Hyman family owned the building that was renovated to make the Omni Hotel (now Charleston Place), and they had the foresight to hang onto the two streetfront properties that now comprise Hyman's and **Aaron's Deli,** right next door to Hyman's, and one of our favorite places for breakfast. This place is usually *packed,* with waits that can easily last an hour or more. It doesn't take reservations, so the best you can do is put your name in with the staff person outside on Meeting Street when you first start sensing that you might be starting to think about getting hungry—then go sightsee or shop some more until you reach the time your name should come up.

Better yet, if you're a local, be sure to ask your waiter for a VIP card, which will enable you to slip past the hordes of out-of-towners next time.

For a true locals' haunt, visit the **Blind Tiger Pub/Four Corners Cafe,** at 38 Broad St., tel. (843) 577-0088. Live music and Lowcountry cooking.

Another place to grab some reasonably priced seafood is up King Street, just past where it starts looking dicey. At 467 King St. is **The Bubble Room,** a simply appointed restaurant with occasional live music and outrageous specials like a whole Maine lobster dinner for $8.95 on Monday, and all-you-can-eat snow crab legs for $10.95.

Like Hilton Head's Salty Dog Cafe, **Poogan's Porch** is named after a dog—in this case, the pooch that once graced its porch. Founded in 1976, praised in *Gourmet, Bon Appétit,* and *Cuisine,* Poogan's, 72 Queen St., tel. (843) 577-2337, is set in an old house on a side street and boasts "authentic Southern Cooking." Lunch 11:30 a.m.-

Hyman's Seafood, a deserved Charleston institution, was voted best seafood restaurant in South Carolina in 1997 (and second-best in 18 southern states).

2:30 p.m., dinner 5:30-10:30 p.m. Be sure to try the triple-layer chocolate cake, fried Carolina alligator, Charleston chicken, and anything with shrimp in it. During the warm weather they throw open the windows and you can sit out on the porch; during the winter, they light fires in the fireplaces and the restaurant takes on an intimate, romantic feel. Dress is casual. Reservations are a good idea. About $15 an entrée for dinner.

Anson, 12 Anson Street, tel. (843) 577-0551, tucked back off Meeting St. facing one of the public parking lots, with Orleans railings and torches flickering outside, is one of the prettiest and most expensive restaurants in Charleston, a very romantic spot serving up regional recipes, heavy on the seafood. Open for dinner only, seven days a week. Dinner'll cost you about $15 an entrée.

Over in an old house at 18 Pinckney Street, you'll find **Pinckney Cafe & Expresso,** owned by a husband and wife who live upstairs. A versatile spot: bright and cheery in the morning (you can eat out on the porch), casual at lunch, romantic at night, with full wait service. You'll find creative menu items including some tasty pasta fritters. The espresso and cappuccino are first-rate. And two other important words here: smoke free. Dinners cost around $12 an entrée, but lunch is considerably cheaper, and you don't need to leave a tip. Open Tues.-Sat. Lunch is served 11:30 a.m.-2:30 p.m., dinner 6-10 p.m.

Slightly North of Broad, 192 East Bay St., tel. (843) 723-3424, is one you'll remember; it offers relatively healthy items, plenty of creative seafood and meat entrées. Nice atmosphere; a bit pricey. Dinner should run you about $13 a plate.

Another good spot for seafood downtown is **A.W. Shucks,** 35 Market St., just off East Bay, tel. (843) 723-1151. Casual; a good place for families or large groups. Open Sun.-Thurs. 11:30 a.m.-11 p.m.; open at noon Friday and Saturday. Dinner'll run you anywhere from $6 or $7 on up to over $15.

When Bradley O'Leary wrote his *Dining By Candlelight: American's 200 Most Romantic Restaurants,* he named **Louis's Charleston Grill at Charleston Place** South Carolina's most romantic restaurant. And it is a beautiful, formal spot, looking out on Charleston Place's courtyard. Dinner entrées average around $17, but

the price is worth it if you're tired of conventional Lowcountry fare. You'll find Charleston Place at 139 Market St., tel. (843) 577-4572. It recently won a Mobil Four Star rating. Chef Louis Osteen himself is not there anymore, however: he and wife Marlene have opened their own place, **Louis's Restaurant,** atop the Nations Bank building right across from Charleston Place, tel. (843) 722-6274. You won't go wrong at either place.

Magnolia's 185 East Bay St., tel. (843) 577-7771, describes itself as "Uptown, Down South," and I can't think of a better way to put it. It's located at the site of the original Customs House, overlooking Lodge Alley. Lunch can be downright cheap; dinner easily runs upward of $15 a plate. Reservations are suggested. Open daily 11:30 a.m.-11 p.m., till midnight on Friday and Saturday. A good place to find some worthy Lowcountry dining late at night. Did I mention that it's an entirely nonsmoking restaurant?

Houlihan's at 39 John St., tel. (843) 722-2400, offers dependably good American/Southern fare not far from the visitors center.

One final spot I can't *not* mention: **82 Queen** (82 Queen St.), tel. (843) 723-7591, Web site: www.82queen.com, is a wonderfully romantic spot right between King and Meeting Streets. The She Crab Soup's widely praised; the entrées include everything from crab cakes to Southern Comfort BBQ Shrimp and Grits to a mixed grill of filet mignon, lamb loin, and Carolina quail. Bring a good appetite, nicer casual clothes (no jacket required, though one certainly wouldn't look out of place), and by all means, the plastic. *Southern Living* readers recently voted this the "Best City Restaurant" in the entire South.

Continental

Long considered one of, if not *the* finest dining experience in Charleston, **Robert's of Charleston,** 183 East Bay St., tel. (843) 577-7565, closed down in the early '90s so that owner/chef Robert Dickson could take a break. He reopened in 1998 to a very grateful public. Dickson sings as well as he cooks, and so you'll be treated to operatic selections and songs from Broadway musicals as you dine on the prix fixe; expect to pay $65 a person, not including tax and tip. You needn't worry about what to order; Robert will decide that for you. As you might guess, you'll need advance reservations.

Fast & French Gaulart & Maliclet French Cafe, 98 Broad St., tel. (843) 577-9797, is a very unique, very *narrow* restaurant that feels like a quick trip to the Continent. A good place for lunch.

Italian

If you've been bustling about the historic district all day and can use a little tranquillity, head on over to **Fulton Five** at 5 Fulton St., tel. (843) 853-5555. Here's one of the most intimate restaurants in town. Tucked back off King St. south of Market, Fulton Five offers very fine Northern Italian cuisine. You can dine outside if the weather's nice, or inside. Either way, the ambience is impeccable. Dinners run around $15. Reservations suggested. Open Sun.-Thurs. 5:30-10:30 p.m., till 11 p.m. Friday and Saturday. The owners close the place sometime in mid-August when it gets too hot and open again in early September.

You'll find **Bocci's,** another slightly off-the-beaten-path Italian joint, over at 158 Church St., tel. (843) 720-2121. It serves lunch and dinner daily, but for ambience, come at night, when the soft lighting looks nice on the darkened street.

Steak and Ribs

Sticky Fingers, begun just in 1992, is constantly voted Charleston's "Best Ribs, Barbecue, and Family Dining" joint. Find it at 235 Meeting, at the Market, tel. (843) 853-7427.

The small regional chain, **TBonz Gill and Grill,** is famous for its grilled steaks. The Charleston location is 80 N. Market St., right on the Market, tel. (843) 577-2511. Opens daily at 11 a.m. and closes "late"—so if Dave Letterman gives you a hankering for a rib eye, you may be in luck. Seafood too. Afterward, head next door to the connected Kaminsky's for a rich dessert.

Charleston Chops, 188 E. Bay St., tel. (843) 937-9300, knows how to put out a wonderful piece of meat—including 21-day aged Angus beef. Expect to pay for the high quality—toward or upward of $20 a plate. Nice candlelit ambience; piano music, chandeliers, fountains.

Barbecue (Beyond Charleston— But Worth the Travel)

For a true barbecue joint you'll need to leave the peninsula. One of the oldest (1946) and most revered greater-area spots is **Bessinger's Bar-**

becue, 1124 Sam Rittenberg Blvd., tel. (843) 763-0339, run by Thomas Bessinger and featuring his mustard-based sauce. Hours are Mon.-Wed. 11 a.m.-7 p.m., Thurs.-Sat. until 8 p.m. You'll find another location in West Ashley at 1602 Savannah Hwy., tel. (843) 556-1354.

You'll also find **Melvin's Barbecue,** owned by Thomas Bessinger's brother Melvin, at 538 Folly Rd., right on the way to Folly Beach, tel. (843) 762-0511.

In East Cooper you'll find another **Melvin's,** at 925 Houston Northcutt Blvd., tel. (843) 881-0549. This is probably my favorite barbecue spot in the Charleston area; it's been down here for some 50 years. Much to the surprise of everyone here, in 1999 *Playboy* Magazine voted Melvin's *hamburgers* the best in all the United States. But I'd still go for the barbecue—it's that good.

I have friends who swear by newcomer hole-in-the-wall **Momma Brown's Barbecue,** 1471 Ben Sawyer Blvd., tel. (843) 849-8802. Momma's features a North Carolina–like pepper and vinegar sauce (Melvin's excels with its South Carolina hickory mustard and hickory red sauces). They'll sell it to you by the sandwich, the plate, or the pound. Also, Momma opens at 6 a.m. and serves breakfast.

Mexican/Southwestern

Arizona's, set over at 14 Chapel St., tel. (843) 577-5090, is off the beaten path, toward the north end of the peninsula, and really too far to walk from the Market. Nonetheless, it's the city's oldest Mexican restaurant, famous for quesadillas, ribs, and other spicy meals. Features live music.

For more casual surroundings, head up King St. to **Juanita Greenberg's Burrito Palace,** 75 1/2 Wentworth St., Charleston, tel. (843) 577-2877, and another location at 439 King St., tel. (843) 723-6224, both great places to shake off the formality of Charlestonian living and the glaze of tourist life.

Pub Grub

Right down on the Market, at 36 N. Market St., tel. (843) 722-9464, you'll find one of my favorite places to catch a USC game: **Wild Wing Cafe,** which features Chernobyl Wings. They're actually quite delicious. The only downside, of course, is that years after you eat these, your kids will be sterile. But who needs grandkids when you can eat wings like these? In fact, isn't there an old saying about giving your children wings?

Tommy Condon's, on the other hand, is one of my favorite places to catch a Notre Dame game. It's an essential Charleston eating place, at 160 Market Street, tel. (843) 577-3818, owned by the pillar-like (and verifiably Irish) Condon family. This is the kind of neighborly place that Applebee's tries to make you believe you're in. Come to hear live Irish music Wed.-Sun. nights. The food—featuring local seafood—is good, but maybe the main reason to eat here is that this is, after all, *Tommy Condon's.* Tell Charlestonians you ate there and they won't have to ask, "Where's that?" Family friendly.

At 288 King St., tel. (843) 577-0123, on the way toward the College of Charleston, **Mike Calder's Pub** is one of those dark places that seems to have been around forever: a good place for cheap fish and chips, fried shrimp, wings, bangers and mash, and steaks. Not to mention beers, Bloody Marys, and other libations.

Other

Easy-to-miss local favorite **Vickery's Bar and Grill,** 15 Beaufain St., tel. (843) 577-5300, sits between King and Archdale Streets, where it serves up fine Cuban/Lowcountry cuisine. The interior is Havana, circa 1959; at any moment, you'll expect Ricky Ricardo and the boys to break into "Babalu." The jerk roasted chicken with black beans and rice is a favorite. Appropriately, the martinis here are widely considered tops in town. Lots of light meals, black beans, and salads; Charlestonians like the relaxed outdoor patio seating. Open every day except Christmas and July 4, 11:30 a.m.-1 a.m.

Sonoma, 304 King St., tel. (843) 853-3222, is a relaxed spot with over 30 wines to taste and lots of hip, mature people to enjoy it with. In fact, the patrons tend to be older than the proprietors, Jessica and Grant Dees, both in their 20s. Fancy food here for the gourmet palate bored with Charleston cuisine. The jerked rib eye ($17) and chipotle marinated duck breast ($18) are popular menu items.

Diner Food

Mickey's used to be *Fannie's* Diner before it was sold. Call it what you will—this 1950s' throwback at 137 Market St., tel. (843) 723-7121, is im-

portant as one of the only 24-hour food joints in the downtown district. You can order breakfast all day, and, most important, there is a jukebox. Lots of seafood and sandwiches. Try the shrimp and grits ($6.45) or the Beach Boy Po'Boy ($5.95). Definitely one of the more reasonably priced spots in the Market area.

A classic locals' breakfast spot in town is **Jack's Cafe,** 41 George St., tel. (843) 723-5237, featuring top-notch waffles, grits, home fries, decent coffee, eggs, and of course, Jack himself behind the grill, as he has been since around 1973.

At the City Marina

At 17 Lockwood Dr., on the waterfront at the City Marina, **Pusser's Landing,** named Charleston's best waterfront dining experience by one local newspaper, features fresh seafood and Caribbean cuisine, as well as Pusser's Rum drinks. Beautiful view of the Ashley. For the Sunday brunch (11:30 a.m.-3 p.m.), children under 12 eat for half price. Thurs.-Sat. there's live music in the bar. Monday and Tuesday nights there is a lobster clambake for $19.95.

One of the best possible ways to spend a night in Charleston is to take a dinner and dancing cruise on the *Spirit of Charleston* at the marina, tel. (843) 722-1691. Tickets run around $35 each for an excellent prime rib dinner. When you think about what you'd pay for dinner at a waterfront restaurant and cover to get into a club with dancing, this really is a great deal.

OUTLYING AREAS

West Ashley

California Dreaming, 1 Ashley Pointe Dr., tel. (843) 766-1644, has one of the best waterfront views in the whole Charleston area, right at the Ripley Light Marina. Set in a replica of an old Civil War fort on the Ashley River, this is a very good-looking branch of the small Carolinian chain; if you can forgive the name of the place (who comes to Charleston to dream about California?) you'll probably have a good time here. Pricier than it needs to be, and the portions won't require you to purge before dessert, but by and large a nice location with tasty (if all-too-precious) food. Try the babyback ribs—the various salads provide a (here's the Californian influence) healthy alternative to the good but cardiac-arresting alternatives in most of the local restaurants.

The Charleston Crab House is one of my favorite places in West Ashley to enjoy a relaxed dinner with friends. Located at the foot of the Wappoo Creek Bridge (145 Wappoo Creek Dr.), tel. (843) 795-1963, this is a place where you can pull the boat up to the dock, tie up, and come inside to eat. Good food—the crab's excellent and plentiful, and the shrimp's fresh and flowing.

Also on the way out to Folly Beach is **Bowen's Landing,** over on Bowen's Island at 1870 Bowen Island Road, tel. (843) 795-2757. Actually, the place, a slightly dolled-up hut of sorts, isn't all that hard to believe, since the Lowcountry is full of such hovels. What's hard to believe is that this is one of the best spots in the Lowcountry to eat authentic South Carolina seafood.

On the beach at the foot of the Folly Beach Pier is the **Starfish Grille,** 101 E. Arctic Ave., tel. (843) 588-2518, featuring indoor and outdoor seating, creatively prepared seafood, and an unbeatable view. The **Sea Shell Restaurant** is a cute place at the end of the drive into Folly—across from McKevlin's Surf Shop and the Holiday Inn.

Shem Creek

Locals normally avoid most of the restaurants at Shem Creek (on Hwy. 17), feeling that the prices have been hiked up for the tourists. That said, there's some very good eating to be done out here on the creek. My favorite is the casual, creekside **Shem Creek Bar and Grill** at 508 Mill St., tel. (843) 884-8102. Local restaurant icon John Avenger and company make some mean milk shakes, as in Dreamsicle (vanilla ice cream, orange juice, amaretto) and the Oreo (vanilla ice cream, Oreo cookies, kahlua), for $5.95. But the true star here is the seafood; every day brings new specials, but you won't go wrong with the basic shrimp dinner ($12.99) or Carolina Deviled Seafood, a baked casserole with crab, clams, and shrimp, topped with Swiss cheese. All dinners are served with creek shrimp and vegetables. Good place for a cheap lunch, too. At night you can have a drink down on the dockside bar. Great place for sunsets. Arrive by boat if you like. Next door you'll find **John's Oyster Bar,** 508 Mill St., tel. (843) 884-8103,

also owned by Avenger, but a little less casual.

Some good news came to fans of the downtown Vickery's in the winter of 1999—the Cuban-American restaurant opened another location in Shem Creek, replacing Reagan's at 1313 Shrimpboat Ln., tel. (843) 849-6770.

If even the Shem Creek Bar and Grill's not casual enough for you, try out **The Wreck (of the Richard and Charlene),** 106 Haddell St., tel. (843) 884-0052. This truly used to be a place that no one but a handful of locals knew about, but once everybody heard about this great undiscovered place in a rundown ice house with big portions and reasonable prices, The Wreck became, well, *discovered.* But that doesn't mean it's not still good. Deep-fried shrimp and fish are the specialties. Expect to pay $12 for dinner.

Mount Pleasant

Captain Guild's Cafe is one of the quaintest places in East Cooper, in the midst of old Mount Pleasant at 101 Pitt St., tel. (843) 884-7009. Dinner here will run you around $10, though specials can go higher. Creative menu with "New Cuisine" touches. Closed Monday.

Though it doesn't look like much from the street, **Locklear's,** 427 W. Coleman Blvd., tel. (843) 884-3346, has been a favorite seafood spot with East Cooper locals for some time now. Sample authentic Lowcountry eats at **Gullah Cuisine,** 1717 Hwy. 17 N, tel. (864) 881-9076, with entrées for $8-11.95. **The Mustard Seed** is a friendly, heartfelt hole-in-the-strip mall that you might well miss if you aren't looking for it. Good vegetarian and American food with a twist, for $5-8.

You'll find the best, and best-priced, Mexican food in East Cooper at the unassuming-looking **Chili Peppers,** 426 Coleman Ave., tel. (843) 884-5779, closed Sunday. Another choice is **La Hacienda,** 1035 Johnny Dodds Blvd., which features a happy hour 4-8 p.m. How authentic is the food? Last time I visited, the restaurant was temporarily closed after a raid by Immigration.

Over at 341 Johnnie Dodds Blvd., you'll find the original **Sticky Fingers Restaurant and Bar,** tel. (843) 856-9840. Open Mon.-Thurs. 11 a.m.-10 p.m., Fri.-Sat. till 10:30 p.m., Sunday 11 a.m.-9:30 p.m. Closed Thanksgiving, Christmas Eve, and Christmas. Loud, hip, fun. You can order out as well as eat there. Memphis and Texas wet and dry ribs, as well as Carolina sweet ribs. Reservations accepted.

For a better-than-average country breakfast, try **Billy's Back Home** at 1275 Ben Sawyer Blvd., tel. (843) 881-3333.

Sullivan's Island

Sully's has long been a favorite place to head to after a day at the beach. Get here late in the afternoon on a day in July and you'll find lots of sunburned, salty families catching a good meal before hitting the road home. Big wood tables, paneled walls. This place—despite having been shut down for a year a while back after a fire—has been around forever, doing simple things in the right way. Which is not to say that the food is simple or unrefined. They can do some wonderful things with shrimp and fish here, and the hush puppies are some of the best around. The shrimp po'boy sandwiches have long been a favorite of mine. Expect to spend around $12 to get full here, less for sandwiches.

Station 22 has also been around for years, at 2205 Middle St., tel. (843) 883-3355, serving soft shell crabs and local grouper. Eat here and you feel as if you've come to know something vital about Sullivan's Island.

Atlanticville Restaurant and Cafe, 2063 Middle St., tel. (843) 883-9452, is set in and above what used to be a fairly unassuming produce stand here on the island. The restaurant is upstairs, complete with piano music and a deck, serving "contemporary American" cuisine. Downstairs you'll find a café with coffee and sandwiches. It's all gourmet, for people who insist on the best for themselves and don't mind paying for it.

Bert's Bar and Grill, 2209 Middle St., tel. (843) 883-4924, is everybody's favorite secret place on Sullivan's Island. It's more an enigma than a secret, really—it's a *dive,* is what it is. And we're all darned glad to have a dive out here among the pricey restaurants and multimillion-dollar homes. This is a place where if you came often enough, everybody really would know your name.

Dunleavy's Pub, 2213 Middle St., tel. (843) 883-9646, is a great place to eat fairly cheaply out on the island. The hot dogs are stellar. I believe they may serve some beer as well. A great place to watch the game.

Isle of Palms

When I lived on the Isle of Palms, our favorite place to go was **Banana Cabana,** 1130 Ocean Blvd., tel. (843) 886-4361. Even if you don't hear it playing while you're here, you'll leave singing Jimmy Buffet. The bar area itself, when you first walk in, is small and friendly, but walk on through to the enclosed porch and outside patio, where you'll find good seating and wonderful ocean views. Order the chicken nachos, the drink of your choice, and enjoy. Owned by John Avenger, of Shem Creek Bar and Grill fame.

Right upstairs from the Cabana, you'll find the pricier **One-Eyed Parrot,** tel. (843) 886-4360. Fresh seafood, Caribbean style.

The other great restaurant on IOP is **The Sea Biscuit Cafe,** 21 J.C. Long Blvd., tel. (843) 886-4079, which has great grits, great biscuits, and an exemplary collection of hot sauces. Another of those great secret places that everybody knows about; if you get here late for breakfast on the weekend, bring or buy a paper, sit down outside, and prepare for a (worthwhile) wait. Another great place for breakfast or lunch is the low-key **Hearts of Palm Cafe,** tel. (843) 886-9661, in the red-roofed pavilion facing the beach. Tables outside, and occasional live acoustic music to accompany your eggs.

Farther North

A wonderfully authentic place out on Hwy. 17 N is **Seewee Restaurant,** 4808 Highway 17 N in Awendaw, tel. (843) 928-3609. A great homey, tasty spot, set in a circa 1920s general store. Owner Mary Rancourt opened it up as a restaurant in 1993, but didn't—thank goodness—remove the red tin roof, old shelving, worn

flooring, and tongue and groove paneling. Most dinners include a fish, three sides, and hush puppies. The fried fish is excellent. The roast pork loin is great as well, and if you've been saving up your fat intake, now is the time to splurge and get the country fried steak—you won't find better. Make sure one of your sides is the spicy fried green tomatoes. If you've never tried them, you won't find a better example.

The seafood is wonderfully (and simply) prepared. Each piece of fish is so fresh that its next of kin have yet to be notified. It's as casual as going to the house of a country uncle (a popular country uncle—it gets very crowded most nights, so you might want to head out there for a late lunch or early dinner). The lunch buffet, open 11 a.m.-3 p.m., usually runs about

$5. For dessert, try the pineapple cake or the peanut butter pie.

Unfortunately, the front steps aren't particularly amenable to wheelchairs, and there's no ramp. But call ahead and maybe Miss Mary can work something out for you—even if it's just a carryout.

SUPERMARKETS

If I have a favorite chain supermarket in the world, **Harris Teeter** has got to be it. Set in an old warehouse on East Bay St., this is the way supermarkets should look—brick on the outside, brick on the inside. Over in East Cooper you'll find a **Publix** in Mount Pleasant, containing a first-rate seafood section.

ENTERTAINMENT AND EVENTS

The *Post and Courier* **Preview** is the weekly entertainment guide of note, featuring movie listings and reviews, as well as previews and reviews of Charleston area theater.

FESTIVALS

Historic Charleston Foundation's **Annual Festival of Houses and Gardens,** mid-March to mid-April, gives you the chance to visit privately owned historic sites during its festival. The monthlong program includes afternoon and evening walking tours and special programs and events. Call (843) 723-1623 for reservations. Or visit the foundation at 108 Meeting Street.

The Preservation Society of Charleston, founded way back in 1920, runs the **Annual Fall Candlelight Tours of Homes and Gardens,** which are much like the Annual Festival of Houses and Gardens tours, only darker. Visit the society at 147 King St., tel. (843) 722-4630.

Spoleto Festival U.S.A.
This world-famous international arts festival—originally established in historic, aesthetically blessed Spoleto, Italy—chose Charleston when establishing its America-based festival back in 1977. For two weeks in late May and early June each year, the streets and parks of Charleston fill with experimental and traditional works by artisans from as far away as Kingston and as near as King Street. The festival's producers pack more than 100 dance, music, and theatre performances into these exhilirating weeks, usually 10 or more events per day—enough to satisfy even the most Faustian traveler.

For information on the Spoleto Festival, call (864) 722-2764.

Piccolo Spoleto Festival
For folks on a budget, the good news is that Piccolo Spoleto runs concurrently with Spoleto, offering local and regional talent at lower admission prices (most performances are free) and generally appealing to a broader audience than the Spoleto events proper. Call the City of Charleston Office of Cultural Affairs, tel. (843) 724-7305, for a schedule of acts and exhibits.

MOJA Arts Festival
Talk about taking a lemon and making lemonade: Charleston served as the port of entry for a majority of the slaves imported to the U.S.; from this grim historical fact each fall arises this joyous festival focusing on the area's rich African-American and Caribbean heritages. The festival's events are mostly free, but some require tickets. For information, call the Charleston Office of Cultural Affairs, tel. (843) 724-7305.

CONCERT VENUES

The 13,000-seat **North Charleston Coliseum,** 5001 Coliseum Dr. N, tel. (800) 529-5010 or (843) 529-5050, catches most of the big rock and country acts these days, as well as ice shows and various other events. Tickets to Coliseum events are available at the Coliseum Ticket Office and at all SCAT outlets. Be sure to visit the South Carolina Entertainer's Hall of Fame, on the premises. It honors world-famous celebrities with a South Carolina connection, including Spring Gully's Ernest Evans (Chubby Checker). See the Hall of Fame online at: members.tripod.com/SCME_Hall_of_Fame. Charge tickets by phone at (843) 577-4500.

The **Music Farm,** 32-C Ann St., tel. (843) 853-3276 (concert line) or (843) 722-8904 (business office), is legendary in the area for giving local bands a place to open for traveling college-circuit bands, and for attracting nationally known acts. **Cumberland's** and **Windjammer** over on Isle of Palms are other major places to find live acts—though they're certainly not the only ones. Check the *Post and Courier's Preview* insert (or one of the free entertainment weeklies in newsstands) to find out who's playing where.

CLUBS AND BARS

Clubs

One of the best places to catch live acts in town is also the oldest: small and smoky **Cumberland's Bar & Grill,** 26 Cumberland St., tel. (843) 577-9469. Monday is open mike night; the first Saturday of the month at 10 p.m., Cumberland's hosts the Lowcountry Blues Society Monthly Blues Jam emceed by "Breeze" DJ Shrimp City Slim. For information, e-mail: emusic@mindspring.com.

Love the nightlife? Got to boogie? A place with a reputation as a college-age pick-up joint on the Market is **Level 2,** 36 N. Market St. (between Mesa Grill and Wild Wings), tel. (843) 577-4454, blasting everything from oldies to the latest dance mixes over the ever-present hum of come-on lines. Also rumoured to earn a significant percentage of its income from its condom dispensers is **Wet Willie's,** a neon daiquiri bar at 209 E. Bay St., tel. (843) 853-5650.

But if luck deserts and you're still unaccompanied (or hungry) when the disco balls stop spinning, stumble over to small, smoky, off-beat late-night Charleston standard **AC's Bar and Grill,** 338 King St., tel. (843) 577-6742. Or head upstairs over Clef & Clef for raw local blues at **Red, Hot and Blues,** 102 N. Market St., tel. (843) 722-0732. **Mistral Restaurant,** 99 S. Market St., tel. (843) 722-5708, features live blues on Tuesday nights and Dixieland jazz on Thursday, Friday, and Saturday.

After closing for a few weeks back in 1998, the legendary Charleston showcase **Music Farm,** 32-C Ann St., tel. (843) 853-3276 (concert line) or (843) 722-8904 (business office), re-opened under new owners Craig Comer and Yates Dew, who vowed not to change anything major, other than adding bluegrass, jazz, and swing to the club's repertoire, and considering weeknight shows with earlier start times, stage and sound improvements, and a high-quality menu. Ticket prices vary but range as low as $5 for over 21 and $7 for under 21. They are available at the club ticket window at 32-C Ann Street. **The Blind Tiger,** 38 Broad St., tel. (843) 577-0088, attracts a slightly more mature crowd attracted to its secluded ambience and beautiful deck.

Finally, a time-honored hangout for Citadel cadets is **Your Place,** 6 Market St., tel. (843) 722-8360.

Over on the Isle of Palms, **Coconut Joe's,** 1120 Ocean Blvd., tel. (843) 886-0046, is a great place to sit up top and listen to reggae on the roof with the crashing of waves in the background. At **Windjammer,** 1008 Ocean Blvd., tel. (843) 886-8596, also right on the beach, it's always spring break. Downstairs there's a fenced in outdoor area with volleyball courts, where various professional volleyball tournaments are held. Live music here most nights—Hootie and the Blowfish have been known to try out new music here, and sometimes the club even hosts local theater.

In West Ashley, **J.B. Pivot's Beach Club,** Savannah Hwy., tel. (843) 571-3668 (just behind Shoney's), offers a Breeze Night on Tuesdays, with free beginner's shagging lessons. Thursday night is ballroom night and Saturday usually features live entertainment.

A Bit Dressy

If you brought some nice clothes, Charleston offers a number of nice places to show them off, such as **Pusser's Landing,** in the Rice Mill Building, 17 Lockwood Dr., tel. (843) 853-1000, fax 853-2750. Mind you, you're welcome to come in wearing shorts and a ball cap, but the ambience—the old brick, the fireplace, the lavish live jazz—begs for something a bit dressier. Set in a semi-refurbished, honest-to-Uncle-Ben rice mill, Pusser's interior reminds me of the 1990s' "haunted house" set for *Saturday Night Live,* back when they had the lead guitarist who looked a bit like Lurch from the *Addams Family.* Get yourself an overpriced drink and listen to the classy jazz/blues. The night I was there, the lounge singer was belting out Frank Sinatra tunes while well-dressed 40-something couples danced around him and retro-dressed 30-something singles sucked cigarettes on the sofas. The back of the building faces the marina; a beautiful location.

One hates to make any claims in advance about the hipness of a place—these things change so quickly—but at press time, one of the hippest spots in Charleston was along the same brick way as Houlihan's at 39 John St. up by the visitors center. **Tango** is owner Leo Chakeris's three-story, atrium-themed club, which has been drawing the notice of the city's dress-to-impress crowd, though the dress code is technically fairly lax—no T-shirts, ball caps, or flip-flops. Women get in for free; men hoping to have access to these women must pay between $5 and $10 (depending on the quality of the women?). Open Thurs.-Sat. 9 p.m.-3 a.m.

If you're old enough to remember looking *forward* to the American Bicentennial, you're old enough to enjoy **Fannigan's,** 159 E. Bay St., tel. (843) 722-6916, a fine place to see (or participate in) shagging, or to just get out there and shake your groove thing. DJ most nights. Open Tues.-Thurs. 5 p.m.-2 a.m., Friday 5 p.m.-4 a.m., Saturday 8 p.m.-2 a.m. Minimal cover charge.

Along with Pusser's, two of the cocktail spots with the most romantic ambience in town are Clef & Clef and The Library at Vendue. **Clef & Clef,** 102 N. Market St., tel. (843) 722-0732, is a very elegant club on the market, featuring live jazz. A wonderful place to stop for late drinks or dessert. **The Library at Vendue,** 23 Vendue Range, tel. (843) 723-0485, features a rooftop bar that provides a wonderful view across Charleston Harbor.

Pubs

McGrady's Tavern, established in 1778, is the oldest tavern in Charleston. Bartender Steve is as friendly and knowledgeable a host as you're likely to meet. McGrady's is a great place to come to on a rainy or foggy day. It's a warm, friendly place, with a long history.

Mike Calder's Pub at 288 King St., tel. (843) 577-0123, is the kind of dark, friendly neighborhood place that Applebee's and Co. pretend to be. **Tommy Condon's,** 160 Market Street, tel. (843) 577-3818, features live Irish music five days a week.

One of the hippest (and smokiest) spots to get a cocktail near the Market is **Club Habana,** 177 Meeting St., tel. (843) 853-5008, upstairs from the Tinder Box cigar shop. Photos of famous carcinogen-blowers grace the walls.

Gay and Lesbian

Gays generally feel welcome at most clubs in the Charleston area, but gay-specific spots include **Dudley's,** 346 King St., tel. (843) 723-2784, downtown (a private club, so call ahead for information); **The Arcade,** 5 Liberty St., tel. (843) 722-5656; and **Deja Vu II,** 335 Savannah Hwy., tel. (843) 556-5588.

Brewpubs

Southend Brewery and Smokehouse, 161 East Bay St., tel. (843) 853-4677, features handcrafted microbrewed beers, smoked ribs and chicken, and a third-floor cigar lounge, with billiard tables. I never pass up a chance to ride in a glass elevator, so up I went to the third floor, tracing the brass path of the steam vent of one of the brewing tanks as we rose. Up on the third floor they've got TVs tuned to sporting events and a nice view of the entire restaurant. It's really a wonderful location, and a good place to watch the game. Expect to spend $7-18 for some worthy burgers, pizza, pasta, and "brew-b-que." Southend has become so popular that today you can find sister locations up in North Carolina in Charlotte, Raleigh, and Lake Norman, as well as Jacksonville, Florida, and Atlanta, Georgia.

Sure, Charleston is chic, but can these people really be South Carolinians? This is what runs through my mind sometimes while visiting **Zebo,** 275 King St., tel. (843) 577-7600. It seems like somewhere Michael J. Fox might have partied in *Bright Lights, Big City*—hip and slick. These are pretty much the types of adjectives a lot of us seek out brewpubs to avoid, but Zebo *is* technically a brewpub, meaning that it features its own brews—including a pretty decent American Pale Ale. Good pasta and wood-fired pizza. Maybe best is the jazz/gospel brunch it has started up on Sunday.

The small regional chain, **TBonz Gill and Grill,** 80 N. Market St., right on the Market, tel. (843) 577-2511, already locally famous for its grilled steaks, has savvily started up its own TBonz Homegrown Ale to cash in on the brew boom. Food is served late here, so if Dave Letterman gives you a hankering for a rib eye, you may be in luck.

What to Do if You Find Yourself Headed for a Chain Restaurant

Yes, the Applebee's in downtown Charleston is warm and cozy. But the very sort of thing—a warm, been-there-forever sort of neighborhood bar—that Applebee's (and TGIFs and Ruby Tuesdays) attempts to re-create is the very sort of place Charleston has in abundance. So if you find yourself walking across East Bay toward Applebee's, turn around and head back to at the very least a smaller chain—TBonz or Wild Wing Cafe—or, better yet, to Tommy Condon's. You bought this book to avoid the Applebee's and the Shoney's of the world.

THEATER AND DANCE VENUES

The **Charleston Stage Company,** the state's largest theater company, offers first-rate theatrical performances at the historic Dock Street Theater, producing over 120 performances a year. For the box office, call (800) 454-7093 or (843) 965-4032 Mon.-Fri. 9 a.m.-5 p.m. Shows are held Thursday, Friday, and Saturday at 8 p.m., Sunday at 3 p.m.

The **Have Nots!** comedy improv company plays at the ACME downtown at 5 Faber St., tel. (843) 853-6687. All shows 8 p.m.; $8 per adult, $6 for seniors and students.

The **Footlight Players Theatre,** 20 Queen St., tel. (843) 722-7521 (office) or (843) 722-4487 (box office) has box office hours Mon.-Fri. 10 a.m.-5 p.m., or till curtain on performance days.

CINEMAS

The **American Theater Cinema Grill,** 446 King St., tel. (843) 722-3456, Web site: www.vr-south.com, e-mail: info@vrsouth.com, allows you to eat while you enjoy your choice of two first-run films. A virtual reality game center on the premises allows you to play games along with surfing the Internet or checking your e-mail. A fine "art" theater is **The Roxy,** 245 E. Bay St., tel. (843) 853-7699. For a nice clean suburban theater, head over to Mount Pleasant and attend **Movies at Mt. Pleasant,** 963 Houston Northcutt Blvd., tel. (843) 884-4900. And for one of the cleanest, finest second-run theaters you'll ever find, head up into North Charleston and get off at the Northwoods Mall; head over to the **Northwoods 10** at 2055 Eagle Landing Blvd., tel. (843) 553-0005. So reasonable, you can even afford popcorn.

COFFEE SHOPS AND CAFÉS

The **Horse and Cart Café,** 347 Kings St., tel. (843) 722-0797, is run by Ken Newman, an escaped New Yorker who is very glad to be down here. How glad? He puts his testimony on every menu, encouraging others to likewise "Follow Your Dream." What's obvious about this place is Ken's very self-conscious attempts—the board games, the shelf of used books, the low prices—to create a warm, human place where a community of regulars would naturally take root—a café rather than just another place to pick up a bagel and coffee. He's succeeded wonderfully, and no doubt for a lot of folks the 113 different kinds of beers don't hurt. Menu items range from a bagel ($1.17) to a $2.54 refillable bowl of soup to sandwiches—around $4.50—and lasagna for about $6.50. Note too how the menus list not only the proprietor, but the chef, cook, waitresses, and bartender. Drumming on Monday at 8:30 p.m., Irish folk jam on Tuesday at 8:30 a.m., poetry readings on Wednesday, and live music Thurs.-Sunday. Open 9 a.m.-2 a.m. A light brunch served here on Sunday 10 a.m.-1 p.m., for $3.74.

Kaminsky's Most Excellent Cafe, on the Market, is constantly voted the best place to get dessert in Charleston. And if you have the money to spend and the time to wait out the usual line outside, it is. Beautiful dark wood paneling, incredibly indulgent desserts, wide selection of wine. Open seven days, afternoon till 2 a.m. If you're going to go off your diet, you may as well do it here.

Mirabel, on East Bay St., tel. (843) 853-9800, is something like a quieter version of Kaminsky's.

wired & fired: a pottery playhouse, 159 East Bay St., tel. (843) 579-0999, fax 579-0311, e-mail: wiredchas@mindspring.com, is the result of a great idea—it's a coffee house/pottery studio, where you pay $8 an hour for studio time, $2-50 for the pottery you want to paint, $3 a piece for the paint, supplies, glazing, and firing. And yes, you have to pay for the coffee, too. A perfect, unique place for a date. Of course, you'll need to leave your pottery for a couple days for the firing, so if you're only in town for a few days, try to hit this toward the beginning of your stay.

Hit hard by hurricane Hugo, the lovely 1924 Francis Marion Hotel has undergone a $12 million renovation.

Port City Java is a chain of coffeehouses with two Charleston locations: one at Saks 5th Avenue and one at the Francis Marion Hotel at 387 King St., tel. (843) 853-5282. In addition to the coffee made from beans roasted on the premises (good but not spectacular), Port City offers a juice and smoothie bar—a very healthy, tasty way to go. Interesting coffeehouse cuisine includes the usual baked goods, hot crab dip crostini ($6.95), wraps ($6.50), and salads ($4.25-8.95).

Old Colony Bakery 280 King St., tel. (843) 722-2147, puts on no airs, but it's the scents it puts *into* the air—pastries, muffins, cookies— that you need to watch out for. Here you'll also find benne wafers, an authentic Charleston food derived from West Africa and named after the Bantu word for sesame seeds—from which the wafers are made.

Bakers Café at 214 King St. offers a variety of coffees; **Coffee Gallery**, 169B King St., allows

you to view (and, if you desire, purchase) local art while high on caffeine purchased on the premises. Finally, if not surfprisingly, **The Bookstore Café**, 412 King, tel. (843) 720-8843, fax (843) 853-9446, e-mail: cater@mindspring.com, combines a bookstore and a coffeehouse, just a block north of the Francis Marion and around the corner from the Hampton Inn and Music Hall. An upscale, clean, well-lighted place serving breakfast and lunch (try the roasted pork and fried green tomato sandwich for lunch), along with scones, croissants, and other caffeine-den favorites. Open for breakfast and lunch only, seven days a week.

Like every other town big enough to have a stoplight, Charleston now has its share of **Starbucks.** Both downtown locations, in fact—one on King St. and one on a side street down by College of Charleston—are uniquely situated inside pre-existing buildings. It's your call, obviously, but you might want to patronize a local establishment.

MORE PLACES TO MEET PEOPLE

Charleston is such an active city that there are plenty of ways to meet local people who share your interests. The best place to look for a comprehensive menu of what's going on is in the *Post and Courier*'s Thursday *Preview* insert, but here's a quick overview of some of the more permanent groups.

Special Interest Groups
Books-a-Million locations in West Ashley and Northwoods Mall hold singles nights on the second Thursday of each month 7-10 p.m., featuring discounts, giveaways, live music, and (I suspect) lots of awkward pickup lines. Call (843) 556-9232 for more information.

The local **Sierra Club** gets together to explore, enjoy, and protect what's left of the world the way we found it. Meetings held on the first Thursday of every month. Call Pat Luck at (843) 559-2568 for more information.

Or take the Village People's advice and give the **YMCA** a call at (843) 723-6473 to hear more about their tai chi, seniors' exercise, massage therapy, hatha yoga, bridge, bingo, modern dance, and swimming programs.

Of course, one of the best ways to use your

free time, and to meet people who share your values, can be to spend it helping someone else. **Charleston Habitat for Humanity,** builds homes to eliminate poverty housing. If you can pound a nail or even carry water to those who do, call (843) 747-9090.

Recovery Groups
Smokers Anonymous meets every Monday at Roper North, at 7:30 p.m., tel. (843) 762-6505.

SPORTS, RECREATION, AND SHOPPING

IN THE WATER

Surfing
The single best, most dependable surf spot in the Charleston area, if not in the entire state, is **The Washout** at the end of East Ashley Ave. in Folly Beach. If the waves are small everywhere else, they may still be decent here. If they're good everywhere else, they'll be pounding here. Of course, if the swell's good, it's also going to be *crowded* here, and while the localism among area surfers isn't as bad as it is down in Florida or out in California, you might want to let the tube-starved locals enjoy themselves and head to another beach.

Another popular spot at Folly is **10th Street,** where you can count on smaller but cleaner—and less-crowded—waves than you'll find up at the Washout. Beside the Holiday Inn at East Atlantic Ave., the **Folly Beach Pier** sometimes offers cleaner waves and longer rides than the Washout, but you'll need to keep an eye out for The Law: though not always enforced, it's illegal to surf within 200 feet of the pier.

Over in East Cooper, a lot of folks like surfing at the **Sea Cabins Pier,** right at 21st and Palm Boulevard. If the wind's blowing out of the northeast, you may want to head over here, or to **Bert's** at Station 22, Sullivan's Island. Named in honor of the venerable nearby bar, this is one of the best places to surf at low tide.

McKevlin's Surf Shop's 24-hour surf report, tel. (843) 588-2261, is updated several times throughout the day. The Charleston *Post and Courier* offers its own **InfoLine Surf Report,** updated a minimum of three times a day, tel. (843) 937-6000, ext. 7873.

Founded in 1965, **McKevlin's** are fine surf shops in both Folly (8 Center St.) and Isle of Palms (1101-B, Ocean Blvd.). Both of owner Tim McKevlin's locations sell and rent both new and used boards and body boards. They also feature the most knowledgeable and courteous counter folk in the area. **Pura Vida,** 1419 Ben Sawyer Blvd., Mount Pleasant, also rents boards.

Water-Skiing
The **Bohicket Boat Adventure and Tour Company,** 1880 Andell Bluff Blvd., tel. (843) 768-7294, offers water-skiing, knee boarding, and tubing trips along the backwater creeks of West Ashley. **Tidal Wave Runners, Ltd.** has two locations, one at the Wild Dunes Yacht Harbor on 41st Ave., Isle of Palms, tel. (843) 886-8456, the other at the Charleston City Marina, 17 Lockwood Dr., tel. (843) 853-4386, offering water skiing trips as well as water ski school. They also rent powerboats.

Sailing
The **Bohicket Boat Adventure and Tour Company,** 1880 Andell Bluff Blvd., tel. (843) 768-7294, offers sailing trips and rentals both inland and out on the ocean.

Jet Skis and Parasailing
Tidal Wave Runners, Ltd. has two locations, one at 69 41st Ave. Isle of Palms, tel. (843) 886-8456, and another at the Charleston City Marina, 17 Lockwood Dr., tel. (843) 853-4386. Jet Ski rental costs $55 an hour single, $15 per passenger; more for high performance models.

For parasailing, it runs $50 for a 10-minute ride at 600 feet. If you'd like to go higher, for $70 they'll take you up to 1,200 feet for 10-14 minutes.

Kayaking and Canoeing
The **Bohicket Boat Adventure and Tour Company,** 1880 Andell Bluff Blvd., tel. (843) 768-

7294, offers a three-hour guided kayak tour along the remote saltmarsh adjoining the North Edisto River.

Over in East Cooper, **Coastal Expeditions,** 514-B Mill St., next to the Shem Creek Bar and Grill at the Shem Creek Maritime Center in Mount Pleasant, tel. (843) 884-7684, is the best place to rent a kayak or canoe, or to sign up for a guided tour of the Lowcountry's barrier islands, the cypress swamp, and Charleston Harbor. Since you'll be paddling a sea kayak, larger and much more stable than other kayaks, you don't need prior training for most of these trips. Half-day trips cost $45 in Shem Creek and Morgan Creek behind Isle of Palms. Full-day tours are 5-10 miles long and cost $85; one is a trip to undeveloped Capers Island, accessible only by boat. Overnight trips to Capers Island-State Wildlife Refuge are also available. One unusual option is the Edisto River Treehouse Trip, where you'll get to sleep in a treehouse on a 130-acre nature preserve. If you do want lessons, call to book a class or find out when one's scheduled.

If you'd like to get over to Bull Island in the Cape Romain National Wildlife Refuge, Coastal Expeditions sends a ferry over there that you can catch. Call for rates and schedule. If you don't need no stinking tour leader, rent a single kayak for $25 half day, $35 full day. Double kayak rental: $35 half day, $50 for a full day. Store hours are Feb. 15-Oct. 31 daily 9 a.m.-6 p.m.; Nov. 1-Dec. 23 closed Monday; open Dec. 24-Feb. 14 by appointment only. **Tidal Wave Runners, Ltd.** with two locations, one at the Wild Dunes Yacht Harbor on 41st Ave., Isle of Palms, tel. (843) 886-8456, another at the Charleston City Marina, 17 Lockwood Dr., tel. (843) 853-4386, rents kayaks.

Boat Rentals

The **Bohicket Boat Adventure and Tour Company,** 1880 Andell Bluff Blvd., tel. (843) 768-7294, offers everything from little johnboats to speedboats, 15-foot Boston whalers, and 22-foot Catalina sailboats. Rental for a full-size boat runs around $100-200 a half day, $150-350 for a full day. Open year-round except for January and February. **Tidal Wave Runners, Ltd.,** with two locations, at the Wild Dunes Yacht Harbor on 41st Ave., Isle of Palms, tel. (843) 886-8456, and at the Charleston City Marina, 17 Lockwood Dr., tel. (843) 853-4386, rents powerboats and leads guided jet-ski tours.

Diving

With history comes shipwrecks; off the coast you'll find great wreck diving. If you're here in the winter, beware that rough, cold waters can make offshore diving here pretty inhospitable between October and April or May. But people dive in the historic rivers year-round; one Lowcountry favorite is the Cooper River, filled with fossilized giant shark teeth, bones, mammal teeth, as well as Colonial and prehistoric artifacts. Expect water temps in the 50s.

Contact **Charleston Scuba,** 335 Savannah Hwy., tel. (843) 763-3483, Web site: www.charlestonscuba.com, or the **Wet Shop,** 5121 Rivers Ave., tel. (843) 744-5641.

Cruises

One of the best possible ways to spend a night in Charleston is to take a dinner and dancing cruise on the ***Spirit of Charleston,*** tel. (843) 722-1691, 205 King Street. Tickets run around $35 each for an excellent prime rib dinner; the night we went, the alternative plate was chicken cordon bleu, which, along with the She Crab Soup that proceeded it, was some of the best food I've ever eaten.

Over in West Ashley, the **Bohicket Boat Adventure and Tour Company,** 1880 Andell Bluff Blvd., tel. (843) 768-7294, offers dolphin watching and sunset cruises, water-skiing trips, eco tours, shelling shuttles, and tours of the ACE Basin. Open March-December.

Gray Line Water Tours, 196 Concord St., tel. (843) 722-1112, behind the Customs House, offers gourmet dinner cruises, harbor tours, and private charters aboard a paddlewheeler. Dinner tours include live music.

Fishing

If you get to South Carolina and realize you forgot to bring your yacht or trawler with you, don't panic—it happens to all of us. Fortunately, a number of companies specialize in getting fisherfolk out to where the deep-sea fish are biting. Most will also rent you the tackle you left back

A dance band enlivens dinner cruises of Charleston Harbor.

home on the yacht as well. Out in the Gulf Stream you can fish for marlin, sailfish, tuna, dolphin, and wahoo. Closer in, you can still hope to land mackerel, blackfin tuna, cobia, and shark. The **Bohicket Boat Adventure and Tour Company,** 1880 Andell Bluff Blvd., tel. (843) 768-7294, offers in-shore fishing trips and offshore fishing trips on a fleet of six passenger boats, running from 25 feet to 55 feet in size. Open March-December.

For tackle, try **Captain Ed's Fly Fishing Shop,** 47 John St., tel. (843) 723-0860, Web site: www.atlantic-boating.com, open Mon.-Fri. 9 a.m.-5 p.m. and Saturday 9 a.m.-1 p.m., or **Silver Dolphin Fishing,** 1311 Gilmore Rd., tel. (843) 556-3526, open 7 a.m.-5 p.m. daily.

Shrimping and Crabbing
The **Bohicket Boat Adventure and Tour Company,** 1880 Andell Bluff Blvd., tel. (843) 768-7294, offers crabbing and shrimping outings. Open March-December.

Water Parks
Splash Island in Palmetto Island County Park in Mount Pleasant and **Splash Zone** in James Island County Park are open every weekend in the summer 10 a.m.-6 p.m. Cost is about $8 for Charleston County residents, $10 for noncounty residents. These fees are in addition to the $1 park entrance fee. Call (843) 795-4386 for information.

HIKES

Just north of Steed Creek Rd. in Awendaw at Hwy. 17, you'll find the trailhead for the 27-mile **Swamp Fox Passage of the Palmetto Trail,** tel. (843) 336-3248, fax (843) 771-0590. It connects with the **Lake Moultrie Passage** up at Moncks Corner, tel. (843) 761-8000. Bring insect repellent. Believe it or not, you could have walked through some parts of this area just after Hurricane Hugo and been the tallest thing in the forest. Today, you'll find lots of pine trees, some Carolina bays, the famous insect-gulping pitcher plant, and cypress swamp. Pack a lot of water, since the primitive campgrounds along the way won't provide any. Don't do this hike in the summer, unless as some type of penance—the humidity, heat, and insects will take most the fun out of the excursion. Bikers use this trail as well, but most of the time you should have the trail to yourself. Three primitive campsites along the way. Bring a hand trowel.

BIKING

If you want to bike around downtown Charleston, check out **Mike's Bikes** at the corner of St. Philips and Wentworth, tel. (843) 723-8025. Rates run $4 hourly, $12 daily, $25 for three days, and just $35 for an entire week.

Of course, no one says you have to keep your rental bike confined to downtown. One of the joys of Carolina beaches is that the flat landscape allows the ocean to creep up quite a ways along the beach, leaving a cement-hard, flat surface behind, perfect for long bike rides on the beach. It's possible to park on Isle of Palms at the county park and ride all the way to the north end of the island, giving you a look at the Wild Dunes boardwalk and Rainbow Row. Or you can head south, take the bridge across Breach Inlet to Sullivan's Island, and check out some of unique houses there. Stop at Dunleavy's or Sully's for lunch, and turn back.

You can also mountain bike the 27-mile **Swamp Fox Trail.**

GOLF

Charleston was home to the first golf course in America (Harleston Green) and organized the first golf club, the South Carolina Golf Club, in 1786. But that's no surprise. In 1998, Kiawah Island Resort and Wild Dunes were both named as two of the top 100 golf resorts in North America by *Links* magazine.

The first thing a duffer will want to do is stop in at the Charleston Visitors Center and pick up a *Charleston Area Golf Guide,* an annual publication by **Charleston Golf, Inc.,** a nonprofit organization dedicated to promoting the Charleston area as a golf destination. Call these people at (800) 774-4444 (get it?), and they'll help you arrange your golfing on your next visit. This will give you a listing and ranking of every course in the area.

Charleston boasts courses by Pete Dye, Tom Fazio, Arthur Hills, Jack Nicklaus, Rees Jones, and Robert Trent Jones Sr., among others. Dye's **The Ocean Course** at Kiawah Island has been ranked by *Golf Magazine* as one of the top 100 courses in America, and *Golf Digest* has dubbed it "America's Toughest Resort Course," as well as one of its "100 Greatest Courses." Taking up more than two miles of oceanfront beach dunes, this is one of the most beautiful courses in the world. Local hotels offering golf packages include Charleston Harbor Hilton Resort, Dunes Properties, Francis Marion Hotel, Hampton Inn, Holiday Inn: Riverview, Island Realty, Kiawah Island Resort, the Mills House, Kiawah Island Villa Rentals, Seabrook Island Resort, Wild Dunes Resort. See accommodations listings for address and phone numbers.

TENNIS

If you're looking for tennis lessons, try the **Charleston Tennis Center,** 19 Farmfield Rd., tel. (843) 724-7402; **Wild Dunes Resort,** tel. (800) 845-8880 or (843) 886-2113; or **Kiawah Island Resort,** tel. (800) 845-2471 or (843) 768-2121, which offers tennis clinics for adults and kids in two tennis complexes with 23 clay courts, three hard courts in all.

MORE RECREATION

In 1998, a **bowling** alley opened up on Coleman Ave. in Mount Pleasant.

You can also shoot **pool** at **Southend Brewery,** or head over to **Salty Mike's** at the Marina, where you can challenge any Citadel candidates who come in.

Sand Dollar Mini Golf, 1405 Ben Sawyer Blvd., Mount Pleasant, tel. (843) 884-0320, seems to have been there on the way to Sullivan's Island forever. This is humble compared to Myrtle Beach's towers of stucco, but with its lighthouse and Willie the Whale, and especially with the souvenir shop, Carolina Gifts and Sea Shells, on premises, this is one of those quaint, time-past spots that will give you an idea of what the area was like before the world discovered the Lowcountry.

PROFESSIONAL SPORTS

Baseball
Charleston has long hosted some estimable minor league ball teams. In the early 1990s, the team was called the Charleston Rainbows, a name that not only featured some pretty goofy-looking logos but also made it rather hard to cheer for them as they battled such tough-sounding teams as the Hickory Crawdads or Capital City Bombers. No one ever felt really comfortable standing up in a tense late inning, beer in hand, and shouting, "Go *Rainbows!*"

Today, fortunately, they're called the **Charleston Riverdogs.** Class A affiliates of the Tampa Bay Devil Rays play at the recently completed Joseph P. Riley Park, named after the city's innovative and generally beloved mayor.

If you want to see a game at this fine, old-timey-styled stadium—designed by the same folks who created Baltimore's famed Camden Yards—call (843) 577-3647, check online at www.riverdogs.com, or head down to "the Joe," 360 Fishburne St., and buy tickets in person. They run $4-8. The great thing about parks this small is that there really aren't any bad seats; 10 or so rows may be the only difference between high-end and low-end tickets. The highest priced seats feature wait service, which could be helpful if you're physically disabled. Most games start at 7:05 p.m.

Hockey
The **South Carolina Stingrays,** 3107 Firestone Rd, tel. (843) 744-2248, play Oct.-May in the North Charleston Coliseum as members of the East Coast Ice Hockey League. They won the 1996-97 Kelly Cup and have posted winning records every season since their inception in the mid-'90s. They also average over 7,500 fans a game. If you haven't ever caught a live hockey game, give it a try. A fun time, even if you haven't watched a hockey game since the 1980 Winter Olympics. You'll find Stingrays games on the radio at 98.9 FM, Charleston's "The Breeze" affiliate.

Soccer
The **Charleston Battery,** who play at Daniel Island stadium over on Daniel Island (right off I-526), tel. (843) 740-7787, do battle April-Sept. in the U.S. International Soccer League.

SHOPPING

King Street is the single best shopping street, especially if you include the back entrance to the Shops at Charleston Place, which opens out onto the street. The shops down here include most tourist town standards—the Audubon Shop, Banana Republic, Liz Claiborne, Victoria's Secret, the Gap, and so forth, but they also include some unique locally owned shops much worth visiting.

To sample or take home some local music, visit **Millennium Music,** 269 King St., tel. (843) 853-1999, a very worthwhile, locally owned (franchise) music store featuring lots of listening stations, at least one of which always contains releases by local artists. Also a good place to find out who's playing where while you're in town.

Chili Chompers is a fun little shop at 333 King St., tel. (888) 853-4144, fax (843) 853-4146, within easy walking distance of the visitors center. What's for sale? Basically anything that will singe your palate. Owner Chesta Tiedemann's extensive hot sauce collection covers an entire set of shelves and includes at least two brands that require customers to sign a written waiver before purchasing a bottle. Here too you'll find the spicy Blenheim Ginger Ale and Ginger Beer (nonalcoholic).

Artists' Galleries
Showcasing the work of more than 50 local craftspersons, **Charleston Crafts,** 38 Queen St., tel. (843) 723-2938, is a fun place to browse for baskets, clay, glasswork, jewelry, paper, photos, wood, and more. Open Mon.-Sat. 10 a.m.-5 p.m., Sunday 1-5 p.m. Inside Charleston Place you'll find **Rhett Gallery,** tel. (843) 722-1144, featuring the watercolors of Nancy Ricker Rhett, along with a wide collection of antique prints. **Gallery Chuma/African American Art Gallery,** 43 John St., tel. (843) 722-7568, Web site: Chuman@galleryChuma.com, features—you guessed it—works created by African-American artists. Occupying both floors of a historic building, covering a total of some 2,900 square feet, Chuma claims to be the largest African-American gallery in the South. Gullah artist Jonathan Green's works are a permanent fixture, as are those of several other renowned artists. Open Mon.-Sat. 10 a.m.-6 p.m., or by appointment. **Gullah Tours** of Charleston leave from the gallery daily—call for information. Finally, with all the great birding in the area, it's only proper that you'll find **The Audubon Shop and Gallery** over on 245 King St., tel. (800) 453-2473 or (843) 723-6171, offering exhibits of wildlife art by regional artists, and featuring the work of Vernon Washington, as well as prints by Old Man Audubon—no stranger to Charleston—himself. You'll also find handcrafted birdhouses and feeders, binoculars and telescopes, and old decoys for sale here.

Farmer's Markets

Charleston's Farmer's Market is held every Saturday at the Maritime Center on Concord St., down by the South Carolina Aquarium, April 18-Oct. 31.

Antiques

Charleston is so old that people throw away as "too new" items that would be antiques anywhere else in the country. King St. is a favorite place to hunt antiques, since between 152 King St. (152 A.D. Antiques) and 311 King St. (Wilson & Gates Antiques), you'll find no less than 33 antique shops, specializing in everything from venerable old rugs to rare maps.

When seeking cheaper prices folks head out to the suburbs to **Page's Thieves Market,** 1460 Ben Sawyer, Mount Pleasant, tel. (843) 884-9672, or the **Hungryneck Antique Mall** at 401 Johnnie Dodds in Mount Pleasant, tel. (843) 849-1733.

Great Bookstores

For new books, try **Chapter Two** in downtown Charleston, tel. (843) 722-4238. This is the bookstore where Albert Finney stocks up on reading material in *Rich in Love.* It's also a good place to pick up a copy of *Sandlapper,* the best magazine available on South Carolina.

For used books, **Atlantic Books'** two locations —310 King St., tel. (843) 723-4751; 191 East Bay St., tel. (843) 723-7654—are the best places in town. If, however, all you want is a paperback for beach reading, you might be interested in **Trade-a-Book,** 1303 Ben Sawyer Blvd., tel. (843) 884-8611.

Pawn Shops, Book Exchanges, Flea Markets
If you drive into Charleston from Columbia on I-26, at Hwy. 17A in Summerville, you'll pass the garish **Money Man Pawn** on your left, tel. (843) 851-7296. But this is only one in a chain; you'll find another in Mount Pleasant, at 1104 Johnnie Dodds Blvd., tel. (843) 971-0000.

TRANSPORTATION AND INFORMATION

GETTING THERE

Airlines

Continental Airlines flies into Charleston International Airport. Delta Airlines' **US Airways** has a city ticket office at 135 King St., tel. (800) 428-4322, (800) 221-1212, or (843) 577-0755. Open Mon.-Fri. 9 a.m.-5 p.m., closed daily for lunch 1:30-2:30 p.m.

GETTING AROUND

One Word of Advice: Walk

A few years back, country singer Dwight Yoakam was slated to play the North Charleston Coliseum. That day it rained, which added to the deluge on the city streets caused by unusually high tides. The embarassed Yoakam finally arrived and rolled onstage more than an hour late. He'd been staying downtown somewhere, and the flooded streets had exacerbated the already dreadful tangle of narrow one-way streets, gawking

tourists, and horse-drawn tour coaches that is downtown Charleston's traffic—making it all but impossible for his car to get through the logjam.

The moral of this story? PASAP. Park As Soon As Possible. Rain or no rain, you don't want to drive around downtown Charleston any longer than you have to—especially if you're a first-time visitor. Charleston was designed to be walked, not driven.

The city has a number of public and private parking lots. Most are reasonably priced. A good place to stop on your way downtown is the **Charleston Visitors Center** at 375 Meeting St., right across from the Charleston Museum. Here, ask the person at the information window for a *Visitors' Guide Map,* which labels quite clearly the places where you can legally park your car. If you want to play it really safe, just leave your car there at the center and take one of the tourist trolleys farther down the peninsula.

DASH

The Downtown Area Shuttle (DASH) is just one segment of the City of Charleston's public transportation system. DASH buses look like trolleys, and they're really pretty nice ways to get from one end of the peninsula to another. Fare is 75 cents, exact change required. A one-day DASH pass costs $2, and the perfect-for-a-weekend-visit three-day pass costs $5. Purchase passes and DASH schedules at the Visitor Reception and Transportation Center and all city-owned downtown parking garages. Seniors and riders with disabilities pay just 25 cents during the week 9 a.m.-3:30 p.m., after 6 p.m., and all day Saturday and Sunday. DASH does not operate on New Year's Day, July 4, Labor Day, Thanksgiving Day, or Christmas Day. You'll notice DASH shelters, benches, and trolley stop signs located throughout the city. These are the only places you'll be able to get on or off a trolley—DASH drivers aren't allowed to make any special stops.

After you pay your fare and climb on board, don't sit in the seats directly behind the driver unless you are a senior or a passenger with a physical disability. For more information, call (843) 724-7420.

You'll also find DASH stops at the Folly Island, North Charleston, and Mt. Pleasant/Isle of Palms Visitors Centers.

Another way to get around is by rickshaw: the **Charleston Rickshaw Company,** tel. (843) 723-5685, provides human-powered service Mon.-Thurs. 6 p.m.-midnight, Fri.-Sat. 6 p.m.-2 a.m., and Sunday 5-11 p.m. The cost is $3 per 10 minutes per person, or $32 per hour per bike. A great, cheap way to see downtown without having to hunt for parking. Call ahead for reservations if you'd like.

By Boat
The **Harbor Intra-Transit System,** tel. (843) 209-2469 (209-AHOY), offers an intriguing alternative to land travel. For $8-12 a roundtrip, you can take a boat from any dock to any dock. It's cheaper, generally faster, and, depending on how much drinking you're doing, safer than driving yourself.

ORGANIZED TOURS

Walking Tours
Charleston Strolls, tel. (843) 766-2080, and **Charleston Walks,** tel. (843) 577-3800, both offer organized walking tours.

Carriage Tours
One fun way to learn the history of the historic buildings of Old Charleston without having to walk around, nose-in-book, is to take one of the city's many carriage tours. And here's a tip—the folks who run these tours love to know they have customers lined up in advance, so all the ones mentioned here will give you a lower price for reserving spots ahead of time. **Palmetto Carriage,** 40 N. Market St., tel. (843) 723-8145, of-

Rich with history, Charleston's Custom House was built in 1767 on top of the 1680 Old Exchange and Provost Dungeon—preserving the basement in which, among other things, pirate Stede Bonnet was imprisoned in 1718.

fers one-hour tours daily from 9 a.m. Kids will appreciate the small petting zoo at the Red Barn.

Charleston Carriage Company, 14 Hayne St., tel. (843) 577-0042 or (843) 723-8687, has been at this longer than anyone, and offers hour-long tours by well-trained guides.

Finally, offering similar services and more unnecessary e's than any other company in town is **Olde Towne Carriage Company,** over on Anson St., tel. (843) 722-1315. **Old South Carriage Tours** is nearby at 14 Anson St., tel. (843) 723-9712.

Minibus Tours
For all the romance of the horse-drawn carriage, there are days in Charleston when you feel the town is best seen from the inside of an air-conditioned vehicle. **Talk of the Towne,** tel. (843) 795-8199, boasts of being able to take you past 250 historic buildings in just two hours. And that's not including all the nonhistoric buildings thrown in as gimmes. All tours leave from the visitors center. The tour company offers complimentary pickup at downtown hotels, inns, and the Market. Fares for the shorter, 75-minute tour run $13 for adults, $8 for children 12 and under. The two-hour your includes a visit to either the 1808 Nathaniel Russell House or the 1828 Edmondston-Alston House. Fares run $21 adults, $14 for children.

Harbor Tours
For a memorable tour of Charleston Harbor, contact **Gray Line Water Tours,** 17 Lockwood Dr. S, tel. (800) 344-4483 or (843) 722-1112. The daytime 90-minute 20-mile Charleston Harbor Tour departs from the City Marina at 2 p.m. daily year-round, plus additional cruises at 9:45 a.m. and 3:45 p.m. March-November. Fares are $8 adult, children 6-11 $4. For another few bucks you can have a meal while you motor past Fort Sumter and the houses on the Battery. The two-and-a-quarter hour, 30-mile Charleston Harbor of History and Cooper River Tour departs from the marina at 11:30 daily year-round. Cost is $10 adults, $5 children 6-11. Lunch onboard for just a few dollars more. Or take the Harborlites Dinner Cruise. You'll cruise 7:30-9:45 p.m., eat a fine dinner while you go, and then dance it off to live music afterwards. If you're here in the sum-

mer, you'll still be able to sightsee around the peninsula as you go. Adults $25, children 6-11 $18, 5 and under $14. Reservations required.

INFORMATION AND SERVICES

Tourist Offices and Visitors Centers
The **Charleston Visitors Center,** 375 Meeting St., tel. (843) 723-5225, is a great place to stop in and get some background and a bagful of brochures and coupon books. Or check the **Charleston Area Convention and Visitors Bureau,** 81 Mary St., tel. (800) 868-8118 or (843) 853-8000, fax (843) 853-0444, Web site: www.charlestoncvb.com; for golf tee times and info, call (800) 744-4444.

Kiawah Island visitors will want to call the **Kiawah Island Visitor Center,** 22 Beachwalker Dr., Kiawah Island.

Mt. Pleasant/Isle of Palms Visitor Center you'll find at Hwy. 17 N at McGrath Darby Blvd. in Mount Pleasant.

Hospitals, Police, Emergencies
The top hospital in the region is the **Medical University of South Carolina Hospital** on the peninsula, tel. (843) 792-2300, but you should be in good hands at **Roper Hospital,** tel. (843) 724-2000, or **Charleston Memorial Hospital,** tel. (843) 577-0600. In North Charleston, call **Trident Regional Medical Center,** tel. (843) 797-7000. In East Cooper, call (843) 881-0100, and in West Ashley, call **Bon Secours St. Francis Xavier,** tel. (843) 402-1000.

In an emergency, reach the police, fire department, and ambulances by dialing 911. The **Poison Control Center 24 Hr. Help Line** is (800) 922-1117.

To reach the police for a nonemergency, call the **Office of Tourism Services** at (843) 720-3892.

Child Care
The **Charleston Nanny,** 1045-F Provincial Circle, Mount Pleasant, tel. (843) 856-9008 or (843) 813-6717, e-mail: tmorris.413@aol.com, offers professionally trained, CPR-certified, insured and bonded babysitters who will watch the kids while you enjoy a day or night on the town.

Post Office

You'll find the main post office downtown at 83 Broad St., tel. (843) 577-0690, and another at 557 E. Bay St., tel. (843) 722-3624.

Public Libraries

The **Charleston Public Library**'s main branch does business at 68 Calhoun St., tel. (843) 805-6802. You'll find the **Edgar Allan Poe Library,** 1921 I'On St. Sullivan's Island, tel. (843) 883-3914—the coolest little branch library in the state—on Middle Street on Sullivan's Island, built into an old defense bunker.

Newspapers

Post and Courier is the paper of record in Charleston, as it has been for many years. Every Thursday, it includes an insert called the *Preview,* which provides pretty much all the current movie, play, and music listings you could need.

The Upwith Herald is a freebie you'll find around downtown, providing pretty much the same information as the *Preview,* as is *Charleston Free Times.*

The Charleston Weekly actually comes out only two times a month, runs two pages long, and features listings only—no articles or full reviews in this other freebie.

Radio Stations

The local "Breeze" affiliate—**98.9FM**—plays "Beach, Boogie, and Blues"—a great soundtrack for your Charleston stay. **96 WAVE** is the big "alternative" station here; you'll see its bumper stickers stuck to everything that's not tied down around here, including traffic signs. A good place to hear local rock. **WBBA—"THE BIG BUBBA,"** is one of the better country stations in the state, featuring some very corny jingles. **WSCI FM 89.3** is the local NPR affiliate. Saturday at 9 p.m., listen for "Vintage Country," with Roger Bellow. If it's talk you want, listen to **WTMA 1250 AM** in the mornings for Dan Moon, a local celebrity and a Charleston institution, to get a sense of the inner workings of the city, as he broadcasts live from store openings, flea markets, and just about any event with room for parking a mobile broadcast unit. Libertarian Scott Caysen hosts a local call-in talk show 3-5 p.m., which occasionally touches on local issues. Midday is filled with the normal syndicated talk shows.

BEYOND CHARLESTON

NORTHWEST ON I-26

Summerville

Summerville's quiet, old-resort-like feel, with its meandering azalea- and pine-shaded streets, is no accident: this burg of 22,000 used to be a place where Lowcountry planters and Charleston residents would hide from the summer fevers. Apparently the distance from the coast and the "high" elevation (75 feet) kept down the mosquitoes.

Summerville is home to author Effie Wilder, whose manuscript was discovered in the slush piles of Peachtree Press. This long-time resident of Presbyterian Home of Summerville became a first-time novelist at age 85 in 1995 with *Out to Pasture: But Not Over the Hill,* and tossed out two other novels (*Over What Hill: Notes from the Pasture,* and *Older But Wilder: More Notes from the Pasture—My Final Short Novel*) before she was 89. She's retired again. For now.

One good place to stay here is the **Bed & Breakfast of Summerville,** 304 S. Hampton St., tel. (843) 871-5275, set in a one-room cottage in a garden behind the 1865 **Blake Washington House,** on S. Hampton Street. Emmagene and Dusty Rhodes' place features a pool, grill, bicycles for touring the town, and a greenhouse. This place is privacy incarnate. Infants

THE BATTLES FOR FORT WAGNER

Folly Island first appears on history's radar during the Civil War, when Union troops stationed at Hilton Head waded through waist-high water onto the south end of Folly Beach as part of their attempt to capture Fort Wagner, the nearly impregnable Confederate fort on Morris Island, north of Folly Beach. Once it captured Fort Wagner, the Union planned to turn the fort's guns on Fort Sumter, the island fortress in the midst of Charleston Harbor—the disabling of which Northerners saw as the key to capturing Charleston. Capturing Charleston, in turn, was the key to crippling Southern importation and shipment of arms and supplies to its armies throughout the South.

First, however, the Yanks had to capture the southern end of Morris Island, just across Lighthouse Inlet from them. From April 7, 1863, until July 6, 1863, the Union soldiers spent their time building up earthworks to protect their gun batteries and constructing barges for an amphibious assault. When the battle actually began, the hard-pressed Confederates holding down the south end of the island eventually ran for the safety of Fort Wagner, leaving 17 dead, 112 wounded, and 67 missing. The Union, though it suffered similar losses, had won the south end of the island.

The next day the Union assaulted Fort Wagner and suffered terrible casualties. A week later, as immortalized in the movie *Glory,* the black 54th Massachusetts Volunteer Infantry, led by Colonel Robert Shaw, attempted to take the fort and was bloodily repulsed, costing 40% of the 54th's lives. Over 1,500 men were lost in both attacks. The fort was never taken. However, the men stayed on Little Folly Island, and the black 55th Massachusetts and 1st North Carolina landed on Folly on August 3rd. The Northern army believed, apparently, that the African-Americans could naturally work better than whites in the extreme heat and humidity. Unfortunately, nature had no such preconceptions, and the men started dropping like flies as they dug trenches, cut timber, built wharves, loaded and unloaded goods, and hauled heavy guns to the front on Morris Island. Most of this work was done under heavy Confederate fire. As if this weren't enough, the Northern whites took advantage of their black cohorts, using them to police and lay out the white camps. In the first seven weeks on Folly, 12 members of the 55th Massachusetts died; 23 had perished by December.

Eventually the Southerners withdrew from Wagner to defend Charleston itself, and the Northerners quickly moved in and turned their guns onto Sumter, which nonetheless hung in there until reduced to rubble. Eventually, the surviving members of the 55th Massachusetts would get the honor of marching into Charleston to bring the Day of Jubilee to the African-Americans of Charleston.

GULLAH CULTURE OF THE SEA ISLANDS

On the quiet Sea Islands south of Charleston, a centuries-old culture is passing away. Like most African-Americans in the state, the Gullah people are descendants of West Africans who made the horrific passage to South Carolina as slaves. (The name of both the people and their language, "Gullah," was long thought to be a derivation of "Angola." Today, many believe it evolved from the words Gola and Gora, both tribal names in modern-day Liberia.) Yet even from the first, the Sea Islander slaves lived notably different from those of their enslaved contemporaries. For one thing, most Sea Islanders lived on isolated plantations where one could commonly find 100 or more Africans for every white person; a Gullah field worker might go months without coming into contact with a European. Consequently, Sea Islanders retained their West African language, culture, and crafts much more coherently than on the mainland.

After the outbreak of the Civil War, Federal ships swept down upon the Sea Islands, establishing the area as a base of operations as they set about shutting down Southern ports. Sea Island slave owners fled, leaving their rice, cotton, and indigo plantations to their slaves. Though President Andrew Johnson nullified General William T. Sherman's order setting aside the Lowcountry for former slaves, many former white planters did not reclaim their lands, and after a number of deadly hurricanes in the late 1890s, many remaining whites left the islands. Few black Sea Islanders interacted at all with whites, and many had never even been to the mainland in their lifetimes. The truth was, despite the hardships their isolation brought them, the Sea Islanders knew they had a good thing.

Things might have stayed like this indefinitely if mainlanders hadn't woken up to the fact that the islands featured some of the best beaches on the East Coast. The Fraser family from Georgia had bought up much of Hilton Head Island for logging, but then one of them got the idea of turning some of the cheap farmland into golf courses. Snowbirds from places like Jersey and Pennsylvania—as sick of Florida as they were of flurries—flocked to the "new" paradise. As quickly as you could say "Please remove your golf shoes," Hilton Head Island became a Northern beachhead in the area—for the second time in a century.

Land prices for the remaining Sea Islanders on Hilton Head and surrounding islands shot up from around $100 an acre in the 1940s to over $100,000 for some oceanfront acres today. In the intervening years, many of those who didn't want to move have found they can't keep up with the higher property taxes and have been forced to sell. Many of those who have somehow remained have discovered that they aren't adequately trained for the higher-paying jobs the resorts had brought to the islands. Consequently, while mainlanders from around the country move in to take many of the managerial and technical positions, the lower-paid service positions have fallen to the Sea Islanders. For many, these become life-long jobs.

And yet, while native Gullah islanders are losing much of their physical and spiritual world to encroaching resorts, network television, and the public schools, the culture lives on, preserved in the still-strong extended families and church-based community.

---

okay, pets are not. Around $50 without breakfast, $60 with. Reservations a must.

While in town, you may want to visit the **Summerville Dorchester Museum,** 100 E. Doty Ave., tel. (843) 875-9666, which features exhibits on Dorchester County and Summerville history, with an emphasis on medical, natural, and plantation history. Open Wed.-Fri. 10 a.m.-2 p.m., Saturday 2-5 p.m. Admission. And just a couple blocks from the downtown district, you'll find the **Azalea Park and Bird Sanctuary.**

At **Old Dorchester State Historic Site,** on Hwy. 642 (Dorchester Rd.) about a quarter mile north of Old Trolley Road Rd. and six miles south of Summerville, tel. (843) 873-1740, you'll find the spot where, in 1697, Massachusetts Congregationalists founded a bluff-top town overlooking the Ashley River. Most of them moved on to the town of Midway, Georgia, by the 1750s, but the British soldiers, after their evacuation of Charleston, took out their wrath on what remained of Dorchester in the 1780s. Today, you'll still find the bell tower of St. George's Church and the tabby walls of the old town fort. Open Thurs.-Mon. 9 a.m.-6 p.m.,

Culture

Perhaps the best-known craft to the casual Carolina visitor is **basketweaving.** In the Charleston Market and along Hwy. 17 north of Mount Pleasant, Gullah women sit in their stands making and selling their wares, the products of a tradition passed down from African ancestors and carried across the Atlantic in the minds and hands of women locked in the holds of slave ships. Most of the baskets you'll see for sale bear European influences as well—the relatively lightweight baskets found for sale are for show, not for carrying clothing, food, or babies, as are the heavier "work" baskets, which are more uniformly African in origin.

Both the "show" and "work" baskets, woven from the Lowcountry's sweet grass, pine straw, bulrushes, and palmetto leaves, contain patterns and designs similar to those found in Nigeria, Ghana, Togo, and Benin. Both boys and girls learn basketmaking at a young age, though primarily women continue weaving as adults.

Another celebrated element of the Gullah culture is the **storytelling** tradition passed down from time eternal. Many of the traditional Gullah stories (still told today) appear to have African parallels. One popular series features "Brer Rabbit," a wily rabbit who stays one step ahead of those who are physically bigger than him through his quick wits. A lot of historians have theorized that this reflects the slaves' own strategies for outwitting the dominant white class during antebellum times, but as scholar Patricia Jones-Jackson points out in *When Roots Die: Endangered Traditions on the Sea Islands,* Brer Rabbit-like characters abound in West African cultures, suggesting that though slaves may well have found it easy to identify with the Brer Rabbit character, the character itself predates American slavery.

Other common Gullah stories feature Jesus as a character, and always contain some sort of moral lesson. Call-and-response relationships between storyteller and audience, in fact, resemble the ones between Gullah preachers and their congregations. Most Sea Island churches tend toward emotive Baptist and Methodist services with the call-and-response forms found in many African-American cultures. One interesting Gullah belief—progressively less common—perceives the human as divided into body, soul, *and* spirit. At death, the body dies, the soul travels to heaven or hell, but the spirit is left behind to do either good or harm to people here on Earth.

Language

Technically speaking, the Gullah tongue is considered a creole rather than a dialect like inland Black English or American Southern English. Linguists consider a dialect a variant of standard English particular to a specific region or social environment, whereas a true creole descends from a "pidgin," a combination language created by people speaking different languages who wish to communicate with one another. Technically, a pidgin has no native speakers; when because of isolation the pidgin is allowed to become the dominant tongue in a region (as has Gullah on the Sea Islands), the tongue is considered a creole.

While the vast majority of Gullah words come from English, a number of words (one linguist estimates 4,000) derive from African languages, including *gula* for "pig"; *cush* for "bread" or "cake," nansi for "spider," and *buckra* for "white man."

Jones-Jackson points out a number of grammatical elements to listen for when conversing with a Gullah speaker; they include pre-marked verbs

(continues on next page)

free tours on the weekends at 2 p.m. On-site archaeological excavation every Thursday and the first and third Saturdays of the month.

SOUTHWEST ON HIGHWAY 17

Charleston Tea Plantation

On Wadmalaw Island at 6617 Maybank Hwy., tel. (800) 443-5987 or (843) 559-0383, fax (843) 559-3049, this is the only tea plantation in America, home to American Classic Tea. Here you

can learn about the process of tea making. Generally, the plantation is open to visitors only on the first Saturday of the month May-Oct. 10 a.m.-1:30 p.m. Free walking tours begin on the half hour starting at 10 a.m., with the last tour at 1:30 p.m. Recently, however, co-owner William Hall announced that the plantation would be offering group tours on weekdays by appointment. So if you have a minimum of 19 friends who would like to join you for a tour, for $5. a person you can get a one-hour tour in which you learn about the world of tea production and take a short walk to

GULLAH CULTURE OF THE SEA ISLANDS
(continued)

("I don shell em" instead of "I shelled them"), verb serialization ("I hear tell say he knows," instead of "I hear it said that he knows"); and adjective and verb reduplication for emphasis ("clean clean" rather than "very clean"). All of these characteristics seem to have roots in African languages.

Where to Experience Gullah Culture
Near Beaufort: The 49-acre, 16-building Penn Center on St. Helena Island stands as perhaps the world's foremost center of information on Gullah culture and on the connections between West Africa and the Sea Islands. The first place to visit is the **York W. Bailey Museum,** tel. (843) 838-8562, on the right side of Land's End Rd. as you come in from Hwy. 21. Admission runs $2. Museum hours run Tues.-Fri. 11 a.m.-4 p.m., Saturday 10 a.m.-4 p.m.

If you can make it here in November you may get to take part in the **Heritage Days Celebration,** a three-day festival celebrating African-American Sea Islands culture. Call (843) 838-8563 for information.

Right at the intersection of Hwy. 21 and Land's End Rd., you'll find the **Red Piano Too,** tel. (843) 838-2241, an old plank grocery store on the National Register of Historic Places, which has reopened as an art gallery for Gullah artists. A great place to pick up a one-of-a-kind (literally) souvenir, including painted furniture, mobiles, regional landscapes, and books written in Gullah. You'll also notice the **Gullah House Restaurant,** next door, tel. (843) 838-2402, with items like "Hot Ya Mout Swimps," and "Uncle Woolie's Crab Cake Dinner," along with meat dishes.

For Beaufort-area tours focused specifically on the Gullah culture, call **Gullah-n-Geechie Mahn Tours,** tel. (843) 838-7516 or (843) 838-3758.

In May, Beaufort hosts a **Gullah Festival** with traditional storytelling, music, and other events. Call (843) 525-0628 for information.

Charleston Area: You'll find Gullah basketweavers selling their baskets along Hwy. 17 north of Mount Pleasant, around the Market area, and sometimes at other known tourist haunts like the visitors center or at Patriots Point—though prices at the latter tend to be more expensive. The **Avery Research Center for African-American History and Culture,** at the College of Charleston, 125 Bull St., tel. (843) 727-2009, features a reading room and archives dedicated to documenting and preserving the cultural history of Lowcountry African-Americans. **Gallery Chuma/African American Art Gallery,** 43 John St., tel. (843) 722-7568, e-mail: Chuman@galleryChuma.com, features Gullah artist Jonathan Green's works as a permanent fixture, along with those of several other renowned African-American artists. Open Mon.-Sat. 10 a.m.-6 p.m. or by appointment. **Gullah Tours** of Charleston leave from the gallery daily—call for information. For authentic Sea Island cooking, try **Gullah Cuisine,** 1717 Hwy. 17 N, tel. (843) 881-9076.

Media
Well-regarded books on Sea Island culture and the Gullah tongue include the very informative *When Roots Die: Endangered Traditions on the Sea Islands,* Patricia Jones-Jackson, Athens, GA: UGA, 1987, which is highlighted by the inclusion of several transcribed Gullah folk tales, sermons, and prayers. SC ETV, tel. (800) 553-7752, Web site: www.scetv.org/scetv/mkthome.html, offers a number of video titles that touch on Gullah and Sea Island subjects.

The bookstore in the museum at the Penn Center is one of the best places in the state (and the world) to find books, music, and videotapes relating to Sea Island culture.

---

see the tea fields and the plantation's unique tea harvester in action—something not seen by the folks who show up for the Saturday open houses. You can stock up on tea bargains or special gift baskets not available in stores. And of course, lots of tea sampling, along with Charleston benne wafers and the plantation's unusual line of tea jellies.

Call for information. Fully accessible.

Kiawah Island
This 10,000-acre island, tel. (800) 992-9666, features some 10 miles of beautiful beach (though only the area at Beachwalker County Park is accessible to those not staying in one of the island's resort villages).

The island features four championship golf courses and is also popular with the tennis crowd. Ice skaters like it, too, apparently: not long after the 1998 Winter Games, Olympic gold medalist Tara Lipinsky and her family announced that they were buying a house here on the island.

Seabrook

Seabrook, 1001 Landfall Way, tel. (843) 768-0880, is located 23 miles south of Charleston off Hwy. 17. It's all villas and a beach club with swimming pools, restaurants, lounges, tennis courts, two golf courses, an equestrian center, trails, fishing gear, sailboats, and bicycles.

EDISTO ISLAND

In 1861, as South Carolina's statesmen gathered in Charleston to debate whether to secede from the Union immediately or wait for other Southern states to come along, the delegate from Edisto Island leapt to his feet and shouted that if South Carolina didn't vote to secede from the Union immediately, then by God, Edisto Island would secede by itself.

This gives you a little insight into the independent, the-hell-with-the-rest-of-the-world feel of this little Sea Island. Coming out here for a vacation stay is a little bit like seceding from the rest of the world.

Archaeologists have found numerous sites used by Edisto Indians in the centuries before the Europeans arrived. In 1674, the British bought the island off the tribe for a few tools, cloth, and some really neat trinkets. Indigo and Sea Island cotton plantations covered the island for quite a while, but after the boll weevil plague in 1920, the land ws reduced to mostly small farming and, near the water, tourism.

The island could call itself "The Last Unresort"—it remains largely resortless, and most of the locals seem committed to keeping it that way. The Edisto Island Historical Preservation Society opened up the Edisto Island Museum in 1991 to combat encroachment (see below).

Edisto is a great spot to rent a beach house or just camp and relax. The waves are pretty decent; the few restaurants range from perfectly decent to quite good, and the people are friendly.

Sights

On your way into town, keep a sharp eye out on your right for the **Edisto Island Museum,**

"WE PAPA" ("OUR FATHER"): THE LORD'S PRAYER IN GULLAH

Jedus tell um say, "Wen oona pray, mus say:
<u>And he said unto them, When ye pray, say:</u>
We Papa een heaben,
<u>Our Father which art in heaven,</u>
leh ebrybody hona you nyame
cause you da holy.
<u>Hallowed be thy name.</u>
We pray dat soon you gwine
rule oba all ob we.
<u>Thy kingdom come.</u>
Wasoneba ting you da want,
leh um be een dis wol,
<u>Thy will be done.</u>
same like e be dey een heaben.
<u>On earth as it is in heaven.</u>
Gee we de food wa we need dis day
yah an ebry day.
<u>Give us this day our daily bread.</u>
Fagibe we fa de bad ting we da do.
<u>And forgive us our sins—</u>
Cause we da fagibe dem people
was do bad ta we.
<u>As we forgive those who sin against us.</u>
Leh we don't have haad test
wen Satan try we.
<u>And lead us not into temptation.</u>
Keep we from e ebil.
<u>but deliver us from evil.</u>

—*Translation from* De Good Nyews Bout Jedus Christ Wa Luke Write, *prepared by the Sea Island Translation and Literacy Team, 1995.*

Hwy. 174, Edisto Island, tel. (843) 869-1954. They've done a wonderful job there with a small building, presenting a number of exhibits interpreting the unique ingredients of Sea Island life. A few books and old posters here for sale, and very helpful workers. Admission is $2 for adults, free for kids under 10.

The oldest home still standing on the island was built around 1735, but most seem to have been built in the '50s, '60s, and '70s, before land prices raced upwards. The **Zion Baptist Church** you pass on your left as you enter Edisto Beach was founded in 1810 by Hepzibah Jenkins, a strong-willed woman raised by her family's slaves after her mother died and her father was impris-

camping on Edisto Island

oned during the American Revolution. So grateful was she to these people that she built this church for them in 1810.

Edisto Island State Park

Edisto State Park, Hwy. 174, tel. (843) 538-8206, may just be the best shelling beach in South Carolina. My wife and I once scored about a dozen conch (here pronounced "conk") shells in a 20-minute walk. However, the no-see-ums are equally legendary here: bring Skin-so-Soft and Deep Woods OFF! and you should be okay. Better yet, pick up one of those screened-in tents to put around the picnic table. Of course, if you're at one of the sites that faces the ocean and not the marshes, you'll be better off. But these are usually reserved in advance, so call ahead.

The amount of shells in the sand at Edisto is incredible. But look a little closer and you might realize that some of them are actually fossils; their presence in this area is attributed by some to the theory that this area was once under the Atlantic Ocean. Back then, Upcountry rivers and streams poured directly into the ocean, depositing the shark teeth, horse, and mastodon bones found here today.

Events

Every July, the **Edisto Summer Fest** celebrates the warm weather with a raft race, shag contest, street dance, music concert, boat poker run, and lots of food. Call (843) 869-3867 for information.

On the second Saturday in October, the Edisto Island Historical Preservation Society's **Tour of Historic Plantation Houses, Churches and Sites** is held. Call (843) 869-1954 for tour information.

When the weather gets colder in November, folks all gather for the **Edisto Oyster Roast,** a one-day festival featuring live entertainment, games, and the namesake shellfish, along with other seafood. Call (843) 869-3867 for information.

Accommodations

If you're not camping, see if you can't reserve one of the five air-conditioned cabins at Edisto Beach State Park. Generally, you'll need to get one months and months in advance, but you might get lucky. Call (843) 869-2156 or (843) 869-2756. Moderate. Otherwise, the traditional way to stay on Edisto Island (practically the only way, given the determined lack of hotels and motels) is one of the hundreds of beach houses lining the shore.

A number of rental companies service the island. Here are a few: **The Lyons Company,** 440 Hwy. 174, tel. (800) 945-9667 or (843) 869-2516; **Edisto Sales and Rentals Realty,** 1405 Palmetto Blvd., tel. (800) 868-5398; or **Fairfield Ocean Ridge,** 1 King Cotton Rd., tel. (800) 845-8500 or (843) 869-2561.

One warning: Rent a house too far south on the island and the water nearest your house will contain inlet currents that make it unsafe to enter. Which means you'll need to hop in the car every time you want to go swimming—not everyone's idea of a relaxed week at the beach.

The reason I say "practically the only way" is because Edisto Island features two B&Bs: the four-story, four-bedroom 1847 **Cassina Point Plantation B&B,** 1642 Clark Road, tel. (843) 869-2535, and the two-unit **Seaside Plantation,** 400 Hwy. 174, tel. (843) 869-0971. Cassina Point features a creek outside and huge old trees with plenty of Spanish moss dripping off its branches. Full breakfast. Premium.

Food

Since the closing of a beloved Hwy. 174 restaurant called the Old Post Office, a lot of people have pointed to the waterfront **Pavillion** restaurant at the corner of Hwy. 174 and Palmetto Drive as a decent place to catch a meal. My experience here was that I sat for 20 minutes on a busy night and didn't even get my water. But people claim the all-you-can-eat shrimp is a good deal, so if you're down and looking for an ocean view, you might want to give it try. On the other side of the island, facing the marshes, you'll find **Dockside Restaurant,** 3730 Duck Site Rd., tel. (843) 869-2695, featuring fresh shrimp, hush puppies, crab, shrimp, and shrimp. Moderately priced.

There's a gas station across from the Pavillion. Inside, you'll find a sandwich counter. The sandwiches are good deli food—if you're looking to cut corners, this is a good place to do it.

Shops, Rentals

Right at the point where Hwy. 174 bends at the BP station and becomes Palmetto Blvd., you'll find **Island Rentals,** 101 Palmetto Blvd., tel. (843) 869-1321, renting four-wheel bikes, Island Cruisers, Waverunners, SeaDoos, 17-foot rental boats, and all the umbrellas, beach chairs, crab traps, fishing rods, rafts, tubes, strollers, and pull carts you'll ever need for a good time on the beach. You can rent by the hour, by the half day, full day, three days, and by the week. Reserve ahead if you can. The young entrepreneur owner, Tony Spainhour, says he'll deliver, too.

You'll come across Karen Carter's **The Edisto Bookstore** at 547 Hwy. 174, tel. (843) 869-1885 or (843) 869-2598, on the right on your way into town. Karen's a friendly, helpful person who keeps her shelves well-stocked with both new and used books.

Information

For more information on this unique little island, contact the **Edisto Chamber of Commerce** at P.O. Box 206, Edisto Beach, SC 29438, tel. (843) 869-3867.

BEAUFORT
AND THE LOWCOUNTRY

To understand the just-growed feeling of the South Carolina Lowcountry today, consider what the area was like just a couple decades ago. Residents of the Sea Islands used to have an arduous time traveling around from island to island, much less from island to mainland. To get from Beaufort to Savannah, a 45-minute trip today, used to require a drive from Beaufort to Sheldon, Sheldon to Ridgeland, Ridgeland to Garden City, Georgia, and then on to Savannah—taking up the good part of a day. Add this to the fact that not many Sea Islanders owned a car in the first place, and it's no wonder that many people in Beaufort never set foot in Savannah, and vice versa. People living on the smaller islands traveled even less, and some part of nearly any trip they *did* take was sure to involve a boat. In the late 1960s when Pat Conroy taught there, Daufuskie Island was so isolated from the mainland that the Gullah children

Conroy took across on Halloween to trick or treat in Port Royale came away believing that on the Mainland, all one had to do to get candy was knock on a door.

Today, in the world of satellite television, car phones and pagers, you'd be hard-pressed to find anyone that innocent down here. But while the modern world of air-conditioning and cappuccino has found the Sea Islands, their character is imbedded enough that it will never wash away entirely—at least not until the last shrimp boat has been beaten into a golf cart.

Despite the bridges that connect most of the islands now, the Lowcountry is still a land where, what with all the shrimping, crabbing, and fishing to be done, boats are considered essential equipment. As Jackie Washington of the little village of Broad River puts it, "If you don't own a boat around here, you're living half a life."

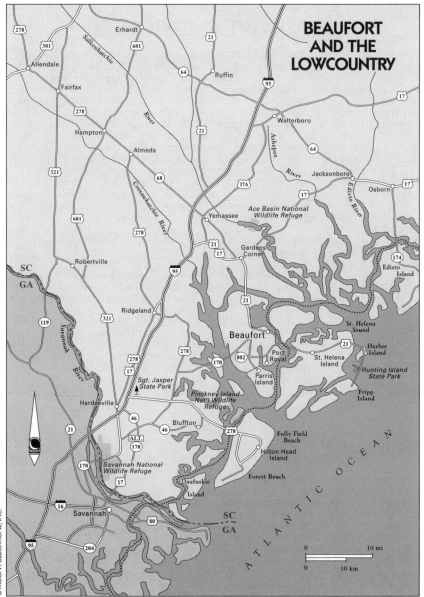

BEAUFORT
AND THE
LOWCOUNTRY

BEAUFORT AND VICINITY

A scene in *The Big Chill* captures Beaufort beautifully: Kevin Kline and William Hurt jog/walk down Bay St. in the early morning fog, longtime friends reunited after years, middle-aged men, T-shirts drenched with the humidity and their efforts to remain potent into old age. Old business blocks lean over the men's shoulders like kindly merchants, potential gleaming in the wet early morning asphalt; this is Beaufort, and, given the high number of people moving from other parts of the country to live here, these—or something else similarly comforting—are things that Beaufort says to many others.

Beaufort is a quiet, romantic poem of a town, a town best absorbed, rather than "done." It's a historic town—second oldest in the state, founded in 1710, only 20 years after Charleston, and, because it sits far from the heavily trafficked path beaten flat by the 20th century, Beaufort remains a town where many of the differences between 1840 and 2000 seem trivial, somehow, and the visitor immediately feels either desperately out of place or home at last.

Orientation

You'll probably want to stop in the visitor information center at 1006 Bay St., tel. (843) 524-3163, for tour maps, information on lodging and dining, and plenty of brochures. But here's a general overview of the town.

Some 65 islands make up Beaufort County. Named after one of Carolina's lords proprietors, Henry, Duke of Beaufort, the town of Beaufort (pronounced "BYOO-fort") is the county seat, its 12,000 residents making it the biggest town on Port Royale, one of the biggest islands in the county. The historic downtown district is called "Old Point." The reason you see so many old buildings still standing here is that Union troops occupied this region early in the Civil War, meaning that it was already Union-held for more than three years by the time Bill Sherman and his 8,000-man incineration squad came to the Carolina coast.

HISTORY

Six flags—or eight, counting the flagless Westoes' and Yamassees' earlier claims to the land—have flown over the people living their lives out in this location: the French, Spanish, English, Scottish, American, and Confederate flags have all waved overhead. Though the French and Spanish both failed to successfully settle the area, Scottish subjects pouring into already-crowded Charleston in the late 1600s asked the lords proprietors if they could try to settle the bad-luck region and were given permission. Thus, in 1684, Lord Cardross founded the city as a haven for

Beaufort's Bay Street Inn, a former Civil War hospital, featured prominently in the films Prince of Tides *and* Forrest Gump.

Scottish immigrants. Two years later, Cardross and his fellow settlers were all dead, murdered by an army of Spaniards and Westoes.

The Yamassee
As early as 1684, the Yamassee Indians of Georgia, who had had trouble getting along with the Spanish, asked for asylum in Carolina. The Carolinian settlers granted the Yamassees' request, figuring that it couldn't hurt to have this warlike tribe who hated the Spanish between St. Augustine and themselves. In the next decades, 10 different Yamassee towns were founded between the Savannah River and Charleston. In 1711, Yamassee warriors joined with British troops under Colonel Barnwell in aiding North Carolinian settlers in their fight against the Tuscarora Indians.

But by this time the Spanish threat had fairly subsided, and the town of Beaufort had already been laid out in 1710, to become home to a number of seasoned Barbadian planters, along with other immigrants who had arrived in Charles Town to find all of the best land there already purchased. Unfortunately, the new settlers' homesteads infringed on the lands granted earlier to the Yamassee, and, worse, some of the British Indian traders cheated the Native Americans and allowed them to run up oppressive amounts of credit that gave them every reason to want to do whatever it took to be free from their debts.

LOWCOUNTRY HIGHLIGHTS

- Beaufort Historic District
- Edisto River Canoe and Kayak Trail
- Gullah House Restaurant (St. Helena Island)
- Harbour Town (Hilton Head Island)
- Hunting Island State Park
- Laurel Hill Wildlife Drive (Savannah National Wildlife Refuge)
- Pinckney Island National Wildlife Refuge
- Sheldon Church ruins (Sheldon)
- Shrimp Shack (St. Helena Island)
- South Carolina's Artisan's Center (Walterboro)

Thus it was that when Beaufort was just five years old, Yamassee Indians wiped out most everybody in the town—most everybody south of Charles Town, in fact. But after the Yamassee and other hostile tribes were chased away and killed (many ran south and joined the defiant Seminole confederation in Florida), settlers came back to the old Second City and began settling here again. The British conquered and occupied the town during the Revolution.

The War between the States
In the War of 1812, English gunboats sailed into range but found the port city too strongly fortified to attack, but 50 years later, during the Civil War, the Union Army was not so intimidated. And they had little reason to be, since most of Beaufort's fighting men had already left town to join the Confederate Army elsewhere. The Yankees attacked the Sea Islands in early November 1861, beginning with an amphibious landing at Hilton Head; they took Beaufort, the wealthy planters' town, on November 7.

The women and children—horrified at the rapacious Northern men bursting into their homes—fled the city, leaving only one white citizen of Beaufort—a pro-Union Northerner who'd moved down just prior to the war. Though some slaves left with their white owners' families, thousands upon thousands of field hands were left behind. Some acquired plats of land subdivided by the Northern Army for farming; some acquired the huge empty houses in town. The Penn School was opened on Saint Helena Island by Quaker missionaries from Pennsylvania to educate the former slaves.

After the War
When the railroad came to town, Beaufortians insisted it be built a mile away from downtown, to reduce the noise and soot. As the 19th century wound down, the strong Northern presence in the area refused to fade. By 1940, one-third of the taxable land of Beaufort County had been purchased by Northerners for hunting preserves. Today, in new "Old South" developments like Newpoint on Saint Helena Island, many of the residents are emigrated Northerners, many living in large mock plantation homes modeled after those owned by the slaveholders their ancestors came to undermine during the Civil War.

THE YAMASSEE WAR

The Carolina settlers had experienced animosities with the indigenous peoples as early as 1671, when they declared open war on the Kussoes, a Lowcountry tribe who had been stealing corn from the settlers' public holds—and whom they believed to be in league with the Spanish conspiring against the English settlement. But by and large, Carolina's Indians and settlers got along in an interdependent fashion, as Charles Town merchants sold and shipped the furs that traders acquired farther upstate. Unfortunately, the men who lived among and traded with the various indigenous tribes, as one settler admitted, "were not (generally) men of the best morals." Many tended to cheat the Indians in financial dealings and were known to seduce Indian women and use violence against the men. Against the pleas of the village chiefs, they continued to sell whiskey to the men of the tribe. And worst, perhaps, was the fact that traders—against the wisdom of most other Carolinians—liked to extend credit to the Indians, allowing them to run up cumulative tabs as high—some estimate—as 50,000 pounds sterling. Hence, even if they forgave the Europeans' other harassments, the Indians now had a strong financial motive for throwing off the strangling yoke of the English.

On top of all this, some of the Lowcountry tribes were concerned about squatters who had begun encroaching on land they hadn't first purchased from the Indians. So universal in fact was Indian resentment against them that one tribe—some suspect the Upcountry Creek, though most believe it to have been the Lowcountry Yamassee—went about spreading word of an upcoming intertribal massacre of the traders and the rest of the non-Indians in Carolina. Odds are also that the Spanish, always trying to present themselves as the Indians' true friend, egged on the violence.

Initial Violence

In 1715, a number of settlers in the Port Royal area heard from Indian friends that such a plot was taking shape, especially amongst the local Yamassees, a tribe who had moved up from the Spanish-held Georgia coast with the Carolinians' permission in the 1680s and settled on and near Coosawhatchie Island. The planters were well aware of the unscrupulousness of many traders—something like the used-car salesmen of the Colonial era—and promptly sent a delegation to the Yamassee town of Pocotaligo to promise redress of their grievances and let them know that the governor himself was on the way to negotiate treaties with them. On April 14, the Yamassee welcomed the Carolina diplomats, received their message, fed them dinner, and then, the following dawn, murdered most of them. A few were taken prisoner. Among these were Indian agent Thomas Nairne, whom they subsequently burned at the stake in a prolonged torture that took several days.

All told, the Yamassee killed somewhere around 90 settlers who were living with them at Pocotaligo. Then they moved on to Port Royal, where they killed 100 more whites and Africans.

The First Stage

South Carolina Governor Charles Craven was en route to the Yamassee negotiations when word of the slaughter reached him. He immediately called out the meager state militia and, leading the troops himself, attacked in retaliation. He stopped them at the Stono River, and while they faced off, Craven sent a company of riflemen up by water to Port Royal, from where they sailed up the river to Pocotaligo and destroyed the town.

When Craven had sent the delegation to Pocotaligo, he'd also dispatched messengers to each of the other tribes supposedly involved in the conspiracy, sending conciliatory messages, along with pleas for help in standing against the Yamassee. One by one, each of Craven's messengers drifted back into camp with grim news: their assigned tribe had massacred every or nearly every white man, woman, and child among them.

Though an estimated 16 Indian nations, reaching as far as present-day Alabama, began the war as part of a coalition with the Yamassee and Creeks, most of these tribes were more concerned with exacting vengeance on the scurrilous traders than with wholesale genocide. Given the overwhelming ratio of Native Americans to Europeans and Africans, only the humanity of these reluctant warriors spared the Carolinians from complete annihilation.

After the first wave of killing, frightened settlers came fleeing to the walled city of Charleston. One thing Carolina had on its side was a shrewd governor. Craven realized quickly that this was not going to be a brief campaign. He also knew well that once the initial excitement had died down and the most obvious threat had passed, his untrained militiamen were going to want to head back home—and that this was just what the Indians would be waiting for. To prevent this, he declared martial law and ordered militia deserters put to death. He also sent messengers to the other colonies—and to England—pleading for assistance.

By June 6, Craven and an army of 250 Carolinian militiamen and Native Americans, in cooperation with another party of men led by Colonel Robert Barnwell (who sailed south past Beaufort and approached from the rear), decisively defeated the Yamassee at Pocotaligo, at the head of the Cumbahee (Salkehatchie) River.

The Second Stage

Now the Cheraws and Creeks grew more aggressive in the north, marching southeast toward Charles Town. North Carolina's Colonel Maurice Moore headed down with a small army to help, and Craven and his militia marched north to join them. But no sooner had Craven and his now 700-man militia crossed the Santee River than a party of 700 Native Americans attacked European settlements from the south, pouring across the Edisto River and burning and slaying their way up the coast until only a few miles stood between them and the cowering city of Charles Town. Fortunately for the Holy City, when word came that Craven was returning, the Indians retreated.

In fact, the number of men who could legally take up arms to defend the colony—white men, free blacks, and loyal Native Americans—stood at only 1,400-1,500, and men not yet burned out of their homes were understandably torn between staying to support and defend their houses and families and joining the militia to battle the aggressors directly elsewhere. The Indians numbered an estimated 15,000. The Colonial Assembly voted to raise a "standing army" of 1,200 men, to include 600 white Carolinians, 100 Virginian mercenaries, 100 loyal Indians, and (here you can hear the collective "gulp!" of Lowcountry planters) 400 African-Americans or other slaves. The move to arm the African-American slaves—who, their advocates noted, were after all just as concerned about their families' safety as anyone else—was a wise one, though it understandably made a lot of slave owners nervous.

Craven sent agents to Virginia, New York, and Boston to get men, guns, and ammunition. Virginia, by far the strongest colony and most able to help, was making a fortune while South Carolina was preoccupied and unable to trade with the Indians. Finally, Virginia Governor Alexander Spotswood convinced his stingy burgesses to send 130 men. The burgesses agreed but demanded that South Carolina send up 130 African-American slave women to take these men's places at their jobs.

Virginia dragged its gutters to come up with its 130 men—many of them derelicts and malcontents whom they were just as glad to get out of the state. South Carolina knew it shouldn't look a gift horse in the mouth, but it also realized that to take the 130 women Virginia wanted away from their slave husbands for a prolonged period was a good way to start a slave insurrection. Wisely, South Carolina never made good its part of the deal.

Up in New York, the governor of New York and New Jersey attempted to get the Seneca Indians to come down and help fight on the side of the English, but they proved unwilling. Most colonies were hesitant to send along their best fighting men when, for all they knew, a riot might break out among Indians in their own region. To forestall this eventuality, the British government sent along 1,000 muskets, 600 pistols, 2,000 grenades, and 201 barrels of gunpowder, but no soldiers.

The lords proprietors (in some cases the heirs of the original grantee) helped very little at all. They provided some money but weren't able to ship any arms or ammunition. The British Parliament told them to hand over the province if they couldn't defend it; the lords told the king he could buy the property if he wanted, but that they would never give it up without getting paid the fair price. Just what the "fair price" for a colony full of butchered colonists and their slaves was, the lords did not say. So, while the Carolinians sweated and looked longingly eastward for their deliverance, a debate arose in England about what the proper price of South Carolina should be, and about whether or not England really needed a colony in Carolina, after all.

The Cherokee to the Rescue

Fortunately for the Carolinians, their salvation didn't depend upon the actions in England. In truth, it rested in another nation, just a few hundred miles away. North Carolina's Colonel Maurice Moore took 300 men up the eastern side of the Savannah River and into the homeland of the Lower Cherokee peoples. The Cherokee were old trading partners with the British, and aside from murdering a few corrupt traders, they had taken no part in the violence thus far. They wavered back and forth between remaining neutral and joining the British to help them defeat

(continues on next page)

THE YAMASSEE WAR

(continued)

the other tribes. If the Cherokees helped the English and the English won, the Cherokees would be in a great position to demand land rights they coveted. And if they did *not* help the English and the Creek and Yamassee—the Cherokees' longtime adversaries—won, the Cherokees would probably be the coalition's next target. In fact, though, this was true whether or not the Cherokees helped the English. So it was ultimately in the Cherokees' best interest to protect their trading partners.

Finally, an incident between the Cherokees and the envoys sent by the nearby Creeks, who wanted to murder the English in the woods on the way back to Charleston, decided the issue. On January 27, 1716, the red "war stick" was sent throughout the Cherokee villages to announce that the Cherokees would fight on the side of the English.

A Hostile Peace

This Cherokee/Carolinian combination was unstoppable—and the other tribes knew it. Most of them quickly made peace upon the Cherokees' arrival. The Lower Creeks bolted from their Georgia homes and fled clear to the Chattahoochee. The Cherokees also put an end to the Cheraws' bartering for guns with Virginia traders.

Knowing the war was essentially won, Craven sailed that April for the mother country, leaving Colonel Robert Daniel to serve as governor in his stead. Isolated killings of settlers continued for another year or so, but by the summer of 1717 even these had tapered off to a prewar level. All told, 400 settlers had been killed during battle, many of them in the initial ambushes. History doesn't record how many Native Americans died, but the number was horrendous. The once-great Yamassee tribe was devastated, and its members drifted south, eventually becoming part of the hodgepodge Seminole people.

South Carolina, which had generally tried to help the "loyal" tribes get along, was now confronted with the threat of a united Indian coalition attacking them. From now on, the Carolinians' theory was divide and rule.

Perhaps the most profound result of the Yamassee War was the way it proved the lords proprietors' inability, or unwillingness, to protect the lives and livelihoods of those to whose labor they owed much of their wealth. When the colonists had come to them for help, the proprietors had passed the sixpence. It was something the Carolinians would not forget.

In the 1960s and '70s, Beaufort gained a bit of renown as the hometown of Smokin' Joe Frazier, heavyweight boxing champion of the world. And then Beaufort native Pat Conroy started broadcasting the town's beauties, foibles, and sins to the world via such novels as *The Great Santini, The Prince of Tides,* and *Beach Music.*

Southern Archetype

Today, Beaufort is a beautiful antebellum town, something of an archetype for Southern splendor, given the town's high profile in a host of recent movies set in the South, including film versions of Conroy's novels and *The Big Chill, Forrest Gump,* and *Something to Talk About.* In fact, *The Big Chill's* Tom Berenger liked it so much here he bought a home on the Okatie River for himself and his family. Costar William Hurt was later sued by his then-live-in, Sandra Jennings, who claimed that while the couple had

lived here together during the filming, they had qualified for "common-law marriage" status under South Carolina state law.

Many South Carolinians come here to visit Hunting Island State Park, preserved for decades by a hunters' collective and later grabbed by the state and reserved for public use. Here you'll see subtropical flora at its best. Speaking of Hollywood, Hunting Island was recently used (along with Fripp Island) as the location for Disney's recent live-action version of *The Jungle Book.*

SIGHTS

Beaufort Museum

The brick and tabby arsenal building at 713 Craven St., tel. (843) 525-7077, looks like a small-town satellite campus of the Citadel. The two brass guns outside were captured from the

British in 1779 and seized by Union soldiers after the fall of Fort Walker in 1861. They were returned to Beaufort in 1880. This 1798 building—rebuilt in 1852—makes a great place for a museum. This is a nice, small museum. Granted, the sheer amount of history in the town seems to deserve a grander reckoning, but the museum does a good job of documenting day-to-day life in the early days of the Sea Islands. In Barbra Streisand's *The Prince of Tides,* this building doubled as a Greenwich Village loft for the dinner party scene.

Open Mon.-Tues. and Thurs.-Sat. 10 a.m.-5 p.m. Admission is about $2.

St. Helena's Episcopal Church

Founded in 1712 and built in 1724, this church at 505 Church St., tel. (843) 522-1712, has seen a lot of history. It survived the Yamassee War in 1715, the Revolution in the 1770s and '80s, and even the Civil War—when army doctors performed surgeries using the churchyard's flat tombstones as operating tables. Stop by and pay a visit Sept.-May 10 a.m.-4 p.m., June-Sept. 10 a.m.-1 p.m.

National Cemetery

Right on Hwy. 21 in Beaufort, you'll come upon the National Cemetery, established by Abraham

ROBERT SMALLS, BEAUFORT'S SAVIOR SLAVE AND UNION WAR HERO

In 1862, Confederates dismantled an old fort on the southern end of Folly Island to take the guns to another fort that needed them. They loaded the Confederate guns onto the CSS *Planter,* piloted by African-American slave Robert Smalls. That night while the others slept ashore, Smalls loaded his family and a group of other slaves aboard and slipped the Confederate ship past rebel guns, through the mines he and his crewmates had helped place, and delivered the boat to the Union soldiers in Charleston.

Smalls' heroism made him an instant cause célèbre for the North. He was given a reward for "capturing" an enemy craft and sneaking it through the mined harbor and sent north to meet with President Lincoln and Secretary of State Edwin Stanton, where he pleaded for the arming of black troops. Upon his return to the South he continued to serve aboard the *Planter.* In 1863, while plying the waters of Folly River, the ship came under such heavy fire from Confederate guns that the ship's captain abandoned the wheelhouse and hid in the coal storage. Smalls—who faced certain death as a traitor if captured—took over the ship and sailed her clear of the enemy's guns. For this he was named captain of the *Planter.* He served the Union forces for the duration of the war, providing the Federals with invaluable information about the Lowcountry coast. His service also included a stint with the Beaufort Light Infantry, during which he was stationed in the Beaufort Arsenal—now the Beaufort Museum.

After the war, the Union honored Smalls by asking him to take part in the ceremonies at the re-raising of the Union flag over Fort Sumter. He was later voted the U.S.'s first African-American congressman, and he purchased the home of his former owner.

Smalls served in the South Carolina house of representatives, the state senate, and eventually the U.S. Congress. Though convicted of taking a bribe and removed from office, Smalls was later pardoned by Governor Wade Hampton III.

He was appointed collector of the Port of Beaufort by the Republicans and served almost continuously in this position from 1889 through 1913. In 1895, he served as a delegate at the South Carolina Constitutional Convention, where he attempted—unsuccessfully—to stop the disenfranchisement of African-Americans. Here, in response to the charge that he was a Confederate deserter, Smalls testified:

I stand here the equal of any man. I started out in the war with the Confederates; they threatened to punish me and I left them. I went to the Union army. I fought in 17 battles to make glorious and perpetuate the flag that some of you trampled under your feet.

Until his death in 1915, Smalls lived in his former master's home in Beaufort. The Robert Smalls Parkway and Beaufort's Robert Smalls Junior High School are both named for this remarkable man.

BEAUFORT

The Northman comes no longer there,
With soft address and measured phrase,
With bated breath, and sainted air,
And simulated praise.

He comes a vulture to his prey;
A wolf to raven in your streets;
Around on shining stream and bay
Gather his bandit fleets.

But, ready with avenging hand,
By wood and fen, in ambush lie
Your sons, a stern, determined band,
Intent to do or die.

—*W.J. Grayson (1864)*

Lincoln in 1863 for burying the Northern Army's victims of its war against the South. Some 9,000 Union boys lie here, along with 122 Southerners who died defending their homeland from the Northern invaders. Relatively recently, in 1989, 19 Union soldiers from the African-American Massachusetts 54th Infantry were reburied here after having been discovered on Folly Island in the wake of Hurricane Hugo.

John Mark Verdier House Museum

Over at 801 Bay St., tel. (803) 524-6334, John Mark Verdier, a wealthy merchant, built this Federal-style home in the 1790s. In 1825, when the Marquis de Lafayette visited town on his triumphant return tour of the U.S., he was welcomed here as a house guest. Union soldiers received a less cordial welcome, but nonetheless, they made this home their headquarters during the Northern occupation of Beaufort during the Civil War. Who can blame them? Each of the eight guest rooms has its own fireplace. Open for viewing Mon.-Sat. 11 a.m.-4 p.m. Admission charged.

Henry C. Chambers Waterfront Park

Concerts take place all the time on the outdoor stage, and weekdays find mothers and nannies sitting on the porch swings while their children play on the mock-Victorian jungle gym. A pleasant place to bring a snack and have an impromptu picnic.

Tidalholm

Sam and Sarah Cooper (Kevin Kline and Glenn Close) lived in this 1856 home in *The Big Chill;* apparently they bought it from the Santini family after Bull Meachum (Robert Duvall) crashed his plane off the coast at the end of *The Great Santini.* The real-life, current owners have signs up to remind you that Bull, Sam, and Sarah can't come out to play—this is a private home. But for fans of these films, it can be fun to peer through the gates to see where Kline, Jeff Goldblum, Tom Berenger, and Meg Tilly played football during half-time for the Michigan game, or the porch where Duvall sat reading the paper and cussing out Fidel Castro.

The privately owned 1856 Tidalholm house was the primary setting for the film The Big Chill *and the home of the title family in* The Great Santini.

Tidalholm actually carries a wonderful story. James Fripp owned the house at the outbreak of the Civil War. When he returned from battle at war's end he found it occupied by a Frenchman and in the process of being auctioned off to pay his estate's back taxes. Fripp watched as the French stranger outbid the others and purchased the home. Then the Frenchman walked over to Fripp, kissed him on both cheeks, handed him the deed to the house, and walked away forever.

Tours

Carriage Tours of Beaufort, tel. (843) 521-1651, leave from the visitors center at Henry C. Chambers Waterfront Park on the Intracoastal Waterway, providing you with a narrated history of the city. Prices run $15 and up. For tours focused specifically on the Gullah culture, call **Gullah-n-Geechie Mahn Tours,** tel. (843) 838-7516 or (843) 838-3758.

Shopping

I can never stop into Beaufort without having to browse through **Bay Street Trading Co./The Book Shop,** 808 Bay St., tel. (843) 524-2000, which offers plenty of rare, locally written books and wonderful souvenirs. **Fordham Hardware** is an fun place to poke around in as well.

EVENTS

On an early spring weekend, St. Helena's Episcopal Church offers its self-guided **Spring Tours** of the city's gorgeous Colonial homes and plantation estates, a tradition since the 1950s. Call the church at (843) 524-0363 for information. In May, the annual **Gullah Festival** features dances, live music, storytelling, and art displays in an all-out celebration of the Sea Island's unique African-American culture. Call Rosalie Pazant at (843) 525-0628 for dates and information. If you missed the Spring Tours, then maybe you can make the late-October **Beaufort Fall Festival of Homes and History,** sponsored by the Historic Beaufort Foundation and featuring home tours, lectures, and special events. Give Isabella Reeves a call at (843) 524-6334 for more information, or stop in and see her at 801 Bay Street. Over on St. Helena Island, November brings the annual **Heritage Days Celebration,** a three-day festival celebrating African-American Sea Island culture. Call (843) 838-8563 for information.

LODGING

Motels/Hotels
Beaufort features a fine **Days Inn,** at Hwy. 21 and Hwy. 802, tel. (800) 329-7466. If you call, ask for rate code "LRO," which will supposedly get you the lowest possible rate. A **Holiday Inn** is at 2001 Boundary St., tel. (843) 524-2144. You'll also find a very nice **Hampton Inn** at 2342 Boundary St., tel. (843) 986-0600, and the **Best Western Sea Island Inn** at 1015 Bay St., tel. (843) 522-2090, as well as a number of other chains along Boundary Street. Also worth a look is the 20-room **Battery Creek Marina and Inn,** 19 Marina Village Ln., tel. (843) 521-1441.

On St. Helena Island, the **Royal Frogmore Inn,** at 864 Sea Island Pkwy., tel. (843) 838-5400, offers 50 units.

Bed and Breakfasts
You just know a cute town immortalized in the baby boomer classic *The Big Chill* is going to have its share of B&Bs. The **Rhett House Inn,** at 1009 Craven St., tel. (843) 524-9030, offers 10 rooms, each featuring its own mini-library to complement a larger one downstairs. It's here that "fire-eater" Robert Barnwell Rhett is said to have written up a draft of the Ordinance of Secession which led to the Civil War. Nick Nolte and avowed champion of the underprivileged Barbra Streisand stayed here in these regal furnishings during the filming of *Prince of Tides.* Owners Stephen and Marianne Harrison hail from Manhattan originally, so perhaps it's understandable why Babs felt at home here. Premium-Luxury.

The **Beaufort Inn,** 809 Port Republic St., tel. (843) 521-9000, offers 13 units, of which all are handicapped accessible. Even if you're staying elsewhere, try to poke your head in to see the unique atrium wrapped by a curving stairway. In fact, if you're not staying here, you ought to consider eating here at the restaurant, named by *Country Inns Magazine* as one of the top 10 restaurants in the country. Breakfast or dinner only. Private balconies, private baths. Rooms with small jacuzzis are available. Premium.

At 601 Bay St., the **Bay Street Inn,** tel. (800) 256-9285 or (843) 522-0050, enjoys a lot of popularity, partly because the eight-room former Civil War hospital faces the river and partly because the inn was featured prominently in the motion picture version of *Prince of Tides* and in *Forrest Gump.* All but one of the guest rooms has its own fireplace. Private baths, antique furnishings. Premium.

Other B&Bs include the five-unit **Craven St. Inn,** at 1103 Craven St., tel. (843) 522-9000 (Premium); the six-unit 200-year old **Cuthbert House Inn,** 1203 Bay St., tel. (800) 327-9275 or (843) 521-1315, where General Sherman once stayed (Premium); the **Old Point Inn,** 212 New St., tel. (843) 524-3177 (Moderate-Premium); and the **Scheper House,** at 915 Port Republic St., tel. (843) 770-0600.

At the fully accessible, five-room 1917 **Two Suns Inn Bed & Breakfast,** 1705 Bay St., tel. (800) 532-4344 or (843) 522-1122, each room features a view of the bay and salt marsh. Expensive-Premium.

Camping

The place to camp in the Beaufort area is **Hunting Island State Park,** 2555 Sea Island Pkwy., tel. (843) 838-2011, but you'll also find two campsites over at **Coosaw Plantation** on Hwy. 21 N, tel. (843) 846-8225, and another 15 at **Kobuch's Campground,** about two miles from the Parris Island Gate on Hwy. 802, tel. (843) 525-0653.

FOOD

Coffee

For coffee and baked goods, you won't find a better spot than **Firehouse Books and Expresso Bar,** 706 Craven St., tel. (843) 522-2665, set, as you might guess, in an old firehouse. Offers sandwiches, espresso, flavored coffees, muffins, and other such coffeehouse favorites. A very good book selection upstairs.

Casual Eats

Banana's, at 910 Bay St., tel. (843) 522-0910, is right on the waterfront, offering sandwiches, the famous Banana's Burgers, fresh shrimp, and hot dogs. Gimmicky enough to draw the tourists,

but tasty enough to draw the locals. A good place for late-night eats. **Plum's,** tel. (843) 525-1946, facing the park, is a casual café serving up giant salads, omelettes, sandwiches, stir-frys, shrimp rolls, and pancakes, along with meats and pasta for dinner. Live blues, Motown, groove, funk, and reggae music on Thursday, Friday, and Saturday nights, beginning at 10 p.m.

A true locals' hangout is **Boundary Street Clubhouse,** 2317 Boundary St., tel. (843) 522-2115, featuring a sporty atmosphere—TVs on the wall show sporting events—and reasonably priced seafood, chicken, ribs, and steak. Open for lunch and dinner, till 11 p.m. on Friday and Saturday, till 10 p.m. on weekdays. Nice Sunday brunch here as well 10 a.m.-2 p.m.

Lowcountry

Along Hwy. 21 on St. Helena Island, you'll run across the famous **Shrimp Shack,** tel. (843) 838-2962, a place that keeps getting written up in major national magazines, but somehow manages to retain its casual-meal-on-the-back-porch charm. Fried shrimp is king of the menu, but they've got shrimp cooked other ways, and other types of seafood, chicken, and steaks that contain no shrimp whatsoever.

But when in Rome, act as the Romans. When in Shrimp Shack, eat shrimp. My favorite is the shrimp burger.

Gadsby Restaurant, 822 Bay St., tel. (843) 525-1800, offers one of the prettier views in town, overlooking the park and the river, and featuring soups, salads, and sandwiches—including a grouper melt you won't believe. Scenes from the Julia Roberts/Dennis Quaid film *Something to Talk About* were shot here in the mid-'90s.

The **Beaufort Inn,** 809 Port Republic St., tel. (843) 521-9000, was named one of the U.S.'s top 10 restaurants by *Country Inns* magazine; lots of people like to come here for the elegant atmosphere, fine wine list, and fresh seafood. It'll cost you quite a bit to eat here, but you won't forget the experience anytime soon.

For another true Southern experience, take the bridge from Beaufort to Lady's Island, take the first sharp right at Whitehall Dr., and turn right into the grounds of the **Whitehall Plantation Inn Restaurant,** (843) 521-1700. This old plantation was owned by Colonel John Barnwell, who now resides yonder in the burial grounds of the St. Helena's Anglican Church. Set on the waterfront, amid pecan trees, camellia bushes, live oaks and cedars, and a gardenful of flowers, Whitehall serves up authentic Southern dishes—crab cakes, She Crab Soup, and the Shrimp Beaufort (baked in sweet butter, shallots, garlic, herbs, spices, lemon and sherry) would be a good place to start, though you'll also find Maine lobster, lamb, and veal here. Try to time it so you're here at sunset—the view is spectacular. Expect to spend around $20 a dinner, less at lunch. Kids' prices available. Open Tues.-Sat. 11:30 a.m.-2:30 p.m. for lunch, 5:30-9:30 p.m. for dinner, closed Sunday and Monday.

Over at 1103 Bay St. you'll find **The Anchorage,** tel. (843) 524-9392, offering seafood and steaks, mostly for under $20.

Steamer's Restaurant on Hwy. 21, tel. (843) 522-0210, is another pricey but tasty place for seafood. Rumor has it that Nick Nolte favored this place while filming *Prince of Tides* here in town.

Over on St. Helena, you'll find the **Gullah House Restaurant,** tel. (843) 838-2402, next door to Red Piano Too art gallery (see below). Breakfast here features a $4.95 buffet—a wonderful place to stop on your way to points west. Lunches and dinners are about what you'd expect from a Lowcountry restaurant next door to an art studio—items like "Hot Ya Mout Swimps," and "Uncle Woolie's Crab Cake Dinner," along with meat dishes. Live jazz on the weekends. Featured in *Southern Living* a while back.

Mexican

Some of the best (and only) Mexican food you'll find in the area is **La Posada Mexican Food,** an outdoors restaurant at the intersection at Frogmore. Open 8 a.m.-11 p.m. Food is served in terra-cotta bowls. I ate outside under an awning. How down-home Mexican style is this? I ordered a Gatorade and they handed me a bottle of Gatorade and a cup with ice in it. This place had just opened up when I was there, but hopefully it will do well and be there for you to try when you visit.

Fast Food

If you're in a hurry or low on cash and you're tempted to eat fast food, at *least* head over to the **Sonic Drive-In** over at 340 Robert Smalls Pkwy.,

tel. (843) 522-8378, in the Wal-Mart Shopping Center. Be sure to get the cheese-covered tater tots instead of the fries.

If you want to cook your own shrimp, go even farther on Hwy. 21 toward Fripp Island and you'll come across **Gay Fish Incorporated,** owned by a guy named Charlie Gay, who will sell you fresh shrimp by the pound.

Barbecue

In this part of the state, it seems like the best barbecue joint in just about every town is a Duke's. This **Duke's** is at 3531 Trask Pkwy., tel. (843) 524-1128, and features a large buffet and a half-mustard, half-tomato-based sauce. An all-you-can-eat buffet. Open Fridays and Saturdays only, 11 a.m.-9 p.m. You'll see it on your left if you're headed down Hwy. 21 into Beaufort.

NIGHTLIFE

Plum's and **Banana's** (see above) are two of the warmer spots at night ("hot spots" is putting it too strongly). This is a casual town where there are lots of places to have a couple drinks with friends, and nowhere, really, to boogie down and get rowdy. Both fruits have live music on the weekends; Banana's tends toward the more laidback Jimmy Buffett '70s' middle-of-the-road crowd; Plum's offers live blues, Motown, groove, funk, and reggae music on Thursday, Friday, and Saturday nights, beginning at 10 p.m. Over at the **Days Inn** on Boundary St., they whir up the karaoke machine in the evenings for a sing-along.

John Cross Tavern, upstairs above Harry's at 812 Bay St., tel. (843) 524-3993, has served spirits on the waterfront since about 1720. Fortunately, they've been washing their glasses all along, so it's quite safe. They serve dinners here as well, but the lounge is a real treat. It's not often you can quaff a glass of ale in a place old enough to have carded George Washington. Enter from the side of the building.

Ping's Sportsbar & Grill at 917 Bay St., tel. (843) 521-2545, is a good sports bar. Popular happy hour, decent pizza. The **Boundary Street Club House,** tel. (843) 522-2115, offers large-screen satellite sports in every room, as well as good prime rib, ribs, seafood, and chicken. A real locals' hangout.

When war come, Missus take me and two more niggers, put we and chillun in two wagon, and go to Barnwell. My mother been one of the nigger. We stay in Barnwell all during the war. My father, he been with the Rebel. . . . When Freedom come, Missus didn't say nothing; she just cry. But she give we a wagon and we press [stole] a horse and us come back to St. Helena Island. It take three day to get home.

When we get home, we find the rest of the nigger here been have Freedom four year before we. . .

My father come back and buy twenty acre of land, and we all live together.

—Former Fripp family slave Sam Polite, a resident of St. Helena Island, interviewed in the 1940s by the WPA

INFORMATION

For more information on the Beaufort area, contact the **Greater Beaufort Chamber of Commerce** at P.O. Box 910, Beaufort, SC 29901, tel. (843) 524-3163.

ST. HELENA ISLAND

Frogmore

Frogmore is a tiny town—officially part of St. Helena—intersected by Route 21. You can't miss it if you're headed in from Beaufort. Also unavoidable is the **Red Piano Too,** tel. (843) 838-2241, an old wooden grocery store on the National Register of Historic Places that has reopened as an art gallery for African-American artists. A great place to pick up a one-of-a-kind (literally) souvenir, including painted furniture, mobiles, regional landscapes, and books written in Gullah. Be sure to stop in at the Pat Conroy Room, where you can pick up an autographed book by Beaufort's most famous native son. You'll also notice the **Gullah House Restaurant** next door.

If shopping's got ahold of you, head across the intersection over on the left across from the park, near **La Posada,** and see what they're selling today over at the vendors' booths, a roadside stand that offers some unique Africa-themed clothing and knickknacks.

Penn Center Historic District

Here on Martin Luther King Dr. stands one of the first schools established for the recently freed slaves of the South. The Penn School was founded by two white Quaker women, Laura Towne and Ellen Murray, and supported by the Freedman's Society in Philadelphia, Pennsylvania. Later that year, African-American educator Charlotte Forten joined the team. In the early 1900s, Penn began to serve as a normal (teachers'), agricultural, and industrial school. The school graduated its last class in 1953.

Every January 1963-67, Dr. Martin Luther King met here with the biracial Southern Christian Leadership Conference to plan strategies for overturning segregation and Jim Crow laws. The **Retreat House,** which still stands at the end of a dirt road on the waterfront, was built for Dr. King in 1968, but he was assassinated before he could stay there.

Today, the 49-acre, 16-building center continues as something of a spiritual homeland for those devoted to civil rights in general and the betterment of African-Americans in particular. Its mission statement states that the Penn Center's purpose is to "preserve the Sea Island's history, culture, and environment." Ironically, the school

LUKE 9:23-25 IN GULLAH

23. Jedus tell um all say, "Ef anybody want fa folla me, e mus don't do jes wa e want fa do no mo. E mus cyah e cross an be ready fa suffa an die cause ob me, ebry day. 24. Anybody wa da try fa sabe e life, e gwine loss e true life. Bot anybody wa loss e life cause ob me, e gwine habe de true life. 25. Wa good e do a man ef e own ebryting een de whole wol an gone ta hell wen e ded? E done loss e true life, ainty?"

23. And he said to them all, "If any one will come after me, let him deny himself, and take up his cross daily, and follow me. 24. For whosoever will save his life shall lose it: but whoever will lose his life for my sake, the same shall save it. 25. For what is a man advantaged, if he gain the whole world, and lose himself, or be cast away?"

From De Good Nyews Bout Jedus Christ Wa Luke Write, *1995*

built for the movement of Gullah blacks into mainstream American society has become something of a shrine to the unique African-American culture the original Northern teachers came down here to "educate" the freed persons out of.

The center, deemed a national historic landmark district in 1974, consists of some 19 buildings. The first one to visit is the **York W. Bailey Museum,** tel. (843) 838-8562, on the right side of Land's End Rd. as you come in from Hwy. 21. Admission runs $2. This is one of the world's centers of information on the Gullah culture and the connections between West Africa and the Sea Islands. Be sure to peek into the book shop, where you'll find a number of hard-to-find books, including a couple penned by Penn Center alumni. You'll also find recordings by the **Hallelujah Singers,** the gospel group featured in *Forrest Gump* and renowned throughout the country for their powerful vocal harmonies. The singers are based here at Penn Center and perform frequently in the area.

Ms. Lola Holmes, an alumna (class of 1939) of Penn Center School and author of *An Island's Treasure,* says plans are underway to move the museum to a bigger, climate-controlled building where its treasures can be better preserved. Museum hours run Tues.-Fri. 11 a.m.-4 p.m., Saturday 10 a.m.-4 p.m.

If you can make it here in November you may get to take part in the **Heritage Days Celebration,** a three-day festival celebrating African-American Sea Island culture. Call (843) 838-8563 for information.

Newpoint

If the shiny new shopping centers on the Sea Island Expressway are making you feel a bit queasy, it may help a bit to take a walk through the Newpoint development, on Sam's Point Road. When you see the quality craftsmanship on the old-style homes, with their front porches within conversation's distance of the sidewalk, you'll swear that the neighborhood comes from the 1820s, but these homes are generally less than 10 years old.

Interestingly, the folks in the real estate office here say that only about one-fifth of Newpoint's population is native South Carolinian. The rest are people looking for the South of their imaginations, who have found that it's easier

(and cheaper) to re-create it than to buy into The Point in Beaufort itself. The riverbank here, though fronted by huge multimillion-dollar homes, is a public waterfront, open to all.

The strength of a place like this is that when people move here they are signing on to a code of conduct, to a view of life, and promising to share a set of values—neighborliness, respect for others' property and privacy—with the rest of their neighbors. The downside? The homes here run $207,000-364,000 and on up to $1.4 million. A lot of others who would love to live in a place with this sort of lifestyle simply can't afford to buy a home here.

Nonetheless, to see a new development done right, head over to St. Helena Island, turn left on the first light onto Sams Point Road (Hwy. 802), and drive for a mile and a half until you see the brick columns on the left, heralding Newpoint's entrance.

HARBOR ISLAND

This 1,700-acre island is the latest to receive developers' dehydrating, blood-powdering touch. Homes and villas rent out here; call Harbor Island Rentals at (800) 553-0251 or (843) 838-5800 for information. Or call **Harbor Island Sales and Accommodations,** tel. (800) 845-4100 or (843) 838-2410.

HUNTING ISLAND STATE PARK

Take Hwy. 21 east of Beaufort for 16 miles and you'll finally reach the ocean at Hunting Island State Park, tel. (843) 838-2011. Native tribes used to hunt here, and after Europeans moved in, hunters purchased the land and ran the island as a hunting club. To reward them for their preservation efforts, the government snatched up the land and turned it into a park.

And what a park it is. This is a subtropical forest. Tell the kids they're going camping where the exteriors for Disney's recent live-action remake of *The Jungle Book* were shot.

The 1875 140-foot **Hunting Island Lighthouse** provides a dramatic view—and a mild aerobic workout, getting to the top. Here on the island, you can camp or rent a cabin—though un-

SPAIN'S FAILED COLONIZATION EFFORT

Close your eyes. Imagine you're the first European to set foot in South Carolina. It's 1526: there are no paramedics a phone call away, not even a bottle of peroxide in the ship's doctor's cupboard. The scariest beasts you've ever seen—giant armor-covered, man-eating, lizard-like monsters—cruise the inlets, waiting to tear off an arm idly draped over the gunwales. Beyond the quicksands on shore, deadly water moccasins swim the rivers, ready to strike. There are mosquitoes and no-see-ums, humidity and malaria.

And no beach music, She Crab Soup, or hot boiled peanuts to balance things out.

Had it been me rather than Spaniard Francisco Gordillo to land first in South Carolina, I might have taken a quick look around and headed back across to Spain for some hot paella.

But history is not made by people who head back for paella. Gordillo and, later, 500 Spaniards under commander Lucas Vasquez de Ayllon came, saw, and colonized.

Ayllon had gathered up about 500 men, women, and children from Santo Domingo in the modern-day Dominican Republic for the colonization effort. Ayllon sailed back to the region the natives called Chicora, establishing San Miguel—the first European settlement in what would become the United States.

No one knows precisely where San Miguel was located. Many suspect it may have been in Winyah Bay, though some argue that it was near the Savannah River, and others somewhere in Georgia.

Wherever it was, things didn't work out according to plan. They had landed in August; by mid-October, the visionary Ayllon was dead. His successor proved to have the leadership ability of a mime in a school for the blind, and after a relatively hard Carolina winter, lethal Indian attacks and disease had killed seven out of 10 colonists before a year had passed. The Spaniards decided that San Miguel was after all really a better name for a beer than for a city, and sailed back to Santo Domingo.

Though Spain sent De Soto through in 1540 to explore the area, in general, with a whole New World to rape and pillage, the Spaniards kept themselves busy until 1558, when King Philip II decided that with the hated French eyeing the region it was time to establish a firm, permanent presence in

"Florida." An expedition headed up from Vera Cruz back to the Santa Elena region, near modern-day Beaufort.

Leader Villafañe arrived in Port Royal Sound on May 27, 1561. He sailed up the river but found nothing that particularly interested him, so he sailed northward as far as Cape Hatteras, where a number of troubles sent him foundering back to Santo Domingo.

What Villafañe had seen in his travels convinced Philip II that there was no true French threat, so he put settlement of the region on the back burner.

The French Threat

Which appears to have been precisely what the French had been waiting for. The very next year, France sent Jean Ribaut, leading a group of French Protestants—Huguenots—who were looking for a place to practice their faith without persecution.

Ribaut and 150 faithful—including a Calvinist minister—first reached North America at the site of Saint Augustine, and turned north until they arrived in the Santa Elena area and founded a small colony on what's now called Parris Island in Port Royal—site of present-day Parris Island Marine Base. However, when Ribaut sailed to France and was kept from returning immediately, the men left behind grew restless, built a ship (the first built in America for trans-Atlantic travel), and sailed back to France. When Ribaut finally returned to "Spanish Florida" with reinforcements, not only were his men gone, but the Spanish were there. Ribaut and his men surrendered to the Spaniards and were executed.

"This Time We Really Mean It"— The Spanish Return

The Spaniards' take-no-prisoners attitude toward the French Protestants revealed their newborn seriousness about settling the east coast of North America quickly, before another European power did. In 1566, Philip II established a chain of Spanish forts along the coasts of Florida, Georgia, and South Carolina. Fort San Felipe—named after the same physician-saint for whom their king was named—was built that April on what's now called Parris Island. The Spanish left 110 men to garrison the fort and sent one soldier with each local Indian chief to help spread Catholicism. Soon, the fort was reinforced with another 300 men under Captain Juan Pardo.

That November, Pardo was sent inland from San Felipe with the order to explore and conquer the land clear from there to Mexico, establishing an overland route to the silver mine of western Mexico. Pardo marched upland to the east of the Savannah, stopping by Cofitachiqui. At the foot of the mountains, Pardo and his men built a blockhouse for safety before moving on. By the time he had reached Wateree, a messenger reached him with orders to return to San Felipe. Pardo did so, leaving behind four soldiers and a priest to begin the job of evangelization.

Pardo marched west again the following September, establishing various garrisons and reaching as far as present-day Alabama before returning back to San Felipe. Indians destroyed the small forts soon afterward, massacring the men left behind to guard them.

Two years later, Jesuit priests arrived, and an earnest effort was made to found a permanent settlement on Parris Island. The village of Santa Elena flourished, becoming the capital of all La

Florida Province. Unfortunately, Spain could not effectively defend her far-off colony; the inhabitants had to flee to St. Augustine in 1576 to escape hostile Indians, who burned the vacated buildings. The Spanish returned the following year to rebuild the town and build San Marcos, a new, stronger fort, on the same site. But in 1587, when the English sea captain Sir Francis Drake swept down on the South Atlantic Coast to harass Spanish settlements, the people of Santa Elena decided to cast their lots with their countrymates in Saint Augustine, leaving South Carolina for the final time.

Only a handful of Spanish friars, devoted to their work among the Indians, were left behind. Even after a 1597 massacre by Indians, which only one friar north of the present-day Georgia-Florida border survived, the Jesuits continued their work in the region that includes South Carolina, establishing a number of missions at San Felipe, on the mouth of the South Edisto, on the Ashepoo, and on St. Catherine's Island. The last of these survived 10 years into the British Colonial period, finally disappearing in 1680.

less you get lucky you'll need a lot of advance notice for the latter. Then just spend your days shelling or fishing from the **Paradise Fishing Pier,** tel. (843) 838-7437, the East Coast's longest freestanding pier.

If you're just here for the day, it'll cost you $3 to park your car within the park. It wouldn't be too hard to find parking outside the park, but this is the sort of place where you'll want to make a contribution, even if you're only staying an hour or so. If you want one of the 200 campsites, it'll cost you around $15 a night, but this includes electric and water hookups. The park's facilities include showers, and two of the sites are modified for the physically challenged. Call ahead to reserve one.

FRIPP ISLAND

Captain Johannes Fripp, hero in the British battles against the Spanish, purchased this coastal island between Hunting Island and Pritchard's from the Yamassee Indians, who had come to settle here in the last part of the 1600s. Nowadays it's a developed resort island with con-

trolled access. Very few automobiles get over here, but over 300 homes and villas are for rent. For lodging, golf, or tennis information, call (800) 845-4100 or (843) 838-3535, or check online at www.FrippIslandResort.com.

The **Fripp Island Marina** is a popular place to hook up with charter fishing boats.

Things are changing here quickly. How quickly? Remember the Vietnam sequence in *Forrest Gump*? It was filmed here in 1993. Today, "Vietnam" is a golf course.

PARRIS ISLAND

Stop by the gate when you reach Parris Island Marine Base. If you don't, you may be shot. But seriously (and I was serious), be sure to ask the guard there to tell you how to get to the Douglas Visitor's Center, or call the center ahead of time (tel. 843-525-2650) and get directions. But stop at the gate anyway.

Over a million men and women have trained here before being shipped off to do battle elsewhere. During WW II alone, more than 204,000

Marines were prepared for battle on this island—as many as 20,000 at a time. At the visitors center you can pick up maps and brochures, and tour the remains of some of the earliest European settlements in North America.

Charles Fort, Fort San Felipe,
Santa Elena, and San Marcos

Here in 1564, French settlers under Jean Ribaut attempted to create a settlement they called Charles Fort on the shore of what is today called Parris Island. But after Ribaut was imprisoned during political intrigues on a trip back to France, the suffering Frenchmen left in Charles Fort were miserable, thinking they'd been forgotten. After surviving awhile upon the good graces of the local Native Americans, they built a boat—the first ever built in North America for trans-Atlantic travel—and sailed it back to France, and that was the end of French Carolina. In 1566, the Spaniards built Fort San Felipe and the village of Santa Elena on the exact same site. Indians destroyed the village in 1576 after the Spaniards fled from their hostility, but a year or so later the Spaniards rebuilt the town, protected by a new, larger fort they called San Marcos. For centuries, the exact location of the Charles Fort site was a mystery—until archaeologists realized that some of the artifacts they were finding at San Felipe were French, not Spanish. Those crazy Spaniards had built right on top of the French foundations, more or less. Over behind the clubhouse for the base golf course (a sign in front of the old home says: "Golfer's Dream House"), you'll find the oldest European-style pottery kiln ever found on the continent. Inside the clubhouse itself, you'll find a pretty decent cheese sandwich.

Stop by the visitors center before you come out here to get a driving map.

Parris Island Museum

If you are a fan of things military, you'll need a cold shower after visiting here. Located at Building No. 111, the War Memorial Building, this museum, tel. (843) 525-2951, celebrates the long history of military life on Parris Island—which I suppose is what you'd expect. One exhibit celebrates women Marines, who have served here since 1943 when they arrived as reservists, filling in jobs vacated by men needed in the Pacific. Another room attempts to help visitors understand the grueling regime

of a Marine Corps recruit here at Parris Island. One display allows you to push a button and get an earful of abuse (minus the obscenities) from a mannequin drill instructor. But perhaps most interesting for civilians are the display cases interpreting local history going all the way back to 1564, when Huguenot pioneer Jean Ribaut arrived with settlers to establish an ill-fated French colony in North America. You'll see some neat artifacts from the 500-person 16th-century Spanish town of Santa Elena, built atop—or so researchers discovered just a couple years back—the former French settlement of Charles Fort. The upper echelon Spaniards ate off imported Ming dynasty china, shards of which have been recovered in the soil near the 14th green of the Parris Island Golf Course. Open 1000-1630 hours (10 a.m.-4:30 p.m.) seven days a week.

PORT ROYAL

This relatively undiscovered town of 3,000 gives you an idea of what Beaufort was like before *Santini*. Here you can view one of the new but old-looking neighborhoods, along the lines of Newpoint on Saint Helena.

A fine seafood spot is **11th Street Dockside Restaurant,** 1699 11th St., tel. (843) 524-7433, one of those waterfront restaurants with open-

Having cast anchor, the captain with his soldiers went on shore, and he himself went first on land; where he found the place as pleasant as was possible, for it was all covered with mighty, high oaks and infinite stores of cedars . . . smelling so sweetly, that the very fragrant odor made the place seem exceedingly pleasant. As we passed through these woods we saw nothing but turkey cocks flying through the forests; partridges, gray and red, little diferent from ours, but chiefly in bigness. We heard also within the woods the voices of stags, bears, lusernes [lynx], leopards, and divers other sorts of beasts unknown to us.

—Rene Goulaine de Laudonniére, a French colonizer who accompanied Jean Ribaut on the first French expedition to Spanish "Florida" in 1562, describing Port Royal

beam ceilings, wooden tables and chairs, and tanned waitrons running around in shorts and aprons, with the name of the restaurant emblazoned on their Polo shirts. It is, in fact, what many of the places up in Murrells Inlet and Shem Creek started out as, and still pretend to be. Good seafood and a relaxed, great atmosphere with a view of the boats out on the river.

The restaurant has been around for years, though new owners bought it in 1995 or so. It draws a lot of visiting parents who come to see their gun-toting children graduate from Parris Island on Fridays. For this reason, you'll want to get here early if you're here on a Thursday night.

Keep heading south along Hwy. 281 and you'll come across a quaint location of **Plum's,** a nice place to pick up an ice cream while strolling around town on a warm summer's night toward the sands, which is where the young folk of Port Royal hang out and play volleyball and such. Here you'll find a boardwalk leading to an observation tower, which provides a great view of the harbor and the docks of the Port Authority, where the big hurricane scene from *Forrest Gump* was filmed.

DOVER PUBLICATIONS, INC.

DAUFUSKIE ISLAND

Hilton Head is a creature unto itself (see below). But hop over it and you'd land here, on Daufuskie. After over a century of virtual obscurity as a home for freed slaves who shrimped and farmed on the small island, Daufuskie gained fame as the setting for Pat Conroy's 1972 novel *The Water is Wide,* which later became the Jon Voight movie *Conrack.* Still accessible only by boat, this island remains partially authentic Lowcountry and part generic Golfland, in the form of the Daufuskie Island Club and Resort.

The island is a nice little half-day trip; you can walk or drive a golf cart around the small village and see the 1912 **Daufuskie Island Elementary School.** Over on the south end, you'll find the old 1880 **First Union Baptist Church,** with two front doors, one for women worshippers, and one for men. Down at the end of the dirt road here is the old **Mary Dunn Cemetery,** with tombstones dating back to the late 18th century.

Check with the marinas in Hilton Head for scheduled ferries and tour boats. One, the **Adventure,** sails out of Shelter Cove Harbor's Dock C, tel. (843) 785-4558. For $15 adults, $7.50 children (3-12 years), you get a narrated cruise to Daufuskie's Freeport Marina and a guided bus nature tour, with stops at spots made famous by *The Water is Wide.*

If you'd like to stay in one of the resort's 191 units, call (800) 648-6778 or (843) 842-2000.

HILTON HEAD

In his sequel to *Less Than Zero,* Brett Easton Ellis sends one of his overstimulated-kid-with-too-much-money characters to Hilton Head for the weekend. This alone is a good proof of the island's emergence as a domestic jet-setter paradise.

"Planned communities" of this sort remind me of short haircuts—they never look all that bad, but then, they never look all that great, either. However, Hilton Head still has its attractions.

Annually, about 500,000 people visit 42-square-mile Hilton Head Island, the largest Sea Island between New Jersey and Florida. One of the first communities in the U.S. to bury its phone lines, hence preserving its 19th-century motif, this planned community is conceptually head and shoulders above the Irvines of the world.

The annual Renaissance Gathering is held here, made famous by attendee Bill Clinton.

Most come to stay in one of four main resort communities—Palmetto Dunes, Port Royal Resort, Sea Pines, and Shipyard Plantation—to play the area's 40-plus championship golf courses, play tennis on one of the island's 300-plus courts, and relax on its 12 miles of white-sand beaches.

Orientation
Stop by the **Hilton Head Island Chamber of Commerce Welcome Center** at 100 William Hilton Parkway for information on the island. You can book a room or a tee time there as well. Open daily 9 a.m.-6 p.m.

HISTORY

Hilton Head Island contains two ancient Native American shell rings, one located in the Sea Pines Forest Preserve and the other on Squire Pope Road. Nobody knows quite what they were used for, but their presence here argues for the existence of a people who lived here before the Yamassee, and even before the earlier Ewascus Indians. British captain William Hilton spotted this island in 1663 while scouting for good sugar and indigo-growing land for his Barbadian employers and advertised in London for settlers, though since no one in London knew what a

"golf villa" was, he didn't get any takers. Nonetheless, the island did eventually develop as an agricultural area, becoming the home of several large plantations in the Colonial period and on up to the Civil War.

During the Civil War, this was the site of an amphibious landing of 13,000 Union troops in November 1861—the largest U.S. amphibious landing until World War II. However, despite its use during the Civil War as a major control center and supply base for the Union navy's blockade of Charleston and Savannah, once the Yanks were gone, Hilton Head returned to its old, sleepy ways. It remained isolated from the mainland until 1956,

Internationally recognized as the symbol of Hilton Head, the Harbour Town Lighthouse was constructed by developer Charles Fraser in 1970 to attract attention and publicity to the harbor community.

> *The lands are laden with large tall oaks, wal-*
> *nut and bays, except facing on the sea, it is*
> *most pines tall and good. . . . The Indians plant*
> *in the worst land because they cannot cut down*
> *the timber on the best, and yet have plenty of*
> *corn, pompions, water-melons, and musk-mel-*
> *ons . . . two or three crops of corn a year as the*
> *Indians themselves inform us. The country*
> *abounds with grapes, large figs, and peaches;*
> *the woods with dear, conies, turkeys, quails,*
> *curlews, plovers, teal, herons; and as the Indians*
> *say, in winter with swans, geese, cranes, duck*
> *and mallard, and innumerable other waterfowls,*
> *whose names we know not, which lie in the*
> *rivers, marshes, and on the sands. There are*
> *oysters in abundance, with a great store of mus-*
> *sels; a sort of fair crabs, and a round shell-fish*
> *called horse-feet. The rivers are stored plentifuly*
> *with fish that we saw leap and play.*
>
> —*William Hilton,* A True Relation of a Voyage
> Upon Discovery of Part
> of the Coast of Florida, 1664

when a bridge was built connecting the 12-mile-long island to the mainland.

People didn't catch on immediately. As late as 1961, Hilton Head was home to just 1,000 African-Americans and about 50 whites. The only businesses were a liquor store and a gas station. But Hilton Head landowner Charles Fraser had a vision: a Southerner's utopia, where golf courses, coastal breezes, and casual lodgings went side by side. Fraser built the island's first resort complex. **Sea Pines Plantation** in the 1960s—the island's first resort complex. **Palmetto Dunes, Shipyard, Forest Beach, Hilton Head Plantation**, and **Port Royal** followed over the years. All have things to recommend them, but stick with Sea Pines, Shipyard, Palmetto Dunes, or Port Royal if you want to be on the ocean.

Hilton Head's a unique place with unique problems, the most inescapable of which is traffic. Nearly all of the different massive "plantations" are de facto large cul-de-sacs, traffic-wise, so all traffic eventually spills onto one of the two main through roads on the island—Hwy. 278 (the William Hilton Pkwy.) and the new four-lane Cross Island Expressway ($1 toll), which cuts from Hwy. 278 near Spanish Wells Rd. to Sea

Pines Circle on the south end of the island.

Today, the island offers 3,000 hotel rooms and 6,000 apartments and villas, hosting as many as 55,000 people during a busy spell.

SIGHTS

The island of Hilton Head is divided up into various private and public complexes. **Harbour Pointe Village** is an odd mix of New England seafront, Mediterranean chateau, and 1970s condo tack. Here's where you'll find the famed **Harbour Town Lighthouse.** Developer Charles Fraser built the lighthouse in 1970. Though folks laughed at him at the time, he was building the lighthouse not to help lead ships into port, but rather to lead golfers into real estate offices—he knew that camera operators covering the MCI Classic across the water on the Harbour Town Golf Links would naturally focus in on this red and white lighthouse, perched poetically at the entrance to Harbour Town like a Statue of Liberty for the world's affluent:

Bring me your sires, your well-born,
Your coddled masses yearning to tan deep . . .

And of course he was right. The zoom lenses haven't yet pried themselves from the giant candy-cane lighthouse: it's become the internationally recognized symbol of Hilton Head.

As you ascend the lighthouse to a gift shop and overlook at the top (free, but not wheelchair accessible), you'll find photos and descriptions of each of the 12 other lighthouses on the East Coast.

South Beach is another quaint spot on the island that plays on the New England-seaside-village-with-exceptionally-warm-weather theme. Last time I was here it was almost 105° F— everyone sat around in the chairs and along the seaside bar drinking and talking. A visit to the **Salty Dog Cafe** is a must—something like the Hussong's of South Carolina, where people who don't even eat there feel compelled to purchase a T-shirt in the gift shop. **Captain John's Gallery** is a decent seafood place that's affiliated with the Salty Dog, featuring a good view and the sort of inflated prices you'd expect from a place famous for its T-shirts.

If you get weary of the island's calculated charms, the **Audubon Newhall Preserve,** tel. (843) 785-5775, on your left just before you reach the cross-island tollway, is a wonderful place to disappear into awhile. Here you'll see what the island looked like in its natural sublimity, before it was improved.

Just after you come down onto the island on Hwy. 278 from the bridge, look to your right and you'll see the antebellum **Old Zion Cemetery** and the **Zion Chapel of Ease,** one of a number of chapels serving St. Luke's Parish, established in these parts in 1767, back in the days when the Church of England was the state religion and the state was divided into Anglican parishes rather than counties.

Self Family Arts Center

Over at 15 Shelter Cove Lane stands this $10 million complex, tel. (843) 842-2787, featuring an art gallery and a theater for the Hilton Head Playhouse. Open Mon.-Sat. 10 a.m.-4 p.m. No admission charged to view the art gallery.

The Coastal Discovery Museum on Hilton Head Island

You'll find this natural history museum on the second floor of the Hilton Head Welcome Center, 100 William Hilton Pkwy., tel. (843) 689-6767. The museum also features displays on Hilton Head's roles in the American Revolution and the War between the States. Stop in and see if the folks there have planned any of their historic or environmental tours or beach walks. Open Mon.-Sat. 10 a.m.-5 p.m., Sunday noon-4 p.m. No admission charged.

The neatest thing about the museum is all the tours and events it sponsors, including a Marine Life and Dolphin Study Cruise, Pinckney Island Tour, History of Hilton's Headland Tour, African Americans on the Sea Islands, and Fort Mitchel Tour with Civil War Overview. Call the museum for dates, times, fees, and reservations.

Pinckney Island National Wildlife Refuge

On Hwy. 278, just a half mile west of Hilton Head Island, you'll come across the entrance to the Pinckney Island National Wildlife Refuge, which was named after the land's former owners, U.S.

Chief Justice and Constitution-framer Charles Pinckney and Declaration of Independence signateur Charles Cotesworth Pinckney. Here you'll find over 4,000 acres of salt marsh and small islands, 14 miles of trails to walk or bike, and not a single car beyond the parking lot. Take the 2.9-mile-roundtrip **Osprey Pond Trail,** or, if you really want to experience the refuge's flora and fauna, and have a day to do it in, take the 7.9-mile-roundtrip **White Point Trail.** No charge, closed dusk to dawn.

Waddell Mariculture Research and Development Center

On Sawmill Creek Rd. about three miles west of Hilton Head, near the intersection of Hwy. 278 and Hwy. 46, you'll find both the Waddell Center, tel. (843) 837-3795, and the Victoria Bluff Heritage Preserve. The center researches the cultivation of marketable marine life, and you can tour this facility and ponds to see what they're up to over here. By appointment only. Open weekdays, no charge.

TOURS

Based at Shelter Cove, **Adventure Cruises,** tel. (843) 785-4558, offers dinner and sightseeing cruises, dolphin-watching tours, and even "Murder" cruises. **Discover Hilton Head,** tel. (843) 842-9217, brings to life the history of the island.

The **Coastal Discovery Museum** sponsors numerous tours and events, including the Marine Life and Dolphin Study Cruise, Pinckney Island Tour, African Americans on the Sea Islands presentation, Native Plants and Lowcountry Gardens, a Nature Cruise, and the Fort Mitchel Tour with Civil War Overview. Call the museum for dates, times, fees, and reservations. **Hilton Head Parasail H20 Sports Center,** Harbour Town Marina, Sea Pines, tel. (843) 671-4386, offers "Enviro Tours" in a USCG-certified Zodiac inflatable, specializing in up-close dolphin encounters and birdwatching. Finally, **Outside Hilton Head,** tel. (843) 686-6996, offers two-hour dolphin nature tours leaving from a number of different locations, which run $35 adults, $17.50 for children under 12 when accompanied by adult. A full-day kayak excursion runs $48-60 adults.

SPORTS AND RECREATION

Beaches

At **Coligny Beach Park** on Coligny Circle, **Driessen's Beach Park** on Bradley Beach Rd., **Folly Field Beach** on Folly Field Rd., and down at **Forest Beach,** you'll find parking and public access to some of the most beautiful, pristine white beaches in North America.

Not much in the way of waves, though. But bring your bike and you can ride for miles along the hard-packed sand.

Golf

Hilton Head is well-known as home to the annual MCI Classic, The Heritage of Golf, held on Pete Dye's Harbour Town Golf Links at Sea Pines Plantation the weekend after the Masters Tournament in Augusta. But the island is also known for the renowned Robert Trent Jones, George Fazio, and Arthur Hills courses inside Palmetto Dunes. Call (800) 827-3006 or (843) 785-1138 for information on any of these courses, as well as information on the Arthur Hills II and Robert Cupp courses. For information on the **Pete Dye Harbour Town Golf Links,** call (800) 845-6131 or (843) 363-4485. For any of the other courses in the Sea Pines Plantation, call the same 800 number or (843) 845-6131.

The best thing to do is pick up a free *South Carolina Golf Guide* before you visit or see the Web site www.travelsc.com for information on the state's public golf courses. Call (800) 2-FIND-18 or (800) 689-GOLF to find out about any of the courses at Shipyard Plantation.

Tennis

With some 300 courts, including clay, hard, and grass surfaces, Hilton Head is as much a tennis mecca as it is a holy land for golfers; for more than a quarter century, the Family Circle Magazine Cup has hosted such women's tennis stars as Chris Evert, Martina Navratilova, and Steffi Graf. Stan Smith, Jimmy Connors, and Bjorn Borg have all appeared between the lines here too.

In 1997, Sea Pines was named the "Top Tennis Resort in the U.S.," by no less than *Tennis* magazine, and a number of other island resorts regularly make the magazine's top 50.

The number for the **Sea Pines Racquet Club** is (800) 732-7463 or (843) 363-4495. The **Palmetto Dunes Tennis Center** contains 23 clay, two hard, and eight lighted courts, tel. (800) 972-0257 or (843) 785-1152. For tennis **lessons,** ask at any racquet club—many offer them. Or call the **Van der Meer Tennis University,** tel. (800) 845-6138 or (843) 785-8388.

Horseback Riding

Unfortunately, **Sea Horse Farms** doesn't really raise sea horses. But the ones they do keep there are fun to ride on terra firma. Call (843) 681-7746. **Lawton Stables,** tel. (843) 671-2586, is another place where you can saddle up.

Bicycling

With the growing traffic on Hilton Head, and with the many fine trails laid out across the island, biking is a good idea on Hilton Head. Though the designated paths won't take you far into Hilton Head Plantation or Sea Pines Resort, you can get almost anywhere else in the island by bike. To rent, you might call **AAA Riding Tigers Bike Rentals,** tel. (843) 686-5833; **Fish Creek Landing,** tel. (843) 785-2021; or **South Beach Cycles,** tel. (843) 671-2453.

Diving

In Hilton Head, the folks at **Island Scuba Dive and Travel,** 130 Matthews Dr., tel. (843) 689-3244, offer local river diving, classes, and eco river tours. In Beaufort, call **Outfar Diving Charters,** tel. (843) 522-0151, to arrange a trip.

Paddling

For on-the-island canoe rentals, you'll want to talk to **Outside Hilton Head,** tel. (843) 838-2008, Web site: www.outsidehiltonhead.com; **Moore Canoeing Center,** tel. (843) 681-5986; or **Island Water Sports,** tel. (843) 671-7007.

If you're thinking about venturing off the island, you'll find canoe and kayak rentals, as well as guided paddling tours of the ACE Basin, barrier islands, coastal marshes, and the Edisto River canoe trails, offered at **Carolina Heritage Outfitters** in Canadys, tel. (800) 563-5053 or (843) 563-5051; **The Kayak Farm** on St. Helena Island, tel. (843) 828-2008; and **Tullifinny Joe's** in Coosawhatchie, tel. (800) 228-8420 or (843) 726-4545.

If at all possible, bring your own kayak, since rentals aren't cheap. Outside Hilton Head, for example, charges $15 an hour, $45 a day for a single kayak. You could rent a Ford Escort for that (though they've been known to bog down in the marshes).

Boating
You'll find **Island Watersports of Hilton Head, Inc.,** tel. (843) 671-7007; **Hilton Head Parasail H20 Sports Center,** Harbour Town Marina, Sea Pines, tel. (843) 671-4386; **Lowcountry Water Sports, Inc.,** tel. (843) 785-7368; and **Outside Hilton Head,** tel. (843) 686-6996, Web site: www.outsidehiltonhead.com, willing to help you out.

Parasailing
If you want to be dragged by a speedboat through the Lowcountry sky, **Hilton Head Parasail H20 Sports Center,** Harbour Town Marina, Sea Pines, tel. (843) 671-4386, will do it.

Charter Fishing
With the Gulf Stream so close by, no doubt the true anglers will want to get out and truly angle for something big enough to cover a wall in the den. **Adventure Cruises,** tel. (843) 785-4558; **Drifter Excursions,** tel. (843) 363-2900; and **Seawolf Charters,** tel. (843) 525-1174, can get you started.

ACCOMMODATIONS

Hunting for the best possible room in Hilton Head is like hunting for a bullet casing on Normandy Beach on D-Day plus one—it's easy to become overwhelmed. Most people choose their room based on what they hope to be doing while on the island. You probably ought to contact **Hilton Head Central Reservations** at (800) 845-7018 or (843) 785-9050, Web site: www.hiltonheadcentral.com, and tell them what you're looking for. Open Mon.-Sat. 9 a.m.-6 p.m. Or call **Hilton Head Oceanfront Rentals Company,** tel. (800) 845-6132, Web site: www.oceanfrontrentals.com. Ask for the free literature they'll be glad to send you.

As far as specific resorts go, you might consider **Palmetto Dunes,** a 2,000-acre resort with the aforementioned world-class golfing, a ten-

nis center, and miles of white-sand beach. Check into the Palmetto Dunes Hilton and immediately your biggest worry is choosing where to eat that night—the folks here will take care of everything else. Luxury. Get a room through Central Reservations, or call (843) 785-1138 if you'd like to speak with the folks at Palmetto Dunes directly.

Sheraton Four Points, tel. (800) 535-3248 or (843) 842-3100, has a luxurious lobby, with five floors in the main building providing scenic views of the island. Several amenities. Rooms come with cable, video games, iron, full-sized ironing board, and hair dryer. Expensive-Luxury.

Disney's Hilton Head Island Resort, 22 Harborside Lane, tel. (800) 453-4911 or (843) 341-4100, claims to offer special activities for kids, but other than that, it's hard to imagine how even Walt's minions can improve upon the natural beauty already here. The intricate illusions of nature that seem impressive in downtown Anaheim feel a bit unnecessary here, but you might give them a call to hear Mickey's side of it. Premium-Luxury.

B&Bs
Bed and breakfasts are pretty uncommon on Hilton Head, but here are two: the **Halycon Bed & Breakfast,** Harbormaster 604 Shipyard, tel. (843) 785-7912, features just one unit. The **Main Street Inn,** 2200 Main St., tel. (800) 471-3001 or (843) 681-3001, is way on the other end of the scale with 34 units—many wheelchair accessible. Nice gardens here.

FOOD

Southern and Seafood
The **Old Fort Pub,** tel. (843) 681-2386, stands in Hilton Head Plantation beside Skull Creek. Crouched beneath tremendous live oaks draped with Spanish moss, this historic old house once served (briefly) as Confederate headquarters and later (not so briefly) as headquarters for the Union. Beautiful views of the Intracoastal Waterway, marshes, harbor, sunset, and sailboats from the dining room, lounge, or deck. This same view inspires some of the most uniquely delicious Lowcountry cuisine. Some of the items include blackened salmon with tomato coulis, red rice, crab cakes, and grilled prawns, or triggerfish with crab, zucchini cakes, and sweet potato

crepes. If you choose to dine outside don't worry about the mosquitoes: an army of citronella tiki torches, along with the citronella candle and a bottle of insect repellent at each table, will protect you. Great wine list. Could well be the culinary highlight of your visit.

Over in Harbour Town is **Crazy Crab,** tel. (843) 363-2722, which as you might guess is famous for its crab boil and other seafood dishes. Dinner only. Expect to pay toward $20 for dinner.

Despite some tough competition, the family-owned **Abe's Native Shrimp House,** 650 William Hilton Pkwy., tel. (843) 785-3675, which began in 1968 as a convenience store on the then-dirt road Hwy. 278, has operated as a full-service seafood restaurant since 1975, which is, in Hilton Head restaurant terms, forever ago. Open daily for dinner only at 5 p.m. A Lowcountry Shrimp Boil will cost you $11.95; get there early for the early-bird buffet, offered Mon.-Sat. 5-7 p.m. and Sunday 5-9 p.m. For something light, try a bowl of the fine seafood gumbo and a salad for about $6. For something heavy, go in with someone else on the Charlie Mae's Chaplin Plantation Dinner, which features fried shrimp, fried chicken, and country ham, served with rice and red-eye gravy, green beans, corn, hush puppies, and dessert. It runs $23 for two people, $43 for four. Of course, you'll need nitroglycerin pills afterward, but if you're only going to eat one big, authentic Lowcountry meal on your trip, this'd be a good place to do it.

Barbecue

If you want real South Carolina barbecue, head over to **Southern Soul,** 51 Orleans Ct., tel. (843) 785-7665, where they use an authentic mustard sauce. Otherwise, you'll have to head off the island and over to Beaufort to eat at Duke's. But if good barbecue ribs will do you, then head over to Shelter Cove for **Kingfisher,** 18 Shelter Cove Harbor, tel. (843) 785-4442. Nice view of the water, good tomato-based rib sauce. Open for dinner only, daily 5-10 p.m. Seafood, chicken, and steaks here too. **Great Plains,** 36 Palmetto Bay Rd., tel. (843) 842-8540, includes pork ribs and seafood.

Italian

Set in an uninspiring shopping plaza, **DeVino's,** 5 Northridge Plaza, tel. (843) 681-7700, has a sign out front:

No Pizza
No Iced Tea
No French Fries

In other words, when you head in, expect to meet with some serious Italian food. Shrimp and fettuccine pesto, seafood, chicken, pasta. Expect to spend about $7 for an appetizer, $17 and up for dinner. **Antonio's Restaurant,** at G-2, The Village at Wexford, also offers some authentic Italian in a nice setting.

Rita's Italian Ice, in the heart of Hilton Head, is the local link of a Northern-based chain well-situated to serve all the Yankee resorters. This is the best Italian ice I have ever had (yes, even better than the Sons of Italy booth at the fair). Rita's also serves frozen custard and, for the best of both worlds, "gelati" (Italian ice with frozen custard on the bottom and top). Try the lemon ice with chocolate custard.

French

A casually chi-chi place right beneath the Harbour Town lighthouse is **Cafe Europa,** tel. (843) 671-2299, where you'll spend upward of $20-30 for a full dinner and maybe less for lunch. The café doesn't serve between 2:30 and 5:30 p.m., when it's cleaning up after lunch and preparing for dinner.

Mexican

Aunt Chilada's Easy Street Café, 69 Pope Ave., tel. (843) 785-7100, features both Mexican and Italian meals, along with seafood and steaks. Open every day, but on Sunday they only serve a brunch. **San Miguel's Mexican Café,** tel. (843) 842-4555, offers another south-of-the-border choice for a lower price.

Budget

Cheap spots to enjoy cheap breakfasts on the island include the **Palmetto Dunes General Store,** which has a little kitchen in back where you can buy a basic breakfast for real world (i.e., *not* Hilton Head) prices. One of my favorites—especially since it's open 24 hours—is the **Hilton Head Diner,** where you'll find not only the predictable hamburgers, fries, and shakes, but (oddly) a full bar. So if you've always thought your patty melt would taste better with a screwdriver, here's your chance. Bring change for the jukebox—there's a box at each table.

Of course, the **Huddle House** offers you lots of ways to eat hash browns. You'll also find fast food chains on the island, including what must be the world's most aesthetically pleasing Hardee's, but if you're going there, please don't let anyone see you carrying this book inside.

Brewpubs

When it opened up a few years back, the **Hilton Head Brewing Company,** over at Hilton Head Plaza, 7-C Greenwood Dr., tel. (843) 785-2739, became the state's first brewpub or microbrewery to operate (legally) in South Carolina since Prohibition. The menu features some good brew favorites: babyback ribs, pizza, seafood, steak, and even bratwurst.

In the Northridge Plaza, **Mickey's,** tel. (843) 689-9952, re-creates an old-time pub feel. Open from 11:30 a.m. Mon.-Sat., with happy hour 4-8 p.m. Good solid pub menu, televisions blaring sports . . . the usual. A place where actual locals head to escape the tourists.

Vegetarian

Beatnicks Internet Café, tel. (843) 785-2328, on College Center Dr., is an affordable spot where you'll find good coffee and a vegetarian bent, but pizza and a wonderful chicken salad as well. A fun place to catch up on your e-mail. Other spots with vegetarian menus include the **Main St. Pizza and Bistro,** tel. (843) 689-9100, and **Starfire Bistro and Wine Bar and Grill,** tel. (843) 785-3434.

ENTERTAINMENT AND EVENTS

Hilton Head is a resort, meaning that a lot of people here—especially the retirees—have a lot of free time on their hands. It's no surprise then that some of that free time gets turned toward the planning of various festivals. The **Winter Carnival,** a monthlong festival beginning in mid-January, combines a celebration of Italian culture, Gullah culture, and jazz music. If you're a Gullah jazz saxophonist with a taste for lasagna, this is really a must. The third weekend of March brings on **Wine Fest,** billed as the East Coast's largest tented public winetasting event, complete with a silent auction. Call (843) 686-4944 for information.

During March, the Hospitality Association puts on **Springfest,** a monthlong event celebrating sports, arts, and food. If you're going to be on the island in March, call (800) 424-3387 for information on events. Later in the month, the **Family Circle Magazine Cup,** the nation's top women's professional tennis tournament, features female superstar racketeers. Call (800) 677-2293 for information on getting tickets.

In April, the Harbour Town Golf Links are the site of the **MCI Classic Golf Tournament,** wherein 120 of the world's top duffers battle over $1.4 million in prize money. Call (843) 234-1107 for information on getting in.

Come October, **Bubba's Beaufort Shrimp Festival** barrels into town for a one-day orgy of things crustacean. Tour marine exhibits, check out shrimpboats, listen to music, and eat, eat, eat. Call (843) 986-5400 for information.

SHOPPING

With up to 55,000 folks penned onto an island with discretionary income and lots of leisure time on their hands, you can just see the merchants' register fingers twitching, can't you? There are a number of shopping centers on the island, including **The Mall at Shelter Cove,** 24 Shelter Cove Ln., anchored by **Belk** and **Saks Fifth Avenue,** but also including **Banana Republic,** a **Talbot's** and **The Polo Store,** among many others. Not a bad place to go during a torrential downpour. **The Plaza at Shelter Cove,** also on Shelter Cove Ln., is the requisite parasite strip plaza near the mall, featuring a **T.J. Maxx** and **Outside Hilton Head,** a good sporting-goods store.

Other options include: **The Village at Wexford,** 1000 William Hilton Pkwy.; **Harbour Town,** on Lighthouse Rd. in Sea Pines Resort; **Northridge Plaza,** 435 William Hilton Pkwy.; **Pineland Station,** also on William Hilton Pkwy.; **Port Royal Plaza,** 95 Mathews Dr., which offers a **Sam's Wholesale Club;** and **Shoppes on the Parkway,** 890 William Hilton Pkwy.

You'll find a **Wal-Mart** here—perhaps one of the few you needn't feel guilty about visiting, since there was no cute old downtown for it to usurp. The daughters and sons of Sam do business on Pembrook Drive.

On the island, you'll find two notable bookstores: one is the **Authors Bookstore,** D-4 Village at Wexford, tel. (843) 686-5020, connected with the **Authors Caffé Expresso,** tel. (843) 686-5021. Unfortunately, the bookstore is only open till 6 p.m. The other bookstore of note is the **Port Royal Bookstore** at Port Royal Plaza, tel. (843) 522-1315.

The Hilton Head Factory Stores, on Hwy. 278 at the Gateway to Hilton Head Island, tel. (888) 746-7333 or (843) 837-4339, are divided up into two separate malls, but all told, they offer scores of stores, including **Nike, The Gap, Book Warehouse, Mikasa, Oshkosh B'Gosh, Geoffrey Beene, Eddie Bauer, J. Crew, Laura Ashley, Oneida, Samsonite,** a frightening-sounding store called **Toy Liquidators,** and a crazy little joint called **Perfumania** ("Smellorama" was apparently already taken). It's like a monthful of shopping catalogs come to life. Enter at your own risk.

SERVICES

Information
For more information on Hilton Head Island, stop by the **Hilton Head Island Chamber of Commerce Welcome Center,** at 100 William Hilton Parkway, tel. (843) 689-6767, for information on the island, Web site: www.info@hiltonheadisland.org. You can book a room or a tee time there as well. Open daily 9 a.m.-6 p.m.

Child Care
A number of the resorts offer child care and children's programs. But if you're in an independent villa or hotel and aren't willing to risk taking baby out to a nicer restaurant, you may want to call **Anazubg Creations Child Care, Inc.** tel. (843) 837-5439; **Companions, Nurses & Nannies,** tel. (843) 681-5011; or **EF Aupair,** tel. (843) 342-2044.

GETTING THERE

Driving
Most people drive to Hilton Head, plummeting down from the north on I-95 before hanging a left at Hwy. 278 or the newly expanded Hwy. 46

and arcing over the large bridge that leaves from South Carolina and touches down in Hilton Head. From anywhere on the South Carolina coast, you'll want to drive down Hwy. 17 to get here. From almost anywhere else in the state, you'll want to cut over to I-95; from most spots in the Upcountry, you'll want to find I-26 first, then head south on I-95 when you reach it.

Flying
People coming from out of state normally fly into Charleston or Savannah, Georgia, and then rent a car and drive the rest of the way. See the Charleston chapter for details on the airport and on local car-rental places in that town. For information on the Savannah Airport, call the **Savannah Airport Commission,** tel. (912) 964-0514.

USAir Express, tel. (800) 428-4322, does offer daily commuter flights direct to the Hilton Head Island Airport. You'll find taxi service at the Hilton Head airport to get you to your hotel or villa.

Train
Oh yeah, right—like they're going to allow a noisy train chugging its way onto the island. You can, however, take Amtrak to Savannah, Georgia, just 45 miles away, and then take a shuttle from there. Call Amtrak for information.

GETTING AROUND

Because so many of the island's highlights are spread far apart on this large island, unless you're just planning to hole up in a specific complex, you'll want to consider either biking (see above) or renting a car. Local rental car spots include **Avis,** tel. (843) 681-4216; **Budget,** tel. (843) 689-4040; and **Enterprise,** tel. (843) 689-9919.

Taxicab companies include **Yellow Cab,** tel. (843) 686-6666, and **Palmetto Coach,** tel. (843) 726-8000.

ACROSS THE BRIDGE TO BLUFFTON

Once, when I was 20, I spent a week at Disney World in Florida. About halfway through the week, my friends and I grew so tired of the manicured lawns, overpriced meals, and carefully constructed walkways, spiels, and smiles that we exploded out of Disney airspace just to find a burger joint, talk to the locals, and say we'd actually seen a bit of central Florida.

I suspect that this same sort of reaction against cultural vacuousness is what propels many Hilton Head guests over the bridge and into the little antebellum town of Bluffton. Bluffton has become something of a day trip for people staying at Hilton Head. It was founded in 1825 as a summer resort for Lowcountry planters escaping the fevers in the rice fields and swamps. Poet Henry Timrod, "poet laureate of the Confederacy," taught here in Bluffton for a while in the 1860s. And Simons Everson Manigault, hero of Padgett Powell's *Edisto,* attends school in Bluffton.

Truth be told, there isn't all that much to see here, but at least you know that the old Gothic 1854 **Church of the Cross,** Calhoun St., tel. (843) 757-2661, was built by South Carolinians in a style they felt was appropriate, not one that the marketing department told them would maximize profits. During the Northern invasion, Union gunboat bombardment nearly leveled the town, and the church would have burned down if small detachments of boys in gray hadn't arrived to put out the fires in time.

Visit Bluffton and you've touched the face of the South—though I'd recommend you head over to Beaufort or on up to Charleston to see what Lowcountry South Carolina is really about.

BEYOND BEAUFORT

SHELDON CHURCH RUINS

Between Gardens Corner and the town of Yemasee on Route S-7-21, you'll pass the ruins of this church. The Sheldon church was first built in 1753, but the British burned it in 1779. It was rebuilt, but in 1865 William Tecumseh Sherman came through and burned it again.

At this point, you might guess that many Sheldonites literally "lost their religion." For whatever reason, the church was not rebuilt, and the ruins stand today, an indictment of the violence of the Northern armies of 1865. Memorial services are

held here under the open sky and moss-draped oaks on the second Sunday after Easter—a memorable experience if you happen to be in the area when it occurs.

ACE BASIN NATIONAL WILDLIFE REFUGE

Named for the three rivers draining the basin—the Ashepoo, Combahee, and Edisto—this refuge serves as home to American alligators, the shortnose sturgeon, wood stork, loggerhead sea turtle, blue-winged teals, and southern bald eagle, along

Evocative ruins today, the Sheldon Church was built in 1753, burned by the British in 1779, rebuilt, and burned again, by Sherman, in 1865.

with a number of other endangered or threatened species. Call (843) 889-3084 or (843) 549-9595 for information. If you'd like to tour the area in a 38-passenger pontoon boat, call **ACE Basin Tours** in Port Royal, tel. (843) 549-9595.

The best way to experience the ACE, however, is in a canoe or kayak. For rentals and/or guided tours, call **Carolina Heritage Outfitters** in Canadys, tel. (800) 563-5053 or (843) 563-5051; **The Kayak Farm** on St. Helena Island, tel. (843) 828-2008; **Outside Hilton Head,** on Hilton Head, tel. (843) 838-2008, Web site: www.outsidehiltonhead.com; or **Tullifinny Joe's** in Coosawhatchie, tel. (800) 228-8420 or (843) 726-4545.

YEMASEE

This town is farther off I-95 than the others on this list, but it's close enough. The main thing it offers—that some of the other highway stops don't—is campsites. **Point South KOA,** Hwy. 17, tel. (800) KOA-2948 or (843) 726-5733, offers 53 sites. **The Oaks,** Rt. 1, tel. (843) 726-5728, has 80 more. In fact, Yemasee is the headquarters for the South Carolina Campground Owners Association.

Outside of town and closed to the public stands **Auld Brass,** the one and only plantation ever designed by Frank Lloyd Wright. It's owned today by Wright aficionado and Hollywood producer Joel Silver, of *Die Hard* and *Lethal Weapon* fame.

WALTERBORO

Here's a good-looking town with some vision. With just under 6,000 residents and more a-coming, the Colleton County seat knows it's got enough beautiful old homes and history to draw some bulging pocketbooks on their way down to Hilton Head. Wisely, it recently lobbied for and got the right to open South Carolina's official Artisan's Center here, showcasing (and selling) the best handicrafts from Palmetto State craftspersons.

The story goes that Walterboro's name comes from a tree-felling contest. The rice town, founded in the early 18th century, was first named Ireland Creek, but two prominent citizens, a Mr.

Walter and a Mr. Smith, each believed the burg should be renamed after himself, and a tree-felling contest was used to settle the matter. In truth, there were two Walters, Paul and Jacob Walter, Lowcountry planters who carved out a retreat up here just far enough away from the mosquitoes and sand fleas.

Another local legend says that the 1879 tornado that tore through town only knocked out the churches, leaving all the bars standing.

A lot of people like to walk or drive **Hampton Street** for its old houses, the earliest of which were built in 1824. Another site is the (private) **Jones-McDaniel-Hiott House,** 418 Wichman St., where the most famous person who ever lived in the house somehow managed to not be a Jones, McDaniel, or Hiott. Instead, it was Elizabeth Ann Horry Dent, widow of the commander of the USS *Constitution* during 1804's Battle of Tripoli, which later worked its way into the nation's consciousness through the Marine Corps Hymn:

> *From the halls of Montezuma*
> *to the shores of Tripoli,*
> *We fight our country's battles*
> *In the air, on land and sea.*

The South Carolina's Artisan's Center at 334 Wichman St., tel. (843) 549-0011, features original handcrafted jewelry, pottery, baskets, furniture, and more, all made here in South Carolina, and most of it for sale. Getting this state center located in Walterboro was a major boon for the plucky little city, and finding it is your own boon. Open Mon.-Sat. 10 a.m.-7 p.m., Sunday 1-6 p.m. No admission charged, but bring money.

The **Colleton Museum,** Jefferies Blvd. at Benson St., tel. (843) 549-2303, is set in a restored 1855 jail. Pop inside—no admission—to check out some of the artifacts reflecting the area's importance during Colonial days as a rice-growing region, along with other displays detailing life in this region. Open Thurs.-Fri. 9 a.m.-5 p.m. (closed 1-2 p.m. for lunch), Saturday 10 a.m.-2 p.m., Sunday 2-4 p.m.

The **Colleton County Courthouse,** on Hampton St. in Walterboro, tel. (843) 549-5791, is the site where Robert Barnwell Rhett, the fiery states' rights politician, demanded that South Carolina secede from the U.S.—way back in 1828, during the Nullification Crisis.

West of town, on the other side of I-95 on Hwy. 64, you'll run across **Mt. Carmel Herb Farm,** tel. (843) 538-3505, where you'll find just about everything with an herbal essence, from books to seasonings.

Events

Come to Walterboro on one of the 18 Saturdays each year when it hosts the **Handmade Series,** wherein you can watch artisans creating their works right before your eyes (let's hope no one's making sausage). Call (843) 549-0011 for information and to find out dates. The last weekend of April brings out the **Colleton County Rice Festival,** featuring the world's largest pot of rice and a rice-cooking contest. Call (843) 549-1079 for information.

Practicalities

Walterboro offers a number of chain hotels up on the interstate. Me, I'd recommend the **Walterboro Inn,** 904 Jeffries Blvd., tel. (843) 549-2581, or the two-unit **Mt. Carmel Farm B&B,** Mt. Carmel Rd., tel. (843) 538-5770; or the four-unit **Old Academy Bed and Breakfast,** 904 Hampton St., tel. (843) 549-2541.

If you've brought along a tent or have an RV, **Green Acres RV Park,** 330 Campground Rd., tel. (800) 474-3450 or (843) 538-3450, and **Lakeside Campground,** Brunson Ln., tel. (843) 538-5382, offer nearly 170 sites between them.

As far as eating goes, the **Washington Street Cafe,** at 242 Washington St., tel. (843) 549-1889, is an inexpensive place for excellent Italian. **Duke's Barbecue,** 725 Robertson Blvd., tel. (843) 549-1446, uses a mustard-based sauce that has made them a very popular outfit. Open Thurs.-Sat. only, 11 a.m.-9 p.m. Head west of Walterboro on Hwy. 15, then take a right on Robertson to get there.

Information

For more information on Walterboro, call the **Walterboro-Colleton Chamber of Commerce** at (843) 549-9595, or fax (843) 549-5775.

COLLETON STATE PARK/EDISTO RIVER CANOE AND KAYAK TRAIL

If you go left on Hwy. 17 at Walterboro you'll end up on Hwy. 15. Before long you'll come to the park, hidden among the live oaks growing along Edisto River, flowing black and silent like Waffle House coffee (and tasting much the same). This is the headquarters for the **Edisto River Canoe and Kayak Trail,** which covers 56 miles of blackwater. Stop by or call **Carolina Heritage Outfitters** in Canadys, tel. (800) 563-5053 or (843) 563-5051, to rent a canoe or kayak, or to sign up for a guided tour along the trail. Call the park at (843) 538-8206 between 11 a.m. and noon to catch the rangers in the office and ask them whatever questions you might have.

There are 25 campsites here at the park—it's a good place to sleep before slipping off down the river in the morning.

SAVANNAH NATIONAL WILDLIFE REFUGE

Along the South Carolina shore of the Savannah River, 26,295 acres have been set aside as a sanctuary for migratory waterfowl and other birds, as well as other Lowcountry creatures. With all these tasty morsels around, its no wonder that this is also a good place to see alligators. Open dawn to dusk only; no charge. Off I-95, take Exit 5; off Hwy. 17 S, take Hwy. 170.

You'll want to take the **Laurel Hill Wildlife Drive,** where you're likely to spot some gators—and possibly quite a few. Bring a camera, but don't get too close—they may look like logs with legs, but when they're motivated, for short distances they can move much faster than a human being. Now you've probably heard someone say that the muscles an alligator has to open his mouth with are very weak, so if necessary you can wait until the gator has his mouth closed and then clamp the mouth shut with your hands. This is true. But if you get to the point where you find yourself holding a whipping, writhing six-foot alligator by the mouth, then you have probably gotten too close in the first place.

Be sure to check out the small plantation cemetery, marked by a millstone that once belonged to a nearby mill. The Laurel Hill Plantation, where most of the cemetery's current residents once spent their vertical days, is no more.

Something else many people like to do is to hike or bike along the miles of dikes. Bring insect repellent.

SAVANNAH, GEORGIA

If you've ventured this far down the state, you might as well zip across the border into Georgia and visit Savannah. Then, if nothing else, when you get home and your friends ask you about *Midnight in the Garden of Good and Evil,* you can say, "Oh, Savannah was fine . . . but I *prefer* Charleston." For independent travelers, Kap Stann's *Georgia Handbook* is the best book available on the state.

HARDEEVILLE

From the Georgia line, turn back north and head up I-95 to reach this little town, which has nearly as many rooms for rent (1,500) as it does residents (1,740). It offers 18 restaurants. But the state is busily expanding Hwy. 46 to make the drive to Hilton Head faster and safer, and because it sits at the intersection of these two roads, Hardeeville is set to take off. Also exciting is the arrival of a Disney property, a shopping, food, and hotel complex located adjacent to I-95, which is supposed to feature a few Disney stores, chain restaurants, and a Disney-run/leased hotel.

You'll find about a dozen different chains here, but you may want to try out the **Carolina Inn Express,** tel. (843) 784-3155.

SERGEANT JASPER STATE PARK

This relatively new state park on Exit 8 off I-95 north of Hardeeville serves as both a recreational park for local residents and a deluxe rest stop for folks barreling down the interstate to Florida or up to New York. Call (843) 784-5130 for information. The park's name honors the man who raised the Palmetto flag after it was shot down during the battle of Fort Moultrie; he was killed later in the Revolutionary War.

RIDGELAND

Ridgeland used to be known as something like the Las Vegas of South Carolina—not for its gambling, but for the goggle-eyed Georgians who used to sneak over here and take advantage of South Carolina's relatively lax marriage requirements. Today, Ridgeland is home to the **Pratt Memorial Library** and **Webel Museum,** at 123-A and -B Wilson St., tel. (843) 726-7744, where you'll find 250 rare books on Lowcountry history and culture, Native American artifacts, and other historical displays reflecting life in this part of the world. You'll also find a number of chain motels, along with the **Plantation Inn,** Hwy. 17 N, tel. (843) 726-5510, and the **Lakewood Plantation B&B,** tel. (800) 228-8420 or (843) 726-5141, with just four units. **Duke's Barbecue,** 17 Hwy. S, tel. (843) 726-3882, offers a large buffet with vegetables and fried chicken, and Duke's fine mustard-based sauce. Open Wed.-Sat. only, 11 a.m.-9 p.m. Call for directions.

ROBERTVILLE

This little town, a short jog northwest along arcing Hwy. 652, gets its name from the family of Henry Martyn Robert (1837-1923). The town is proud to claim Robert, who wrote *Robert's Rules of Order,* the world's most popular handbook on parliamentary procedure. (This in spite of the fact that he, a well-known military engineer, made the social faux pas of fighting for the Union during the war.) So if you've ever "had the floor" or "seconded a motion," you may want to tip your hat to the master as you pass through town.

COLUMBIA
AND THE MIDLANDS

Columbia, the capital city, lies in the middle of South Carolina—by design. For years it stood here—like a compromise candidate, pleasing everyone a little, but no one very much. This is South Carolina without the Lowcountry's salt marshes and palmettos, without the Upcountry's granite cliffs and thundering falls. Thomas Taylor, who sold his plantation to the state to build Columbia, afterward concluded, "They spoiled a damned fine plantation to make a damned poor town." And yet the capital city, plush with pines and oaks, built on rolling hills above the broad Congaree, has its attractions.

Set almost exactly halfway between New York and Miami, Columbia itself has 98,000 residents, but the Columbia region, including Richland, Lexington, Fairfield, Newberry, and Kershaw Counties, includes over 552,000 people.

Sometimes you'll see Columbia abbreviated to "Cola" in print. You won't hear many folks *call* it Cola in conversation, however.

Climate

Columbia is warmer than the beach cities and generally warmer than the mountains, averaging highs of 56° F in January and 91° F in July and August. Snow comes nearly every year, but only long enough to take a few snapshots before it melts. It *does* get hot here in the summer—hotter than Charleston, and hotter than the mountains.

HISTORY

Before Europeans arrived, the Congaree River Valley was populated by the Congaree Indians, who lived in a town on the west side of the Congaree River. Captain Juan Pardo, accompanied by a Roman Catholic priest and 125 Spanish soldiers, appeared at the town in 1566, made friendly with the Congarees, and raised the Spanish flag to claim the area for Spain. For a century, as far as the Old World was concerned,

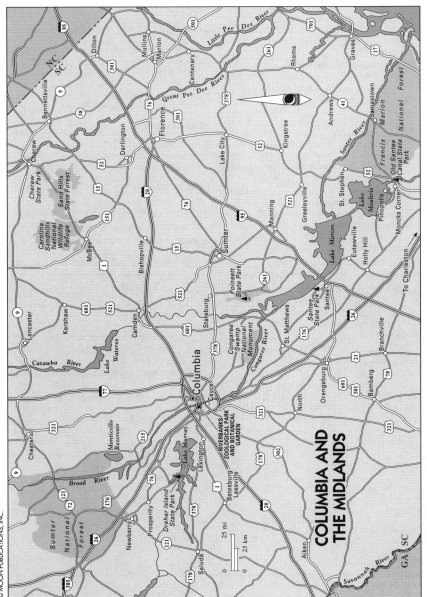

COLUMBIA AND
THE MIDLANDS

© MOON PUBLICATIONS, INC.

HIGHLIGHTS OF COLUMBIA AND THE MIDLANDS

COLUMBIA

- The neighborhood districts of Congaree Vista and Five Points

- Maurice Bessinger's original Maurice's Gourmet Piggie Park Barbecue (West Columbia)—*People* magazine voted this the "Best All-In-One Barbecue Restaurant" in the entire country. Whether you're coming in specifically for barbecue, for eternal salvation, or for a job—and whether you're driving in, driving through, or walking in, this is certainly a one-of-a-kind experience.

- Riverbanks Zoo and Botanical Garden—Either one of these would make the list by itself; joined as they are by a footbridge over the beautiful Saluda River, they comprise a genuine gem of an attraction in the middle of the state.

- The State Museum—Set in what was once the first all-electric mill in America, this is a great place to get yourself started.

- The USC Horseshoe—This is the most beautiful and historic part of one of the nation's most beautiful and historic campuses.

AND BEYOND

- Revolutionary Camden
- Congaree Swamp National Monument— Whether you hike it or paddle it, here's your chance to experience the largest remaining stand of first-growth hardwood cypress swamp in the Southeast.
- Darlington International Raceway (Darlington)
- Duke's BBQ (Orangeburg)
- Edisto Memorial Gardens (Orangeburg)
- Swetman's Barbecue (Holly Hill)

the Spanish essentially ruled the area—though the Congarees would have been surprised to hear of it. John Lawson, a British explorer, visited in 1700, becoming the first Englishman to meet the Congaree. After the settlement of Charles Town in the late 17th century, the Cherokees began to come down from the mountains to trade here with English agents.

During Anne's reign of England (1702-13), the queen bequeathed a large tract of land west of the Congaree and Saluda Rivers and named it Saxe Goth, in honor of the Prince of Wale's marriage to Princess Augusta, princess of the German state of Saxe Goth. Before long, the same coastal planter/upland farmer animosities that eventually split West Virginia from Virginia threatened to do the same to South Carolina. The wealthy slave-owning plantation owners around Charleston and Georgetown feared that the generally non-slave-owning Upcountry, whose voting population (white males) outnumbered the Lowcountry's 4 to 1 in 1790, might well vote for emancipation if given due— which is to say, majority—representation in the state legislature.

Through the earliest years of the colony, the state had been legislatively divided into an upper section and a lower section, with the former sec-

tion containing all of what is today considered the "Midlands" as well as the Upcountry. Because slave owners received three-fifths of a vote for every slave they owned, a man who owned a thousand slaves—a number did—in truth wielded 601 votes. Hence, for example, the scant 226 voters of plantation district St. Stephen's parish near modern-day Moncks Corner received the same number of legislators (three representatives and one senator) as Edgeville, which had 9,785 voting citizens. Later in the antebellum period, the invention of the cotton gin in neighboring Georgia made the Midlands' short-fiber cotton plantations more profitable. Soon, Midland and Upcountry farmers needed all the hands they could get to provide cotton for their gins. As more and more Midlanders became large slave owners, the Lowcountry became more trusting of the upper section.

Which was timely, because by now Upcountry citizens had begun to demand equal representation in the state government in Charleston. Even though by this time the Upcountry had received minimal formal representation—John C. Calhoun's father, Patrick Calhoun, was one of the upstate's first three representatives in the 1750s—the Upcountry folks still found themselves put out by the several-days' ride to the capital—and to the colony's single court of law—there in the midst of Charleston. Some Lowcountry elites responded with the type of condescending attitudes that had caused them to rebel against the British only a decade earlier, but fortunately, more fair-minded heads in the Lowcountry prevailed and voted in 1786 to move the state capital to a compromise place in the center of the state.

THE FOUNDING OF COLUMBIA

The extension of settlements far to the west loudly demanded on republican principles a removal of the seat of government from the vicinity of the Atlantic Ocean. . . . A high and commanding situation about 120 miles from Charleston, and about three miles from the junction of the Broad and Saluda Rivers, commonly known by the name of the plane of Taylors Hill, was selected. In many respects this choice was judicious; perhaps a much better place could not have been made to the east of the mountains. There was sufficient elevation to carry off with management all superfluous water. Some of the defects in the original plan of Charleston were obviated. No lots were to be less than half an acre. The two main streets crossing each other at right angles were to be each 150 feet wide, and none were to be less than 60. . . . The place is sufficiently high to have in it no other than running water; and the streets are wide enough to admit without inconvenience three rows of trees to be planted in each of them. These advantages, with the surrounding woods and vegetation, especially when drained of every drop of stagnant water, may keep the town healthy till the rising value of its lots paves the way for the destruction of pure air by a crowded population. . . . The natural advantages of Columbia and its scattered settlements, together with the improved plan of the town, bid fair, under the direction of a well-regulated police, to preserve it healthy for several years; but from its greater heat it will be more exposed to diseases than Charleston when population, compact settlement, and consequent filth, shall be equal in both.

—David Ramsay, History of South Carolina,
from Its First Settlement
in 1670 to the Year 1808, *1809*

Though several sites were proposed, the South Carolina General Assembly chose a two square-mile stretch of land on the Taylor Plantation just below the point where the Saluda and Broad Rivers came together to form the Congaree.

According to legend, the assemblymen named the capital "Columbia," after the phrase of Senator John Lewis Gervais who, responding to protests that the new capital in the middle of nowhere would become a haven for bandits and rogues, responded that he hoped and believed the city would become a place where even the lowest of the low from around the world would find a safe haven "under the wings of Columbia." Columbia, of course, was an intrinsically American mythical figure derived from Columbus' name, and at that time was as popular a symbol for American liberty as Uncle Sam is today.

The new capital city of Columbia beat out the District of Columbia—not even a glimmer in a bureaucrat's eye until 1790—to become the first community in North America named "Columbia."

After its founding, Columbia shared its capital status with Charleston in all but name; the Holy City still retained its own Court of Appeals—where "lower section" cases were heard, and its own treasurer. This remained the case until the end of the Civil War.

President George Washington visited the new capital in 1791 and was notably unimpressed, but toward the end of the antebellum period, a New York visitor described Columbia as "famed for its fine public buildings, its magnificent private residences, with their lovely flower gardens which savor . . . of oriental ease and luxury."

In fact, had it not been for the events of a night in February 1865, Columbia would stand today as one of the gems of the Old South.

Picking Up the Ashes

As for wholesale burnings, pillage and devastation committed in South Carolina, magnify all I have said of Georgia some fifty-fold, and then throw in an occasional murder . . . and you have a pretty good idea of the whole thing.

—William T. Sherman, quoted by a correspondent for the New York Herald traveling with Sherman's troops

canoeing through the
Congaree Swamp

After the War between the States, with armed Federal troops drilling on Greene Street and a corrupt "carpetbagger" government in the State House, Columbians halfheartedly attempted to rebuild. The family of the Presbyterian Reverend Joseph R. Wilson moved into a newly built home on Hampton St. in 1872, where their bookish son Tommy "Woodrow" Wilson would spend his teenage years amid the war-scorched community. The last Occupational troops left in 1876 with the end of Reconstruction and the rise to power of Wade Hampton III and the Red Shirts. In the last decades of the 19th century, some true progress became evident: electricity and phone lines were installed, a line of streetcars was laid out, and public schools began educating all young people. New textile mills and factories opened up, causing the population of the city to double between 1875 and 1900, as failed farmers poured in to take their spots at the spinning machines. In 1896, Clemson's and Carolina's football squads played the first match of their annual classic. Columbia's first skyscrapers climbed up into the skyline in the first dozen years of the new century.

During the 1920s, a black nightclub over on Hampton St.—the Big Apple, still standing—became the birthplace for a new dance that briefly became the rage across America. During the late '20s and into the Depression, 5,000 residents, three churches, and six schools were moved out, 2,300 graves dug up, and the trees churned into 100 million board feet of lumber,

ODE SUNG AT THE OCCASION OF DECORATING THE GRAVES OF THE CONFEDERATE DEAD

I

Sleep sweetly in your humble graves,
Sleep, martyrs of a fallen cause;
Though, yet no marble column craves
The pilgrim here to pause.

II

In seeds of laurel in the earth
The blossom of your fame is blown,
And somewhere, waiting for its birth,
The shaft is in the stone!

III

Meanwhile, behalf the tardy years
Which keep in trust your storied tombs,
Behold! your sisters bring their tears,
And these memorial blooms.

IV

Small tributes! but your shades will smile
More proudly on these wreaths today,
Than when some cannon-moulded pile
Shall overlook this bay.

V

Stoop angels, hither from the skies!
There is no holier spot of ground
Than where defeated valor lies,
By mourning beauty crowned!

—Henry Timrod, 1867

THE BURNING OF COLUMBIA

Who could command drunken soldiers?

—Gen. William T. Sherman

In the last months of the War between the States, as Sherman, having already completed his famous "March to the Sea" at Savannah, approached Columbia from the southeast. The city had swollen with refugees from coastal towns. General Wade Hampton III and his Palmetto Guard had been charged with protecting the city, but even before the first shells began to smash into the streets from across the Congaree River, Hampton knew his small force was no match for the 40-mile-wide horde of Sherman's men. Hampton's men assisted with the evacuation of those who wanted to evacuate, and rode off onto a hill to glumly watch the occupation take place. Mayor Col. Thomas Jefferson

General William Tecumseh Sherman

Goodwyn walked forward from the Capitol to meet the approaching troops and formally surrendered the capital at what is now Fifth Street and River Drive. A granite marker marks the spot.

Though Columbians had every right to fear that Sherman would take out his wrath on the Confederacy by striking at Columbia, birthplace of the secession movement and capital of the first state to secede, the general's words and behavior after arriving portended a better fate. After setting up headquarters at the Blanton Duncan home on 1615 Gervais St., and handing over command of the city to his lieutenant, General Howard, Sherman rested up between meetings with various women from the city who came to ask that guards be detached to their homes. These early visitors found him "respectful and kindly," according to one woman. Mayor Goodwyn arrived in the late afternoon, and Sherman promised him that the city would not be destroyed. The general took a walk with Goodwyn and had the mayor introduce him to various acquaintances in the city. They paid a long visit to a woman by the name of Poyas, daughter of a family he had known in

Charleston during his pleasant time stationed at Fort Moultrie in the 1840s. Here, he heard a flattering story: earlier that day, when Federal troops had invaded her yard, the shrewd Miss Poyas had handed the soldiers a book that the young Lieutenant Sherman had inscribed years before. The impressed soldiers had immediately stationed a guard at the house and even assigned a young Iowan to take care of a baby in the home.

After a pleasant visit, Goodwyn took Sherman to meet another old acquaintance. Finally, in saying goodbye to the mayor, the general told him, "Go home and rest assured that your city will be as safe in my hands as if you controlled it."

But while Sherman rested, just after nightfall, red, white, and blue rockets exploded over the Columbia sky—a prearranged signal amongst the plotting Union soldiers, who at once set more than a hundred fires across the city. When he awoke because of the flickering light cast through his bedroom window, Sherman rose to look out upon a city ablaze.

Imagine night turned into noonday, only with a blazing, scorching glare that was terrible—a copper-colored sky across which swept columns of black rolling smoke glittering with sparks and flying embers, while all around us were falling thickly showers of burning flakes. Everywhere the palpitating blaze walled the streets as far [as] the eye could reach—filling the air with its terrible roar. On every side the crackling and devouring fire, while every instant came the crashing of timbers and the thunder of falling buildings. A quivering molten ocean seemed to fill the air and sky.

—Emma LeConte, who lived on the South Carolina College grounds

Some claim that the campus of the college (now a university) was preserved because its buildings housed Federal and Confederate wounded, but this is only half true: the drunken mob of Union troops

THE BURNING OF COLUMBIA

(continued)

tried to burn the campus as well—disregarding the yellow hospital flag outside. Cursing, howling men tried to break down the gates on Sumter St., as injured soldiers of both colors did the best they could to evacuate the buildings. Fortunately, three college professors and a doctor stationed themselves at the campus's main entrance, where they somehow held off the horde until (sober) Federal troops arrived.

Realizing that they weren't going to get to burn the college, the mob started looking for the Baptist church where the South Carolina Secession Convention had met back in 1860. They found an African-American man and asked him which of the city's many church buildings was the guilty party, and he misled them—legend has it he was a sexton of the church in question—to the *old* Baptist building, then being used as a Methodist Church. The Yanks burned that, and so the First Baptist Church at 1306 Hampton St., birthplace of the South Carolina's secession—and, hence, the Confederacy—was spared, and still stands today.

If Sherman or one of his subordinates had ordered a large body of men into the city early in the evening, it's possible that they could have kept the incendiaries from spreading the fires. But only four brigades were sent, and these were not enough to control the fire or the ones who kept it burning. Late in the evening, General W.B. Woods' troops began rounding up all the drunken and disorderly soldiers, arresting 370 and shooting two who resisted arrest, including one whom the angered Sherman personally ordered his aide to kill. Even still, only a merciful shift in the wind saved the city from complete annihilation. Too few firefighters were sent too late. By morning, 500 buildings and 84 out of 124 city blocks had burned, including every building on Main Street.

As if that wasn't enough, Sherman and his troops stayed in town for another two days before marching on, tearing up the railroad and all railroad property, along with whatever remained of all state buildings—with the exception of the beautiful, unfinished State House. When they departed, they left behind 500 head of cattle, 100 muskets, ammunition, salt,

and wire for a ferry across the river, along with drugs for the sick and wounded. As the soldiers marched out of town, the bitter Columbians spit upon and verbally accosted them. A number of poor whites and ex-slaves left along with the army.

So whose fault *was* the burning of Columbia? Most Southerners blamed Sherman, who, even if he hadn't explicitly ordered the burning, had nonetheless made statements to his men that might have misled them into thinking that these were his wishes. Too, with the winds blowing and so many angry, exultant Union troops wandering through town, Sherman could have stationed more guards throughout the city, or even made the town off-limits to his troops.

Sherman himself blamed three others, but not himself. First, he blamed Mayor Goodwyn for not removing the city's store of liquor before the Yanks arrived. Later, testifying in court, he accused General Wade Hampton of having caused the fire by ordering the burning of Columbia's cotton bales in the streets before evacuating the city, but Sherman himself later admitted he'd lied about this to destroy the popular Hampton's credibility with his fellow Carolinians. Finally, Sherman blamed God himself, claiming, "I did not do it. . . . God Almighty started wind sufficient to carry that [burning] cotton wherever He would."

After the war, Sherman was called to testify as to his culpability in the burning as part of a lawsuit filed by British and American insurance companies with interests in Columbia. By unjustly blaming Hampton, and because it was proven he had never ordered a direct command to anyone telling them to burn the town, Sherman was cleared of responsibility. But what the general had expected his experienced city-burners to do—the ashes of Atlanta still in their hair—on a boisterous, wind-whipped night in an enemy capital, is hard to imagine.

"Though I never ordered it and never wished it," Sherman later admitted toward the end of his life, "I have never shed any tears over the event, because I believe that it hastened what we all fought for, the end of the war."

GENERAL WADE HAMPTON III~
THE VISIONARY ARISTOCRAT

Born in 1818 into one of the state's leading families, Wade Hampton III was one of the richest men in America before the War between the States. Though he opposed secession, once the war was underway, he organized, bankrolled, and led "Hampton's Legion," with which he fought as a colonel at Bull Run, later attaining the rank of brigadier general. He fought with J.E.B. Stuart's army of Northern Virginia, was wounded five times, and promoted to lieutenant general, served as chief of cavalry under Robert E. Lee, and fought General George Custer at the Battle of Gettysburg before returning to his home state to lead the desperate and largely symbolic defense against Sherman's approaching army. In the wake of Sherman's troops, his country estate, Millwood, lay burned to the ground.

But though the war left him relatively poor, Hampton's aristocratic bearing never left him. For Carolinians, the mere existence of such a noble aristocrat seemed to justify the antebellum social stratification turned on its head by Reconstruction. Hence it was no surprise that white Carolinians saw him as the natural choice to lead them back to "the way things were," and elected him governor in 1876.

Though he subscribed to the white supremacist and upper-class elitist beliefs of his time and place, as governor, Wade Hampton III immediately devoted himself to cooling South Carolina's frothing racial cauldron by assuring African-Americans economic and educational equality, legal rights, and (limited) political representation. Unlike many of his supporters and his Democratic successors in the governor's chair, he argued that blacks deserved a fair deal in life—the opportunity to make a good life for themselves. His "radical" notion was to appeal to black voters' needs and get their votes honestly, rather than (as others, such as Edgefield's General Martin W. Gary, wanted) to merely disenfranchise them out of the equation.

After his victory, though he hadn't received much of the black vote, he felt grateful to the 17,000 African-Americans who *had* voted for him and thereby turned the tide in the close election. He worked to make good on his promises, which included ensuring South Carolina's support and implementation of the 13th, 14th, and 15th Amendments, outlawing slavery, providing nonwhites equal protection under the law, and guaranteeing suffrage for all races. He appointed 86 African-Americans to office, insisted upon the appointment of an honest white Republican as chief justice of the state supreme court, and made certain that black schools had sufficient funds to operate on a par with white schools.

These gestures of fair-mindedness set other white Democrats to howling—especially Gary, the leader of the paramilitary "Red Shirts," who had been largely responsible for getting Hampton elected in the first place. Bitter after 12 years of Northern Republican rule, they wanted no such "concessions to the enemy."

Only the weight of Hampton's personality and popularity allowed him to have his way. Historian Hampton W. Jarrell concludes: "Hampton in two years accomplished more for both races and more nearly harmonized the two than has any other leader, North or South."

He also did a lot for the Democratic Party. Hampton's election marked the establishment of a 99-year hold on the State House by the Democrats; the next Republican governor of South Carolina would be James Burrows Edwards, in 1975.

When he ran for re-election in 1878, the Republicans didn't even bother running anybody against him. Of 169,763 votes cast, he received 169,550. He went on to serve his state as a U.S. senator from 1879 to 1891, and died April 11, 1902.

and the 50,000-acre Lake Murray took their place after the construction of the then-largest earthen hydroelectric dam in the world, 208 feet high and 1.5 miles long. During WW II, Fort Jackson on the east side of town became the world's largest military training camp. Jimmy Doolittle's squadron, famed for its brutal bombing of Tokyo, trained over in Lexington County at the site of the present-day Columbia Airport. In 1951 and 1964 Columbia was named an All-American City; the latter designation was made in recognition of Columbia's peaceful, step-by-step implementation of desegregation. Columbia-raised William Price Fox (1926-) published

> *We have eaten two silver pitchers, one or two dozen forks, several sofas, innumerable chairs, and a huge bedstead.*
>
> —*Poet Henry Timrod in a postwar letter to fellow poet Paul Hamilton Hayne*

his first books of poor-white life in and around Columbia with his acclaimed short story collections *Southern Fried* (1962) and *Southern Fried Plus Six* (1968), and with his novel *Moonshine Light, Moonshine Bright* (1967).

During the 1970s many of the city's historic treasures were buffed up and polished, including the Horseshoe at the University of South Carolina. Riverbanks Zoo was opened, quickly gaining notice as one of the nation's top zoos. Over at the university, George Rogers became the school's first Heisman Trophy winner in 1980.

The 1990s have seen a revitalization of the Congaree Vista District, a booming of Columbia's alternative music scene based in Five Points—much thanks to the worldwide success of former USC students Hootie and the Blowfish—the continuing controversy over the Confederate battle flag flying over the State House, and the long $60 million-plus renovation of the State House, complicated by Sherman's burning of the original plans along with the old State House. (At one point contractors discovered that walls they had thought were two feet thick were in fact six feet thick, making the job of drilling and wiring through the walls much more difficult.)

The State House, with its new copper-colored copper dome replacing the oxidized green one of old, reopened to the public and to the people's business in 1998. As of this writing, the controversial Confederate battle flag still flies above the State House.

SIGHTS

ORIENTATION

Columbia is primarily a government and university town, and most of what's best about the city revolves around this fact. The State House sits at the intersection of Gervais and Assembly Streets. Head north on Gervais or east on Assembly and you're headed to downtown Columbia, the original business district of the city, currently in the process of rejuvenation. Southeast of the Capitol you're deeply entrenched in the University of South Carolina region of the town, where 26,000 Gamecocks live for at least nine months of the year.

Gervais (Highways 1 and 378) is one of the two major streets crossing the Congaree River west of town; Blossom St./Knox Abbott Dr. (Highways 321, 176, and 21) is the other. Follow Blossom east and you'll arrive at a five-way intersection where Blossom meets Devine St. and Saluda Ave.—the reason the area is now known as the Five Points district. This is where many of Columbia's most famous nightspots and best restaurants do business. Devine Street rises up out of Five Points into the residential neighborhood of Shandon.

Five Points

Though downtown and the Vista are increasing in popularity, Five Points is still the liveliest section of Columbia at night, due in large part to the university students who trickle down the Greene Street hill every night and stagger back up after closing hour. Five Points was the place where streetcars click-clacking between downtown and Shandon used to turnabout. Today you'll find over 60 shops and restaurants here, along with hot college-age nightclubs where live bands like Hootie and the Blowfish are the soundtrack to many a game of quarters. Two of Columbia's most notorious crimes took place in quick succession in 1992-93: in 1993, Nancy Thurmond, daughter of Senator Strom Thurmond, was killed by a drunk driver while jaywalking across Harden St. to the Eckerd store, not far from the spot where Dail Dinwiddie was last seen walking home late at night after a 1992 U2 concert. Dinwiddie has never been found.

Shandon

Shandon contains some lovely, tree-shaded streets and some graceful brick and stucco homes. To get a feel for the area, take Harden Street up the hill out of Five Points, and then make a right or left and just walk or drive around. To see some nice homes, turn right off Harden onto Heyward, then right on Saluda. You might want to park at this point and enjoy the walk. Next turn left on Catawba, and then right on Wateree. Follow it as it turns into Myrtle and bends around past a little fountain—note the beautiful city view at this point—and you'll see a newer, Charlestonesque neighborhood that, unlike many newer neighborhoods in town, blends in perfectly with the older homes and should look even better when all the trees have grown tall.

Main Street

Originally, Assembly St., the planned main thoroughfare of Columbia, was called Main Street. Today's Main St. originally was called Richardson St. after a Revolutionary War hero. As it became apparent that the center of business was actually one street over, Main was renamed Assembly, and Richardson became Main. The fire of 1865 destroyed every building on Main Street, but the street rose again through the late 19th and early 20th centuries.

But what Sherman's fires were unable to destroy, the rise of the enclosed shopping mall has seriously weakened. Columbia has been trying to revitalize its Main Street area for years now, but this plan has yet to achieve the success of similar schemes in Greenville and Charleston. On weekends and government holidays, this area can seem markedly dead, but on weekdays it teems with well-dressed businessfolk and politicos. And on any day, you'll find a number of interesting structures here.

Starting from the State House, head north on Main and you'll soon come across the 1871 Brennan Building, which houses **Capitol Restaurant,** here since 1913, and home to many an important informal meeting between legislators over grits and eggs. Open 24 hours. In the middle of the next block on your right, you'll find the fascinating **Arcade Mall,** 1332 Main St., opened in 1912, Columbia's first indoor mall. This ornate L-shaped Renaissance Revival building faces both Main St. and Washington Street. My favorite element is the skylight that illuminates the center of the mall. And be sure to notice the large antique bronze chandeliers. It's no wonder this place is on the National Register of Historic Places.

The downside is that there's simply not much to see inside the mall other than **Gracie's Tea Room,** a nice place to pick up a sandwich or salad for lunch on a weekday—open 11:30 a.m.-2:30 p.m.

Continue down Main and you'll see the 1913 **Palmetto Building,** one of Columbia's two earliest skyscrapers, though at just 14 stories, it doesn't scrape very deeply. With a limestone and glazed terra-cotta facade, a copper cornice, and stone parapet, this is one of the most ornate skyscrapers you'll ever find. The detailed palmetto trees throughout the building's facade make it uniquely South Carolinian.

Down another block you'll see the beautiful **Sylvan's Jewelry** building, built in 1871, the only Second Empire building left in Columbia. It has been run by Sylvan's Jewelry since 1906. The clock out front on the sidewalk has been there since 1908.

Continue on down to Blanding St. and you'll turn right at **Tapp's,** long a major department store in town. Turn right here, head down Blanding, and you'll see an old fire station on the left, across from a Streamline Moderne-style building, now owned by the Lexington State Bank. The 1870s firehouse, the last remaining volunteer firehouse in Columbia, has long been the home of **Villa Tronco,** Columbia's oldest and most revered Italian restaurant.

Congaree Vista District

This area, roughly along Gervais St. between Assembly and Huger, above the river, used to be the bad part of town. Then a trendy spaghetti restaurant opened out here, and pretty soon people realized that these old warehouses can look pretty good if you put enough neon on them. Nowadays this is the chic side of town, the part everyone brags about, the place where students

have their parents take them out to dinner. Antique shops and **Vista Studios** round out the area's attractions.

SOUTH CAROLINA STATE MUSEUM

Set beside the Congaree River at 301 Gervais St., in what was, at its 1894 opening, the world's first all-electric textile mill, the State Museum, tel. (803) 737-4921, is one of the largest museums in this part of the country and is very much worth an afternoon of your time. In fact, I suppose the perfect South Carolina visit would begin with a trip here, so that you could explore South Carolina's past from dinosaurs to desegregation before heading off to experience the state as it is today.

As you tour the museum's four floors, be sure to see the very rare 1922 Anderson touring car, built in Rock Hill by a Tucker-like carriage maker/entrepreneur in the early days of automaking. Also note the full-scale reproduction of the "Best Friend of Charleston," the world's first American-built steam locomotive to offer regular railroad passenger and freight service in the U.S., which used to run the 135 miles between Charleston and Hamburg (near modern-day North Augusta), then the longest railroad route in the world. The history section also contains a permanent exhibit on slave life, with examples of slave housing, slave-made basketry, pottery, and carpentry. You'll also find a reconstructed South Carolina one-room schoolhouse and country store. In the art section, be certain to see the Audubon prints for which naturalist-artist Maria Martin of Charleston, Audubon's assistant and editor during his stay in the Lowcountry, painted the backgrounds.

On the museum's science and technology floor, be sure to see the space suit that Lancaster's Charles Duke wore in 1972 when, as part of the Apollo 16 mission, he became one of only 12 men in history to walk on the moon. The moon rock on display in the space science area is one of only two on public display in the Southeast—courtesy of Charles Duke.

Also here is the world's largest laser exhibit hall, including exhibits on the history, principles, and applications of the laser, as well as the Nobel Prize for Physics, won in 1964 by Dr. Charles H. Townes, a Greenville native and inventor of the maser and the laser.

On the cultural history floor, be sure to see the life-size—or, more accurately, death-size—replica of the CSS *Hunley,* the first submarine in history to sink an enemy ship. And the sizable collection of art here all carries a South Carolina connection, either created by a South Carolina artist or featuring a South Carolinian theme.

Kids will love the hands-on science exhibits and general interactive character of the museum. Admission $4 adults, $3 seniors and college students with ID, $1.50 children 6-17, children under 6 years free. No children under 13 allowed without an adult.

Open Mon.-Sat. 10 a.m.-5 p.m., Sunday 1-5 p.m., closed Thanksgiving, Christmas, and Easter. Open New Year's Day 1-5 p.m.

For souvenirs and some neat books on South Carolina, see the Cotton Mill Exchange, open during regular museum hours.

Fully accessible to the handicapped. See the Web site at www.museum.state.sc.us.

THE STATE HOUSE

This three-story, gray granite Italian Renaissance building was originally supposed to feature a rectangular tower instead of its famous—and far more commonplace—copper dome, but it's a beautiful building nonetheless. In 1851, when space problems stirred up demand for a replacement to the original Capitol building, the state began constructing this structure. Three years later, after its foundations turned out to be unsafe, they were ripped out along with the walls built atop them, and the job was begun again under the architectural oversight of Vienna-born Baltimore resident John R. Niernsee. Most of the granite, pulled from the ground by slaves, comes from the Granby quarry three miles away, conveyed here by a railroad specially laid for the task in 1857.

Progress was slow, but this turned out to be a blessing in disguise. When Sherman rode into Columbia at the end of the war, burning the state house in which secession had drawn its first breaths was

a high priority. Fortunately, since the new state house was not complete—and thus had not been used for the Secession Convention—it was spared. Some say that Sherman couldn't bring himself to demolish the unfinished building anyway, since, according to his aide-de-camp, he considered it a "beautiful work of art"—but considering how many other beautiful edifices fell in his path, this story may well be a bit of 19th-century PR work. Sherman certainly didn't think too highly of the building to train his guns on it: today, you'll find a handful of large brass stars marking the spots where Sherman's cannons pounded the building during the pre-invasion bombardment.

The 1990s' $43 million renovation and refurbishment of this beautiful building cost far more money than it was initially supposed to, but now the interior supposedly looks more like it did 100 years ago. The old green copper on the dome outside has been replaced with shiny new copper. For tour information, call (803) 734-2430.

> *Mr. Sumner, I have read your speech twice, with great care and with as much impartiality as I am capable of, and I feel it my duty to say to you that you have published a libel on my State, and uttered a slander upon a relative who is aged and absent, and I am come to punish you.*
>
> —Congressman Preston S. Brooks, just before beating the bejeezus out of Massachusetts Senator Charles Sumner on the floor of the U.S. Senate, May 22, 1856

On the state grounds outside you'll find some beautiful statues, including a life-size iron *Palmetto Tree,* a monument to the Palmetto Regiment of South Carolinians who raised the American flag in Mexico City during the Mexican War, and who lost a full 900 of its 1,200 members to disease and Mexican bullets—in that order; only about 450 are noted here.

The monument itself has seen some battle. In 1865, Sherman's men destroyed the original plates. These were replaced after the war, but in 1939, a freak tornado tore the statue to pieces. For the time being, however, the unusual work is back in one piece, so be sure to take a look.

North of the *Palmetto Tree* you'll find a bronze statue of 1890s pro-agriculture Governor Benjamin Ryan "Pitchfork Ben" Tillman, unveiled in 1940. Ironically, on Gervais St. in front of the State House in 1903, Tillman's nephew Lieutenant Governor James H. Tillman shot *The State* editor N.G. Gonzales to death for calling him a "proven liar, defaulter, gambler and drunkard," in the newspaper's pages. A change of venue brought the younger Tillman's murder trial to a Lexington jury, which, after listening to the defense's plea of self-defense and the "right of revenge," found Tillman not guilty. The fact that Tillman was a Democrat and Gonzales a known Republican didn't hurt any, either.

On the other side of the Capitol you'll see one of the most touching memorials in the state, a tribute to the women of the Confederacy.

SOUTH CAROLINA DEPARTMENT OF ARCHIVES AND HISTORY

Since Charleston was one of the prime entry ports to North America during the Colonial period, and because it was a primary slaving port, many Americans can trace their ancestors to South Carolina. Consequently, every year, people from all over the United States visit this building at 1430 Senate St., tel. (803) 734-8577, Web site: www.scdah.sc.edu/homepage.htm, as they seek Alex Haley–like after their personal roots. But the Department of Archives and History is about more than that. You can find publications and exhibits on South Carolina history and numerous resources for researching your own genealogy. Business hours run Mon.-Fri. 9 a.m.-5 p.m.; reference hours are Tues.-Fri. 9 a.m.-9 p.m., Saturday 9 a.m.-6 p.m., Sunday 1-6 p.m.

TRINITY EPISCOPAL CATHEDRAL

This huge church on Sumter between Senate and Gervais Streets, tel. (803) 771-7300, was founded in 1812, one of the first Episcopal churches outside the Lowcountry area. The Episcopal church, before the Revolutionary War, had been the government-supported Church of England, and so it was natural that, after the pro-British rectors were run off and taxpayer funding cut, the denomination sagged in influence and attendance, particularly outside of the Lowcountry, where the wealthy planter class still patronized the church. Trinity was founded by a group of Lowcountry Episcopalians dedicated to promoting the growth of the church in the rest of the state.

The current building, listed on the National Register of Historic Places, was constructed in 1845 under the leadership of Dr. Peter Shand, a popular long-time rector at the church, and is modeled after England's York Cathedral, featuring stained-glass windows imported from Munich. The 188-foot steeple once claimed title as the highest point in Columbia.

Though many of South Carolina's movers and shakers continue to come and go from here on Sundays, it's the folks who never leave the church grounds that make it an especially interesting place to visit. Wade Hamptons I, II, and III lie here, along with five (in addition to Wade III) South Carolina governors—amongst them James Francis Byrnes, U.S. congressman, senator, Supreme Court justice, director of war mobilization under FDR during WW II, and U.S. secretary of state under Truman. Nicknamed "the assistant president" by the press during WW II, Byrnes was FDR's choice for vice president in 1944, but Big Labor supported the more liberal Truman, and he got the nod. Hence, upon FDR's death in 1945, South Carolina was deprived of her second native-son president (Andrew Jackson being the first). Also buried here is Henry Timrod, poet laureate of the Confederacy.

The cathedral has a bookstore open Mon.-Fri. 10 a.m.-2 p.m., Sunday 9 a.m.-1 p.m.

HAMPTON-PRESTON MANSION

This home at 1615 Blanding Street was built in 1818 for Ainsley and Sarah Goodwyn Hall. But apparently even this mansion wasn't impressive enough for the Halls. Before they had lived here for five years, Ainsley had Robert Mills design him a new, even more impressive home next door—now known as the Robert Mills House. Before construction was completed, however, Ainsley moved on to that great mansion in the sky. Revolutionary War hero Wade Hampton I and his wife Mary Cantey Hampton purchased the older home from the widow Hall, and the Hampton family occupied the residence until 1873. Many considered Wade Hampton I the wealthiest man in the U.S. at the time of his death in 1835. Hampton's daughter Caroline Hampton married the wealthy barrister/planter/politician John S. Preston, and after 1848 they lived here, making this house the center of life for Columbia socialites. Wade Hampton II, Caroline's half brother, lived at nearby Millwood Plantation. You can see *his* son, Wade Hampton III, preserved in statuary outside the State House. During the War between the States, Wade III raised (and largely bankrolled) the Hampton Legion, which saw battle on the fields of Virginia. At the end of the war, Hampton was reassigned to defend—or attempt to defend—Columbia from Sherman's minions. After the war, even despite the corruption and intimidation that put him into office, it was Hampton who brought some sanity to state politics at the end of Reconstruction.

Despite its strong "se-cesh" connections, the mansion was spared during the war temporarily when Union General John A. Logan made it his headquarters. He planned to burn the mansion when he left, but, according to one story, was talked out of it by a group of Ursuline Sisters, who had taken to living here after Sherman's men burned their Assembly St. convent. Another story has it that Sherman found one of the Ursuline Sisters and the children from the convent school hiding in a Columbia graveyard. Moved by the sight, Sherman offered the nun any house in Columbia to live in, and the shrewd sister picked the Hampton-Preston mansion. Sherman told Logan to pack up, and the nuns moved in. Logan grudgingly obeyed, ordering

his men to remove the barrels of highly flammable pine pitch from the basement, where he'd planned to light them.

The building in fact, after various other uses, served as a convent from 1887 to 1890. "Robber governor" Franklin J. Moses, the state's most notoriously corrupt Reconstruction-era governor, purchased the building from the Hamptons in 1873.

After a number of owners including the Ursuline Sisters, in 1890 the mansion became home to the Presbyterian College of Women—one of the first colleges in the South to provide women with a challenging education. In 1915, it became the Chicora College for Women and served as such until 1930.

The inside of the house includes a gentlemen's sitting room where portraits of the three Wade Hamptons hang. Much of the silverware and valuables here are refugees from Millwood, Wade Hampton III's plantation on the outskirts of town, burned by Sherman. Today the home is owned by Richland County and the City of Columbia. For tours call (803) 252-7742. Or head over to the gift shop at the Robert Mills House for information and tickets.

ROBERT MILLS HISTORIC HOUSE AND GARDEN

This home at 1616 Blanding St., tel. (803) 252-1770, is one of the few residences designed by Columbian Robert Mills, the first Federal architect and designer of the Washington Monument and U.S. Treasury Building in Washington, D.C. The home was originally designed for a Mr. Ainsley Hall in 1823, but he died before he could move in. His wife was forced to sell the house to the Presbyterian Synod of South Carolina and Georgia, which ran the Columbia Seminary there from 1831 on into the 1920s. Woodrow Wilson's father, Reverend John Ruggles Wilson, taught here 1870-74 while the future president was still a gangly teen.

The Columbia Bible College used the Mills House from the 1930s to '60s, at which point it was slated for demolition. Fortunately, a number of historical preservationists banded together to save it. The home features a Federal-Greek Revival style, with columns, ornate ceilings, and curved walls. Inside you'll find crystal chandeliers, marble mantles, and period furnishings.

On the surrounding grounds, the Historic Columbia Foundation has seen to the reconstruction of several outbuildings. You'll also find some nicely kept gardens and a boxwood hedge maze. A carriage house used to stand out here; during the Presbyterian days, it became the chapel for seminary students. Young Woodrow Wilson worshipped there, and in fact devoted his life to divine service there.

Eventually, a college—Winthrop College—was founded in the carriage house. The house was later dismantled and moved to Rock Hill with the college itself.

The caretakers offer guided half-hour tours at quarter past the hour Tues.-Sat. 10:15 a.m.-3:15 p.m., Sunday 1:15-4:15 p.m., closed major holidays. Admission runs $3; half price for students with ID, children 6-18 years old, and members of the military.

WOODROW WILSON BOYHOOD HOME

Young Woodrow's parents, the Reverend John Ruggles Wilson and Jessie Woodrow Wilson, designed and built this home at 1705 Hampton St., tel. (803) 252-7742, while the reverend was preaching at the First Presbyterian church and teaching at the Columbia Theological Seminary, then housed in the Robert Mills House. Though few think of Woodrow Wilson as a Southerner, the nation's future 28th president had been born in 1856 in Staunton, Virginia, and had spent most of his childhood—from 1857 through the Civil War and on through 1870, in Augusta, Georgia, where the elder Wilson pastored a church.

But this house in Columbia would be the only home the Wilsons ever owned for themselves. They spent some $8,500 building this cottage-style Tuscan villa; apparently they planned to live here long-term. Young Woodrow—or Tommy, as he was known—became a member of the Presbyterian Church, attending services at the old carriage house of the Mills House, converted into the seminary's chapel.

Unfortunately, John Wilson's unpopular proposal to have seminary students attend a separate church service from the rest of the Presbyterian congregation made things uncomfortable for him, and by 1874 he had to move on to teach in Wilmington, North Carolina. At this time, Tommy went off to Davidson College, also in North Carolina, and from thence to Princeton, where he rose from student to university president before becoming governor of New York and then two-term president of the United States.

Despite the way things turned out for them, the elder Wilsons apparently always felt that Columbia was the closest thing they had to an earthly home; when they died, they were buried in the plots they'd purchased in the graveyard of the First Presbyterian Church on Marion and Lady Streets.

The home is furnished with a number of original Wilson family pieces, including the bed in which young Thomas Woodrow Wilson was born. The Columbia Garden Club has replanted the gardens outside to resemble the way they looked when Mrs. Wilson puttered about here. The magnolia trees in front of the house are the ones she planted. Open Tues.-Sat. 10:15 a.m.-3:15 p.m., Sunday 1:15-4:15 p.m. Tickets available at the Mills house.

MANN-SIMONS COTTAGE: MUSEUM OF AFRO-AMERICAN CULTURE

In 1860, slave Celia Mann bought her freedom from her Charleston owner and walked the 112 miles to Columbia to start a new life as a freedwoman. Today her humble but comfortable Columbia home at 1430 Richland St., tel. (803) 252-1770, is listed on the National Register of Historic Places, and is home to a museum of African-American culture.

The trouble with historic preservation is that the homes preserved usually belonged to the community's movers and shakers, who, in the 18th and 19th centuries, as today, were usually the wealthy of society. Which means that it's hard for most of us to get an idea of what life was like for the average Joe or Josie. This is one of the many reasons I like to visit the Mann-Simons Cottage: more people, white *and* black, lived in cottages like this than in something like the Robert Mills House. Half-hour guided tours are offered at quarter past the hour Tues.-Sat. 10:15 a.m.-3:15 p.m., Sunday 1:15-4:15 p.m.

Closed major holidays. Admission is $3, half price for students with ID, children ages 6-18, and members of the military.

CONFEDERATE RELIC ROOM AND MUSEUM

At 920 Sumter St., tel. (803) 734-9813, this classic Roman-looking building was built in 1935 to honor South Carolina veterans of (as the inscription reads above the entrance) *the* World War. The collection itself, however, was established in 1895 to honor South Carolina's Confederate veterans. Through the years the collection has expanded to reflect all periods of the state's cultural and military history. The museum contains items from the Colonial period through today, including a vest hand-sewn by former tailor (and then-president) Andrew Johnson. Plenty of Civil War items as well, with a special emphasis on South Carolinian regiments and battles—Civil War buffs from around the world make the pilgrimage here. Open Mon.-Fri. 8:30 a.m.-5 p.m. and the first Saturday of the month 10 a.m.-4 p.m., admission free.

COLUMBIA MUSEUM OF ART

Formerly housed in a historic home on the corner of Senate and Bull Streets, the Columbia Museum of Art, tel. (803) 799-2810, moved to a new $16 million, 20,000-square-foot facility at Maine and Hampton Streets and held a grand reopening in July 1998.

The new building triples the museum's available floor space, and the curators plan to expand its series of public programs. The museum features a permanent collection of Renaissance and Baroque paintings, sculptures, and South Carolinian artists' works. Rotating exhibits here as well. The Samuel H. Kress Collection of Baroque and Italian Renaissance Art is one of the highlights: Kress, owner of the S.H. Kress Store that used to do a booming business on Main Street, generously divvied up his artwork amongst the museums in cities where he'd built stores, and hence the Columbia Museum received such works as Botticelli's *The Nativity* and Claude Monet's joyous *L'Ile Aux Orties, Giverny.*

Museum hours are Tues.-Sat. 10 a.m.-5 p.m., Wednesday until 9 p.m., Sunday 1-5 p.m.

Regular admission is $4 for adults, $2 for students and seniors, and free for museum members and children under 5 years of age.

GOVERNOR'S MANSION AND GOVERNOR'S GREEN

The **Governor's Mansion** was originally built in 1855 as the officers barracks for the Arsenal Military Academy, sister of the Citadel. Both institutes were founded in 1822 in the wake of the Vesey plot to provide training for local men as well as a standing army in case of slave revolts. At the end of the War between the States, while the rest of the school was Shermanized, this building survived. Since 1868, it has served as a home to all but a handful of South Carolina's many governors. Among other notables, FDR and George Bush have spent the night here. To tour the mansion, call (803) 737-1710.

Also on the green is the 1830 Greek Revival **Caldwell-Boylston House,** featuring a five-level garden outside, and the ornate 1855 **Lace House.** The latter was designed by a French architect from New Orleans, and it shows.

FIRST BAPTIST CHURCH

Here at 1306 Hampton St., South Carolina leaders passed through the mammoth brick pillars to meet in this newly built church—replacing an earlier wood frame building constructed in 1811—after the election of Abraham Lincoln. They drew up the Ordinance of Secession that led to the Civil War. According to local legend, when Sherman arrived in 1865, he intended to burn the church as punishment; an African-American sexton deliberately misled Sherman's men to the old wood frame church, which they burned. Open Mon.-Fri. 9 a.m.-5 p.m. No admission charge. Call (803) 256-4251 for more information.

MODJESKA SIMKINS HOUSE

Named after the 19th-century Polish actress Madame Helena Modjeska, Simkins is called by some "The Matriarch of the South Carolina Civil Rights Movement." Here in her antebellum second home, at 1920 Marion St., Simkins met with Thurgood Marshall and John McCray during NAACP strategy sessions.

The classic Gothic Revival **First Presbyterian Church** at 1324 Marion features a beautiful spire above and the graves of President Woodrow Wilson's parents in the graveyard outside.

MILLWOOD RUINS

Out on Garner's Ferry Rd. (follow Devine St. south from Five Points—it'll change to Garner's Ferry eventually) you'll come to this set of columns, which, alas, are all that's left of the antebellum home and plantation of Wade Hampton III, Confederate general and post-Reconstruction governor. Call (803) 252-1770 to reserve a tour, held at 2 p.m. the last Sunday of each month March-October.

THE UNIVERSITY OF SOUTH CAROLINA

We-all were U.S.C. before California was even a state!

—A clerk at the USC
Married Housing Office, 1991

The 242-acre, 26,000-student University of South Carolina regularly appears in the second tier of lists ranking the nation's most beautiful college/university campuses. Enter USC from Sumter St. onto the historic antebellum Horseshoe, and you'll not only agree that South Carolina belongs on *any* list of beautiful campuses, but you'll probably question the second-tier status as well. Continue past the McKissick Museum and across the Pickens Street Bridge to the regrettable 1968 Welsh Humanities Office Center, looming over East Campus like some massive concrete and tinted-glass 3-D salute to the Scantron sheet, and you'll begin to understand. Fortunately, just across the walkway from Welsh is the new **National Advocacy Center,** the architecture of which suggests that the powers that build have woken from their cement and rebar stupor and have rededicated themselves to building new structures that flow

logically from the styles of the original campus buildings.

After the American Revolution, South Carolina Lowcountry planters and merchants who had traditionally sent their children off to Oxford and Cambridge for schooling did not want to send them to England anymore. Too, the visionaries in the infant nation realized that an educated population was needed to provide leadership for the newly freed state. The University of South Carolina was founded in 1801 as South Carolina College. The shrewd legislators placed the college in the newborn capital city of Columbia to quell Upcountry citizens who were threatening secession because of the Lowcountry's domination of state politics. In the South Carolina College, the state had created a place on more or less neutral ground where both Lowcountry and Upcountry citizens could send their young men to learn alongside students from the opposite region, building bridges between the two parts of the state. In 1805, the college opened with 29 young men as its student body.

The school was used as a hospital during the Civil War, one of the main reasons it wasn't burned. African-Americans were legally admitted to the school in 1868 under the Reconstruction government, but no blacks actually attended until 1873, whereupon white faculty members

---

A CLEMSON JOKE SAMPLER

Q: Why did the Clemson fan marry the cow?
A: He had to.

Q: Do you know how to tell which girls at Clemson are level-headed?
A: The snuff runs out of both corners of her mouth.

Q: What do you call a line of John Deere tractors going down the road?
A: The Clemson Homecoming Parade.

Q: Do you know why Clemson fans wear orange?
A: That way they can go straight from the deer stand to the road crew to the ball game and never have to change clothes.

—quoted from Web site www.cockfans.com

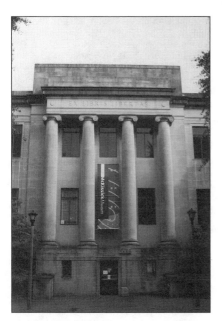

Highlights of a visit to the University of South Carolina campus include the McKissick Museum and other architecturally distinguished buildings located on The Horseshoe.

and students abruptly left the campus. For four years, only African-Americans attended, during which 23 degrees were conferred. In 1877, the college was shut down by Governor Wade Hampton; it re-opened in 1880 as the white-again College of Agriculture and Mechanic Arts, its new focus reflecting the back-to-the-basics attitudes of a people clawing their way back from destruction.

In 1893, the school became coeducational. The college became a chartered university in 1906, after which its history is one of ballooning growth. The campus doubled in physical size and increased 1000% in attendance between 1940 and 1979. Today, students from all 50 states and over 100 foreign countries attend here.

Visitors Center
Now known as *The* USC (to differentiate it from that *other* USC, the University of Southern Cali-

fornia), the university has a pretty helpful visitors center over at the old Columbia Hotel on the corner of Pendleton and Assembly Streets, tel. (800) 922-9755, tel. (803) 777-0169, e-mail: visitor@sc.edu. Here you'll find all the pamphlets you can carry concerning various campus programs, free parking passes, and free phones with which to call various campus departments. You'll also find guided tours departing from here at 10 a.m. and 2 p.m. weekdays during school months, by appointment; exhibits are dedicated to the University's recent notable alumni, including *Entertainment Tonight's* Leeza Gibbons. USC alumna Donna Rice, former model and *Monkey Business* crew member-turned-anti-child-porn crusader, receives no mention.

A Walking Tour of the Horseshoe
Begin by parking along Sumter or down College St. on the west side of campus. As you cross the street, look down to your right and you'll see what looks like a Roman temple, but is in reality the **Longstreet Theatre**. Built in 1855 and long used as everything *but* a theater (the acoustics were terrible), it was remodeled in 1976 and made worthy of its original purposes. Today it's the headquarters for the Department of Theatre and Speech, and features a circular, hydraulic stage. Walk around to the courtyard at the rear of the building to enter.

The Longstreet Theatre was named after Augustus B. Longstreet (1790-1870), author of *Georgia Scenes, Characters, and Incidents,* published in 1835, one of the first recognized pieces of Southern humor and local color, and a major influence on such later writers as Mark Twain and Joel Chandler Harris. Longstreet served as president of the University of Mississippi 1849-1856, then served as the president of the South Carolina College 1857-1861. An ardent secessionist, his passionate speeches were so electrifying that once the War for Southern Independence broke out, the entire student body rushed off to enlist in the Confederate Army after one of his speeches, closing the school for the duration of the war. Longstreet himself, in his 70s by this point, did not enlist, but rather returned to the comforts of the University of Mississippi in Oxford, Mississippi, while his students died on the battlefields of Bull Run, Antietam, and Gettysburg.

If the Longstreet Theatre looks strangely familiar, you may recognize it as the building emblazoned on Hootie and the Blowfish's megaselling CD, *Cracked Rear View.*

Now enter through the gates to the beautiful antebellum **Horseshoe**—the original campus. On your left you'll see the **South Caroliniana Library,** built in 1840 based on a design by Robert Mills. This is the first freestanding college library in the nation. Take a peek upstairs—this *looks* like a library should look, with high windows, paneled walls, and busts of various South Carolina heroes watching over your work. My favorite bust is of General States Rights Gist, a man who wore his politics (and his parents') on his birth certificate. Appropriately, States Rights died in the War for Southern Independence.

This used to serve as the main library for the college, but in 1940 when the McKissick Memorial Library was opened, the focus of the South Caroliniana Library narrowed to documents pertaining to South Carolina and the Confederacy. Consequently, this is one of the best places in the world to find literature on South Carolina and the Civil War.

Continuing along the left leg of the Horseshoe, you'll come across **Elliott College,** a residence hall built in 1837 to deal with a swelling student body, then up to 142 students.

The hall is named for Beaufort-born Stephen Elliott (1777-1830), state legislator, author of the state's Free School Act, cofounder of the *Southern Review,* and author of an important 1808 book, *Sketch of the Botany of South Carolina and Georgia.*

Harper College stands at the other side of Elliott. This is the headquarters of the South Carolina College, the Honors College of the university. Built in 1848, just after the death of William Harper (1790-1847), class of 1808, U.S. senator from South Carolina, noted judge, and member of the board of trustees of the South Carolina College.

Farther down is **McCutchen House,** the Faculty House, built in 1813 as a faculty residence and named for Professor George McCutchen, one of the distinguished faculty who called the building home over the years. Since 1945, the university hasn't provided housing for faculty members, but the building is a meeting place for faculty and high-ranking staff members. The

beautiful wrought-iron courtyard and flanking gardens are used to lure desirable faculty candidates. Be sure to take a peek.

Desaussure College, built in 1809, is the second-oldest building on campus. Today it houses the College of Social Work. It's named after Pocotaligo-born Henry William DeSaussure (1763-1839), longtime jurist and one-time director of the U.S. Mint. The WPA-built **McKissick Museum** stands at the top of the Horseshoe. Named for a former USC president, McKissick is the Horseshoe's newest building by far. For 36 years it served as the campus library, until replaced in 1976 by the Thomas Cooper. The hall now houses a museum featuring a silver collection, gemstone collection, doll collection, geology exhibit, and rotating displays of artwork by regional artists. No admission charge.

Beside the McKissick, as you begin down the eastern fork of the Horseshoe back toward Sumter St., is **Rutledge College,** the original campus building, constructed in 1805. For the university's first few years, it served as dormitory, lecture hall, chapel, library, faculty housing, and laboratory. Today Rutledge still contains the campus chapel and the Department of Religious Studies, as well as student housing. East of the building you'll see the pretty Sundial Garden. The building is named after John Rutledge (1739-1800) and Edward Rutledge (1749-1800), brothers, Revolutionary-era leaders, and former governors of South Carolina.

Next down the row, with U.S. and South Carolina flags hanging outside, is the President's House, built 1810, rebuilt in 1854. The building served as a faculty house until the 1940s, when it became, briefly, a women's residence hall. In 1952 it was converted into a massive, ornate single-family home—the President's House.

Legaré College was built in 1848 and serves as the Department of Military Science, as well as a residence hall. The building is named after Hugh Swinton Legaré (1797-1843), class of 1814, a Charleston scholar, and U.S. secretary of state, and U.S. attorney general under John Tyler. Some say he had the most cultivated mind in the antebellum South.

Crippled for life by a childhood illness, Legaré set to developing his mind. He graduated from the South Carolina College in 1814 at the top of his class. He went to law school in Charleston and then continued his studies in Edinburgh. As a great supporter of Charleston literature, he is credited with quickening the Southern cultural renaissance, especially through his 1828 cofounding (with Stephen Elliott) of the *Southern Review.*

Next along the east fork comes **Pinckney College,** built in 1837 and used today primarily as a residence hall. The building was named after the Pinckney family, whose members have included early indigo planter Eliza Lucas Pinckney (1722-1793); Charles Cotesworth Pinckney (1746-1825), legislator, diplomat, and member of the USC board of trustees; and Charles Pinckney (1757-1824), a framer of the U.S. Constitution. The late Josephine Pinckney (1895-1957), sometime poet and novelist *(Three O'Clock Dinner),* descended from the same family.

Lieber College fronts Sumter. Built in 1837, Lieber is named after political scientist and former professor Francis Lieber (1800-1872), who lived here in the building until leaving USC in 1855.

Lieber was a genius German scholar who had already founded the *Encyclopedia Americana* before taking the job at USC in 1835. A brilliant thinker who offended South Carolinians with his abolitionist views, Lieber was overlooked for appointment to college president because of his controversial opinions. In protest, he left to assume a position at Columbia University, where he spent the rest of his career. During the War between the States, Lieber wrote a paper distributed by the Union government as *Instruction for the Government of Armies in the Field, General Orders No. 100,* which became and remains an international standard for conduct in war.

In the center of the Horseshoe you'll find yourself walking over bricks, many of which were once part of Columbia's Booker T. Washington High School, the first school for African-Americans in South Carolina, which stood across Blossom Street. The bricks are engraved with the names of contributors to the university—look carefully west of the monument standing in the middle of the green and you'll find a brick purchased by USC alums Hootie and the Blowfish.

The monument, the Egyptian-revival **Maxcy Monument,** was designed by Robert Mills in 1827 just before he designed the Washington Monument. It honors Johnathon Maxcy, first president of the university.

Other Notable Buildings

Other buildings worth visiting on campus include the **Thomas Cooper Library,** tel. (803) 777-3145, a 286,000-square-foot building with 40 miles of shelving, considered by most to be the best library between Chapel Hill, North Carolina, and Austin, Texas. A large reflecting pool fronts the building.

The huge rectangular library, built on the old parade ground where the occupying Federal soldiers used to drill during Reconstruction, is much bigger than it appears from the outside: what you see from the street is only the top two floors; five of Cooper's floors are underground, making it an excellent place for bookworms to hide during a nuclear blast.

One of the library's bragging points is its rare-books collections; the Graniteville Reading Room gives you the opportunity to sit and read these rare, noncirculating documents in comfort. You'll find even more old books on the shelves alongside newer titles; it's not uncommon to be able to check out a book that is over 150 years old. Open Mon.-Fri. 7:30 a.m.-midnight, Saturday 10 a.m.-8 p.m., and Sunday 1 p.m.-midnight, the library was named for English-born Thomas Cooper (1759-1839), second president of the college and a prolific writer of everything from political and religious tracts to scientific textbooks and articles.

Just east of Thomas Cooper you'll come across the **Russell House,** 1400 Greene St., another massive (225,000 square feet) building. Opened in 1955 and expanded three times since then, it's one of the largest student unions in the Southeast, and one of the busiest: according to the university, the doors of the Russell House open 18,000-20,000 times a day, and the structure hosts some 5,700 events and meetings a year. The Grand Market Place on the first floor offers better-than-average cafeteria food and a great chance to throw yourself right smack into the middle of student life. On the second floor you'll find some additional food joints including a scaled-down Pizza Hut. Down in the basement is the Carolina Mall, a small mall for students, but not good for much except cheap eats—and haircuts, if you're in the need.

Downstairs on the northwest side of Greene St., facing the street you'll find the **University Bookstore,** a good place to find Gamecock-related books, and T-shirts reading, "GO COCKS!" and just "COCKS!"

You get used to it.

Russell House is named for USC alumni and then-college president Judge Donald S. Russell, one-time U.S. assistant secretary of state, South Carolina governor, U.S. senator, and district judge. For more information on what's here, call the Russell House University Union Information Center at tel. (803) 777-3196.

Continue down Green and you'll see the 1928 **Melton Observatory** on your left. The observatory, tel. (803) 777-4180, is open every clear Monday night 8:30-10:30 p.m., 9:30-11:30 p.m. during daylight saving time.

After the observatory, hook left until you see the Pickens St. Bridge on your right. Cross this and you'll see the **Welsh Humanities Center.** Sure, the tower looks like something from an East German flea market, but the sunken beer garden in front, with the tables and umbrellas, used to look much worse in the early 1990s, when it was filled with litter-strewn water surrounding a god-awful "sculpture" that looked more like what you'd expect if Hurricane Hugo had hit the set of *The Empire Strikes Back.*

On the second floor of the Humanities Classroom Building to your right is where the late poet/novelist James Dickey used to hold court with students, which over the years included (in rapidly plummeting order of accomplishment) novelists Pat Conroy, Ben Greer, and the author of this book.

Though Dickey now seeks his deliverance elsewhere, humorist/novelist/short story writer William Price Fox still teaches here. Humorous chronicler of poor whites in South Carolina in such books as *Southern Fried, Southern Fried Plus Six,* and *Ruby Red,* along with one of the best books to be written about the Hugo disaster, *Lunatic Wind,* a few years ago he took up with a grad student named Sarah Gilbert and helped her see her first book, *Hairdo,* to publication. Before her second book, *Dixie Riggs,* was published, in 1992, Fox and Gilbert were married in front of a large rocket at the State Fair—perhaps the perfect venue for a wedding between two authors famous for their proto-Foxworthian humor.

They've since divorced.

The tower itself is primarily an office building.

Back in the early 1990s, on a school night you might hear poet/novelist James Dickey down the hall, plunking out the theme to *Deliverance* on an old guitar in his office.

The 18-story, gold-capped building towering over the scene is called the **Capstone,** built in 1967 (now there's a surprise), a residence hall that used to have a rotating restaurant at the top. This was the only rotating restaurant in the Carolinas, but the rotating mechanisms have been removed, and the round restaurant (still providing an excellent view of the city) is used only for special events.

Beyond the Capstone you'll see some nice old neighborhoods around the Gregg Street area. Actor/director Robby Benson used to live here when he served as an instructor in the USC film program.

OTHER COLLEGES

Other than USC, Columbia houses a handful of other noteworthy colleges. Historically black Allen University and Benedict College were both founded in 1870 by Christian groups (the African Methodist Episcopal and Baptist churches, respectively) who made it their business to educate former slaves. Today, **Allen University,** 1530 Harden Street, tel. (803) 254-4165, Web site: www.icusc.org/allen/, founded 1870, continues as a private coed college (enrollment 250) affiliated with the AME church. **Benedict College,** located at Harden and Blanding Streets, tel. (803) 256-4220, employs over 300 faculty and staff and enrolls over 1,800 students in a host of fields of study including business, mathematics and natural sciences, humanities, social and behavioral sciences. See the college online at www.icusc.org/benedict/sch_link.htm.

Columbia College, 1301 Columbia College Drive, tel. (800) 277-1301 or (803) 786-3871, is a small (1,300 enrollment) four-year women's liberal arts college, ranked recently as one of the top 10 regional liberal arts colleges in the South by *U.S. News and World Report.* It was here that the state considered establishing a women's military program to avoid having to allow female cadets at the Citadel, but it proved too expensive a proposition. See the school's online site at www.colacoll.edu.

Columbia International University, 7435 Monticello Rd., tel. (803) 754-4100, the new name for the former Columbia Bible College, highlights the school's international-missions focus. Finally, the **Lutheran Theological Southern Seminary,** tel. (800) 804-5233 or (803) 786-5150, serves seminarians of numerous denominations, providing several theological degrees.

RIVERBANKS ZOOLOGICAL PARK AND BOTANICAL GARDEN

Many of us remember the small city zoo of the type now found only in children's books, the kind with the depressed lions and the peanut-snuffling elephants, and the monkeys clanging tin cups against their bars.

Well, Riverbanks is to that sort of zoo what a fresh Maine lobster is to a can of tuna. Most of its 2,000 animals live in "natural habitat" exhibits that use such "psychological barriers" as moats and light to create a setting that's got fewer bars than a Mormon-run county.

Riverbanks, at 500 Wildlife Parkway/Greystone Blvd.—just off I-126 at Greystone Blvd. in Columbia, tel. (803) 779-8917—has been ranked the third-best zoo in all of the U.S.A., topped only by the much larger ones in San Diego and Washington, D.C. In 1993, Riverbanks was named the No. 1 travel attraction in the entire Southeast—which certainly must have made the nose of a certain Floridian mouse twitch. And all this *before* Riverbanks added the beautiful 7,000-acre Botanical Gardens across the river. Now, over 850,000 people a year come here to visit—eight times the population of Columbia, and almost a quarter of the population of the entire state.

The Zoo

The zoo itself is divided up into different continental regions, of which "Africa"—with the zebras, hippos, giraffes, and lions, is a favorite.

One of the highlights of the zoo is the Aquarium Reptile Complex (ARC), an award-winning collection depicting South Carolina, the jungle, the ocean, and the desert.

Although all are fascinating, the unique South Carolina section of the ARC is the most immediately interesting for someone in the midst of exploring the state. From alligators to gar fish and the state's deadly snakes, this is a good place to come in and get acquainted with some of the creatures it would behoove you to be able to identify quickly in the wild.

Elsewhere, the polar bear, pink flamingo, and Bengal tiger areas are all favorites, as is Gorilla Island, a cleverly designed exhibit that allows people to see the leaping, screeching, scratching animals from all angles.

The zoo offers scheduled sea lion feedings at 10:30 a.m. and 2:30 p.m., and penguin feedings at 11:30 a.m. and 3:30 p.m. Kids and city slickers enjoy the milking demonstrations at Riverbanks Farm at 10 a.m.

The Aquarium Reptile Complex diving demonstration (11 a.m. and 2 p.m.) sounds compelling, but forget those images of somebody diving into the alligator tanks. Instead, the diving takes place in the 55,000-gallon Indo-Pacific coral reef tank with colorful tropical fish, sharks, moray eels and other Pacific Ocean species.

After the penguin feedings, my favorite of all the shows is the tropical rainstorm simulation in the birdhouse, which takes place at scheduled times throughout the day—weekdays: 11 a.m., 1 and 3 p.m.; weekends: 11 a.m., 1 p.m., 2 p.m., and 4 p.m. It's possible for these times to change, so stop by the birdhouse early in the day to get the schedule.

The Gardens

This zoo has expanded greatly in the past few years with its addition of the Botanical Gardens, connected by a brick-paved pedestrian bridge over the Lower Saluda River. The walk to the Botanical Gardens visitors center is only 0.3 miles, but the incline on the far side is not for everyone. You might opt for the trams that leave every couple minutes from over by the Burger King. On the other side you'll find lush hardwood forest reminiscent of the Upcountry, with huge oaks, birches, hickories, and maples canopying the native flowering shrubs, vines, wildflowers and ground cover. Spanish moss abounds.

Take the half-mile River Trail and Woodlands Walk and you'll explore the southern two-thirds of the Riverbanks property, all naturally—which is to say minimally—landscaped. You'll also run across the stone ruins of the old Saluda factory, built in 1834. This was one of the first water-powered textile mills in South Carolina, and it helped provide materials for Confederate uniforms during the War between the States.

The Botanical Gardens site features three definite topographic land masses: the floodplain valley, the valley slopes, and the uplands—an area 135 feet above the Saluda River. Of these, the first two have been left largely au naturel, while in the "Uplands," Riverbanks has thus far built a visitors center, a football-field-sized English-style walled garden, and an amphitheater for outdoor arts performances. And they've got even more up their khaki sleeves.

Here in the Uplands you'll also find the visitors center complex, featuring the Garden Terrace Cafe, a gift shop, an art gallery, and spaces for various community events.

Dining

Another nicety of this zoo is that it's taken time to create some ambience in two of its eateries. The former **Kenya Cafe** has been possessed by the flame-broiled spirit of Burger King, a tradeoff for that corporation's providing the trains that run to and from the Botanical Gardens, but no one, including the employees, seems very excited about the new chain. If nothing else, this gives you the chance to see what must be the world's *prettiest* Burger King. There's plenty of outdoor seating on the deck over the "jungle," above the alligators. **The Garden Terrace Cafe** in the Botanical Gardens visitors center provides an attractive setting for a light snack and coffee. There are a couple of other stands around where you can pick up an ice cream or pizza, but they're only open on busy days.

These places are reasonably priced. You'll also find a pizza/submarine sandwich station and several other refreshment stands throughout the park. Or, if you really want to save money, use the free picnic area located at the west end of the park.

Admission

If you need them, you'll find strollers and wheelchairs available for rent near the front gate. Tickets run $5.75 for adults, $3.25 for kids 3-12; ages 2 and under free. In January and February, take advantage of "Free Fridays," which offer just what it sounds like they offer: free admission for all.

Special Events

If you're here in the winter, try to visit the **Lights Before Christmas** (separate admission), where you can ogle more than one million holiday lights (someone counted?) in a myriad of displays throughout the darkened park as you sip hot cider and listen to Christmas carolers. Be aware, though, you won't be able to see most of the animals at this hour—their "natural habitats" are not lit, and many of them are catching shut-eye anyway.

In January and February, head here on a Friday and get in for free 9 a.m.-4 p.m. If you happen to be here in April when they hold the **Taste of Columbia at Riverbanks Zoo & Garden** event, you'll get to sample the specialties of Columbia's best restaurants while listening to live music. Call the zoo for information, tel. (803) 779-8917.

PARKS

Riverfront Park and Historic Columbia Canal

This narrow stretch of land down along the river at 312 Laurel St., tel. (803) 733-8613, is one of the true delights of life in Columbia. Across the old pedestrian bridge you can walk or jog, skate or bike along the paved trail between the Congaree River and the 1824 Columbia Canal. No admission; open 9 a.m.-9 p.m.

The old-fashioned benches that convert into picnic tables are one of the unique touches to this park. A clever design. I wonder why we don't see more of these around. At the entrance to the park, you'll see a pink castle—that's the Columbia Marionette Theatre.

This place is a lot more fun for me since the prison next door closed down a few years back. It used to be you'd see guards up in the tower and hear murderers and rapists at play on the other side of the wall as you walked down these solitary paths. Now the murderers and rapists are off to less time-worn digs and kudzu has taken over the walls and guard towers. And the joggers, walkers, and picnickers have the river and canal all to themselves.

The canal here was originally built in 1824 to allow boats to bypass the rocky shoals where the Saluda and Broad form the Congaree. A few years after it was built, however, the railroad was completed from Charleston to Columbia,

man-made waterfall is one attraction in Columbia's masterpiece Finlay Park

and river traffic decreased. In the 1890s, the canal was refitted and retrenched to generate electricity for local industry—including the world's first all-electric textile mill, now the State Museum. In 1906 the city's waterworks moved into this area, and here it stays. Note the pump house here, long since replaced by more modern equipment, but still here for the viewing.

Finlay Park
Since the early 1800s, visitors to Columbia have raved about the park at 930 Laurel St., tel. (803) 733-8331. Largely destroyed by turn-of-the-century industrialization, Sidney Park became the pet project of Mayor Kirkman Finlay, who envisioned a modern, urban park in touch with both the region's natural heritage and the recreational needs of urban residents. The park was re-opened in 1990 and now contains a man-made waterfall beside a hillside planted with yellow jessamine, the state flower; a snack bar; and an outdoor stage that hosts a summer concert series

(7-10 p.m., Saturday nights June-Aug.), Shakespeare plays, and other performances. Beautiful views of the Columbia skyline here, especially from the platform of the Watermark Cafe. This is where the city's big Mayfest is held each year.

Sesquicentennial State Park
This 1,419-acre park at 9564 Two Notch Rd., tel. (803) 788-2706, is amazing in that it seems to come from nowhere in the midst of tract mall land some 13 miles northeast of downtown Columbia on Two Notch Road. The park provides a good example of natural sand hills flora, featuring a 30-acre lake, nature trails, and picnic areas.

Also here is **The Log House,** a 1756 structure discovered in 1961, when some homes were demolished in the county. Fortunately, whoever was operating the bulldozer that day held off the march of progress long enough for interested parties to dismantle the old house and move it over here. Sesqui ("SESS-kwee"), as it's called, also offers 87 camping sites, a nature center, swimming (in the lake), paddle boats (ditto), and fishing (yet again). A good place to spot fireflies in the summer.

On the park grounds you'll also find a life-size replica of the "Best Friend of Charleston," America's first locomotive, built for service between Charleston and Hamburg on the Savannah River. Open 7 a.m.-9 p.m. April-Oct., 8 a.m.-6 p.m. Nov.-March. Office hours 11 a.m.-noon, 4-5 p.m.

Vietnam Veterans' Memorial Park
Officially titled **Memorial Park,** this park at the corner of Gadsden and Hampton Streets, tel. (803) 733-8331 or (803) 733-8220, is the second-largest Vietnam memorial in the country. It contains a replica of the Washington, D.C., Vietnam Memorial, along with a five-sided pylon carved with friezes portraying contributions by each branch of the armed forces. Two black granite walls contain the names of every South Carolinian who died or disappeared during the war in Vietnam.

Dreher Island State Park
On Rte. 1, 12 miles off I-26 Exit 91 and 25 miles from downtown Columbia, tel. (803) 364-3530, this park offers 12 miles of shoreline and 348 acres of parkland made up of three islands connected by bridges to the mainland and to each other.

Unlike most of the state's parks, Dreher has no supervised beach, but there's plenty of good swimming to be had here—at your own risk. If you can, though, rent a boat on the lake at **The Lake Connection** in Chapin, tel. (803) 781-8083; **Lake Murray Marina** in Ballentine, tel. (803) 781-1585; or **Putnam's Landing** tel. (803) 345-8083.

Once you have a boat, take it out to the former Bombing Range Island, now called Lunch Island (which, you'll admit, sounds safer), and visit the **Purple Martin Audubon Sanctuary,** established by the Columbia Audubon Society, the South Carolina Department of Natural Resources, and South Carolina Electric and Gas. Here the martins—the largest North American swallow extant—arrive in June by the tens of thousands until some 750,000 are crammed onto the tiny island. It's sort of the bird version of Oahu, apparently.

In case you were wondering, the "Bombing Range Island" tag dates to WW II, when this was used for dummy bomb drops by Army Air Corps bomber crews in training from Fort Jackson. Today, I suppose you could still call it Bombing Range Island, but for a different reason. The feathered bombers fly out as far as 75 miles away on sorties during the day when they're staying here, and then venture back to catch some shut-eye.

A great way to experience Lake Murray is to camp or rent one of the lakeside villas at Dreher State Park for a couple of nights. Lots of fishing and boating, a nature trail, and a playground for the kids. Two well-treed camping areas are here, with a total of 112 sites. The five lakeside villas have two to three bedrooms and sleep six to eight people. One of the three-bedroom villas has been designed to accommodate handi-capped visitors. Most of the campsites rent on a first-come, first-served basis, but you can make reservations for 40 of them. Be sure to reserve well ahead for the villas.

FORT JACKSON

Talk to anyone in the U.S. Army and there's a good chance he or she has spent time at Fort Jackson, named for South Carolina's home-grown military leader and president Andrew Jackson. It was established in 1917 as Camp Jackson to train soldiers for WW I. At the start of WW II the slumbering camp swelled as America geared up in 1940. The fort became, during the war, the third-largest city in the state. The father of actress Mary-Louise Parker *(Fried Green Tomatoes, Grand Canyon)* was doing a hitch at Fort Jackson when she was born on-base in 1964.

In 1967, the fort celebrated its 50th anniversary. The City of Columbia paid its respects by donating the large statue of Andrew Jackson that stands at Gate No. 1 on Fort Jackson Boulevard. The next year, Columbia annexed the fort and its 1,700 buildings.

Nowadays, more than 97,000 people live on this 52,303-acre installation at any given time. Some 62,000 soldiers pass through here each year, receiving training in basic combat and advanced individual training. The Fort Jackson Museum, located on Jackson Blvd., contains thousands of military weapons, uniforms, and other memorabilia, dating from the American Revolution on through Desert Storm. The museum is open Tues.-Sun. 1-4 p.m. No admission charge. See the fort online at jackson-www.army.mil.

LODGING AND DINING

ACCOMMODATIONS

Hotels

The **Fairground Plaza Hotel,** 621 S. Assembly St., tel. (800) 220-2752 or (803) 252-2000, fax (803) 779-0026, is located within a couple miles of USC and Five Points, over by the fairgrounds. Inexpensive. A nicer-than-average **Holiday Inn** at 630 Assembly St., tel. (803) 799-7800, offers a pool and excellent location just downhill from the USC campus. Moderate-Expensive. On the premises you'll find **The Shag Club,** a nightclub where many of the Capital City's movers and shakers come here to move and shake.

Over on the other side of the State House on Main Street you'll find **The Governor's House Hotel,** 1301 Main St., tel. (800) 800-0835 or (803) 779-7790, fax (803) 779-7856, which offers some reasonable rates and a fine location, within easy walking distance of the Capitol Restaurant and the State House. Offers 89 clean rooms, free covered parking, a pool, and—important for this location, given the clientele—a large writing desk in each room. Continental breakfast. Cheaper weekend rates.

Motels

Across the Assembly Street Bridge in Cayce at 111 Knox Abbott Dr. is **Best Western Riverside Inn,** tel. (800) 528-1234 or (803) 939-4688. This '60s-style complex, though on a busy street, seems somehow quiet and blissful beneath the many trees near the river. The motel offers continental breakfasts, a pool, nine-hole putting green, and two open-pit grills. Golf packages available. Moderate.

You'll find a cleaner-than-average **Motel 6,** tel. (803) 798-9210 or (803) 772-6580, far away from most anything interesting, off I-26 Exit 106 and St. Andrews Road. The address is 1776 Burning Tree Rd., but by the time you get over there you'll see the sign. Inexpensive. You'll also find a number of chain lodgings near the airport.

Bed and Breakfasts

Claussen's Inn, 2003 Greene St., tel. (800) 622-3382 or (803) 765-0440, fax (803) 799-7924, set in a brick 1928 bakery building, is a favorite place to stay in Columbia, primarily because of its great location close to USC and in the midst of Five Points. The 29 rooms here have private baths, and extras include a jacuzzi, continental breakfast, complimentary wine and sherry in the lobby, and chocolate and brandy at night. Reserve ahead. Expensive.

The **Chesnut Cottage B&B,** 1718 Hampton St., tel./fax (803) 256-1718, offers four rooms in a house once owned by James and Mary Chesnut, just down from Woodrow Wilson's childhood home, in the Expensive-Luxury range. Private baths, no smoking, kids allowed only after the age of 12. Some whirlpool tubs. Features a full gourmet breakfast.

Richland Street Bed and Breakfast, 1425 Richland St., tel. (803) 779-7001, fax (803) 256-3725, offers rooms at prices ranging Moderate-Premium, depending on when you stay here and which of the eight rooms you choose. Two stories tall, smoke-free, children must be approved. No pets. One room equipped for guests with disabilities. Features a gazebo and rockers on the porch.

Right over by the university you'll find the 1894 Victorian **Rose Hill B&B,** at 1006 Barnwell St., tel. (803) 771-2288, featuring queen beds, private baths and fireplaces, along with a full breakfast and a garden courtyard. Children allowed at hosts' discretion. Moderate-Premium.

Villas

The lakeside villas at **Dreher Island State Park,** Rte. 1, 12 miles off I-26 Exit 91 and 25 miles from downtown Columbia, tel. (803) 364-3530, have two to three bedrooms and sleep six to eight people. One of the three-bedroom villas has been designed to accommodate handicapped visitors. A delightful, restful place to stay—but be sure to reserve well ahead.

Campgrounds

Sesquicentennial State Park, 9564 Two Notch Rd. (Hwy. 1), tel. (803) 788-2706, offers 87 spaces on a first-come, first-served basis. Each site has water and electric. Hot showers and restrooms available. **Dreher Island State Park,**

Rte. 1, 12 miles off I-26 Exit 91 and 25 miles from downtown Columbia, tel. (803) 364-4152, offers well-treed camping areas here, with a total of 112 sites. Other local campgrounds include **Putnam's Landing,** tel. (803) 345-3040, in Chapin, four miles southeast off I-76.

FOOD AND DRINK

American/Southern

If you come in **Yesterday's** main entrance on the corner of Devine and Harden, 2030 Devine St., tel. (803) 799-0196, head straight back past the restrooms (on your left) to the booth with a plaque hanging on the wall above it. You'll find the names of a group of writers who used to meet here: Pat Conroy, James Dickey, William Price Fox, and novelist Ben Greer, for starters. In the novel *The Prince of Tides,* Conroy has Tom Wingo's parents take him out to Yesterday's for dinner after a big USC football game. A scene from the 1994 James Caan movie, *The Program,* was filmed here as well.

But all of this name-dropping aside, Yesterday's really is a great, unpretentious, reasonably priced restaurant. Order the Nacho Man Nachos with black bean chili and chicken if you're truly hungry—a large order serves two for under $7—or get the Confederate Fried Steak if you want a real Southern treat. Last time I was there they offered a full pound of crab legs for $6.95 on Monday and Tuesday. Yesterday's also features many microbrews on tap and bottled, and some delicious hot toddies such as the Nutty Nun. Over by the main entrance, while you're waiting for a table, check the photos they've posted of various customers posing with their Yesterday's T-shirts at different unique spots around the globe.

Lizard's Thicket (multiple locations) is one of the most authentic Southern meals you can find in Columbia. For dinner, order the dinner special, which lets you choose one meat (each night features one or two offerings) and three vegetables (which can also vary). Or you can cheat and go for the Country Skillet Apples as one of your veggies.

You'll find more than a dozen Lizard's Thickets in the Columbia area; here you choose between 10 meats and 20 vegetables every day.

Open seven days a week. If you do nothing else, come in the morning for the fish and grits, $3.95. The Thicket chain was founded here in Columbia in 1977 and has expanded over the past 20-plus years, though solely in the greater Columbia area.

And since you were wondering, the name doesn't really mean anything—Bob and Anna Williams, the chain's founders, heard the name in conversation while living in Alabama and figured its country sound fit with their vision of a homey country restaurant. Locations include one near the USC campus at 919 Sumter St., tel. (803) 765-1373, one over at 818 Elmwood Ave., tel. (803) 779-6407, and one at 2240 Airport Blvd. in West Columbia, tel. (803) 796-7820. Since they're all owned by the Williams family, you can call one of the above numbers and ask for the location nearest you.

The only thing I wouldn't recommend is the barbecue, which you'll probably mistake for tuna when you first see it. Lots of locals like it that way though, so you might want to peek at surrounding tables and see if it looks all right to you.

Saluda's, 751 Saluda Ave., tel. (803) 799-9500, is upstairs in Five Points. A pretty veranda overlooking Five Points provides a romantic setting for a more formal dinner.

Longhorn Steaks serves up some serious beef down in the Vista at 902 Gervais St., tel. (803) 254-5100.

Over at Five Points, **Harpers,** 700 Harden St., tel. (803) 252-2222, is your basic $6 hamburger joint, with a nice, right-in-the-middle-of-it atmosphere. Try the tortilla soup—it's delicious.

In the Vista District, **Richard's Fine Southern Cuisine,** 1109 Lincoln at Gervais, tel. (803) 212-7217, got *Southern Living*'s nod when they came through town a while back. Open for lunch 11 a.m.-2 p.m., dinner 6-10 p.m.

Scott Brothers at Lincoln and Senate, tel. (803) 254-8833, features a big porch where you can eat wonderful roast beef sandwiches and babyback ribs. Everything here is smoked in-house. Well, not the *drinks*—but you get the idea. Lunch and dinner.

Seafood

The Blue Marlin, 1200 Lincoln St., tel. (803) 799-3838, is relatively new to the Vista area. The fish is fresh and good, and the Blue Marlin

TWO RECIPES FROM MISS SHARON

Catfish Stew
5 lb. potatoes, diced
2 lb. onions (sweet if available), diced
$1/2$ cup celery, chopped
5 lb. catfish fillet
12 strips bacon
1 lb. fried bulk sausage
2 (15 oz.) cans tomato sauce
24 oz. bottle ketchup
$1/2$ stick margarine
1 tablespoon sugar
1 tablespoon black pepper
hot sauce to taste

Place potatoes, onions, and celery in an 8- to 10-quart pot. Add enough water to cover and boil until fully cooked. In separate pot, boil fish until done. Fry bacon and sausage and save drippings. When ready, add fish and drippings and all other ingredients to potato mixture. Continue to cook 25-30 minutes, stirring frequently to avoid sticking. Hot sauce salt to taste. (If you are using fish with bones, remove bones before adding to potato mixture.)

(To keep bones out of mix, put enough liquid from boiled catfish to cover catfish in blender with deboned catfish and blend on high for two or three seconds.)

Barbecue Hash
(for one hog)
6 lb. onions
8 lb. potatoes
4 lb. beef (an old roast will do)
liver
2 strips of side
1 hog head
28 oz. Worchestershire sauce
1 qt. mustard
2 qt. ketchup
salt and pepper

Cook onions, potatoes, and beef. Grind, and save liquid it was cooked in. Grind other meat. Add all in pot. Cook and stir on low heat and add whatever you need according to taste.

also features many traditional Lowcountry favorites such as shrimp and grits, $9.79, and Carolina deviled crab, $10.95. Thorough wine list and delectable homemade desserts. Lunch prices considerably less expensive than dinner.
La Vecchia's Seafood Grille, 1736 Main St., tel. (803) 376-8888, on the corner of Main and Laurel Streets, serves up such Southern seafood specialties as fried oysters and seared crab cakes as well as unusual entrées like Sesame Salad Yellowfish Tuna served with spicy eggplant, Asian noodles, and wasabi vinaigrette ($17.95), and Pepper-Thyme Crusted Monkfish ($15.95). Live music on the weekends, upbeat atmosphere, and alfresco seating make this a special dining experience. Reservations recommended.

Barbecue

Over in West Columbia, Maurice Bessinger's **Maurice's Gourmet Piggie Park Barbecue,** 1600 Charleston Hwy., tel. (800) 628-7423, stands as an important pilgrimage spot for America's barbecue faithful. No less than *People*

magazine named Maurice's as the "Best All-In-One Barbecue Restaurant" in the entire country.

The Piggie Park, a humble cabin-like building serving up pig beneath a 100-foot flashing pig, has been open since 1953, when Ike was president, Strom Thurmond was still a Democrat, and most of our parents were still strangers. It's really quite a place. It features a wonderful old building where you can drive in, drive through, or park, get out, and do it the old-fashioned way. You'll find a number of Maurice-generated fliers here and there inside, covering everything from Maurice's views on his Southern heritage (one flier retells the story of his grandmother's encounter with Sherman's troops; another postulates that Abraham Lincoln was John C. Calhoun's love child) to his barbecue philosophy and spiritual convictions. You'll also find Xeroxes of every positive review the restaurant chain has ever received.

But that's not all: a one-time outspoken segregationist who underwent a conversion to Christianity and became one of the state's leading integrationists, Maurice has put his money where his mouth is. The Gospel Mission next door is Maurice's, and it features an employment office for anyone looking for a hand up. Everyone working full-time gets full benefits.

Also there is the office for Flying Pig Enterprises, the Maurice's subdivision in charge of shipping the shredded pig meat around the world to feed the barbecue-deprived. Call (800) MAURICE (628-7423), fax (803) 791-8707, or go online to www.mauricesbbq.com. to get some pig sent to you. You can also buy Maurice's sauces ("good on everything—including grits!")—available in many stores in South Carolina as well—along with Maurice's T-shirts.

If you're very lucky, while you're in Columbia you'll hear a Maurice's radio commercial. If you hear one, you'll know what I mean.

Over a million pigs have met their demise at the hands of Maurice Bessinger. Someday, when pigs take over the world, I suppose the Piggie Park will be preserved as a memorial shrine to all those hogs and sows who checked in and didn't check out. But in the meantime, you might as well enjoy yourself. Head in and order a Little Joe Basket. Incidentally, Maurice's barbecue sauce is fat free.

Technically, there are other restaurants serving barbecue in Columbia. They include **Millender's Bar-b-que Place,** which offers a buffet at 1076 Chris Dr., in W. Columbia, tel. (803) 796-9785, and **Gilligan's** at 2006 Senate St., tel. (803) 252-5252, in Five Points, which offers ketchup, mustard, *and* vinegar-based barbecue sauces. Millender's also features a fish night on Thursday, 5-9 p.m. To get there, take Exit 110 off Hwy. 378 and I-26.

Mexican

Little Mexico, 6164 St. Andrews Rd., tel. (803) 798-6045, across from the Seven Oaks Shopping Center, gets my vote for the best Mexican food in the entire Columbia area. From the roast *cabrito* on the menu to the bilingual wait staff—most of it, anyway—this place is authentic. The *cabrito* is my favorite but it's not always available—but whether you order one of the shredded, seasoned beef burritos or the chicken enchiladas, you're in for a treat.

Right next door to Hannah Jane's in Five Points you'll find **Monterrey Jack's,** 733 Santee St., tel.

(803) 256-7764, the spot where Hootie and the Blowfish played their first off-campus gig way back in 1985. Decent Mexican cuisine with a full bar. Darius Rucker of Hootie wore a Monterrey Jack's T-shirt during the band's breakthrough first appearance on the *Late Show with David Letterman,* which didn't hurt business here one bit.

Italian

Mangia! Mangia!, 100 State St., tel. (803) 791-3443, has gotten a lot of press for its Tuscan-style and Northern Italian spreads, with an emphasis on fresh seafood, meat, and pasta. Closed Sunday. **Villa Tronco,** 1213 Blanding, tel. (803) 256-7677, between Main and Sumter Streets, is set downtown in an 1870s firehouse. This is the oldest and most revered Italian restaurant in town, famed for its traditional Italian cuisine, homemade bread, fresh seafood, and wonderful cheesecake.

Al's Upstairs Italian Restaurant, 304 Meeting St., tel. (803) 772-5586, just west of the Gervais St. Bridge, is one of the Columbia area's classiest restaurants, with a number of tables offering a view of Columbia's skyline across the river. Closed Sundays and major holidays. Dressy casual attire. The steaks, seafood, veal, and pasta are the favorites here. Prices range from about $12 to the high teens here.

Garibaldi's, 2013 Greene St. at the corner of Greene and Harden Streets in Five Points next to Claussen's Inn, tel. (803) 771-8888, is considered one of the city's top restaurants with nice atmosphere and art deco decor. Features pasta dishes, seafood, veal, and chicken. Expect to spend $10-20 for a dinner.

Pizza

Notice how I've separated the Italian restaurants from the pizza. For a town with 26,000 college students, Columbia is noticeably lacking in fabulous pie. Nonetheless, the small-chain **Sharky's** at 636 Harden St., tel. (803) 779-7979, has some better-than-average pizzas, as well as some tasty calzones it calls Shark Fins. **Village Idiot,** 2009 Devine St., tel. (803) 252-8646, is a favorite haunt for students desiring cheap beer, decent pizza, and wings. Give them a call and they'll deliver self-same to your door. **Parthenon,** 734 Harden St., tel. (803) 799-7754, is a Greek place, not Italian, but it serves some of the best pizza in town, along with some tasty baklava.

Asian

Is it me, or are Chinese takeout places the hermit crabs of fast food? In a round 1950s-vintage burger stand that surely must have once been called "Satellite Drive-In" or "The Astroburger," the (mostly Latino—go figure) cooks at **Egg Roll Station,** 725 Crowson Rd., tel. (803) 787-6820, voted "Best of Columbia" in the Chinese food category, dish out plentiful portions of excellent, steaming kung pao chicken, chow mein, and egg rolls—in Styrofoam containers. Just follow Devine St. until you pass the Kroger shopping center; Crowson will come up on your left.

Egg Roll Station's main competitor serves up a slightly more traditional Chinese restaurant, though its name—**Red Pepper Seafood House**—would never tip you off to this fact. It's located at 900 Senate St., tel. (803) 252-8228. Or head out to 551 St. Andrews Rd. to **Pepperland,** tel. (803) 798-7377, Web site: www. pepperland.net, home of authentic Sichuan food and a great buffet including chicken, pork, beef, vegetables, shrimp, salads, and ice cream for $4.50 at lunch and $5.95 at dinner. If you're headed over to this part of town to take in a cheap movie at the St. Andrews $1.50 Cinema, the inexpensive dinner buffet will make it a thrifty proposition all the way around. Check the Web site for coupons.

Food Stands, Lunch Counters

I'm really not sure what the name of the place labeled **Restaurant Coffee House 24 Hrs EAT-All-Night** is; it never actually says "Martin's" anywhere on the huge electric sign hailing traffic out on Devine St., but that's how it's generally known in town. (The name "Martin's Restaurant" *does* appear in neon above the front window.) Inside, the front of the menu says, "Martin's Restaurant," but the inside of the menu (and the listing in the phone book) says Martin's Coffee House, tel. (803) 787-8395. Just show up at 4459 Devine St., sit down, and order a breakfast or a Masterburger and a Coke. Relax, play the jukebox, read Martin's business philosophy on the back of the menu, and obey the signs, especially the one that says PLEASE NO PROFANITY. Open 24 hours a day Mon.-Fri., and Saturday till 1 p.m. I took my visiting mother-in-law here once and they had someone in jackhammering the base of one of the counter stools while we ate our grits and eggs. A classic joint.

Two more classic joints in Five Points include **Groucho's,** 611 Harden St., tel. (803) 799-5708, famous for its sandwiches and dips, and the Edward Hopperesque **Frank's Hot Dogs,** where parts of the acclaimed 1978 short subject film *Grits* were filmed.

Over on the other side of campus you'll find **Sandy's,** a nothing-to-look-at, molded Formica 1970s spot that always wins the award for Columbia's Best Hot Dogs in *The State's* yearly poll, much to Frank's consternation. If Frank was this close to the dorms, he'd probably win too—but this is not to dis Sandy's dogs. Try the slaw dog, which is—you guessed it—a chili dog with cole slaw on top. Strange if you've never tried it, but tasty. Ice cream available as well.

Perhaps the heart of Old Columbia is the Tsantrizos family's **Capitol Cafe,** 1210 Main St., tel. (803) 765-0176, fax (803) 254-4509, where they serve up traditional American fare. It's open 24 hours, and if you're wise to South Carolina politics, you'll recognize many of the be-suited men sitting around you.

Cholesterol to Go
Call **Wings on Wheels,** tel. (803) 256-2625 (256-COCK), and order some of the wings that got me through grad school. **Village Idiot** (see above) also delivers both wings and pizza.

Local Foods, Health Foods, Drinks
The Basil Pot, 928 Main St., tel. (803) 799-0928, has some of the best vegetarian food in town, including some so good you forget it's good for you. Try the Portabello Burger. Featuring daily specials and several dishes made with tofu.

Immaculate Consumption, 933 Main St., tel. (803) 799-9053, features Ben and Jerry's ice cream cones. IC also has delicious and inexpensive sandwiches—with your choice of breads—and soups. A fun place. When you get there, see if you can still see the basement through the hole in the floor. Nickelodeon is right next door, so you can stop by before or after the movie.

On College St., downstairs from Caffe Espresso and just a scone's throw from the USC Horse-shoe, **Nice-N-Natural,** 1217 College St., offers some very tasty but never (for me) quite filling sandwiches in a casual environment.

Rosewood Market and Deli at 2803 Rosewood Dr., tel. (803) 256-6410 (deli) or (803) 756-1083 (market), does a good business selling organic, vegetarian, and macrobiotic meals to Columbians with appetites for the healthy. But me, I can never get here because I have to pass the **Rosewood Dairy Bar,** 3003 Rosewood Dr., tel. (803) 252-1662, on the way. Their burgers, chicken, and ice creams are great.

Supermarkets
You'll find all the big Southern chains in Columbia. Perhaps my favorite store in town is the Piggly Wiggly up Devine St. from Five Points, a nice neighborhood market. Continue on down Devine to the big complexes on Garner's Ferry Rd. and you'll see a large Kroger and a mammoth Winn-Dixie, among others. Both have ATMs.

ENTERTAINMENT RECREATION, AND SHOPPING

CONCERT VENUES

The absolute biggest venue in Columbia is the mammoth 80,000-seat **Williams-Brice Stadium.** Super big stars like the McCartney brothers—former-Beatle Paul and Promise Keeper Bill—pack the stadium when they come to town, but that's about it. Call the USC Ticket Office for ticket information at (803) 777-4274, or stop over at the window outside the Coliseum.

The USC Coliseum seats 12,401 people; both men's and women's USC basketball teams play here. When the teams are out of town or out of season, folks like James Taylor and Run DMC and whoever else is currently hip enough to fill the hall come here to play. Call the USC Ticket Office at tel. (803) 777-4274, or stop over at the window outside the Coliseum.

The beautiful glass **Koger Center for the Arts,** 1051 Greene St., tel. (803) 251-6333, is Columbia's primo arts venue; this is where George Winston plays when he strolls into town in his purple socks. The **Township Auditorium** at 1703 Taylor St., tel. (803) 252-6530, is the place for events and acts too big for the clubs and too small for the Coliseum. Check one of the entertainment papers to find out who or what's playing there—sometimes it's a professional wrestling match, sometimes a less well-scripted art form—and then call the number above for tickets.

As for the alternative scene, check www.scmusic.com to find out who's playing where throughout the state. *The State*'s Friday *Week-End!* insert provides the same information, as does the local entertainment freebie, *Free Times.*

CLUBS, BARS, BREWPUBS

If you appreciate acoustic string music, one of the best ways you could spend a Friday night in Columbia is to head over to **Bill's Music Shop & Pickin' Parlor,** tel. (803) 796-6477, for the weekly bluegrass jam. No liquor, no cussin' allowed. If you pick, bring it along.

A big event in Columbia's calendar is the State Fair. . . . On "Big Thursday," thousands fill the football stadium when two traditional rivals, the State University and Clemson College, meet on the gridiron. The governor of the State, with great ceremony, changes his box from one side to the other during the intermission between halves.

The Palmetto State Fair for Negroes follows on the same grounds the next week,when the Negro population of South Carolina enthusiastically gathers to view its own exhibits. Negro domestics make this occasion so complete a holiday that local white restaurants are crowded.

—From WPA's South Carolina: A Guide to the Palmetto State, *1941*

Goatfeathers at 2017 Devine St., tel. (803) 256-3325 or (803) 256-8133, is a dark, croissant-and-soup, dessert-and-brandy sort of place connected to the **Intermezzo Book Store,** the sort of place where the New Age/occult shelves take up twice as much space as the do-it-yourself section. Nearly everybody claims to dislike Goatfeathers because it's full of yuppies, yet nearly everyone eats there—and no one admits to actually *being* a yuppie. Anyway, the desserts are—or so the yuppies tell me—wonderful, and in fact, you can get a full meal here. Intermezzo offers a good selection of out-of-town and international newspapers and literary mags, which you'll probably get a chance to peruse because Goatfeathers nearly always has a crowd. Blame those darn yuppies.

The **Village Idiot,** 2009 Devine St., tel. (803) 252-8646, is a favorite place for students looking for cheap beer and good pizza and wings. They deliver too, so if you're in your bathrobe playing Brian Wilson, give them a call.

Group Therapy, 2107 Greene St., tel. (803) 256-1203, besides sporting one of the best names of any bar anywhere, is one of the more convivial drinking spots in Five Points. The mermaid rising up from the tree roots at the bar's entrance is the work of Dan Berry, the brother of Camden carpenter/artist Joe Berry.

Elbow Room Music Hall, 812 Harden St., tel. (803) 771-1502, is one of the places where alternative music bands play when they come to town. Monday nights feature $1.50 margaritas; Tuesday nights are called "$2 Tuesdays"; on Wednesday nights, bring your own mug and they'll fill it up with beer for a dollar. Cover charges range from zip to about $8.

At the Holiday Inn you'll find **The Shag Club,** a nightclub where many of the Capital City's movers and shakers come here to move and shake. Another popular shag spot that periodically offers lessons is **Mallard's Lounge** in the Ramada Plaza Hotel at the intersection of I-77 and Two Notch Rd., tel. (803) 731-1585. A third spot is the **Malibu Beach Club,** at the corner of Lady and Gadsen Streets, in the Vista District.

Even when it was open, **Rockafella's,** 2112 Devine St., was one of the ugliest spots in Columbia. You'd stop by outside during the day and you'd swear the tiny black-painted brick place had closed down sometime ago, after a particularly ugly riot. But seven nights a week, like a pockmarked vampire, it would kick open again with loud live music. Most of the best regional alternative bands played here, including Hootie and the Blowfish. In January 1998, however, Rockafella's closed for real after a 14-year run. The Charleston *News and Courier* quoted Hootie drummer Jim "Soni" Sonefeld's lament, "It's like your best friend or neighbor has moved and you can't go over or have a beer in his kitchen anymore." In fact, Hootie ended up renting Rockafella's and spending much of early 1998 working up new songs for their third album in the abandoned club.

But don't be surprised if it's reopened by the time you get there—it's hard to keep a good dive down.

Manhattan's, 931 Senate St., tel. (803) 252-1999, features beach music on Wednesday, retro music on Thursday, and '70s and '80s dance music on Friday and Saturday.

Gilligan's, 2006 Senate St. at Harden, tel. (803) 252-5252, features lunch and dinner, volleyball, and a seafood blues theme. Are you following this? Saturday night is open mike/songwriter's night.

Jungle Jim's at 724 Harden in Five Points, tel. (803) 256-1390, lies fairly low these days. Back in 1992, 23-year-old Dail Dinwiddie attended a U2 concert at the Williams-Bryce Stadium with some friends. Afterward, they stopped in at Jungle Jim's to have a few drinks. Through a miscommunication, Dail got left there, and by the time her friends realized their mistake and returned to pick her up, Dail had disappeared. She was last seen walking north on Harden St., as though she intended to walk home. Her picture went up all across the state, and her story appeared twice on TV's *Unsolved Mysteries,* but no one has ever found out what happened to Dail Dinwiddie.

Pizza Bistro, 725 Broad River Rd., tel. (803) 561-0800, and **Alley Cafe,** 911 Lady St., tel. (803) 771-2778, both feature live music.

Hunter-Gatherer Brewery and Alehouse, 900 Main St., tel. (803) 748-0540, huddles one block behind the State House. H-G features a Wednesday night winetasting during the spring and summer 5:30-7:30 p.m. every week. For $10 you can sample four different wines and munch light hors d'oeuvres. No reservations necessary.

A lot of students call the **Publick House,** 2307 Devine St., tel. (803) 256-2207, the best neighborhood pub in Columbia, based largely on its extensive draft beer selection. **Art Bar,** 1211 Park St., tel. (803) 929-0198, offers some of the best people-watching in town.

With a name like "Tombstone," a bar has to feature either country music or medleys of songs by The Cure. Columbia's **Tombstone,** 7315 Garners Ferry Rd., tel. (803) 783-2400, offers the former.

Vista Brewing & Bistro, 936 Gervais St., tel. (803) 779-2739, offers creative, upscale dinners Mon.-Sat. 5:30-10:30 p.m., and a late dinner 10:30 p.m.-1 a.m. Entrées include a house-made lobster ravioli ($16.50) and rabbit à la Moutarde ($15.25). Lunch, served Mon.-Sat. 11:30 a.m.-2:30 p.m., is considerably cheaper, consisting mostly of sandwiches (crab cake sandwich, $5.95) and salads (traditional Greek salad, $5.95).

Vista's handcrafted ales, made here on the premises, include the entry-level, smooth, light Taneyale #18, the amber Scottish Ale, and the brace-yourself-first Pub Porter, along with seasonal selections.

Gays looking to party with other gays favor **Metropolis,** 1800 Blanding St., tel. (803) 799-8727.

Comedy Clubs

Stop by the **Comedy House Theatre,** 14 Berryhill Rd., tel. (803) 798-9898, for live comedy several nights a week. The **Russell House** on the USC campus often draws college-circuit comedians; call (803) 777-3196 for information.

COFFEEHOUSES

At 724 Saluda Ave., **The Gourmet Shop,** tel. (803) 799-3705, offers much more than great coffee: great salads, sandwiches, and pastries, as well as a menagerie of high-end kitchenware—garlic presses, coffee grinders—to covet after. It's a bit of Marin County, California, beamed down into Columbia. A nice place to sit outside on the patio and watch Five Points happen around you, but eating inside with all the gourmet kitchen gear is fun too. Certainly one of the best-*smelling* restaurants around. Breakfast and lunch only.

When the Gourmet Shop closed down at night, **Adriana's Gelateria** used to be about the only place in Five Points to find nighttime high-end coffee. Now, even with a handful of new coffee joints opened up, Adriana's continues to draw folks with its coffee, gelato, shakes, and lunch specials.

Over at 2718 Devine St. you'll come upon **Rising High,** offering pastries (cinnamon swirls) and fresh-baked bread with a smell that'll drive you to your knees. Not far away at 2865 Devine, **Bread and Bagel Cafe,** tel. (803) 256-2001, works its own brand of olfactory magic, adding some fine salads and sandwiches to the mix.

Though Adriana's was already doing a good business, when **Caffe Espresso** opened up at 1217 College St., tel. (803) 256-4246, in the early '90s, it was a godsend to Columbians looking to hang out in public without having to endure loud grunge music and drunk, screaming undergraduates. It was a perfect place to study or talk with friends; it offered about a zillion different flavors of coffee, the first good scones in town, and a second-story view. Not so long ago, the original owner sold the café. Now Caffe Espresso is crammed with loud grunge music and *wired,* screaming undergraduates.

Of course, "deafening" is a subjective term—if this sounds like your cup of joe, head on over.

Immaculate Consumption, 933 Main St., tel. (803) 799-1102, roasts its own coffee as well as providing good sandwiches and Ben and Jerry's ice cream near the Capitol.

THEATER, DANCE, OPERA, CLASSICAL MUSIC VENUES

Theater

The **Town Theatre,** 1012 Sumter St., tel. (803) 799-2510, is the oldest continuously operating theater in America, and is listed on the National Register of Historic Places. This is the mainstream theater in Columbia, featuring Broadway musicals and other crowd-pleasers.

The **Trustus,** 520 Lady St., tel. (803) 254-9732, performs less proven, less mainstream scripts, many of them penned by local playwrights. The performances are normally top-notch.

Puppetry

A lot of string-pulling goes on here in the state capital; some of the most benign variety goes on at the 400-seat **Columbia Marionette Theatre,** 401 Laurel St., tel. (803) 252-7366, one of only 20 marionette theaters in the entire nation. The theater—set in a castle-like building—offers performances of childhood favorites like *Tom Sawyer, Peter Pan,* and *Beauty and the Beast* every Saturday and Sunday at 3 p.m. all year.

Orchestra

The **South Carolina Philharmonic Orchestra** gives eight Master Series concerts and three pop concerts each year, all of them held at the Koger Center. Come Christmas, the Orchestra moves over to the Coliseum for its extremely popular Holiday Concert. For more information, call (803) 771-7937.

Dance

Columbia City Ballet gives three major performances a year, as well as a children's se-

ries—in 1998 they performed a ballet version of the 1964 Newberry Award-winner, *Where The Wild Things Are.* Call (803) 799-7605 for more information.

The **University of South Carolina Dance Company** offers spring and fall dance concerts featuring a variety of ballet, jazz, and modern dance. Call (803) 777-4288 for performance information.

CINEMAS

Movies are big business in Columbia. More than 147,000 cinema tickets were sold in Richland and Lexington Counties in just one month in 1998. **Nickelodeon,** 937 Main St. at Pendleton downtown, tel. (803) 254-3433, offers the film festival-attending, subtitle-reading public a comfortable place to watch films that won't ever make the mall megaplexes. See its Web site at www.scsn.net/users/nickelodeon; e-mail: nick@scsn.net.

For the subtitle-impaired, the **Regal Cinema 7,** located on the rooftop of the Richland Mall, tel. (803) 748-9044, boasts some of the best screens in town. Other area cinemas include the **Carmike 14,** across from the Columbiana Centre, tel. (803) 781-3067, and the **St. Andrews $1.50 Cinema,** on St. Andrews Rd., tel. (803) 772-7469, a good second-run theater where I've caught and enjoyed many a film that I'd never have paid full price for. For $1.50, I'll watch most anything.

PLACES TO MEET PEOPLE

One way to meet folks while you get to know the area is to give **Adventure Carolina** a call, tel. (803) 796-4505. These go-getters are always planning canoeing, kayaking, and hiking trips that you can join for a fee. If you're over in Cayce, stop by at 1107 State Street.

PLACES TO PEOPLE-WATCH

The **Five Points** area is probably the best place in town to watch people—especially those of the university variety. If you want to watch people in suits with briefcases and cell phones, park yourself in front of the Capitol building. Or sit near the Russell House on the USC campus to get a good sense of what's going on at the university. Across from **Williams-Brice Stadium,** tel. (803) 253-4041, you'll find the **Farmers Market,** where producers, produce, and produce-eaters meet. A good place to strike up a conversation with a Carolina farmer.

ORGANIZATIONS

Environmental Organizations
If you'd like to link up with the local Sierra Club, the South Carolina headquarters for the club meets at 1314 Lincoln St., Suite. 211, tel. (803) 256-8487.

Recovery Groups
To hook up with the **Alcoholics Anonymous** chapters in the Midlands area, call (803) 254-5301. **Adult Children of Alcoholics** meet every Wednesday at 5:30 at the Shandon United Methodist Church, 3407 Devine St., tel. (803) 256-8383. **Narcotics Anonymous** has a hotline at (800) 922-6587 or (803) 254-6262.

RECREATIONAL SPORTS

Kayaking/Canoeing
One place to rent canoes is over at **Adventure Carolina, Inc.,** 1107 State St., Cayce, tel. (803) 796-4505. **River Runner,** over at 905 Gervais St., tel. (803) 771-0353, is another.

If you're planning a trip into the area and would like to meet other people interested in exploring the state's waterways with you, you really ought to contact the **Palmetto Paddlers Club,** tel. (803) 771-4329, which promotes the use and preservation of both urban and wild rivers and waterways.

Boat Rentals
With all the lakes around, you'd better believe you'll find people hereabouts willing to rent you a boat. Call the **Blue Heron** and charter a 22-food Cuddy Cabin for 2-4 people for $30 or less. This is for pretty much a whole day, 6:30 a.m.-3:30 p.m. Sometimes you can hook on (figuratively speaking) with other folks and just pay for yourself: this'll run you about $80 a day. Call (803) 364-2971 for more information.

Just Add Water, tel. (803) 345-9682, offers a variety of different boats to rent, from houseboats to Waverunners.

Diving
Yes, diving. **Columbia Scuba,** 1234 St. Andrews Rd., tel. (803) 561-9500, offers complete lessons and equipment rentals, as does the **Wateree Dive Center Inc.,** 1767 Burning Tree Dr., tel. (803) 731-9344. Both of these businesses are always getting together groups to probe the depths of South Carolina's lakes, rivers, and on down to the coast, where a wealth of sunken ships awaits. A third alternative is **Sunset Scuba** at 5339 Sunset Blvd., tel. (803) 808-3483.

Fishing
Fishing is such a major life force in these parts that you'd think folks were pulling gold and not bass, bream, and crappie from Lake Murray. Of course, to freshwater fish in South Carolina, you'll need a fishing license, available at most sporting-goods stores. For information on obtaining a hunting or fishing license, call (803) 734-3833.

Golfing
The Columbia area features some 21 golf courses, including P.B. Dye's heavily bunkered **Northwoods,** and the more classic **Oak Hills,** traditional favorites in the area. Out at Lake Murray, a favorite is the wooded, multilevel **Timberlake.** For other options, call (800) 682-5553 to receive a *South Carolina Golf Guide,* or go online to www.travelsc.com for info.

Tennis
You'll find plenty of tennis courts open to the public in Columbia, including 14 at the **Columbia Tennis Center,** 1635 Whaley St., tel. (803) 733-8440, and four at **Martin Luther King Park** near Five Points, 2300 Greene St., tel. (803) 733-8452. Farther out, you'll find 12 each at the **Caughman Road Park and Tennis Center,** 2800 Trotter Rd., tel. (803) 776-3250, and the **Richland County Tennis Center and Park,** 7500 Parklane Rd., tel. (803) 788-3001.

Bowling
The sport of the gods is available to mortals here in Columbia. You'll find no less than five establishments in the area.

My favorite while I was at USC, and the closest to downtown, was the **AMF Park Triangle Lanes,** in Parkland Plaza in Cayce, just across the Blossom St. Bridge, tel. (803) 796-6300. It's still there, setting 'em up. While you're there, head over to **D's Wings.**

Wherever you bowl, beware of the heavy league bowling that starts around 7 p.m. most nights—you may have a hard time getting a lane.

SPECTATOR SPORTS

Gamecock Football

The Gamecocks play in the mammoth **Williams-Brice Stadium,** named in honor of a bequest by Mrs. Martha Williams Brice, widow of a wealthy former USC gridiron letterman, which paid for a major stadium expansion in the early '70s. With continuing expansions, the stadium now seats 80,250 fans. The Gamecock average of 79,535 per game (in 1997) ranked seventh among all colleges in the United States. Getting tickets can be a challenge, but it'd be well worth your efforts if you got to experience the incredible energy of a college football game in South Carolina. Call the USC Ticket Office for ticket information at (803) 777-4274, or stop over at the window outside the Coliseum.

If you want to keep up with the Gamecocks on the Web, visit www.uscsports.com, www.columbiasouthcarolina.com/gamecocks.html, or www.cockfans.com. The last is my favorite—it even features a 23-page collection of Clemson jokes.

Capital City Bombers

The Columbia baseball team, which plays at **Capital City Baseball Park** at 301 S. Assembly, tel. (803) 254-4487, has gone through many name changes throughout the years. Not so long ago, in the early '90s when now-New York Met Butch Huskey was playing for Columbia, the team was known as the Columbia Mets. But civic pride won over and the team changed its name to honor Jimmy Doolittle's Raiders, who trained near Columbia during WW II before going off to put the fear of Godzilla into Tokyo. At the beginning of the 1992 season, the Columbia Mets became the Capital City Bombers.

This is one of the finer Single A stadiums you'll run across—rumor has it that the extensive 1991 refurbishment was undertaken with the intention of convincing other, higher leagues (AA and AAA) that Columbia has what it takes to support a higher-level ball club. As of this writing it hasn't worked yet, but nonetheless this is an excellent place to watch a well-run ball team play. And though this is only Single A ball, a number of the players that used to play here in the early '90s have already—as of the late '90s—made it to the Bigs. Come out and see them take on such South Atlantic League (Sallie League) nemeses as the Charleston River Dogs, Savannah Sand Gnats, Piedmont Boll Weevils, Cape Fear Crocs, Hickory Crawdads, and (my favorite) Asheville Tourists, whose mascot is a bear wearing a camera around his neck, with a bat in one hand and an overstuffed suitcase in the other. Home games start at 7:05 p.m. except for Sunday games and the rare double header, which begin at 6:05 p.m. The mascot, Bomber the Mouse, is popular with the kids. Strolling vendors—often young kids with powerful voices—roam the stands selling hot boiled peanuts. Tickets run $5-6, cheaper for seniors and military personnel with ID.

Gamecock Basketball

The Carolina Coliseum was built in 1968, and it looks it. The Coliseum seats 12,401 fans; both men's and women's basketball teams play here. Call the USC Ticket Office at (803) 777-4274, or stop over at the window outside the Coliseum.

SHOPPING

The Columbia area features some uncommon shopping venues, including Devine St., Five Points, and the Vista District, which allow you to browse local merchants while getting to know the town better.

Devine St. is an attractive sloping tree-covered road threading the prestigious Shandon area and featuring a variety of small and not-so-small shops—the Rodeo Drive of Columbia, if you will. Upscale clothes shops such as **Willis and Winter,** 2734 Devine St., tel. (803) 254-3990, and **Rackes Direct,** 2930 Devine St., tel. (803) 799-8642, offer fine women's apparel; **Brittons** at 2818 Devine St., tel. (803) 771-2700, is something of local tradition for men's and women's wear. **Bohemian,** at 2738 Devine, tel. (803) 256-0629; **Non(e)Such,** 2754 Devine St., tel. 254-0772; and **Columbia Art Glass Company,** 2712 Devine St., tel. 254-6088, are always worth a browse for unique items. **Morris Gallery,** 2515 Devine St., tel. (803) 254-1640, fax (803) 254-2257, carries the paintings of contemporary Southern artists and also deals in antique collectibles.

In Five Points you'll find some fine, easily spotted places to buy Deadwear, along with the best used record store in the state, **Papa Jazz,** 2014 Greene St., tel. (803) 256-0095. Here you'll find used LPs, CDs, 45s, and cassettes. Just hope they're playing something bearable when you're in there—sometimes the music is wonderful, and sometimes Papa Jazz seems to be trying to scare its customers from the building. Once when I was in there an employee was blasting a sound-effects record—the sounds of various drills, and then of various explosions. But bring earplugs if you must, and check this place out.

Most of the Vista's best stores involve antiques, but poke your head into **Vista Studios** at 808 Lady St., tel. (803) 252-6134, and you may well find some Midlands artists at work. Vista Studios includes 13 studios and one gallery where you can view the work of local painters, sculptors, and print makers. Call ahead to make sure it's open.

Uphill from the Vista District, near the Capitol at 1235 Assembly St., you'll find a Columbia landmark, **Cromers P-nuts,** which has been selling peanuts to Capital City residents since 1935. In part, the company's slogan—"Guaranteed Worst in Town"—is responsible for the company's longevity. Founder Julian Cromer, the story goes, was angered in 1937 by a competitor who told his customers that Cromer's peanuts were "no good." The young entrepeanutre decided he could do his foe one better: he grabbed a piece of cardboard, wrote "Worst in Town" on it, and placed it beside his peanuts. Amused bypassers stopped in their tracks and demanded to taste the worst peanuts in town for themselves. Later, Cromer added "Guaranteed" to let them know he wasn't kidding.

Today, Cromers has three stores, two here in town and one in Myrtle Beach, and sells party goods as well as peanuts.

South Carolina State Farmers Market
Across from **Williams-Brice Stadium,** tel. (803) 253-4041, you'll find the Farmers Market, alive with the tastes and smells of South Carolina's produce. Retail hours are 6 a.m.-9 p.m. Good place to find peanuts, peaches, corn, squash, and okra, along with herbs and house plants.

Department Stores and Malls
Step inside one of Columbia's several megamalls and you leave behind South Carolina for the climate-controlled, fluorescent-lit Republic of American Consumeria. Lose the Chick-Fil-A sites, the Christian bookstores, and the Duck Head shops and you could be in Boise, Vancouver, Syracuse, or Pasadena. Rumor has it the emaciated women at Wet Seal, the clove-smoking kids in the arcades, and the nose-pierced record shop clerks are all shipped to the nation's malls from a central warehouse in Ohio.

Malls are *not* South Carolina. And yet, increasingly, they are.

Like it or not, sometimes one of Columbia's coven of malls contains something you need. Off the Harbison Blvd. exit off the I-26 you'll find the **Columbiana Centre,** 100 Columbiana Circle, tel. (803) 732-6255, fax (803) 732-6262. As denoted by its regal British spelling of the word "center," this is an upscale mall voted "Columbia's Best Shopping Mall" by *The State* readers in recent years. The Centre features **Dillard's, Parisian,** and **JB White** as anchors and more than 100 smaller shops to keep intrepid consumers satisfied while trekking between them.

Richland Mall, tel. (803) 782-7575, fax (803) 782-8779, has long been the up-and-coming mall in town, half-empty for much of the early '90s, but now filled with interesting small shops, anchored by a **Dillard's, JB White, Parisian, Talbot's,** and featuring a **Barnes and Noble, TGIF,** and the **Litchfield Rooftop Cinemas,** some of the best screens in town.

The largest mall in the Midlands (106 stores), **Columbia Mall** over at 650 Two Notch Rd., tel. (803) 788-4676, features a recently opened food court, an indoor kids' play area, a **Dillard's, Sears, JCPenney,** and a **Rich's.** See its site online at www.ShopYourMall.com.

Market Point Mall at I-20 and Bush River

Road, tel. (803) 798-8520, is an outlet mall most noted for its **Waccamaw Pottery** outlet.

Best Bookstores
The Happy Bookseller, 4525 Forest Dr., tel. (800) 787-1503 or (803) 782-2665, Web site: www.happybookseller.com, is one of the best independent bookstores in the state, offering one of the best selections and most ruthless book searches you'll find in the Southeast. This is where a lot of the faculty at USC buy their books, and one of the best places to find local and national authors signing books. Open weekdays 10 a.m.-8 p.m., Saturdays 10 a.m.-7 p.m., Sunday 1-6 p.m.

University bookstores are a lot of fun because you can mix your book browsing with Gamecock paraphernalia ogling. The official **University of South Carolina Bookstore** in the bottom of Russell House on Greene St., contains the best collection of titles, including, often, books signed by visiting authors. The **Addams University Bookstore** at 601 Main St., tel. (803) 256-6666, is a giant private store with loads of fascinating Cockwear and other essentials like license plate frames, "Little Cocky" dolls (and lamps), and some of the hardest hitting bumper stickers available.

SC Book Store, Inc., down the street at 801 Main St., tel. (803) 799-7188, fax (803) 799-5521, offers a similar selection.

Down in Five Points, **Intermezzo,** 2015 Devine St., tel. (803) 799-2276, provides out-of-area newspapers, expensive cigars and cigarettes, slick magazines, and a good selection of literary magazines. Besides its great location, one of the best things about Intermezzo is that it's open late—till midnight daily.

As far as the chains go, **Barnes and Noble,** 278 Harbison Blvd., tel. (803) 749-9009, and **Books-A-Million,** 4850 Forest Dr., Forest Acres, tel. (803) 782-4475, also 275-1 Harbison Blvd., tel. (803) 749-9378, provide some of the best prices and selections available.

Special-Interest Books: An intriguing store downtown is **The Unexpected Joy,** 942 1/2 Harden St., tel. (888) 779-4512 or (803) 779-4512, run by Orthodox Christians and advertising "The South's largest incense selection," along with new and used books, chant CDs and tapes, frankincense and myrrh. Even—or perhaps es-

pecially—if you're ignorant of the difference between a Baptist and a Byzantine, you might want to stop by.

For a true Southern experience, stop into the **Shepherd's Corner Christian Bookstore** over in the old Cedar Terrace Shopping Center on Garner's Ferry Road, across the parking lot from the new Eckerd's. This is a classic little Fundamentalist Christian bookstore, right down to the anti-papist Jack Chick tracts for sale. A visit to the big **Living Vine Christian Bookstores** at 2825 Ashland Rd., tel. (803) 798-6586, and 4617 Forest Dr., between Beltline and Trenholm, tel. (803) 790-4506, provides a more representative look at the contemporary Evangelical Christian subculture. Downtown's historic **Trinity Cathedral,** 1100 Sumter St., tel. (803) 771-7300, has a bookstore open Mon.-Fri. 10 a.m.-2 p.m., Sunday 9 a.m.-1 p.m.

TDIR Books, also downtown at 6920 N. Main, tel. (803) 754-5911, fax (803) 754-4922, Web site: www.tdirbooks.com, specializes in Afrocentric books. Open Mon.-Sat. noon-7 p.m. Ditto for **Books in the Black and Stuff Like That,** 228 Somerset Dr., tel. (803) 865-9252, where they advertise "An Oasis For the Soul." African artifacts, prints, jewelry and fabric here as well.

Used Books: I don't much like the clinical name, but the **Book Dispensary** at the Columbia Mall, 7384 Two Notch Rd., tel. (803) 736-4033, and 1600 Broad River Rd. at the Boozer Shopping Center (love *that* name, too), tel. (803) 798-4739, offers one of the best-organized collections of used books I've ever seen. If you have a little more time to browse, check out the **Antique Mall** at 1215 Pulaski St., tel. (803) 256-1420, or—possibly the best for very rare 19th-century books, though you'll pay more—**The Book Place,** 3129 Millwood Ave., tel. (803) 799-6561.

Antiques
In Five Points you'll run across **Revente** at 733 Saluda Ave., specializing in furniture, home accessories, and vintage clothes, sold on consignment. **Thieves Antique Flea Market** at 502 Gadsden St., tel. (803) 254-4997, contains nearly 50 vendors hawking some great local antiques, along with nostalgic items you kick yourself for having thrown away 15 years ago.

A nice way to spend an afternoon is to grab lunch at one of the Congaree Vista restaurants while puttering around at the **City Market An-**

tiques Mall, 701-709 Gervais St., tel. (803) 232-1587. The **Old Mill Antique Mall** at 310 State St., tel. (803) 796-4229, also offers 75 dealers to tempt you and your charge card. The **Columbia Antique Mall,** at the corner of Huger and Blossom Streets, contains an eclectic mix of toys, books, magazines, and furniture, furniture, furniture.

Charlton Hall Galleries, Inc., 912 Gervais St., tel. (803) 779-5678, fax (803) 733-1701, Web site: www.charltonhallauctions.com, pre-sents periodic auctions of top-end antiques. Call them or stop in to find out when the next one is.

Photo Supplies
Columbia Photo Supply, 2912 Devine St., tel. (803) 254-2982, is a good non-chain photography store. Other than just about any kind of film you could want, it offers full-service processing and computer/digital imaging.

SERVICES, INFORMATION, TRANSPORTATION

BANKS

You'll find banks nearly on nearly every business block of Columbia. You'll find an ATM in Five Points, just past Loose Lucy's heading south, on the corner of Blossom and Harden. There's another ATM behind the Russell House on campus.

POST OFFICES

The city's main post office features a parking lot perched over Finlay Park at the corner of Assembly and Taylor Streets. There's another in Five Points on Greene St., across from Group Therapy.

LAUNDROMATS

If you hate doing laundry, then you might want to do yours at **Soaps: The Good Time Laundry,** 114 Assembly St., tel. (803) 252-0005, where there are televisions, a bar and grill, pool tables, video games, and even tanning beds to keep you from remembering why you're really here. And if you feel trusting, you can leave your clothes unattended and head next door to the full-scale pool hall next door. Open seven days a week, 6 a.m.-11 p.m.

SPECIAL COURSES

Bluegrass Pickin'
If you're a picker, or even just a strummer like myself, you're sure to learn a thing or two at a Friday night bluegrass jam over at **Bill's Music Shop & Pickin' Parlor,** tel. (803) 796-6477. No liquor, no cussin' allowed. These aren't formal lessons, mind you, but pay attention and you'll surely learn something. The picking begins around 7:30 p.m. No charge.

Shagging
No, Austin Powers fans—it's not *that* kind of class. At **Manhattan's** at the Vista you can take free shag dancing lessons with Jo Jo Putnam 8-9 p.m., then stay and dance to beach, boogie, and blues with DJ Woody Windham of the Breeze Radio Network's "Windham Brothers" morning show. At the Holiday Inn at 630 Assembly St., tel. (803) 799-7800, you'll find **The Shag Club,** which also occasionally holds lessons. Call for information.

TOURIST INFORMATION, MAPS

The **Columbia Metropolitan Convention and Visitors Bureau** can be reached at P.O. Box 15, Columbia, SC 29202, tel. (800) 264-4884 or (803) 254-0479, e-mail: visit@columbiasc.net, Web site: www.columbiasc.net. Or contact the **Visitors Center,** 1012 Gervais St., on the corner of Gervais and Assembly, just a few steps from the Capitol. Hours are Mon.-Fri. 9 a.m.-5 p.m., Saturday 10 a.m.-4 p.m., Sunday 1-5 p.m. Closed major holidays. Contact the offices before you leave for Carolina and you can arrive with all the information you need already in hand.

HOSPITALS, POLICE, EMERGENCIES

Call 911 in any physical emergency—it's the fastest way to get you through to the professionals you need. Call "0" if you need a number that's not listed here.

Emergency Medical Service
Call 911 if you need immediate help. Or, in Richland County, call (803) 254-3061. In Lexington County, call (803) 359-2521.

Nonemergency Medical Service
If you've got an ache, pain, or rash that's troubling you, you should call (803) 254-2288 for the **Ask-a-Nurse** program at **Providence Hos-**

pital. They can give you advice and may help you from ruining a good trip by needless worry. If you definitely need a hospital, the two choices are **Baptist Medical Center,** 1330 Taylor St. at Marion St., tel. (803) 771-5010, and **Richland Memorial Hospital,** I-277 and Bull St. at Harden St. Extension, tel. (803) 434-7000. Baptist Medical Center has a Web site at www.bmcc-sc.com. Richland Memorial has one too: www.rmh.edu.

Rape Crisis Network

If you've been sexually assaulted, call the Network at (803) 771-7273. You may also want to call the AIDS Hotline at (800) 342-AIDS.

PUBLIC LIBRARIES

Richland County Library

This is simply one of the most beautiful new libraries I've ever seen, at 1431 Assembly St., tel. (803) 799-9084. Bright and airy, so that reading takes on connotations of discovery and not skullduggery, with a wonderful children's section downstairs, a bookstore, and a tea room, along with a very healthy selection of books and books on tape. Hours are Mon.-Thurs. 9 a.m.-9 p.m., Friday and Saturday 9 a.m.-6 p.m., Sunday 2-6 p.m. You'll find the tiny **Shandon Branch** of the county library on Devine St. in Shandon.

NEWSPAPERS

The paper of record for Columbia (and, some would say, South Carolina) is *The State.* On Friday, *The State*'s *WeekEnd!* insert provides information on most anything you could think to do in the Capital City area over the next few days, telling you what band is playing at what bar, what movie is playing at what theater, and what homeowner is having a garage sale, along with a "Calendar" section telling you about whatever cultural or athletic events are going on in town. The generally well-written *Free Times* covers much of the same ground, with the sort of "subversive" edge endemic to middle-class college towns. (A recent issue discussed the hardships facing young Columbia music consumers forced to drive to Charlotte to catch their favorite performers. Another celebrated gourmet beers.)

LOCAL RADIO STATIONS

Columbia's affiliate of the Carolina "Breeze" network is **WLXC FM 98.5,** featuring beach, boogie, and blues tunes. Definitely worth a listen, especially 6-10 a.m. when the Windham Brothers spin the discs. **WCOS 97.5** is the chief country music station here in town. **WVOC 560 AM** ("The station you're hearing right now!") provides a good morning news show to give you a taste of Capital City life, before giving way to the aural strip mall of nationally syndicated talk shows. Local Libertarian host Scott Caysen holds forth on local and national issues in the afternoons.

At night during the summer, **WIS news radio 1320 AM** broadcasts Bombers' games. At **620 AM** and **1170 AM** you'll find some fiery black Gospel music. At **100.1** on the FM dial you'll find oldies and swing.

Other than these, you'll find the usual mix of rock and adult contemporary stations on Columbia radio, including the NPR affiliate down on the low end of the FM dial, along with the college rock of USC's student-run station.

GETTING THERE

Columbia was literally designed for convenience—its location was chosen to make trips to the capital convenient for both Upcountry and Lowcountry residents.

By Car

I-26 comes down from Spartanburg to Columbia; it rises up northwest from Charleston going the other direction. I-20 comes east from Augusta, Georgia, and I-77 plunges southward down the state into Columbia from Charlotte. If you'll be entering South Carolina from I-95 headed south, wait until you come to I-20 at Florence and head west. If you're headed north on I-95, head north on I-26 at the intersection.

By Air

A new $14.5 million concourse opened at Columbia Metropolitan Airport in Columbia in the mid-1990s, part of a $48 million renovation project unleashed upon the 2,600-acre facility.

Seems like a lot of money until you consider what they spent on upgrading the State House.

Here's the important news: despite all the changes, the 15-minute parking just outside the terminal area remains.

AirTran, Comair, Continental, Delta, Midway, and USAir/USAir Express all service the airport, along with Alamo, Avis, Budget, Hertz, National, and Thrifty car-rental agencies.

The airport is located on Hwy. 302 off I-26 at Exit 113, six miles southwest of Columbia's central business district and not far from the I-20 and I-77. For more information, call (803) 822-5010 or (803) 822-5000.

Incidentally, if you're old enough to remember WW II, or at least old enough to have watched *The World at War,* then you'll be interested to know that on this same ground in 1943, Jimmy Doolittle gathered and trained volunteer B-25 crews for a secret mission that turned out to be the famous Doolittle Raid over Tokyo. It's from this connection that the name of Columbia's baseball team—the Capital City Bombers—derives.

By Bus

If you want to go Greyhound, the number for the Columbia station is (803) 256-6465.

GETTING AROUND

Columbia is *not* the easiest town to find your way around in, however. Except for the down-

town grid, a good bit of the sprawling city winds around hills and bends with rivers, and this causes strange three, four, and (in Five Points) five-way intersections. On top of this, to make things more challenging, city planners like to have streets change names two and three times as they course through the city. If you're just staying close to the USC area, you'll be all right. But if you're planning to head out to one of the malls to catch a movie, or off to Riverbanks Zoo, for instance, you'll want to bring a good map.

Taxi

If you're at the Columbia Airport and need to get to town, call **AAA Airport Shuttle Service,** 2805 Augusta Rd., W. Cola, tel. (803) 796-3626. From anywhere in the area, you can call AAA Taxi Service at the same address and a different number: tel. (803) 791-7282. Other companies include **Blue Ribbon,** tel. (803) 754-8163; **Checker Yellow Cab Co. Inc.,** tel. (803) 799-3311; and **Gamecock Cab Co.,** tel. (803) 796-7700. The last three companies advertise 24-hour service.

Columbia Trolley

Columbia has had a hard time getting Columbians interested in riding public transportation. Currently, the nostalgia-themed Columbia Trolley runs a limited midday route Mon.-Fri. 11:20 a.m.-2:30 p.m., serving Main St. and the Congaree Vista area. Trolley Stop locations are marked with blue and gold signs along the

In Riverfront Park, this pedestrian bridge crosses the historic Columbia Canal, dug in 1824.

route and the trolleys run about every eight minutes. Just wave your hand to show the driver you want to ride. Have your fare ready.

No service is provided on New Year's Day, Good Friday, Memorial Day, Independence Day, Labor Day, Thanksgiving Day, the Friday after Thanksgiving, or Christmas Day. Rates: Adults 25 cents; seniors, 17 and under, disabled, 10 cents; under 6 free.

Car Rentals
This is the state's capital city. All kinds of car rental shops do business here, including **Alamo, Avis, Budget, Hertz, National,** and **Thrifty.**

WEST OF COLUMBIA

CAYCE

Cayce began as the old Saxe Gotha Township, which retained this name until James Cayce bought the home in 1816 on this site and the area became known as Cayce.

The Cayce Museum, 1800 12th St., tel. (803) 796-9020, is within the old Saxe Gotha Township, the earliest settlement in the Midlands of South Carolina. Centered around a reconstruction of the trading post established at Granby Village in 1765, the museum interprets the architectural, social, and cultural heritage of Cayce and other local communities.

The original trading post had quite a history. It was originally founded by important Colonial Carolinians James Chesnut and Joseph Kershaw. British forces seized the post in early 1781, fortified it, and renamed it Fort Granby. Revolutionary hero Emily Geiger was incarcerated here. In 1816, James Cayce bought the former fort and he and his family made it a home.

Today, the Cayce Museum is divided up into six exhibit areas. The first, the Saxe Gotha-Granby Room, contains displays pertaining to the Congaree Indians, including artifacts found on the former site of the Congaree village. The Trading Post Room includes memorabilia from the Revolutionary period, including artifacts of Lord Cornwallis, Commander of the British forces in the South. The Emily Geiger Room was the quarters of Lord Rawdon, commander of Fort Granby in 1781, when Emily was held prisoner in this room as a possible spy. The Victorian Room depicts the years 1837-1901 with household items, period clothing, and military items from the War for Southern Independence, including the interesting sketches of Camp Sorghum, a local Confederate prison camp for Union offi-

cers. The Cayce Room presents the Cayce area's 20th-century history, including Cayce's years as an important railroad town.

The museum also contains a visitors center, a separate kitchen, family dairy, smokehouse, and a railroad caboose containing the Railroad Hall of Fame, which celebrates Cayce's railroad history. The museum grounds also include the 1922 Dixiana Depot, once an important stop between Savannah and Columbia. Finally, near the museum you'll find **Granby Gardens Park,** with picnic facilities, and **The Granby Botanical Gardens** beside the creek. The garden includes plants the first settlers brought into the Saxe Gotha Township from 1737 on.

Open Tues.-Fri. 9 a.m.-4 p.m., Sat.-Sun. 2-5 p.m. Closed Monday except by appointment. Small admission charge.

LEXINGTON

Lexington's been growing quickly over the past few years as folks have started commuting to Columbia from here, but it's still got the reputation of being a great town, and a friendlier place to live than the Capital City. Famed Harlem Globetrotter **Meadowlark Lemon** was born here.

Lexington County Museum Complex
Head out I-20 to Lexington until you come to Hwy. 1, then follow that into Lexington until you turn right onto Columbia Avenue. You'll come to an Ace Hardware on your right—the museum is just behind the store.

On the corner of Fox St. and Hwy. 378, tel. (803) 359-8369, this interesting collection of buildings includes three 18th-century cabins, two antebellum houses, a post house, and other outbuildings. When you get here you can take the Antebellum Tour, where you'll be guided around the complex and allowed to view the **John Fox House,** furnished with locally crafted furniture from the antebellum period.

Those interested in roots music will want to stop by the pre-1820 **Hazelius House,** once owned by the Lutheran Synod of South Carolina as a seminary—making it the second-oldest seminary in the United States. In the office of this home, itinerant preacher Charles Tillman returned from a tent meeting where he'd just held forth. Earlier in the day, an African-American congregation had used the tent. Tillman had joined their worship and heard the local faithful sing a rousing spiritual he'd never come across before. Here in the Hazelius House, he wrote

---

EMILY GEIGER: REVOLUTIONARY HERO

An exciting Revolutionary story here focuses on Emily Geiger (1760-?), a woman in her early 20s who volunteered to courier an important message to General Thomas Sumter for General Nathanael Greene in 1781. When captured by suspicious British troops on alert for just such a message-bearer, Emily demanded that a woman be found to conduct the body search the redcoats wanted. She was locked in Lord Rawdon's room at Fort Granby while the soldiers sent for a Tory woman to search her for possible messages. As she waited, Geiger removed the message from her bodice, memorized it, and ate the paper. When the Tory matron arrived and searched her, she found nothing.

Once Emily was released, she rode all night and all the next day before reaching Sumter's camp and delivering the message. Within an hour after her arrival, Sumter's troops were on the march to Orangeburg to join Greene's soldiers and take part in the Battle of Orangeburg—an important American victory.

A life-size model at the Lexington County Museum re-creates the event in one of the museum's central displays. And though it's never been made official, some have suggested that the woman holding the branch of laurel on the South Carolina state seal should rightly be called Emily Geiger.

---

out the words and music as best he could recall them, and within a few years, the song, "Give Me That Old Time Religion," had become a gospel standard.

Tours are given by guides in antebellum costumes. Open Tues.-Sat. 10 a.m.-4 p.m., Sunday 1-4 p.m. Last tour at 3:30 p.m. daily. Admission. Limited handicapped access.

On Main St. in Lexington, you'll find **Lexington Antiques,** 711 W. Main, tel. (803) 356-7111—normally worth a stop. So is **Miller's Back When,** 877 S. Lake Dr., tel. (803) 957-1205.

NEWBERRY

Newberry is one of South Carolina's small-town gems. This community of 10,000 features a renovated 1882 Opera House, the 1998 rebirth of which has symbolized and instigated the resurrection of Newberry's delightful downtown.

Founded the same year that the American Constitution was written, 1789, Newberry was first "settled" when British troops camped here just before the Battle of Cowpens.

Throughout the railroad era, Newberry was a railroad stop between Columbia and Greenville, which caused the town to grow.

Back when the Opera House and Newberry Hotel were first built, Newberry was rejoicing from its emergence after years of war and (for whites, at least) enemy occupation. Reconstruction was particularly bitter in the area. During the late 1860s, Newberry was one of the local hot spots of Ku Klux Klan action: "bands of persons generally disguised, having on false faces, and with white sheets around them" terrified local Republicans, black and white. But the Klan didn't have any monopoly on political violence: during the election of 1870, when it was discovered that an African-American man had voted for a Reform Democrat, a number of other blacks attacked him. Whites and other Reform African-Americans took up his defense, and a riot nearly ensued.

Today, plans are underway to open commuter train service between Newberry and Columbia, which will make this a perfect place to live while working in Columbia, and will also make a train ride, play, and dinner a perfect night out for Columbians. Meanwhile, the same folks who brought the return of the Opera House are now setting their sights on restoring the 19th-century Newberry Hotel.

Sights

On the town square, the **Old Court House,** now the Town Hall, is most famous for the bas-relief on its front, which provides a quick lesson on Reconstruction-era politics. It features an upturned palmetto tree, symbolizing the uprooted South Carolina culture; the eagle clutching the scales of justice in its beak represents the federal government, and a strutting gamecock represents the still-proud South Carolinian people.

The relief was added to the 1851 courthouse in 1876, at the end of the Northern occupation.

The restored **Opera House** on Main St. once saw such performers as Tallulah Bankhead and the Barrymores (not Drew). Today it is again center of artistic action here in Newberry, attracting various shows and performers. Call (803) 276-8685 for information.

On College St., pretty little **Newberry College,** enrollment 700, is a national historic district, and fun to walk around. Affiliated with the Lutheran Church, the college was created in 1856 and used as a Confederate hospital and later as a U.S. garrison during the War between the States.

You'll find a number of gracious old **antebellum homes** worth ogling on Boundary Street. A lot of people also come here to visit **Carter & Holmes, Inc.,** tel. (803) 276-0579, open 8 a.m.-5 p.m. and Saturday 8 a.m.-noon, one of the Southeast's largest indoor orchid nurseries, and the **Wells Japanese Garden** on Lindsay Street.

Downtown you'll find plenty of interesting shops and restaurants, many of which have only recently opened. **Cabana Cafe** features deli sandwiches, beer, and crab cakes. **Hal's** features good country breakfasts; **Vivian's** is the place for deli lunches.

While on Main St., you might want to visit **Leslie's Antiques & Auctions,** which features antique medical equipment. Nearby is **Showcase Early American Art & Antiques,** owned by Jim Putnam, who moved here after living at such other chic spots as Palm Springs and Jackson Hole.

Accommodations

Barklin House, 1710 College St., is a recently refurbished Queen Anne furnished with family heirlooms, a wraparound porch with rockers and swing, and a private garden. Barklin House is also home to the working art studio of Barbara and Franklin Miller, the hosts. Two rooms here, Inexpensive. Smoking on the porch only. One room has a private bath; the other has a shared bath. Full breakfasts. Children allowed at host discretion.

If your kids don't pass muster with the Millers, the **Best Western Newberry Inn,** at 11701 Hwy. 34, tel. (803) 276-5850, offers 113 units. You'll also find a **Days Inn** at 50 Thomas Griffen Rd., tel. (803) 276-2294.

Information

Stop by the **Newberry County Visitors Center** right on 1109 Main St., tel. (803) 276-0513.

PROSPERITY

The town of Prosperity has one of those great names that reveals the optimism of a different day. The town's name used to be Frog Level, but when the railroad came through here the townspeople decided it needed something a little more auspicious-sounding. Preacher's kid Erskine Caldwell, author of *Tobacco Road,* lived here for several years while his father was pastor at the local Associate Reformed Presbyterian Church.

The Back Porch is a wonderful café and bakery here in town.

EAST OF COLUMBIA

ALONG US 378

Stateburg

Here on Hwy. 261 you'll find the **Church of the Holy Cross,** a unique Gothic Revival building. Buried in the graveyard outside is Joel Roberts Poinsett, one of the best-traveled men in the antebellum South. Born with poor health in 1779 in Charleston, Poinsett traveled to England with his family shortly after the Revolution ended and lived there until 1786, returned there for school, and managed to travel throughout Europe, Asia, South America, and the American West before truly settling down to live in South Carolina. On his Western trip he met Nashville's Andrew Jackson, who later, as president, entrusted Poinsett with leadership of the state's Unionists during the 1828 Nullification Crisis. Later, while serving as U.S. Ambassador to Mexico, Poinsett introduced a red-leaved plant to America that came to be called the poinsettia in his honor.

Poinsett married late and divided his last years between homes near Georgetown and Greenville. When he took ill again, he started out from Georgetown and attempted to make a long trip for his health. He made it only as far as Stateburg, where a friend, a Dr. Anderson, convinced him to stop and rest until he regained his strength. Poinsett never regained his strength, but rest he did—and continues to, in the Anderson plot in the Church of the Holy Cross graveyard. At Christmastime, local residents decorate his grave with poinsettias.

Sumter

Sumter is the birthplace of Bobby Richardson, former Yankees second baseman during the late '50s and early '60s, longtime Gamecock baseball coach, and one-time South Carolina gubernatorial candidate. In his autobiography, *The Bobby Richardson Story,* Richardson recalls the day in 1953 that the entire town—and a local radio remote unit—showed up at the bus station to see off Sumter's great pinstriped hope.

As I sat down and looked out at the crowd— still waving, still shouting, "Best of everything, Robert!" "Show 'em you're from Sumter!" "Keep in touch, Bobby!"—I felt a big lump rising in my throat.

What could the Yankees offer me that could match this?

The five-foot eight-inch, 158-pound Richardson went on to replace Billy Martin at second base, and played on several World Series teams during the Mantle and Maris years, setting a number of World Series records in the process. After retirement, Richardson enjoyed long success as baseball coach at the University of South Carolina. More recently, Richardson appeared briefly as a reporter in *Forrest Gump,* filmed in the area. When his former teammate and old friend Mickey Mantle died in 1993, the devout Richardson counseled the slugger in his last hours and later officiated at his memorial service. Each year, the state's athletic coaches compete with one another in the Bobby Richardson Lowcountry Open Golf Tournament.

Country singer-songwriter Rob Crosby, who hit the country charts with a handful of sensitive, pro-woman songs ("She's a Natural," "Love Will Bring Her Around," "Working Woman") in 1990-92, also hails from Sumter, as does actress *(Dancer, Texas)* and former Miss South Carolina Shawn Weatherly.

For years, the Sumter Telephone Manufacturing Company produced many of the world's telephones and switchboards from South Carolina white oak, walnut, and sweet gum. Other than that, the Sumter area is known for having been home to the Ellison family, who were wealthy African-American industrialists and slave owners, and for being home to the **Swan Lake Iris Gardens,** West Liberty St., tel. (800) 688-4748 or (803) 778-5434, a 150-acre swamp-side collection of over 25 varieties of iris, and home to every one of the eight swan species in the world. No admission charge—open daily.

Sumter isn't always the prettiest town in the world, but it has its beauties, including the

Sumter Opera House, an 1890s clock-towered stone masterpiece, at 19-21 N. Main St. It's open during the day—feel free to pop inside for a look around. Also worth a peek is the **Sumter County Museum,** 122 N. Washington St., set in an 1845 Victorian home featuring formal gardens outside and period furnishings, local artifacts, and genealogical research materials inside. Both the gallery and the museum are wheelchair-accessible.

If you find yourself needing to spend the night in Sumter, consider **The Bed and Breakfast of Sumter,** 6 Park Ave., tel. (803) 773-2903, fax (803) 775-6943, where Suzanne and Jess Begley rent out five rooms, all with private baths. A nice old 1896 home with its Victorian parlor and big front porch with rocking chairs. Moderate.

The Calhoun Street B&B, 302 W. Calhoun St., tel./fax (800) 355-8119, tel. (803) 775-7035, Moderate-Expensive, and **Magnolia House,** 230 Church St., tel. (803) 775-6694, Moderate, offer alternatives. The Magnolia House is probably the most stately of the three, with its huge pillars outside and its walled English garden. Call and inquire about children.

For eats, try **Ward's Barbecue** on E. Liberty St., locally known for its barbecue and hush puppies (weekends only), or **Big Jim's,** tel. (803) 773-2323, a combo coffee shop/restaurant/tavern downtown on Hwy. 76.

If you'd like to see—and possibly buy—some of what the area's artisans have been up to lately, stop by the **Sumter Gallery of Art,** 421 Main St., tel. (803) 775-0543, featuring local, regional, and national works in an antebellum home, and **Dees Handmade** at 755 Bultman Dr., tel. (803) 773-9710.

ALONG I-20

Camden

Camden, the oldest inland city in South Carolina and one of the true gems of the state, properly belongs to the Old English District, but it's closer to Columbia than to any city in the district.

Shortly after assuming power over South Carolina, as part of his push to create a wall of British settlement around his prized colony at Charles Town, King George II issued instructions in 1730 for the establishment of a township to be located on the "River Watery (Wateree)." Surveyors laid out the township of Fredericksburg during the winter of 1733-34, but those who came to populate the town called it Pine Tree Hill.

In 1750-51, a number of Irish Quakers arrived at Pine Tree Hill, and for the next 10 years, Scotch-Irish settlers began to populate the area. In 1758, young mover-and-shaker Joseph Kershaw arrived in town to establish a store for a Charleston mercantile firm. He soon, however, developed a vision for the area, and with his leadership, saw, grist, and flour mills soon provided industry for the small town, mainly a collection of log houses. In 1768, he persuaded his fellow citizens to rename the town Camden, after Charles Pratt, Lord Camden, a member of Parliament who championed the rights of the colonies.

Before long, however, Camden had become prosperous enough to witness the building of a number of prestigious homes, including Joseph Kershaw's own home, begun in 1777, in the optimistic period after Colonel Moultrie and his men had thwarted the British attempt to take Sullivan's Island down near Charleston, and it looked to the Carolinians as if the redcoats weren't coming back.

RUSHING RIVERS

A weight of wide red water hurls
Itself upon itself, and whirls
Downward, muscled—leonine,
Wrenching rubble and log and vine,
Gathering all it washes by
Color of earth—color of sky
Churned to mauve up river reaches,
Boiling red in sun-struck patches,
Or chemistried to angry purple
In the blue shadow of a maple.

. . .

But when the mighty summer rains
Ring silver coins that jump and gleam
On the dark metal of the stream,
Resounding like a copper gong
It drags the clinging town along—
Columbia on the Congaree—
Camden on the Wateree—
The High Hills of the Santee
Draining from the watershed.

—Josephine Pinckney, 1927

Unfortunately for Kershaw, when the British came back in spring of 1780 and captured Charleston, one of the first things General Lord Charles Cornwallis did was head off to establish a number of posts in the interior of the state, to thus stabilize any political unrest. On June 1, the British arrived to occupy Camden, and General Cornwallis chose Kershaw's comfortable new home as his headquarters.

The summer of 1780 passed slowly. On August 16, American Continentals and militiamen under General Horatio Gates attempted to retake the town, but all they succeeded in doing was causing the bloody Battle of Camden, in which the Brits sent the untrained Yank militia—Gates included—running through the thickets where a rabbit wouldn't go. The better-trained Continental troops under mercenary German Baron de Kalb held their ground . . . until de Kalb was shot and bayoneted to death. The town of DeKalb is named in his honor.

After the Battle of Camden, the British took fortification more seriously. They surrounded the entire town with a stockade wall which comprised six small forts along its perimeter.

By the following April, General Nathanael Greene, new Commander of the American Forces, thought about having another crack at Camden. By now, Cornwallis was gone, having led the larger part of his army off to Virginia, and Lord Francis Rawdon was now in command of the remaining garrison at Camden. Greene, however, took a good look at the British fortifications and decided that attack would be suicide.

Rawdon, on the other hand, took a look at the puny force of Yankees at their encampment one mile outside town on Hobkirk Hill and decided that an attack would be bloody good fun. Unfortunately for the Brits, the Yanks fought like cornered wildcats. The Brits chased them off the hill, but the Yanks killed so many of the British during the process that afterward, the British took a head count and realized that there weren't nigh as many as there was a while ago. They could not continue to hold the fort with the number of men still alive, so reluctantly, they burned their fortifications and hightailed it for Charleston.

Actor Samuel E. Wright, most famous for his role playing Cheraw's Dizzy Gillespie in *Bird,* and for providing the voice for the crab Sebastian in Disney's *The Little Mermaid,* is from Camden. Wright rose to fame playing the purple grapes in the old Fruit of the Loom underwear commercials. Pioneer African-American baseball player Larry Doby, who followed just 11 weeks after Jackie Robinson to become the first black player in the American League, was born in Camden as well.

South of downtown on Hwy. 521 (Broad Street) stands **Historic Camden,** a historical park containing a mix of original and replica structures from the Revolutionary era, some of which have been moved here from elsewhere in the state. Open daily except Monday for a nominal admission fee. The small store at the end of the parking lot contains a number of small press books of historical interest, along with replica period coins and other knickknacks.

Joe and Kellie Berry's **Old Gin Woodworks,** 909 Market St., tel. (803) 432-0394, sits on a small side road, so it's easy to overlook it. But don't—the Berrys are fascinating people and Joe's woodworking—all by hand—is the sort of work that will be collector's items in our grandchildren's generation. Come over and take a look at their garden of wooden cutouts—golfers, cowboys, coyotes. But don't stop there. Go on inside (you'll pass a pen of rottweilers—also for sale) and take a look at some of the Camden native's handiwork—one-of-a-kind furniture that no factory could ever make. It's open Mon.-Fri. 10 a.m.-6 p.m., sometime Saturday, but these are just approximations. You'll find the real policy hand-painted on a sign beside the door:

OPEN—When I'm here
CLOSED—When I ain't

What strikes you most about Joe Berry is his craftsman's integrity. Joe doesn't advertise—he's got all the work he can handle now, and he's not about to contract out.

Be sure not to take photos of any of Joe's works (his cutouts are particularly attractive subjects) without asking his permission first. They're his livelihood, and he's understandably sensitive about people stealing his designs.

Next time you visit Columbia, stop into Group Therapy, the Five Points bar, and take time to admire the metalwork mermaid emerging from the tree roots at the transom. Joe's brother Dan created this—he's an artisan in his own right.

CUPS, right downtown at 1040 A Broad St., tel. (803) 425-9900, fax (803) 425-9922, is a deliberately comfy spot to drink some coffee. Plenty of readings and book signings here, as well as alternative bands and acoustic musicians, some local, some who head up after playing Columbia. Hours Mon.-Tues. 7:30 a.m.-6 p.m., Wed.-Thurs. 7:30 a.m.-10 p.m., Friday 7:30 a.m.-11 p.m., Saturday 9 a.m.-11 p.m., Sunday 9 a.m.-5 p.m. Plenty of baked goods and desserts, including Häagen-Daz ice cream. Reasonably priced soups, salads, and sandwiches served Mon.-Sat. 11 a.m.-3 p.m.

Bishopville

Sometime DJ, sometime country performer Jim Nesbitt hails from Bishopville. If you're old enough, you may remember his novelty songs, "Mother-in-Law" and "A Tiger in My Tank," both country top 20 hits, and his string of political satire hits, "Please Mr. Kennedy," "Looking for More in '64," "Still Alive in '65," and "Heck of a Fix in '66" (all top 40). Word has it that Jim—inching toward 70 years of age—has gone into the mobile home business over in Florence.

Bishopville was founded as Singleton's Cross Roads, named after Bill Singleton's tavern, which served the stagecoach passengers on the road between Georgetown and Charlotte. On Main St. you'll see the Lee County Courthouse and the Opera House, which has never in all its 80-something years actually been used as an opera house. Here in town at 115 N. Main St. you'll see what used to be the Copeland Grocery Store, since reborn as the **South Carolina Cotton Museum,** tel. (803) 484-4497, fax (803) 484-4270. To understand the cotton subculture that was, and to some extent still is, an important part of this corner of the state, you'll want to visit the museum. It features cotton-picking and weaving tools, an enlarged model of a boll weevil, an antebellum spin ginner, and several different types of cotton gins. The museum is open Mon.-Fri. 10 a.m.-5 p.m. Adults $2, discounts for students and seniors. Pre-schoolers free.

And if you haven't pulled over to the side of the road and done it already, this will give you the chance to feel "raw" cotton.

Located at 165 Broad Acres, Bishopville, one mile north of I-20, off Exit 116, tel. (803) 484-5501, **Fryar's Topiary Gardens** feature three acres of trees and shrubs formed into imaginative spirals, pom-poms and other curious shapes by gardener Pearl Fryer.

If you get hungry in these parts, consider heading over to **Charlene's Taste of Country,** east of town on I-20, tel. (803) 662-1030. Seriously filling country cooking here. A sign outside commands you to "EAT"—I suggest that you obey it.

For more information on Bishopville and Lee County, write the **Lee County Chamber of Commerce,** P.O. Box 187, Bishopville, SC 29010, or call (803) 484-5145.

NORTHEAST: THE PEE DEE

Most folks up here will tell you that Stephen Foster's "Way Down Upon the Swanee River" was originally "Way Down Upon the Pee Dee River," until he changed the lyrics at the last minute—purely, so far as anyone can tell, for reasons of aesthetics. That's okay—when Barry Gifford wrote *Wild at Heart* in 1987 (later made into the Nicholas Cage film by David Lynch), he sent the main character to Pee Dee State Penitentiary, primarily, one assumes, because he liked the sound of the word "Pee Dee."

Florence

At the **Pee Dee Farmers Market,** one mile west of I-95 on Hwy. 52, you'll not only find farm fresh produce, but also the **Red Barn Visual Center,** tel. (803) 673-1766, featuring two art galleries, a gift shop, and an exhibition gallery, offering works for sale by different local artists each month. You can usually also find artists and artisans at work.

Located at 558 Spruce St., tel. (843) 662-3351, **Timrod Park** is named for Henry Timrod, poet laureate of the Confederacy, who once taught in the little one-room schoolhouse on the park grounds. **The Florence Museum** here features regional history and art exhibits, along with an interactive Children's Gallery and activity area.

According to Bo Bryan in *Shag: The Legendary Dance of the South,* shag pioneer Billy Jeffers and his friends spent the summer of 1937 around the swimming pool here swimming and sunbathing, and dancing the dances of the day, including the "wild jitterbug." Because he had asthma, Billy slowed the jitterbug down, an important step toward the development of the casual coastal dance. The next summer, Billy was living at Myrtle Beach, spreading his bit of the puzzle that would become the shag of today.

If you'd like to try some great (albeit Northern-style) ribs, stop in at **House of Ribs,** 220 N. Cashua Dr., tel. (843) 317-9821, open Mon.-Sat. 11 a.m.-6 p.m. The House is run by Major Pickard, a 50-something retired bus driver and nowadays pastor of the People United Missionary Baptist Church. The ribs are made with a vinegar sauce, and you can order baked beans, fries, and slaw on the side if you like. A slab of ribs'll cost you $15, $7.50 for half a slab.

For more information on Florence and surrounding areas, write the **Greater Florence Chamber of Commerce,** P.O. Box 948, Florence, SC 29503, or call (803) 665-0515. Or check in at the **Florence Convention and Visitors Bureau,** 3290 Radio Rd. in Florence, tel. (803) 664-0330.

South of Florence on US 52

If you can find an excuse to take this road on a Thursday, Friday, Saturday, or Sunday, be sure to stop by at **Schoolhouse Bar-B-Que,** tel. (843) 389-2020, in the tiny town of Scranton, about 2.5 miles north of the town of **Lake City.** Then continue on down into little Lake City to the **Moore Memorial Museum,** 111 Singletary Ave., tel. (803) 394-3368, set in a 1928 home, featuring a room for children, exhibits of each of South Carolina's 85 governors, and other small-town collectibles.

Darlington

Like Daytona and Indianapolis, Darlington is a sacred city for auto-racing buffs—here's where the Southern 500 is run each year, and where numerous NASCAR stock car races take place throughout the year. But its history goes back centuries. European immigrants first settled here in 1798, and some of its buildings date to before the Civil War.

In 1894, a policeman and two civilians were killed during the "Darlington War." Governor Benjamin Tillman's harsh (and ineffective) liquor regulations allowed for the search of private homes without warrant if the residents were suspected of concealing liquor within. After the initial violence, in which three were killed, a trainload of consta-

bles was sent into Darlington. Local residents fired on the train, while other locals harassed every cop they could find. Finally, Tillman ordered the state militia to establish order in Darlington and Florence Counties, but many companies—including the one from Charleston—refused to turn their guns on their fellow citizens. Tillman ordered these conscientious objectors dishonorably discharged. Fortunately, the Darlington Guards were able to establish order on their own, and no one else was killed.

Today, besides its NASCAR attractions, Darlington draws visitors for its historic downtown, which features antebellum buildings and a charming mural of 1930s Darlington (on N. Main St.) by South Carolina artist Blue Sky.

Just outside the gates of the massive **Darlington International Raceway,** Route 157, you'll find the **NASCAR Stock Car Hall of Fame,** formerly named the Joe Weatherly Museum, featuring videos of famous races, old racing cars, photos and bios of all the inductees into racing's hall of fame. If you know the sport, this will get your engines revving. Open year-round 9 a.m.-6 p.m.; $3 admission, 12 years and under get in free.

Of course, twice a year, the *inside* of the raceway is much more exciting than the museum

---

DARLINGTON'S COUNTRY-WESTERN PIONEERS

Dorsey and Howard Dixon, pioneer country performers of the 1930s, were raised in Darlington, though they had to move on to East Rockingham, North Carolina to find mill work after WW I. With their reedy harmonies and original songs—including "I Didn't Hear Anybody Pray," better known as "Wreck on the Highway"—the Dorseys recorded some 55 sides in the mid-1930s. Many of the best—"Weave Room Blues," "Spinning Room Blues," and "Weaver's Life is Like an Engine" reflect life in the textile mills of the Upcountry.

Both returned to their mill jobs in East Rockingham when the music quit paying well enough. Howard died in 1961, but Dorsey lived long enough to be honored for the brothers' contributions to American music, and to be asked to play the Newport Folk Festival. He died in 1968.

outside: when the mid-March Transouth 400 and Labor Day Weekend Mountain Dew Southern 500 (also known as the Darlington 500) are run. The latter is one of the most famous races in the sport and is South Carolina's single-top-drawing event.

If you want to peek at the track, walk over to the security building and ask the guard for permission.

On Spring Street, 60-acre **Williamson Park** features a five-mile boardwalk swamp trail dripping with azaleas and camellias and draped with Spanish moss.

Marion

Here's a pretty little courthouse town just perfect for an afternoon's walkaround. Once an Indian trading post on America's first frontier, Marion was known as Gilesboro from the mid-1700s until the 1830s when it, like the county, was named after General Francis Marion. The four-part public square at the intersection of Main and Godbold was donated by the area's first English settler, Thomas Godbold. The **Marion Courthouse,** with its Doric columns and curving iron railings, stands on the southwest corner of the square. Built in 1853-4, it's the third courthouse built on the site. It looks out over a square with a small fountain.

The **Marion Museum,** 101 Wilcox Ave., tel. (843) 423-8299, is open Tues.-Fri. 9 a.m.-5 p.m. (closed noon-1 p.m. for lunch). The two-story brick **Old Town Hall and Opera House,** at 109 W. Godbold St., was built in 1892. Most of the rest of the town's notable buildings can be found south on Main St. and up E. Godbold Street.

Mullins

Native Americans resentful of the disease, forced removal, massacres, and alcoholism can take some comfort in remembering that it was Native Americans who initially introduced Europeans and European-Americans to tobacco.

Mullins is a town that has long made much of its wealth off of tobacco money, and was long the largest tobacco market in the state. This tobacco-based town of 6,100, the boyhood home to former Olympic and professional boxing champ Sugar Ray Leonard, celebrates the **Golden Leaf Festival** on the fourth weekend of September each year, featuring a "Tot Trot," arts and crafts booths and demonstrations, a parade, and a husband hollerin' contest—something like a hog hollerin' contest, but with slower response times. The nice little downtown contains a number of shops, restaurants, and antiques. For more information, call the **Mullins Chamber of Commerce** at (843) 464-6651.

In the ugly days of Reconstruction, it's rumored that about five miles east of town was something called the "Dead Line," which Horry County farmers, few of whom had ever owned slaves, drew as a boundary for African-Americans, as a response to the rising crime of the newly emancipated people. If a black was found on the east side of the line, the legend goes, he would be killed. As late as 1940, WPA writers noted that blacks still avoided the Dead Line area.

If you're thinking of staying for the night, visit **O'Hara's Century House Inn,** 123 E. Wine St., tel. (843) 464-7287, offering seven units. **Webster Manor,** 115 E. James St., tel. (843) 464-9632, offers six. Inexpensive. For a little less, visit the **Imperial Motel** at 109 Legion Rd., tel. (800) 264-5004 or (843) 464-8267 (Budget); or the 50-room **Martin's Motel,** 1001 N. Main St., tel. (843) 464-7894 (Budget).

Dillon's "South of the Border"

No one who's ever driven I-95 can forget the billboards. For hundreds of miles north and south of Dillon, South Carolina, you can't miss them:

Keep Yelling, Kids (they'll stop)

You're aways a WIENER at Pedro's!

Mullins changes in late summer from a lackadaisical little town to a bustling metropolis. . . . landowners and tenants settle up, and merchants are busy from daylight till dark selling clothes and supplies for the winter. Nights are almost as busy as days, with trucks, trailers, "pickups," and wagons roaring and rattling into town. While the farmers' tobacco is being unloaded, their wives and children window shop, the men gossip and settle national problems, and take naps on their piles of tobacco.

—*WPA's* South Carolina: A Guide to the Palmetto State, 1941

They increase in frequency mile after mile as you near the South Carolina/North Carolina state line, until you see a giant sombrero floating 200 feet in the air beside the freeway. This is the strange world of South of the Border.

Eightysomething Alan Schafer, mastermind of the SOB empire, started over 40 years ago with a small roadside beer stand that has metastasized on both sides of the interstate. Looking to eat dinner in a sombrero-shaped restaurant? This is the place. Wanna buy some candy? Some firecrackers? Some pornography? Pedro's got what you need.

Pedro is Schafer's long-time cartoon spokesman, comedian to children ("YOU NEVER SAUSAGE A PLACE!" he used to intone on billboards, in his native Pedro-speak), and bane to Latino activists concerned about the effect a 97-foot-tall Mexican caricature wearing a sombrero and a poncho and talking like Jose Jiménez might have on the racial beliefs of American motorists. Consequently, over the past few years, the "Pedrospeak" signs have been disappearing all along the East Coast.

But though he's been forced to learn a second language, Pedro still manfully straddles the parking lot—you can even drive your car between his legs. With over a dozen shops full of touristy goodies, five restaurants, 300 guest rooms, a golf course, an RV park, and, of course, Pedro's Pleasure Dome—an enclosed pool area accessible to anyone staying in Pedro Airspace—South of the Border takes in road cash from more than eight million people a year.

You've got to stop here at least once, and if all the plaster burros and M-80s don't entice you, here is one good, unobjectionable reason: Schafer's the man responsible for resurrecting the Blenheim Ginger Ale label a few years ago, so you can find good Blenheim in all its fiery flavors at various shops across the 135-acre SOB empire.

Griping about South of the Border's being "tacky" is like griping about Tokyo's being crowded—of *course* it is, but that's beside the point. You can't miss it.

CHERAW

Pronounced "chuh-RAW," this is the hometown of jazz great Dizzy Gillespie. This area was originally occupied by the Cheraw Indians, the chief tribe up here near the upper part of the Upper Pee Dee region, who kept a well-fortified village on the riverside hill near present-day Cheraw. After European diseases decimated their numbers, the surviving Cheraws left to join the Catawba Confederation, leaving the town site open for European settlement. Brits and their African slaves began moving in as early as the 1730s; once the British government awarded a group of Welsh Baptists a large land grant downriver near present-day Society Hill, commerce and settlements began working their way up the Greater Pee Dee, eventually centering at its head, or northernmost navigable point, at what was then widely called "Cheraw Hill." James Gillespie and Thomas Ellerbe opened a water mill and trading center here in 1740. Thomas and Eli Kershaw formally laid out the town in 1768, a plan that included broad streets, a village green (still there) and the Anglican church building (still standing) for the newly established St. David's Parish. The Kershaws, who actually held the grant to the center of present-day Cheraw, renamed the settlement Chatham in 1775—after William Pitt, the Earl of Chatham. But alas, the local residents took to this about as warmly as the U.S. took to the metric system in the 1970s, and when local leaders incorporated the town in 1821, they wisely chose the name most everyone had insisted on calling the town for years.

During the Revolution, Cheraw was occupied by both the British and American armies; St. David's Church was used as a hospital by both. After Independence, located at the spot where the old Indian paths met the river, Cheraw quickly became a major shipping center for cattle and cattle products, as well as corn, tobacco, indigo, and rice grown in the area, and this prosperity only grew once bridges and steamboats made traveling across and along the Pee Dee easier. In fact, by the start of the War for Southern Independence, Cheraw was home to the largest cotton market between Georgetown and Wilmington, North Carolina, and the largest South Carolina bank outside of Charleston. The affluent town planted oak trees in triple rows along its streets for shade; you can still see some of the median oaks on Third Street.

Cheraw agitated for secession; once the war came, its streets, homes, and buildings were

DIZZY GILLESPIE

Jazz great Dizzy Gillespie was born John Birks Gillespie in Cheraw in 1917, the youngest of the nine children of Lottie Gillespie and her brickmason and sometime-musician husband, James. The Gillespie home—now a vacant lot—stood on the west side of the 300 block of Huger Street.

As a young boy, Dizzy would dance for money upstairs in the ballroom at the Chiquora Club, where he was normally the only black allowed inside. The 1910 building still stands just behind Town Hall, where Dizzy is also said to have performed. When Dizzy was 10, his father died suddenly from asthma. Now the reasonably prosperous Gillespies were plunged into severe poverty; Lottie took on work as a maid and laundress, and each child tried to make whatever money he or she could. When he wasn't out dancing for money, Dizzy had taken to sneaking into the Lyric Theatre (now the Theatre on the Green) and watching cliffhangers. He got so good at it that the theater owner finally hired him to keep other kids from doing the same thing. As payment, Dizzy got to watch all the movies he wanted.

Later, Dizzy appeared in minstrel shows put on by his music teacher at the all-black Robert Smalls School on Front St. (no longer there), and played his first paid gig for the white high school. In 1933 Gillespie graduated from Robert Smalls School, then moved to the Laurinburg Institute in North Carolina on a band scholarship.

Not long after he left, Lottie Gillespie finally left for the north to live with her sister. When Dizzy graduated from Laurinburg, he reunited with his family, joined a band, and the rest is jazz history.

Dizzy didn't pick up his famed nickname until after he left Laurinburg—old friends and family in Cheraw still refer to him as "John Birks." And though Dizzy never lived in Cheraw again, he came back numerous times to visit old friends. He also often opened his performances by announcing, "I'm Dizzy Gillespie from Cheraw, South Carolina."

filled with fugitives from less-secure areas, along with their valued possessions. In March 1865, General Sherman and friends came a-calling. Fortunately, they didn't burn the place down, which is why many fine old antebellum homes survive today. In 1867, the Reconstruction-era Union troops even allowed the local citizens to erect a monument in Old St. David's cemetery—first in the state—to those Confederates who had died in the war. The original inscription could not directly mention the Confederates themselves.

Unfortunately: a) before the Yanks even got to town, an accidental explosion leveled the business district over on Front St., which is why most of the buildings on Front are post-bellum; b) Sherman's boys *did* torch the Chesterfield Courthouse, burning most of Cheraw's records, which is why most dates for antebellum houses are preceded by "circa"; and c) like the rest of the state, Cheraw's fortunes took a postwar nosedive and didn't really look back up until the turn of the century, when Victorian and Revival buildings reflected an improved economy.

Modern Cheraw

Today, Cheraw is home to about 5,500 people and boasts one of the largest historic districts in the state—214 acres—built around the original town green and including over 50 antebellum homes and buildings. Stop in at the **Greater Cheraw Chamber of Commerce,** beside the green on 221 Market St., tel. (843) 537-7681, to pick up a self-guided tour of the historic district.

The place to start is at the intersection of Church and Front Streets, where you'll find the highlight of the historic district: tall, simple, clapboard **Old St. David's Episcopal Church,** named after David, patron saint of Wales. Authorized by the South Carolina General Assembly in 1768, completed in 1744, St. David's was the last Anglican parish established in South Carolina under George III, before the Revolution came along and thrust a sword between church and state. In the courtyard, in unmarked graves, lie the bodies of 50 members of Cornwallis's 71st Regiment of British regulars, men who died from smallpox while keeping Cheraw's British subjects safe from the ravages of rebellion. Services are held in a more modern building now: "New" St. David's, circa 1916, over on Market Street. But Old St. David's stands yet. If you'd like to see inside, call Sarah Spruill over at the Cheraw Visitors Bureau, tel. (843) 537-3387.

Facing the church from Church St., to the left you'll find **Riverside Park,** the old site of Kershaws Ferry, the steamboat landing, and a covered bridge. A plaque marks the point of the old bridge built by Horace King, born a slave here around 1807 and sold to a bridge builder at the age of 22. King mastered his master's craft and was released from bondage in 1846. He formed his own construction company and built bridges throughout the South before the war. During the war, King served the Confederate cause by building bridges for its armies and transports. After the war, the King Brothers Bridge Company made good money rebuilding the many bridges ruined during the hostilities. Today, though few Horace King bridges are still around, you can see a portion of one in the Lyceum Museum.

Now head away from the river on Church for a block, turn right on 2nd St., and soon you'll come upon the chamber of commerce on your left, just across from the town green. If you're visiting during business hours, now's the time to pick up a map of the historic district. If not, here's a brief tour.

Right on the town green, at the southwest corner of Market and 2nd, you'll see **Market Hall,** circa 1836, once used as a public market, slave market, and (ironically) a court of equity. Next door stands the **Inglis-McIver Office,** circa 1820, a small white frame Greek Revival building that used to be on Front St. and was fortunate enough to survive the big explosion during the war. John A. Inglis chaired the committee that drew up South Carolina's Ordinance of Secession.

Across Market St., opposite the Inglis house, you'll see the **Lyceum Museum,** a small brick Greek Revival building, circa 1820. Originally a library, this was also used by the Cheraw Lyceum as a meeting place for its lectures, concerts, and other cultural events. Today, the museum houses various local artifacts and includes a Dizzy Gillespie exhibit and a portion of Horace King's bridge. Ask the folks at the Cheraw Visitors Bureau, or call Sarah Spruill at (843) 537-3387 to get inside.

Right next door on the corner is **Town Hall,** circa 1858, built in part by the local Masonic lodge, which used it as a meeting place. Now the city keeps several offices there, which means you can pop in during business hours to take a look. Among its many employments, the building has served time as an opera house.

Continue up 2nd and turn left on Kershaw. At the southeast corner of Kershaw and 3rd, at 230 3rd St., you'll see "The Teacherage," said to be the oldest house within the original town limits of Cheraw. Teachers—you may have guessed—boarded here in the first part of the 20th century; before that, the Malloy family used to entertain the Reverend Wilson—Woodrow Wilson's father—when he'd come up from Columbia. General Sherman used the home as his headquarters after the town was captured by Union soldiers.

Directly across 3rd St. at 235 3rd is "The Lafayette House," site of a public reception for General Lafayette during his triumphant 1825 return to the United States. Head north up 3rd to 321 3rd Street. This circa 1820 home, believe it or not, was moved back from the street in the 1940s with one mule. What makes it interesting, though, are the remaining slave cabins behind the main structure. Continue on around past the Dutch Colonial Revival home (circa 1901) at the corner, turn left on Greene St., and soon on your right you'll pass a fish-out-of-water Charleston "single-house" (circa 1860), a late Queen Anne (circa 1895), and the Wesley United Methodist Church, 307 Greene Street. Dizzy Gillespie attended here as a child. Turn right on Kershaw, head down a block to Huger, and you'll find a plaque erected in honor of Gillespie, who was born about a quarter mile northwest of where you're standing.

Now head on down Huger back to Church, turn left, and enjoy a nice picnic at Riverside Park.

Cheraw State Park
Four miles southwest of Cheraw on Hwy. 52, you'll find 7,361-acre Cheraw State Park, tel. (843) 537-2215. This is the state's oldest park, established in 1934. Plenty of swimming and fishing in 332-acre Eureka Lake, with eight rental WPA-era cabins, 17 campsites, an archery range, and—this *is* South Carolina, after all—a championship 18-hole golf course. For day visitors, the park's open April-Oct. 6 a.m.-9 p.m., Nov.-March 7 a.m.-7 p.m. Office hours 11 a.m.-noon, 4-5 p.m.

At the Dogwood picnic area you can take a nice 0.9-mile loop around the lake, allowing you to view longleaf pine, juniper, dogwood, yellow jessamine, trumpet plants, and other regional flora.

Sand Hills State Forest
This state forest, 46,000 of sandhills, was the result, so some scientists believe, of a prehistoric period when, if anything around had had a developed enough brain to come up with the idea, building beachfront condos in McBee would have been a good idea. Along with the adjacent Carolina Sandhills National Wildlife Refuge, the state forest preserves a huge tract of little-visited land. If you're looking to get away from it all, this is a good place to start; you can camp here on the side of the trail, but you'll need to get permission from forest headquarters. A good place to start out is at Sugarloaf Mountain, where you'll find a well-marked trail leading to the top of the 513-foot monadnock. Beautiful striated sandstone along the way. Also in the park is the rare, pink-blooming pixie moss, which thrives in the sandy soil. A new 6.7-mile mountain biking trail

gives bikers a chance to leave even the infrequent passing auto behind. Call (843) 498-6478 for more information.

Cheraw Fish Hatchery and Aquarium
Just a little farther down the road on Hwy. 1, you'll come upon the **Cheraw Fish Hatchery and Aquarium**, tel. (843) 537-7628, which raises bass, blue gill, sun fish, and catfish for stocking in ponds and reservoirs around the state. In the aquarium, you'll see the critters in re-created natural environments. Call before coming between December and early March, since the ponds are likely to be dry during these months.

Carolina Sandhills National Wildlife Refuge
Continue on down Hwy. 1 and you will come to this 45,586-acre property of once-barren, overcut, mismanaged land, established as a wildlife refuge in 1939. After 50 years of forward-thinking management, the land looks almost completely restored, with pine and scrub oak everywhere, providing homes for many species of wildlife including migrating ducks and the red-cockaded woodpecker, and even the rarely spotted eastern cougar. Because the area is dedicated to assisting the reestablishment of wildlife to the area, you'll find some 30 man-made ponds for fishing and birdwatching, and the many miles of paved and unpaved NWR service roads provide excellent mountain biking opportunities. The refuge also includes hiking trails, observation towers, photography blinds, picnic shelters, and interpretive displays. You can fish and canoe (bring your own) on Lake Bee, Martins Lake, and Mays Lake, three of the larger ponds.

It's easy to get yourself off on a road or trail and not see another person for hours. A great place to disappear for a day. Pick up a brochure from the sign board at Refuge Visitors Dr., a right turn off Hwy. 1 well-marked by signs. The refuge office there is open 8 a.m.-4:30 p.m. Call the refuge manager at (843) 335-8401.

Woodland Pond Trail: You'll find the parking area and trailhead for this 0.9-mile hike by driving one mile past the NWR headquarters on Hwy. 1 to Pool A, on the north side of Little Alligator Creek. This is a nice little trail with boardwalks and footbridges and a beautiful view of the serene pond and the wildfowl it attracts.

Whitetail Trail: If you want a slightly longer trail, keep driving north 3.2 miles past the Woodland Pond Trail parking area to a boat ramp, where you'll also find the trailhead. This 5.8-mile hike (2.9 miles each way) will likely give you a peek at some whitetail deer, yellow jessamine, pines, ferns, and mosses. You'll also pass an observation deck and a wildfowl photography blind, so bring along the camera and zoom lens. When you come to the junction with a loop trail around Lake 12, take the loop and head back the way you came.

Area Practicalities

If you're here to camp, you'll find 17 camping sites with water and electrical hookups, plus hot showers and generally clean restrooms at **Cheraw State Park,** tel. (800) 868-9630, and some primitive camping at **Sandhills State Forest,** tel. (843) 498-6478; pick up a permit from forest headquarters. If you'd rather sleep with a roof over your head, you might see if you can get one of the cozy WPA **cabins** over at Cheraw State Park, tel. (843) 537-2215. If at all possible, call well in advance and make a reservation.

For a more cosmopolitan stay, close to the river and downtown you'll find the motel called **Inn Cheraw,** 321 2nd St., tel. (843) 537-2011, fax (843) 537-1398. It offers friendly service and well-kept rooms. Inexpensive. Cheraw has a **Days Inn** at 820 Market St., tel. (843) 537-5554, fax (843) 537-4110. It's inexpensive, but rather far off the beaten path—away from the historic downtown, and subject to some heavy traffic noise. If you stay here, ask for a room facing the Sonic Drive-in—the traffic noise is quieter in that direction.

If a B&B in the midst of Cheraw's historic district sounds more appropriate, see if you can get a room at the circa 1850 **Spears Guest House,** 501 Kershaw St., tel. (888) 424-3729 or (843) 537-7733, fax (843) 537-0302. Kay and Larry Spears rent out four rooms. One room is furnished with antiques. Inexpensive-Moderate rates; $56 a night will get you golf privileges at the Cheraw Country Club. If you're traveling with a large group, or just really, really, want to be alone, you can rent the whole house for $200 a night. Continental breakfast. The Spears restored this home in 1985, enclosing the rear porches and adding a new wing on the right. At 314 Market Street, Janice and Jim Galletly have opened up the **Market Street B & B,** tel. (843) 537-5797, in a Colonial Revival home built in 1906. Inexpensive, offering two rooms with a shared bath and double bed, and another room with a queen-size bed; a light breakfast of fruit juice and cereal is included, and there are four porches from which to man a rocker and peer out upon the historic district.

Locals' favorites in Cheraw include **Tommy's Coffee Cafe,** 156 Market St., tel. (843) 537-2274, where you can get very good coffee, egg-and-bagel sandwiches, and just about anything else you could want to get you going in the morning. **The Country Kitchen,** Hwy. 9 W, serves up breakfast and a Southern buffet lunch featuring corn muffins, biscuits, peach cobbler, and strawberry pie. **El Pico de Gallo** serves up authentic Mexican fajitas and flautas over at 165 2nd Street. Or try **El-Sherif's House of Pizza,** 215 2nd St., where the stromboli and salads are said to be wonderful. If the weather's nice, you might want to just grab a chicken salad sandwich or some bread and cheese over at **Market St. Deli** at 17 Market St., carry it out to the Riverside Park at the end of Church St., and have a picnic. On Thurs.-Sat. only, you can get supper out at **Cabin Creek,** Hwy. 1 S, tel. (843) 537-4195, highly recommended by locals for its fish and steaks.

For a treat at an authentic old-fashioned ice cream fountain, be sure to stop in at **Wannamaker's Drug Store** at 154 Market Street.

Shopping

Cheraw, like many restored downtowns these days, features a number of cute and unusual gift and antique shops. Head down to 2nd St. and you'll find a number of shops, including **Palmetto Gifts,** 181 2nd St.; **Sunflowers, etc.,** 236 2nd St.; **Sentimental Journey Antiques, 242 2nd St.;** and **The Flag Shop II,** 247 2nd St., all worth a browse.

ORANGEBURG AND VICINITY

A weed-filled Confederate graveyard lies in downtown Orangeburg, on a square intersected by John C. Calhoun Drive. The name of this street reflects the entrenched stance of Orangeburg's white power-wielders: in most Southern towns, the Calhoun Drives and Jeff Davis Parkways became Martin Luther King Boulevards sometime in the late '60s or early '70s. But even Orangeburgians agree that if the South is 10 years behind the rest of the country, Orangeburg is 10 years behind the rest of the South.

Orangeburg, a pretty antebellum town of about 13,000, today serves as the commercial center for the numerous agricultural burgs that surround it. Set on a combination of rolling hills and river plain, it's also an area of great natural beauty, including a wonderful boardwalk-crossed swamp park right beside old downtown, a world-renowned rose garden, and moss-strewn oaks shading huge planters' homes. The North Edisto River, flowing right through downtown, is the world's longest blackwater river. The town's annual South Carolina Festival of Roses attracts thorn-and-petal devotees from around the country to Edisto Gardens, and the rod and reel set thrives on the extensive fishing opportunities in the area's many ponds, swamps, lakes, and rivers.

For all its scenery, Orangeburg is also a town with a heartbreaking racial history. Though traditionally moderate (when the play version of Thomas Dixon's *The Clansman* came to South Carolina in 1911, Orangeburg's city fathers banned it from being performed in town) the infamous 1968 "Orangeburg Massacre," the Kent State of the Civil Rights Movement, marked a low point for black-white relations in the Palmetto State. The violence occurred when state troopers and highway patrolmen opened fire on a crowd of protesting African-American students on the campus of South Carolina State College (now University), wounding 31 and killing three.

The resentments remain. Today, despite a number of biracial reconciliation projects, Orangeburg is for all practical purposes two homogenous towns living side by side. In a town roughly half of whose citizens are blacks and half white, very few public events draw anything close to a balanced racial mix; many locals seem to view events as "black" or "white" and attend accordingly.

Despite a downtown rejuvenation project begun in 1993, Orangeburg remains a frustration to those who see the potential in the moss-draped streets and classic brick downtown set on rolling hills. Though lying in a strategic spot between Charleston and Columbia and poised to provide countless rural towns with restaurants, shops, and entertainment, it has never developed as the tourist destination and commerce center it could, largely—by all accounts—due to the lack of cooperation between black and white business leaders. Consequently, most new development is occurring north of town: developers are ripping out pine woods for Wal-Marts and new upscale chain restaurants, while the center of town comes undone into a row of whitewashed windows, wig shops, and secondhand stores.

No, Orangeburg is not what it could be. But what is here (including three of the best barbecue places in the state!) is worth seeing, and given Orangeburg's central location just off I-26, there's no reason to miss it.

HISTORY

George Sterling moved into what would become the Orangeburg District in 1704 to trade with the local Indians. The district became known as Orangeburg in honor of William, Prince of Orange. After the colonists in Charles Town pushed to have the royal government take control of the colony from the lords proprietors, the royals began pushing for settlement inland along the rivers of the Lowcountry and Midlands, including along the black, slow-moving Edisto River. The General Assembly of the province created the township of "Edisto" in 1730 along the banks of the North Edisto River, and in 1735, 200 Swiss, German, and Dutch settlers formed a colony there. They soon changed the name to Orangeburgh, after William, Prince of Orange. At first, settlers shipped agricultural and lumber products along the river, but within a couple of

THE ORANGEBURG MASSACRE

One of the darkest moments in South Carolina history came in February, 1968, on the campus of South Carolina State College (now University), in Orangeburg. The events leading to what came to be known as the Orangeburg Massacre began when students of the nearly all-black college—and also-black Claflin College, next door—began protesting Harry Floyd's refusal to admit African-Americans to his All Star Bowling Lanes, on Russell Street, five blocks from campus.

It was an old complaint. Members of Orangeburg's white establishment had already opened their formerly "whites only" restaurants to black customers, and white civic leaders had attempted to persuade the crusty Floyd to desegregate, but Floyd argued that desegregating would cost him his white clientele. Besides, no one was exactly sure that the 1964 Civil Rights Act covered bowling alleys. Floyd told the students that if they disagreed with his policy, they could take him to court.

But the students didn't wait for the courts. After a couple of failed protests, campus activists led a sit-in. Some 50 highway patrolmen and policemen showed up to arrest the trespassers. In the parking lot, as the lawmen prepared to take the students away, some 300-400 more State and Claflin College students, having heard that their classmates were being arrested, poured into the parking lot. Some shouted racial slurs at the policemen; others threatened to burn the city. A fire truck was brought to the scene, reminding students of the 1960 incident when State and Claflin students had been blasted with fire hoses. As police moved to provide cover for the firefighters, the students surged against the un-protected bowling alley door, smashing through the window. When police attempted to arrest the student they thought responsible, violence broke out. One student sprayed a caustic solution into a policeman's eye, permanently damaging his vision. The police started swinging their billy clubs, knocking male and female students to the ground. An officer was hit with a piece of lead pipe and drew his gun—but didn't fire.

The officers regained control and pushed the students back toward campus. But the angry students ravaged white-owned businesses along the way, throwing bricks, rocks, and firewood; smashing windows; and damaging automobiles at a car lot. Back at campus, seething students stood on College Avenue, hurling rocks and other objects at passing cars driven by anyone with white skin—including a police car. The officer stopped and fired a warning shot into the air, momentarily driving the students back but also fueling on-campus paranoia.

National Guardsmen and State Law Enforcement Division officers poured into the city. For two nights, delegations from the city and state parleyed with student leaders. Anonymous phone calls lit up police switchboards, threatening to burn the bowling alley, the shopping center, and/or the whole town. A white news photographer reporting the story had his car pelted by rocks and pieces of brick. A white man, his deaf-mute son, and women and children in two other cars were nearly killed by bottles, rocks, and bricks that shattered their car windows. National Guardsmen moved in and blocked off Hwy. 601.

And that's the way it stayed for the next two days. On the dark evening of Thursday, February 8, students taunted the officers and pelted them with rocks and bottles. Small arms fire echoed from campus. Firebombs exploded against buildings and in the middle of Hwy. 601. Students dragged lumber from an unoccupied house adjacent campus and threw it onto an impromptu bonfire.

Patrolman David Shealy was struck in the face and dropped to the ground, his face bloodied and his body convulsing. Word spread quickly along police lines that he had been shot—though in truth he had been hit with a banister torn from the vacant house. The fire had been put out and the students had retreated into the campus, but some lingered behind close to the street, and this brought many of the others back down toward the street. To the patrolmen—many of whom believed the students were bent on marching out to wreak havoc on the town—the approach of 200 angry students apparently looked like a charge. At least one officer, dodging rocks and bricks, shouted repeatedly for them to stop. But the students—if they could even hear his shouts in all the confusion—ignored the warnings, confident that the police would never shoot real bullets at unarmed college students, and certainly not on their own campus.

But when the students came within 25 yards, one of the patrolmen fired a carbine loaded with buckshot. Suddenly, other officers opened fire on the students, some of them firing over the students' heads, some of them attempting to fire low to hit

(continues on next page)

THE ORANGEBURG MASSACRE

(continued)

them in the legs. The barrage lasted less than 10 seconds before shouts to stop firing and the students' screams were left alone to fill the night air. But in those few seconds, 30 students had been hit—including one standing outside a campus building nearly a quarter of a mile away. Students were rushed to Orangeburg Hospital—where they had to wait for aid in segregated waiting rooms. Three—Henry Smith, Samuel Hammond, Jr., and Wilkinson High School student Delano Middleton—died from their wounds. A pregnant female student who claimed to have been beaten by police in the aftermath of the shootings eventually suffered a miscarriage.

Though evidence did show that there indeed *had* been small arms fire from campus earlier in the evening, over half of the massacre's victims had been shot either in the side or in the back. No indictments were issued against the nine officers who admitted to firing their weapons toward the crowd—but they were charged in federal court with violating the students' civil rights. The jury—which included two African-Americans—took less than an hour to find all the defendants not guilty by reason of self-defense.

Of all the rioters, Cleveland Sellers, a veteran of the Student Nonviolent Coordinating Committee, was alone indicted on charges of participating in a riot, incitement to riot, and conspiracy to incite others to riot. Officials from Governor Robert McNair on down labeled him as the "outside

agitator" (he had been raised in nearby Denmark) responsible for the student unrest. Sellers eventually served seven months in state prison for inciting students at the bowling alley two nights before the massacre but later went on to earn a master's degree from Harvard, a doctorate from the University of North Carolina, and a spot on the South Carolina Board of Education. The state pardoned him of the riot charge in 1993.

The FBI's interest in the case waned quickly in the aftermath of Orangeburg, as Martin Luther King's assassination that April—and the ensuing riots nationwide—took up much of their investigative manpower. A year later, the deaths of four white students at Kent State would become forever etched in the collective baby boomer consciousness, while outside the civil rights community, Orangeburg and its black victims became something little spoken of, or even known. On campus, the Smith-Hammond-Middleton Memorial Center health and physical education building bears the names of the three dead men, and near the center of campus stands a granite marker commemorating the young victims.

A federal judge ordered the All-Star Bowling Lanes desegregated shortly after the shootings. Much to Harry Floyd's surprise, it continued to do a healthy business, with white bowlers as well as black.

All Star Bowling, flashpoint of the Orangeburg Massacre

years, a public road was constructed between Orangeburg and Charleston, bringing prosperity to the small farming community. Despite the fact that Orangeburg became the scene for Revolutionary War carnage,

Orangeburg County went on to become the top cotton-producing county in the world.

During Sherman's March at the end of the Civil War, 600 Confederate troops dug in where the Edisto Gardens now lie, defending the Edisto River bridge against the advancing Union Army. Though they were able to delay the Yanks, providing precious time for fleeing citizens, the Federals outflanked them and they were forced to retreat to Columbia. After the war, Orangeburg became the site of Claflin University and South Carolina State University, both historically black schools, established in 1878 and 1896, respectively.

In recent years, when movements were made to bring a representation of white students into the student body at the state university, many black students protested, desiring a continuance of the current de facto segregation.

The rest of the city serves as an important commercial center for the surrounding farming communities.

SIGHTS

Edisto Memorial Gardens and Horne Wetlands Park

Each year, over 400,000 visitors tour Orangeburg's beautiful gardens, Hwy. 301, four blocks west of downtown, tel. (803) 534-6821, consisting of 150 acres of azaleas, camellias, roses, and other flowers spaced among giant oaks and century-old cypress trees. The gardens' landscapers keep more than 4,000 plants on display here, including 75 varieties of roses. Edisto also contains one of only 23 official test gardens in the United States sanctioned by All-American Rose Selections, Inc. You should find roses in bloom here anytime between mid-April and the first killing frost, normally in November. No charge

Built in 1992-94, a 2,600-foot walkway leads into the Horne Wetlands Park, a wetland that lies between the Display Garden and the north fork of the Edisto River. Absolutely beautiful—especially considering this is downtown Orangeburg, more or less. The waterwheel is used to provide water to the nearby pond.

The ornate fountain at the main entrance to the park memorializes soldiers who died in the U.S. wars of this century. This is where the "Memorial" in the gardens' name comes from.

A prime time to see Orangeburg at its best—and most unified—is during the South Carolina Festival of Roses, held in the gardens the last week of April. From late November through the

end of December, the gardens are decorated with Christmas lights for the Children's Garden Christmas, open 5-10 p.m.

South Carolina State University

Founded in 1872 as the Colored Normal, Industrial, Agriculture and Mechanical College by the African-American and "Carpetbagger"-run Reconstruction-era General Assembly, the historically black South Carolina State University is now integrated, and features **I.P. Stanback Museum and Planetarium,** named in honor of the university's first black chairman of the board of trustees, Columbia businessman/philanthropist Isreal Pinkney Stanback. The museum's main gallery features African and African-American works, including art by the Bambara, Mende, and Yoruba peoples. It's open weekdays during the school year. Shows are offered Sundays in the planetarium's 40-foot dome Oct.-April at 3 and 4 p.m.

Claflin College

Right next door to South Carolina State is the state's first black college, Claflin. Opened as a Methodist Episcopal University in 1869, it was founded by and named after philanthropist Lee Claflin and his son William. Today it continues as a coed private college affiliated with the United Methodist Church. It enrolls some 950 students in 24 different majors and programs. Recently, the college established a Center for Excellence in Science and Mathematics to recruit and graduate students in science, engineering, mathematics, and technology. Find out more online at www.icusc.org/claflin/campus.htm.

Donald Bruce House

Take Hwy. 301 four miles southeast of Orangeburg and you'll come upon the Donald Bruce House, built in 1735. This two-story white frame house with its double piazza is the oldest home in the county. Both South Carolina president John Rutledge and Lord Rawdon used this as headquarters during the Revolution, and Union officers did the same during the Civil War.

EVENTS

In early January, some 600 coon hunters and 25,000 spectators come to Orangeburg for the

Grand American Coon Hunt, now over 35 years old, recently named one of the Southeast Tourism Society's "Top Twenty Events in the Southeast." This is the largest field trial for U.S. coon dogs, and it's a qualifying event for the World Coon Hunt.

Now wait a minute, you say—what about the poor raccoons? Officials for the contest assure us that while the wild raccoons in the woods outside Orangeburg do perhaps need to take some Tagamet at the end of the hunt, they aren't actually shot or torn apart by the sharp teeth of the hunting dogs. As soon as a dog runs a coon up a tree, the masked house cat of the forest is considered "treed," giving the dog points for his tracking ability.

For more details, contact the Orangeburg County Chamber of Commerce, tel. (800) 545-6153 or (803) 534-6821.

In the spring, another of the Southeast Tourism Society's "Top Twenty Events in the Southeast" takes place here in Orangeburg. Some 20,000-30,000 people attend the South Carolina Festival of Roses each year to view the roses and arts and crafts, and cheer on participants in the blackwater river race, road races, and sports tournaments, as well as the Princess of Roses Pageant. Local bands play continuously on the outdoor stages.

For more details, contact the Orangeburg County Chamber of Commerce, tel. (800) 545-6153 or (803) 534-6821.

FOOD AND DRINK

The bad news: Orangeburg has traditionally lacked quality restaurants. Locals think nothing of making the 40-mile trip through the pines to patronize the finer restaurants up in Columbia.

Up until a couple years ago, the town's only Mexican restaurant was Taco Bell. Older, Chinese-American-run **China Garden,** 725 John C. Calhoun Dr. SE, tel. (803) 534-3434, is worth noting. In 1994 and 1995, Orangeburg received a nod from the upscale chain gods and was granted a **Red Lobster** and an **Applebee's,** both built north of town near the Prince of Orange Mall and the new Wal-Mart center. Even more recently, a good new **Mr. Fatz** opened up down by I-26 on St. Matthews Road.

For something that won't make your cardiologist wince, try one of the grilled chicken sandwiches or Greek salads at the **House of Pizza,** 591 Calhoun Dr., tel. (803) 531-4000, located in the San Diego-esque, tile-roofed Chestnut Shopping Center on Chestnut.

But again, none of these will make you forget about your last meal in Charleston.

Barbecue
Now, the good news: If you're looking for the Southern culinary experience, you are in some luck. Orangeburg hosts four superb barbecue joints (remember, "barbecue" down here is a noun, not a verb), and three of them contain "Duke" in the name. It's no wonder the franchise location of Maurice's Gourmet Piggie Park Barbecue on West Calhoun Drive closed down; you'll want to hit the original Maurice's Gourmet Piggie Park Barbecue when you're in Columbia, but Orangeburg is Duke Country. The Duke family is one of Orangeburg's most prominent; a father and two of his sons own the individual restaurants, all run separately. For country atmosphere, you'll want to head south out of town on the Charleston Highway to **Earl Duke's BBQ.** This Duke's charges $4.95 for all you can eat, and the strength here is variety. You'll find hash, collard greens, mustard greens, and black-eyed peas in addition to the bottomless pitchers of sweet tea. Earl Duke, the owner, is a 50-ish Nashville nearly-was who came back home to take part in the family industry, and he's filled the restaurant's entryway with signed glossies of Burt Reynolds, beauty queens, and other Southern icons. Once you're inside, you'll notice a set of doors on the far side of the main paneled room. If they're open, be sure to poke your head in; Earl's got a karaoke machine in there, and if you're lucky, he'll sing you a song or two. He really does have a fine voice for country or adult contemporary music. He may even ask you to sing a duet.

When you get around to eating, make sure you take only what you can eat of the fixin's at the food bar; a nice gray-haired woman will drift by before you're done to check your plates. If they're clean, she'll write "20% off" on your check. Seriously. And you won't have to feel guilty about the starving kids in China, either.

Another Duke's stands just on the other side of

the railroad tracks on Chestnut Road, near the county jail. This Duke's, a windowless cinder-block building with a cement floor and wooden picnic tables inside, puts loaves of locally baked Sunbeam bread (white) on the long red-checkered tables, along with pitchers of sweet tea. The whole deal costs $4.50—slaw and all—and you're welcome to eat as much as you can, a policy most people seem to take as a personal challenge. You can take the food to go here—a one-plate take-home (or, in your case, take-motel) deal costs only $3.75. The Duke family (or maybe some of their friends from the First Baptist Church, who sometimes fill in) will pile it on for you. There's only one rule here, noted by a hand-written sign above the self-serve meat bin: "Please do not use bare hands." Is it more disconcerting that Duke's has hung such a sign, or that it needed one?

The third Duke's—also called just plain "Duke's"—is located on the other side of John C. Calhoun Drive, on Five-Chop Rd., set inside a cinder-block building with false windows, frilly curtains and all. Prices run $5.75 for all you can eat; here this includes top-notch potato salad with the tea and Sunbeam bread. You'll also find friendly servers, inspirational plaques, and evangelical tracts positioned at strategic locations throughout the restaurant.

Earl Duke's is open Mon.-Sun.; the other two Duke's are more classic barbecue spots in that they open only on Fridays and Saturdays. For many Orangeburg natives, stopping by to "pick up some Duke's" on the way home from work on Friday is a lifelong tradition. For the latter two restaurants, get here early after they open at 4:30—on a busy night, the Dukes may run clean out of pig by 8, and since it's a once-a-week ordeal, they're not going to fire up a second.

Breakfast
More good news: Fine basic breakfasts abound in Orangeburg. One of the cheapest is at the **Waffle House,** 3695 St. Matthews Rd., tel. (803) 536-5481, out on Highway 20. The best thing here—or any of the countless Waffle Houses—is always the potatoes, which you can order with an imaginative number of mixings—my favorite is a mix of ham, cheese, and sliced tomatoes. Though a chain—and a near-national one at that—Waffle Houses, like Dairy Queens, somehow transcend

their origins by meeting the needs of, and thus reflecting the personality of, South Carolinians.

Fast Food
Every small Southern town worth its grits offers a venerable old hamburger-and-ice cream joint where the kids spend Friday and Saturday nights (and every night in summer) perched on car hoods, talking; in Orangeburg the "strip" has become the stretch between the Burger King on the corner of Old St. Matthews Road and Chestnut and the McDonald's on St. Matthews and Highway 301. Fortunately, the hometown **Dairy-O,** 1504 Russell St., tel. (803) 536-4205, thrives in the middle of this stretch, turning out excellent pimento cheeseburgers, chicken livers (don't knock it till you've tried it), and slaw burgers. As with most places of this ilk, steer clear of the token Mexican items on this menu, which are only a little less authentic than the egg roll-on-a-stick at the county fair. *Do* consider indulging in the ice cream. Dairy-O's local claim to fame, its frostees and shakes, run less than two dollars. Tip: If you like your shakes thick, ask them to put in a little less milk. They won't put in more ice cream.

NORTH AND EAST OF ORANGEBURG

North (Northwest)
Just northwest of Orangeburg, North, South Carolina, has one of the worst names of any town in the state. It's also one of the more ironic: North lies in central South Carolina, whereas the town of Central, South Carolina, lies in the northernmost reaches of the state (near Clemson).

In truth, North gets its name from John F. North, who in 1891 contributed 100 acres of land to establish a town and railway depot. Two other donors contributed the same amount of land, but North was the oldest of the three, and a Confederate veteran to boot. He became North's first mayor.

Singer, actress, and sometime sex kitten Eartha Kitt was born and spent her first years in an alcoholic household outside of North, raised by her cotton-picking grandparents. While here, the future Catwoman (she replaced Julie Newmar on the *Batman* TV show) went to a school in the yard of St. Peter's Church. Though she left after the death of her mother to live with an aunt in New York City at the age of seven, her 1956 autobiography, *Thursday's Child,* includes memories of life in North, including a tragic Southern moment involving a chain gang:

One day my sister and I were sitting in the yard playing when we heard the chanting of the chain gang, building a new road near our house. We sat and listened, humming along with them when it was a familiar song. The chain gang was a natural thing, so no one paid much attention until one of the men, with chained feet, came riding a horse into the yard. He had a pail and asked for water from our well. He was very dark and wore a torn sun hat. He looked at us with eyes that envied our freedom. His shoulders were broad and strong. His chest and arms were muscled. His trousers were dirty and worn. The stripes were faded, so it was hard to tell which were supposed to be black and which white.

He slumped over to take the water the old man gave him, turned his horse around, and headed back. As he reached the road that led back to the others, he swiftly turned his horse and headed for an opposite trail. He took off like a bat out of hell. Everyone in the house, my sister, and I sprang up to watch as he galloped off. The guards soon caught up with him. The ringing of the rifles reached our ears with a deathlike tone. We all bowed our heads and went back to our affairs, as if this too was all very natural.

St. Matthews

St. Matthews is an interesting-looking town of 2,600 on the west bank of the Congaree. It was one of the first areas cultivated by plantation owners with the courage to stray far above the Charleston region.

At 303 Butler St., you'll find the **Calhoun County Museum,** tel. (803) 874-3964, a good place to get a feel for what life was like here before you arrived. Open Mon.-Fri. 9 a.m.-4 p.m. No admission charge. Wheelchair accessible.

Congaree Swamp National Monument

Located 20 miles southeast of Columbia off Hwy. 48, 200 Caroline Simms Rd., Hopkins, tel. (803) 733-8440, this designated site on the United Nations International Biosphere Reserve Program is the last large tract of old-growth bottomland hardwood forest in the entire country. The park covers 22,200 acres and 18 miles of hiking trails. Fishing, canoeing, and kayaking are excellent. Bring insect repellent.

Primitive camping permits are available from the ranger's office. Open 8:30 a.m.-5 p.m. daily. Admission free. The park service provides wheelchair access on a couple of boardwalks. During the rainy season, the majority of the boggy trails are tough to get around even for hikers. However, the rainy season—usually in the summer and fall—is when the swamp looks the most swamplike. Otherwise, when the forest floor on either side of the boardwalks is dry, the swamp can look pretty much like a wood with cypress knees, though it's still a beautiful place to explore.

If you've come to hike, the 4.6-mile Weston Lake Loop Trail will give you plenty of swamp—and a beautiful black lake—for your effort. The 11.1-mile Kingsnake Trail will get you far past the last dabblers, the sort of people who hike carrying Hardee's cups.

I love this swamp, but one thing hikers new to this sort of terrain might find is that there is a certain repetitiveness to swamp hiking. There's no astonishing overlook at the midway point of this trail, just beautiful trees, water, and lots of knees to trip over.

If this is your first time in the swamp you might want to take the 0.7-mile self-guided boardwalk tour.

I've never seen a gator in this swamp, but I'm told they're out there. Keep your eyes out for snakes. If you see one and you're not sure it's not poisonous, leave it alone. Wear hiking boots and long pants, if possible. Wear footwear you don't mind getting wet, too. Best yet, check in with the ranger at the station near the entrance to sign in and check on trail conditions. The most popular times to visit the park are in the spring and fall. Christians wanting to impress children with the concept of hell may wish to visit in July or August.

Poinsett State Park

This park is named for Joel Roberts Poinsett, antebellum U.S. Ambassador to Mexico and the man who introduced the U.S. to the poinsettia—named in his honor. The 40-mile-long High Hills of Santee Passage of the Palmetto Trail threads through the park now, running from the 301 bridge over Lake Marion, through Clarendon and Sumter Counties to the Wateree River. Some sections are open to equestrians and mountain bikers, allowing you to explore a very interesting landscape where the Lowcountry and sandhills meet in an explosion of red cedar, oaks, dogwoods, mountain laurel, and loblolly pine.

TO THE SOUTH

Branchville
Think of every railroad junction you've ever seen or heard about. Then reflect on this—Branchville is the first railroad junction ever in the world. Ever. Branchville, 16 miles south of Orangeburg on Hwy. 21, grew along a major junction on the line from Charleston to Hamburg, near Augusta.

To celebrate this fact, Branchville holds its "Railroad Dayze" every year and operates a small **Railroad Museum**, in the old depot.

Bamberg
The seat of Bamberg County, Bamberg (pop. 4,000) was long home to the Carlisle Fitting School, a military prep school. A WPA writer in 1940 wrote of finding the local soda fountains crowded with uniformed cadets during the afternoons. Today, it's hard to imagine anything particularly crowded here in Bamberg, which lies about 25 miles south of Orangeburg along Hwy. 301/601.

Founded as a turnout on the stagecoach route between Charleston and Augusta, Bamberg takes its current name after the man who bought the railroad station here. Today, the blocks surrounding the station make up Bamberg's historic district, featuring a number of attractive pre-Civil War homes. Be sure to see the 1938 New Deal program painting by Dorothea Mierisch, a mini-mural on canvas hanging in the Bamberg post office on Hwy. 78.

SOUTHEAST:
THE SANTEE-COOPER REGION

Santee State Park
This 2,496-acre park at 251 State Park Rd., three miles northwest of I-95 off Hwy. 6, is for lake-lovers, best known for its unique pier-based cabins and two lakefront camping areas (174 sites total). Catfish and largemouth and striped bass frequent the waters here. Of course, this is camping Carolina-style, meaning you'll find 30 cabins, tennis courts, rental pedal boats, and so on. The cabins are two-bedroom with heating and a/c, furnished kitchens, bed and bath linens, and cable TV—just like the pioneers had. The park also has a restaurant open year round, three meals a day, seven days a week.

Santee
In the late 1960s, rumor had it that Walt and Roy Disney were fixin' to make the Santee area the home of their new amusement park, which some rumored was going to be even bigger than Disneyland. A couple savvy Santee residents set to buying up lots and building hotels in the sleepy highway town. And then Walt and Roy chose to buy farther south, in Florida, leaving some people hereabouts in the lurch—or bankruptcy court.

Some 30 years later, tiny Santee seems to be benefiting from the trickle-up theory, however. Through the years, a number of folks who have barreled down I- 95 to and from Orlando in station wagons have looked up from Santee's gas pumps long enough to notice that, by gosh, this wouldn't be a bad place to retire and golf and fish oneself silly. The town now features a large number of restaurants, outlet shops, and the Santee Cooper Resort—which features the Santee National Golf Club and two other courses.

Eutawville
This tiny burg of 382 was founded in the 1840s as a summer resort for Santee River plantation owners. It grew up around Eutaw Springs, which had been a strategic spot along the British supply line extending west from British-held Charleston in the latter part of the war. On September 8, 1781, the Battle of Eutaw Springs was fought here, scene of the last major Revolutionary War battle in the state.

Holly Hill
At **Swetman's Barbecue**, just grab a paper plate and pile it up as high as possible—unlike most barbecue joints, here you're only allowed one trip down the line. But it's about as good a

ketchup-based barbecue as you're going to find. And if it's your first time here (don't ask how they know if you're a returning customer—they just *know*), you're allowed a second trip.

Pinopolis

Pinopolis is most important to the traveler as home of **Blackwater Adventures,** tel. (800) 761-1850 or (803) 761-1850, providers of paddling instruction ($65 per hour), guided tours ($35 and up), kayak, canoe, and trailer rentals ($35-50), and tent rental ($30). They also sell canoes and kayaks.

Moncks Corner

On 9th Avenue in New York City, there's a restaurant named Moncks Corner that does carryout-only items like smothered chicken, oxtail stew, and baked short ribs with side items like macaroni and cheese, collards, and black-eyed peas. Columbia-based humorist William Price Fox has set some of his better stories here in Moncks Corner.

Something about the name, and about the odd town itself, makes it something like the capital of the Hell Hole region.

Anglers Marina and Restaurant

Behind the Anglers Minimart off Hwy. 52, tel. (843) 899-6120, just off the banks of the Tailrace Canal, Anglers offers happy hour specials in the Brass Bass Lounge 4-7 p.m., as well as New York strips, prime rib, oysters, shrimp, and (on Sundays) wings. Thursday night is shag night. It's technically a private club. Don't think you can just waltz into a fancy place like this. No sir—you've got to pay a $1 membership fee, presumably to establish your solvency.

Old Santee Canal State Park

In the years before the American Revolution, farmers in the Upcountry became troubled by the long trip they had to take to get their crops to the markets in Charleston. If they took the overland route, the trip was excruciatingly long, and the need for numerous wagons to carry the shipments made it an expensive proposition. Farmers could float their crops down the Santee River, but it let out south of Winyah Bay near Georgetown, from which the crops had to be loaded onto ocean schooners that would then attempt the perilous, unpredictable southward passage along the coast.

The solution, it seemed, was to create a canal between the Santee River—which flowed through the Upcountry—and the Cooper River, which flowed right into Charleston Harbor.

Though postponed by the Revolution, in 1793 work began, financed in part by Battle of Sullivan's Island hero William Moultrie. The 22-mile long, 30-foot-wide, five-and-a-half-foot-deep canal was shovel-and-picked between the rivers over the next seven years by African-American slaves under the supervision of Colonel Christian Senf, a Hessian engineer who had served in the Revolution. Through a series of rises and drops, the 10 locks allowed boats to navigate the 35-foot-drop between the rivers. The canal immediately became the toast of the young country, and through the first decades of the 19th century, it showed a profit. In 1830, over 700 barges and boats—by now loaded with Upstate cotton—floated through the canal, moved along by the muscle work of polemen who would jab the ends of poles into the canal bed, then walk along to the back of the boat, thus providing a steady source of propulsion.

In the 1840s, the spread of the quicker, even-more-direct railroads across the state snuffed out the economic life of the canal. Today, most of the canal lies beneath the waters of Lake Moultrie. What you see at the park are the lower reaches of the canal, where Charleston-bound barges would join the Cooper River.

The park features a number of interesting sites. Start off by visiting the **Berkeley County Historical Society Museum** to the right after you enter the parking lot (entry fee). The museum, tel. (843) 899-5101, houses various historical exhibits and displays. Open Mon.-Sat. all day, Sunday afternoons.

Mepkin Abbey

Today, you can visit Henry Laurens' grave site and old plantation grounds at Mepkin Abbey. Originally recorded under the name of Sir John Colleton, one of South Carolina's original lords proprietors, Mepkin became Laurens' home in the 18th century, when he ran the Mepkin Plantation here. After Laurens' death (he's buried

HELL HOLE SWAMP

Several stories circulate as to how Hell Hole Swamp got its name. The most probable one concerns General Francis Marion, the French-American partisan fighter known as "The Swamp Fox." Legend has it that British troops chasing Marion during the Revolutionary War watched him disappear into the swamp. After hours of slogging around through the muck, they couldn't find him. One of soldiers marveled, "That's a helluva hole." And so the area got its name as Hell Hole Swamp. (Had the soldier watched his tongue, the place might have become Heck Hole Swamp.)

While folks often refer to the towns of Jamestown, Huger, Bethera, and Shulerville as being set in Hell Hole Swamp, the name technically refers only to an area of the Francis Marion National Forest—2,000 acres of wilderness, uninhabited by anything but swamp critters. But Hell Hole Swamp is more than a physical locale—it's a mythical place, "its whereabouts always designated as 'just a piece down the road,'" as the 1941 WPA guide described it. Here, far from the eye of the law, and equipped with souped-up automobiles for racing over the crude dirt and mud roads to and from hidden stills, bootleggers ruled the swamp, churning out the Prohibition-era "liquid corn" that was not only tippled in the blind tigers of Charleston and on front porch stoops of Berkeley County, but was sold across the country.

Like today's drug lords, rival bootleggers battled over turf—two competitors shot it out on Moncks Corner's Main Street one day in 1926. Al Capone is said to have visited Hell Hole Swamp once, to check on the production end of his illegal whiskey empire. Sometimes illegal whiskey would also be brought up from Cuba, along the Santee River, and stored in Hell Hole Swamp until it was smuggled aboard trains bound for Chicago.

The Hell Hole brand of shine even advertised its low iodine content with the bold slogan "Not a Goiter in a Gallon." The moonshine industry continued strong even after FDR's revocation of Prohibition, providing cheap (because untaxed) and powerful intoxicants for the rural poor.

Mendel Rivers, St. Stephen–born chairman of the House Armed Services Committee, liked to boast that he was a member of the "Hell Hole Swamp Gang," a group of Berkeley County boys who had gone on to gain national or state political prominence, including Governor Robert E. McNair, State Senator Rembert Dennis, and Columbia Mayor Lester Bates.

Recently when local counties decided to pitch in and create a high school for students of St. Stephens and surrounding towns, one of the first names suggested (and quickly voted down) would have established Hell Hole High.

But the average folks around here (if not the average school board member) remain powerfully proud of the Hell Hole name. Each May, Jamestown holds the annual **Hell Hole Swamp Festival,** featuring a tobacco-spitting contest, 10K Gator Run, greased pole climb, snake and reptile show, parade, pig cook-off, beauty contest, softball tournament, and other events. Contact Jean E. Guerry, P.O. Box 176, Jamestown, SC 29453, tel. (843) 257-2234, for information.

General Francis Marion, "The Swamp Fox"

DOVER PUBLICATIONS, INC.

on the grounds), the land passed through a number of owners, including Henry and Clare Boothe Luce—respectively, the publisher of *Time* and *Life* and the former ambassador to the United Nations. In 1949, Clare donated the plantation to the Trappist Abbey of Gethsemani in Kentucky, best known as home of author Thomas Merton.

These days, life at the abbey follows a regular rhythm of meditation and scripture reading, communal prayer, periods of "grand silence," and times of physical labor.

The abbey's new church and gardens are open to visitors 9 a.m.-4:30 p.m. daily. No charge. All liturgical services are open to the public as well. If you're interesting in disappearing here for a few days, call (843) 761-8509 or see the monks online at www.mepkinabbey.org.

You'll find Mepkin Abbey south of Bonneau and 5.8 miles south of Hwy. 402 on Road 44.

St. Stephen

St. Stephen was the childhood home of the famed congressman Mendel Rivers (1905-70), who anchored a seat in the U.S. House of Representatives for 30 years and served as Chief of the House Armed Services Committee during Vietnam, bringing lots of taxpayer-funded goodies to his district (his slogan in the 1968 campaign was, fittingly, "Rivers Delivers!"). Not for nothing did the appreciative Naval Yard town of North Charleston, way back in 1948, name one of its main arteries "Rivers Avenue."

The two-mile stretch of road from the historic St. Stephen's Episcopal Church (which Rivers attended as a child) to the site of his childhood home on the road to Bonneau was renamed "Mendel Rivers Road" in 1964.

Though the death of his father caused Rivers' family to move to North Charleston before he reached his teen years, the Congressman always liked to boast about his membership in the "Hell Hole Swamp Gang," which consisted of politicians from rural Berkeley County who had gone on to statewide prominence: Rivers, Governor Robert McNair, State Senator Rembert Dennis, and Mayor Lester Bates of Columbia.

Jamestown

The area around Jamestown used to be known as the French Santee, since French Huguenots had settled hereabouts along the Santee River as far back as 1685, becoming wealthy quickly through their raising of indigo and rice. You'll pass the town hall on Hwy. 41 as you pass through. Nowadays, the chief attraction of the town is its placement in the midst of the 250,000-acre **Francis Marion National Forest,** rich in wildlife and in places to fish, paddle, bike, and hike. The 27-mile Swamp Fox National Recreation Trail, now part of the Palmetto Trail, runs through the forest. For information on the forest, call the National Forest Service's South Carolina office at (803) 561-4000.

About 90 people live hereabouts.

Each May, during the **Hell Hole Swamp Festival,** Jamestown swells like a week-old alligator carcass in the sun. The festival includes a snake and reptile show, various exhibits, a 10K "Gator Run," a greased pole climb, a parade, and the Miss Hell Hole Swamp beauty pageant. Call (843) 257-2234 for information.

AIKEN AND
HORSE COUNTRY
AIKEN

Aiken is a pretty town in the heart of South Carolina's thoroughbred-raising country. Years ago it was rated one of the best small towns in America. In 1997, it was selected as one of the U.S.A.'s top 10 "All-America Cities." That same year, both *Money* and *Golf* magazines listed it as one of the top 10 places to retire in the U.S.

Today, this town of 25,000 has little crime, great health care, award-winning schools, remarkable public recreation facilities, and plenty of upscale shopping. It has the largest municipal park—the 2,000-acre Hitchcock Woods—smack in the midst of town. It has exclusive streets still unpaved to make things nicer for the horses who often amble along them, and its famed Triple Crown races draw tens of thousands of spectators each year.

What Aiken has, in other words, is plenty of money, and plenty of people who can afford both the time and the funds to make certain it remains a nice place to live.

Climate

Weather is a bit cooler here than at the beach. In January, the average minimum temperature hovers at around 33° F, while the average high in July is a hot 91° F. The area receives about 50 inches of rainfall a year.

HISTORY

The story goes like this: In the late 1820s, Andrew Dexter, one of the engineers laying out the South Carolina Canal and Railroad line, became enamored of the daughter of a Captain W.W. Williams, who owned a plantation in the area where Aiken now stands. In order to win permission for Sarah's hand, Dexter had to redirect the railroad line to bring it past Williams' land (causing it to skyrocket in value). Despite the inferior nature of the soil in the area, Dexter thought enough of the superior nature of Sarah

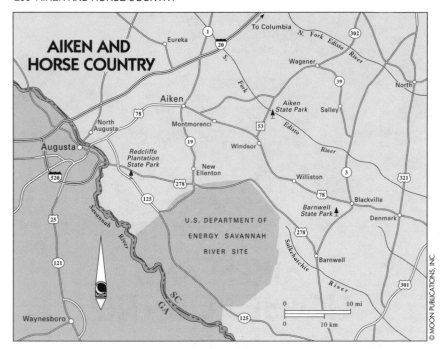

AIKEN AND HORSE COUNTRY

To Columbia

Eureka

Wagener

Aiken

Aiken State Park

Salley

North Augusta

Montmorenci

North

Augusta

Redcliffe Plantation State Park

New Ellenton

Windsor

Williston

Blackville

U.S. DEPARTMENT OF

ENERGY SAVANNAH

RIVER SITE

Barnwell State Park

Denmark

Barnwell

Waynesboro

Savannah River

SC

GA

0   10 mi

0   10 km

© MOON PUBLICATIONS, INC.

that soon he and co-engineer C.O. Pascalis were laying out a railroad town, named "Aiken" after William Aiken, the president of the railroad and father of the future governor of the state. The town was chartered in 1835.

Colonists had begun to settle Aiken even before the Revolution. Most of them were loyal to the king during the war, which made them unpopular with the rest of the state. At Dean Swamp in Aiken County, revolutionists attacked

---

AIKEN AND HORSE COUNTRY HIGHLIGHTS

- Aiken County Historical Museum
- Downtown Aiken
- Healing Springs (near Blackville)
- Hitchcock Woods
- Montmorenci Vineyards
- Redcliffe Plantation State Park

---

and killed a number of the Tories. After the war, George Washington passed through here on his 1791 Southern tour—on Two Notch Road—while traveling between Columbia and Augusta.

In the early 1800s, cotton became the staple crop in the area. Rather than send it eastward through the swamps to far-off Charleston, wagons carried the cotton to nearby Augusta, Georgia, just 20 miles away, where much of it was taken down the Savannah River to Savannah and shipped off to Europe. In an effort to reclaim this lost shipping revenue, William Aiken, one of South Carolina's leading cotton merchants, hired engineer Horatio Allen—later the designer of the Brooklyn Bridge—to build a railroad from Charleston to the town of Hamburg, forming on the South Carolina side of the Savannah River. Work began in Charleston in 1830, and on October 2, 1833, the first train rolled into the newly established town of Aiken, about 16 miles from Hamburg. The rails then continued on to the end of the Charleston-Hamburg line, at that time the longest railroad line in the world.

In 1845, William Gregg built a cotton mill and a workers' village about five miles west of town from granite in the Horse Creek Valley six miles from Aiken, and called it Graniteville. People moved into the Graniteville area to work the mill. At the same time, people from the Lowcountry had noticed Aiken's drier, cooler climate, and began to stay here in the summer to escape the malarial season. Noted Charleston poet James M. Legaré moved year-round into the house at 241 Laurens St. in the late 1840s, seeking a drier climate for his tuberculosis; he was able to survive another 10 years by doing so.

For most of the Civil War, Aiken's mills provided equipment for Confederate troops, and the rails running through town kept busy shipping materials and soldiers to wherever they were needed. In February 1865, Aiken was the site of the last Confederate victory of the War between the States when troops under General Joseph Wheeler held off a body of Sherman's troops sent out from conquered Savannah to destroy the mills at Graniteville. Much of the battle took place in the front yard of Chinaberry, the main

One of Aiken resident's James M. Legaré's best poems describes a (presumably African-American) boatman crossing from the Lowcountry woods for Charleston's Market, and turns this nature-to-marketplace transition into a picture of the compromises of manhood—specifically, the compromises of a poet forced to make a living by other means, concluding that the river's message to him is a reminder of man's post-Fall curse:

Oh son of toil, whose poet's heart
Grieves from thy quiet woods to part,
And yet whose birthright high it is, to labor
    in the mart,

To thee, a child, the bloom was sweet;
But manhood loves the crowded street,
And where-in closes, loud and clear, the forging
    hammers' beat.

But even there may bloom for thee
The blossoms childhood loved to see;
And in the cinder of thy toil, God's fairest
    flowers be.

plantation house owned by Captain W.W. Williams. One of the Union soldiers who died of wounds after that battle is buried beside the Baptist Church on Richland Ave.; you'll find many others of both armies buried in the Williams's cemetery on Grace Ave., just before Magnolia.

When the war was over, wealthy Northerners began to visit the region in the wintertime, building huge "cottages"—most with over 20 rooms, and some up to 90—to escape the cold northern winters. When these families began bringing down their strings of horses to ride through the woods, the city quickly became an equestrian center.

But the combination of wealthy, powerful Northerners, armed Union occupational forces, freed slaves, and disgruntled, hungry white Carolinians was an explosive one. Two bloody race riots occurred in Hamburg and nearby Ellenton. In 1876, rioting African-Americans burned down the Baptist Church on Aiken's Richland Avenue. Soon, former Confederate Army General Wade Hampton held rallies at Aiken's Kalmia Hill, beginning the Democrats' "Red Shirt Campaign" to wrest power back from the hands of the Republicans—mainly carpetbaggers and blacks—and put it back in white power.

Despite all the unpleasantness, by 1882 Northerners—known as the "Winter Colony" because they a) came in winter, and b) remained self-contained, rarely deigning to interact with the year-round residents other than those in their employ—had introduced the sport of polo to Aiken. In December of that year, a number of German astronomers attempting to see the transit of Venus between the sun and the earth came to town, fed up with cloudy German conditions. They remained in the city for six weeks, setting up their telescopes in the garden of the E.P. Anderson home at the corner of Laurens St. and Edgefield Ave., so that no passerby would jostle their lenses. Later, the German government built a marker in the garden to commemorate the successful observations.

But this is not to say that the colonists weren't interested in the community: by the early 1890s, the widow of Thomas Hitchcock—who had graciously donated the 2,000-acre Hitchcock Woods to the city—looked around at the needs of Aiken and decided that what the town really needed now was a boys' polo school. She founded one.

AIKEN'S HEROIC ABOLITIONIST EDUCATOR

The Schofield School was founded by Martha Schofield, a Pennsylvanian Quaker born in 1839, who had been raised on a farm that served as a station on the Underground Railroad. Her childhood included visits by such luminaries as Lucretia Mott and William Lloyd Garrison. After becoming a teacher in New York, she dedicated herself to a solitary life of service. When the Civil War broke out, she volunteered at a hospital.

In October of 1865, Martha's abolitionist leanings drew her to working for the Freedmen's Bureau. She was assigned to Wadmalaw Island north of Charleston. Here she taught some 1,500 blacks who had followed Sherman's army and been more or less dumped on the island. When President Andrew Johnson restored plantations to former owners, the Freedmen's Bureau was greatly weakened. Martha served at Edisto and John's Island, as well as Charleston.

Eventually, after a trip back north, she was assigned to Aiken, a hotbed of anti-Northern resentment. Nonetheless, Martha taught the African-Americans of the city and became popular among Aiken's blacks, working in conjunction with J.E. Hayne, pastor of the freedmen's Baptist church. Many of the wealthy Northerners wintering in Aiken would also deign to visit the school, and many contributed large sums of money to the school.

As the Quakers back home in Philadelphia became more interested in the plight of the American Indian, Martha scrambled to put together her own school, using inherited money, newly available state funds, and donations from those back home who still believed in what she was doing. She built a school in Oakwald, where she lived.

Before the war it had been illegal to educate blacks in South Carolina; now, Schofield knew it was imperative for blacks to become educated in order to compete in the postwar world. Though originally she'd wanted to train blacks to become teachers themselves, and thus exponentially speed up the education process, most of her students had to quit and return to work before they could graduate. Eventually Schofield added trade courses that would educate her students in the various trades in which they were likely to end up. She established programs at the Schofield Normal and Industrial School in shoe repair, printing, carpentry, chair caning, and blacksmith work, as well as in domestic duties.

Schofield was also involved in the Local Republican Club and took an active part in the fight for women's suffrage and the Women's Christian Temperance Union.

Today, though the Schofield School remains, the only original part of it built by this dedicated Northerner is a cupola on the school grounds.

In the 1890s the first holes to the Palmetto Golf Course were laid out, the Willcox Inn opened for those socialites who couldn't find friends with a spare room, and the Southern Railway passenger station was built. In 1897, Henry Dibble planted the oak trees you see today along South Boundary.

In the 1940s, the Savannah River Site was built south on 19 to produce nuclear weapons materials during the Cold War. Now that war is over but the plant keeps on, employing some 15,000 employees, a number of whom are employed at the Savannah River Site Defense Waste Processing Facility, trying to condense and stabilize the huge volume of radioactive waste by getting it into solid form. Of course, the end of the Cold War brought many sleepless nights to a lot of employees here; Westinghouse, which operates SRS for the U.S. Department of Energy, has actively sought out new ways to use the existing infrastructure and well-trained personnel.

Today, Aiken sees a $20 million annual economic impact from its horse industry and plans to increase its tourism base by improving the public landscape, building a new Visitor Reception Center, and an expanded arts district, all by 2010. Aiken even plans to host the Olympics in 2010—the Senior Olympics.

SIGHTS

Nearly all of Aiken's notorious "cottages" are still privately owned and off-limits to the public, but if you like big old mansions, this is a great town to walk about, guide in hand. Pick up the pamphlet *Presenting the Charm, Grace and El-*

egance of Aiken's Past at the chamber of commerce for an easy-to-follow map to the city's historical landmarks.

If the chamber is closed or you're short on time, I've provided a short listing of the city's highlights.

One old (circa 1900) mansion you can visit is **Rose Hill College,** recently—1996—converted into a classics-oriented Eastern Orthodox college after years as a retreat center. As of 1998, the student body counted 16. (No plans at present for a football program.) Before the 10,000-square-foot building and estate were donated to Owen and Julie Jones in 1991, they were owned by the Phelps family, an affluent brood from New Jersey.

You can also visit the enormous 1931 **Banksia,** 433 Newberry St., a 14,000-square-foot house off South Boundary, now the home of the **Aiken County Historical Museum,** tel. (803) 642-2015. The former estate of Richard Howe, Banksia also includes a circa 1808 log cabin and an 1890 schoolhouse on the grounds. The exhibits inside the museum include a small-town drugstore, Native American artifacts, and a 1,700-piece miniature circus. Hours are Tues.-Fri. 9:30 a.m.-4:30 p.m., weekends 2-5 p.m. Closed holidays. No admission charged, but donations appreciated.

The final old winter estate open to the public—at times—is the **Rye Patch,** 100 Berrie Rd., tel. (803) 642-7630, a circa 1905 winter home complete with stables and a tea cottage, adjacent to Hopeland Gardens on Whiskey Road. When the previous owner died, she deeded it to the city. Though there are no formal tours of the building on a regular basis, it is available to rent for meetings and celebrations. To view the collection of restored vintage carriages in the carriage house, make an appointment at the number above.

Hopeland Gardens is a 14-acre park on Whiskey Rd., the former home of a Mr. and Mrs. Iselin. Mrs. Iselin, who died a widow at 102 years of age, left her estate to the city in the hope that it would always be preserved. Eventually, the city removed the house and added a Touch and Scent Trail for the visually challenged. Open year-round, dawn to dusk.

Within Hopeland Gardens you'll find the **Thoroughbred Racing Hall of Fame,** at the corner of Dupree Place and Whiskey Rd., tel. (803) 642-7630. No admission charge. Set in what used to be the Iselin family's carriage house, since 1977 this building has contained displays commemorating stars of equestriana. The hall features a gallery of champion thoroughbred flat racers and steeplechase horses trained in Aiken from 1942 to today. Pleasant Colony, the 1981 Kentucky Derby winner, is among those so honored. If you're a horse racing fan, you won't want to miss the displays of racing silks, trophies, and numerous paintings and sculptures, all related to equestrian sports from polo to the steeplechase. Open Tues.-Sun. 2-5 p.m., October through May.

The Willcox Inn (Whiskey Rd. and Colleton Ave.), tel. (803) 649-1377, is a beautiful inn built in 1898 to service the Winter Colony guests. Though in its golden era the inn housed such luminaries as FDR and Winston Churchill, it closed down for some 40 years before it reopened in 1985. Known as the "Queen of Aiken," it's really worth taking a look. Better yet, you can actually sleep and eat here if you like (see below).

The 2,000-acre **Hitchcock Woods,** located smack in the center of Aiken, are supposedly the largest urban forest in the country, a 2,000-acre preserve of horse and hiking trails, and paths used by carriages. No bikes, and certainly no motorized vehicles permitted. You'll find a number of gates around the perimeter of the park, which closes at sunset (not that anyone who ever saw *Psycho* would want to visit a place called Hitchcock Woods at night anyway).

At 122 Laurens St. SW, you'll find the **Aiken Center for the Arts,** tel. (803) 641-9094, featuring monthly gallery exhibits by local, state, and regional artists, and hosting a variety of local artists and center members year-round. Open Wed.-Fri. 11 a.m.-5:30 p.m., and Saturday 10 a.m.-3 p.m.

The **Legaré-Morgan House** was begun in the late 1820s, when Charleston poet James M. Legaré moved into this town and this house to cure his tubercular lungs. Legaré lived another 10 years before succumbing to the disease and is buried in the graveyard of St. Thaddeus Episcopal Church at the corner of Richland and Pendleton.

Let's Pretend was a house owned by the novelist Gouveneur Morris, who here entertained such luminaries as Rudyard Kipling and Stephen Crane's old rival, Richard Harding Davis, and his wife, novelist Rebecca Harding Davis.

Of course, to truly experience Aiken, you'll want to visit some of the city's equestrian sites. The **Whitney Polo Field** on Mead Ave. features matches during the week and on Sunday afternoons. The weekday matches are free, the Sunday matches cost $2. If you just want to see some of the world's most promising thoroughbreds training to race and jump, head over to the **Aiken Training Track,** site of the annual Aiken Trials, on Two Notch Road; the Steeplechase Track, site of the **Aiken Hunt Meet** held in March; and the **Aiken Mile Track,** located on the 77-acre training center, which is actually three different tracks: a one-mile red clay track, a seven-eighths-mile all-weather track, and a half-mile clay track. You'll also find 150 stables and nine separate barns.

The Alley, off Richland Ave., is one of the most charming sections of this charming town. It features several fine restaurants and fun shops.

EVENTS

On the last weekend of February, some 10,000 people swarm into town for the **Battle of Aiken Reenactment,** held at Rivers Bridge State Park in Bamberg County. The event commemorates the Feb. 11-12, 1865, battle between Union and Confederate troops—the last Confederate victory of the war, when General Joseph Wheeler ambushed Sherman's advancing troops and stopped them from advancing west.

Aiken was once home to some 17 polo fields and was known by many as the "Polo Capital of the South," and even the "Polo Center of the World." While compared to its heyday, today finds Aiken with a comparative absence of mallets, **polo season** still comes twice annually to Aiken's five remaining polo fields: the spring season, from March to July, and the fall season, from September to Thanksgiving. Matches are held at Whitney Field off Hwy. 19 (Whiskey Rd.). You'll find club matches played here as well as medium goal tournaments. Sunday games are $2 a person, but there's no admission charge for games during the week. Call the Aiken Polo Club at (803) 643-3661 for information.

Each spring, the **Aiken Triple Crown Horse Races** extend over three consecutive weekends, normally the last three weekends in March,

drawing an average of 20,000 people to little Aiken. They provide viewers with the chance to watch three separate events. The first race is the Trials, held since 1942 on the Aiken Training Track, the first public viewing of some of the finest thoroughbreds in the world. The horses come here for an annual training in Aiken, and the Trials is something like the horses' debutante ball; two- and three-year-olds get to race for the first time under "full grandstand conditions," competing against each other in timed flat races. Nominal admission. Bring tail-gating goodies and join the crowds that always gather to picnic and party down in the parking lot before the races. The Steeplechase is run at Conger Field the following weekend, complete with a massive tent party. The final weekend features harness racing at the Aiken Mile Track.

You'd think all this excitement would tucker little Aiken out, but by the first week of May, Aikenites are at it again with the annual **Lobster Race and Oyster Parade.** In case you were wondering, this is the world's only known Running of the Lobsters. It's a great time, featuring the aforementioned race, live beach music, and the inevitable shagging, along with the seafood-themed Oyster Parade. Slip on a pair of claws and join the procession. Lots of gourmet and just regular food from booths set up by local restaurants. Jugglers, magicians, and kiddy rides entertain the shorter set. The festivities start on Friday and take place downtown.

Come to town during the second full weekend in September and join some 25,000 other people for **Aiken's Makin',** an annual celebration of Aikenite and Southern arts and crafts held in the downtown parkways. Lots of good food here, along with a juried arts and crafts show and live entertainment. Perhaps the most popular event is a race between the waiters and waitresses of the town's many restaurants.

If you find yourself in town on Thanksgiving Day, head to the Memorial Gate at the South Boundary entrance to Hitchcock Woods at 11 a.m. for the annual **Blessing of the Hounds.** The dogs, followed by some 50 horses and riders, take part in the ensuing drag hunt—the first of the season—in Hitchcock Woods. Trust me—unless the Gamecocks are playing, this is well worth pulling yourself away from the television for. Incidentally, an unconfirmed rumor has it that a less-publicized counter-ceremony, the Damning of the Hounds, is held simultaneously in the woods by area foxes.

From the second Saturday of December, through the fourth, Hopeland Gardens is transformed into a wonderland of holiday lights. Enjoy lighted walkways and holiday displays, and partake in the holiday refreshments, on many nights to the sound of live holiday concerts. The city offers tours of the Thoroughbred Racing Hall of Fame and Rye Patch, which also contains crafts displays on some nights. About 16,000 people manage to make this a part of their holiday season each year.

For information on any of the preceding events, contact the **Aiken Chamber of Commerce** at 400 Laurens St. NW, tel. (800) 542-4536 or (803) 641-1111, fax (803) 641-4174.

Tours

If you're here on a Saturday and can spare 90 minutes, head over to the Aiken Municipal Building in the Alley at 10 a.m. and take the air-conditioned guided bus tour ($5) sponsored by the City of Aiken Parks and Recreation Department and the Aiken Chamber of Commerce, tel. (803) 641-1111, which features stops and admission to Hopeland Gardens, the Thoroughbred Racing Hall of Fame, horse-training areas, and a lot of interesting stories concerning the many historic homes and assorted other structures. For a first-time visitor, it's a great way to get the lay of the land.

ACCOMMODATIONS

Hotels and Inns

Aiken is the perfect-sized town for anything from a weekend or weeklong stay. While you'll find a number of the chain lodgings north of town on I-20, unless it's a race weekend or other major event, you really ought to try to stay closer in to town. **The Holley Inn-Holley House,** at 235 Richland Ave. W, tel. (803) 648-4265, calls itself the "Center of the City, Capturing the Charm and Character of Old Aiken." And they have it just about right: this 1929 hotel enjoys a great location, just around the corner from the Aiken Brewery and a number of other restaurants, theaters, and shops, and featuring a courtyard garden

Built in 1898 and known as "The Queen of Aiken," the Willcox Inn counts among past guests Franklin Delano Roosevelt and Winston Churchill.

and swimming pool. Courtyard rooms, suites available. Continental breakfast comes with the room. The place had become run-down over the years, but the last few years have seen a fine renovation. Moderate.

Founded in 1898, the venerable, national registered historic **Willcox Inn,** 100 Colleton Ave. SW, tel. (800) 368-1047 or (803) 649-1377, e-mail: wersdl@connect.reach.net, is set in a wonderful old Second Empire/Colonial Revival building that offers you the chance to sleep where Winston Churchill, FDR, and Elizabeth Arden all once slept. Owned by the **Someplace Different** company, holders of 22 "distinctive inns, small hotels, and resorts" in the eastern U.S. and Canada, the Willcox goes full bore, with an elegant grand lobby, poster beds, decorative fireplaces, nightly turndown service, complimentary shoeshine, and the morning paper. Special packages include golf packages, gourmet dining tours, and honeymoon specials. A pub and the Pheasant Room restaurant are on the premises.

B&Bs

The Briar Patch, 544 Magnolia Ln. SE, tel. (803) 649-2010, is a good-looking two-story home offering two former tack rooms that have been converted to detached guest rooms. Each room features a private bath and fireplace. You'll enter the property along a gravel courtyard. The site includes a tennis court. Morning means continental breakfast, featuring pecan muffins. Children welcome, smoking allowed outdoors only. Inexpensive-Moderate. The **New Berry Inn,** 240 Newberry St. SW, tel. (803) 649-2935, is a Dutch Colonial-style home decorated with antiques. Four rooms here, children allowed at hosts' discretion. Smoking allowed outdoors only. Inexpensive-Moderate.

Motels
On the cheaper end of the scale, you'll find **Comfort Inn and Suites,** 3608 Richland Ave. W, tel. (803) 641-1100, with 68 rooms. Inexpensive. **Days Inn Downtown,** 1204 Richland Ave. W, tel. (803) 649-5524, (there's another up by I-20) runs just a little less than Comfort Inn.

FOOD

Barbecue
At long last, you'll find a **Duke's BBQ** in Aiken, what used to be Whiskey Road Bar-B-Q, 4248 Whiskey Rd., tel. (803) 649-7675 (649-PORK). Here you'll find a ketchup-based sauce and a big buffet, with lots of vegetables. Open 11 a.m.- 9 p.m., Thurs.-Sat. only. Or dial (803) 649-OINK and speak to the good folks at **Hog Heaven Bar-B-Que,** 1050 York St., NE. Featuring a mustard-based sauce in addition to three tomato-based sauces of various temperatures, Hog Heaven is open Wednesday as well as Thurs.- Sat., 11:30 a.m.-8:30 p.m. each day. It features a buffet, but carryout is available.

Other Restaurants
For some great Italian cuisine and a peaceful outdoor setting, visit **Olive Oils,** 233 Chesterfield St., tel. (803) 649-5817. Open for dinner only, 5-10 p.m.

If you'd like to dine in a warm, historic setting— in this case, four dining rooms, each with fireplaces, inside the former home of noted poet James M. Legaré—try **No. 10 Downing St.,** 241 Laurens St., tel. (803) 642-9062. A bakery serves up goodies 10 a.m.-6 p.m. Lunch is served Tues.- Sat. 11:30 a.m.-2:30 p.m., dinner 6-9:30 p.m.

If another meal rolls around and you're still feeling historical, head over to the **Willcox Inn,** 100 Colleton Ave. SW, tel. (803) 649-1377. You'll find a pub here and a fine restaurant.

For something more formal, try **Up Your Alley,** 222 The Alley, tel. (803) 649-2603, featuring meat dinners—steaks, lamb chops, filet mignon—for around $20 and seafood and fowl dishes for somewhat less. Up Your Alley also has a lounge.

Pubs
A warm, friendly spot downtown—and the city's only microbrewery—is Mark Findlay and Dan Beavers' **Aiken Brewing Company Grill and Bar,** 140 Laurens St. SW, tel. (803) 502-0707, fax (803) 502-0407, where the specialties are the homemade brews, the ale-braised baby-back ribs ($13.95 for a whole rack), and the wings ($5.25 a dozen). The bartender, Randy, knows his beer—as well he should, since he heads up the local home brewers' group in his spare time and has personally designed many of the pub's popular brews, which include a Sierra Nevada-like Aiken (Pale) Ale, the zestier Thoroughbred Red, and a fine Oatmeal Stout.

If the ground floor of the brewery seems too crowded, head back outside and turn left. The first door you'll come to on your left leads to a second dining room and bar, where you can order everything you can get downstairs. Karaoke up here a couple nights a week.

Another spot to grab a meal and or a drink is **The West Side Bowery,** 151 Bee Ln., tel. (803) 648-2900, where dinners run anywhere from $6 for a bleu-cheese burger to $15 for calf's liver. Come 5-6:30 p.m. for early-bird specials, including a prime rib dinner for $8.95. The Bowery has been here since 1981, back when Reagan was still learning his way around the White House, and the Alley was just, well, an alley. The Bowery, which has grown from a small friendly pub to a large friendly restaurant, now features two dining rooms, named Clay Court and Tulip Garden for the former occupants, Southeastern Clay Co. and Holland Architects. Best of all, if weather permits, you can enjoy eating outside in a fenced courtyard—one of the more pleasant spots in a very pleasant downtown.

Coffeehouses
If you're thinking more about coffee than about a full meal, consider **The New Moon Cafe,** 116 Laurens St., tel. (803) 643-7088, specializing in

gourmet coffee, espressos, cappuccinos, mochas, lattes, and a bunch of other words that you didn't hear much in these parts until just recently. The milk shakes ($2.50)—including a blueberry and a chocolate chip—are delicious. Breakfast includes toast, bagels, muffins, "humungus" cinnamon buns with icing, and fruit bowls. Lunch starts at $2 for a bowl of soup; various sandwiches on your choice of good bread start around $5. Try the Cajun roast turkey on spring herb bread with Swiss cheese and a side of the red potato salad and some brown mustard. Or the turkey special, with bacon and sun-dried tomato cream cheese. New Moon is open Mon.-Wed. 7 a.m.-5 p.m., Thurs.-Fri. 7 a.m.-10 p.m., Saturday 8 a.m.-10 p.m., and serves Sunday brunch 9 a.m.-2 p.m.

Another spot for coffee is **Mud and Stogies,** on The Alley, a coffeehouse that encourages the combination of caffeine and carcinogens, along with desserts that wouldn't make your doctor happy either. But at least while your cardiopulmonary system goes to heck in a handbasket, you'll have fun in this relaxed establishment. Open late nights for dessert and (more) coffee.

SHOPPING

Art Galleries

You'll find a number of artists' galleries in Aiken. The place to start is the **Aiken Center for the Arts,** 122 Laurens St. SW, tel. (803) 641-9094, where in addition to the gallery of local art for sale you'll find monthly gallery exhibits by local, state, and regional artists, and variety of local artists and center members year-round. Open Wed.-Fri. 11 a.m.-5:30 p.m., Saturday 10 a.m.-3 p.m. Next door you'll find **The Garret Fine Framing and Prints,** 116 E. Laurens St. SW, tel. (803) 641-9094. Down the street you'll find the **Artists'**

Parlor, 126 Laurens St. NW, tel. (803) 648-4639. Or head north and a block west on Richland Ave. to visit the **Arnold Gallery,** 321 Richland Ave. W, tel. (803) 502-1100, or another block farther south to Hayne Ave. and the **Art Works Studio,** 337 Hayne Ave. SW, tel. (803) 643-8335.

Antique Stores

With all the fine old mansions—er, "cottages"—around, you had better believe that the buying and selling of antiques is a major occupation in Aiken. You'll find the **Aiken Antique Mall,** 112-114 Laurens St. SW, tel. (803) 648-6700, and **Sanford-Oakes Ltd.,** 146 Laurens St. SW, tel. (803) 641-1168, a block from each other on Laurens Street. South of town on Hwy. 278 you'll find the quaint **Memory Lane,** 2483 Williston Rd., tel. (803) 652-3096, which offers a lot of antique advertising collectibles, furniture, pottery, and toys. Neat location and interesting collection, but it's open odd hours during the week—it's better to call first. On the weekend, it's almost always open Saturday 10 a.m.-5 p.m. **Market Place Antique Mall,** 343 Park Ave. SW, tel. (803) 648-9696, hosts some 48 dealers who offer used and rare books, furniture, various collectibles. **York Cottage Antiques,** 409 Hayne Ave., tel. (803) 642-9524, and the **Swan Antique Mall,** east of town on Hwy. 1, 3557 Richland Ave. W, tel. (803) 643-9922, are also worth a browse.

INFORMATION

The **Aiken Chamber of Commerce** can provide plenty of information to help you fill out your itinerary. Contact the chamber at P.O. Box 892, Aiken, SC 29802, tel. (800) 542-4536 or (803) 641-1111, fax (803) 641-4174, or Web site: city.aiken.net

BEYOND AIKEN

EAST AND SOUTHEAST

Montmorenci

Down Hwy. 78 in the tiny town of Montmorenci, once known for its asparagus fields, you'll find the family-owned, award-winning **Montmorenci Winery,** one of only two South Carolina wineries presently open for business. Winemaker Robert E. Scott Jr. and family open up the tasting rooms Wed.-Sat. 10 a.m.-6 p.m., closed major holidays and the first two weeks of January. They feature over a dozen varieties of whites and reds, from the dry, drinkable Savannah White to the fruity Triple Crown Blush. Call (803) 649-4870 for information on tours and winetasting. Here you'll also find the delightful **Annie's Inn Bed and Breakfast,** Hwy. 78, five miles south of Aiken, tel. (803) 649-6836, fax (803) 642-6709, set in a home built in the 1830s as the main house on a 2,000-acre cotton plantation. Originally built as a three-story building, a Civil War cannonball courtesy of General Sherman rendered a quick renovation—today it's two stories.

Each of the good-sized rooms comes with pine plank floors, a fireplace, and a private bath. The motif here is country: rocking chairs on wraparound porches, wood-burning stove, rooms decorated in country antiques, quilts. Concessions to the post-WW II era include a swimming pool, telephones, and televisions. Full breakfasts served in the dining room or kitchen each morning. No pets. Annie's also offers two guest cottages for rent by the week. Moderate-Expensive.

Aiken State Park

Get to Aiken State Park, about 16 miles east of Aiken, by heading down Hwy. 78 until you come to the tiny town of **Windsor,** then follow the brown signs north onto State Park Road. Before long, you'll see signs for the park on your left, at 1145 State Park Rd., tel. (803) 649-2857. The park contains four spring-fed lakes and the black South Edisto River, a fine river to fish and canoe. There are just 25 campsites in this 1,067-acre park, so you know there's lots of undeveloped land. You can rent canoes here and fishing

boats. Hiking trails, picnic areas, playground for the kids. Unlike most South Carolina state parks, this one has no lake swimming. It's open year-round, April-Sept. 9 a.m.-9 p.m., Oct.-March 9 a.m.-6 p.m. Office hours for the rangers are 11 a.m.-noon—that's when you'll want to call to make your reservations.

Wagener

From Aiken State Park, Hwy. 53 leads north to Kitchings Mill, from which Hwy. 302 takes you nine miles farther to this small town of just over 1,200 people. Once called Pinder Town, and later Gunter's Cross Roads, the town was renamed for George Wagener, a Charleston merchant largely responsible for bringing the railroad to the area. On Earle St. in Wagener you'll find the **Wagener Museum** in an old jail, interpreting the history of the area. Open Sunday 1-4 p.m. or by appointment. For an appointment, call Mr. Leister at (803) 564-3520 or Wagener Town Hall at (803) 564-3412.

Salley

About 10 miles southeast of Wagener along Hwy. 39 you'll find this little town. In 1735 Henry Salley received the land where Salley now stands in a grant from King George II himself. The town of Johnston stood here before the Civil War, but Sherman's troops—apparently overestimating the microburg's threat to the safety of the Union—burnt nearly all of it down. Salley was founded under its current name by Captain Dempsey Hammond Salley in 1887, the same year it became a whistle-stop on the railroad.

In town you'll see **Salley Town Hall** on Railroad Ave., housed in the former 1887 train depot. Over at 218 Pine St., you'll find the **Salley Old School Museum,** housing Salley family memorabilia dating back to the 1730s, as well as Sardis Baptist Church Black History. Open by appointment only. Call (803) 258-3230 or (803) 258-3321.

About 1.2 miles west of Salley, on Hwy. 394 at Rd. 52, you'll find a **memorial** to the Battle of John Town, fought here May 4, 1782. In the battle, Carolinian Revolutionists bent on defending the British and Tory prisoners they were keeping in two bull pens fended off the attack of a superior body of Tory troops.

Increasingly since the mid-1960s, Salley has been much better known for its annual odoriferous **Chitlin' Strut,** held annually the Saturday after Thanksgiving. This one-of-a-kind event features a parade, hog-calling contests, live music, arts and crafts, and all the fried chitlins you can eat. It also features the strut, a contest held each year.

For information on the Chitlin' Strut, call Peggy Yon over at the Salley Town Hall, tel. (803) 258-3485.

Blackville

Head south on Hwy. 39 and then Hwy. 3 to find this tiny town. Named for Alexander Black, an early railroad executive, Blackville boasts some good-looking old buildings such as the brick 1910 **Shamrock Hotel,** in the 300 block of Main Street. If it hasn't reopened by the time you pass through, it surely will be open before long—it's a crime to keep fine old buildings like these boarded up.

Beside the Healing Springs north of town off Hwy. 3 N, you'll find the **1772 Healing Springs Baptist Church.** In this area you'll also find a number of Mennonite families who settled here in the early '60s, from other parts of the country. A Mennonite school, church, and many Mennonite farms stand close to Healing Springs.

At 202 Solomon Blatt Ave. in Blackville, you'll come across the neat little **Depot Library,** formerly the town's train depot, moved over here onto the old high school campus. The library also contains a small museum. Incidentally, the

---

BLACKVILLE'S HEALING SPRINGS~ TRULY GOD'S PROPERTY

North of Blackville off Hwy. 3 N, look for the signs leading to Healing Springs. These springs had long been noted by local Native Americans for their curative powers. During the Revolution, a company of British troops returning to Charles Town from the battle of Slaughter Field in 1781 left six wounded soldiers here beside the spring. The two least-injured soldiers were ordered to wait until the other four had died from their clearly mortal wounds, bury them, and then head back to Charles Town. Half a year later, all six of the men reappeared in Charleston.

Native Americans had revealed their secret healing springs to an Irish trader shortly before the wounded soldiers came to drink and heal. Which, supposedly, they did at an alarming rate. Many local citizens believe in the power of the springs, and you may well see folks showing up with jugs and bottles in which to take home some of the water. Apparently this is all right with the owner. That would be God himself, who has legally owned the springs and the acre plot around them since they were deeded to him by L.P. "Lute" Boylston in 1944. Boylston didn't want anyone buying the spring and closing it off to the public, and now it's legally impossible for anyone to do so.

The downside of this is that God doesn't keep up the yard the way some folks would like. And since no mortals are responsible—or legally allowed—to perform maintenance . . . Well, you can see the problem. The Barnwell Historical Society, which would like to "improve" the lot, is attempting to step in and become the legal guardians of "God's Little Acre." What the courts—both human and otherwise—have to say about this remains to be seen.

railroad bed you see passing through town is the railroad bed of the "Best Friend of Charleston," the name of the train that ran on the Charleston-Hamburg railroad line—the first commercial railroad in America and the longest commercial line in the world at that time.

Two miles west of Blackville on Hwy. 78, you'll come across the new Clemson University-run **Edisto Research Center,** tel. (803) 284-3343, which includes a museum with exhibits on the historical and cultural influences of agriculture on the area, an interactive learning facility focusing on the past and on the future, and a visitors information stop along the South Carolina Heritage Corridor. Open by appointment only.

About 3.3 miles south of town on Hwy. 3, you'll come across beautiful 307-acre **Barnwell State Park,** tel. (803) 284-2212, a popular place for picnicking and camping. Like most of the state parks, Barnwell has a lake with a designated swimming area and boat rentals. You can also rent one of the five cabins here for $40 a night, $120 a weekend, or $240 a week, or camp at one of the 25 campsites for $10 a night. Call ahead for reservations, especially for the cabins.

Miller's Bread Basket, 322 Main St., is owned by a Mennonite and is locally—and nationally, since the folks from *Good Morning America* paid them a visit—famous for its hot pastries, fresh-baked bread, and home-cooked meals. Next door, you'll find a shop selling Mennonite crafts and quilts.

Right on Hwy. 78 you'll notice the town's only public lodging, **Miss Lillian's Bed and Breakfast,** tel. (803) 284-4710, fax (803) 284-4815. Miss Lillian keeps five rooms in what used to be the manor house of an 8,000-acre plantation. Each room comes with air-conditioning, television, and in-room phones.

Denmark

Eight miles east of Blackville along Hwy. 78 is another child of the Charleston-Hamburg railroad—this small town, established back in 1837 as Graham's Turnout, later simply Graham, and finally Denmark, after the president of a construction company. Denmark's claim to fame is that it is the home of artist **Jim Harrison,** whose rural-themed paintings are popular throughout the region. He has a gallery here that's worth a visit.

Denmark's other claim to fame is as home to the historically black **Voorhees College,** a fully accredited four-year liberal arts college founded in 1897 by African-American teacher Elizabeth Wright as Denmark Industrial School but later renamed after local resident Ralph Voorhees, who donated 400 acres of land and provided for the construction of the first school buildings. The 1940 WPA guide reported, "Officials of the school assert that no graduate has ever been on relief."

BARNWELL

From Denmark, double back on Hwy. 70 about 15 miles southwest to reach Barnwell. This is the birthplace and early childhood home of the troubled R&B legend and Rock and Roll Hall of Fame inductee Reverend James Brown, "The Godfather of Soul." But you'd never know it—there's nothing in town to commemorate the fact. This quiet county seat of 5,600 set amongst the swamps and pine forests of Barnwell County was settled by Virginians who moved down and founded the community as Red Hill. It was renamed for Colonel John Barnwell, an Irish Carolina settler who had traveled to London as an agent for the colony in trying to persuade the Lords of Trade to pay for a string of forts to prevent against the encroachments of the Spanish and French. Though the lords shared Barnwell's concern, they were only willing to spring for a

> *I was a stillborn kid. . . . When I appeared, they did all the usual things, gave me the usual spanking, all that, but I didn't respond. . . . After a while, they just laid me aside. . . . While Aunt Estelle tried to comfort my father, Aunt Minnie picked me up and started blowing breath in me. She just wouldn't give up. She patted me and breathed into my mouth and rubbed my back. Just about the time my father busted out crying, I did too.*
>
> *He waited until he was sure I was all right, and then he walked nine miles into Barnwell to record my birth: May 3, 1933.*
>
> —James Brown,
> James Brown: Godfather of Soul, 1986

> We lived in a series of shacks all around the Barnwell and Elko areas. . . . The shacks were unpainted, didn't have windows except for shutters that you could pull together; and there was no electricity or indoor plumbing. . . .
>
> Being alone in the woods like that, spending nights in a cabin with nobody else there, not having anybody to talk to, worked a change in me that stayed with me from then on: It gave me my own mind. No matter what came my way after that—prison, personal problems, government harassment—I had the ability to fall back on myself.
>
> —James Brown,
> James Brown: Godfather of Soul, 1986

fort at the mouth of the Altamaha River, which Barnwell himself was put in charge of constructing in 1721. The fort, Fort King George, was garrisoned for the next 15 years against Spanish encroachment.

Some 144 years later, after wading through the three-mile swamp of the Salkehatchie, Union troops under General Kilpatrick—one part of Sherman's army—flanked the Confederate brigade guarding Rivers' Bridge two miles south of Barnwell. Legend has it that as the city burned that night, the Union soldiers decided they wanted to celebrate, and with musicians playing and confiscated spirits flowing, the Yankees began to eye the local women. At this point, according to the WPA account, "When General Kilpatrick invited the Barnwell ladies to dance, they took the invitation as a command. Proud and unsmiling, they went through the figures while their homes burned."

If you've come into town on Hwy. 278/Jefferson St., you'll come smack upon Barnwell's pretty **Courthouse Square.** Be sure to see the town's claim to fame—the **vertical sundial,** in front of the courthouse. Captain Joseph D. Allen of Barnwell had this sundial made in Charleston and presented it to his hometown in 1828. Since then, this timepiece has kept accurate standard time—even though it was erected two years before standard time was even established. Though they burnt the county courthouse, Sherman's troops left the sundial intact—they apparently weren't here to kill time. Despite the

sundial's stellar record of dependability, however, word has it this is the only vertical sundial left in the nation.

Incidentally, the story on the good Captain Allen is that he was, well, a bit eccentric, and had a special fetish for monuments. When his parents died, they each received ornate treatments in stone. When his childhood nanny died, she too was memorialized with a stone marker. He believed that everybody must get stones—he even left his mark on his dog's grave. But the Civil War ruined Allen financially, and when he died he was buried in an unmarked plot.

Behind the sundial stands the **Barnwell County Courthouse,** built after Reconstruction in 1878. It succeeds several earlier buildings here, including the one that Sherman's troops burned in 1865.

The **Bethlehem Baptist Church,** on Wall St., is one of the handful of pre-Emancipation churches organized by and for African-Americans. It was built in 1829 by a white congregation, then donated to African-American Baptists in 1860. The building you see today is an 1889 reconstruction that used much of the original materials.

The Church of the Holy Apostles, over on Hagood Ave. at Burr St., was built in 1856 from local cypress wood to serve the Episcopalians of the area. The England-born Reverend Edwin Wagner himself donated the medieval stone baptismal font from Europe for their christenings. In 1865, when General Sherman and his acolytes came to town for their firelight procession, the parishioners buried the church's stained-glass windows to protect them from the troops. But Holy Apostles was spared from burning, because the Yanks decided to use the big church as a stable for their horses. The huge medieval stone baptismal font from Europe was used as a watering trough for the animals.

Out in the church's graveyard you'll see the inscription of William Gilmore Simms Jr., namesake son of the novelist and a distinguished soldier, lawyer, and community pillar in his own right. Note, too, the grave of Congressman James O.H. Patterson near that of Charlotte, his family's loyal slave, and the grave of South Carolina Congressman Solomon Blatt. Here too lies Confederate general and later governor (1880-82) Johnson Hagood, for whom Hagood Ave. is named. The story goes that when Hagood was asked whether he preferred to be called "General" or "Governor," he answered, "Call me 'General.' I fought for that and begged for the other."

Barnwell was a fairly wealthy town before the Civil War, an important commercial center for the Midlands plantations. As such, it was surveyed for inclusion on the original South Carolina railroad, but the local plantation owners refused to grant the railroad right of way—they were worried that the noise would disturb the peace and the train would run over their slaves and livestock.

Nonetheless, despite its inland location, Barnwell has often been noted as a town that looks more Lowcountry than Upcountry. The **Banksia Hall,** 2108 Reynolds Rd., is a good example of the sort of buildings that give the town this reputation. During Reconstruction, this building served as headquarters for the local federal occupation forces. In the drawing room, all Southern white men had to take an oath of allegiance to the U.S. government before being allowed to regain their rights as citizens.

Iris Hill, the circa 1815 home on Perry St., was owned by Lewis O'Bannon, who laid out the town of Barnwell and named its original streets. Over on Academy St., you'll see the **Old Barnwell Presbyterian Church,** now the **Circle Theatre.** When Union soldiers burned the county courthouse in 1865, the Presbyterian Church served in its place. These days, the Circle Theatre presents a half-dozen events here annually. If you'll be in the area overnight, call (803) 259-7046 for performance information.

The **Barnwell County Museum,** at Hagood and Marlboro Ave., tel. (803) 259-1916, is a good little local museum, with displays on the history of—what else?—Barnwell County. No admission charged. Open Tues.-Thurs. 3:30-5:30 p.m., Sunday 3-5:30 p.m.

Practicalities

If you're going to spend the night here in town, try the **Days Inn,** 1020 Dunbarton Blvd. (Hwy. 78), tel. (803) 266-7001. For food, you might enjoy **Ballard's Cafe,** 1618 Main St., tel. (803) 259-1245, right there on the circle, or **The Winton Inn** at 1003 Marlborough Ave., tel. (803) 259-7181, featuring prime rib and a good seafood buffet on Thursday, Friday, and Saturday.

SAVANNAH RIVER SITE ENVIRONMENTAL RESEARCH PARK

In the 1940s, the Savannah River Site was built to produce nuclear weapons materials during the Cold War. Though that war is over, the plant keeps on, employing some 15,000 people. A number of these work at the Savannah River Site Defense Waste Processing Facility, trying to condense and stabilize the huge volume of radioactive waste by getting it into solid form.

But all is not lead canisters and half-lives. Though the U.S. Department of Energy oversees the Savannah River Site, the U.S. Forestry Service's Savannah River Forest Station oversees the forest management program for SRS's 198,000 acres. You can arrange a group tour with the Forest Service by calling Wilma Marine at (803) 725-8718, fax (803) 725-1807.

On-site, too, the Savannah River Site Ecology Lab conducts ecological research—which I suspect involves counting a lot of extra toes on alligators. Call Dr. Whit Gibbons at (843) 725-2752, fax (843) 725-3309 to book a group tour with him.

New Ellenton, population 2,500, is what they call the town of Ellenton since they had to move it back in the 1950s to make room for SRS. The "old" Ellenton was the site of a bloody race riot on May 15, 1876, when, in a time when severe political antagonisms exacerbated racial tensions, a mob of armed blacks came to defend two black men arrested for beating a white woman. In the melee that ensued, 15 blacks—one of them Simon Coker, a Barnwell County legislator—and two whites were killed.

WEST OF AIKEN

At Hwy. 278, about two miles below Beech Island, at the entrance to Redcliffe Plantation State Park, you'll see **All Saints Episcopal Church.** The building was constructed in 1836 for the nine-year-old Beech Island Presbyterian Church, pastored first by a Rev. Nathan H. Hoyt from Vermont. Hoyt's son-in-law, Rev. Edward Axson, also served here. Axson's daughter, Ellen Axson, was baptized here. In 1885, she went on to marry another preacher's kid from Columbia— Woodrow Wilson—and eventually became first lady of the United States. She died in 1914, while Wilson was still president.

The church was rechristened as All Saints in 1950.

Redcliffe Plantation State Park
Located about seven miles southeast of North Augusta on Hwy. 278, Redcliffe Plantation State Park, 181 Redcliffe Rd., Beech Island, tel. (803) 827-1473, is the former home of Governor James Henry Hammond, credited with popularizing the phrase, "Cotton is King." The plantation was last owned by John S. Billings, great-grandson of Hammond and former editor of Time-Life publications. The grounds include hiking, fishing, and picnicking. Admission to the grounds is free; they're open Thurs.-Mon. 9 a.m.-6 p.m. Touring the house, open Thurs.-Sat. and Monday 10 a.m.-3 p.m., Sunday noon-3 p.m., costs a nominal fee.

North Augusta
North Augusta sits across the river from its namesake, Augusta, Georgia. North Augusta is a relatively new city, founded by brothers Walter and James Jackson in 1906 as a resort town on the trolley line between Augusta and Aiken. However, the railroad/port town of Hamburg stood near here in the early 1800s, and a number of pre-1900 homes remain in the area, including the circa-1790 **Charles Hammond House,** 908 W. Martintown Road. Next door you'll find a family cemetery featuring a granite pyramid honoring the Hammonds' contributions to the fight for American Independence. The home was put on the Register of Historic Places back in 1973.

Farther west along Martintown Rd. you'll pass **Elm Grove,** a large home with six chimneys and fronted by what are said to be the first Spanish cork oaks brought to the New World. This land was originally granted to the Hammonds before the Revolution by King George III; Major Andrew Hammond built the home here in 1840.

Another interesting historic spot is **John C. Calhoun Park** at the intersection of Georgia and Carolina Avenues. Here, in addition to a monument to North Augusta's war victims, you'll also find a monument to the victims of the Riot of Hamburg on July 8, 1876.

The Godfather of Soul, James Brown, lives here. So does Frank Wills, one of the security guards who foiled the Watergate burglars, touching off the scandal that led to the fall of President Richard Nixon in 1974.

If you're looking for a place to stay, consider **Rosemary Hall** and **Lookaway Hall,** both at 804 Carolina Ave., tel. (800) 531-5578 or (803) 278-6222, a restored pair of remarkable old antebellum mansions holding 23 rooms combined. Expensive-Luxury ($125-250).

Across the Savannah: Augusta Proper
Augusta is Georgia's second-oldest city, a classic Southern river town featuring tree-lined streets, regal antebellum homes, and calming views of the mighty Savannah River. The **Riverwalk** is a celebrated pedestrian mall with a plaza of restaurants and specialty shops.

What Augusta is most famous for, however, is hosting the annual **Masters Tournament,** the famed golf tournament that draws the world's best golfers—and most avid golf fans—to the city. The day after the tournament, Columbia-based band Hootie and the Blowfish hosts its own golf tournament, Hootie after the Masters, with proceeds going to charity.

SOME NOTED CATAWBAS: KING HASLER GEN NEW-RIVER GEN AYERS GEN JIM KEGG COL DAVID HARRIS MAJOR JOHN JOE GAP BILLY GEORGE LIEUT PHILLIP KEGG SALLIE NEW-RIVER POLLIE AYERS PETER HARRIS THE LATTER BEING MADE AN ORPHAN BY THE SMALL POX SCOURGE WAS RAISED BY KANAHWA HE RECEIVED A PENSION FOR SERVICES IN THE REVOLUTION OF 1776 AT 70 YEARS OF AGE. HE DIED AT THE SPRATT'S HOMESTEAD AND AT HIS OWN REQUEST WAS BURIED IN THE FAMILY GRAVE YARD

YORK COUNTY AND THE OLD ENGLISH DISTRICT

Someone in the South Carolina Department of Tourism cooked up the label "Olde English District" to describe the seven-county area fanning out from Charlotte as far south as Camden (which I've included in the Columbia chapter for its geographic proximity to the capital), as far west as Kings Mountain National Military Park, and as far east as Cheraw—Dizzy Gillespie's old stomping grounds (olde stompeing groundes?). Like Camden, Cheraw (less than 30 miles from Darlington in the Pee Dee) is covered in the Columbia chapter.

In truth, back when those who used the king's English tagged on the extra "e," this region would have been rightly called the Brand-Spanking New English District—or perhaps the Olde Native American District. Today the name fits well enough—this part of the upstate was, after all, settled during British Colonial days, and stood (Camden being a notable exception) as a Tory stronghold during much of the Revolution. It's a fitting name for a cohesive region, even if I

move the tourism department's boundaries just a bit, and jettison that bloody *e*.

HISTORY

The Catawbas lived in this region when the Spanish explorers first arrived; DeSoto, who cut through this part of South Carolina during his 1540 expedition up from Florida, reported meeting a people called "Esaws" or "Eswau"; the Catawba originally called themselves Ye Iswa, meaning "River People." The current name, "Catawba," seems not to have developed until after the arrival of the Europeans; since no Siouan word sounds like this, the meaning of "Catawba" remains a mystery. During the Yamassee War of 1715, the Catawba fought alongside the colonists against the Tuscarora (1711) and the hated Cherokee (1760s), with whom they often battled over mountain lands. After the ravages of the Yamassee War, the relatively isolated Catawbas offered sanctuary to other Native American groups like the Waxhaws, Wateree, Sarahs, and Sugaree, devastated by war and disease and unable to fend off assimilation into Carolinian culture any longer on their own. Some 30 different Native American groups ended up joining with the Catawba.

The Catawba realized quickly that to continue to survive, and to prosper, the tribe would have to make the British their allies. When the Revolution came, they fought on the side of the Carolina patriots (the Cherokee fought with the loyalists).

As with the Upcountry proper, the Old English District was resettled by British-Scotch-Irish-French religious independents (which is to say, non-Anglicans) during the 18th century. In fact, these folks seem to have been generally cantankerous out of sheer principle; many of those who chose to settle in the Old English District drifted down here dissatisfied with life in Pennsylvania; consequently towns like York, Chester, and Lancaster honor the Penn State towns the disgruntled

farmers had left behind and, apparently, began to miss immediately once they arrived here. They worked hard to scratch a living from their small red-dirt farms. Ever conscious of the Lowcountry's condescending monopolization of Colonial politics, they kept to themselves and remained loyal to the royal government that had allowed them to come here in the first place.

Pitting the Factions

In fact, the British army actually counted on the Upcountry/Lowcountry rivalry as an important part of its Revolutionary War strategy. By getting the loyalist upstaters to keep the Lowcountry patriots in check, the British would have enough trained British troops to march north and engage Washington. All seemed to go well; the first major battles in South Carolina were in truth a sort of Civil War as Carolinian fought Carolinian, with only a handful of British officers on the field. Then a certain British colonel slipped up.

The first thing that made the erstwhile loyalists blink was when General Henry Clinton sent

Colonel Banastre Tarleton after Colonel Buford, who had brought a body of Virginia patriots with the intention of defending Charles Town, but had turned back as soon as he realized they had arrived too late. Tarleton gave chase and caught up with them on May 29, 1780, near Lancaster. The Americans were told to surrender and refused. The British attacked with fury. Realizing quickly that they had no chance of escape, the Americans finally threw down their arms and begged for quarter. But the enraged British refused to hear them, butchering the unarmed Americans. Of 350 men, only 30 escaped capture, wounding, or death. For the rest of the war, Southern patriots would charge to the cry of "Tarleton's quarter!" which meant, "Let's kill every last one of them."

Another mistake the British made was in harassing the invalid wife and burning the Stateburg home of a rather inconsequential colonel named Thomas Sumter. In his fury at this outrage, "The Gamecock" became one of the fiercest and most devastating guerrilla leaders of the war. The combined efforts of guerrilla leaders Sumter, Andrew Pickens, and Francis Marion greatly interrupted supply lines and weakened British troop strength and morale. Defeats at King's Mountain and Cowpens made it clear to the British that the South could not be won.

With the loss of the South, the British knew they could never muster enough troops to capture all of the colonies. When it became apparent they couldn't win, they cashed in their fish and chips and went home.

Reconstruction Racism

Though English settlers had lived in these part since the 1700s, Rock Hill was settled as a rail-

> We lived in a log house during the Ku Klux days. They would watch you just like a chicken rooster watching for a worm. At night, we was scared to have a light. They would come around with the dough faces on and peer in the windows and open the door. If you didn't look out, they would scare you half to death. John Good, a darky blacksmith, used to shoe the horses for the Ku Klux. He would mark the horseshoes with a bent nail or something like that; then after a raid, he could go out in the road and see if a certain horse had been rode; so he began to tell on the Klu Klux. As soon as the Ku Klux found out they was being give away, they suspicioned John. They went to him and made him tell how he knew who they was. They kept him in hiding, and when he told his tricks, they killed him.
>
> —Brawley Gilmore of Union, South Carolina, as reported by Caldwell Sims

road textile town in 1852. During the Civil War, towns like York and Chester served as refuges for Lowcountry whites—Mary Boykin Chesnut spent time in Chester. After the war, whites disgusted with Reconstruction-era political corruption and incensed by the presence of black militia began making night raids as local members of the Ku Klux Klan.

When the federal government passed the Ku Klux Klan Act and decided to prosecute South Carolinian Klan members as an example to those in other states, Dr. Rufus Bratton of York, a KKK leader, escaped from federal troops and fled to Canada. The U.S. sent operatives into Canada to kidnap him and bring him back to stand trial. In 1904, Thomas Dixon based part of his novel, *The Clansman,* on the incident, setting much of the action in the York County village of Sharon. The novel served as the basis for D.W. Griffith's groundbreaking movie *The Birth of a Nation.*

Common Culture

Despite the racial fireworks in the area during Reconstruction, the Old English District never had anything like the percentage of black residents found in the Lowcountry. Even into the 1900s, one of the most notable aspects of the

---

YORK COUNTY AND OLD ENGLISH COUNTRY HIGHLIGHTS

- Chester Historic District
- Historic Brattonsville
- Kings Mountain National Military Park
- Paramount's Carowinds (Fort Mill)
- York Historic District

area was its homogeneity. Though the cotton boll weevil may have driven the small farmer into the textile mills, that farmer still shared the same culture. In 1948, Lancaster's Elliott White Springs described the average Old English mill worker thus:

Two-hundred and fifty-six have been with the company twenty-five years or more. Ninety-nine and forty-four one-hundredths per cent of the textile employees are great-great-grandchildren of American citizens, the majority of whom came to Lancaster, Pennsylvania about 1720 from Scotland via North Ireland, and joined with the Lutherans from Bavaria to come South between 1740 and 1770.

They fought with Braddock on the Monongahela; they killed Ferguson at Kings Mountain; they went with their Cousin Andrew Jackson to New Orleans; they went to Mexico for Cousin James K. Polk; they flung the gauntlet at Cousin Abe Lincoln, and they refused to be reconstructed by Cousin Andrew Johnson; they joined their North Carolina and Tennessee cousins in the Thirtieth Division to break the Hindenburg Line; they saddled Halsey's white horse at Tokyo; and they are ready to take on Joe Stalin or any one else who attempts to exploit them. Every spinner could be a Colonial Dame, a D.A.R. or a U.D.C. if she wished.

They have never since lived anywhere but Lancaster, York, and Chester Counties, and each family still owns a farm, and expects to return to it when wages go down and cotton goes up.

Today, the largest city in the Old English region is Rock Hill, 47,000 and growing, growing, growing as Charlotte, North Carolina, overflows her suburbs, spilling BMWs and cell phones into York County. Nearly all the towns up here—Rock Hill, Fort Mill, York ("The Charleston of the Upcountry"), Chester, Camden, and Cheraw—boast lively, renovated brick downtowns with antique stores, gourmet coffee, and horse-drawn carriagefuls of ambience.

ROCK HILL

Established in 1852 as a railway stop between Charlotte and Columbia, and named after the hill of flinty white rock encountered by Charlotte, Columbia, and Augusta Railroad workers, Rock Hill quickly attracted farmers who shipped their produce and cotton to the big cities on the railroad, and counted about 250 residents by the end of the Civil War. As the Industrial Revolution began revolting, locals built water-turned mills to process the area's cotton; before long, the impoverished small farmers who swarmed upstate to fill the mill jobs swelled the town's population to over 5,500. Downtown Rock Hill sprouted handsome brick business blocks.

Things stayed pretty much status quo until the 1960s, when the business-minded community briefly became center stage for the Civil Rights Movement. In 1961, nine black Friendship College students took seats at McCrory's (now Vantell Variety, on Main St.) whites-only lunch counter and refused to leave. When police arrested them, the students were given the choice

civil rights battleground: the interior of Vantell Variety, in Rock Hill

THE ANDERSON~
THE CAR OF THE SOUTH

The Anderson car was created by Rock Hill's John Gary Anderson, owner of the Rock Hill Buggy Company, largest buggy manufacturer in the Southeast. With the growing popularity of the horseless carriage, Anderson shrewdly decided to create his own vehicle—a deluxe automobile on a par with his renowned buggies. Designed by a New York engineer, the Anderson deluxe model cost around $1,600—about five times the price of Ford's basic black Model T. Advertising with the slogan "A Little Higher in Price, But—Made in Dixie," Anderson sold over 6,000 cars throughout the country beginning in 1916 (with a production break during WW I). Eventually, the company also introduced the Anderson Light Six—a less expensive model.

Andersons were built of ash and oak logged from Anderson's own forests and covered with light aluminum. Propelled by powerful six-cylinder engines, the cars could reach up to 50 mph. Unfortunately, by 1925 the company had ceased production and gone bankrupt. In 1939, a warehouse fire burned all but 13 of the remaining cars, as well as all the car parts and company records.

Consequently, it's not too often you'll have the chance to see an honest-to-goodness Anderson. The one on view in the Federal Building in Rock Hill is on loan from the Museum of York County. You can see another one down at the State Museum in Columbia.

The Anderson automobile from Rock Hill: "A Little Higher In Price, But—Made in Dixie"

of paying $200 fines or serving 30 days of hard labor in the York County jail. The "Friendship Nine" chose the latter, becoming the first sit-in protesters of the Civil Rights Movement to suffer imprisonment.

As the '60s progressed, supermarkets, suburbs, and shopping malls drained the life of Rock Hill's downtown, just as they did across the country. The city took action and blocked off a two-block area of Main St. to vehicular traffic, creating a pedestrian mall. Unfortunately, as happened to many such efforts in other cities (Eugene, Oregon, for example), the pedestrian mall ended up becoming an economic dead spot; downtown continued to spiral. By the 1990s, the city reopened the "mall" to traffic, and—along with other redevelopment efforts—this breathed life back into the district. Today downtown Rock Hill still has a way to go, but good signs—old buildings under refurbishment—abound. As with York and Fort Mill, Rock Hill is attracting people who are transferring to Charlotte from other large cities but who refuse to get stuck in another big urban area. Some—though not all—of these folks truly appreciate these small towns for the slower, smaller way of life they offer, and they—more so, in some cases, than the lifetime residents—are making efforts to preserve and to some degree, restore, traditional Upcountry living to these towns.

Downtown

Rock Hill's downtown district, though not as old as many in the state, is still a nice place to walk around and get the feel for the town that is, and the town that was.

The first place to stop is the **York County Visitors Center/Tom S. Gettys Center,** 201 E. Main St., tel. (800) 866-5200 or (803) 329-5200, where you'll find helpful staff and pamphlets galore. Hours are Mon.-Fri. 9 a.m.-5 p.m., Saturday 10 a.m.-4 p.m., Sunday 1-4 p.m. Look for the blue flyer *Strolling through Historic Downtown Rock Hill, South Carolina.* You'll want this for your walk. If the center's closed or out of maps, here's a shortened version:

Start out at the **Center for the Arts Building,** 121 E. Main St., tel. (803) 328-2787. Set in a building completed in 1900, formerly home to a furniture company and dry goods store, Rock Hill's Center for the Arts opened in 1996 with a housing office, classroom, and artist studio spaces for local artisans. The Dalton Gallery, which features local, regional, and national artists, opens to the public for viewing Mon.-Fri. 9 a.m.-5 p.m. Which is sort of curious, since these hours effectively keep the average employed Rock Hillian from ever seeing the inside of the gallery.

As you stand outside the arts center, facing Main, turn left and walk past the **Peoples Building,** circa 1909, a former bank, and then (still on your left) on into **Vantell Variety,** 135 E. Main St., tel. (803) 327-0545. You'll find a lunch counter on your right; go in, sit down at the counter, and order yourself a soda or malt. Enjoy your drink. Linger awhile. And then reflect: For doing exactly the same thing, nine black Friendship College students were dragged off to jail in 1961.

McCrory's sold out a few years ago, and the folks who now own the diner seem like nice people. One of the family was manning the grill when I visited; he said they're always having magazine and newspaper reporters come down to photograph the famous lunch counter.

When you've finished your soda, head back outside (pay your bill first), turning left again. You'll pass the 1908 Lyric Building and the 1925 Professional Center, now the Citizens Bank. At 154 E. Main St., across the street, you'll find **Central Newsstand and Bookstore,** one of those essential small-town newsstands (with a surprisingly good selection of magazines) where, if you listen hard enough, you can hear the rush of the town's lifeblood as it pumps through the building. You'll also find a cooler of drinks here with—most importantly—*three* varieties of South Carolina's own Blenheim Ginger Ale.

Cross Caldwell St. and you'll come to the **Tom S. Gettys Center,** 201 E. Main St., circa 1931, at the corner of Main and Caldwell. Once the central post office in town, the Federal Building at 201 E. Main St., tel. (800) 866-5200 or (803) 329-5200, currently houses the **How We Got Here From There** exhibit.

It's more interesting than it sounds, since the exhibit includes Indian dugout canoes used on the Catawba River, a covered wagon, buggy, and, perhaps most fascinating, a genuine Anderson automobile, built here in Rock Hill. Open Mon.-Fri. 10 a.m.-5 p.m., Saturday 10 a.m.-4 p.m., Sunday 1-4 p.m.

Next door, at 215 E. Main, you'll see the 1920 **First Baptist Church,** and across Oakland St. is the large **Guardian Building** at 223 E. Main St., originally built in 1926 as the Andrew Jackson Hotel. The spot has hosted countless community receptions and dances in its second-floor ballroom over the years. Now turn left on Oakland. Halfway down the block, you'll pass the 1906 U.S. Post Office building on your right. St. John's Methodist Church, a good-looking brick building completed in 1924, is home to the area's oldest organized church body (1856). Next come two other venerable old churches: on your left, **The Episcopal Church of Our Savior,** built in 1872 and featuring some excellent stained glass; and to your right across White Street, the **First Associate Reformed Presbyterian Church** (1897). Turn right on White St. and then right again on Elizabeth Ln. to see **The White House,** at 258 E. White Street. Built in the 1830s, it's one of the oldest homes in the city; it served as a shelter for Lowcountry Carolinians fleeing General Sherman.

Now make your way back down to Main St., turn right., and head back to your car. Before you drive off to wherever you're going, head over to White St., turn left, and cross Dave Lyle Boulevard. On your right, you'll see the 1881 **Rock Hill Cotton Factory,** the first steam textile mill in South Carolina, still in use today.

Winthrop University

You can enter the Winthrop campus from Oakland Avenue. Founded in 1886 as the South Carolina Normal School for Women down in Columbia, the school transferred up to this beautiful shaded brick Georgian campus in 1895. The campus is now a registered U.S. Department of the Interior Historical District, with 5,000 men and women attending. The Winthrop Galleries, in the Rutledge Building and McLaurin Hall, exhibit work by children, Winthrop students, and local and national artists. And, of course, the Departments of Music, and Theatre and Dance perform regularly throughout the year.

The Winthrop Chapel used to stand in Columbia, where it began as a carriage house at the Robert Mills House, and in the 1870s it was used as the student chapel for Columbia Seminary, where young Thomas Woodrow Wilson's father taught. Tommy Wilson worshipped between these walls, and here became a member of the Presbyterian church. In 1886, Winthrop College was founded in the same old carriage house. Winthrop moved to Rock Hill in 1895, and years later, Winthrop alumni paid to have the building disassembled and moved up here.

To find out what's going on at the university, call the Arts Hotline, tel. (803) 323-3000. To set up a campus tour, call (803) 323-2211.

Glencairn Garden

Dr. David and Hazel Bigger began what is now Glencairn Garden when they planted a few azaleas they'd received as a gift. One thing led to another, and by 1940, the garden had grown so large and so beautiful that the Biggers decided to share it with the public. They named it Glencairn Garden in honor of the good doctor's Scottish heritage. Eighteen years later, after Dr. Bigger died (there were apparently no little Biggers), Mrs. Bigger deeded Glencairn to the City of Rock Hill.

Today, Glencairn Garden contains a beautiful fountain, a Japanese footbridge, winding trails, a tiered fountain, and year-round blooms. For the very peak bloom season, the garden keepers recommend a visit from the last week of March through mid-April when you'll likely see blooming azaleas, tulips, pansies, dogwood, periwinkle, wisteria, and other flowers and shrubs. Come in summer for the crepe myrtle, Kwanzan and Yoshino cherry, and various annuals. Fall brings sassanqua and an annual pansy. Winter brings the camellia, Bradford pear, daffodil, and winter honeysuckle.

To get to Glencairn Garden, head along Charlotte Ave. until you reach Edgemont. Open dawn to dusk, every day of the year.

The Rock Hill Telephone Company Museum

If you have an insatiable curiosity about things in general, or if you just find the subject of telephones and telephone repairs fascinating, then you might want to pay a brief visit here. What makes this place nifty is the work that's gone into some of the displays; clearly, the folks at RHTC are proud of what they do. Lots of interactive displays: use an original magneto telephone to call a friend, or try out an old pay phone in a mockup of a 1930s hotel lobby. At 117 Elk Ave., tel. (803) 324-4030, the museum is open Monday, Wednesday, Friday, and Saturday 10 a.m.-2 p.m.

Museum of York County

This surprising, offbeat (and off-the-beaten-path) little museum, at 4621 Mt. Gallant Rd., tel. (803) 329-2121, exhibits the largest collection of mounted African mammals anywhere in the world, featuring life-like dioramas to show what the animals looked like when they were alive and in their native environments. The museum also contains African artifacts, three changing art galleries with work by regional and national artists, and the Vernon Grant Gallery, a permanent exhibit of the Rock Hill artist/illustrator who designed spokes-elves Snap, Crackle, and Pop for Kellogg's Rice Krispies cereal. To get here from downtown Rock Hill, follow the signs: take Hwy. 274 northwest to Mt. Gallant Road. Head east until you come to Museum Road. Admission $2 adult, $1 seniors, students. Children under 5 free. York County residents half price. Open Tues.-Sat. 10 a.m.-5 p.m., Sunday 1-5 p.m. Closed on major holidays.

Cherry Park

At 1466 Cherry Rd., this landscaped 68-acre park features playgrounds, picnic areas, and a huge statue of Casey, title character of Thayer's famous baseball poem, "Casey at the Bat." Many community picnics take place here, and local softball teams battle it out in the summertime.

Golf

The **Crystal Lakes Golf Center,** 195 Crystal Ln., tel. (803) 327-3231, is a nine-hole lighted course; **Pinetuck Golf Course,** 2578 Tuckaway Rd., tel. (803) 327-1141, offers 18 holes.

Shopping

Up here in textile country, it's no surprise that you can find some good bargains on things made out of cloth. Rock Hill features two outlet stores: **Plej's Textile Mill Outlet,** 215 Chatham Ave., tel. (803) 328-5797, where you can find household linens and window treatments, and **Rock Hill Factory Outlet,** at the intersection of Oakland Ave. and Cherry Rd., tel. (803) 327-7276, which features women's apparel.

If all these old homes have put you in the mood for antique shopping, Rock Hill won't disappoint. Mary Ann Walker's **Vintage Antiques and Collectibles** does business over at 137 E. White St., tel. (803) 329-0866, specializing in pre-Depression furniture and home decorations; another specialty is Depression glass. At **Furniture Plus,** 104 S. Oakland Ave., tel. (803) 324-1855, Jack Lee specializes in estate items.

Lodging

Over by Winthrop University, **The Book & the Spindle,** 626 Oakland Ave., tel. (803) 328-1913, is a brick Georgian home overlooking the campus. You can choose between two rooms and two suites here; all boast private baths, cable TV, and coffeemakers; suites include kitchens and a patio. By reservation only, so call ahead.

East Main Guest House, 347 Park Ave., tel. (803) 366-1161, is set in a renovated circa 1900 Craftsman home in the historic district. Hosts Melba and Jerry Peterson, who oversaw the renovation of the property in 1990, now offer three upstairs rooms. The Honeymoon Suite and the East Bedroom both contain fireplaces and connecting private baths. The bright, airy Garden Room contains twin beds, a private bath, and a view of the back garden. Breakfast is served downstairs in the dining room—or under the patio arbor, weather permitting—and normally includes fresh-baked muffins and breads. Come evening, it's wine and cheese in the parlor.

Camping

You'll find a number of sites at **Ebenezer Park,** 4490 Boatshore Rd., tel. (803) 366-6620. **Chester State Park,** tel. (803) 385-2680, has 25 shaded sites, all with electricity and water hookups.

Food

Jackson's Cafeteria, 1735 Heckle Blvd., tel. (803) 366-6860, serves basic, though better-than-average, cafeteria-style grub; it's been here forever and is really part of the downtown scene. Another good spot downtown for basic American standards is **Watkins Grill,** 123 Elk Ave., tel. (803) 327-4923, a lunch counter with old photos on the walls. Take a peek to see the Rock Hill of yesterday.

For something more upscale, and certainly dimmer, try another old favorite, **Tam's Tavern,** 1027 W. Oakland Ave., tel. (803) 329-2226. Tam's serves grilled chicken, burgers, sandwiches, and casseroles for lunch Mon.-Sat. 11 a.m.-3 p.m., and fresh seafood, meats, and pasta for dinner Mon.-Sat. 5-10 p.m. A strong wine list. If you're looking for something with a little zest to it, try **Tropical Escape Cafe,** 590 N. Anderson Rd., Hwy. 21 Bypass, tel. (803) 366-3888, where the cooks serve up Filipino and Chinese foods along with broiled seafood and American dishes. Or head over to the town's best Mexican restaurant, **El Caribe,** 886 S. Anderson Rd., tel. (803) 985-7272.

Coffee

For fancy coffee, try **D.C. Stickies,** 113 E. Main St., Suite 10, tel. (803) 366-0423.

FORT MILL

Fort Mill is one of the towns that the Charlotte/Rock Hill urban sprawl will someday likely swallow up, but for now the community of 5,931 retains its small-town ambience. The name comes from the town's location: it once stood between a British fort and a grist mill on Steele Creek. Though the fort, built to protect Catawba women and children when Catawba men were off warring with the Cherokees, and the mill have disappeared, Fort Mill continues, now as home of Springs Industries, one of the country's largest textile manufacturers.

Of course, if the name "Fort Mill" is familiar to you, you may remember the town as the former home of Jim and Tammy Bakker's famed **Heritage** amusement park and resort complex. Bakker and Bakker have long since lost the park. Members of their PTL ministry sought Jerry Falwell's help to keep the ship afloat, and the park reopened briefly as New Heritage USA before folding again. A couple years later, the Radisson Corporation reopened the park and resort, but this only lasted a few years before folding. When I was last in Fort Mill, the big news was that four new players had bid on the old Heritage properties. All four deals have since fallen through, and at press time the acreage's future was still uncertain.

Downtown

Fort Mill still has a nice downtown, which includes little **Confederate Park,** home to a Confederate monument, and a very interesting monument to the Catawba Nation. After the initial Indian attacks of the Yamassee War, the Catawbas switched sides and helped save the lives of many Back Country Carolinians. The monument also pays tribute to the number of Catawbas who served as Confederate soldiers and officers.

At 205 White St. you'll see the **Founders House,** the refurbished Victorian home of Captain Samuel E. White, now used by Springs Industries as a guest home for visiting business guests. On Hwy. 160 stands the two-story brick Georgian home of William Elliott White, where President Jefferson Davis of the Confederate States of America held a final cabinet meeting after the fall of Richmond at the end of the War between the States. Davis had spent the previous night at **Springfield** (on Hwy. 21, 2.5 miles north of town), a graceful old frame home now employed as center of operations for the Springs Company. Call (803) 547-1000 for tour information.

AAA Baseball

The **Charlotte Knights** play in Fort Mill at, appropriately, "The Castle," a very fine stadium on 2280 Deerfield Dr., tel. (803) 548-8050. The Knights, a AAA farm team for the Florida Marlins, battle such International League nemeses as the Richmond Braves, Syracuse Sky Chiefs, and Toledo Mud Hens. The season runs from April through early September; if the Knights are in town when you are, try catching a game. Most games start Mon.-Sat. 7 p.m., Sunday 2 p.m. Thursday nights are "Thirsty Thursday," offering half-price draft beer and $1 soft drinks. Sunday is Kids Day, with attractions for the younger set, but at any home game the kids will probably light up when they see Homer the Dragon, mascot for the team.

Christian Epics

Once the main outdoor stage at Jim and Tammy Faye Bakker's theme park Heritage USA, **Kings Arena,** tel. (888) 437-7473 or (803) 802-2300, e-mail: NarroWay@FMTC.net, is now owned by NarroWay Productions. This non-Bakker-affiliated group produces various Christian musical dramas based on the life of Jesus—huge epics fea-

turing live camels, horses, and huge casts. These are reenactments of the Christ story by people who believe that no other chain of events in history has carried such import. They're a unique, non-threatening way to learn more about how most South Carolinians understand the universe. Tickets run about $12 for adults, less for children.

Golf

Fort Mill Golf Course, 101 Country Club Dr., tel. (803) 547-2044, offers 18 holes. Over at the old Bakker/Radisson place you'll find **Regent Park Golf Club,** tel. (803) 547-1300, on Hwy. 21, and **Regent Park Practice Complex,** tel. (803) 802-2053, a 25-acre lighted facility including practice tees, putting green, chipping area, and on-site golf instruction.

Lodging

Whether or not you plan on visiting Carowinds, you might as well benefit from the flood of budget lodging and dining options that have accompanied it. The **Comfort Inn** right at I-77 and Carowinds Boulevard, 3725 Ave. of the Carolinas, tel. (803) 548-5200, offers 153 rooms and suites. You'll find it right at the entrance to Carowinds, and right beside the Outlet Marketplace, in case you feel like shopping. **Holiday Inn Express,** located more or less across from Carowinds, at the point where Ave. of the Carolinas tees into Carowinds Blvd., 3560 Lakemont Blvd., tel. (803) 548-0100, is clean, and fancier than you'd think it would be. And right next door you'll see **Sleep Inn,** 3540 Lakemont Blvd., tel. (803) 547-2300. It's only a few years old; a safe bet for a good night's sleep.

Steer clear of the Days Inn-Carowinds: it's too far out from anything worth seeing, the service I received was marginal at best, and the on-the-property restaurant is now closed down. The rooms were the poorest I've seen in the chain. Days Inn has many fine properties, but this is not one of them.

Camping

An intriguing place to stay is **Lakeside Lodges,** I-77 Exit 88 and Gold Hill Rd., half a mile west at 940 Gold Hill Rd., which not so long ago was known as the New Heritage USA Campground. Lakeside, tel. (803) 547-3505, has 127 sites. A stay at **Lazy Daze Campground,** over on Gold

Hill Rd., tel. (803) 548-1148, is camping South Carolina-style, which is to say that when you pay for your site (full hookups) you're also paying for a pool, recreation director, miniature golf, game room, and so on. A good place to stay with the family. **Paramount's Carowinds Campground** at 3900 Ave. of the Carolinas, tel. (704) 588-3363 or (800) 888-4FUN, will get you closest to the park itself; this part they have got right, with a nice, wooded campground, tent sites, RV sites with full hookups, private showers, a "trading post," and a swimming pool.

PARAMOUNT'S CAROWINDS

On the I-77, this 83-acre theme park, tel. (800) 888-4FUN (4386), is more conceptually interesting than your average Six Flags. Straddling the North Carolina-South Carolina border so that you'll spend the day crisscrossing from North to South and then back again, the park

The worthy wooden Hurler is the centerpiece of the Wayne's World section of Paramount's Carowinds theme park.

was originally designed to celebrate the history and culture of the Carolinas, with "lands" named Plantation Square, Carolina RFD, Blue Ridge Junction, and so forth.

Then Paramount, the movie company, moved in, bringing along Scooby Doo, the Flintstone's dog Dino, a host of other Hanna Barberra characters, and a prerecorded music soundtrack (piped throughout the park via hidden speakers) composed entirely of Muzak versions of movie themes. When Wayne's World opened up, it was the first land specifically dedicated to a Paramount movie.

Carowinds also includes a water park, featuring water slides, a wave pool, wading pools for little ones, and even a volleyball court. Not a bad idea on a hot day—be sure to pack a swimsuit, or wear one beneath your clothes. Your admission ticket to the park allows you to use the water park as well.

Some local boosters might tell you that Carowinds is a lot like Disneyland and Disney World, but it's a lot closer to a Six Flags than anything else—more an amusement park than a true "theme" park. At a *theme* park, you need to have some effective theming, not just to separate the inside of the park from the outside world, but to separate the individual themed "lands" within the park from one another. If you've left Tomorrowland for Frontierland, there had better be no mistaking it.

But here at Carowinds, despite the atmospheric names given to different regions of the park, the planners spend little effort or money to make you feel that you're anywhere but at an amusement park. It's easy to step from Wayne's World (supposedly suburban Aurora, Illinois, in the late 1980s) to Blue Ridge Junction and not know you've switched lands.

There's very little to do at parks like this if you're not standing in line, riding a ride, or watching a show, but Carowinds holds one major plus over Six Flags: while Paramount hasn't put much time or money into making the queue areas themselves (where, after all, you spend most of your time) interesting parts of their attractions (as Disney does on most of its newer rides), at least Paramount doesn't follow the lead of Six Flags Over Georgia and have music videos blaring in those areas. At the end of a day at Six

Flags over Georgia, you feel as if you've spent 10 hours watching MTV.

What Carowinds *does* have is a bang-up selection of thrill rides. Here are the best the park has to offer:

The Hurler: Set in Wayne's World—a great name for the ride. The video playing in the boarding station features Mike Myers and Dana Carvey in their roles of Wayne and Garth. This is about as heavily themed as Paramount gets; it adds to the ride and certainly makes the last part of the queue area a lot more fun. The ride itself is a hurtle down an unpainted wooden roller coaster. It *moves.*

Thunder Road: Another fine wooden roller coaster, featuring a gutwrenching first drop. The first seat's a good one, but so is the back. Very, very shaky. Put your head against the headrest if you can, or bring aspirin. You can choose between trains that ride forward, and those that ride backward. While the latter may sound more daring, a lot of people find that without being able to see where you're going, all the tantalizing anticipation of drops evaporates. If you're only riding once, go forward.

Carolina Cyclone: This is a good, fast, violent metal coaster that makes the most out of its ride time and does a good job exploiting the possibilities of metal tracks: a nice first drop into two 90-degree loops, then a hard right into a corkscrew, before a big round-up and a final fling into the station. At the end you'll feel so abused you'll be tempted to slap the ride operator.

Vortex: This usually has the biggest line; it's a stand-up coaster, which, according to the commercials, is supposed to make it scarier. But while standing up in a sit-down coaster *is* scary (and stupid), the way you're locked in here, it's more like taking a ride while clapped in the village stocks. The other problem I have with this breed of coaster is that if you aren't in the front row, the view never changes. And by the way, stocks or no stocks, you're not really standing—there's a bike-seat thing jammed up into your crotch to keep you from squatting down and out of your overhead shoulder restraint. At best, instead of a "standing coaster," they should call this a "coaster with your legs straight under you." Some people swear by this one, but I don't get it. Imagine being in a van you can drive standing up versus a sleek sports car in which you have to slide your legs way forward. Now which vehicle do you think would make the quicker, sharper turns? But if the line's short enough, by all means squat aboard and judge for yourself.

Drop Zone: Hop into a chair and get jerked several stories into the air. Then plummet to the ground, slowing just in time to keep from running up Paramount's liability rates. If you're afraid of elevators, this will either cure you or send you into therapy. My favorite moment is that few seconds when the seat carriage stops at the top, all of Carowinds beneath you, the wind in your hair, waiting for the little click that means you're about to plunge back to Earth. Yes, it's very basic and as subtle as a hurricane. But it's a heck of a lot cheaper than skydiving, and you don't have to remember to pull any cords.

Rip Roaring Rapids: This ride isn't scary one bit, certainly not compared to a true Level IV or above whitewater rafting trip. But it's fun: bumping along in a big wheel of a raft, feeling like a number on a roulette wheel as you face the other members of the boat at the center as the boat spins this way and that, bouncing off each artificial rock. Some people get drenched, with a bathtubful of water pouring onto their laps, while others leave the ride relatively dry. That's what makes this a fun ride for me—especially if I'm with a crowd of friends, and it's warm, and I'm not wearing white pants.

Carolina Goldrusher: This is just a basic runaway train-type roller coaster, with no big drops but a lot of fast turns as you whoosh around the side of a hill, pines and bridge beams flying past—essentially like watching an old Burt Reynolds chase scene in 3-D. A great ride for those who like a little thrill but aren't quite sure if they're ready for the Hurler and Thunder Road.

Powder Keg Flume: Carowinds' flume ride is a step above those "what-you-see-is-what-you-get" flume rides you sometimes find at third- and fourth-rate parks, where the ride essentially consists of a loading area, a lift, and a drop, the latter two connected by about 50 feet of flume track with no theming. Powder Keg Flume (technically, not a *log* ride—you're riding in mock wooden barrels) gives you a bit of a ride up there at the top; winding about in the flume amongst the tops of the pines, you can almost forget for a moment and think you're up in the mountains somewhere. Well, for a few seconds, anyway. Then it's down the final drop with you. Another good one to ride if it's hot—maybe not such a great idea if it's chilly.

When it comes to food, I'm afraid, the best advice is eat outside the park, if possible. You'll see a gas station on your right just as you begin to head onto the Paramount property; it includes a Blimpie's restaurant at the food mart. That's as good a place as any to stock up on sandwiches at a much more reasonable price than you'll find after you pay $30 a person to get into the park.

Usually, when I go to a Disney park, I'm surprised by how decent the food is, and how reasonably priced it is—compared to what they *could* charge if they wanted to. Well, I'm afraid that Carowinds food *is* that poor, and that overpriced. By all means, eat up before you get here. If you *must* eat in the park—and the food lines can get dreadfully Soviet-esque—then try the Subway, just to the left of the Plantation Entrance.

CLOVER

Tiny Clover has no antebellum homes—it was founded in 1874 as a railroad town, though the area had been used as a "preaching point" for itinerant Presbyterian ministers long before that. You'll find some antique shops here on the old main street. Every spring, the town celebrates **Feis Chlobhair, A Clover Kinntra Gatherin'**, a festival honoring the town's Scottish-Irish heritage with music, games, and food.

KINGS MOUNTAIN STATE AND NATIONAL MILITARY PARKS

On this rugged mountain in October 1780, a band of Appalachian pioneers—including Joseph Crockett, David's father—surprised the left wing of Lord Cornwallis' army and changed the course of the American Revolution.

Before the battle, British Commander Lord Charles Cornwallis, fresh from a victory at Camden, was geared up to invade North Carolina. The defeat at King's Mountain turned popular sentiment against the British, thwarting British hopes of arousing loyalist support in the Carolinas and forcing Cornwallis to split his forces—half to hole up in Charleston and keep an eye on Southern malcontents, and half to march up-

ward toward Washington, Yorktown, and defeat. A film at the visitors center and a 1.5-mile self-guided battlefield trail help to sketch in the rest of the tale. Limited camping; the adjacent Kings Mountain State Park offers more. Kings Mountain National Military Park is near Blacksburg on Hwy. 216, between Hwy. 161 and I-85, 12 miles northwest of York, tel. (864) 936-7921, fax (864) 936-9897. Off I-85, take North Carolina Exit 2. Open daily 9 a.m.-5 p.m. Labor Day to Memorial Day, daily 9 a.m.-6 p.m. Memorial Day to Labor Day. Closed Thanksgiving Day, Christmas Day, New Year's Day.

YORK

The county seat of York County, York (pop. 7,610) is nicknamed both the "White Rose City" and "The Charleston of the Upcountry." A good place to stop when you get downtown is **The Historical Center of York County,** 212 E. Jefferson St., tel. (803) 684-7262, fax (803) 684-7262.

York Historic District
To start off your tour of this 340-acre historic district, one of the largest in the country, and the second-largest in the state, after Charleston's, you'll want to stop at **Ferguson & Youngblood,** 30 N. Congress St., tel. (803) 684-6461. This is a classic general merchandise store, with an emphasis on the word *general.* Tracy Ferguson Jr. sells everything from lock washers to real estate and roasted peanuts here. Stop in, keep an ear open, and you'll soon overhear what's going on in town.

Ivy Hill Gift Shoppe, 8 N. Congress St., tel. (803) 684-7614, fax (803) 628-0847, is one of those stores where you walk in and feel your pulse rate drop immediately. It's that warm and serene inside; all scented candles and garden stones, that sort of thing. Native Yorkers say that this store is such a great place to buy gifts that it's picked bare a week before Christmas. Don't forget to say hello to Squirrel, the black cat, who lives here.

Food
Former Cheeseheads Mike and Linda Peavy's **Roadside Grille,** 307 W. Liberty St., tel. (803)

628-5415, is a fun place with a road-trip theme: the to-go menu folds like a road map; the food categories include "Start Your Engine" (appetizers), "Light Trips" (salads and soup), "Pick-Ups" (finger food), and "Lubricants" (drinks). The burgers and "freeway fries" are scrumptious, the malts are super thick. Best of all are the diverse entries from the eateries of roadside America: western caviar from the Big Texan in Amarillo; muffaletta from New Orleans, hot brown (an open-face hot turkey sandwich topped with a cream sauce, Parmesan cheese, and bacon strip) from Louisville, Kentucky, and, of course, Southern barbecue. Karaoke over in the lounge at night.

Wait—*best* of all is the free CD jukebox stuffed with vintage rock, country, and big-band music.

For good steaks, locals point to **The Coal Yard,** set right next to the York Chamber of Commerce at what used to be the train depot, 105 Garner St., tel. (803) 684-9653. **The Garden Café,** 8-C N. Congress St., tel. (803) 684-7019, offers sandwiches, quiche, pasta, homemade soups, gourmet coffees, and tasty desserts. Come on the weekend for live music and prime rib, chicken, and seafood. For lunch this is a pretty cheap place to go; for dinner, you're looking at the high teens per plate. Open Tues.-Sat. 10 a.m.-3 p.m.; dinner on Fri.-Sat. only. Closed Sunday and Monday.

HISTORIC BRATTONSVILLE

So many historic villages are marred by the intruding modern skylines and traffic noise. Which makes Brattonsville all the more special. This 25-acre reconstructed historic farm community, located in the country on a narrow, winding Piedmont road, gives you the feeling that you've really left behind today and found yesterday. The period-costumed staff and volunteers participate in 18th-19th century activities like butter churning and sheep shearing, which can be an education for kids and adults alike. (Sometime in the future, tourists will flock to a reconstructed late-20th-century suburban home to watch re-enactors make espresso or rebuild a computer desktop.) Here, too, you'll see 24 restored structures, some native to the farm, some moved here from elsewhere: a restored plantation house (circa 1823), the Colonel Bratton Home (circa 1780),

slave cabins, a 19th-century doctor's office, a pioneer cabin, homestead house, and other examples of bygone architecture, art, and tools and farm equipment, dating from 1750 to 1900.

If you're planning to visit a Lowcountry plantation or two, you should really visit Brattonsville if only on the equal time principle: after all, for every one huge Lowcountry plantation that ever existed, there were a dozen of these small to midsize Upcountry farms.

If you know something about farming, you'll find Brattonsville especially interesting since, as part of its Heritage Farm Program, Brattonsville raises varieties of mid-19th century livestock and grows crops from seed stock unique to the region, using historically accurate agricultural techniques.

The Battle of Huck's Defeat was fought here on July 12, 1780, a skirmish that was the first chink in the armor of the loyalist and British forces, an omen of what was to come that autumn and winter at Kings Mountain and Cowpens. Reenactors run through the historic paces each year to show you what it looked like in case you missed the original. Living History programs are held monthly, and once a year you can come up for Euwabu, an African-American celebration. If you're here in the fall you may catch the Red Hills Heritage Festival and the Christmas Candlelight Open House, but you'll find special reenactments held out here sporadically throughout the year. When I visited in June, they were reenacting an 1840s political stump meeting.

Getting out here takes a little patience, but it's a pretty drive. Brattonsville is in McConnells, off Hwy. 322, 10 miles west of Rock Hill, tel. (803) 684-2327. Open March-Nov. Tuesday and Thursday 10 a.m.-4 p.m., Saturday and Sunday 2-5 p.m. Closed Easter, Memorial Day, July 4, Labor Day, and Thanksgiving. Admission $5.

UNION

Here's another one of those towns whose names just sound out of place in South Carolina. But Union gets its name not from the federal Union but from Union Church, a Colonial-era church that served the needs of many different frontier congregations: Presbyterian, Episcopalian, and Quaker, all of whom worshipped there together.

If you're trying to remember where you've heard the name "Union," it's (sadly) probably in connection with the Susan Smith case a few years back. Smith drowned her two sons in the family car in nearby Lake John D. Long. After Smith was arrested, another family visiting the boat launch to pay their respects to the victims were drowned when their vehicle's transmission slipped and they too plunged into the lake's waters. The twice-deadly launch has since been removed.

But don't let this tragic chain of events keep you from visiting this historic town. The **Union County Courthouse** is a beautiful neoclassical building on Main Street. You'll find memorials to John Pratt—inventor of the ptereotype, a predecessor of the typewriter—and to the Confederate army. Next door to the courthouse you'll see the 1823 granite **jail,** designed by Robert Mills, architect of the Washington Monument. Down at 418 E. Main St. you'll see the **Wallace House,** former residence of Confederate general and Reconstruction-era South Carolina Speaker of the House William Wallace.

Accommodations

To camp in the Union area, head over to **Woods Ferry Recreation Area,** tel. (864) 427-9858, which has 32 sites. Open May-Jan. only.

With the assistance of J.D., the cat, Peggy and Jim Waller run **The Inn at Merridun,** 100 Merridun Place, tel. (864) 427-7052, fax (864) 429-0373, five rooms in a circa 1855 Greek Revival mansion located on nine wooded acres five minutes from downtown Union. This is a nice place to get away from it all if just being in Union itself doesn't do the trick. A full country breakfast and evening desserts come with the room; dinners can be arranged in advance. No kids under 12 allowed; smoking on the porch only. Private baths. On the National Historic Register. Expensive-Premium.

Mike Doyle's **The Inn of Fairforest,** 2403 Cross Keys Hwy., tel. (864) 429-3950, fax (864) 427-8598, is set in a hillside Scottish manor home featuring mahogany ceilings, hardwood floors, and six fireplaces. Three of the four rooms are two-room suites. Features full breakfasts, rocking chairs, walking paths, and a large hot-springs hot tub. I don't know about you, but I've got my day planned out already.

ROSE HILL PLANTATION STATE PARK

Eight miles south of Union on Rd. 16 (Sardis Rd.), you'll come to Rose Hill Plantation State Park, former home of William Gist, the governor of South Carolina at the time of secession. The Gist plantation was famous in its day for its rose garden and 44-acre lawn, and you can see both of these, still alive and well, today. Mansion tour hours are Monday, Thursday, and Friday 1-4 p.m., Saturday 11 a.m.-4 p.m., and Sunday noon-4 p.m.

CHESTER

This is a good-looking little town, its simple brick business blocks bending and sloping with the hills. Locals call the hilltop public square and brick downtown area simply, "The Hill." Here you'll see the 1891 opera house, now used as city hall. A handful of antiques and gift shops also make the area worth a stop.

Home to around 7,400 citizens, Chester is Chester County's county seat, named by settlers who came from Pennsylvania not long after 1755. Grab a self-guided walking tour of historic downtown Chester at the **chamber of commerce,** 109 Gadsen Street.

the Sanitary Barber Shop

The Chester County Historical Society Museum, tel. (803) 385-2330, offers local artifacts for viewing in a 1914 jail behind the county courthouse on McAlily Street. Hours are Wednesday 11 a.m.-3 p.m., last Saturday each month 11 a.m.-3 p.m. Free admission.

Collins Bantam Chef is a no-frills small-town fast-food restaurant featuring good fried chicken and real malts. Stop by for a peek at where you would have hung out if you'd gone to Chester High.

LANCASTER

Named by settlers who came from Lancaster, Pennsylvania, Lancaster is home to the largest southern textile mill under one roof, Springs Industries, Inc., founded by early 20th-century renaissance man Elliott White Springs, a WW I flying ace, successful novelist, and industrialist. The 1825 Robert Mills courthouse may be the most remarkable building in town. My favorite thing about Lancaster, though, is the mural painted on a downtown building depicting famous Lancastrians of years gone by, including Andrew Jackson; 1920s, '30s, and '40s black movie actress Nina McKinney, raised here in Lancaster; and James Marion Sims, 1813-83, the father of modern gynecology, who was born in Lancaster.

Efforts are underway to revitalize Lancaster's downtown, but for now, **Howell's Art and Antiques,** 121 S. Main St., tel. (803) 285-7971, fax (803) 283-4498, is one of the few businesses of interest to most travelers. See the store's Web site at www.antiqunet.com/da/howell.html.

ANDREW JACKSON STATE PARK

This 360-acre park nine miles north of Lancaster, off Hwy. 521, 196 Andrew Jackson Park Rd., tel. (803) 285-3344, attempts to mark the very spot where the powerful populist president and scourge of the British, Cherokee, and (during the Nullification Crisis of the 1820s) South Carolina itself was born and raised. In a pioneer-style log building, you'll find a museum displaying Jackson papers, Native American artifacts, and pioneer household equipment such as a spinning wheel and loom, which would have been part of the young Jackson's boyhood.

The centerpiece of the park is Anna Hyatt Huntington's *Boy of the Waxhaws,* which shows young Andrew before the Trail of Tears was even a glimmer in his eye.

If you'd like to camp here, the park offers 25 campsites with water and electricity, a bathhouse with hot showers, a picnic area, playground, fishing, and a boat rental. You can bring a pet if it's on a leash.

GREENVILLE AND THE UPCOUNTRY

You wanna talk about the vanishing wilderness? . . . You push a little more power into Atlanta, a little more air conditioners for your smug little suburb, and you know what's going to happen? We're gonna rape this whole goddamned landscape!
—Lewis (Burt Reynolds), in James Dickey's screenplay of his novel Deliverance

To get a rough understanding of the Upcountry, take most everything you know about the Lowcountry and reverse it. Instead of lying gentle and flat, the Upcountry stands ruggedly mountainous. Instead of subtropical, the Upcountry is alpine and piedmont; instead of warm, slow black rivers stained with tannic acid the Upcountry is cut through with clear mountain whitewater rivers and creeks roaring their way down into the valleys below. Rather than the Lowcountry's soft dirt and swampy marsh, picture hard red clay; instead of endlessly shifting sand

dunes envision monadnocks—granite outcroppings that refuse to wash away with the rest of the mountain.

The people, too, are different here, though less so these days than before. As opposed to the High Church British who settled the Lowcountry, Scotch-Irish Protestants settled most of this region—Low Church (Methodist, Baptist) folk who believed in egalitarianism—among whites, at least—with all their hearts. As Clemson's Ben Robertson wrote in his 1942 *Red Hills and Cotton:* "We did not call ourselves old Southern planters— we were old Southern farmers. We were plain people, intending to be plain. We believed in plain clothes, plain cooking, plain houses, plain churches to attend preaching in on Sunday."

Where the constant comings and goings in the ports kept racial, ethnic, and intellectual diversity afoot in the Lowcountry for most of its history, the Upcountry—with notable exceptions in such summer resorts as Greenville—became known for its homogeneity.

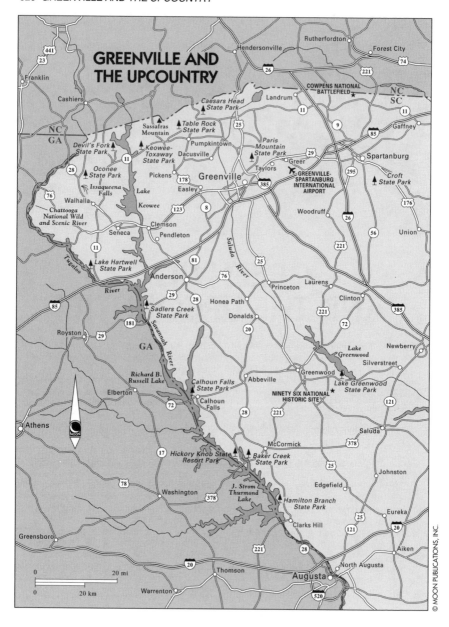

GREENVILLE AND
THE UPCOUNTRY

Climate

Average highs in an Upcountry summer range around 88°; average lows drop down to 31° in January. The region receives about 50.5 inches of rain a year—much of it in the summer, when the lightning strikes from convectional rainstorms.

For current weather conditions and forecasts, call (864) 848-3859.

HISTORY

After the French and Indian War of the 1750s, the victorious British government took control of all of the present-day United States from the Mississippi River east. This land they divided between their European colonists and their Native American subjects, giving the Indians the larger share. Though Governor Nicholson had sought to pacify the Cherokee—the dominant Upcountry tribe—with gifts and trade preferences, the Native Americans had nonetheless become less than satisfied with the arrangements. In 1730, Sir Alexander Cuming treated with the Cherokee and arranged for them to open up their lands for settlement. By 1753, however, the Cherokees' animosities with the neighboring Creek led Governor James Glenn to act as Jimmy Carter at Camp David, stepping in to bring peace between the two. The Cherokee rewarded Glenn by granting South Carolina a few thousand acres of land, on which the Carolinians built Fort Prince George on the Keowee River as

a British outpost to protect British citizens and interests in the area, and to protect the Cherokee from the Creek. Two years later, Old Hop, top Cherokee chief, sat down with Glenn at Saluda Old Town, midway between Charles Town and the Indians' town of Keowee, and deeded the Carolinians the 96 District, a region that now includes parts of 10 separate counties.

The Cherokee War

By January 19, 1760, the Cherokee, angered at British encroachments and unkept promises, began massacring white settlers in just this region. Carolinians acted quickly, spreading their own brand of terror into the Cherokee villages and burning out their crops and winter stores. In 1761, a number of Cherokee chiefs led by Attakullakulla petitioned for peace.

With the Cherokee finally "pacified," new settlers—including the future parents of one-day president Andrew Jackson, born in 1767—flooded into the Upcountry through the Waxhaws in (now) Lancaster County. As in most frontier communities, lawlessness soon ensued. Robbery, arson, and looting became common.

Unfortunately, South Carolina's sole court of law was in Charles Town. Without any real formal law to protect them, Upcountry residents formed a group of "Regulators," vigilantes who took law into their own hands.

Now with over 50% of the state's white population, the Upcountry sent representative Patrick Calhoun and others before the Charles Town state legislature, where they appealed for representation, courts, roads, and provisions for churches and schools. Fortunately, fairer minds prevailed in Charles Town and before long, Calhoun and Moses Kirkland were sitting in the legislature as Upcountry representatives.

Despite the tribe's loss in the Cherokee War, the Cherokee still held deed to the extreme southeast of the state until the middle of the American Revolution. The Cherokee remained faithful to the British and paid for it—after patriots repulsed Cherokees allied with the redcoats, the Indians found themselves in a bad position. In 1777, they ceded the tribe's remaining South Carolina lands to the young state.

Despite their democratic leanings, the Upcountry largely sided with the loyalists for most of the American Revolution. The reason for this

---

GREENVILLE AND THE UPCOUNTRY HIGHLIGHTS

- Caesars Head and Raven Cliff Falls
- Chattooga National Wild and Scenic River
- Cherokee Foothills Scenic Highway
- Cowpens National Battlefield
- Downtown Greenville and the Peace Center
- Foothills Trail
- Issaqueena Falls and Whitewater Falls
- Pendleton Historical District
- Spartanburg's live music scene
- South Carolina State Botanical Gardens, Clemson
- Table Rock State Park

comes at least partly from that other defining attribute of Upcountry-dwellers—their distaste for their powerful Lowcountry neighbors. Only when the atrocities of the British army violated the Upcountrymen's strong sense of right and wrong were the Lowcountry Revolutionists able to get a majority of Upcountrymen to their side.

The British and American armies had fought to a virtual stalemate up north, and Lord Cornwallis, British Commander of the South, in 1780 began a second attempt at capturing the South (the first attempt had ended after the defeat at Sullivan's Island) and raising an army of loyalists with which to both hold the Carolinas and sweep north to pin Washington in the north. In June, the British marched to the Star Fort at Ninety Six to secure the Upcountry for England. At the end of that summer, leaving a loyalist New York officer in charge of the fort, Cornwallis headed to Camden and crushed the American forces there. With these two key towns under control, Cornwallis felt he was ready to leave the Back Country in the hands of loyalist troops and march northward and take on Washington.

In October 1780, a group of backwoodsmen poured over the Appalachians from Tennessee and defeated the loyalists at Kings Mountain. Down in Ninety Six, the British staved off a siege by General Nathanael Greene long enough for reinforcements to arrive.

HENRY LAURENS:
THE HERO SWAPPED FOR CORNWALLIS

Most people know that the American Revolution ended at Yorktown, where Lord Charles Cornwallis surrendered to General George Washington. But few know that when Cornwallis sailed back to England, the Americans exchanged him for diplomat Henry Laurens of South Carolina (for whom the town of Laurens and Laurens County are both named).

Born the son of a French Huguenot saddler in Charles Town in 1724, Laurens made much of his wealth in exports and imports in the busy port city. Many of his imports included Protestant Irish workers and African slaves.

After his wife's death in 1770, Laurens took his sons to England for schooling and attempted to persuade his English business associates that English mistreatment of the colonies could only mean trouble. When war became imminent, he sailed back to the colonies to take his stand with his neighbors, who quickly named him president of the first Provincial Congress in South Carolina in 1775. He was one of the handful of delegates the colony sent to the Continental Congress; he succeeded John Hancock as Congress president.

During the Revolutionary War, Laurens sailed to Holland to negotiate a badly needed $10 million loan for the Colonial armies. He was intercepted by the British and taken prisoner; the letters he was carrying at the time caused a war between Holland and England.

Laurens was thrown into the Tower of London and charged as a traitor against the Crown. Despite the lobbying of his friend Lafayette, as well as Edmund Burke, the gout-ridden Laurens wasted away inside the prison, month after month. On top of everything, the Brits charged him room and board, and required him to pay his jailers' salaries.

Finally, his son John Laurens—one of Washington's officers—arranged the elder Laurens' release from the Tower of London, and Henry sailed to France to assist Benjamin Franklin, John Adams, and John Jay in their armistice negotiations with Great Britain.

Laurens' involvement in the importation of both indentured servants and African slaves made him sensitive to the inhumanities of both practices, and he became one of the first powerful Americans to speak out against slavery. To his fellow elites he made clear his longing to see the new vaunting of liberty in the States lead to the abolition of slavery in the new country.

Though he served for a number of years as a de facto ambassador to England after the war, Laurens never fully physically recovered from his imprisonment, and his frailty no doubt was exacerbated by the senseless death of his beloved son John, in an unimportant skirmish at the tail end of the Revolution. Of 12 children born to Henry and Elinor Laurens, only three outlived their father. Laurens lived out the rest of his life in relative serenity on his plantation, Mepkin, in Berkeley County. He is buried there.

GREENVILLE

In no other place are Baptists likely to remind a stranger of Verdi.

—Novelist Rebecca West, on Greenville

Situated in the heart of the Upcountry, Greenville calls itself the "Textile Center of the World." Greenville and the Upcountry north of it were in land claimed by the Cherokee, though most of the Cherokee actually lived farther up in what is now North Carolina. Richard Pearis, an Irishman, came around 1765 from Virginia. He married a Cherokee woman and became so popular among the tribe that they deeded him, eventually, a 10-mile-square plot of land. Pearis built a gristmill and trading post at Reedy Falls, now in the midst of downtown Greenville.

With the outbreak of the Revolutionary War, both the colonists and the British, respecting Pearis' influence with the mighty Cherokee, sought his favor. Though he thought first of fighting for the Continentals, he ended up choosing to fight for the British, and sure enough, the Cherokee sided with the British as well. Were it not for this fact, "Pearis" might be one of the great South Carolinian names today, and the Cherokee might have remained a strong presence in the upstate. As it was, the colonialists threw Pearis into the Charles Town prison for nine months, during which time Continental troops captured and destroyed his plantation as an enemy stronghold. When he was released, Pearis fought for the loyalists as an officer. When the war was over, the British government granted Pearis a large plot of land in the Bahamas, far away from the turbulence and bitterness back in his old hometown. Paris Mountain, near Greenville, is named in his honor.

The English leaned on the Cherokee, and in 1777 the tribe deeded their remaining South Carolinian lands to the state.

Lemuel J. Alston, brother of Governor Joseph Alston of Beaufort, the son-in-law of Aaron Burr, purchased a portion of Pearis' land in 1788 and within 10 years had laid out the village of Pleasantburg. In 1816, Alston sold his properties to Vardry McBee, who is generally considered the "father of Greenville." McBee built a cotton mill on the Reedy River and gave land for the construction of the town's first churches and schools.

Though Scots-Irish drifting down from the colder climes up north were some of the first settlers, a sizable minority was made up of wealthy Lowcountry plantation owners who wanted somewhere to hide away from the fevers during the summer.

The town's name was changed in the early 19th century to match the name of the county for which it serves as seat. Greenville County had been named back in 1786 to honor—so most believe—Isaac Green, a pioneer settler.

In his 1826 *Statistics of South Carolina,* architect Robert Mills wrote of the city:

The village of Greenville is . . . beautifully situated on a plain, gently undulating. The Reedy river placidly leaves its southern borders previous to precipitating itself in a beautiful cascade, over an immense body of rocks. . . . The public buildings are: A handsome brick courthouse, lately erected; a jail; a Baptist meeting house; an Episcopal church; and two neat buildings for the male and female academy.

During the Civil War, the isolated town became a refuge for Lowcountry residents burned or simply frightened out of their homes. The mountains surrounding the city were filled with

---

I worked jes' as long when I lived in the country—and it was harder work, too. . . . I like it here. We live in a nice house, lots better'n than that cabin in the country. And there's always people around to talk with. Me and my gals—between the four of us we make from $25 to $30 a week, and that ain't to be sneezed at, let me tell you. And we get it in good, hard cash every Saturday, without any ifs and ands about it.

—A Graniteville cotton mill worker and former sharecropper in the 1880s, quoted by W.E. Woodward in The Way Our People Lived: An Intimate American History, 1944.

deserters from both armies, and these men formed gangs that for a time conducted raids of travelers and isolated farms. Greenville was also the home of a number of hospitals for injured Confederates.

Because Greenville and the upstate in general had been an oasis of pro-Union sentiment before and during the war, the region rose in statewide influence during Reconstruction. Benjamin F. Perry, a Greenville resident, was named provisional governor of the state by President Andrew Johnson—himself a former resident of Laurens. James L. Orr of nearby Anderson County succeeded Perry.

In the last part of the 19th century, Greenville recovered to become the the de facto capital of the Carolina textile belt.

Today, Greenville enjoys its role as gateway to Appalachia, and the town has received praise in several national magazines for its renovated downtown. It's a dynamic city with a growing population—people who believe in "progress," and believe they know how to achieve it.

SIGHTS

Greenville County Museum of Art

At 420 College St., tel. (864) 271-7570, this is arguably the world's best collection of works by Andrew Wyeth, along with pieces by Georgia O'-Keeffe, Jasper Johns, and America's first female professional artist, Charleston's Henrietta Johnson. Large collection of Southern art. Nice gift shop here with reproductions of some of the museum's most popular works. Open Tues.-Sat. 10 a.m.-5 p.m., Sunday 1-5 p.m. Best of all, it's free.

Reedy River Falls Historic Park and Falls Cottage

At 123 W. Broad St., tel. (864) 421-0042, this rich green oasis of a park marks the spot where Greenville began in 1776 when Richard Pearis, the area's first white settler, built a gristmill and trading post. Falls Cottage has been here since 1838, when it was a combination rental home and shoemaker's shop. Nowadays it's home to a catering business that also serves lunch (see below).

Greenville Cultural Exchange Center

Stop in here, at 700 Arlington Ave., tel. (864) 269-1549, to view displays on upstate African-Americans, including Jesse Jackson, and one-legged dancer "Peg Leg Bates." Open Saturday 11 a.m.-5 p.m., Sunday 2-5 p.m., and other times by appointment. Donation requested.

Beattie House

At 8 Bennett St., tel. (864) 233-9977, the Beattie House, built in 1834, is listed on the National Register of Historic Places for its beautiful early Italianate Gothic design. The building is now home to the Greenville Women's Club and open to the public. Free admission.

Christ Episcopal Church

At 10 N. Church St., tel. (864) 271-8773, this Gothic-Revival structure, the oldest church in

Built in 1838, Falls Cottage was once a rental home and shoemaker's shop; nowadays, it's a great spot for lunch.

Greenville, features a rare brick spire. Founded in 1820 by summertime visitors from Charleston, Christ Episcopal is on the National Register of Historic Places. Town founding father Vardry McBee lies in the churchyard.

Furman University Thompson Gallery
Furman University's Roe Art Building is home to this gallery, 3300 Poinsett Hwy., tel. (864) 294-2074, featuring the work of local and regional artists. Open 9 a.m.-5 p.m.

Kilgore-Lewis House
This historic home and five-acre gardens at 560 N. Academy St., tel. (864) 232-3020, is listed on the National Register of History Places. Open Mon.-Fri. 10 a.m.-2 p.m.

Bob Jones University, Museum, and Gallery
If you live outside of the state, it's quite possible that the only time you've ever heard of Bob Jones University was in the early 1980s, when BJU was threatened with losing its tax-exempt status if it didn't agree to admit black students, which some of the arch-conservative leaders of the school believed would violate a God-ordained separation of the races. But that was 20 years ago; today, the photos on the university's promotional literature are as consciously multiracial as those found at every other college, and this is gradually being reflected in the student body's demographics.

Bob Jones founded Bob Jones College in 1927 in College Point, Florida; by 1933 the college had moved to Cleveland, Tennessee, and by 1947 it had become a university and moved here to Greenville. Today the school has over 1,500 faculty, offers over 100 degrees, and serves some 8,000 students. It may not be the most conservative Christian school in the country, but it is certainly the most conservative *large* Christian school.

How conservative is it? Female students may not wear pants on campus (as a guest, just make sure you're not wearing "short shorts"). Male students must wear ties.

In other words, if you've got a rebellious bone in your body, this is just the sort of place that will bring it out in you. Even the young Billy Graham spent only one semester at BJU (then in Tennessee) before rejecting its stern doctrinairism based upon Dr. Bob's (and only Dr. Bob's) interpretation of Scripture. After talking with Dr. Bob Sr., who called him a quitter who would never amount to anything, Billy moved down to Florida to finish his seminary training.

And yet while many Fundamentalist schools find artistic expression to be superfluous at best, Bob Jones University is notable in its attention to the arts. The late Bob Jones Jr. (Dr. Bob III is now head of the college) was a gifted Shakespearean actor, and the university to this day maintains an acclaimed Shakespearean troupe.

Even more famous is the **Bob Jones University Museum and Gallery**, 1700 Wade Hampton Blvd., tel. (864) 242-5100, ext. 1050. which the university advertises as containing "one of the most important collections of religious art in America." But since for many the term "religious art" summons up images of black-velvet crucifixion scenes and those old paintings of a blond-haired, blue-eyed Jesus holding a lamb on his shoulders, perhaps BJU should advertise that, as Paul Richard of the *Washington Post* admitted, "When it comes to baroque painting . . . Bob Jones wins hands down." Dutch, Spanish, and Italian masters are all featured here, including works from Dolci, Rembrandt, Rubens, Titian, and Van Dyck. No wonder art lovers and Biblical scholars visit here from around the world. If you visit, set aside a full afternoon to do the place justice.

You will notice, as you start to browse, that in each gallery (there are more than a dozen), a museum host will stand in the doorway, keeping an eye on you. These "hosts" may seem a bit oppressive at first, but keep in mind that they are here instead of the usually ever-present security cameras and Plexiglas canvas shields. And who can blame the curators for taking precautions? After all, there aren't many museums in the world where you can stand face to face with a Rembrandt with nothing between you but air and your good intentions.

Be sure to pick up the pamphlet *On Looking at Old Master Paintings,* in which the university explains its rationale behind presenting these oft-times biblically inaccurate paintings to the viewing public. "When looking at religious art," the pamphlet explains, "we should not simply enjoy it," but ask ourselves, "Is the subject scriptural;

SHOELESS JOE JACKSON: BASEBALL'S NOT-SO-TRAGIC FIGURE

Greenville prodigy Shoeless Joe Jackson has become something of an icon over the years, the subject or a character in at least two motion pictures and a one-man play all in the past 15 years.

In 1888, Joseph Jefferson Jackson was born in Pickens County, the oldest of George and Martha Jackson's eight children. When little Joe was five years old, his father took a job with the Brandon Textile Mill in West Greenville and moved the family down from the hills into one of the Brandon Mill textile villages. A year later, at the age of six, Joe Jackson began working in the textile mills himself.

By age 13, in 1901, Joe made the Brandon Mill baseball team. After five years in the mill leagues, Joe was signed to the semi-pro Greenville New Leaguers. Two years after that, he was hired by the Carolina Association team, the Greenville Spinners. He hit .346 and led the league in batting.

It was while playing for the Spinners at nearby Anderson that Joe got his famous nickname. He found that his new shoes had given him painful blisters on his feet, but because the team only carried 12 players to begin with, and a number were already hurt, his manager insisted that he play. Joe slipped out of his shoes and played the rest of the game—the only game in which he ever did this—in his stocking feet. When he rapped out a triple, an Anderson fan stood up and shouted, "You shoeless son of a gun, you!" The name stuck, though Jackson never did like it.

In 1908, Jackson married his sweetheart Katie Wynn. And later that summer, the Philadelphia Athletics signed him and brought him up to the major leagues.

Joe played the next two years in the minors, but in 1910 he was called up to the Cleveland Indians and hit .387 over the last 20 games of the season. In 1911, his first full season, he batted .408, the highest average ever by a rookie. Amazingly, he didn't even win the batting crown that year, since Ty Cobb picked that same year to hit .420.

Jackson dominated the league for the next seven years. In 1919, while playing for the White Sox, he roomed with a member of the team who conspired to throw the World Series. Though Jackson himself batted .375 and set a record for number of hits, and fielded a perfect 1.000 fielding average, he was named as a co-conspirator in the 1920 Black Sox trial and, though found innocent, was banished for life from organized baseball.

Though Joe did continue to play organized baseball for a number of teams through the '20s and '30s, he never considered himself the tragic figure that the press—and, later, novelist Thomas Kinsella and filmmaker John Sayles—made him out to be.

I have read now and then that I am one of the most tragic figures in baseball. Well, maybe that's the way some people look at it, but I don't quite see it that way myself. I guess one of the reasons I never fought my suspension any

and if so, is it treated *in light of Scripture* and not according to some traditional formula?" Somehow, among these lofty questions, the author manages to include a quick critique of the Roman Catholic doctrine of Transubstantiation.

You'll find a gift shop with miniature reproductions of many of the prints. The museum's open Tues.-Sun. 2-5 p.m. Closed Dec. 20-25, January 1, and July 4. Free admission. Unfortunately (though understandably), the museum staff will not suffer the little children to come unto them; kids under six are not allowed.

Also here is another important collection, the small (seven paintings) but significant **Benjamin West Collection,** in the War Memorial Chapel on campus—the largest assemblage of this pioneer American painter's works in the world. Born in 1738 into the then-frontier region of Pennsylvania, West is said to have learned to use color from local Native Americans, and to have begun painting using brushes made from the hair of the family cat. As a young man, West won the admiration of Philadelphia businessmen who sent him to Europe for further training; after three years in Italy, he settled in England at the age of 25 and later went on to cofound the Royal Academy and influence American painting by influencing a number of famous U.S. artists, including Gilbert Stuart. The paintings here were created for King George III as part of a proposed

harder than I did was that I thought I had spent a pretty full life in the big leagues. I was 32 years old at the time, and I had been in the majors 13 years; I had a lifetime batting average of .356; I held the all-time throwing record for distance; and I had made pretty good salaries for those days. There wasn't much left for me in the big leagues.

First of all, the conception of Shoeless Joe Jackson as a barefoot mill-town hayseed is way off. True, Jackson's education was limited; his signature is widely prized—partially because he only shakily signed his name a few times in his life—but many often ignore Joe's business success. Even before the scandal, Joe owned a successful valet business in Georgia. After the scandal, Joe and his wife moved to Augusta, and she ran the business while Joe played for the local ball club. After his mother died in 1935, the Jacksons returned to Greenville for the funeral—and stayed for the next 16 years, living at 119 E. Wilborn St. on the south side of Greenville, while Joe became successful owning a liquor store—though he didn't drink—and a dry-cleaning business.

Why did he allow folks to think he was dumb in his baseball days? Shoeless Joe himself explained:

All the big sportswriters seemed to enjoy writing about me as an ignorant cotton-mill boy with nothing but lint where my brains ought to be. That was all right with me. I was able to fool a lot of pitchers and managers and club owners I wouldn't have been able to fool if they'd thought I was smarter.

When Jackson died of a massive heart attack in December 1951, he was buried in Woodlawn Memorial Park on Wade Hampton Blvd. in Greenville. You'll find his grave in Section V, plot 333. If you want to visit the site, stop by the office at Woodlawn and they'll be glad to give you directions.

In March 1996, the Shoeless Joe Jackson Memorial was dedicated at the old Brandon Mill baseball field. Later that year, the South Carolina legislature passed legislation to change the name of the road that runs near the Brandon Mill Baseball field to "The Shoeless Joe Jackson Memorial Highway."

On May 5, 1998, state legislator J. Verne Smith proposed—and the South Carolina state legislature passed—legislation asking the commissioner of baseball to reinstate Joe Jackson as a member in "good standing" of professional baseball. This is one of the necessary steps that must be accomplished before Jackson can be considered for the Hall of Fame.

To celebrate the 110th anniversary of his birth, Greenville Mayor Knox White declared July 1998 "Shoeless Joe Jackson Month." Plans were made for a public display all month at City Hall of Jackson memorabilia.

For an excellent Web site on Joe Jackson, see www.blackbetsy.com, home of the Virtual Hall of Fame. To see Joe portrayed by D.B. Sweeney as an "ignorant cotton-mill boy," watch John Sayles' fine film *Eight Men Out.* To see him played by Ray Liotta speaking with a Brooklyn accent, see *Field of Dreams.*

chapel at Windsor Chapel; the series of works was supposed to represent the Judeo-Christian faith from its inception to its end in the book of Revelation. When the king's ill health kept the chapel from being completed, the paintings were returned to West.

If time permits, explore the campus bookstore just to get a feel for the place and the counterculture of which this school is an expression.

Greenville Zoo

Home to over 250 animals from all around the globe, the Greenville Zoo, 150 Cleveland Park Dr., tel. (864) 467-4300, doesn't hold a torch to the Riverbanks Zoo down in Columbia, but it's

certainly worth a visit if you have kids and aren't planning on stopping in Columbia. Open daily 10 a.m.-4:30 p.m. Closed Thanksgiving, Christmas, New Year's. Children under 13 must be accompanied by an adult. The grounds here include tennis courts, playgrounds, and picnic facilities, so even after you've viewed your last ocelot, you're free to break out the rackets and eats and make a full day of it.

Nippon Center Yagoto

You'll find this cultural curiosity at 500 Congaree Rd., tel. (864) 288-8471. Where else in the Appalachian foothills can you take part in an authentic Japanese tea ceremony? (That's a rhetorical question, but if you find an answer, do let me know.) This cultural center features a rock garden, Japanese artwork, and wonderful furnishings. The tea ceremony costs $5, and guided tours cost $3. There's also a restaurant on site (see below).

Poinsett Bridge

Completed in 1820, this is the oldest bridge in South Carolina, and it used to be an important crossing on the original state road between Greenville and Asheville, North Carolina. From Hwy. 25 N, two miles northwest of Hwy. 11 turn onto Old Hwy. 25, travel 3.2 miles, and turn right onto Callahan Mountain Road. Travel 2.2 miles up the road and you'll see the bridge on your left.

Roper Mountain Science Center

Up here on Roper Mountain, 504 Roper Mountain Rd., off I-385, tel. (864) 281-1188, stands the state's only science center and its largest planetarium. The telescope here is the seventh largest in the country. The center consists of a living history farm, discovery farm, sea life room, observatory, planetarium, and health education center. Open on the second Saturday of each month 9 a.m.-1 p.m. Planetarium shows are generally offered Fridays at 7:30 p.m., but call for current program information. The nature trails are open 8:30 a.m.-5 p.m. daily, and they're free.

Shoeless Joe Jackson Memorial Park

This park on West Ave., tel. (864) 288-6470, marks the site where Shoeless Joe Jackson and countless other mill workers spent their off-days in the sun, playing at the home diamond for Greenville's Brandon Mill neighborhood in the first decades of the 20th century. Now this is a Greenville County Recreation District park, and countless Little League and softball games are played here every summer.

16th SC Volunteers
Museum of Confederate History

Located in Greenville's Pettigru Historic District, this museum, 15 Boyce Ave., tel. (864) 421-9039, houses a collection of Confederate relics and military and personal artifacts, as well as a small research library. Open Friday 5-9 p.m., Saturday 10 a.m.-5 p.m., Sunday 1-5 p.m.

Whitehall

Built in 1813 by Henry Middleton, Whitehall, 310 Earle St., tel. (864) 421-0042, was renovated to look like a Lowcountry home in the 1870s. During the Spanish-American War in the last years of the 19th century, the house was used as a nurses' quarters. It's listed on the National Register of Historic Places.

Hollywild Animal Park

The park, on Hampton Rd., tel. (864) 472-2038, allows you to visit lions, elephants, chimps, and tigers, many of them used in actual Hollywood films, where they portray wild versions of themselves. Open April 1 to Labor Day daily 9 a.m.-6 p.m., Labor Day to October 31 Saturday and Sunday 9 a.m.-5 p.m., late November to January 1 6-9 p.m. Admission $6, children $4. Safari rides are $2.

Tours

For tours of Greenville, contact the folks at the award-winning volunteer program, **A Glimpse of Greenville,** located in the WestEnd Market above Reedy Falls at 1 Augusta St., tel. (864) 421-0042.

The guides here are well-informed and a tour with them will not only show you the past of Greenville, but give you a peek at the city's plans for the future. Tours of the Peace Center for the Performing Arts are available.

SPORTS AND RECREATION

Hiking

Of all the hundreds of miles of trail up here, the **Foothills Trail** is the definitive hike. A nearly 90-mile stretch of trail from Table Rock State Park to Oconee State Park, the trail crosses some of the most rugged and beautiful terrain in the Southeast, and includes a chance to climb Sassafras Mountain, the highest peak in the state, along the way.

Other popular hikes include the 14-mile Table Rock trail at Table Rock State Park and shorter ones at Caesars Head, Jones Gap, Paris Mountain, Oconee and Keowee-Toxaway State Parks. Call the park you're planning to visit for more information, or call South Carolina State Parks at (803) 734-0156.

For more information on these trails, contact the **Foothills Trails Conference,** Greenville, tel. (864) 233-903, or the **South Carolina Department of Parks, Recreation and Tourism** at (803) 734-0122, or visit www.sctrails.net.

Biking
Four of the most scenic—and challenging—biking paths up here include the 130-mile **Cherokee Foothills Scenic Highway,** the **Issaqueena Dam** area off **Old Six Mile Highway** in Pickens County, and the **Fant's Grove** area near the Twin Lakes Campground in Anderson County. For an informative booklet on biking the upstate, call the South Carolina Department of Parks, Recreation and Tourism at (803) 734-0122.

Horseback Riding
Horse trails are plentiful in these parts; rental horses, however, are not. If you happen to have your own horse, probably the best place to go riding is the **Rocky Gap Trail,** which begins at Whetstone Horse Camp and goes on for 12.5 miles before connecting with the Willis Knob Horse Trail in Georgia, providing some 26 miles of riding near the Chattooga. Call Andrew Pickens Ranger District Office at (864) 638-9568 for information.

Beginners and families might want to amble on over to **Circle R Trails Inc.,** at 550 Circle R Trails Dr., Mountain Rest, tel. (864) 638-0115, where you can take guided rides over some 150 miles of trails. **Foxcroft Farms,** 175 McConnell Rd., in Taylors, tel. (864) 244-2636, fax (864) 322-7993, offers horse rentals and 500-plus acres laced with scenic trails. Lessons here too. Call ahead for reservations.

Croft State Park, 450 Croft State Park Rd., tel. (864) 585-1283, features horse trails and offers a show ring and stable to rent, but it's strictly BYOH, as is **Riverbend Equestrian Park,** 175 Riverbend Rd., in Travelers Rest, tel. (864) 288-6470, fax (864) 288-6499, South Carolina's only public equestrian park. Instructional classes offered, but again it's BYOH.

Leaf-Viewing and Apple Tasting
In the entire state, one of my favorite things to do is drive around up here on a crisp fall day, stopping at the many roadside stands and sampling their hot boiled peanuts and hot apple cider.

During the late summer, you can do the same thing in Cherokee and Spartanburg Counties, but you'll be tasting peaches. Get on up to the two-lane 130-mile Cherokee Foothills Scenic Highway (Hwy. 11) and prepare for a pleasant day. One good place to stop is **Perdue's Mountain Fruit Farm,** Hwy. 11 at N. Tigerville Rd., tel. (864) 244-5809, fax (864) 292-9326. You'll find nearly 30 varieties of apples, as well as plums, peaches, nectarines, grapes, berries, and cider. Open July 1 through Halloween.

Cherokee Foothills Scenic Highway (Hwy. 11)
You'll note this specially marked road on your map; this 130-mile two-lane road follows the route once used by the Cherokee and by English and French fur traders as they traveled in this area. In 1998, President Clinton recognized the route as one of the nation's 30 National Scenic Byways. On a clear fall day, with the leaves turning color, there aren't many prettier drives in the world.

Whitewater Rafting
Call **Wildwater Ltd.,** tel. (800) 451-9972 or (864) 647-9587, or **Nantahala Outdoor Center,** tel. (800) 232-7238 or (864) 647-9014, for guided rafting tours down the Chattooga. Book well in advance.

Golf
You'll find more than 40 semiprivate and public courses in Upcountry. Certainly one of the most beautiful courses anywhere is the cleverly named **Tom Jackson's Links O'Tryon** course, framed within seven different mountains; **Cobb's Glenn** (which periodically hosts a Nike tour event) and **The Gauntlet** are beautiful, challenging places to play a round as well.

Call (800) 682-5553 for a *South Carolina Golf Guide,* or see www.travelsc.com for information on the state's public golf courses.

Ice Skating
On Scottswood Dr., tel. (864) 322-7529, you'll find the **Greenville Pavilion Ice Rink,** one of only two public indoor rinks in the state.

Baseball
The **Greenville Braves,** 1 Braves Ave., tel. (864) 299-3456, fax (864) 277-7369, play such AA

opponents as the Carolina Mudcats, the Knoxville Smokies, and Mike Jordan's old team, the Birmingham Barons, at some 70 home games here between April and August each year. A good chance for Atlanta Braves fans to spot out the team's future stars. Tickets run between $5.50-7.25, less for seniors and children. Games start at 7:15 most evenings, 5:15 p.m. Sundays. Hear the games on WPJM 800 AM and WPCI 1490 AM.

The **Clemson Tigers,** 103 Tillman Hall, Clemson University, tel. (800) 253-6766 or (864) 656-2118, play their NCAA season from February to May, so if you're here in spring and want to catch a game, call to see if they're in town.

Football

You'd never know it, of course, because nobody up here likes to talk about it, but Clemson University does field a football team. The NCAA Division I team plays in the Atlantic Coast Conference over at Clemson Memorial Stadium, nicknamed "Death Valley" for the long dry stretches between victories over USC. The stadium seats 81,474 people—one of the largest on-campus stadiums in the U.S. If you're planning a trip here between September and November and would like to be one of these people, call (800) 253-6766 or (864) 656-2118 for ticket information and prices.

Basketball

To see Clemson hoops in the 11,020-seat Littlejohn Coliseum, call (800) 253-6766 or (864) 656-2118 for ticket information and prices.

Soccer

The **South Carolina Shamrocks,** tel. (864) 585-5009, fax (864) 585-0083, started in the mid-1990s up here, playing in the USIAL professional league. The team name makes reference to the strong Irish heritage in this area. The Shamrocks play at Shamrock Stadium in Greer.

ACCOMMODATIONS

If money's no object—or someone else's object—then my top pick in town would be the 327-room **Hyatt Regency** at 220 N. Main St., tel. (864) 235-1234, right in the middle of everything

downtown, with a large, beautiful eight-story atrium enclosing a fountain and gardens, a health club, and good-sized rooms. Premium-Luxury. The Hyatt, along with the **Embassy Suites** at 670 Verdae Blvd., tel. (843) 676-9090 (Expensive-Premium), and the **Greenville Hilton and Towers,** 45 W. Orchard Park Dr., tel. (843) 232-4747 (Moderate-Premium), make up the city's premier lodgings. At all three places, the prices are considerably cheaper on Friday and Saturday nights. The Hilton and Embassy Suites have indoor pools.

The rest of the week, for about 50% of the price of the Hyatt, you can stay at father and son Thomas and Steve Moore's **The Phoenix: Greenville's Inn,** a much nicer-than-average motor lodge with outdoor corridors at 246 N. Pleasantburg Dr., tel. (800) 257-3529 or (864) 233-4651, fax (864) 233-4651, e-mail: phoenix-inn@aol.com, off I-85 Exit 51. This place looks like just about what you'd get if a Best Western mated with a really nice B&B. A pretty courtyard garden here, with a pool and a very nice pub and restaurant. Moderate.

You'll also find a **TraveLodge** nearby at 1465 S. Pleasantburg, tel. (843) 277-8670. Inexpensive. At the airport, the cheap-but-safe place to stay is the **Microtel Inn,** 20 Interstate Court, tel. (888) 771-7171, Inexpensive. You'll also find most of the chains right off the I-85. A very friendly little motel, run by Bill Patel, is **Clemson Suites,** Hwy. 123 and Hwy. 93 N, 106 Liberty Dr., tel. (864) 654-4605. Inexpensive.

Bed and Breakfasts

Over at 302 Pettigru St. you'll find the five-room **Pettigru Place B&B,** tel. (864) 242-4529, fax (864) 242-1231, set in a renovated 1920s Georgian Federalist home on the National Historic Register. Here, Gloria Hendershot and Janice Beatty serve up home-baked breads and muffins, fruit, some sort of entrée, and afternoon refreshments. The rooms each have different themes, from Victorian to Charlestonian, and some come with private phones—all include private baths, some with whirlpool tubs. Expensive-Luxury. Children 12 and older only. Smoking in outdoor area only.

The **Blue Veranda,** 409 Wilton St., tel. (864) 271-5047, offers a single room in a 1924 home in the historic Earle St. area, about five blocks from downtown. The decor is neo-traditional but, the large bay window overlooking the front yard is peaceful and pretty. The room also includes a queen-size bed, private phone line with an answering machine, and a large private bath with an antique pedestal sink and a transom window. Full Southern breakfasts served (though innkeeper Judy Bikas will alter the menu if you have health considerations). The veranda is the centerpiece of this home; a great place to sit and think about how glad you are you're not in a chain motel by the freeway. Pets welcome here; smoking on the veranda only. Ask about children. Expensive—cheaper rates for multiple-night stays. To get there, take I-385 into Greenville, take the Stone Ave. exit, turn right on Stone Avenue. The second right past Main is Wilton—turn right. You'll find the B&B on the third block, on the left.

East of town on the way to the airport, Jayne and Jerry Frye are the innkeepers at **Creekside Plantation Bed and Breakfast,** 3118 S. Hwy. 14, tel. (864) 297-3293. Luxury, but if you've got the money and aren't traveling with children (forbidden) or pets (ditto) and want to spend the night in one of the four bedrooms in this white, pillared manse, well, then go ahead. Nice front porch, complete with rockers. Healthy, gourmet breakfasts.

FOOD

American/Southern
On the West End, overlooking Reedy Falls, you'll find **Cottage Cuisine,** 615 S. Main St., tel. (864) 370-9070, set in Falls Cottage, built back in 1894 as a rental house. Since Cottage Cuisine is also a catering establishment, you'll find carryout available 9 a.m.-4 p.m., but to eat lunch at the restaurant, you'll need to be here 11 a.m.-2:30 p.m. Creative sandwiches around $6.50. Local artwork also on display here; take some home and the commission will go toward the further development of Reedy River Falls Historic Park. The folks at Cottage Cuisine have started serving dinner, too, but not here in the cottage. You'll find them over at the Peace Center.

On the romantic side, the perennially candlelit **Stax's Peppermill,** 30 Orchard Park Dr., tel. (864) 288-9320, offers secluded tables surrounded by plants. Low lighting. Visit Stax's Wed.-

Sat. for live lobster and entertainment. Expect to spend upwards of $20 for one of the meat or seafood dinners; about half that for lunch.

For something more specifically Southern, head over to 44 Pendleton St. and the **McBee Diner,** tel. (843) 235-2559, where you can eat better-than-average "soul" food.

Seafood
Seafood's not a real strength in Greenville (when asked to vote for the best seafood place in the upstate, *Greenville Times* readers voted **Red Lobster** the winner). But there are some exceptions: **Alley Gator Rawbar and Grille,** 115 Pelham Rd., tel. (864) 370-1857, not only serves up good seafood, but serves it up late. You can get a six-ounce filet mignon with béarnaise sauce and a baked potato and salad for just $6.95 4-11 p.m. A Cajun crawfish boil will run you $6.25 a pound, and sometimes they serve live Maine lobsters for under $12. For those culinarily curious about carnivores, the menu also includes alligator.

Italian
Vince Perone's Restaurant at 1 E. Antrim Dr., tel. (864) 233-1621, features steak, seafood, or pasta in a casual but classy atmosphere. Recently voted "Best All-Around Restaurant in the Upstate" by readers of the *Greenville News.* This is one of those places where the waiters are such professionals that they don't have to pretend to be actors or struggling writers anymore—they're just waiters, at the top of their field. Be sure to try the Killer Pie.

Ristorante Bergamo, in the center of town at 100 N. Main St., tel. (864) 271-8667, serves nouvelle Italian in a casual, hip atmosphere. Dinner only, 6-9:30 p.m. Plates average out to around $15.

Asian
If you'd like a break from barbecue, or from South Carolina in general, you have a handful of options in Greenville. In the midst of downtown, **Lemongrass,** 106 Main St., tel. (864) 241-9988, serves up authentic Thai cuisine. Lunch is usually under $8, and dinner can vary from about $7 to about $18. Beer, wine, and liquor available. Open for lunch Mon.-Sat. 11:30 a.m.-2:30 p.m.; for dinner Mon.-Wed. 5:30-10 p.m., Thurs.-Sat. 5:30-10:30 p.m. No smoking.

The **Nippon Center Yagoto,** 500 Congaree Rd., tel. (864) 288-8471, is open for dinners only (Mon.-Sat. 6-9:30 p.m.) This beautiful restaurant features a waterfall, planted gardens, and a variety of dining areas, including tatami rooms. When you step outside at the end of the night, you'll have to pinch a forearm to remind yourself that you're in upstate South Carolina. Dinners range from around $15 to around $40. Bring some yen.

European
One of the classic downtown alfresco spots is **Bistro Europa,** 219 N. Main St., tel. (864) 467-9975, offering a wonderful vegetarian pasta primavera, and during "Sinatra Sunday" the smoky voice of the Chairman of the Board oozes through the speakers while diners eat open-faced omelettes and smoked-salmon eggs Benedict.

Coffeehouses
Coffee fans and caffeine addicts may wish to stumble over to the **Coffee Underground,** 1 E. Coffee St. at the intersection of Main and Coffee Streets, tel. (864) 298-0494, an upscale spot with European blends, gourmet teas, rich desserts, and deli sandwiches, running from $3 to about $6. Late dinners possible here; wine and beer served. The Underground is also home to the local art-house theater. Call for show times. Hours: Mon.-Wed. 8 a.m.-11 p.m., Thursday 8 a.m.-11:30 p.m., Saturday 8 a.m.-12:30 a.m., Sunday 3-8 p.m. No smoking.

Coffee Underground does bean battle with **The Coffee Beanery Ltd.** just down across from the Hyatt Regency at 225 N. Main St., tel. (864) 241-0474, fax (864) 241-0433. Gourmet coffee bar offers international coffees. Deli sandwiches, salads, and scale-denting desserts; just about everything's under $6. Open Mon.-Fri. 7:30 a.m.-11 p.m., Saturday 8:30 a.m.-midnight. Wheelchair accessible from Main St. entrance. Nonsmoking.

Brewpubs and Sports Bars
In a region where so many families originated in the land of Blarney, it's not surprising to find some authentic Irish eats. Perhaps the most authentic around is **Connolly's Irish Pub,** 24 E. Court St., tel. (864) 467-0300. Try the Irish stews and shepherd's pie. Oh, and the place serves a bit of beer as well.

Also downtown is the **Blue Ridge Brewing Company Brew Pub,** 217 N Main St., tel. (864) 232-4677, across from the Hyatt, tel. (864) 232-4677 (232-HOPS), fax (864) 232-4680. This place has a less-forced feeling to it than many of the new brewpubs popping up here and there around the country—the lack of neon is refreshing. A fairly broad food menu; lunch will cost you around $6 and dinner will cost you on up to around $15. Extensive wine list and a full bar here too, so tipplers of all stripes will be happy. Open Mon.-Fri. 11 a.m.-2 a.m., Saturday 11:30 a.m.-midnight. Those in wheelchairs can access the first floor only. Smoking section. Take a peek at the menu online at www.blueridge.com.

Big River Grille and Brewing Works, 211 E. Broad St., tel. (864) 370-1118, fax (864) 467-0001, a 12,000-square-foot historic brewery, is a good place to spend the entire evening, from appetizers to after-dinner beverages on the patio, listening to the live bands. Price range runs from $6 to $13 or so; it's a great place to catch an after-the-play meal. Open Mon.-Sat. 11:30 a.m. till they feel like closing. Closed Sunday. Ramp for those in wheelchairs.

The menu here is extensive, but not expensive. You've got salads. You've got your creative, eclectic menu: chicken fajitas for $11.95, cedar plank trout (trout baked on a cedar board and served with wild rice pilaf and fresh-cut vegetables) $12.95. If you're doing penance for last night's barbecue, try the vegetable enchiladas in vegetarian green chili, topped with chipotle mayonnaise and sided by Spanish rice and black beans, $7.50. The menu goes on and on, including everything from Lowcountry shrimp 'n' grits and jumbo coconut shrimp to pork ribs.

And then you've got the beer, made here. Varieties include the Southern Flyer Light Lager, Upcountry Amber Ale, Golden Peg Legs Special Ale, hoppy, dark brown Iron Horse Stout. If you're a hops-chewing, dyed-in-the-kidneys microbrew connoisseur, try the copper-colored Walhalla Ipa. Its powerful taste'll knock a Coors drinker halfway to Easley, but you'll probably like it.

At **Bailey's Sports Grille,** 2409 Laurens Rd., tel. (864) 281-9347, wings and sandwiches dominate the menu. This sports bar/full-service restaurant features over 25 televisions (two of them wide screens), and you had better believe that none of them are tuned to PBS—

we're talking sports, sports, sports. On a Clemson game day, we're talking Tigers, Tigers, Tigers. If all this vicarious competition gets your endorphins pumping, spring to your feet between innings or quarters, swagger over to the pool felts, ping-pong tables, and video games, and take on all comers.

Barbecue
One of the best barbecue joints in the Upcountry is **Henry's Smokehouse,** 240 Wade Hampton Blvd., tel. (864) 232-7774; here you'll find ribs, barbecue hash, and even—to please the North Carolinians dripping over the border—Brunswick stew. Another Henry's location does business south of Greenville, on Main Street in Simpsonville.

Over by the Haywood Mall, you'll find **Diggers Barbecue,** 1175 Woods Crossing, tel. (864) 627-1050, serving up barbecue the way it's supposed to be, smoked over a charcoal pit, with lots of fixings on the side. Meals go for $4.50-7.50. Open 11 a.m.-9 p.m. Mon.-Sat. Wheelchair accessible. Smoking section.

Hamburgers
Carpenter Bros. Ol' Timey Soda Fountain & Gift Shop is a great old high-ceilinged soda shop downtown at 123 S. Main St., tel. (864) 232-2416. As long as Carpenter Bros. stays in business, Greenville will keep its small-town feeling: founded in 1883, Carpenter Bros. still dishes out ice cream sodas and shakes and other fountain good-

ies and sandwiches; order a BLT and a chocolate malted and watch the crowd shuffle by outside. Or better yet, listen to the banter between other patrons and the staff, and get the inside scoop on local events. They invite customers to "Visit Downtown . . . the way it used to be," and when they say this, they're playing on a nearly universal nostalgia for a slower-paced, friendlier era—but this of course is made complicated by the South's particular history. Ask Jesse Jackson if he wants to visit downtown Greenville "the way it used to be": Under Jim Crow laws, as an African-American, he would have been arrested for sitting at the counter.

But don't let semantics keep you from coming in and enjoying a light meal or dessert.

Northgate Soda Shop, down the street at 918 N. Main St., tel. (864) 235-6770, cooks up a mean pimento cheeseburger—if you haven't had one yet, you really do need to eat one before you leave the state. And if you like your milk shake here (you will), be sure to tell the person working the fountain that you think he or she's a born jerk.

Over at 598 Pendleton St., tel. (864) 271-2970, you have **Pete's Original,** which has been churning out fine basic pancake breakfasts, chili-cheeseburger plates, onion rings, and hot dogs since 1950, before we even knew they were bad for us.

Down on 2921 White Horse Rd., tel. (864) 269-7661, across from PYA Food Distribution, you'll find **The Clock Drive-In,** the original lo-

Greenville's Carpenter Brothers soda fountain, founded in 1883, harks back to a bygone era of small-town America.

cation in a six-link Upcountry chain. Open 9:30 a.m.-midnight. Though it's possible to get carhop service, you can also use drive-through. Cheap breakfasts; Clock's makes good bacon and eggs and burgers and onion rings and fries, but the barbecue's especially good—especially for a place without a prominently displayed pig on the premises.

ENTERTAINMENT AND EVENTS

The Upcountry's prime large-scale arena for sports and entertainment is the **Bi-Lo Center,** 409 E. North St., tel. (864) 241-3800, fax (864) 241-3872, seating anywhere from 2,500 to 16,000.

Sure, the name of the **Peace Center** may sound very high-minded, but in truth, the name is as high-minded as that of the Trump Towers—the center is named for the Peace family, which donated money for this massive complex at 300 S. Main St., tel. (800) 888-7768 or (864) 467-3000, fax (864) 467-3040. But that doesn't mean you won't find some very groovy operas, classical concerts, Broadway productions, and pop shows here. Call ahead to see who'll be in town when you're here.

Music
To find out what's going on in town, grab the *Greenville News* on a Friday and pick up the weekly entertainment insert. Or, for a high quality "alternative" entertainment paper, pick up a copy of *Creative Loafing,* which you'll find in racks and in stacks in various businesses—especially downtown.

If you're in town on a Wednesday night in the summer, head over to the Peace Center Amphitheater 7-9 p.m. for a free outdoor concert, part of the **Reedy River Nighttime Series** sponsored by the city and the *Greenville News.* Musical styles vary from folk to jazz to "patriotic" to reggae. Call (843) 467-6627 for information.

Clubs
Creative Loafing will also tell you what's going on in the upstate in music (and in stage and film), but for starters, **Henni's,** right downtown at 103 N. Main St., tel. (864) 370-1090, Web site: www.hennibar.com, features live music on Fridays, including a live "Unplugged" series. You'll

---

FAMOUS UPSTATERS

- Pink Anderson, blues legend (Spartanburg)
- David Ball, country music star
- Joe Bennett and the Sparkletones, rockabilly pioneers (Cowpens)
- Reverend Gary Davis, blues legend (Laurens)
- Esquirita, rock pioneer, major influence on Little Richard
- Jesse Jackson, civil rights leader, U.S. presidential candidate (Greenville)
- President Andrew Johnson (Laurens, briefly)
- "Shoeless" Joe Jackson, baseball legend (Greenville)
- The Marshall Tucker Band (Spartanburg)
- Aaron Tippin, country music star
- Ira Tucker, lead singer of gospel music's Dixie Hummingbirds
- Josh White, blues legend (Greenville)

---

also hear live acoustic Thurs.-Sat. at **Lemongrass Lounge,** on the other side of the street beneath Lemongrass Restaurant at 106 N. Main St., tel. (864) 241-9954.

Gametime Riptide, 5 Webb Rd., tel. (864) 297-6500, boasts over 50 televisions (let's all scream together), 19 pool tables, darts, virtual-reality games, karaoke and live bands in a huge 20,000-square-foot warehouse o' stimulation . . . like an adult *Less Than Zero*-themed amusement park for adults. But it's very, very popular, and (so I am told) prime huntin' grounds for Vics and Vixens. **Blue Ridge Brewing Company,** 217 N. Main St., 232 Hops, has live music most nights (closed Sunday). **The Handlebar** is a pub and café in the Mills Center, 500 Mills Ave., tel. (864) 233-6173, offering a Tuesday night bluegrass jam, occasional Wednesday night alternative country series, live bands most every night, and occasional afternoon poetry "slams." **Tidewater,** 233 N. Main St., tel. (864) 271-1400, usually has jazz of some sort; **Occasionally Blues** presents mostly live vintage Delta blues. **The Thirsty Dog Saloon,** 2640 Poinsett Hwy., tel. (864) 235-4469, provides some live "alternative" bands and much cheap beer. **The 858,** 7700 Pelham Rd., tel. (864) 458-8443, features more alternative. In other words, this is a pretty hip town.

Mountain Music Venues

For some "alcohol-free family entertainment," visit **The Barn** on Depot St., over in Greer, tel. (864) 801-1999. If you'd like to see some live mountain music up here in the mountains, or would just like to see what an alcohol-free family looks like, stop on by 8-11:30 p.m. On Saturdays, you'll usually catch Ernest Harvey and the Ernest Harvey Band there. Guest singers are welcome to join in: think of it as karaoke, pioneer style.

Also out of town—and also alcohol- and smoke-free—is **Uptown on the Square** in the tiny town of Belton, tel. (864) 226-9719 or 224-5058. Live bluegrass and gospel music at 6 p.m. Free admission.

Finally, if it's a Saturday night in summer, and you're really looking for a true Southern experience, bring your blankets, picnic baskets, chairs, and jug of sweet tea on down to **Blue Ridge Gospel Park** at 80 W. Tyger Bridge Road, tel. (864) 246-7820 or (864) 895-6457, for a 6 p.m. gospel concert. No charge.

Comedy Clubs and Theater

858 Restaurant (see above) features a comedy club Friday and Saturday. Over at the Holiday Inn at I-85 and Augusta Rd. you'll find **Mac's Comedy Scene**, tel. (864) 299 6227 (299-MACS). Tickets run $5 on Wednesday and Thursday, $7 on weekends. Call for show times. Downtown, **Cafe and Then Some**, 101 College St., tel. (864) 232-2287, features local original comedy and musicals Wed.-Saturday. Call ahead for reservations. Head over to the **Greenville Little Theater,** 444 College St., tel. (864) 233-6238, for Saturday Night Improv, where they take a topic and just run (hop, skip, jump, and only occasionally belly flop) with it. Shows begin at 8:30 p.m.

SHOPPING

You'll find plenty of places to shop throughout the Greenville area. One of my favorites are the **WestEnd Market,** at 1 Augusta St., overlooking Reedy Falls Park. In what was formerly an old marketplace, the city had the foresight to re-open as a public marketplace in 1994. Today you'll find a genuine farmers market featuring

upstate produce and local jellies, herbs, and spices; the **Atrium Shops,** on the Augusta St. level, featuring specialty gifts and curious arts and crafts; and the **Artists Underground,** where you can watch artists working or examine their work. You'll also find a number of spots to eat. Nearby you'll find the **Little Stores of West End,** at 315 Augusta St., tel. (864) 467-1770, a village of sorts featuring antiques, textiles, paintings, beads, and all the other necessities of modern life. Open Mon.-Sat. 10 a.m.-5:30 p.m.

Another neat idea become Greenville reality is the log-cabin **Senior Citizens of Greenville Country Store,** at 102 E. Park Ave., tel. (864) 467-4344. Here, the city's elders are able to supplement their incomes by utilizing their lifetimes of skill in creating homemade crafts—afghans, crochet work, dolls, toys, quilts, and so forth. It's a great way for these folks to raise money for themselves, and a great way for them to share the skills of an earlier generation. The store stands in McPherson Park: take the Stone Ave. exit off I-385, turn south on Main St. and east (left) on Park. You'll see the park and store on your right.

Other spots to shop in Greenville include the **Augusta Road Business Association,** on Augusta Rd., just south of Church St., tel. (864) 281-0604. You'll find some 75 specialty stores and restaurants.

Downtown at 5-B E. Coffee St., you'll find **The Map Shop,** tel. (864) 271-6277, fax (864) 235-7031, Web site: www.themapshop.com, where you'll find travel guides, DPS, and USGS topo maps. The shop can even customize maps if you need one.

INFORMATION

Stop by the **Greenville Convention and Visitors Bureau** downtown at 206 S. Main St., tel. (800) 717-0023 or (864) 233-0461. Or check online at www.greenvilleonline.com.

MEETING PEOPLE

Regular Events

If you like reading poetry or hearing it read, open mike night at **Sarrai's Gallery and Gourmet Coffee,** 305 N. Main St., Anderson is a great spot. **TZ's Fine Wines and Spirits** holds periodic winetastings. Reservations required; admission runs $12. Call (864) 288-1849 for information.

Shared-Interest Groups
Carolina Singles Hiking and Adventures Club offers hikes, day trips, and parties. Call Kathy at (864) 233-1082 or Robert at (864) 244-6244 and find out if they've got something planned while you're there. A more sedentary group—the **Greenville Chess Club,** meets 7:30-11 p.m. every Thursday night at the Bobby Pearse Center, 820 Townes St., tel. (846) 246-6363. All ages welcome. For a true Southern experience, head up to the Quincy's on the Hwy. 123 Bypass in Seneca, where at 7 p.m. every first Tuesday of the month the **Sons of the Confederate Veterans** break yeast rolls and listen as one of the members holds forth on a given history topic. Call Frank Axson for information, tel. (864) 882-1650.

Support Groups
Recovering alcoholics who want to link up with others while on the road can call **AA Hotline,** tel. (864) 233-6454. Or call **Narcotics Anonymous** at (800) 922-5305. The **Rape Crisis Council of Greenville** has a 24-hour help line at (864) 467-3633.

GETTING THERE

By Air
The **Greenville-Spartanburg International Airport** (GSP), 2000 GSP Dr., Greer, tel. (864) 877-7426, fax (864) 848-6225, has recently doubled in size thanks to a $40 million renovation. GSP provides passenger service on Continental, Delta, Norwest, USAir, and a number of smaller airlines. You can get from here to most domestic and international destinations, though in most cases you'll stop at a hub city first. Of course, you can also land in Columbia and drive up here in an hour and a half, or drive down from Charlotte, North Carolina in two hours. Atlanta's only two and a half hours to the west.

By Train
Amtrak stops in Greenville, Spartanburg, and Clemson. At Greenville, the stop's at 1120 W. Washington Street. In Spartanburg, Amtrak stops at 290 Magnolia St., and the Clemson stop is at the intersection of Hwy. 123 and Hwy. 133. For information on all of the above, call (800) 872-7245.

By Bus
Greyhound will get you to the Upcountry if that's what you really want. Call (800) 231-2222 for schedules and rates. To speak directly to the folks at the Greyhound station in Greenville, call (864) 235-4060 or (864) 235-4741.

By Car
I-385 and I-85 intersect at Greenville; from Columbia, head north on I-26 toward Greenville. From Atlanta, take I-85 east. From Charlotte, head west on I-85. From Charleston, as always, head north to Columbia first.

If you work out your itinerary so that you're down in Aiken before you head up to the Upcountry, you've got a nice drive ahead of you through the Old 96 District. Take Hwy. 19 to Eureka, then take Hwy. 25 through Edgefield (see below), parts of the Sumter National Forest, and into Greenwood (see below). At Greenwood you have three choices, all with some merit, depending on what you're looking for: 1) veer left (west) along Hwy. 178 and pass through tiny Hodges, Shoals Junction, Honea Path, and into Belton (see below), where you'll take Hwy. 20 north to the I-85 and on into Greenville; 2) take Hwy. 25 all the way into Greenville, passing mostly through Upcountry farmland and the tiny crossroads of Princeton; or 3) take Hwy. 72 east until you come to Hwy. 221 and take it north into the historic old town of Laurens (see below). From Laurens, either head east and join the I-385 north into Greenville, or take Hwy. 14 through the small farm towns of Barksdale, Gray Court, Owings, Fountain Inn, Simpsonville, and Mauldin before entering Greenville from the south.

GETTING AROUND

Rental Cars
Call **Budget Rent-A-Car** at 458 Woodruff Rd. in

Greenville, tel. (864) 297-0395, fax (864) 288-2946. Budget offers free customer pickup and operates a location at the GSP Airport.

Another option is **Fairway Ford/Isuzu/Saab,** 2323 Laurens Rd. in Greenville, tel. (800) 344-3673 or (864) 242-5060, fax (864) 233-1301, Web site: Fairwyfrd@aol.com.

Bus

The number for the **Greenville Bus** system is (864) 467-4287. For Spartanburg's **SPARTA Transit** system call (864) 583-5789. If you're in Anderson, call the **City of Anderson Transit Division** at (864) 231-7625. In Clemson, call (864) 654-2287 (654-CATS).

EAST OF GREENVILLE

GREER

Take Exit 60 off the I-95 at Greer and you'll come to the **BMW Zentrum,** a one-of-a-kind visitors center at the first non-German plant the Bavarian Motor Works has ever built. South Carolina was so delighted at being the recipient of this plant that the locals even came up with a country song that became popular on Upcountry radio stations, which asserted that the acronym BMW now stood for Bubba Making Wheels.

Here at the Zentrum you'll see exhibits chronicling BMW engineering, including a virtual tour demonstrating the building of a Z3 automobile. Tours are available spring to fall, but not during the winter except for groups of 15 or more (call to make reservations). Open Tues.-Sun. 9:30 a.m.-5:30 p.m., Thursday 9:30 a.m.-9 p.m. To take in this interactive commercial for BMW's luxury vehicles, there's currently no admission charge, but this may change. You'll find a café and gift shop on the premises.

Located in the downtown historic district of Greer, the **Greer Heritage Museum,** 208 Trade St., tel. (864) 877-3359, features a number of artifacts conveying the history of Greer. Open Wed.-Thurs. 11 a.m.-4 p.m. and by appointment. Out on S. Suber Mill Rd., **Suber's Mill,** tel. (864) 877-5616, was built back in 1908 to grind corn using water power. Today, it's still a-grinding. Open for visitors Mon.-Fri. 8 a.m.-5 p.m., Saturday 8 a.m.-noon.

A good place in Greer to find a cheap breakfast or lunch (open till 6 p.m.) is **Broadway Bagels,** 2426 Hudson Rd., tel. (864) 292-6200. The **Arlington House,** 104 W. Arlington Ave., tel. (864) 877-3201, is a bed and breakfast offering two rooms with private baths. Children welcome. Inexpensive.

SPARTANBURG

This city of 45,000 was founded in 1785. Over the past decades, the area has developed into an industrial center; people have moved here from all over the world, giving this once inbred town a more diverse feel.

But this is not to say the town has been devoid of culture all these years. Spartanburg was one of the towns where the mountain people who trickled down from Appalachia to work the mills congregated. The blend of mountain music with blues influences has bred such musicians as Don Reno of the famous bluegrass duo Reno and Smiley, and guitarist Hank "Sugarfoot" Garland; '70s country-rock pioneers The Marshall Tucker Band live in the Spartanburg area. Charlie Daniels went to junior high here. Current country star Aaron Tippin has roots here and now owns a farm outside of town. All this action from such a small town has earned Spartanburg the nickname "Hub City."

Spartanburg is increasingly becoming a city of contrasts: the city is home to **Westgate Mall,** South Carolina's largest, and yet Spartanburg County is also an intensely agricultural region that produces more peaches than any other part of the state. South Carolina ranks second in the nation in peach production, behind only California (Georgia, "The Peach State," runs third). That means there are a lot of peaches here, and if you're visiting at the right time of year this is a nice area to pull over to a roadside stand and load up on juicy, fuzzy balls of peachy goodness.

Information

For more on Spartanburg, give the folks at the **Spartanburg Convention and Visitors Bureau** a call at (800) 374-8326 or (864) 595-5050, or fax them at (864) 594-5055.

Sights

Walnut Grove Plantation, 1200 Ott Shoals Rd., in nearby Roebuck, tel. (864) 576-6546, is an 18th-century plantation furnished with antebellum antiques and available for touring. From April to October you can tour the home Tues.-Sat. 11 a.m.-5 p.m. Year-round you can visit on Sunday 2-5 p.m. and by appointment.

At 501 Otis Blvd., the **Regional Museum of Spartanburg County,** tel. (864) 596-3501, offers various changing exhibits on the history of the Spartanburg region. Open Tues.-Sat. 10 a.m.-noon, 3-5 p.m., Sunday 2-5 p.m. Admission $1, 12 years and under free. One of the oldest and most interesting is the Pardo Stone. In 1566, Spanish King Philip II called for the establishment of a chain of Spanish forts along the coasts of modern-day Florida, Georgia, and South Carolina. The first of these was Fort Felipe on Parris Island, and in autumn of the same year, Fort Felipe's commander, Captain Juan Pardo, was ordered to explore and conquer the land inland. Before long, Pardo was recalled to the coast. He journeyed again in September 1567, reaching as far as present-day Alabama before heading back to San Felipe, but the small garrisons of men he left in his wake were soon massacred by Indians.

Hatcher Gardens, on Reidville Rd., tel. (864) 582-2776, features more than 10,000 plants, numerous ponds, and trails from which to view the prodigious wildlife.

THE PARDO STONE

In 1935, a bogged tractor 12 miles northwest of Spartanburg exposed a large stone marked with carvings of a parallelogram, an arrow, a rising/setting sun, two parallel lines, and the number "1567." Captain Juan Pardo's journal shows he passed through the area in that very year. Given that at that time a major Indian trail cut through the area—and that nobody in the vicinity in 1935 knew anything about Pardo's journeys—scientists are pretty well convinced the stone is authentic.

Today, you can see the stone at the **Regional Museum of Spartanburg County,** 501 Otis Blvd., Spartanburg, tel. (864) 596-3501.

Accommodations

If you find yourself up in this neck of the woods and need a place to stay, the **Nicholls-Crook Plantation House,** 120 Plantation Dr. in the nearby town of Woodruff, tel./fax (864) 476-8820, provides one of the most relaxing nights in the area. This circa-1793 Georgian plantation house features three rooms (two of which share a bath), a tavern room, as well as period gardens and some huge pecan trees outside. Children six and over allowed, pets allowed at hosts' discretion. Moderate-Expensive.

Food

If you go to Rome, you *must* visit the Vatican. If you're in Spartanburg, you *must* stop at the **Beacon Drive In,** 255 Reidville Rd., tel. (864) 585-9387, an increasingly famous old-time carhop drive-in featured in 1989's *Shag.* The second-largest drive-in in the nation.

For Mexican food in a family atmosphere, head over to **Corona Mexican Restaurant,** 404 McCravy Dr., near Western Auto, tel. (864) 585-9980. Nice family-owned place to take your own family—reservations a good idea. Mariachis on the premises. Open Mon.-Thurs. 11 a.m.-2 p.m. and 5-10 p.m., Friday 11 a.m.-2 p.m. and 5-11 p.m., Saturday noon-10:30 p.m., Sunday noon-10 p.m. Smoking section. A good place for a cheap breakfast or lunch (open till 6 p.m.) is **Broadway Bagels,** 1200 E. Main St., tel. (864) 591-0058. Salads.

Nightlife

Magnolia Street Pub, 261 Magnolia St., tel. (843) 948-1777, is something of an institution here. Shows vary in content: one week in 1998 had 1970s rappers Sugar Hill Gang on Wednesday, a local Battle of the Bands on Thursday, and Southern rock/surf/punk/funk band Southern Culture on the Skids on Friday.

Ground Zero, 3059 Howard St., tel. (864) 948-1661, caters to the Gen-X crowd with compound-word bands like "Skinnerbox," "Bongzilla," and so on.

If you tend toward less-piercing music from less-pierced musicians, head on out to the alcohol-free **The Jamboree,** Old Sky City, Hwy. 221, Whitney Road, tel. (864) 271-3079. Features country music on Fridays and Saturdays, TVs for watching the games, complete with live half-time concerts. **Abby's Grille,** tel. (864) 583-4660, also provides live acts.

CROFT STATE PARK

Just three miles southeast of Spartanburg on SC 56, you'll discover Croft State Park, tel. (864) 585-1283, with 50 campsites.

GAFFNEY

Gaffney is known for raising a lot of peaches, and for one peach that was raised years ago and stayed raised—**The Peachoid,** a peach-shaped water tower that has become something of a landmark for folks passing through town on the I-85. The town's name comes from a famous crossroads tavern that used to operate here, owned by Michael Gaffney. Today, Gaffney has blossomed into a town of 16,000, and the Peachoid has to share notoriety with the town's **Carolina Factory Shops** on I-85.

Gaffney was the childhood home of actress Andie MacDowell, she of *Sex, Lies and Videotape, Multiplicity,* and *Groundhog Day* fame.

In town at Irene Memorial Park on S. Logan St., you'll find the **Cherokee County Veterans Museum,** tel. (864) 489-4404, which displays some 400 artifacts from the nation's wards. Open

Saturday 10 a.m.-noon, Sunday, 2-4 p.m. Here at 105 Hillside Dr., by I-85 Exit 90, you can see a restored one-room schoolhouse built in 1880 and enclosed by a split rail fence made of chestnut—a rarity.

COWPENS NATIONAL BATTLEFIELD

Twelve miles northwest of Gaffney, at the intersection of Hwy. 11 and Hwy. 110, you'll find Cowpens National Battlefield, P.O. Box 308, Chesnee, SC 29323, tel. (864) 461-2828, fax (864) 461-7077. During the American Revolution, loyalist-leaning Upcountry residents believed the well-drilled redcoats would throttle any makeshift army the colonialists put together—until Daniel Morgan's rustic backwoods Continentals decimated Banastre "No Quarter" Tarleton's British regulars at this site.

A fine visitors center, exhibits, a walking trail, and marked driving tour tell the story. Be sure to catch the audiovisual presentation, *Daybreak at Cowpens*—well worth the $1 admission (50 cents for children). And don't forget to browse the center's interesting and hard-to-find small-press regional-history books. Visitors center open daily 9 a.m.-5 p.m., battlefield open daily 9 a.m.-8:30 p.m. from Memorial Day to Labor Day. Closed Thanksgiving, Christmas Day, New Year's Day. No admission to the park or visitors center.

NORTH OF GREENVILLE

LANDRUM

Just before you cross the North Carolina border headed north on Hwy. 176, you'll pass through the little foothills town of Landrum. Founded around the turn of the century as a railroad town, Landrum today contains a wealth of antique stores and restaurants. The **Foothills Equestrian and Nature Center** (FENCE), located between Landrum and Tryon, North Carolina, off I-26, offers riding trails and equestrian events on its 200 acres. Every year a Revolutionary War reenactment takes place. A lot of people like to bike up here as well. Call the chamber of commerce at (864) 457-5315 and they'll be happy to give you plenty of information.

CAMPBELL COVERED BRIDGE

If you're a sucker for covered bridges—as I am—you'll want to see this one—the only covered bridge in South Carolina, built in 1909. North of Travelers Rest on Hwy. 25, take Hwy. 414 through Tigerville, turn right on Pleasant Hill Rd., then right on Campbell's Bridge Road. Drive about a quarter of a mile and you'll come to the bridge, which is no longer open to traffic, though you can cross it on foot.

PARIS MOUNTAIN STATE PARK

This mountain was once part of the land owned by Richard Pearis, one of the pre-founding fathers of Greenville; "Paris" is a transmogrification of his name. The campground here on Hwy. 253, just nine miles north of Greenville, tel. (864) 244-5565, offers 50 sites for tents or RVs, plus two for handicapped persons. Water and electrical for all sites.

DACUSVILLE

Although it was only opened in 1991, Terry Taylor's **Dacusville Smokehouse B-B-Q** is the kind of pretenseless country-road barbecue that all those smokehouse-themed places in Columbia and Charleston pretend to be. It's also a good place to find mustard-based shredded, hickory-smoked, tuna fish-looking barbecue. Good hash. On Hwy. 135, 2.5 miles north of the intersection at Highway 183, tel. (864) 855-5431. Open Thurs.-Sun. only, 11 a.m.-9 p.m. Carryouts available. I'd recommend the large barbecue plate ($6.50). On Thursday, you can get minced turkey instead of pork; rib specials Friday and Saturday. Every evening has great specials—one meat, two vegetables for only $3.75! On Sunday, choose from a special Sunday lunch menu that changes every week.

PUMPKINTOWN

The small town got its name just the way you'd figure—from the pumpkin-growing that goes on in these parts. Cattlemen used to drive their herds from Tennessee and western North Carolina through here on their way to Atlanta. Local Native Americans raised a lot of pumpkins in the area, and the drivers took to resting their herds there.

Nowadays about 30 people live in Pumpkintown, but some 40,000 come to visit each fall for the annual Pumpkintown Festival. Whenever it is that you visit, be sure to stop in the old Pumpkintown General Store on Hwy. 11 and say hey to owner Harry Monroe.

Up here on Scenic Hwy. 11 two miles east of Table Rock State Park, you'll also find **Aunt Sue's Country Corner,** tel. (864) 878-4366, a cross between an Appalachian village and a strip mall, featuring **The Christmas House, Pop's Rock Shop, The Wood House, The Gospel House, The Candle House, The Stamp House,** and **The Dream House,** a jewelry shop. These stores are all individually owned. Aunt Sue moved up here back in 1984 from Florida with her husband and kids; they opened up a little place selling ice cream cones and sandwiches, and the place did well enough that they built gift shops, occupied by tenants ("cousins").

Aunt Sue's also features **The Ice Cream House,** with deli sandwiches, salads, and home-made ice cream cones and fudge. Closed Monday, unless it's a holiday. The parlor's open April through Thanksgiving. On the second Saturday of October, be here for the **Pumpkintown Festival,** featuring a parade, music, and clogging. But any old weekend (and most weekdays), you ought to find Miss Phyllis Cannon out on the porch cranking out such classics as "The Elephant Walk" on an organ—perfect ice-cream-licking music if ever there was any. Makes you want to strap on some wheels and free skate. You can even purchase personal tapes of Miss Phyllis. Her husband is "Pop" of "Pop's Rock Shop," which you really ought to stop into if only to see some of the Native American crafts; one of the artists, Tommy Hawk Sloan, was recently invited by the Smithsonian to create works for its Cherokee Nation Exhibit. See them online at www.auntsues.com.

MOUNTAIN BRIDGE STATE NATURAL AREA

The State Parks Department has recently combined **Caesars Head State Park** and **Jones Gap State Park** to form this natural area. The Jones Gap Environmental Education Center stands at 303 Jones Gap Rd., tel. (864) 836-3647, featuring exhibits on the history of the Mountain Bridge region. The park is open 9 a.m.-6 p.m., office open 11 a.m.-noon. The "gap" in the mountains is the Saluda River Gorge. It was named for pioneer Solomon Jones, who blazed the road along here.

At 3,266 feet, the **Caesars Head Station,** 8155 Greer Hwy., on Hwy. 276 at the border between South and North Carolina, tel. (864) 836-6115, offers a wonderful panoramic view of the Blue Ridge Mountains. The visitors center is open year-round, daily 9 a.m.-5 p.m. In addition to the state parks, the preserve is also home to 420-foot Raven Cliff Falls (off Hwy. 276), Cleveland Cliffs, and Ashmore Heritage Preserve. You'll need to hike in two miles to see Raven Cliff, but this is one of the prettiest sights in the entire state, so try to make it if you can. The trailhead is about a mile north of the visitors center.

A lot of people also like hiking the Jones Gap Trail, a five-mile hike between Jones Gap and Caesars Head.

Five miles off Hwy. 276 near Caesars Head, you'll find **Symmes Chapel,** a YMCA camp chapel, which is also known as "Pretty Place," because . . . well, you know. The gorgeous view of Standing Stone Mountain draws 100 couples a year who say their vows up here. Call (864) 836-3291 for directions and admission to the camp.

TABLE ROCK STATE PARK

The rounded monadnock called Table Rock may well be the Upcountry's most famous attraction. Certainly, Table Rock State Park is one of the state's most popular parks, with camping, hiking, fishing, boating, swimming, miniature golf. There's a restaurant up here and rental cabins.

SASSAFRAS MOUNTAIN

Those who make it a point to climb the highest peak in every state will want to head to Sas-

upstate landmark monadnock Table Rock

safras, on Hwy. 199 off Hwy. 178 in Pickens County. You'll reach the dizzying height of 3,554 feet at the summit, which is not very tall compared to the mountains in Colorado or California—or even North Carolina, for that matter.

But nonetheless, you'll be able to see four different states from the summit: both Carolinas, Tennessee, and Georgia. Some say that on a really clear day you can also see Iowa, but this sounds just like a rumor to me.

WEST OF GREENVILLE

PICKENS

Named for Upcountry Revolutionary hero Andrew Pickens, the 5,000-person town of Pickens includes the 1828 **Hagood-Mauldin House,** 104 N. Lewis St., formerly the county seat and currently home to the **Irma Morris Museum of Fine Art,** tel. (864) 878-9459. Open on weekend afternoons 2-5 p.m. from April to early December, featuring displays of 17th- and 18th- century furnishings and art.

The **Pickens County Museum,** Johnson and Pendleton Streets, tel. (864) 898-5963, is set in the historic old turreted Pickens County Jail. The first floor features a worthwhile historical collection; you'll find art upstairs. Open Tues.-Fri. 9 a.m.-5 p.m. No admission charged.

If you've a mind to stay the night here, see if you can get one of the six rooms at **The Schell House,** 117 Hiawatha Trail, tel./fax (864) 878-0078, a Victorian home offering views of Table Rock, along with the private baths (some jacuzzis). Children allowed by hosts' discretion. Gourmet breakfasts and afternoon refreshments served.

On the same road, you might want to stop in and browse a bit at **Rain Barrel Antiques & Gifts,** tel. (864) 878-0097.

EASLEY

Surrounded by mountains and lakes, the foothills town of Easley is home to over 20,000 people. At 201 Enon Church Rd., tel. (864) 859-1958 (a.m.) or (864) 843-6320 (p.m.), you'll find a beautiful old **19th-century mill** with waterwheel powered by Golden Creek. If you're here around mealtime, eat at **Joe's** on E. Main St., tel. (864) 859-9186, locally famous for its hot dogs, hamburgers, and ice cream. Or pick up a barbecue sandwich. Whatever you get, if you spend more than six dollars it means you left a very generous tip. This is the kind of small-town place where everybody ends up after the football game. Really worth a stop. Open daily at 11 a.m., except Sunday, when it doesn't open up until 5 p.m. for the dinner crowd.

You may also want to visit **Mountain View Hotel Antiques,** 108 N.W. Main St., tel. (864) 306-1069; **Adams Attic,** 223 W. Main St., tel. (843) 859-4996; or **Lost in the Past Antique Mall,** 6811 Calhoun Memorial Hwy., tel. (864) 859-2288.

Continue west on Hwy. 93 and you'll soon come upon **Liberty** and **Central** (so named because the lunch-stop railroad town was in the center between Atlanta and Charlotte).

West of Central you'll come upon Issaqueena Trail, which you can use to cut south and on down to Hwy. 28 and then east into Pendleton. Or you can continue along Hwy. 93 on into Clemson.

KEOWEE-TOXAWAY STATE PARK

Don't let the name keep you away. No matter what it sounds like, Toxaway is *not* a toxic-spill cleaning product. Keowee and Toxaway are both names of rivers now immersed in Lake Keowee. You'll find an interpretive center and a boardwalk with artifacts and exhibits commemorating the Lower Cherokee, who once had their capital on the banks of the Keowee. This lake is about a third the size of Lake Hartwell, but some say it's prettier.

This state park on Hwy. 11 at Lake Keowee, tel. (864) 868-2605, features 24 camping sites, 10 for RV, 14 for tents, and two handicapped. Boating, fishing, water-skiing, swimming, and camping are all popular up here. To rent boats or boating gear, contact **Lake Keowee Marina,** tel. (864) 882-3111, fax (864) 882-1026.

You really ought to stop by the **Cherokee Indian Interpretive Center** to get a better understanding of the Cherokee. Located inside the Keowee-Toxaway State Park, tel. (864) 868-2605, the center traces the history and culture of the Keowee Valley's first inhabitants. Stop by Wed.-Sun. 9 a.m.-5 p.m. June-Aug., or Wed.-Sun. 10 a.m.-noon and 4-5 p.m. the rest of the year, and by appointment. No charge.

LAKE JOCASSEE STATE PARK

This beautiful lake gets its name from the legend of a young Cherokee woman, Jocassee. Jocassee's lover was murdered, and Jocassee drowned her sorrows by drowning herself. However, she didn't drown here, since the lake's only been in existence since 1974. Less than a tenth the size of Lake Hartwell, Jocassee features 7,500 acres of water and 75 miles of shoreline. The good news recently has been that the state has begun acquiring property in the Jocassee Gorges, above the lake.

DEVIL'S FORK STATE PARK

The Blue Ridge Mountains make a beautiful backdrop for this park at 161 Holcombe Circle, on Lake Jocassee, tel. (864) 944-2639. Fifty-nine sites for RVs, 20 walk-in tents-only sites. Two are set aside for visitors with disabilities. Water and electrical on the RV sites. Carolinians really like the 20 fully furnished mountain villas here, which are available for rent—reserve well ahead of time.

The park also includes a picnic area with shelters, a park store and tackle shop, laundry facilities, a nature trail, a swimming beach, and bathhouse. Lake Jocassee itself is very cold and deep, making it a popular place for catching brook, brown, and rainbow trout.

WHITEWATER FALLS

A few miles north of Devil's Fork, this falls descends in two stages, totaling nearly 700 feet—making it the highest series of falls in the eastern U.S. You can drive right up to the overlook for these. The North Carolina-South Carolina border actually runs right between these falls—the Upper Falls are in Tarheel Country; the Lower Falls are in South Carolina. For more information on the falls or to get a guide to 25 Upcountry waterfalls, call the South Carolina Department of Natural Resources at (803) 734-3944.

ELLICOTT ROCK WILDERNESS

If you really want to get away from it all in South Carolina, this may be the place to do it—it doesn't get much more pristine than this. In 1975, the U.S. Congress designated this area as South Carolina's first wilderness area, covering 9,012 square miles and even lapping over into North Carolina and Georgia.

To get there, take Hwy. 325 off Hwy. 107. For more information, contact the Forest Service at 112 Andrew Pickens Circle, Mountain Rest, or call (864) 638-9568.

Ellicott's Rock itself is a large rock marked by surveyor Andrew Ellicott in 1811 to signify the exact spot where South Carolina, North Carolina, and Georgia all meet. Unfortunately, he got it wrong by a few feet—Commissioners Rock, which extends into the river, bears the true inscription: Lat 35, AD 1813 NC-SC.

You can reach it by taking the 16.7-mile Sumter Section of the Chattooga Trail. The trailhead is at Russell Bridge on Hwy. 28. Stop by the Stumphouse Ranger Station just five miles north of Walhalla on Hwy. 28 to pick up a map. Or call (800) 862-1795 or (864) 646-3782 to have one sent to you.

THE CHATTOOGA NATIONAL WILD AND SCENIC RIVER

Made famous (and popular) by its starring role in the Dixophobic classic, *Deliverance,* the Chattooga was named the South's first national wild and scenic river just a year after the film's release, saving it from certain overdevelopment and overuse. However, even though (and perhaps because) the National Park Service limits the number of paddlers allowed to blast down the river's gorges, the Chattooga remains a big one of the biggies for rafters and kayakers. It drops an average of 49.3 feet per mile.

Toward the upper part of the river you'll find **Chattooga Town,** a major Cherokee archaeological site. The fishing's good as well. For information on the river, call (864) 638-9568.

THE CHAUGA RIVER SCENIC AREA

South of the Chattooga runs the short, fierce Chauga, a great whitewater-rafting area that drops some 46 feet per mile for a good stretch and features the beautiful Chauga Narrows and Riley Moore Falls. Primitive trails lead to fishing and primitive camping areas. Call (864) 638-9568 for information.

OCONEE STATE PARK

This WPA-era park on Hwy. 107, 12 miles northwest of Walhalla, tel. (864) 638-5353, has always been a favorite base camp for people looking to explore the Upcountry. You can camp here or rent one of the cabins, though to do that you'll usually need an advance reservation. Neat little camp store. Camping includes 150 sites, 10 specially set aside for tenters, and two specially set aside for campers with disabilities. Water and electrical hookups. Open year-round, though in winter the park does get snow.

STUMPHOUSE MOUNTAIN TUNNEL AND ISSAQUEENA FALLS

Call (800) 862-1795 or (864) 646-3782 for information on this unique little park. Here on Hwy. 28, five miles north of Walhalla, you'll find these two interesting sites. The tunnel was begun in the 1850s in the spirit of Southern pride—an attempt to connect the ports of Charleston with the wheat and cattle of the Midwest. It was abandoned during the Confederacy and never finished. For a number of years, Clemson University used to age its famous blue cheese in the tunnel here, back before climate-controlled lockers became common.

The legendary 200-foot Issaqueena Falls is one of the prettiest and most accessible cataracts in the state. You can practically drive to the very top of the falls, and a very short, steep hike will get you to the bottom. Apparently, it's a good party spot as well for the locals; you may want to play Woodsy Owl by bringing a garbage bag and wading around for the cans that usually end up down here. But don't let the litter scare you away—this is a beautiful fall, with a small cave up at the top just beneath the sheet of water. Legend has it that a young Cherokee woman named Issaqueena was being pursued by fellow Cherokees—angered because she'd warned nearby settlers of a planned attack. She shook off pursuers here by pretending to jump from the falls, while in reality hiding behind them. No doubt the bad guys figured she'd shredded herself on the beer cans at the bottom and died.

The 12-mile stretch of road north of the park on Hwy. 413, on to the North Carolina border, is called the **Wiginton Scenic Byway.**

On Hwy. 107, 5.8 miles north of Oconee State Park, lies the **White Rock Scenic Area,** a 3,416-acre zone containing some of the most rugged land in the state and a number of waterfalls, along with the **Winding Stairs Hiking Trail.** The name might make you breathe heavily just thinking about it, but this is at most a moderately challenging trail. Start from the Cherry Hill campground entrance.

WALHALLA

Founded by German immigrants, Walhalla ("Pleasant Hill") features some pretty old buildings including **Walhalla Presbyterian Church** at the corner of Main and South Johnson, and **St. John's Lutheran Church,** on Main, featuring the town clock.

Oconee Station, just over 8.5 miles north of Walhalla on Rd. 95, tel. (864) 638-0079, is the oldest building in Oconee County. It was built in 1792 as one of a chain of blockhouses erected along the western frontier of South Carolina to protect against Indian attacks. Troops were kept here for seven years, until 1799. The **William Richards House,** next door, was built in 1805, thought to be the oldest brick house in the upstate.

If you're parked here, follow the winding trail that leaves from the house to 60-foot Station Cove Falls, a two-step waterfall about a mile down the trail. The park is open Thurs.-Sun.

March through December. You may tour the buildings 1-5 p.m. on Saturday and Sunday. Free admission.

The area at the base of the waterfalls has been designated the **Station Cove Botanical Area.** In spring, you'll find some colorful and rare wildflowers down there.

Most people heading up into the country around Walhalla sleep at one of the campgrounds, but there's something to be said about being able to look forward to a comfortable bed and a shower at the end of a long day on the whitewater. The **Liberty Lodge B&B,** 105 Liberty Lane, tel. (864) 549-3232, fax (864) 549-6913, offers a large Victorian manor with a wraparound porch and hiking trails right on the premises. The lodge serves up a full country breakfast, and dinner's available upon request. Six rooms; bathrooms can be private or shared. Children and pets at hosts' discretion. Moderate-Expensive.

SENECA

The first Seneca was a Cherokee town called Sah-Ka-Na-Ga ("Great Blue Hills of God"), which English ears and tongues turned into "Seneca." The current town, formally chartered in 1874, was built up around the railroad.

Today, most folks who drop by Seneca do so as a stop on a Sunday drive or as a jumping-off place for the surrounding mountains. But don't rush off too quickly: much of town—the entire historic district, in fact—is listed on the National Register. Pick up a self-guided tour map at the **Lumney Museum,** tel. (864) 882-4811. For other information, contact the **Seneca Chamber of Commerce,** P.O. Box 855, Seneca, SC 29679, tel. (864) 882-2047.

CLEMSON

Note the giant orange tiger tracks painted onto the asphalt as you drive into town. The town of Clemson, with its 11,100 full-time residents, is greatly influenced by the large numbers of Tiger faithful who migrate here on weekends during football season.

Clemson has a cute—almost too cute—downtown. People keep sitting on the curbs and ask-ing when the electrical parade starts. On the other hand, it seems like just about the perfect-sized town to go to school in, and there are just enough good restaurants to keep you busy.

Clemson University

This 1,400-acre campus was founded in 1889 and named after Thomas Green Clemson, John C. Calhoun's son-in-law, who donated the plantation—Fort Hill—which he had inherited from Calhoun, to the state for an agricultural college. Located on the shores of Lake Hartwell, the campus itself is surrounded by another 17,000 acres of university farms and forest used for research. The college has 16,000 students, 4,000 of them graduate students, the rest undergrads.

To pick up information and campus publications, and to find out about guided tours, stop by the campus **visitors center,** tel. (864) 656-4789, open Mon.-Sat., afternoons only on Sunday, closed weekends in December and January. To reach the center from 93, take a right at the first traffic light onto N. Palmetto Blvd., then go approximately two-tenths of a mile to the stop sign where the road forks. Take the left fork; this will lead to a cul de sac at the new center.

One spot you must stop at while on campus is **Uniquely Clemson,** inside Newman Hall, tel. (864) 656-3242. You can purchase ice cream, blue cheese, and other dairy products whipped up right here at the Agricultural College. Open Mon.-Sat. 9 a.m.-9 p.m., Sunday 1-9 p.m. For information check online at www.clemson.edu.

South Carolina State Botanical Gardens

On campus you'll find this 270-acre master garden, tel. (864) 656-2458, featuring 2,200 varieties of ornamental plants including azaleas and camellias, wildflower, fern, and bog gardens, and many indigenous plants. You'll find the Azalea and Camellia Trail especially pretty in the spring. The re-created Upcountry homestead features a waterwheel, wagon, and cabin, along with a garden featuring the sorts of varieties of vegetables and herbs a pioneer family would have planted. In the summer of 1998 the Wren House, a *Southern Living* Showcase Home, was opened. By the time you get there, the home will have finished its tenure with *Southern Living* and become the **Fran Hanson Center,** a visitors center for the garden, and the Discovery Center

On the Clemson University campus, the South Carolina State Botanical Gardens include this cabin, part of a re-created upcountry homestead.

for Region I of the South Carolina Heritage Corridor. This home was largely built with South Carolina products and decorated with South Carolinian art. Be sure to see the mural that illustrates the natural history of the state, showing the changes from the terrain of the mountains to the coast. Open daily. Free admission to both the home and the garden.

Fort Hill

This Nationally Registered Historic Landmark on the Clemson University campus, tel. (864) 656-2475, was the plantation home of former U.S. Vice President John C. Calhoun, and later home of Thomas Green Clemson, Calhoun's son-in-law, and donor of the land that became Clemson University. In the State Dining Room you'll see a beautiful mahogany sideboard made from paneling salvaged from the officers' quarters of the USS *Constitution,* which had been condemned in the late 1820s. Calhoun received the sideboard as a gift from Henry Clay, who was taken with a speech Calhoun gave defending the U.S. Constitution. Ironically, back in Boston, Oliver Wendell Holmes ended up writing the famed poem "Old Ironsides," which stirred up public sentiment to restore and refurbish the old ship. Calhoun was allowed to keep his sideboard.

While you're here, also poke your head into the master bedroom to see the huge mahogany bed. Supposedly, the Marquis de Lafayette slept in this bed while a guest at the Calhouns' Washington home. Unfortunately, when the Agricul-

tural College was built in the 1890s, most of Calhoun's books were moved from his attached office to a safe new brick building, which promptly burned. Nonetheless, a few books have come back to the home over the years, donated by the descendants of those to whom Calhoun gave them.

Open weekdays 10 a.m.-5 p.m., Saturdays 10 a.m.-noon and 1-5 p.m., Sunday 2-5 p.m. No charge to tour the house, but you really ought to leave a couple bucks as a donation.

Lodging

Clemson features an abundance of reasonably priced lodging designed for visiting Tiger faithful. On the cheap but tidy side is **Clemson Suites,** 106 Liberty Drive (at Hwy. 123 and 93 No.), tel. (864) 654-4605, with kitchenettes available and a pool. You'll also find a **Days Inn** at 1387 Tiger Blvd., tel. (864) 653-4411, fax 654-3123, on Hwy. 123, 0.4 miles south of the junction of 123 and US 76.

Food

Sardi's on Hwy. 93 specializes in great, fall-off-the-bone ribs. Anderson's well-traveled Geoff Grafton swears they're the best he's had anywhere. No cute country ambience here—you come for the rack, not the tack. Hole-in-the-wall rib place. Sardi's opened up a new location in Anderson.

Calhoun Corners, 103 Clemson St., tel. (864) 654-7490, was named for John C. Calhoun. A nice brick restaurant owned by the same folks who own Pixie and Bill's, Calhoun Corners features a pub up on the third floor. Open for lunch and supper.

One of the classic places for alumni in town on football weekends and students letting their visiting parents treat them is **Pixie and Bill's,** 1058 Tiger Blvd., tel. (864) 654-1210, where the seafood and steaks get raves. My favorite is the chicken parmesan artichoke bake. Or for something more casual, try **Keith Street Pub and Grille,** at 101 Keith St., tel. (864) 654-2274, where you'll find some good sandwiches and salads and over 200 different beers, including 14 on tap.

To plunge deeply into the orange seas of Tigermania, take a meal at the **Tiger Town Tavern,** 368 College Ave., tel. (864) 654-5901.

Reading the menu is half the fun—it's divided up into such categories as "Preseason" (appetizers), "The ACC" (sandwiches), "Olympic Sports" (light soups and salads), and "Bowl Game" (house specialties). Or you can throw cardiopulmonary health to the wind and order a "William Refrigerator Perry" (a double hamburger), named for the former Tiger who went on to become a Chicago Bear. The description of the Gamecock—a chicken salad sandwich—notes, ". . . these chickens have been sliced, diced and shredded by opponents regularly, a favorite of the big CAT."

You'll find live music here some nights. This place is over 20 years old—something of a Clemson tradition, as is **Mac's Drive-In,** 404 Pendleton

JOHN C. CALHOUN

In 1754, Patrick Calhoun—father of John C. Calhoun—made his home across Long Cane Creek in Indian territory, one of the Scottish-Irish emigrants from northern states who began to settle in the perilous region. John C. Calhoun was born into the rugged frontier of western South Carolina in 1782.

Calhoun's parents sent him to a log-cabin school where he learned the classics, Bible study, and discipline. Calhoun's mind was exceptionally sharp. He was able to enter Yale as a junior in 1802 and graduated two years later—a member of Phi Beta Kappa. (Yale would go on to name one of its colleges in his honor.)

Calhoun went to Connecticut and studied law, completing his studies in Charleston. In 1807, he moved to Abbeville and opened a law firm on the square.

In 1808 and 1809, he served in the state legislature in Columbia. In 1811, he was sent to Washington as a member of the U.S. House of Representatives. Speaker of the House Henry Clay put Calhoun on a committee where his anti-British feelings helped lead the country into the War of 1812.

After the war, Calhoun served as secretary of war under President James Monroe for eight years. He served as vice president under Quincy Adams and Jackson, resigning partway through Jackson's first term to run for (and win) a South Carolina seat in the Senate, where he was author of the Nullification Crisis. Though many of his upstate constituents felt Calhoun had sold them out

through his politically important hobnobbing with the Lowcountry elites and his focus on their obsession with the slavery issue, Calhoun always considered the Clemson area his home.

Despite Northern disapproval of his staunch states' rights stand, he's even today widely considered South Carolina's greatest statesman of all time. It is Calhoun's statue that represents South Carolina in the Capitol rotunda in Washington, D.C.

Rd., tel. (864) 654-2845, featuring one counter, 15 stools, and plenty of Clemson orange paint.

Nightlife

Pick up a copy of *The Clemson Weekly,* which you'll find in most bars, coffeehouses, and so on. **Los Hermanos** has live bands on the weekends, the **Esso Club,** 129 Old Greenville Hwy., tel. (864) 654-5120, on Thursdays and Fridays. **McP's,** 1393 Tiger Blvd., tel. (864) 654-9072, has some of the best live music in town, except on karaoke Sundays, when it varies considerably.

PENDLETON

This city was founded as the capital of the Pendleton district in the late 1770s, after the Cherokee—who had sided with the British in the Revolution—ceded the region to South Carolina. At the time, this was the only town built west of Camden. Pendleton was named after Judge Henry Pendleton, a Virginia militia leader whose minutemen helped defend the patriot cause in South Carolina. The region became an important trade and government center, which helps explain the number of large old beautiful buildings here.

Pendleton's extensive and well-preserved historic district has made it a popular place with visitors. It features numerous antique and specialty shops, as well as restaurants and B&Bs, all in addition to some 40 structures of historical interest.

Sights

On the town square, the **Farmers' Society Hall,** tel. (800) 862-1795 or (864) 646-3782, is the focal point of the old part of town. This is the oldest farmers' hall in continuous use in the nation—it was built on the site of the old courthouse.

At 125 E. Queen St., the 1850 **Hunter's Store,** tel. (800) 862-1795 or (864) 646-3782, now houses the Pendleton District Historical, Recreational and Tourism Commission. You'll also find a bookstore, research library, arts and crafts shop, and an exhibit area. Open Mon.-Fri. 9 a.m.-4:30 p.m.; closed holidays. Free admission.

If the history of this agricultural region interests you, stop by the **Pendleton District Agricultural Museum,** Hwy. 76, tel. (800) 862-1795 or (864) 646-3782, where in addition to early farm equipment and tools you'll see Cherokee arti-

facts, a surrey with a fringe on top, and the first !#*!&@!! boll weevil ever found in South Carolina. Open by appointment only. Free admission.

Ashtabula and **Woodburn,** one on Hwy. 88 east of Pendleton and one on Hwy. 76 west of Pendleton, tel. (800) 862-1795 or (864) 646-3782, are two beautiful old Upcountry mansions built by Lowcountry planters who moved up here to the healthier summer climate in the foothills. Both are furnished with period antiques and open Sundays only, 2-6 p.m. April-Oct., or by appointment. A small admission is charged.

Accommodations

A favorite spot for leisure travelers these days is the 10-room **Liberty Hall Inn,** 621 S. Mechanic St., tel. (800) 643-7944, tel./fax (864) 646-7500, an antebellum home set on four acres, where a distinct "country" feel emanates from the quilts and pine floors. Continental breakfast buffet and complimentary wine. If you like, you can dine by candlelight in the restaurant. Moderate-Expensive.

Food

On the town square in the old courthouse, you'll find the **Farmers' Hall Restaurant,** tel. (864) 646-7024, where you can eat outside under a huge oak, or inside. Dinners run about $16, half that for lunch. Open Wed.-Sat., lunch and dinner only, closed 1:30-5:30 p.m. between meals.

Shopping

Two spots for antiquing and locally made crafts are **Mountain Made,** right on the square at 150 Exchange St., tel. (864) 646-8836, featuring South Carolina utilitarian pottery and estate finds, and **Village Curio,** 124 Exchange St., (864) 646-8600, carrying a variety of small antique pieces, including crystal and china.

LAKE HARTWELL STATE PARK

Right on the state line, Lake Hartwell State Park, 19138-A S. Hwy. 11, Fair Play, SC 29643, tel. (803) 972-3352, is one of the Southeast's largest, most popular lakes. It was built 1955-63 to control flooding and provide more power for the "smug little suburbs" Burt Reynolds berates at the beginning of *Deliverance* (and this chapter). The lake features 962 miles of shoreline encircling 56,000 acres of water, campgrounds, boat access ramps, and recreation areas.

For boat rentals, contact **Hartwell Lake Ma-** **rine Rentals,** 4439 Hwy. 24, tel. (864) 260-9712; **Portman Marina,** 1629 Marina Rd., tel. (864) 287-3211, fax (864) 882-1026; or **Big Water Marina,** 320 Big Water Rd., tel. (864) 226-3339.

SOUTH OF GREENVILLE

SADLERS CREEK STATE PARK

Sadlers Creek State Park, on Hwy. 187, tel. (864) 226-8950, is also on Lake Hartwell and the state line. The sites here are close together—if you're in an RV and tend to leave your TV volume cranked up to drown out your generator anyway, then this probably won't bother you. But if you're looking for a quiet, back-to-nature tenting experience, I'd pick the Corps of Engineers' **Springfield Campground,** nine miles southwest of Anderson off Hwy. 187, with 79 sites, many of them on the waterfront. If you have a boat, you can actually park it at the front of your site.

ANDERSON

The county seat of Anderson County, Anderson now boasts over 27,000 residents. Greenville's Shoeless Joe Jackson played the only baseball game he ever played shoeless here. Hampered by blisters, he chose to play in his stocking feet in the game against the Anderson team. When he rapped out a triple in the seventh inning, a large Anderson fan stood up and shouted, "You shoeless sonofagun, you!" which caught on with his teammates, branding him with the name for life, and on into legend.

Sights

Anderson's 16-block **historic district** isn't the prettiest in the Upcountry, but it does include the old county courthouse, a brass cannon used in the Revolutionary War and in the War of 1812, and an old passenger station for the Blue Ridge Railway.

Set in an original Carnegie Library building, the **Anderson County Arts Center** at 405 W. Main, tel. (864) 224-8811, displays various exhibits and hosts a number of programs throughout the

year. Open Mon.-Fri. 9:30 a.m.-5:30 p.m.; Sunday 1:30-3:30 p.m. No admission fee. Also downtown is the **Anderson County Museum,** 1 Court Square, tel. (864) 260-4737, which contains a number of artifacts and photos pertaining to the county. Open Mon.-Fri. 10 a.m.-4 p.m.

Accommodations

The **Days Inn,** at I-85 Exit 19A, tel. (864) 375-0375, is a good, safe, clean place to stay out by the freeway. Expensive.

The city also offers a selection of B&Bs. The **Evergreen Inn,** at 1109 S. Main St., tel. (800) 241-0034 or (864) 225-1109, is right next door to the 1109 Restaurant, which has its benefits. Here you'll find six plush rooms, owned by the same Swiss family that makes the restaurant next door so nice. Built in 1830 and seated on a three-acre lot, this is one of the oldest homes in Anderson, and it's listed on the National Historic Register. Moderate. For something a little fancier, head on over to **Centennial Plantation,** 1308 Old Williamston Rd., tel. (864) 225-4448, where Georgann and Ed Fontaine rent out three rooms on a 10-acre turn-of-the-century plantation, complete with gazebo, horse, goats, and geese. Kids are welcome, and they love the farm atmosphere. Breakfast includes homemade bread covered with homemade jams and jellies. Moderate-Expensive. Finally, **Anderson's River Inn,** 612 E. River St., tel. (864) 226-1431, fax (864) 231-9847, offers three rooms on the "freshwater coast." Children and smoking (in restricted areas) both allowed, though smoking children are frowned upon. Moderate-Premium.

Food

If you liked the TV show, you'll love the restaurant: **Friends,** at 112 N. Main St. in downtown Anderson, tel. (864) 231-0663, is only just a little less trend-conscious than the TV show. But don't let that keep you from the good beef stroganoff and grilled salmon here. Lunches served Mon.-Sat. 11 a.m.-6 p.m., dinners Fri.-Sat. only, 5 p.m.-late. Live entertainment on the weekends, and a late-night menu. Word has it the owners are planning to open up a less-intimate joint called Acquaintances, but this may only be a rumor.

Probably my favorite restaurant in Anderson is the **Ole Country Smokehouse BBQ,** 3819 Hwy. 81 N, tel. (864) 375-0050, where you'll find lots to eat, lots of memorabilia on the walls, and both mustard-based and tomato-based sauces on the table. On Wednesday nights, a local Baptist church holds services on the screened porch on the side.

If you get a hankering for real Mexican in the upstate, you really ought to head over to **Don Pablos,** 3730 Clemson Blvd., tel. (864) 261-7250. This small East Coast chain knows what it's about. Big burritos, chicken flautas.

In the hamburger department, the burgers at **Fireside Restaurant,** at I-85 and Hwy. 81, tel. (864) 224-6454, come highly recommended. Sure, **Skin Thrasher's,** 203 Hudgens St., tel. (864) 231-0370, sounds like a punk nightclub (at best), but this landmark dive serves beer-soaked hot dogs. And can you say that about your average French restaurant?

For something fancier and even more romantic than Skin Thrasher's, head over to the restored 1906 Greek Revival mansion reborn as **1109 South Main Restaurant,** tel. (864) 225-1109, located inside the Evergreen Inn. The very name of the place tells you these folks don't take anything for granted. Expect to spend about $15 for dinner.

The Swiss-born chef/proprietor here serves up some unique gourmet entrées, which have become popular enough around these parts to make reservations a very good idea. Open for dinner only, 6-10 p.m.

Nightlife
You'll find live music at **Friends,** 112 N. Main St., Anderson, tel. (864) 231-0663, where "We're just friends" isn't just an alibi, but a corporate mission statement. But the **Vintage Blues Cafe** offers live entertainment most nights; Monday is live DJ tunes, Tuesday and Thursday are open jam nights, and Friday and Saturday feature Cocktail Frank. Pay the $5 cover ($10 for under 21), order a martini, and relax.

DUE WEST

Along with other strange-but-true South Carolina town names like Central (in the northern part of the state) and North (in the central part of the state), you've got to include this little town. You might well look at Due West on a map and wonder, "Due west of *what?*" In truth, the town resulted from a misunderstanding on the part of Scottish-Irish immigrants after the Revolution, who arrived at what was then known as DeWitts Corner, built a church, and called it, "The Church at Due West Corner." Rather than embarrass their new neighbors, everybody nodded and went along with it.

Due West's claim to fame is **Erskine College,** the first four-year church college in South Carolina, affiliated with the Associate Reformed Presbyterian Church.

This small town is slow-paced and tree-shaded; a walk around Erskine Campus is a nice way to spend an hour or so. Perhaps the most famous building there is the three-story brick **New Erskine Building** (1893), erected on the site of the first brick college building built here in 1842. The building's two towers look almost like a compromise design created by committee with different aesthetic values—one tower holds a town clock, the other is capped by a dome. For more information on Erskine, see the Web site www.erskine.edu.

The **Somewhere in Time B&B** at 1 Abbeville St., tel. (864) 379-8671, offers five rooms.

ABBEVILLE

Arguably, the Confederacy was both born and ended in this picturesque little town. On November 22, 1860, at what is now called **Secession Hill,** a mass meeting voted unanimously to approve South Carolina's Ordinance of Secession. It was signed a month later in Charleston at a convention of delegates all around the state, and South Carolina began its maverick secession, which, when followed by other Southern states, led to the American Civil War.

On May 2, 1865, C.S.A. President Jefferson Davis presided over the War Council of the Confederate Forces, where it was decided to formally disband the Confederate States Armies.

Of course the town is much older than the War between the States. In 1754, Patrick Calhoun—father of John C. Calhoun—made his home across Long Cane Creek in Indian territory. Scotch-Irish immigrants from northern states began to settle in the perilous region. In 1764, over 200 French Huguenots moved into the region. One of them, Dr. John De La Howe, named Abbeville after his hometown in France.

Due largely to cotton planting, the town prospered over the next hundred years. The railway came to town in 1860, coinciding with the construction of the spired "Pink Church," **Trinity Episcopal Church,** and in 1896 the first textile mills were built here.

The historic district includes some 300 Victorian-era homes and churches, including the pink one, whose spire shoots up 125 feet.

Today, the town of 6,000 has become the cultural center of the region. The historic district includes downtown—including the revitalized town square—as well as part of the surrounding residential area.

Sights
Right in the center of the town square, you'll find the new obelisk honoring Civil War veterans. The old obelisk was destroyed by fire.

How does a block of granite get destroyed by fire? Each Christmas, the folks of Abbeville used to turn the obelisk into the core of an artificial Christmas tree. A few years back, the tree caught fire; when fire hoses doused the raging Yuletide inferno, the cold water cracked the heated granite, and the obelisk shattered faster than you can say "Robert E. Lee."

Sarah Bernhardt, Fanny Price, Jimmy Durante, and Groucho Marx are among the many famous lights who played the **Abbeville Opera House** in its day. Or, I should say, in its *old* day—because the opera house is still a regional hot spot for live theater—playing host to performances 45 weekends a year. Stop by at town square, tel. (864) 459-2157, and take in a live show. A nice way to spend an evening here in town. Call for shows and times. Wheelchair accessible.

At the corner of N. Main and Greenville Streets you'll come across the **Burt-Stark House,** tel. (864) 459-4600. This is where, shortly after Lee's surrender to Grant at Appomattox, the War Council of the Confederate Forces met with C.S.A. President Jefferson Davis and formally disbanded the Confederacy's armed forces, though of course Grant, Sherman, and company had already accomplished a good deal of informal disbanding by this point. Open Friday and Saturday 1-5 p.m., or by appointment. Admission $3. At 203 S. Main St., you'll find the **Abbeville County Library,** tel. (864) 459-4009, which houses the Poliakoff Collection of Western Art. Unless you head to the museums of Albuquerque and Santa Fe, you won't find a better collection of contemporary Native American ceramics, weavings, paintings, and bronzes.

historic, picturesque little Abbeville

Accommodations

To stay right on the square, and not a hundred yards from the Abbeville Opera House, reserve one of the 25 individually decorated rooms at the 19th-century **Belmont Inn,** 106 E. Pickens St., tel. (888) 251-2000 or (864) 459-9625. (Moderate-Expensive). After scores of years of underuse and disuse, the Belmont reopened in the 1980s due to the efforts of forward-looking preservationists. This is a beautiful old inn; at night you can sit on the veranda and listen to the piano player as you watch folks walking around the square. Ask about theater packages in connection with the opera house.

If you're coming into town from the north on Hwy. 28, you'll drive right by Jim and Gail Ulrich's turn-of-the-century **Vintage Inn,** 909 N. Main St., tel. (800) 890-7312 or (864) 459-4784, which offers three rooms. One has a double bed and one has a queen, which share the same bath (Moderate). There's also a Master Suite (Luxury) that includes a jacuzzi bathtub and a king-size bed. Quiche breakfast included. Theater packages available.

The circa-1860 **Abbewood B&B,** 509 N. Main St., offers three more rooms a little closer to downtown, along with a wraparound veranda armed with rocking chairs and ashtrays, tel. (864) 459-5822 (Moderate). One room has a private bath, the other two share one. Continental breakfasts are served, and if you're planning to take in a show at the opera house, proprietors Ruth and Charles Freeman can sell you a theater package.

If you want to save a little money, check into the **Abbeville Motel,** Hwy. 72 E, tel. (864) 459-5041. Inexpensive.

Food

For the best macaroni and cheese you've ever tasted, head over to the Mennonite-run **Dutch Oven,** 112 N. Main St., tel. (864) 459-5513. Lunches (only) served here, cafeteria-style. No frills, just as-good-as-it-gets comfort food and friendly people, not far off the square. Dirt cheap.

Another spot for great, cheap down-home cooking is **Yoder's Dutch Kitchen,** on Hwy. 72 E, tel. (864) 459-5556. Try the Shoo-fly pie for dessert.

For something less traditional, try the **Village Grill,** 114 Trinity St., tel. (864) 459-2500, a mid-priced Appalachia-meets-Marin sort of place where you can eat healthy if you've a mind to. Some very good rotisserie chicken and pasta. Dining outside.

Finally, for a slightly more formal South-meets-France dinner, head over to **Timothy's** in the Belmont Inn, tel. (864) 459-9625. Reservations are a good idea here; dress is "dressy casual." Open for lunch (true Southern cooking) and dinner (fine Southern cuisine); closed 2-5:30 p.m. between meals. Eat alfresco on the marble-floored veranda overlooking the square if you choose.

"THE MAJOR OF ST. LO": ABBEVILLE'S THOMAS HOWIE

In July 1944, in the shell-shocked weeks after D-Day, the survivors of the initial invasion at Omaha Beach set their sights on their next objective: the communications and traffic crossroads town of St. Lo. One of these men was Abbeville native and Citadel graduate Major Thomas Howie, commander of the 3rd Battalion, 116th Infantry.

After five weeks of brutal battling against tenacious German forces, Howie's division found itself positioned outside the city, ready for the final assault on the city. Howie gave his men a rousing speech, promising them, "I'll see you in St. Lo!"

As fate would have it, a mortar shell killed Howie immediately afterward, and he never saw the successful taking of the town the following day. When the smoke cleared, General Charles H. Gerhardt ordered the column to carry Howie's body into the town square, where he lay in state on a pile of toppled wall beside the church of Ste. Croix. There, his division passed the casket in somber review.

A New York *Times* correspondent on the scene wrote an article that spread the story of the "Major of St. Lo" around the world. The people of Abbeville erected a granite marker on the lawn of their courthouse.

When you're visiting the Citadel Military College in Charleston, be sure to note the Summerall chapel's 90-foot carillon, named in honor of Howie (class of 1929) in 1954. Howie's story also serves as subject of the mural *The Major of St. Lo* inside the Daniel Library.

Expect to spend between $13 and $17 a plate for dinner, though it's possible to go cheaper if you order one of the small plate entrées like brown rice and scallop pilaf with woodsy mushrooms and bacon, which runs just $6.95. Downstairs, the **Curtain Call Lounge** serves food and drinks in a more casual setting.

Shopping

This is the kind of town that makes even the most rootless Modernist want to go antiquing. Stop by **The Uptown Exchange** on the Square, tel. (864) 459-2224, and **Miriam's Southern Accents,** 128 Trinity St., tel. (864) 459-5995. Another fascinating place is **The House of Times Past,** on the square at 102 E. Pickens, tel./fax (864) 459-0325, Web site: www.thepast.com, purveyors of authentic reproductions of Confederate and Union uniforms, weapons, and other period items. If you're from out of state and interested in catching a battle reenactment while here, stop in and talk to David "Injun" Ward (he's half-Cherokee), who seems to know everything about all the different reenacting groups in the state.

Information

Stop by the **Abbeville Chamber of Commerce,** 17 Court Square, tel. (864) 459-4600, to view an audiovisual preview of the town and receive a printed self-guided tour to the area.

CALHOUN FALLS

Don't do what I did years ago and come up here looking for waterfalls—there aren't any. There *used* to be some falls, but they're long buried beneath Lake Richard Russell. However, you will find a nice place to stay in the 17-room **Latimer Inn,** right on Hwy. 81, tel. (864) 391-2747.

Founded in 1890, this town, and the nonexistent falls, are not named for John C. Calhoun but for Colonel James Edward Calhoun, a wealthy relative of the statesman's.

CALHOUN FALLS STATE PARK

Situated on scenically named 46 Maintenance Shop Rd., tel. (864) 447-8267, Calhoun Falls State Park offers 438 relatively untouched acres

along the freshwater coast, 86 campsites (14 tents only), tennis courts, a swimming area, nature trail, and good fishing.

HICKORY KNOB
STATE RESORT PARK

This park, about six miles west of McCormick on Hwy. 378, tel. (800) 491-1764 or (864) 391-2450, fax (864) 391-5390, sits on the banks of Strom Thurmond Lake. It's a good example of the traditional Southern idea of what a state park should be, featuring an 18-hole championship golf course, swimming pool, tennis and volleyball courts, and other such "improvements." Here you choose between staying in lodge rooms or suites ($40-80), cabins ($300 a week), or renting the Guillebeau House for $480 a week. Staying here will give you access to the swimming pool, tennis courts, and lodge.

Campsites all include water and electricity. Most important are the golf course, driving range, and putting green. You can rent johnboats here for just $10 a day.

Before you get to the turnoff for Hickory Knob, another turnoff leads to **Baker Creek State Park,** tel. (864) 443-2457. Both Baker Creek and **Hamilton Branch State Park** (south on Hwy. 221/28, tel. 864-333-2223) offer plenty of camping sites, fishing, and boating access.

McCORMICK

Q. What does the land here have in common with the Spanish-American War?
A. They were both purchased with Hearst money.

Granted, this town of just under 2,000 is named after Cyrus H. McCormick, inventor of the reaper and founder of International Harvester, who donated the land where most of the town stands today. But he had bought up the land from Dr. J.W. Hearst, a relative of William Randolph Hearst, who had the good fortune to own it in 1852 when gold was discovered here. McCormick never lived in the town he named for himself; when he found the mine was unprofitable, he decided to plan a town here. He bought enough

SOUTH CAROLINA'S HEROES OF THE ALAMO

At one time a popular bumper sticker in the Saluda area read "Texas Starts Here." Saluda County was, after all, birthplace and childhood home of two of the Alamo's biggest heroes, William Barrett Travis and James Butler Bonham. Travis was the commandant of the makeshift fortress when the Mexican Army led by General Santa Anna arrived in San Antonio. A lawyer by trade, Travis was a fiery, handsome redhead with a restless spirit. Before coming to Texas in 1831 he had already tried Alabama, where both he and his childhood friend from Saluda County, James Bonham, had practiced law. When it became clear that there would be a fight in Texas, Travis asked his friend Bonham to join him as a second lieutenant.

Travis was a complicated sort. When he moved out to Texas he had pretended to convert to Catholicism (a requirement of Mexican citizenship) and declared himself single, though he had left behind a son and a pregnant wife in Alabama. Shortly before his death at the Alamo, his wife came from Alabama to get his consent to a divorce. He kept written documentation of his extramarital conquests. And yet he was considered a fair man, and well-disciplined. Though he had been sent to the Alamo to destroy it so that the Mexicans couldn't use it,

he became so convinced of its importance in the war that he refused to leave. To Travis's mind, the Alamo was the one thing keeping Santa Anna from the vulnerable East Texas settlements.

Bonham was related to the important Butler family of what would become Saluda County. He attended South Carolina College in Columbia (he didn't graduate) and practiced law as late as 1830 in Pendleton. By 1835 he had moved to the Old Southwest, opening a practice in Montgomery, Alabama. Then, before the year was out, his old friend Travis invited him to join him in Texas.

Six other South Carolinians perished at the Alamo, but the roles of Travis and Bonham are legendary. Toward the beginning of the Mexican siege, Travis is said to have drawn a line in the sand with his sword, telling the 184 or so men inside the fortress that every man ready to commit to fight to the death should cross the line. All but one man stepped across the line. It was this bold gesture that President George Bush (a sometime Texan) was alluding to when he spoke of "drawing a line in the sand" during the Gulf War.

Bonham is reckoned a heroic figure for his having twice left the doomed garrison to courier Travis' pleas for help to the Texans under the command of

stock in two different railroads to be able to influence them both to pass through the town. With the property values now rising, he had the town divided into lots, donated land for churches, a school, and a cemetery, and from there on let his wife Nettie concern herself with the town as a sort of hobby. She was involved in the Temperance movement, and part of the town's 1882 charter included the provision that no alcohol was to be sold here for 100 years.

In 1994, John Villani ranked McCormick as one of "The 100 Small Art Towns in America." Stop by the visitors center at 100 S. Main St. for more information, including a self-guided walking tour, or call (843) 465-2835.

A big draw in town today is **The MACK Art Gallery**, 115 S. Main St., tel. (864) 465-3216, set in the old Keturah Hotel (the acronym stands for "McCormick Arts Council at the Keturah"). You'll find it where Hwy. 378 crosses S. Main St., next door to Fannie Kate's Inn. In the first

floor gallery you'll see a changing exhibition of locally produced oils, watercolors, quilts, photographs, and pottery pieces. The town also uses the first floor for art classes and as a general reception hall. Here too is the Gallery Shop, where you can purchase the work of local artists. Up on the second floor you'll find the Folklife Archives—worth taking a peek. There's a darkroom for local photographers, and this is also where the scouts meet and music lessons are given. The adjacent park and amphitheater are site of other right-brain hijinks, including plays and a summer concert series. Free admission. Open Mon.-Fri. 9 a.m.-5 p.m. Feel free to call the above number for more information.

You wanna see something *really pretty?* Head about 10 miles south on the Hwy. 28 out of McCormick and then turn left on S-33-138. You'll come to **Price's Mill,** an old-fashioned water-powered gristmill built in 1890 on Stevens Creek. Bring your camera.

Colonel James Fannin in nearby Goliad. Both times, Fannin refused Travis' pleas, but Bonham did round up 32 men from the DeWitt colony willing to help. Under cover of darkness, Bonham and the others fought their way back through the Mexican lines to join the doomed men at the Alamo.

By the following night, all 183 defenders of the Alamo were dead, along with somewhere between 200 and 600 Mexican soldiers.

Today, numerous place-names throughout Texas honor William B. Travis, including Travis County, home of the state capital of Austin, and nearby Lake Travis. But Travis' legacy goes beyond that. Though he lived in Texas for just over four years, the name of this South Carolinian has become synonymous with the American West in general and Texas in particular. Countless Texan boys are given the rugged first name of "Travis" each year. The countless Western films throughout the years have used the name "Travis" for their protagonists (in the recent *Executive Decision*, Steven Seagal took no chances; his character was named Colonel Austin Travis). Actors from Lawrence Harvey to Alec Baldwin have portrayed Travis throughout the years; in 1991, a bioflick called *Travis* traced his entire life, from South Carolina onward.

While James Butler Bonham hasn't exactly become a household name, head north of Fort Worth, Texas, not far south of the Red River and the Oklahoma border, and you'll find the 10,000-person city of Bonham, Texas, named in honor of Saluda County's James Butler Bonham. Home to legendary U.S. Speaker of the House Sam Rayburn, Bonham ironically serves as the seat of Fannin County, named after the very man who refused to save Bonham's life. In the John Wayne film *The Alamo,* Wayne chose his son Patrick to play the heroic role of Bonham.

In South Carolina, you'll find a monument to Travis and Bonham on the lawn in front of the Saluda County Courthouse. The Red Bank Baptist Church on 309 E. Church St., where the Bonham and Travis families worshipped, still stands today. Bonham's birthplace, now called **Bonham House,** still stands as well, and the Saluda County Historical Society is working on restoring it. To get there, take Hwy. 178 east 3.5 miles to Rd. 328. Take 328 north seven-tenths of a mile to Rd. 329, and follow this road east for two-tenths of a mile until you see the old house on the west side of the highway.

You'll also find a monument to Travis on Hwy. 121, erected jointly by Saluda County and the State of Texas.

Next door to the MACK is the 1884 **Fannie Kate's Country Inn and Restaurant,** 127 S. Main St., tel. (800) 965-0061 or (864) 465-0061, fax (864) 465-0057, another old railroad hotel renovated in 1991 and once again serving the public. Book ahead for one of its nine rooms (Moderate), which include queen-size beds, fireplaces, private baths, and breakfast at the full-service restaurant downstairs. Children welcome.

Even if you're not staying at the inn, you ought to stop by Fannie Kate's for some good country cooking. And as long as I'm passing out bad diet tips, be sure to stop by **Strom's Drug Store** on Main St., an old-fashioned soda fountain where you can still get ice cream sodas and cherry Coke.

CLARKS HILL

This tiny resort town features **La Cantina,** Hwy. 28 Fury-F Rd., tel. (864) 333-5315, a unique restaurant out among the trees serving Central and South American meat dishes and seafood. Occasional live (Spanish) music. Open Wed.-Sat. for dinner only.

EDGEFIELD

For some reason, this small town of 2,644 has been home to no fewer than 10 South Carolina governors and five lieutenant governors. Among the most noted are **Preston Brooks,** famous for caning Massachusetts senator Charles Sumner in the Senate in 1857, and Strom Thurmond (not quite old enough to have witnessed the attack).

A good first place to stop in town is the **Courtesy Center and Archives** at 104 Courthouse Square, where you can get information on Edgefield and view the historic collection.

At 320 Norris St. you'll see **Magnolia Dale,** tel. (803) 637-2233, a home built in the 1830s and featuring the Strom Thurmond Room. Open by appointment only.

Another old home—just five years younger than Magnolia Dale, is **Oakley Park** at 300 Columbia Rd., tel. (803) 637-4027. After the War between the States, General Martin Witherspoon Gary, the organizer of the Red Shirts movement, lived here. Open Wed.-Fri. 10 a.m.-4 p.m., or by appointment. Admission charged.

Old Edgefield Pottery at 230 Simkins St., tel. (803) 637-2060, exhibits Edgefield pottery, a traditional, alkaline-glazed type of pottery made in this area in the 1800s. A potter here will usually work the wheel as you watch. Donations appreciated. Wheelchair accessible.

At **Starview Farms** on Old Stage Rd., six miles south of Edgefield off Hwy. 25, tel. (800) 820-9276, you can tour a working sheep farm and see sheep sheared (when it's time for shearing) and demonstrations on spinning and dyeing wool. Garden tours are by appointment only.

The **Wild Turkey Center** on Hwy. 25 is headquarters for the National Wild Turkey Federation (do some people have more free time than we do?) where turkey conservation is stressed.

Architecture in the Old South has featured **Cedar Grove Plantation of Edgefield,** on Hwy. 25, 5.5 miles north of Edgefield, tel. (864) 637-3056, one of the oldest plantations in the Upcountry (1790). Visits are by appointment only, and the owners ask that you not bring children along—apparently since this would ruin the Old South ambience (were there no children before the war?). Admission charged. You'll want to view this to see the hand-carved moldings and mantels, and the original kitchen, complete with quarters for the kitchen slaves.

Edgefield offers a number of good places to stay—including two rooms at the **Cedar Grove Plantation** itself (see above). Call ahead at (864) 637-3056. No children allowed. Inexpensive-Moderate.

Other upscale but affordable options include four rooms in the former home of Bourbon-era Governor John Sheppard, now called the **Carnoosie Inn,** 407 Columbia Rd., tel. (800) 622-7124 or (803) 637-5107 (Inexpensive), and the six-room storefront **Inn on Main,** 303 Main St., tel. (803) 637-9915 (Inexpensive). If you're shut out in town, head east of Edgefield to the town of **Johnston,** where you'll find the **Cox House Inn,** at 602 Lee St., tel. (803) 275-2707.

SALUDA

This crossroads town is a convenient spot to spend the night on your way to Aiken or the Upcountry. **Cree Hall B&B and Gift Shop,** RR2, tel./fax (803) 445-7029, is set in an 1870s Victorian farmhouse with a wraparound porch and four rooms with fireplaces—though you may have to share a bath. The rates include a full breakfast. Inexpensive.

OLD 96 DISTRICT HILLTOWNS

The 96 District was so named after the old British fort at a point 96 miles south of the lower Cherokee capital of Keowee. In the 18th century, this was South Carolina's western frontier, a wild land filled with soldiers, Indian traders, and Cherokee Indians. In 1785, the state General Assembly broke the 96 District into three counties: Abbeville, Edgefield, and Laurens. In 1895, these counties were again subdivided, creating the new counties of McCormick and Greenwood.

General Andrew Pickens comes from here. John C. Calhoun does, too. In the 1820s, future president Andrew Johnson lived here before moving farther west, to Greeneville, Tennessee.

Information
For information on the Old 96 District, contact the **Old 96 Tourism Commission,** 104-1/2 Public Square, Laurens, tel. (864) 984-0096, Web site: www.scold96.org.

NINETY SIX
NATIONAL HISTORIC SITE

Located two miles south of Ninety Six on Hwy. 248, tel. (864) 543-4068, this national historic site commemorates the frontier community and Revolutionary battle site here. Visit and you'll see a historic star fort, where British troops held out against the siege of General Nathanael Greene's troops. Open daily, free. Most of the site is wheelchair accessible.

In May 1781, American General Nathanael Greene led 1,100 men to surround the British-held, star-shaped fort at Ninety Six. The 550 soldiers inside were Americans as well—but loyalists, devoted to preserving the king's rule in America. Lieutenant-Colonel John Harris Cruger, a fair-minded native of New York, was the British commander, popular with the local citizenry.

Greene ordered his men to build a tower from which they could fire down into the fort, as well as give protecting fire to the American troops who began digging trenches to safely get closer to the fort. In mid-June, before the zigzagging trenches could get to the fort, word came that British reinforcements were on the way. Greene's troops attempted an all-or-nothing attack, but before his work parties of axmen and hookmen could make a hole in the fort for the American infantry to rush through, Cruger sent out skirmishers into the trench surrounding the stockade who drove back the work parties, slaughtering many in the process. Greene held the rest of his men back in the trenches; when the men returned he evacuated his troops before the loyalist rescue column arrived. When the British reinforcements came, they helped the loyalists evacuate the doomed fort and village and hightail it for the safety of British-held Charleston.

GRACE AND RACHEL MARTIN~
HEROES OF THE REVOLUTION

It may read a little like an episode of *I Love Lucy,* but the story of the Martin women is a true tale of heroism from the Revolution.

Grace and Rachel (history forgets their maiden names) married the Martin brothers of the 96 District in the years before the Revolution. When their husbands joined the American army, the women moved in with their mother-in-law.

One night, word came to them that a British courier would be coming along the road by their mother-in-law's house, bearing an important message to the loyalist partisans stationed farther up the road. The courier, the informant told them, would be guarded by two armed British officers.

If only their husbands—or, for that matter, any men—had been anywhere nearby, the women thought, the men could waylay the courier, steal the information, and pass it along to patriot General Nathanael Greene. Then one of them got an idea.

That night, dressed in their husbands' clothing and bearing guns, the women stood in the darkness beside the moonlit road and waited. Finally it came: the unmistakable clomping of hooves on dirt road, echoing through the blackened woods.

When the three men rode closer, Grace and Rachel jumped out in front of their horses, each gun barrel pointed at a man's chest. They shouted in their lowest voices for the men to hand over the dispatches. Shaken and frightened out of their minds, the officers didn't dare reach for their pistols. The courier threw down his dispatches and the three rode off. Grace snatched up the important parchments and the women pulled their horses out from behind the trees, leapt upon them, and raced back to their mother-in-law's house via a shortcut. They got home and handed the messages to a young pro-patriot messenger, and he raced the valuable information off toward General Greene's army.

The women put away their husbands' guns and, after telling the story to their mother-in-law, went to their rooms and changed out of their husbands' clothes.

Then they heard it—hoofbeats and male voices, the voices of the British officers and courier. Someone rapped upon the door. Their mother-in-law answered.

The redcoats were friendly—they asked if three of the king's men might not ask room and board from a loyalist woman.

"But you passed here a short while ago, did you not?" Mrs. Martin asked.

The officers explained that the letters had been intercepted by "two rebel lads" who had come upon them so quickly that they didn't even have time to defend themselves.

By now, Grace and Rachel appeared, wearing their frilliest. They served the men a late supper, made up beds for them in a spare room, and, in the morning, rose early to cook them breakfast. The courier and escort thanked them profusely, doubtless thinking it fortunate that on a mission where they had completely failed, they had also met such hospitable women.

GREENWOOD

Actor Bo Hopkins *(American Graffiti, The Wild Bunch)* comes from Greenwood. So does 1960s party band The Swinging Medallions, whose raucous "Double Shot of My Baby's Love," was named the "Greatest Party Song of the 1960s" by *Rolling Stone Magazine.* The Medallions are still around, a noted force in the beach music scene.

This town of 23,000 was founded by two Irish settlers in 1802; a judge from Ninety Six moved up in 1823 and founded a summer home that he called "Green Wood," and which the post office simplified to "Greenwood." The town grew up around the railroad that arrived later in the century, and even made room for it on its main street; today, Greenwoodians claim that their town boasts the "widest Main Street in the world," at 316 feet.

Lander University, a four-year coed state university founded in 1872, is here. Greenwood has been listed as one of the best towns of its size in America, and each June it draws floral types from around the country for the six-day **South Carolina Festival of Flowers,** which centers around Park Seed's gardens and includes private garden tours but also features golf and tennis tournaments, demonstrations, and a flotilla on Lake Greenwood.

Sights

The first stop you want to make in any of these hilltowns (other than at a barbecue joint) is the local museum. Greenwood's got a good one.

The **Greenwood Museum,** 106 Main St., tel. (864) 229-7093, features a fascinating "village street" exhibit, wherein you can visit an old-fashioned general store, a one-room school, and an old apothecary's shop. Also here are Native American artifacts and natural-history exhibits. Open 10 a.m.-5 p.m. Wed.-Sat. Admission. Wheelchair accessible.

Gardeners may want to head seven miles north of town on Hwy. 254, where they'll come across **The Gardens of Park Seed Co.,** tel. (864) 223-8555. It's most breathtaking here between May and July, but anytime's a good time to stop by the Garden Center and see the 70,000 trial plants and pick up some of the plants or tools you've been ogling in its catalog. No admission charge. Gardens open dawn to dusk

Mon.-Sat., Garden Center open 9 a.m.-6 p.m. the same days.

Accommodations

Top of the line in this department would be the turn-of-the-century charmer **Inn on the Square,** 104 Court St., tel. (864) 223-4488 or (864) 231-9109, fax (864) 223-7067. Greenwood's top lodging offers courtly ambience in its 46 rooms furnished with handsome period reproductions including mahogany carved rice beds and brass nightstands. The inn features a three-story skylight atrium, a Charleston courtyard with pool, and the dining room. Moderate. Price includes a full breakfast in the dining room downstairs.

Food

At the **Inn at the Square** you can pick up a Southern-style breakfast buffet and lunch buffet. Or stop by the inn's **English Fox & Hound Pub** for nightly meals and snacks.

Shopping

Somewhere in Time Antiques and Collectibles, 1312 Hwy. 34, tel. (864) 227-3380, specializes in antiques and collectibles having to do with racing. Since 1960, Mrs. Evelyn Dodgen has been selling collectibles, antiques, and handmade furniture at **Rainbo Antiques,** 2720 Hwy. 25 S, tel. (864) 227-1921 or (864) 227-3508.

Information

For information on Greenwood and Greenwood County, contact the **Greenwood County Chamber of Commerce,** tel. (864) 223-8431.

LAKE GREENWOOD STATE PARK

Head farther along Hwy. 35 to 914-acre CCC-era Lake Greenwood State Park, 302 State Park Rd., tel. (864) 543-3535. Besides the lake, the park offers a camp store, 125 camping sites (five are tents only), and lake fishing.

CLINTON

Arthur "Guitar Boogie" Smith came from Clinton. Smith played on Spartanburg radio station WSPA in the 1930s, and brought his Dixieland back-

ANDREW JOHNSON IN LAURENS

Andrew Johnson is no longer the only president in American history to be impeached by Congress, but he was the only president who had a criminal past. Johnson had run away from an abusive tailor in Raleigh, North Carolina, and bore a price of $10 on his head when he wandered into the sleepy cotton town of Laurens in 1826 and began asking around about prospects for a skilled tailor in the area.

When the 18-year-old discovered that there was no competition around, he rented a shop on the northeast corner of the Laurens town square, and he immediately became successful with the planters in the area. Once or twice a week, he'd ride 38 miles to Abbeville, where he opened a second shop.

Before long, Johnson fell in love with Sarah Word, the daughter of a wealthy Laurens cotton farmer, and proposed to her, but Word and her family rebuffed him, telling him that they knew he'd never amount to anything.

Johnson left Laurens shortly afterward, returning to Raleigh to officially buy his freedom from his old master and persuade his poor white mother, stepfather, and alcoholic older brother to come west with him to Tennessee, where he planned to purchase a farm and open up a new shop with the money he had made off the citizens of Laurens. There, Johnson's political career began as town alderman of Greeneville, rising upon Lincoln's assassination to the presidency of the United States.

Laurens historian Libby Rhodes says that the descendants of Sarah Word—the Crews family—kept a quilt that Sarah and Andrew had made together in their possession for many years before donating it to the State Museum in Columbia.

Andrew Johnson

ground into his country guitar stylings. His 1945 "Guitar Boogie" has become a standard. In the 1950s, he and guitarist Don Reno wrote a song called "Feudin' Banjos," which they later proved in court was the basis for the 1973 *Deliverance* theme song and pop hit "Dueling Banjos."

LAURENS

With 11,000 residents, Laurens is one of the larger towns in the Old 96 District. Named for the Revolutionary-era Carolinian Henry Laurens, who was captured in Europe while on a diplomatic errand for the colonies and imprisoned in the Tower of London, Laurens is where a young Andrew Johnson operated a tailor shop in the 1820s before moving on to Greeneville, Tennessee, where he began his political career. At the end of the same century, blues legend Reverend Gary Davis was born and raised here.

The 1812 **James Dunklin House** at 544 W. Main St., tel. (864) 984-4735, features antique Southern furnishings. Open by appointment only; admission charged. Just a couple doors down, with the Doric columns, is the **W.D. Simpson House,** home of post-Reconstruction Governor W.D. Simpson, and on the National Register.

The gray stone **Laurens Courthouse,** built in 1838, dominates the town square. In 1870, at the National Guard Armory across from the courthouse, an army of armed African-Americans attempted to burn the town but were thwarted by white townsfolk.

For information on Laurens and Laurens County, contact the **Laurens County Chamber of Commerce** at (864) 833-2716.

BOOKLIST

For addtional recommendations, please see the special topic "A South Carolina Syllabus" in the Introduction.

Battaile, Andrew Chandler, Arthur W. Bergernon Jr., et. al. *Black Southerners in Gray: Essays on Afro-Americans in Confederate Armies.* Edited by Richard Rollins. Redondo Beach, CA: Rank and File, 1994. Fascinating studies on this little-known minority group in the Civil War.

Bodie, Idella. *South Carolina Women.* Orangeburg, SC: Sandlapper Publishing, 1991.

Brown, James (with Bruce Tucker). *James Brown: The Godfather of Soul,* New York: Macmillan, 1986. Brown on Brown; a bit dated now, but nonetheless a powerful rags to prison to riches story, beginning in the little town of Barnwell.

Bryan, Bo. *Shag: The Legendary Dance of the South.* Beaufort, SC: Foundation Books, 1995. The single best reference on the dance and the surrounding subculture.

Cohodas, Nadine. *Strom Thurmond and the Politics of Political Change.* New York: Simon and Schuster, 1993. A look at Thurmond's long, bending career.

Cooper, Peter. *Hub City Music Makers: One Southern Town's Popular Music Legacy.* Spartanburg, SC: Holocene Publishing, 1997. Cooper, a Wofford graduate and upstate resident, provides in-depth coverage of a number of residents with Spartanburg roots, including blues guitarist Pink Anderson, country rockers the Marshall Tucker Band, and early rockabillies the Sparkletones. A fun, fascinating read.

Dickey, Christopher. *Summer of Deliverance: A Memoir of Father and Son.* New York: Simon and Schuster, 1998. A heartwrenching and insightful look at the rough-edged career of the late James Dickey—poet, novelist, screenwriter, critic, and longtime USC professor.

Edgar, Walter. *South Carolina: A History.* Columbia: USC Press, 1998. A long-needed 700-page comprehensive history by a longtime Carolina scholar.

Federal Works Project. *South Carolina: A Guide to the Palmetto State,* 1941. The definitive old-time guide, created during the WPA years.

Hudson, Charles, and Carmen Chaves Tesser, eds. *Forgotten Centuries: The Indians and Europeans in the American South, 1521-1704,* Athens, GA: UGA Press, 1994.

Hurmence, Belinda, ed. *Before Freedom, When I Can Just Remember: Twenty-seven Oral Histories of Former South Carolina Slaves.* Winston-Salem: John F. Blair, 1989. Absolutely fascinating accounts of life under slavery and during Reconstruction.

Johnson, Michael P., and James L. Roark. *Black Masters: A Free Family of Color in the Old South.* NY: Norton, 1984. Details the experiences of William Ellison, African-American cotton-gin builder in Stateburg before the Civil War.

Jones-Jackson, Patricia. *When Roots Die: Endangered Traditions on the Sea Islands.* Athens, GA: UGA, 1987.

Kitt, Eartha. *Thursday's Child.* New York: Duell, 1956. Covers Kitt's early childhood in North, near Orangeburg.

Kovacik, Charles F., and John J. Winberry. *South Carolina: A Geography.* Boulder, CO: Westview Press, 1987. Reprinted by USC Press in 1989 as *South Carolina: The Making of a Landscape.* The definitive look at the various geographies of the state.

Lippy, Charles H., ed. *Religion in South Carolina,* Columbia, SC: USC Press, 1993. Fourteen essays shed light on the tangle of denominations that make up organized religion in South Carolina. Like touring the engine room of the Queen Elizabeth II.

Martin, Floride Milner. *A Chronological Survey of South Carolina Literature.* Self-published. A representative sampling of the state's literature, from early explorer records to present-day Carolinian authors.

McCloud, Barry. *Definitive Country: The Ultimate Encyclopedia of Country Music and Its Performers,* New York: Berkley, 1995. A wonderful reference for the student of country music.

Miller, Mike. *Hootie! How the Blowfish Put the Pop Back into Pop Rock.* Columbia, SC: Summerhouse Press, 1997. The definitive book on the mid-'90s pop icons by a USC graduate and *The State* reporter.

Nelson, Jack, and Jack Bass. *Orangeburg Massacre,* New York: World, 1970.

Pinckney, Elise, ed. *Letterbook of Eliza Lucas Pinckney, 1739-1762.* Chapel Hill: University of North Carolina Press, 1972. Along with Mary Chesnut, the indigo pioneer Pinckney is one of South Carolina's most interesting women.

Powers, Bernard E., Jr. *Black Charlestonians: A Social History: 1822-1885.* Fayetteville: University of Arkansas, 1994. A much-needed accounting-for of the important contributions of the black citizens—slave and free—to one of the most important Southern cities of the 19th century.

Rhyne, Nancy. *Carolina Seashells,* Orangeburg, SC: Sandlapper Publishing, 1989. Learn to know your conch from your limpet.

Shepard, Charles E. *Forgiven: The Rise and Fall of Jim Bakker and the PTL Ministry.* New York: Atlantic Monthly Press, 1989. The author, who won a Pulitzer Prize for his reporting of the PTL scandal, provides an exhaustive and troubling account.

Simpson, Lewis P. *Mind and the American Civil War,* Baton Rouge: LSU, 1989. Studies American history's foremost conflict in terms of the collision of two distinct philosophies and the cultures that spawned from them.

Smith, Gregory White, and Steven Naifeh. *On a Street Called Easy, in a Cottage Called Joye: A Restoration Comedy.* A humorous accounting of the authors' adjustment from New York to Aiken life and their experiences overseeing the refurbishment of one of the town's grand "cottages."

Smith, Michael B. *Carolina Dreams: The Musical Legacy of Upstate South Carolina.* Beverly Hills: Marshall Tucker Publishing, 1997. An enjoyable, informal look at the musical roots of the upstate, with a special focus on the Marshall Tucker Band.

Smith, Reed. *Gullah.* Edisto Island, SC: Edisto Island Historical Preservation Society, 1926. Reprinted 1993.

Starobin, Robert S., ed. *Denmark Vesey: The Slave Conspiracy of 1822,* Englewood Cliffs: Prentice-Hall, 1970. A collection of essays and original documents pertaining to the aborted revolt.

Wallace, David Duncan. *South Carolina: A Short History 1520-1948.* UNC Press, 1951. Until Walter Edgar's book, this was the most recent large work on the entire state. Still worth reading for its compelling storytelling.

Woodward, C. Vann, ed. *Mary Chesnut's Civil War.* New Haven: Yale, 1982. The Pulitzer-prize winning collection of letters by a witty, shrewd eyewitness to the inner workings of the Confederacy.

INDEX

AFRICAN-AMERICAN HERITAGE

1251

1341

114235

2721

43152

61328

321; Splash Island 184; Splash Zone 155, 169, 184
Anderson: 355-356
Anderson, Alvin "Pink": 46, 65
Anderson automobile: 314-315
Anderson, Bill: 64
Anderson County Arts Center/Museum: 355
Andrew Jackson State Park: 324
Andrews Gospel Music and Storytelling Festival: 96
Angel Oak Park: 154
Annual Fall Candlelight Tours of Homes and Gardens: 177
Annual Festival of Houses and Gardens: 177
Antebellum Old South: 31-36; Tour 271; *see also* historic homes/buildings; plantations; slavery; *specific place*
antiquing: general discussion 68; Abbeville 359; Aiken 303; Charleston 187; Cheraw 283; Columbia 265-266; Easley 348; Georgetown 131; Greenwood 364; Lexington 271; Newberry

272; Rock Hill 317
apple industry: general discussion 43; Apple Harvest Festival 97; apple tasting 335
aquariums: Cheraw Fish Hatchery and Aquarium 282; Ripley's Aquarium 61, 110-111; Riverbanks Zoological Park and Botanical Garden 249; South Carolina Aquarium 61, 158
archaeology: 21-22, 163-164, 195
area codes: 91
Arthur, John, House: 130
Artists' Parlor: 303
Ashtabula: 354
ATMs: 93-94
Audubon Newhall Preserve: 218
Audubon Swamp Garden: 153
Augusta, Georgia: 309
Auld Brass: 225
Aunt Sue's Country Corner: 346-347
auto racing: 60
Autumnfest: 97
Avery Research Center for African-American History and

Culture: 156, 194
Awendaw: 175-176
azaleas: 16; Azalea Park and Bird Sanctuary 192; *see also* gardens/botanical parks; *specific place*

B
backpacking: *see* hiking/backpacking
Bailey, York W., Museum: 194, 211
Baker Creek State Park: 359
Bakker, Jim and Tammy: 317-318
Ball, David: 64
Bamberg: 291
banks/banking: 93-94, 267
Banksia Hall: 308
Barbadian settlement: 23-24
Barefoot Landing: 105, 107, 109
The Barn: 341
Barnwell: 306-308
Barnwell County Courthouse: 307
Barnwell County Museum: 308
Barnwell State Park: 306

ART VENUES

Aiken Center for the Arts—Aiken: 299, 303
Aiken's Makin'—Aiken: 300
Anderson County Arts Center—Anderson: 355
Arnold Gallery—Aiken: 303
Artisan's Center—Walterboro: 225
Artists' Parlor—Aiken: 303
Artists Underground—Greenville: 341
Art Works Studio—Aiken: 303
The Audubon Shop and Gallery—Charleston: 186
Bob Jones University, Museum, and Gallery—Greenville: 61, 331-333
Center for the Arts Building—Rock Hill: 314-315
Charleston Crafts—Charleston: 186

Columbia Art Glass Company—Columbia: 264
Columbia Museum of Art—Columbia: 243
Furman University Thompson Gallery—Greenville: 331
Gallery Chuma/African American Art Gallery—Charleston: 186, 194
Gibbes Museum of Art—Charleston: 61, 156
Greenville County Museum of Art—Greenville: 330
Handmade Series—Walterboro: 226
Harborwalk Festival—Georgetown: 97
Howell's Art and Antiques—Lancaster: 324
Irma Morris Museum of Fine Art—Pickens: 348

The MACK Art Gallery—McCormick: 360
McKissick Museum—Columbia: 246
MOJA Arts Festival—Charleston: 177
Morris Gallery—Columbia: 264
Piccolo Spoleto Festival—Charleston: 97, 177
Red Barn Visual Center—Florence: 276
Rhett Gallery—Charleston: 186
Self Family Arts Center—Hilton Head: 218
Sloan, Tommy Hawk: 347
Spoleto Festival U.S.A.—Charleston: 97, 177
State Museum: 61
Sumter Gallery of Art—Sumter: 274
Vista Studios—Columbia: 264
West, Benjamin: 332-333

BED AND BREAKFASTS, INNS, AND GUESTHOUSES

CHURCHES, CHAPELS, AND SYNAGOGUES

COFFEEHOUSES

HISTORIC HOMES/BUILDINGS

MOVIE LOCALES

PLANTATIONS

STATE PARKS

ABOUT THE AUTHOR

A graduate of the University of South Carolina, Mike Sigalas has served as a writing instructor at the USC, The Citadel Military College, and Orangeburg-Calhoun College.

The one-time rock roadie and Jungle Cruise pilot's poetry has appeared in various literary journals over the past decade and is featured in Kim Weir's *Southern California Handbook*.

A former resident of Columbia, Isle of Palms, and Orangeburg, Sigalas currently writes from a small town in California's Sacramento Valley.

ACKNOWLEDGEMENTS:

Thanks to my wife, reader, editor, research assistant, and coach, Kristin, who made this book possible; and to my son Noah, whose arrival made it necessary.

Very special thanks to the wonderful folks of South Carolina, and in particular, to Geoff and Tammy Grafton and family for the van; to Tant and Sharon Ehrhardt for showing us where the key was and learning us about hospitality; to Billy and Anita Bryan for the recipe, the babysitting, and the restaurant tips; to Kendall and Meredith Buckendahl for the golf assistance and for giving us the big bed. To Tom and Debbie Caverly and family for the shrimping, swimming, and beach house. Also to George Sigalas, horticulturalist at Reynolds Plantation resort in Greensboro, Georgia, for his help with the flora; and to his wife wife Kristin for the gracious hospitality and photo assistance.

Thanks as well to S.C. Hockey expert, Stephanie A. Kavanaugh; to Lisa Hammersley of the Myrtle Beach Area Chamber of Commerce; to the helpful folks at the Historical Charleston Chamber; Tammy Norris, Rock Hill Area Chamber; Diane Wilson at Greenville Chamber of Commerce; Vicki Loughner of the Old 96 District Tourism Commission; to Sarah Spruill at the Cheraw Visitors Bureau; Rebecca Temples and the rest of the crew at Ripley's; Karen Carter at the Edisto Bookstore, the Wilts at the Rice Museum in Georgetown; the crew at Judy's House of Oldies in Ocean Drive Beach; and to Shaggin' Czar Barry Thigpen for his research assistance.

Also to my parents, George and Sue Sigalas, who drove instead of flying.

And to my mother, sister Mary, and Jeanette Pelak, for being flexible and giving me time to write.

AVALON
TRAVEL
publishing

How far will our travel guides take you? As far as you want.

Discover a rhumba-fueled nightspot in Old Havana, explore prehistoric tombs in Ireland, hike beneath California's centuries-old redwoods, or embark on a classic road trip along Route 66. Our guidebooks deliver solidly researched, trip-tested information—minus any generic froth—to help globetrotters or weekend warriors create an adventure uniquely their own.

And we're not just about the printed page. Public television viewers are tuning in to Rick Steves' new travel series, *Rick Steves' Europe*. On the Web, readers can cruise the virtual black top with *Road Trip USA* author Jamie Jensen and learn travel industry secrets from Edward Hasbrouck of *The Practical Nomad*.

In print. On TV. On the Internet.

We supply the information. The rest is up to you.

Avalon Travel Publishing

Something for everyone

www.travelmatters.com

Avalon Travel Publishing guides are available at your favorite book or travel store.

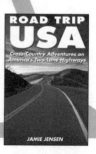